# SEGEDUNUM

Published in the United Kingdom in 2016 by
OXBOW BOOKS
10 Hythe Bridge Street, Oxford OX1 2EW

and in the United States by
OXBOW BOOKS
1950 Lawrence Road, Havertown, PA 19083

Hardcover Edition: ISBN 978-1-78570-026-2
Digital Edition: ISBN 978-1-78570-027-9


A CIP record for this book is available from the British Library

Library of Congress Cataloging-in-Publication Data

Names: Rushworth, Alan. | Daniels, Charles (Charles M.) | Bishop, M. C. |
    Caruana, I. D. (Ian D.) | Moffat, P. (Pete)
Title: Segedunum : excavations by Charles Daniels in the Roman fort at
    Wallsend (1975-1984) / by A. Rushworth ; with contributions by M.C.
    Bishop, I.D. Caruana, C.M. Daniels, P. Moffat ; illustrated by C. MacRae,
    M. Johnstone.
Description: Oxford : Oxbow Books, 2015- | Includes bibliographical
    references and index.
Identifiers: LCCN 2015039327| ISBN 9781785700262 (volume 1 : hardcover) |
    ISBN 9781785700279 (volume 1 : digital)
Subjects: LCSH: Segedunum Roman Fort Site (Wallsend, England) | Excavations
    (Archaeology)--England--Wallsend. | Fortification--England--Wallsend. |
    Material culture--England--Wallsend. | Animal remains
    (Archaeology)--England--Wallsend. | Wallsend (England)--Antiquities, Roman.
Classification: LCC DA690.W2214 R87 2015 | DDC 936.2/879--dc23 LC record available at http://lccn.loc.gov/2015039327

Printed in the United Kingdom by Short Run Press, Exeter


For a complete list of Oxbow titles, please contact:

UNITED KINGDOM
Oxbow Books
Telephone (01865) 241249, Fax (01865) 794449
Email: oxbow@oxbowbooks.com
www.oxbowbooks.com

UNITED STATES OF AMERICA
Oxbow Books
Telephone (800) 791-9354, Fax (610) 853-9146
Email: queries@casemateacademic.com
www.casemateacademic.com/oxbow

Oxbow Books is part of the Casemate Group

*Front cover: Portable lead shrine.*
*Back cover: Copper alloy ramshead skillet.*

# SEGEDUNUM

## EXCAVATIONS BY CHARLES DANIELS IN THE ROMAN FORT AT WALLSEND (1975–1984)

## Volume 2: The Finds

## Edited by A. T. Croom

*With contributions by*
L. Allason-Jones, D. Allen, R. Brickstock, P. J. Casey, B. Dickinson, L. J. Gidney, W. B. Griffiths,
K. F. Hartley, M. Henig, R. McBride, J. Tipper, R. S. O. Tomlin, R. G. Willis

*Principal illustrator*
G. Hodgson

OXBOW | books
Oxford & Philadelphia

# CONTENTS

## Volume 2

# PART 6

# THE FINDS

Many of the specialist reports were first written in the late 1980s and then revised, where necessary, in the late 1990s. Most have not been updated since. Occasionally extra finds not included in the original reports have turned up after further work on the collection (such as after the processing of the coarse wares) and these finds have been added to the original reports. These are indicated by (AC) after the entry. Some finds have been lost or have deteriorated since their recovery, and where possible these are illustrated by drawings based on the sketches in the original site finds books, although it should be noted these were not always drawn to scale and can only give an approximate idea of the object. The catalogue entries for the finds include, in order, location, period, context number, site small finds number, museum record number, and sometimes also accession number.

# 21. BUILDING MATERIAL

## by A. T. Croom

## Architectural fragments and other objects of stone

### Prehistoric (Fig. 21.01)

1. Cup marked stone (L:220mm W:210mm B:90mm). Unstratified, Site 18, 2640, WSS44.
Roughly triangular piece of sandstone with two cup marks on one surface. A portable example of rock art such as this may originally have been used in a burial cairn. Bronze Age.

### Sculpture (Figs 21.02–4)

2. Statue (L:130mm W:80mm B:90mm). L08:50, *Via principalis*, 2518, WSS1.
Incomplete head from a sandstone statue of a woman shown with her hair rolled back on either side of

Figure 21.01: Cup-marked stone. Scale 1:2.

her face wearing a helmet with a peaked front and a central plume. The statue was not large, probably only approximately 0.5m tall. This is most probably Minerva, although a relief from Birrens depicting a goddess with a number of Minerva's attributes was dedicated to Brigantia, the local regional deity (*CSIR I.6*, no. 12). Minerva was one of the three most important state gods, but she would also have appealed to soldiers in her role as goddess of war, and a fragment from a large statue of Minerva has been found to the west of the fort at Wallsend (*CSIR I.I*, no. 208).

3. Bas relief (L:320mm W:140mm B:120mm). Levelling between Buildings Q and R, late third/fourth century, F11:18, 1210, WSS2.
Rectangular sandstone block. Carved in relief on one of the wide surfaces with a T-shaped object below a pendant loop. On one of the adjoining faces is an incised fish.

4. Incised figure (L:370mm W:360mm B:75mm). Building 4, officer's quarters, Period 2, F04:07, WSS4. A large flat sandstone slab with a smooth upper surface, used as a flagstone. To one side is an incomplete incised line figure. It can be interpreted as a standing figure of man holding a long object, but while there are three lines on the right-hand side, all or some of which might be depicting an arm, there is only a single line on the left-hand side, and any head (now missing) was not shown attached to the 'body'. Very simple incised figures are known from a number of sites Roman, including, in the northern frontier zone, Great Chesters (*CSIR I.6*, nos 81, 360), Willowford (*ibid.*, no. 365), South Shields (unpublished, SF no. S407), Newcastle (Ross 1967, pl. 52a), and Maryport (*ibid.*, pl. 63c). On these examples, however, the figure tends to occupy the whole face of the stone, and the Wallsend example may be closer to

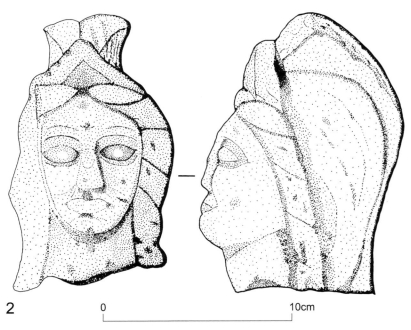

2

0           10cm

*Figure 21.02: Sculpture of female head. Scale 1:2.*

the hunting or gladiatorial scenes on the stones from Chesters (*CSIR I.6*, 401–3).

5. Phallic symbol (L:250mm W:160mm B:130mm). Road 3, K14:15, 1584, WSS21.
Sandstone block with incised phallic symbol, re-used in a road. On the opposite face there is an incised roughly rectangular shape, perhaps an abortive attempt at a second phallus.

### *Altar* (Fig. 21.04)

6. Altar (H:240mm W:290mm B:150mm). Building 3, south wall, Period 2, P08:11, 2515, WSS5.
Incomplete sandstone altar base, showing signs of burning, with a complete width or breadth of 290mm (both of the other measurements are incomplete). This was built into the wall of an Antonine building, and is therefore likely to be Hadrianic in date. The simple base with a moulding wider at the top than the bottom is also found on Antonine altars at Birrens (*CSIR I.4*, nos 3, 15).

### *Architectural* (Figs 21.05–6)

7. Bench leg (H:630mm W:440mm B:100mm). F09:55, Road 8, 2382, WSS40.
L-shaped sandstone seat support with concave mouldings on the front of the leg. Flat-topped examples were used as bench legs to support wooden or stone seats (Croom 2007, 112). They are frequently found in bath-houses as changing-rooms were often lined with benches as seating for bathers getting changed. This example is unusual in having an extension above the seat, which reduces the width of the support available for the seat by half. It may have been intended as a decorative feature for the end of a bench, or to act as a divider in the middle of a long bench.
Parallels (without extension): Mumrills: Macdonald and Curle 1929, 453 and fig. 11b;
Pentre Farm, Flint: J. Webster 1989, fig. 32, no. 4;
Chesters: *in situ* in bath-house

8. Latrine seat (L(surviving):660mm W:380mm D:120mm). Building 8, room 2, mid-third century?, WSS63.
Incomplete sandstone latrine seat with two key-hole shaped holes set *c.*480mm apart. The top surface is very smooth and slopes down towards the holes which are approximately 130mm in diameter. The interior face of the holes and the front face of the block are only roughly worked. Stone latrine seats, often in marble, were commonly used in Mediterranean-region large multi-seater public toilets, but they are rare in Britain. As stone seats would have been unpleasant to use much of the year (especially for sick patients in a hospital), wooden seating set on stone uprights usually seems to have been preferred. This example was found re-used in the latrine channel in the final phase of remodeling in the hospital, the stone seating of an earlier phase having apparently been replaced by wooden seating.

9. Guttering (L:630mm W:390mm B:190mm channel W:140mm). E08:50, Road 5, 2436, WSS30.
Large sandstone guttering block, tapering slightly to one end. Possibly originally from the headquarter's building.

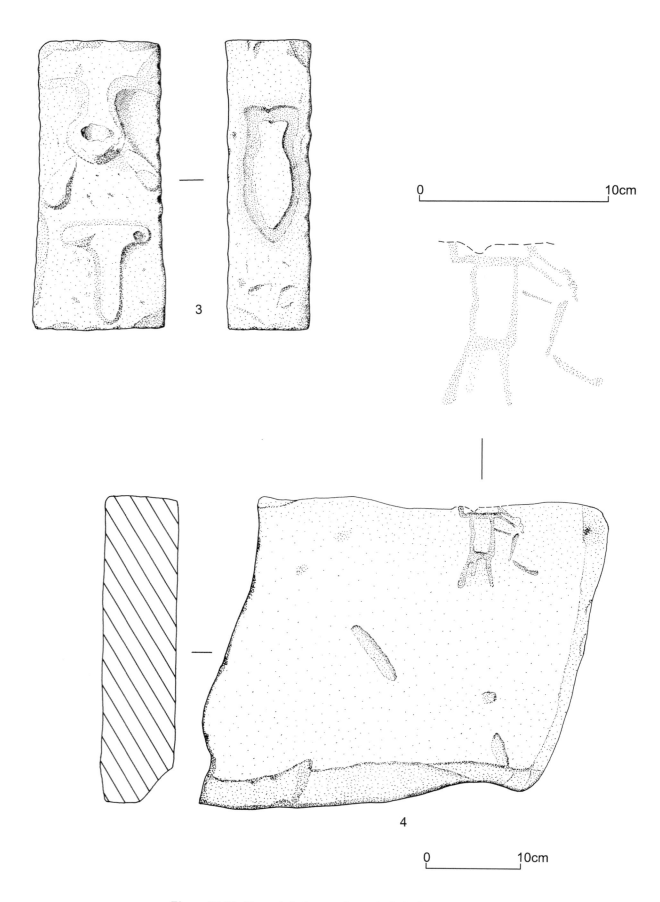

*Figure 21.03: Decorated stonework nos 3–4. Scale 1:4 and 1:2.*

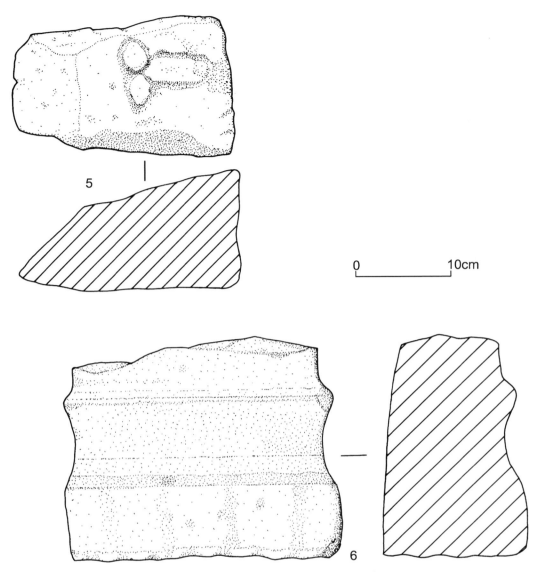

*Figure 21.04: Architectural stonework nos 5–6. Scale 1:4.*

10. Guttering (L:140mm W:190mm B:130mm channel W:90mm). Surface round Cistern 1, Period 2 or 3, E08:64, 2440, WSS24.
Small sandstone fragment, from a block with a narrower channel than no. 9 above.

The hospital has 14 surviving guttering stones *in situ*. These vary in length, but most are about 0.9–1.0m. The floor of the channel also varies in width from 60–100mm, but generally about 80mm. The guttering in the courtyard of the headquarter's building is generally in poor condition, but complete examples are longer (up to 1.5m) than those from the hospital, slightly wider, and with a much wider channel base (*c*.170mm).

11. Circular guttering (D:480mm overall L:630mm). *In situ*, hospital courtyard.
Two examples (out of a probable four) were uncovered *in situ* set in the corners of the courtyard of the

hospital. The circular basin itself is 360mm in diameter and 50mm deep, with a small, lower central section 200mm in diameter and 20mm deep. A channel leads off one side to connect to the stone guttering set round the edge of the courtyard. The circular basin would have collected rain water falling from the corner valleys of the portico roof and fed it into the guttering, although this is not a common feature of courtyard gutters (they were not, for example, used in the headquarter's building).

12. Block with clamp holes (L:570mm W:300mm B:180mm). L08:50, *Via principalis*, 2522, WSS39.
Large sandstone block with one surviving flat face, with clamp holes at either end. Block from a substantial building, re-used in a road surface.

13–15. Armchair voussoirs
Sandstone voussoirs, used in hollow roofing for a

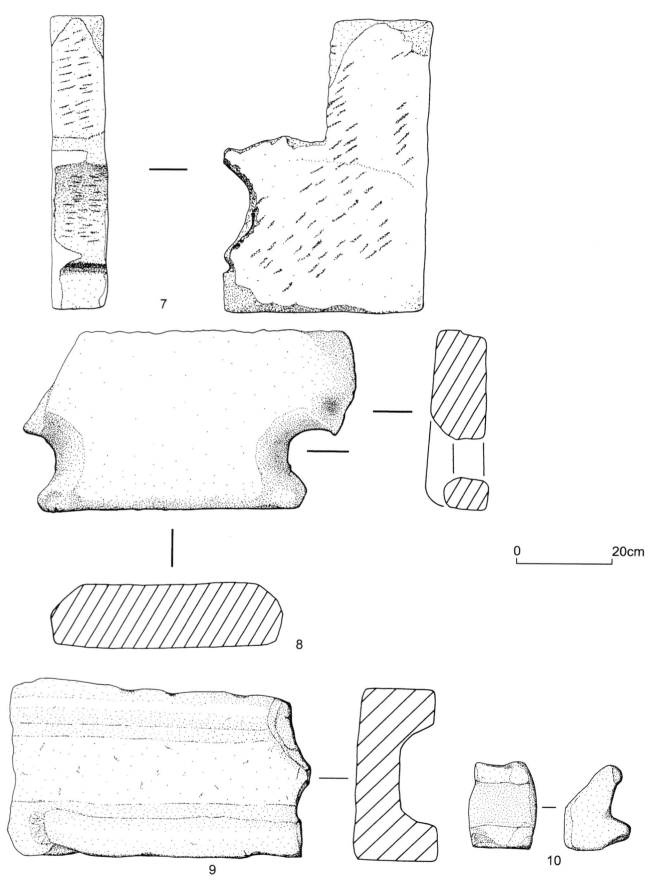

*Figure 21.05: Architectural stonework nos 7–10. Scale 1:8.*

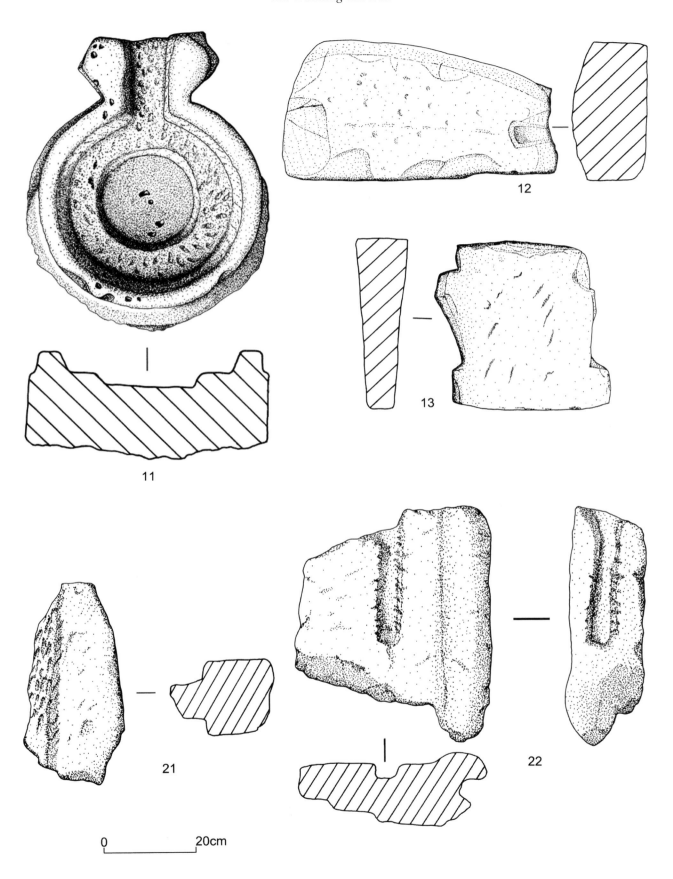

*Figure 21.06: Architectural stonework nos 11–22. Scale 1:8.*

bath-house. Other re-used debris from the bath-house found inside the fort includes a fragment from an inscription found near the *porta quintana* (Tomlin 2003, fig. 128), and possibly the bench leg (no. 7 above).

13. (L:390mm W: 350mm B:120mm). Building BK, mid-third century?, N13:04, 1915, WSS37.

14. (L:350mm W: 380mm B: 90mm). Unknown context, 1913, WSS36.

15. (L:380mm W: 290mm B: 70mm). Building BK, mid-third century? N13:04,1914, WSS45.

16–17. Roofing slates
Incomplete examples of sandstone slates.

16. (L:190mm W:180mm B:30mm). Unstratified, WSS14. With nail-hole.

17. (W:230mm B:45mm). Building 13, room 6, Period 4, H12:66, 1916, WSS42. With rounded lower edge.

18–20. Troughs

18. L:410mm W:180mm B:220mm depth:120mm). Lower fill of north-south drain in Alley 9, F10:29, 2282, WSS26. Incomplete.

19. (L:390mm W:300mm B:170mm depth:100mm). Area over *Via principalis*, unstratified, M08:01, 2381, WSS27. An almost complete small rectangular sandstone trough.

20. (L:280mm+ W:290mm B:190mm depth: 90mm). Unstratified, WSS28.

21. Screen (L:450mm W:220mm B:150mm). Area of Cistern 1, unstratified, E08:16, 2294, WSS31.
Fragment of fine sandstone block with a roughly worked tongue 60mm wide on one side. Probably from a flat panel used in a screen or water-tank.

22. Screen (L:540mm W:430mm B:170mm both slots W:50mm DT:30mm). Area of Building 14, unstratified, J12:04, 2469, WSS32.
Incomplete sandstone block with a groove cut into one face *c.*220mm from one edge. This edge has a thicker ridge running down its length, and a groove cut into its side. Both grooves are of the same dimensions, and presumably one of them belongs to some moderation or alteration of the structure.

23. Pier base (L:300mm W:330mm B:150mm). Granary, north west loading steps robber trench, G08:39, 2616, WSS38.
Weathered pier base, two sides surviving.

### *Other* (Figs 21.07–8)

24. Worked stone (L:370mm W:120mm B:27mm). Building 13, courtyard, Period 3–4, M11:08, 1918, WSS46.
Incomplete flat sandstone block with two projections on one side.

25. Panel and bas-relief (Panel L:800mm W:450mm). Building H, 941, J05:25.
An unusual combination of a stone panel and carved relief was found in the interior of Building H (the end contubernium of a third-century barrack), in or on a rough rubble 'surface' that could post-date the use of the building. The panel, which has been left *in situ*, was finished on three sides with a rounded moulding and a deep groove. The fourth side was cut straight, but roughly finished. In the centre of the top surface there was a depression about 150mm by 120mm. Found sitting within this, and of similar dimensions, was a stone with a bas-relief, which cannot now be located. It is a roughly rectangular block, which appears to show the defaced head and shoulders of a person.

## Ceramic building material

The assemblage as it now exists consists only of selected tile fragments, and although all the common tile types are represented, there is a heavy bias in favour of box tile fragments with their interesting keying patterns.

### *Fabrics*

The stamped tiles show that the collection includes tiles made by three different units. There are three tiles stamped by *Legio VI*, 16 stamps from *Cohors IIII Lingonum*, who garrisoned the fort from the 170s/180s through to the fourth century, and a single tile stamped by the *Ala I Asturum*, based at Benwell fort. There is little noticeable difference in the fabrics used by the different units, even though the *Cohors IIII Lingonum* tiles are the only ones likely to have been made in the vicinity of the fort, and the non-stamped tiles cannot be assigned to units.

### *Fabrics groups*

Fabric 1: orange fabric with mixed inclusions, most noticeably occasional rounded sandstone pieces, usually less than a centimetre across, but sometimes up to 20mm. A number are over-fired, with a wide grey core and occasionally purple/grey surfaces as well. Some examples have a thin red wash over the exterior surfaces. Used for all tile types. This is the most common fabric.

Fabric 2: This is fired to a cream colour. It has frequent small soft red inclusions, also seen in Fabric 1 but never so noticeable as in this fabric. Most frequently found as *imbrices*, but also used for *tegulae* (eg. an example from J10:45).

Fabric 3: A very fine, micaceous fabric, with few visible inclusions. Occasionally has a silky feel. Most frequently used for box tiles, but occasionally used for roof tiles as well. This fabric must come from a different source to that used for the other tile types, suggesting perhaps that the box tiles were imported ready-made.

## Quality

Many of the fragments give an impression of quite careless tile-making, with warped tiles, twisted flanges, uneven thicknesses and a variety of finishes. Colours range from cream, cream/pale orange, orange, red-washed and overfired to purple or grey. Although some of these (in particular the cream) may have been deliberately fired to produce those colours for use in patterned roofs, others give the impression of being purely accidental.

### Tegula (Fig. 21.09)

Dimensions of complete or near complete tiles (in mm)

| | L | W (top) | W (lower) | B | Details |
|---|---|---|---|---|---|
| 1. | 340 | 290 | 270 | 40–50 | Area over Building 14, post–Roman debris?, H10:32, WST1 |
| 2. | – | – | c. 300 | 40–50 | Building 14, water tank, fourth century?, J10:18, WST2 |
| 3. | – | 300 | – | | Tile drain south of Building 13, Period 4, L12:08 |

The complete tile from H10:32 is a good example of a poorly made tile (Fig. 21.09, no. 1). It is overfired to grey and warped to a height of 10mm so that it does not lie flat. The flange on one side varies from 20–35mm in thickness, and the nail hole is at least 50mm from the top edge. The height of the tile with the flange varies from 50mm on one side to 40mm on the other. All three of the tiles with surviving complete widths have a width of 300mm or less, which is at the lower end of tile size for *tegulae*. Other small examples come from Piddington villa, Dorchester, Caistor by Norwich and Silchester (Brodribb 1987, 12). As these are the only complete tiles from the site, it is impossible to determine whether all the *tegulae* were this size, or if by co-incidence the only surviving tiles are the smaller examples of tiles of graduated size (cf. Warry 2006, fig. 6.5).

#### Decoration

This consists of a large cross from edge to edge, each arm consisting of two+ finger grooves, found on tiles stamped by the *IIII Lingonum*. The cross, although common on square construction tiles, is rare on *tegulae*. There is no evidence for the use of the more common semi-circle on the lower edge. There are a few possible signatures, all of which are fragmentary.

There are a number of *tegulae* with very narrow

*Figure 21.07: Sculpture no. 25 in situ.*

*Figure 21.08: Sculpture no. 25.*

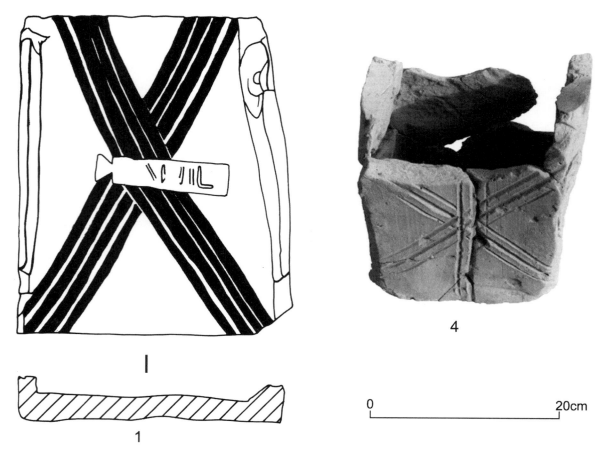

*Figure 21.09: Complete tegula, scale 1:4, and box tile, not to scale.*

flanges *c.*15mm thick, that are often also low in height (for example, 12mm tall: H05:12). The typical dimension of a flange on a normal tile is approximately 25mm wide with an overall height of flange and base of 40mm.

### FLANGES

On some examples the flanges are very roughly cut away at the top end of the tile, sometimes apparently done by hand rather than with the aid of a knife. The undercuts on the lower ends of the tile either extend up to top of flange (reducing the width of flange by half), or until only half way up (Warry 2006, fig. 1.2, types B and C).

## *Imbrices*

### DIMENSIONS

There are no surviving examples with complete width or length. The normal thickness is *c.*15mm, but there are a number of example of thicker ones, of *c.*20–5mm (Q04:02), which were possibly ridge tiles.

## *Box (Fig. 21.09)*

Dimensions of near complete tiles (in mm)

|     | L    | W      | B   | Details |
|-----|------|--------|-----|---------|
| 4.  | 200+ | 150    | 150 | Building 1, Period 3–4, M05:02 Height surviving to bottom of vent; star pattern with 3–toothed comb (Fig. 21.9, no. 4) |
| 5.  | –    | *c.*120 | –   | Area over Building 5 and Alley 4, unstratified, H05:01 |

There are a large number of box-tile sherds within the fort, found in all periods.

### SURFACE TREATMENT

The sherds show a range of different surface treatments for keying; from leaving the surface deliberately rough, incised lattice (Fabrics 1 and 3), comb, and one example of wavy finger grooves (M05:13). The combing takes the form of lattice, star, along the edges with a central cross, diagonal and wavy lines.

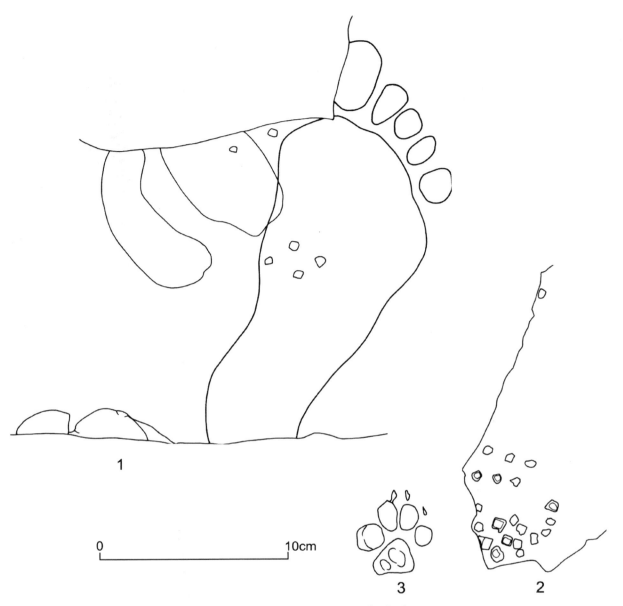

*Figure 21.10: Impressions on tile. Scale 1:2*

The combs can have up to seven teeth, but there is one example of a two-teethed comb lattice (E14:06). One fragment has keying on two adjoining sides, with spaced wavy finger decoration on one face, and incised lattice decoration on the other (F04:19).

VENTS
Both rectangular and with a curved edge (presumably circular, but there are no complete examples) have been found. Both types of vents are found in both Fabrics 1 and 3.

*Bricks*

Dimensions of complete or near complete tiles (in mm)

| | L | W | B | Details |
|---|---|---|---|---|
| 6. | 195 | 180 | 45 | Building AZ, Period 4, L13:42, WST6 |
| 7. | 250 | – | – | Structure C, Period 3–4, F05:24 |

The fragments divide into tiles of approximately 35, 45 and 60mm thick. Those that are *c.*35mm thick were probably mainly *bessales*, used to make tile underfloor piers, and the thicker fragments from larger tiles such as *pedales*. However, some examples vary quite

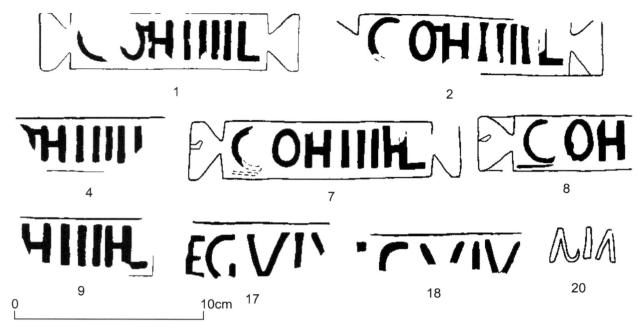

*Figure 21.11: Tile stamps. Scale 1:2.*

considerably in their thickness. Some are thicker towards the centre of the tile, such as one 45mm at the edge and 60mm towards the centre (P08:28), or one 35mm at the edge and 55mm in the centre (F05:24), while others the thickness at the edge of the tile changes along its length, such as one 40mm at a corner, and 60mm further along the edge (P08:28). The complete *bessalis* from L13:42 (cat. no. 6) has one corner 10mm shallower than the others.

Another unstratified tile, probably but not certainly Roman, is made in a quartz-rich red fabric, with a rough incised lattice on one surface. It is 85mm wide and 200mm long, breaking off at a point where it reaches a corner. The other end is bevelled (N05:16).

### Keying

One has a finger arc across one corner (45mm, P04:08), and another wavy finger line on one surface and knife-cut lattice on the underside (F04:19). There is at least one other example of a brick with incised lattice on the lower, sanded face (E14:01). These are possibly facing tiles of the type used to line walls.

## Impressions (Fig. 21.10)

Few of the surviving fragments have any impressions on them, but since the more 'interesting' tiles were kept, it is likely this reflects the true number from the site. Four of the impressions come from a single *tegula* (L12:08). There is a cow hoof-print, a possible dog, four hobnails (although it is unclear why only so few are visible) and a bare human foot-print (Fig. 21.10, no. 1). The foot-print is probably not complete, but the surviving length is 23cm long, suggesting an adult, probably male (allowing 10% for tile shrinkage during firing). There is a *bessalis* with an incomplete impression of a hobnailed sole (Fig. 21.10, no. 2: M05:11) and a *tegula* with a dog's paw print (Fig. 21.10, no. 3: H15:12).

## Stamped tiles (Fig. 21.11)

Wallsend has produced a total of 24 stamped tiles from inside the fort (21 from the 1975–84 excavations and three examples from the 1987–8 excavations), and six from outside the fort. The collection includes both legionary and auxiliary stamps.

### Cohors IIII Lingonum

There are 16 examples from these excavations, another three from the later excavations (McBride 2003, 189), as well as one certain and two possible examples from outside the fort. Most of these stamps came from *tegulae*, with no examples at all on *imbrices*. There is one stamp on a *bessalis* (the complete tile surviving, 40mm thick) and another also probably on a *bessalis* (the fragment is overfired and uneven, 34–9mm thick). Stamps on *bessales* are generally rare (Brodribb 1987, 35).

Two different dies were used although the shape, size and spacing of the letters are very similar. The stamps measure approximately 145mm by 30mm.

Die 1 (*RIBII* 2476.1) has a line connecting the 0 and H of COH. There are five certain and one probable example of this die, all on *tegulae*. Two are overfired and are purple/brown in colour through-out.

Die 2 (*RIBII* 2476.2) has a line connecting the last I of IIII and the L. This die also has a final mark,

*Table 21.01: Stamped tiles*

| Die | Cat | Type | context and period |
|---|---|---|---|
| *Cohors IIII Lingones* | | | |
| 1 | 1 | T | *RIBII* 2476.1. Area over Building 14, unstratified, H10:32, WST1 |
| | 2 | T | *RIBII* 2476.1. Building 14, water tank, fourth century?, J10:18, WST2 |
| | 3 | T? | Building 14, courtyard, late third/early fourth century, J10:02, WST3 |
| | 4 | T | Area over Building 14 and Road 3, unstratified, K12:01, WST4 |
| | 5 | T | Area over Building 13, unstratified, M11:01, WST5 |
| ?1 | 6 | T | Area over Building 8, unstratified, E12:01, WST10 |
| 2 | 7 | B | Building AZ, Period 4, L13:42, WST6 |
| | 8 | T | Area over Road 3, unstratified, M13:15, WST7 |
| | 9 | T | Area over Building 7, unstratified, G10:11, WST8 |
| | 10 | B? | Area over Building 14 and Road 3, unstratified, K12:01, WST9 |
| ?2 | 11 | T | Building 14, water tank, fourth century?, J10:18, WST11 |
| | 12 | T | *RIBII* 2476.2. Area over Building 13 and Alley 7, unstratified, L10:01, WST12 |
| Un | 13 | T | Building 14, water tank, fourth century?, J10:18, WST13 |
| | 14 | T | Building 14, water tank, fourth century?, J10:18, WST14 |
| | 15 | T | Building 14, water tank, fourth century?, J10:18, WST15 |
| | 16 | T | Area over Building 16 and Road 1, unstratified, N08:01, WST16 |
| *Legio VI Victrix* | | | |
| | 17 | T | Building 13, east hypocaust, mid-third century, M12:17, WST17 |
| | 18 | I | Area over Building 2 and Alley 1, post-Roman dereliction, M05:04, WST18 |
| | 19 | I | Area over Building 12, unstratified, L14:01, WST19 |
| *Ala I Asturum* | | | |
| | 20 | T | Area over Building 2 and Alley 1, unstratified, M05:01, WST20 |
| Unclear | | | |
| | 21 | T | Building 14, water tank, fourth century?, J10:18, SF no. 1960, lost |

Key
B       *bessalis*
I       *imbrex*
T       *tegula*
Un      unidentified

probably a peg-mark, on the left-hand end, while the clearest impression of this die also has a line, presumably accidental, under the C. This feature may well also appear on Die 1 stamps but there are few good impressions of this end of Die 1 stamps. There are four certain examples of Die 2 stamps, and two further possible examples. One of the stamps is on a *bessalis*, and a second fragment that may possibly come from a *bessalis* is overfired like the two Die 1 examples.

There are a further four incomplete or faint stamps which cannot be assigned to either die with certainty.

Five of the *tegula* fragments with stamps include an end or edge to the tile, and in general the stamps appear to have been placed parallel to the end. There is one example of a complete *tegula*, and almost half of a second one, with Die 1 stamps; both have a cross of grooves made by the fingertips with the stamps about half way up the tile (*c*.160mm from the lower edge) and upside down in relation to the tile. A Die 2 stamp in a similar position was the other way up, but whether the position of these stamps is significant cannot be shown from such a small sample.

LEGIO VI VICTRIX
The 1975–84 excavations produced three fragmentary *Legio VI* tiles, and a further two examples have been found in excavations outside the fort. They are all on *imbrices* except for one example. The exception is the most complete of the stamps, and can be identified as an example of *RIBII* 2460.50. There is one stamp of an unknown die, and two too fragmentary for identification.

ALA I ASTURUM
There is one example of this stamp on a *tegula*, identified as having been produced by a metal die in incuse letters without a frame (*RIBII* 2464). Almost 70 examples of this have been recovered from Benwell Roman Fort, where *Ala I Hispanorum Asturum* was in garrison in the third century.

*Dating*
Only nine of these tiles are unstratified, and six of these came from a single context, the fill of the water-tank of Building 14 (fourth century?). Another came from the same courtyard, and the remaining two

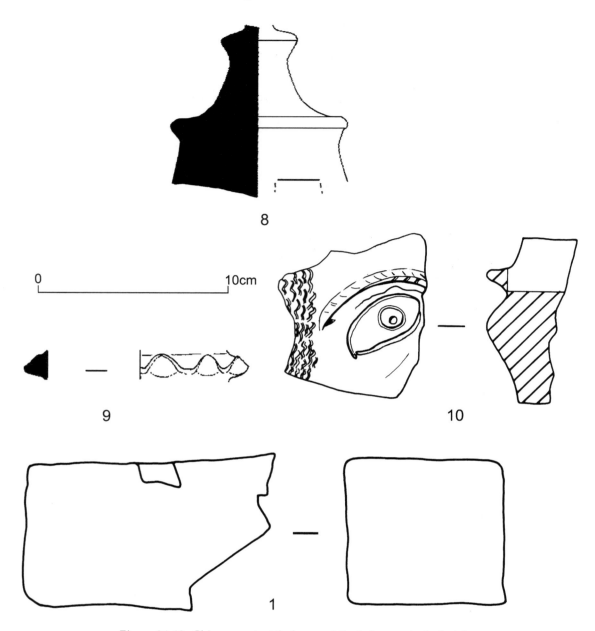

*Figure 21.12: Chimney pots, tile face, and fired clay no. 1. Scale 1.2*

came from the backfill of the hypocaust in Building 13 (mid-third century), and re-used in a possible hearth in Building AZ (Period 4).

### Chimney pots (Fig. 21.12)

8. Terminal. Area of Road 3 and Building 12, unstratified, N14:01, WST28
Sherd from near the pot of the chimney pot, missing the very top of the terminal. The body expands into a ridge which is very battered, but appears to be plain. There are traces of two vents.

9. Body sherd. Alley 8, H11:36, WST25
An applied ridge with pie-crust decoration which has separated from the body of the pot.

Only two fragments of chimney pot have been recovered from the entire site, in contrast to the many fragments known from South Shields Fort (Bidwell and Speak 1994, fig. 5.11).

### Face (Fig. 21.12)

10. Area over Building 14 and Road 3, unstratified, J12:01, 2077, WST24
The tile assemblage also included a fragment of tile with elaborate applied decoration. The decoration consists of a human face, although only a projecting eye and eye-brow survive. The shape of the eye, the iris and pupil, and the hairs on the eyebrow are all picked out in incised lines. The hair on the side of the head is shown as a series of interconnecting Ss,

drawn using a split stick. The tile is slightly curved and sanded on the interior surface, with finger grooves smoothing over a join in the clay behind the eye. Above the level of the eyebrow the join was either less well keyed and the clay has split along the join, or else there was an opening in the centre of the forehead and this section is the edge of the opening. Too little of the tile survives to be certain of its original use. Antefixes, which normally have moulded rather than applied decoration, are rare in Britain, and are usually associated with the legions. It is thought that the antefixes may have been used only on the corners of roofs or on ridge-ends rather than in the Mediterranean fashion at the ends of each run of *imbrices*, and it is possible this hand-made version was intended as a similar architectural detail. Just such an individual approach to roof decoration was found at the fortress at Lauriacum, where a crude face was applied to a crescent-shaped piece of tile that was perhaps designed to fit over the roof-ridge (Braithwaite 2007, fig. S12 and pl. S27). The Wallsend piece is unstratified, but comes from an area covering a section of road 3 and the back range of the Headquarters building.

### Discussion

Tile-making near the fort would have been inter-mittent, being set up only when major changes were intended within the fort and new supplies were needed (Frere and Tomlin 1992, 196). The presence of tiles stamped by *Legio VI* and *Ala I Asturum* could therefore reflect batches of tile being brought in from elsewhere when small-scale repairs were required during those periods when the kilns were not in production and any stock-piled spares had been used up. At least one of the legionary stamps is a type that has also been found at Catterick, Corbridge, Ebchester, Netherby and Vindolanda but not at York, implying a tilery set up somewhere in the region of the Wall. The *Ala I Asturum* stamp suggests another shipment also came from Benwell sometime in the third century. However, it has also been suggested that in the late Roman period complete tiles from sites were salvaged and redistributed over long distances, perhaps after local tile-making had come to an end (Caruana 1997, 268), in which case the *Legio VI* and *Ala I Asturum* tiles may have been part of less formal shipments to the site.

The number of complete tiles at Wallsend is small and their date of production is unknown, so it is difficult to say whether those that survive are typical examples, but it is of interest that they are unlike those made at the nearby forts at South Shields and Newcastle. The Wallsend *tegulae* made by the *Cohors IIII Lingonum* are smaller in size and make use of a different type of decoration that has no immediate parallels. It seems that the tile-makers at Wallsend were allowed to follow a slightly different tradition of tile-making, and were apparently not obliged, or trained, to make a standard product.

## Other building material

### Fired clay (Fig. 21.12)

1. Support (L:130mm+ W:80mm B:70mm, expanding to 80mm). F09:66, post setting related to Building AP, SF 2481, WSIM36
Incomplete rectangular block of fired clay, tapering slightly. Roughly made with grass impressions on the surfaces and a patchy and uneven colouring; along the edge of one side there is an inscribed alphabet (Graffito no. 29). The appearance of the clay is very similar to the fragments of burnt daub from the site, and some pieces which have identified as daub but which have apparently straight external edges may come from similar blocks. Tapering rectangular blocks were used to support the containers used in salt production over the source of heat (Morris 2007, fig. 5, no. 17), but similar supports were probably used elsewhere round hearths for other industrial or domestic purposes.

### Burnt daub

Fragments of burnt daub were recovered during the excavations but little was retained for study.

### Opus signinum

The fragments that survive come from a number of different mixes, including pieces with coarse tile fragments as well as upper layers with a pink colouration and finely crushed tile inclusions. The largest surviving assemblage comes from Building 13, the commanding officer's house (M12:07) and contains at least four different types of *opus signinum*. A fragment with very fine tile inclusions recovered from the robbing of the granary has a convex surface and is likely to come from a quarter-round moulding between floor and wall (G09:07).

### Painted plaster

Very little painted plaster has survived. The painted plaster found in room e of Building 14 is very fragmentary, with the largest piece only about 20mm long. Pieces show traces of red, black and grey paint, and black alongside red. Some seem to have been over-painted with white (K12:32). Better preserved pieces of plaster from the drain south of the building, the majority of which show a red zone or band over white probably come from the same room (H12:09, associated with late third century or later pottery).

# 22. THE POTTERY

## by B. Dickinson, A. T. Croom, K. F. Hartley and R. McBride

The pottery from Wallsend shows that the site had the same sources of supply as the forts at South Shields, Newcastle and Benwell, but is of particular interest in having some large early assemblages, such as those from Alley 1 and the possible Rampart building, that are absent from the other three forts. This report looks at these, and a number of other assemblages of interest in detail. It does not, however, include a detailed discussion of the overall supply of pottery to the site, as this will be addressed in a later overview of all the Lower Tyne Valley sites. As with the other finds reports (see p 1), most of the pottery was catalogued and studied some years ago, resulting in the lack, in places, of the full quantification now expected (such as the lack of sherd count in the coarse wares), and the absence of the most up-to-date references or parallels.

## The samian ware
*by B. Dickinson*

*Table 22.01: Quantification of the samian by phase*

**South Gaul**

| | PERIOD | | | | | | |
| | 2 | 3 | 4 | mC3+ | post R | uncert | TOTAL |
|---|---|---|---|---|---|---|---|
| FORM | | | | | | | |
| 15/17 or 18 | 1 | – | – | – | – | – | 1 |
| 18 or 18/31 | – | – | – | – | – | 1 | 1 |
| 18R | – | – | 1 | – | – | – | 1 |
| 18/31 | 1 | – | – | 1 | – | – | 2 |
| 18/31R | – | – | 1 | – | – | – | 1 |
| 33 | – | – | – | 1 | – | – | 1 |
| 37 | 3 | – | 1 | – | – | – | 4 |
| Jar | – | 1 | – | – | – | – | 1 |
| Total | 5 | 1 | 3 | 2 | – | 1 | 12 |

**Central Gaul (Les Martres-de-Veyre)**

| | PERIOD | | | | | | |
| | 2 | 3 | 4 | mC3+ | post R | uncert | TOTAL |
|---|---|---|---|---|---|---|---|
| FORM | | | | | | | |
| 18/31 | 4 | 4 | 2 | – | 3 | 4 | 17 |
| 18/31 or 31 | – | – | – | 1 | – | – | 1 |
| 27 | – | – | – | – | – | 1 | 1 |
| 30 or 37 | 1 | – | – | – | – | – | 1 |
| 31 | – | – | 1 | – | – | – | 1 |
| 33 | – | – | 1 | – | – | – | 1 |
| 37 | 1 | – | – | 2 | – | – | 3 |

| | | | | | | | |
|---|---|---|---|---|---|---|---|
| Bowl | – | – | 1 | – | – | – | 1 |
| Dish or bowl | 1 | – | – | 1 | – | 1 | 3 |
| Cup | – | – | 1 | – | – | – | 1 |
| Total | 7 | 4 | 6 | 4 | 3 | 6 | 30 |

### Central Gaul (Lezoux)

| | PERIOD | | | | | | |
|---|---|---|---|---|---|---|---|
| | *2* | *3* | *4* | *mC3+* | *post R* | *uncert* | *TOTAL* |
| FORM | | | | | | | |
| 18/31 | 5 | 7 | 9 | 7 | | 4 | 32 |
| 18/31 or 31 | 7 | 12 | 9 | 14 | | 12 | 54 |
| 18/31-31 | – | – | – | 1 | – | – | 1 |
| 18/31R | 2 | 3 | 10 | 2 | 3 | 5 | 25 |
| 18/31R or 31R | 1 | – | 4 | 2 | | 4 | 11 |
| 18/31R-31R | 1 | – | – | 2 | – | 1 | 4 |
| 27 | 1 | 3 | 3 | 3 | – | 4 | 14 |
| 30 | 2 | – | 4 | – | – | 2 | 8 |
| 30 or 37 | 4 | 4 | 7 | 8 | 3 | 7 | 33 |
| 31 | 11 | 2 | 47 | 34 | 9 | 37 | 140 |
| 31R | 3 | 8 | 29 | 17 | 1 | 27 | 85 |
| 33a | 1 | – | – | – | – | – | 1 |
| 33 | 12 | 5 | 35 | 19 | 9 | 27 | 107 |
| 35 | – | 1 | – | 1 | – | – | 2 |
| 36 | 1 | 3 | 7 | 5 | | 1 | 17 |
| 37 | 14 | 14 | 39 | 34 | 4 | 30 | 135 |
| 38 | 1 | 1 | 2 | 4 | – | 4 | 12 |
| 38 or 44 | 1 | 2 | 1 | 4 | 1 | | 9 |
| 45 | – | – | 1 | 2 | 1 | 3 | 7 |
| 46 | – | – | 2 | – | – | – | 2 |
| 68? | – | 1 | – | – | – | – | 1 |
| 79 | – | – | 2 | 2 | 1 | 1 | 6 |
| 79 or Tg | – | – | 1 | – | 1 | – | 2 |
| 80 | – | – | 2 | – | – | – | 2 |
| 81 | – | 2 | 1 | – | 1 | 1 | 5 |
| Curle 11 | 1 | – | 2 | – | – | – | 3 |
| Curle 15 or 23 | – | 2 | 4 | 5 | – | 1 | 12 |
| Curle 21 | 1 | – | 2 | 1 | – | 3 | 7 |
| Curle 23 | – | – | – | 1 | – | – | 1 |
| Dish | 4 | 4 | 10 | 15 | 1 | 7 | 41 |
| Dish or bowl | 4 | 3 | – | 13 | 7 | 10 | 37 |
| Bowl | 1 | – | 3 | 2 | – | 1 | 7 |
| Cup | – | 1 | 2 | – | 1 | 2 | 6 |
| GSM | – | – | 1 | 3 | – | 2 | 6 |
| Jar | – | – | 1 | 2 | – | – | 3 |
| Enclosed | – | – | 1 | – | – | – | 1 |
| Total | 78 | 77 | 242 | 203 | 43 | 196 | 839 |

### East Gaul[1]

| | PERIOD | | | | | | |
|---|---|---|---|---|---|---|---|
| | *2* | *3* | *4* | *5* | *post R* | *uncert* | *TOTAL* |
| FORM | | | | | | | |
| 18/31 | – | 2 | 1 | – | – | – | 3 |
| 18/31 or 31 | 2 | – | 1 | – | – | – | 3 |
| 18/31R | 2 | – | – | – | 1 | 1 | 4 |
| 18/31R or 31R | – | – | 1 | – | – | – | 1 |
| 27 | – | – | 1 | – | – | 1 | 2 |
| 30 or 37 | – | – | 2 | 2 | – | 4 | 8 |

|  |  |  |  |  |  |  | Total |
|---|---|---|---|---|---|---|---|
| 31 | 2 | 1 | – | 2 | 2 | 4 | 11 |
| 31 or 31R | 1 | 1 | 1 | – | – | – | 3 |
| 31R | 4 | 2 | 10 | 4 | 3 | 4 | 27 |
| 32 | – | 1 | 1 | 1 | – | – | 3 |
| 32 etc. | 2 | – | – | 2 | – | – | 4 |
| 33 | – | – | 3 | 4 | – | 5 | 12 |
| 36 | – | – | 2 | – | 1 | – | 3 |
| 37 | – | 2 | 18 | 9 | 5 | 4 | 38 |
| 38 | 1 | 1 | – | 1 | – | – | 3 |
| 38 or 44 | – | – | 1 | – | – | – | 1 |
| 40 | 1 | – | – | – | – | – | 1 |
| 40? | – | – | 1 | – | – | – | 1 |
| 45 | – | – | 4 | – | – | 2 | 6 |
| 79R or TgR | – | – | – | 1 | – | – | 1 |
| Curle 15 | – | – | – | – | – | 1 | 1 |
| Curle 21 | – | – | 1 | – | – | – | 1 |
| Dish | 1 | – | 2 | 2 | 1 | 1 | 7 |
| Dish R | – | – | 1 | – | – | 1 | 2 |
| Dish or bowl | – | 1 | 4 | 6 | 1 | 3 | 15 |
| Bowl | – | – | 1 | – | – | – | 1 |
| GSM | 1 | – | – | 1 | – | – | 2 |
| Total | 17 | 11 | 55 | 35 | 14 | 31 | 164 |

[1.]Comprises: Argonne (8); Chémery-Faulquemont? (1); La Madeleine (22); Rheinzabern (66); Trier (16); East Gaul unassigned (52).
GSM = Gritted samian mortarium

When this report was written in the early 1990s, only the stratified contexts were quantified. Consequently, the forms which occurred in unstratified groups were counted as single examples within their groups. The phasing also represents that known at the time, and does not take into account later modifications

## Introduction
### by A.T. Croom

The site produced 50.807kg of samian, over half of which was unstratified, consisting of 4789 sherds from 1045 vessels.

*Table 22.02: Samian sources shown as percentages of vessel numbers*

| Source | 1975–84 | +1997–8 |
|---|---|---|
| South Gaulish | 1.1 | 0.9 |
| Central Gaulish (Les Martres) | 2.9 | 2.5 |
| Central Gaulish (Lezoux) | 80.3 | 82.7 |
| Central Gaulish (Vichy) | – | 0.3 |
| East Gaulish | 15.7 | 13.6 |
| Total | 1045 | 1443 |

The second column relates to the pottery recovered 1975–84, while the third column also includes both the 1975–84 samian and the samian recovered during the 1997–8 excavations

There were at least 50 sherds of South Gaulish samian, mainly of Flavian or Flavian-Trajanic date, but with two Flavian survivals (cat nos D64, D91). Most of the vessels were bowls or dishes, but there were also sherds from cups and jars, and a single sherd from an inkwell (K12:01). This was unstratified, but came from above or near the back range of the headquarters building. The type is most often associated with military sites, and has occasionally been found from the area of the *principia* of other forts (Willis 2005, 108; 110).

The majority of the samian came from Central Gaul, with over 80% coming from Lezoux. Almost 50% of the Central Gaulish decorated ware dates to the late Antonine period.

The major supplier of East Gaulish samian is Rheinzabern, with small quantities from other sources. The high proportion of East Gaulish ware (15.7%) is typical of sites on Hadrian's Wall; at South Shields Roman Fort, the average from excavations inside the fort and from the *vicus* is approximately 15%, while at Newcastle Roman Fort (constructed in the late second or early third century) it makes up 20% of the samian (Dickinson 2002, 147). A number of sherds, including those from vessels in the style of Iulius viii, indicate samian was still arriving at the site in the third century (cat. no. D93; cf. D114).

The proportion of decorated ware in the assemblage

Table 22.03: Samian vessel types, shown as percentages of vessel numbers

| Type | % |
|---|---|
| Cup | 14.5 |
| Beaker | 0.6 |
| Dish | 50.8 |
| Decorated bowl | 22.0 |
| Plain bowl | 4.0 |
| Mortarium | 2.8 |
| Inkwell | 0.1 |
| Unknown | 5.3 |
| Total | 1046 |

Table 22.04: Samian vessel types, shown as percentages of EVEs

| Type | % | Total | Typical %* |
|---|---|---|---|
| Cup | | 30.0 | 25.6 |
| 27 | 3.1 | | |
| 33 | 26.0 | | |
| 40 | 0.1 | | |
| 80 | 0.8 | | |
| Dish/platter | | 48.5 | 39.8 |
| 18/31 | 9.0 | | |
| 18/31 or 31 | 6.4 | | |
| 18/31R | 2.3 | | |
| 18/31R or 31R | 0.3 | | |
| 31 | 21.5 | | |
| 31R | 8.8 | | |
| Curle 15 | 0.2 | | |
| Decorated bowl | | 15.8 | 27.1 |
| 30 | 0.6 | | |
| 30 or 37 | 6.2 | | |
| 37 | 9.0 | | |
| Plain bowl | | 1.4 | 3.7 |
| 36 | 0.3 | | |
| 38 | 0.4 | | |
| 38 or 44 | 0.6 | | |
| 44 | 0.1 | | |
| Mortarium | | 2.3 | 0.1 |
| 45 | 2.2 | | |
| Curle 21 | 0.1 | | |
| Bowl/dish | | 1.8 | |
| Total | 6220 | | |

* by vessel number: Willis 2005, table 45

Table 22.05: Dated samian, shown as a percentage

| | Wt (kg) | Sh | EVE (%) |
|---|---|---|---|
| Pre-Hadrianic | 1.9 | 2.8 | 3.0 |
| Trajanic-Hadrianic | 0.8 | 1.2 | 1.3 |
| Hadrianic | 7.4 | 6.1 | 8.3 |
| Hadrianic-early Antonine | 9.9 | 9.6 | 9.6 |
| Hadrianic-Antonine | 15.4 | 20.6 | 14.8 |
| Antonine | 22.8 | 26.4 | 34.2 |
| Early Antonine | 0.2 | 0.3 | |
| Mid to late Antonine | 25.6 | 19.7 | 20.6 |
| Late Antonine | 9.7 | 6.6 | 2.8 |
| Late second century/third century | 6.3 | 6.6 | 5.4 |
| | 38.853 | 3453 | 5186 |

## Decorated ware (Figs 22.01–7)

D1.   Form 37, Central Gaulish. The mould is probably by Rogers's X–9, one of the potters at Les Martres-de-Veyre who supplied Medetus, but the bowl itself is in Lezoux fabric. A panel or upper zone contains a spiral in a double festoon. The rosette-tongued ovolo is probably Rogers B38. Hadrianic (area over west fort wall and gateway, unstratified, D08:11, 2253). (Not illustrated.)

D2.   Form 37, Central Gaulish. The ovolo (probably Rogers B155) and arcade are on a stamped bowl of Severus iv from York (S. & S., pl. 128, 1, but supported by caryatids, instead of columns), and the astragalus at the top corner of the panel is on a bowl in his style from Verulamium. However, the zig-zag borders (Rogers A26) are more typical of Servus iv (S. & S.'s Servus 2), whose style is close to that of Severus. The Pan (D.412 = O.710) is on a bowl in his style from Lauriacum (Karnitsch 1955, Taf. 7, 6). A range c.AD160–200 would fit either potter (area of Building 8 and *Via quintana*, unstratified, D12:01).

D3.   Form 37, East Gaulish, with ovolo (Ricken-Fischer, E11) and rosette (*ibid.*, O38a) used at Rheinzabern by Cerialis v. c. AD160–190 (Building N, D12:08). (Not illustrated.)

D4.   Form 37, Central Gaulish. The ovolo (Rogers 208), large beads and Bacchus (O.768) were all used by Casurius ii, but the astragali across the borders and inaccurately placed at the top are more typical of Docilis i, who also used the ovolo. Nevertheless, the bowl is more likely to be by Casurius. c.AD 160–190 (Chalet 9, Building W, D13:55; joining D13:03 (area over Building 9, unstratified)).

D5.   Form 37, East Gaulish, with mould-stamp of Belsus of Rheinzabern ([BE]LSVSF retr., see no. S16 below). The scroll has a striated double medallion (a more complete version of Ricken-Fischer, KB136), leaf (*ibid.*, P61) and bird (*ibid.*, T250) in the upper concavity and the same medallion in the lower concavity. c.AD175–200 (area over Building 10, unstratified, D14:01).

(22% by vessel numbers, 16% by EVEs) is not as high as the average for military sites as noted by Willis (2005, table 45), but it is very similar to the decorated ware from the *vicus* at South Shields Roman fort at 18% and from the fort at Newcastle at 17% (Wild 2010, 89–90, 94; Dickinson 2002, tables 15.2–3).

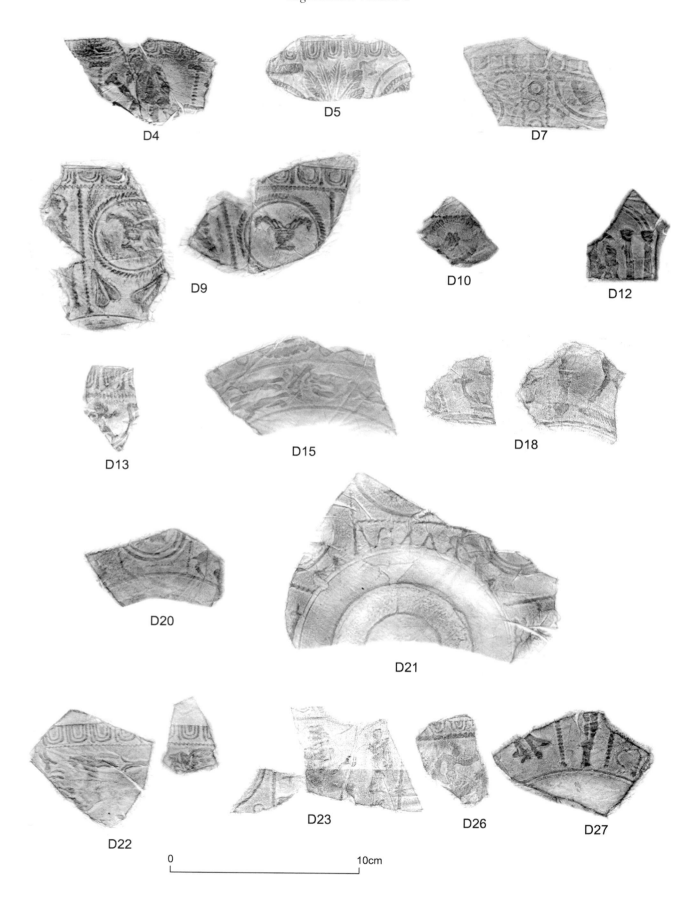

*Figure 22.01: Decorated samian nos D4–D27. Scale 1:2.*

D6. Form 37, Central Gaulish. The rosette-tongued ovolo was used at Lezoux by Sacer i. Both zones of decoration contain chevron festoons (Rogers F60), with small masks between them in the upper zone and rosette tassels (Rogers C25) in the lower. Two festoons in the lower zone have the same kneeling horse and another has a hare (O.2061?). A stamped bowl of Sacer from Dragonby, Lincs, is almost certainly from the same mould (Dickinson 1996, 594, 1542–3). *c.* AD125–145 (area over *intervallum* road (Road 4), unstratified, E04:01, with a sherd from the soil layer west of Building 18, *contubernium* 1, Period 3–4, F05:08 and from Building 5, F05:31). (Not illustrated.)

D7. Form 37, Central Gaulish, with panels: 1) a single medallion, ring and astragali. 2) A vertical series of rings. 3) A bird to left, looking back, and small beaded ring (Rogers C120) in a single festoon, over an astragalus. The ovolo (Rogers B247), zig-zag borders, both types of ring and random astragali are all on a bowl in the style of Tetturo in a pit of *c.*AD150–160 at Alcester (Hartley, Pengelly and Dickinson 1994, fig. 50, 275). The rings and borders are on a signed bowl from Corbridge (S. & S., pl. 131, 3). *c.*AD130–160 (Area over *intervallum* road (Road 5), E04:01 (with F05:02, area over Alley 4, unstratified).

D8. Form 37, East Gaulish. The ovolo is on a stamped bowl of Satto ii from Chémery-Faulquemont (Delort 1953, pl. 45, 9322). Here it has a straight line below, instead of beads. Hadrianic? (area over Road 5 and Building 5, unstratified, E04:07). (Not illustrated.)

D9. Form 37, Central Gaulish. The ovolo (Rogers B223, or a version of it) was used at Lezoux by Casurius ii. The panels include: 1) a caryatid (D.657 = O.1206). 2) A medallion (Rogers E25), containing an acanthus in a cup (similar to Rogers K3), over heart-shaped leaves (Rogers J56 variant). The caryatid and acanthus are on a stamped bowl of Casurius from Wels (Karnitsch 1955, Taf. 7, 4). For the medallion and leaf, cf. a bowl from Leicester (S. & S., pl. 133, 17). *c.* AD160–190 (area over Road 5 and Building 5, unstratified, E04:07, with sherd from area over Alley 4, unstratified, F05:02).

D10. Form 37, Central Gaulish, with a six-petalled rosette (Rogers C30) in a medallion with looped border (a fuller version of Rogers F74?). Acaunissa used the rosette, but is not known to have used the medallion. The fabric and glaze suggest Hadrianic or early-Antonine date. The bowl is unusually thick for its size (area over Alley 4, unstratified, E05:01).

D11. Form 37, East Gaulish. The ovolo (Ricken 1934, Taf. VII, B), used at La Madeleine, has a double groove above and a bead-row below. *c.*AD130–160 (area over Road 1, unstratified, E07:03, 2291). (Not illustrated.)

D12. Form 37, probably Central Gaulish. An arcade with fluted columns contains an identical column and a figure or figures. Not closely datable, in the absence of parallels, but probably Hadrianic or early-Antonine (area over Road 8, unstratified, E08:01, 2227).

D13. Form 30, Central Gaulish. The ovolo (Rogers B161),

festoon with beaded outer border (Rogers E8, in partial impression) and Cupid (O.440 variant) were all used by Do(v)eccus i. Cf. a stamped bowl from Silchester (S. & S., pl. 148, 14). *c.*AD165–200 (rerouted *Via principalis*, E08:13, 2275, with two sherds in E09:13, area over Road 8, unstratified).

D14. Form 37, Central Gaulish, with plainware stamp of Reginus iv on the rim (see S84 below), and an ovolo used at Lezoux by Advocisus and some of his associates (Rogers B103). *c.*AD160–180 (area over Cistern 1, unstratified E08:20, 2295).

D15. Form 37, Central Gaulish, with a leafy festoon (Rogers F16), rings and perhaps a figure in the upper zone, and a pair of dogs (not in D. or O.), a snake on rock (probably a double impression of D.960 bis = O.2155) and a bear (D.818 bis = O.1616) in the lower zone. There are no close parallels for the decoration as a whole, but Attianus ii used the bear and snake and the festoon is on an unprovenanced bowl in his style in the British Museum (M1347). The bowl could almost equally well be by his associate Martio i, who favoured hunting scenes and is known to have used the snake *c.*AD125–145 (Cistern 1, fill, E08:29, 2359).

D16. Form 37, Central Gaulish, with panels: 1) a seated Bacchus (D.534a = 0.571) in a double medallion and astragali in corners. 2) A tier of cups (Rogers Q27). The medallion, cups and astragalus were commonly used by Cinnamus ii. The Bacchus is less usual for him, though it occurs on one of his earlier bowls with a small label-stamp, from Colchester. *c.*AD140–170 (Cistern 1, fill, E08:29, 2344). (Not illustrated.)

D17. Form 37, Central Gaulish, in the style of Advocisus. The panels include: 1) a Pudicitia (D.548 = O.935). 2) A leaf (Rogers J49). 3) A double medallion over trifid motifs (Rogers G70), impressed stem-to-stem. This may well be from the same mould as a bowl from Silchester (S. & S., pl. 112, 6). *c.*AD160–190 (rubble round Cistern 1, E08:30, 2298). (Not illustrated.)

D18. Form 37, Central Gaulish. A panel contains a Pan (D.412 = 0.710) over a large striated spindle, with a caryatid (D.656 = O.1199) on the left and perhaps also on the right. Another panel shows the caryatid at the right with a sea-bull over the partly-impressed spindle. The Pan, sea-bull and spindle are on a bowl from Wels (Karnitsch 1959, Taf. 62, 4) which is probably by Servus ii (S. & S.'s Servus 3). His style is related to that of Docilis i and Casurius ii and he has Casurius's large beads, but he often omitted the terminal beads, as here. *c.*AD160–190 (Cistern 1, fill, E08:29; with area over Cistern 1, unstratified, E08:08, 2231, and area over Building 8, unstratified, E10:13, 2262).

D19. Form 30 or 37, Central Gaulish, with ovolo and bead-row used at Lezoux by Iullinus ii (Rogers B164). *c.*AD160–190 (Cistern 1, fill, E08:29, 2342). (Not illustrated.)

D20. Form 37, Central Gaulish. A bowl in the style of Banuus, with panels: 1) a crab, as on a stamped bowl from Lezoux and on another in his style, also from Lezoux (S. & S., pl. 140, 13). 2) A double medallion, over a partly-impressed striated spindle. 3) A hare to right (0.2057A?). The panel borders lack terminal beads. The hare is on a stamped bowl from Roanne, but with an ovolo which Banuus probably used only at the Terre-Franche kilns at Vichy. The fabric of the Wallsend piece suggests origin at Lezoux, however. *c.*AD160–200 (Cistern 1, fill, E08:29, 2410).

D21. Form 37, Central Gaulish, with stamp of Banuus (see no. S14 below) and panels: 1) a candelabrum (Rogers Q27), lying flat. 2) A double medallion over a leaf (Rogers H69, partly impressed). 3) A hare (O.2057A?) in a single festoon, over the stamp. 4) = 2?. 5) = 1? The bowl is mended with a lead cramp and the footring, which must have been added after the bowl had been removed from the mould, has broken off. *c.*AD175–250 (Cistern 1, lower fill, E08:44, 2393, 2401, 2402; upper fill, E08:27, 2365; and probably N05:04, Building 1, demolition).

D22. Form 37, Central Gaulish. The ovolo with bent tongue (Rogers B245) was used by some members of the Paternus v group. The freestyle scene includes a boar (D.835 = O.1674), stag (D.860 = O.1732), goat (O.1849 variant) and dog (O.1926A). The closest connections are with Paternus himself, though the wavy line below the ovolo is rather unusual for him and may indicate that this is one of his earlier bowls. *c.* AD155–170 (Building O, portico, E09:09, 2315: with F10:01 (area over Buildings 7 and 8, unstratified) 2200, and G14:01 (area over Building 7, unstratified)).

D23. Form 37, Central Gaulish, with one of the ring-tongued ovolos used at Lezoux by the Paternus v group. The panels include: 1) a double medallion. 2) A wide panel, with an athlete (D.377 = O.650) and a Pudicitia (a variant of D.541 = O.930), over a leaf (of the type Rogers J146–149). The bead-row under the ovolo and the vertical border of rhomboidal beads suggest Paternus v, though the rosette half-way up the border (Rogers C194) is unusual for him. *c.*AD160–195 (area over Road 8, unstratified, E09:13, 2236).

D24. Form 37, Central Gaulish. A small bowl, with beaded borders and a groove below the decoration. The panels include: 1) a bear to left (a smaller variant of D.775 = 0.1615). 2) A caryatid (perhaps a smaller version of D.656 = O.1199, with the mask impressed twice). 3B) Dolphins on a basket (Rogers Q59) and a Pan-mask (a smaller version of D.675 = O.1214). All the details were used at Lezoux by Iullinus ii. *c.*AD160–190 (rerouted *Via principalis,* E09:22, 2309). (Not illustrated.)

D25. Form 37, Central Gaulish, with panelled decoration. The ring-tongued ovolo (Rogers B105), borders of squarish beads and the vertical border topped by a leaf (S. & S.1958, fig. 30, 6), suggest the work of Paternus v (Rogers's Paternus II), though the surviving figure, an athlete (D.386 = O.663), is not otherwise known for him. *c.*AD160–195. (Assembly area, E09:44, 2331). (Not illustrated.)

D26. Form 37, East Gaulish. A bowl by a potter of Trier Werkstatt II, with ovolo Fölzer 1913, Taf. XXXII, 956?) and erotic group (*ibid.,* Taf. XXIX, 528, perhaps without the couch). Cf. Taf. XXI, 3. *c.*AD160–200 (Building N, E11:06; probably joining a sherd in E11:22 (Building 8, courtyard)).

D27. Form 37, Central Gaulish. A panelled bowl in the style of Casurius ii, with: 1) Minerva (D.77 = O. 126). 2) Satyr on a pedestal (D.369 = O. 599). 3) Leaf tendril. The satyr is on a stamped bowl from Naples (S. & S. 1958, pl. 133, 19). The Minerva is on a bowl in Casurius's style in the Wroxeter Gutter hoard (Atkinson 1942, pl. 36, G9). For all three elements see a bowl from Leicester (S. & S. 1958, pl. 137, 55). *c.*AD160–190 (Building 8, courtyard, E11:22).

D28. Form 37, Central Gaulish. A bowl by a member of the Sacer i group, with ovolo Rogers B185 = B205 (very blurred) and a beaded border below. The freestyle scene perhaps includes a bear to right and heavy foliage (as on a bowl from Caerwent: S. & S.1958, pl. 82, 5). There may also be a stag to left. Another sherd of the same date, with a lioness (D.793 = O.1537) may be from this bowl, though the wall is thinner. *c.*AD125–145 (Building 8, courtyard, E11:35). (Not illustrated.)

D29. Form 37, East Gaulish, with mould-stamp of Cobnertus iv of Rheinzabern (see S32 below). The ovolo is Ricken-Fischer 1963, E44, with a corded border below (*ibid.,* O244). The freestyle scene includes a boar to right (*ibid.,* T70a), lion to left (*ibid.,* T4), stag to left (*ibid.,* T92) and bifid motif (*ibid.,* P150). *c.*AD160–180 (Building 8, courtyard, E11:35, with two sherds (joining) in F11:01 (area over Building 7) and two sherds in F12:01 (area over *Via quintana),* 1104).

D30. Form 37 East Gaulish (La Madeleine). The ovolo is impressed over a straight line, with a border of separate square beads below. The decoration includes an acanthus and a saltire with diagonals of rectangular beads, and leaves (Ricken 1934, Taf. VII, 44) at the sides. Cf. Taf. XI, 13a and X, 17 for the line and beads, respectively. *c.*AD130–160 (area over Building 9, unstratified, E13:01). (Not illustrated.)

D31. Form 37, South Gaulish, with a Diana (D.63 = O.104B), used at both La Graufesenque and Banassac, and a hare. This bowl is probably from La Graufesenque. Flavian-Trajanic (Building 9, *contubernium* 1, Period 1, E13:20). (Not illustrated.)

D32. Form 37, Central Gaulish, with panels: 1) a vine (Rogers N1, with a variant of the leaf H119), bird (D.1019 = O.2252?) and Bacchus (O.566, without boots). 2A) Festoon (Rogers F16), probably containing a sea-cow (D.29 = O.42?); 2B) trifid motifs (Rogers G56) stem-to-stem, joined by a vertical astragalus. The Bacchus and vine are on a stamped mould of Sacer i from Lezoux (Simpson 1977, pl. 1) and the rosette junction-masks are on bowl with the same stamp from Vienne (*ibid.,* pl. II). The trifid motif is on a signed bowl from Corbridge (S. & S. 1958, pl. 83, 13) and the same arrangement as in 2B, but with a different trifid motif, occurs on a signed bowl from Holt (*ibid.,* 12). *c.*AD125–145 (Area over Building 9, unstratified, E14:01, with joining sherd in F14:01 (area over Building 10 and Alley 5, unstratified)).

D33. Form 37, East Gaulish (Rheinzabern). The ovolo is probably Ricken-Fischer 1963, E39. The decoration includes one panel with warriors (*ibid.,* M207–8) and a bush (*ibid.,* P9) and another with a large

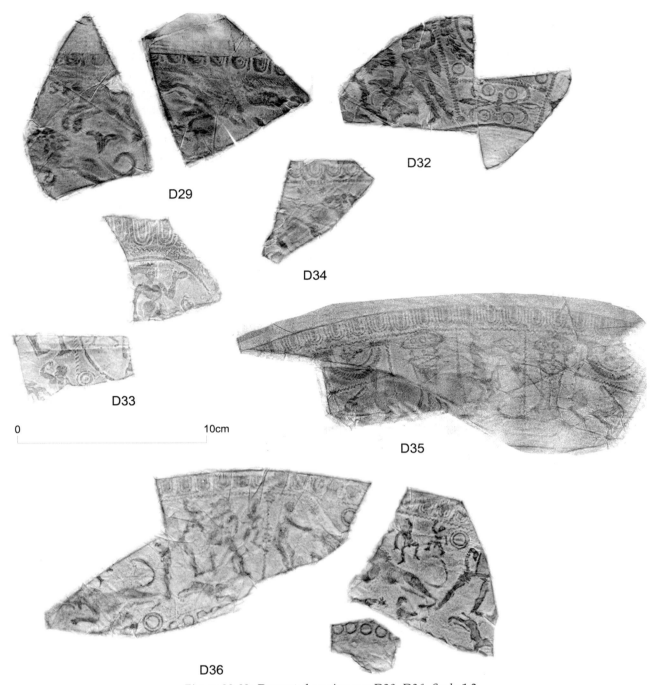

D29

D32

D34

D33

0 ────────────── 10cm

D35

D36

*Figure 22.02: Decorated samian nos D29–D36. Scale 1:2.*

roundel and a single medallion containing a Venus (*ibid.*, M44), between two figures to left (*ibid.*, M260). The use of wavy-line and corded borders is common in Cobnertus iv's work and they and many of the motifs appear on a stamped bowl from Osterburken (Ricken 1948, Taf. 31, 1). *c.* AD160–180 (area over Building 10 and Alley 5, unstratified, E14:01).

D34.　Form 37, Central Gaulish. The ovolo (Rogers B231) was used by potters associated with Sacer i and Cinnamus ii and appears on bowls in the style of Paternus iv, a Hadrianic-Antonine associate of

Sacer, who stamped moulds in the nominative. The decoration includes a lion (D.727 = O.1379), as on a bowl in his style from Watercrook (Wild 1979, 287, 76), a panther (D. 799 = O.1518) and seven- or eight-petalled rosettes. *c.*AD130–155 (area over Building 10 and Alley 5, unstratified, E14:06).

D35.　Form 37, Central Gaulish, with panels: 1A) festoon (Rogers F70), containing a fan-shaped plant (Rogers G259, impressed sideways); 1B) hare to left (O.2119?). 2) Tripod (Rogers Q7). 3) Scarf-dancer (D.217 = O.354). 4) = 2). 5A) = 1A; 5B) hare to right (O.2057A?). The ovolo (Rogers B31) was used by

X–5 and most of the details appear on other bowls in his style, the hares at Wels (Karnitsch 1959, Taf. 34, 4) and Wroxeter, the festoons and ovolo at Bingen (S. & S.1958, pl. 67, 1), the dancer at London (BM M1272) and the tripod at Wanborough, Wilts. *c.*AD 125–140 (Alley 3, F04:33; with sherd from Road 1, Period 4 to mid/late third century, L08:13).

D36.    Form 37, Central Gaulish. The single-bordered ovolo (Rogers B28), with guide-line below and then a wavy line, suggests a member of the Quintilianus i group. Two unusually wide panels, repeated, both have a pair of gladiators (O.1003–4) and a lion to left (not in D. or O.). The other details are a pygmy (D.440 = O.699), Pan (D.424 = O.723), panther to right (O.1516), athlete (O.682A variant), naked man to right, bird to left, looking back, double medallion, basal wreath of rings with a guide-line above and an eight-beaded rosette (Rogers C281). Most of the details are on signed bowls of Paterclus ii, the ovolo, gladiators and rosette at Silchester (S. & S. 1958, pl. 72, 33) and the bird, panther to right, medallion and basal wreath at Caerwent. *c.* AD 125–140 (Alley 3, F04:33 (three sherds), with others in F04:01 (area of Building 5, unstratified), F04:11 (wall tumble over Alley 3), and F05:01 (area of Alley 4, unstratified)).

D37.    Form 37, Central Gaulish, with panels: 1) a leaf (Rogers H105?), hanging down. 2) A fleur-de-lys (Rogers G88), hanging down, and an athlete to left over a row of rings. In two adjacent panels on the other sherd the fleurs-de-lys points upwards. The decoration is closely paralleled on a bowl with an ovolo of Pugnus ii from a pottery shop at Castleford burnt down in the 140s (Rush *et al* 2000, fig. 24, no. 465). The leaf, wavy lines and horizontal astragali are on a signed Pugnus bowl from excavations at Carlisle. *c.* AD 130–150 (Alley 3, F04:33, with a sherd, slightly burnt, from the Assembly area, F09:58).

D38.    Form 37, East Gaulish. The ovolo replacement (Ricken-Fischer 1963, R8) has been impressed on top of a guide-line. The medallion with beaded outer border (*ibid.*, K57) contains a Pan-mask (*ibid.*, M17a). All the details are on a bowl from Rheinzabern in the style of Reginus vi (Ricken 1948, Taf. 17, 13). *c.* AD 160–180 (area over Alley 5, unstratified, F05:01).

D39.    Form 37, from the East Gaulish factory of La Madeleine. The decoration, with a guide-line for laying out and a closing bead-row, includes an acanthus (Ricken 1934, Taf. VII, 25), on a double astragalus. *c.* AD 130–160 (rubble round Cistern 1, F08:25, 2475). (Not illustrated.)

D40.    Form 37, from one of the East Gaulish factories in the Argonne. The ovolo (probably Chenet and Gaudron 1955, fig. 54 bis, third example on Row X) has a tongue turning to the right at the bottom. The decoration includes a bird (a debased version of Fölzer 1913, Taf. XXVIII, 385) and a double medallion, probably both in the upper concavity of a scroll. Mid- to late-Antonine (area over Road 8, unstratified, F09:01).

D41.    Form 37, from the East Gaulish factory of La Madeleine. The decoration, closed by a bead-row,

includes a warrior to left (Ricken 1934, Taf. VII, 90) and a bear to right (perhaps the one on Taf. Vll, 115). *c.* AD 130–160 (pit in Assembly area, F09:23, 2259). (Not illustrated.)

D42.    Form 37, Central Gaulish. The rosette-tongued ovolo (Rogers B7) was used at Les Martres-de-Veyre, but sometimes occurs on bowls in Lezoux fabric, like this one, in the style of Sacer i. The panels include: 1B) Cupid to right (D.247 = O.405). 2A) Double festoon containing a bird (O.2317); 2b) a row of rings; 2C) an erotic group (a variant of Oswald, pl. XC, B). 3A) Apollo (D.55 = O.92) and Cupid to right (D.245 = O.403). Another sherd has a figure over a hare (O.2061?), both to right. The panel junctions are masked by hollow rosettes, with ten or eleven petals. *c.* AD 125–145 (pit in Assembly area, F09:59, 2377, (3) and 2388, with 2373, (2) from the Assembly area, F09:63).

D43.    Form 37, Central Gaulish. The panels include: 1) a draped figure (D.372 = O.365). 2) A Cupid (D.252 = O.417) on a tripod (Rogers Q7). 3) A Jupiter (D.1 = O.1). On the other sherd both the larger figures are in the same panel. D.372 and the tripod are on a stamped and signed bowl of Docilis i from Néris-les-Bains (Piboule 1977, 100) and he is known to have used the other details. *c.* AD 130–165 (Alley between buildings 7 and 8, F10:29, area over Road 3, unstratified, 2245).

D44.    Form 37, Central Gaulish, with a ring-tongued ovolo (Rogers B105) and a candelabrum (Rogers Q40). The ovolo suggests a member of the Paternus v group, though none is known to have used the candelabrum. *c.* AD 150–190 (Road 3, F11:73, 2422).

D45.    Form 37, Central Gaulish. One panel has a vertical series of spirals, with an astragalus separating two of them, and another spiral in the adjacent panel. Cf. signed bowls of Mox(s)ius from Birdoswald and Chester (S. & S. 1958, pl. 152, 3, 4). Hadrianic or early-Antonine (area over *Via quintana*, unstratified, F12:01).

D46.    Form 37, East Gaulish, probably from La Madeleine, on the evidence of the fabric. The square-bottomed ovolo has a short tongue on the left. Arcades separated by rhomboidal beads rest on an arrow-head motif. The Cupid is on a bowl from the Saalburg, which has the beads and arcade (used as a festoon) and perhaps the same ovolo, though in a more complete version (Ricken 1934, Taf. X, 12). *c.* AD 130–160 (area over *Via quintana*, unstratified, F12:01).

D47.    Form 37, East Gaulish. The tongueless ovolo (one of the series Ricken-Fischer 1963, E55–7), here impressed over a guide-line, and leaf (*ibid.*, P81) were used at Rheinzabern by Reginus vi. *c.* AD160–180 (area over *Via quintana*, unstratified, F12:01).

D48.    Form 37, Central Gaulish, with the large label-stamp of Paternus v, [PΛTER]NFE retr. in the decoration (see no. S77 below). The ovolo is probably Rogers B105. The panels, divided by astragalus borders (Rogers A10), include: 1) a (double?) medallion. 2A) A single festoon with a leopard (D.789 = O.1509), over an astragalus (Rogers R60); 2B) perhaps a column on its side. Another sherd has the tripod,

Rogers Q16. *c.* AD 160–195 (area over *Via quintana*, unstratified, F12:01).

D49. Form 37, Central Gaulish. The ovolo, with bifid or trident-tongue, is on a signed bowl of Attianus ii from Canterbury. The horseman (D.158 = O.249) and snake on rock (D.960 bis = O.2155) are on a stamped bowl from Verulamium (S. & S. 1958, pl. 86, 12). The incurving festoon in the adjacent panel is on a stamped bowl from Corbridge (*ibid.*, 10). *c.* AD 125–145 (Building Row 20, building T, F12:04).

D50. Form 37, Central Gaulish. The bold basal ridge between two slighter ones is typical of X–6 and the leaf in the upper concavity of a scroll (Rogers H26?) is on one of his bowls, from Carlisle (May and Hope 1917, pl. VII, 91). The lower concavity contains a pygmy (D. 422 = O.703, with right foot broken). *c.* AD 125–150 (Chalet 9, robbing and post-Roman dereliction, F13:16).

D51. Form 37, East Gaulish, with an ovolo (Ricken-Fischer 1963, E69) and roped border used at both Rheinzabern and Heiligenberg by Ianus ii. The hard fabric and good glaze of this piece suggest origin at Heiligenberg. *c.* AD 140–160 (area over Building 10 and Alley 5, F14:01). (Not illustrated.)

D52. Form 37, from the East Gaulish factory of La Madeleine, with ovolo Ricken 1934, Taf. VII, C and a border of square beads. *c.* AD 130–160 (*intervallum* road (Road 6), F15:04). (Not illustrated.)

D53. Form 37, Central Gaulish, in the style of Cettus of Les Martres-de-Veyre. The ovolo resembles Rogers B97, but the tongue is on the other side of the egg. It occurs, together with the lion (a smaller version of D.769 = 0.1457), on two of his bowls, from London and Corbridge (S. & S.1958, pl. 144, 49–50). The lion and astragalus are also on a bowl from Camelon. *c.* AD 135–160 (Alley 4, G05:07, with a sherd from F07:01 (area of *Via principalis*, unstratified)).

D54. Form 37, Central Gaulish, with ovolo Rogers B231 and panels: 1) ?. 2A) Double medallion; 2B) Hercules (D.446 = O.753). 3A) Chevron festoon (Rogers F8); 3B) Europa and sea-bull (D.28 = O.43). 4A) Double medallion; 4B) kilted man. On another sherd the festoon contains a dolphin to left above the Europa and the medallion in the adjacent panel contains a bird (O.2317), probably above the kilted man. The junction-masks are seven-beaded. The style, though not the figure-types, suggests the Sacer i-Attianus ii group, which almost certainly used the ovolo. *c.* AD 125–145 (robbing of street drain or north wall of Building 18, G05:18, with a sherd from the area over Building 5 and Alley 4, unstratified, J05:03).

D55. Two fragments of form 30, Central Gaulish, with ovolo 2 of Cinnamus ii (Rogers B231) and panels: 1) a double medallion and an astragalus. 2) A candelabrum (Rogers Q43). The other sherd shows the motif Rogers Q27 and the astragalus and medallion. *c.* AD 150–180 (Building 5, *contubernium* 2, G05:25).

D56. Form 37, Central Gaulish. One panel has a single festoon containing an animal and an astragalus with chevrons of unequal size at the ends. Below is a saltire with the astragalus in the top and at the sides. The beads in the diagonals and the panel border are square. The arrangement of the panel is paralleled on a bowl in the Oswald-Plicque Collection which is possibly by the late-Antonine Lezoux potter, Marcus v (area over Building 7, unstratified, G09:01).

D57. Form 37, East Gaulish, from Lavoye. The decoration includes a standing figure, perhaps a Venus with mirror (Chenet and Gaudron 1955, fig. 60, J), over a trifid motif (Fölzer 1913, Taf. XXVIII, 399). Second half of the second century (area over Building 7, unstratified, G11:01).

D58. Form 37, Central Gaulish, in the style of Casurius ii, with ovolo Rogers B208 and panels: 1) a festoon, containing a sea-horse (D.33 = O.33). 2) A leaf (Rogers H47). One of the vertical borders continues into the ovolo zone, without a junction-mask, and two panels have leaf-tendrils attached to the bottom of their borders. *c.* AD 160–190 (Building Row 20, Building AX(N), south wall, G11:38; with two joining sherds in G11:17 (Building Row 20, Building R)).

D59. Form 30, Central Gaulish, with ring-tongued ovolo (Rogers B105) and panels: 1) a medallion and corner astragalus. 2) A double festoon, containing a dolphin to right (D.1050 = O.2382). The type of beaded border below the ovolo suggests Paternus v, who used all the other motifs. *c.* AD 160–195 (Building Row 20, Building AX(N), south wall, G11:38).

D60. Form 37, Central Gaulish, with a variant of Cinnamus ii's ovolo 3 (Rogers B143). However, the decoration is slightly unusual for him, with a single medallion or scroll and a leaf (Rogers U161), pointing upwards. Possibly by Paternus iv, who used the leaf and the same beads. Riveted. *c.* AD 130–150 (Building Row 20, Building R, G11:13).

D61. Form 37, East Gaulish. The ovolo (Ricken-Fischer 1963, E46), rosette (*ibid.*, O48) on top of a divider (*ibid.*, O271) and medallion (perhaps a full version of *ibid.*, KB105) were all used at Rheinzabern in the late second and first half of the third century. Cf. Ricken 1948, Taf. 159, 13 (Disturbance/levelling north-east of Building R, G11:44).

D62. Form 37, East Gaulish. The figure to left (a variant of the right-hand figure in the group Fölzer 1913, Taf. XXIX, 519) appears singly on a bowl of Criciro vii of Trier, from Neuss. Above is an ovolo-replacement of rosettes (*ibid.*, Taf. XXXI, 850?). The mould was presumably made at Trier, but the fabric and glaze suggest that the bowl may have been made elsewhere, perhaps at one of Trier's smaller satellite potteries, such as Haute-Yutz or Daspich-Ebange. Late second century or first half of third century (area over *Via quintana*, unstratified, G12:01).

D63. Form 37, Central Gaulish. The single-bordered ovolo (Rogers B12), tree (Rogers N7) and rosette at the top of a panel border (Rogers C23) were all used by Attianus ii. *c.* AD 125–145 (area over Road 3, unstratified, G12:15, and area over Building 9 and Road 3, unstratified, G13:01).

D64. Form 37, South Gaulish. The lower zone includes a panel containing rows of leaf-tips and a saltire with a five-bladed plant with striated outer petals in the bottom, over a basal wreath. The plant is on

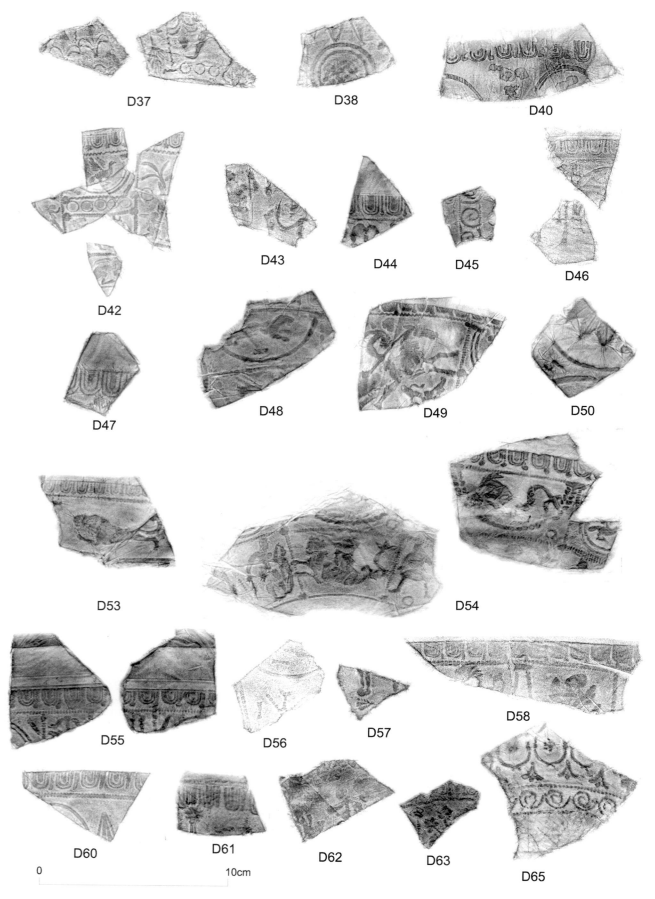

*Figure 22.03: Decorated samian nos D37–D65. Scale 1:2.*

a stamped form 37 of Frontinus from Canterbury. *c.* AD 70–85 (Chalet 9, robbing and post-Roman dereliction, G13:03). (Not illustrated.)

D65. Form 37, from the East Gaulish factory of La Madeleine. The decoration includes at least two rows of festoons (Ricken 1934, Taf .VII, 51), the lower containing seven-beaded rosettes (*ibid.*, 1), and a row of pendant trifid motifs (*ibid.*, 11). The basal wreath consists of spirals (*ibid.*, 33). The wreath, festoon and rosette are on a bowl from Corbridge and the wreath also occurs on a bowl from Camelon. *c.* AD 130–160 (Chalet 9, robbing and post-Roman dereliction, G13:03).

D66. Form 37, Central Gaulish, with ovolo Rogers B102 and panels: 1) a composite motif (Rogers Ql). 2) A Cupid (D.275 = O.503). The ovolo, neat beads and six-petalled rosette (Rogers C122) were all used by Advocisus. The Cupid is unusual for him, but occurs on a stamped bowl from Corbridge (Simpson 1953, fig. 16, no. 29). The composite motif is on a bowl from Little Chester which is in a style related to that of Advocisus but is probably not by him. Another sherd, which may belong to this bowl, has concentric double medallions in the manner of Divixtus i (cf. S. & S.1958, pl. 116, 15), one of whose styles is close to that of Advocisus. Mid- to late-Antonine (area over Alley 5, unstratified, G14:03).

D67. Form 37, Central Gaulish. The ovolo (S. & S.1958, fig. 9, 1) and double arcade or medallion occur in moulds in the so-called Medetus style, mainly from Les Martres-de-Veyre, though some may have been made at Lezoux. This bowl is in Lezoux fabric. *c.* AD 125–140 (Building 9, *contubernium* 8, G14:17). (Not illustrated.)

D68. Form 37, Central Gaulish, with ovolo Rogers B228 and a kneeling stag (a variant of D.847 = O.1704) in a double festoon. The ovolo was normally used in the Hadrianic and early-Antonine periods, but the fabric of this piece and the coarse zig-zag border suggest mid- to late-Antonine date (Chalet 10, Building X, G15:16).

D69. Form 37, Central Gaulish. Two panels are divided by a wavy-line border. The hand of an unusually large figure, holding something, stretches over the border into a panel with a *quadriga* (similar to O.1169 or 1170) and, perhaps, an animal. Hadrianic-Antonine, perhaps by Sissus ii, who is one of the few potters of this date to have used large figure-types (area over Tower 1, unstratified, H02:03).

D70. Form 37, Central Gaulish. One sherd shows a Vulcan (D. 39 = O.67), over two rings. The other shows the top part of a panel, with a lion's head (perhaps an incomplete impression of D.741 = O.1389) in a chevron festoon (Rogers F41). The zig-zag borders (Rogers A24) and rings suggest Arcanus and the festoon and Vulcan are on a signed bowl from Rottenburg (S. & S.1958, pl. 78, 1). *c.* AD 125–140 (area over Road 4, unstratified, H03:03).

D71. Form 37, Central Gaulish, with panelled decoration. The ovolo (Rogers B76), recumbent lion (perhaps D.754 = O.1422) and double astragalus are on form 30 from London(?), in the style of Geminus

iv (Walters 1908, M1062). The beaded borders and rosette junction-mask (Rogers C28) normally appear in his later style, while the rest of the details go with his earlier style. *c.* AD 125–145 (Building 4, make up material, H04:07).

D72. Form 37, East Gaulish, with ovolo Ricken-Fischer 1963, E39b, ornamental medallion (*ibid.*, K48), including a Cupid (*ibid.*, M121) and a flute-player (*ibid.*, M167), dividers with bifid motifs at the bottom (*ibid.*, P142?) and six-petalled rosettes in the middle and a bifid motif in the field. A V in the decoration is probably not a signature, but a badly applied motif. Most of the details are common to Ianus i and Cerialis v, but only Ianus used the double border of rectangular beads below the ovolo. The fabric suggests origin at Heiligenberg rather than Rheinzabern. The bowl is mended with a lead rivet. Early-Antonine? (Cistern 2, upper fill, H07:03).

D73. Form 37, East Gaulish (Rheinzabern), with ovolo Ricken-Fischer 1963, E19 and corded borders defining a zone with corded festoons (*ibid.*, KB115), one with a pygmy (*ibid.*, M152), another with a panther (*ibid.*, T47). The cord of the tassel (*ibid.*, O242, as in the zonal borders) has a blob half-way down and a bifid motif (*ibid.*, P142?) at the bottom. A stamped bowl of Ianus ii from Straubing (Walke 1965, Taf. 23, 5) offers a close parallel. *c.* AD 160–180 (Cistern 2, modern(?), H07:03; joining sherd from Building 16, N08:24, 2514).

D74. Form 37, Central Gaulish. A bowl in the style of Casurius ii, with ovolo Rogers B208. A panel contains a double festoon with a hare (O.2119A) and small leaves (Rogers H167). A stamped bowl from Corbridge (S. & S. 1958, pl. 132, 11) has all the details. *c.* AD 160– 190 (area over Road 3 and Building 9, unstratified, H13:06).

D75. Form 37, from the East Gaulish factory of La Madeleine. The basal wreath consists of trifid motifs (Ricken 1934, Taf. VII, 24), impressed sideways, between two bead-rows. *c.* AD 130–160 (Chalet 9, robbing and post-Roman dereliction, H13:09).

D76. Form 37 Central Gaulish, with mould-stamp [PΛTER]NFE retr. (see no. S78 below). This bowl of Paternus v has a border of rhomboidal beads dividing two panels. One perhaps contains a warrior (D.117 = O.188); the other has a festoon or medallion. *c.* AD 160–195 (area over Alley 5 and Building 9, unstratified, H14:04). (Not illustrated.)

D77. Form 37, Central Gaulish. A centaur (D. 431 = O.732) is an uncommon figure-type. Leaf-tips in the field suggest a member of the Cerialis ii-Cinnamus ii group. *c.* AD 135–170 (area over Alley 5 and Building 9, unstratified, H14:30). (Not illustrated.)

D78. Form 37, Central Gaulish. The ovolo (Rogers B108?), wavy line below it and horse and rider (D.152a = O.258) are all on a stamped bowl of Maccius ii from Lezoux (Oswald-Plicque Collection). *c.* AD 130–160 (area over Building 10, unstratified, H15:01). (Not illustrated.)

D79. Form 37, Central Gaulish, with a saltire panel with diagonals of large, square beads, cut through by a basal groove. Perhaps by Marcus v. Cf. D103.

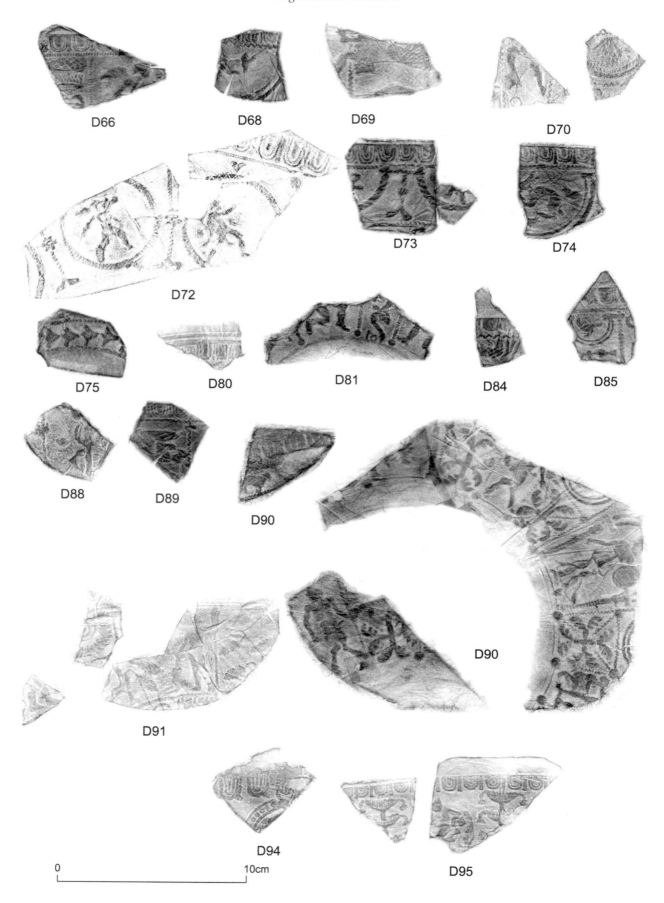

*Figure 22.04: Decorated samian nos D66–D95. Scale 1:2.*

Late-Antonine (area over Road 9 and Building 10, H15:03). (Not illustrated.)

D80. Form 37, South Gaulish. The single-bordered, square-bottomed ovolo is on a second-century Montans bowl from Cramond. There is a double internal groove above the level of the ovolo. Hadrianic or early-Antonine (area over Road 9 and Building 10, H15:10, and sherd from area over Building 8, unstratified, E11:11).

D81. Form 37, Central Gaulish, in the style of Advocisus. The panels contain: 1) a sea-horse (D.35 = O.52A). 2) A Cupid to right (D.282 = O.508). 3) A vine-scroll (Rogers M50). 4) A Cupid to left (D.277 = O.504). Both Cupids are on a stamped bowl from the Wroxeter forum destruction (Atkinson 1942, pl. 33, H3) and the scroll is on another, from Caerwent (S. & S. 1958, pl. 112, 12). The sea-horse is on a bowl in his style from Wroxeter (unpublished). *c.* AD 160–190 (area over Building 10, unstratified, H15:10).

D82. Form 37 from the East Gaulish factory of Chémery-Faulquemont. There is a mould-stamp SATVRNFECIT (see no. S94 below) in the decoration and a fragmentary cursive signature below the decoration (see no. S146 below), from a mould signed before firing. Stamps of Saturninus i are often associated with signatures of Satto ii on moulds, but the signature here, ....fe, upside-down, does not seem to fit, to judge by the remaining letters. The decoration includes a scroll, with a putto (O.439 or 439A) and small rosettes. Trajanic or Hadrianic (area over Building 5, unstratified, J05:03). (Not illustrated.)

D83. Form 37, East Gaulish (Trier). The decoration includes a medallion with dotted border (Fölzer 1913, Taf. XXXI, 830) and two blurred rosettes above the basal ridge. The medallion is on a stamped bowl of Censor ii from Bonn (*ibid.*, Taf. XVI, 12). Mid- to late-Antonine (area over *Via quintana*, unstratified, J12:01). (Not illustrated.)

D84. Form 37, Central Gaulish. The ovolo (Rogers B147), zig-zag border (Rogers A26) and large striated spindle, impressed horizontally, were all used by Servus iv (S. & S.'s Servus 2). *c.* AD 160–200 (Road 3, J12:33).

D85. Form 30, Central Gaulish, in the style of Do(v)eccus i, with his large beads (Rogers A3), ovolo Rogers B160 and panels: 1) a small double festoon with a bird (O.2298) over a tier of cups (Rogers Q49?, impressed sideways). 2) A beaded ring (Rogers E58?) in the top corner and, probably, a double medallion. The bird and columns are on a stamped bowl from London (S. & S. 1958, pl. 149, 31). *c.* AD 165–200 (area over Building 12 and Road 9, unstratified, J14:01).

D86. Form 37, Central Gaulish. A bowl in the style of Banuus, with a blurred ovolo, leaf (Rogers H69) in the top part of a panel and a rosette (Rogers C165) at the top of a border. *c.* AD 160–200 (area over Gate 3 and *intervallum* road (Road 6), unstratified, J16:01). (Not illustrated.)

D87. Form 37, East Gaulish. A cockerel (Ricken-Fischer 1963, T236) and rosette (*ibid.*, O49) were used at Rheinzabern by Reginus vi. *c.* AD 160–180 (area over Gate 3 and *intervallum* road (Road 6), unstratified, J16:01). (Not illustrated).

D88. Form 37, Central Gaulish. A bowl in the later style of Geminus iv, characterised by beaded borders and six-petalled rosette junction-masks (Rogers C28). One panel is divided across the middle. The adjacent panel contains a Venus at an altar (D.184 = O.322) and a trifid motif (Rogers G112). All the details except for the figure are on a bowl in this style from Scole (Hartley and Dickinson 1977, fig. 71, D19). *c.* AD 130–145 (area of Gate 1, unstratified, K03:02).

D89. Form 37, Central Gaulish. The ovolo (Rogers B18) was occasionally used by X–5. His characteristic striated spindle is across a wavy-line border which continues into the ovolo zone. One panel contains a boar (D.826 = O.1641). Cf. S. & S. 1958, pl. 67, 12. *c.* AD 125–140 (Gate 1, robber trench, K03:22).

D90. Form 37, Central Gaulish. The greater part of the bowl, with ovolo Rogers B231 and panels: 1A) a sheep (O.1857A variant); 1B) Pan (D.419 = O.717). 2A) A double medallion; 2B) a saltire with acanthi (one of the series Rogers K16–36) in all four quadrants. 3) Minerva (D.77 = O.126), in a double arcade supported by pillars (Rogers P10). 4B) = 2B. 5) Scarf-dancer (D.217 = O.354). 6) ? 7) = 5, but in an arcade, as in 3). 8B) = 2B). 9) Pan, as in 1B). 10) = 2). 11) = 3). 12) = 2. 13) Two figures, one kneeling, the other standing (D.150 = O.238). The rosette junction-masks have twelve petals (Rogers C229). The style is that of the potter X–9, who supplied moulds to Medetus at Les Martres-de-Veyre and perhaps also at Lezoux. The micaceous fabric suggests that the bowl, at least, was made at Lezoux. Most of the details are on bowls in the 'Medetus-Ranto' style, from Cambridge and London (S. & S. 1958, pls. 30, 355 and 31 368). The bowl is mended with lead rivets and much of the external glaze has been removed, presumably by chemical action in the soil. *c.* AD 125–140 (Building 4, *contubernium* 9, K04:25).

D91. Form 37, South Gaulish. The bowl has no ovolo, though it could have been removed when the rim was finished. There are at least three zones of decoration; the top one contains a Bacchus (Hermet 1934, pl. 19, 71) between vines, and a Pan (*ibid.*, 90); the next zone includes a chevron festoons with spirals, either in panels or separated by tassels; no decoration is visible in the third zone. The design is closely paralleled on a bowl from La Graufesenque with one of Germanus i's commoner ovolos (*ibid.*, pl. 100, 12). *c.* AD 70–90 (Building 16, floor, K07:08 (with more in Building 16, occupation/levelling, Period 3, K08:33).

D92. Form 37, Central Gaulish. A bowl in the style of Criciro v, with a panel containing a double medallion, followed by a narrow panel with a caryatid (not closely identifiable), The panel borders are closed by Criciro's characteristic beaded rings (Rogers C125). *c.* AD 135–165 (Building 14, courtyard, K10:28).

D93. Form 37, East Gaulish, in the style of Iulius viii (Ricken-Fischer 1963's Julius II) of Rheinzabern. Two arcades, one containing a cockerel (*ibid.*, T239b) have a cross between them (*ibid.*, 053a) and rest on a support (*ibid.*, O182). The general arrangement is paralleled on a stamped Rheinzabern mould (Ricken 1948, Taf. 207, 9). Probably early third-century. *c.* AD 225–250 (area over Building 14 and *Via quintana,* unstratified, K12:01). (Not illustrated.)

D94.     Form 37, East Gaulish. The ovolo (Fölzer 1913, Taf. IX, 6F, reversed) is on a stamped mould of Criciro vii from Trier and a stamped bowl (unpublished) from Neuss. The arcade (*ibid.*, Taf. XXXI, 800) is on a bowl from Bad Godesberg (*ibid.*, Taf. XVI, 33), with Ipigenia inscribed retr. in the decoration, indicating the legend depicted. *c.* AD 190–210 (area over Building 14 and *Via quintana,* unstratified, K12:01).

D95.     Form 37, East Gaulish, in the style of Cerialis v of Rheinzabern, with ovolo Ricken-Fischer 1963, E44, fisherman (*ibid.*, M173) and tiers of acanthi (*ibid.*, P112). Cf. Ricken 1948, Taf. 54, 10. *c.* AD 160–180 (Building 12, unstratified, K14:01).

D96.     Form 37, Central Gaulish, with panels: 1) and 2) Venuses (D.193 = O.339 and D.173 = O.278). 3) A double medallion, containing an urn (Rogers T5). All the details are on stamped bowls of Iullinus ii (S. & S. 1958, pls. 125, 7, 2; 126, 11). *c.* AD 160–190 (area over Building 11, unstratified, K15:01).

D97.     Form 37, Rheinzabern ware, showing the upper concavity of a scroll, with a dolphin (Ricken-Fischer 1963, T194a), a sea-monster (*ibid.*, T183) and perhaps a dog to left. Both identified figures appear on 'Ware mit E8' (Ricken 1948, Taf. 165, 2). Late second century or first half of third century (area over Building 1, unstratified, L04:11). (Not illustrated.)

D98.     Form 37, South Gaulish, with a joining sherd in H13:24 and another in Q04:05. The panels show: 1) a Cupid (?) to right and a Bacchus with leopard (Hermet 1934, pl. 19, 71). 2) Repeated partial impressions of a four-bladed plant (a smaller version of *ibid.*, pl. 14, 49). 3) A Victory (*ibid.*, pl. 20, 102). The plants are repeated in another panel and one sherd has a Cupid to right. The mould was stamped and part of the stamp (illegible) remains below the decoration, as does part of a rosette. *c.* AD 90–110 (area over Building 2 and Alley 1, unstratified, L05:03).

D99.     Form 37, Central Gaulish, with a fourteen-petalled rosette (Rogers C243) over a double medallion containing a figure with raised left arm. The medallion and rosette are on a signed bowl of Acaunissa from Heerlen. *c.* AD 125–145 (area over Building 2 and Alley 1, unstratified, L05:03). (Not illustrated.)

D100.    Form 37, East Gaulish, with motifs used at La Madeleine and comprising an ovolo (Fölzer 1913, Taf. XXV, 119), a small medallion with corded outer border (*ibid.*, Taf. l, 42?) and a seven-beaded rosette (*ibid.*, Taf. XXV, 107). *c.* AD 130–160 (area over Building 16, unstratified, L07:01, 2454).

D101.    Form 37, East Gaulish. The scene, a grape-harvest, is common at Chémery-Faulquemont (Delort 1953, pls. 53–59), but the details, a grape basket, Cupid and six-beaded rosette in a basal wreath are not precisely paralleled on published bowls. Trajanic or Hadrianic (Building 16, L07:10).

D102.    Form 37, East Gaulish, abraded on the outside and with some of the glaze ground off on the inside. Trier ware, with decoration including a captive (O.1154) and two lions (O.1413). The decoration is closed by a double groove. The captive is on a bowl from Niederbieber (Oelmann 1914, Taf. VIII, 21); the lion is on a bowl from Zugmantel (Fölzer 1913, Taf. XIX, 1). The figure-types were used by more than one potter at Trier, which does not make dating easy, but the example from Niederbieber will not have reached the site before the late second century (Road 1, L08:63). (Not illustrated.)

D103.    Form 37, Central Gaulish. One panel has a double medallion (containing an eagle?) with beaded diagonals below, crossing at the groove below the decoration. Sherds in H15:03 and G09:01 may be from bowls by the same potter (Marcus v?). Late-Antonine (yard south of Building 13, L12:14; almost certainly from the same bowl as D79).

D104.    Form 30, with large label-stamp of Cinnamus ii, CINNAMI retr., (see no. S28 below), in a narrow panel. The next panel contains corner astragali and a double medallion with a scarf-dancer (D.220 = O.348). A third panel contains a candelabrum (Rogers Q43). *c.* AD150–180 (area over Building 12, unstratified, L14:01, 1406). (Not illustrated.)

D105.    Form 37, East Gaulish, showing a chariot race. The *meta* (Ricken-Fischer 1963, 04) and *quadriga* (*ibid.*, M164) are both on bowls in the style of Cerialis vi from Rheinzabern (Ricken 1948, Taf. 65, 4 and 7). The ovolo is probably one of his (Ricken-Fischer 1963, E11?). *c.* AD 160–180 (area over Building 12, unstratified, L14:01).

D106.    Form 37, from the East Gaulish factory of La Madeleine. A figure with a staff (Ricken 1934, Taf. VII, 97) stands between medallions with beaded inner borders. The basal wreath consists of trifid motifs (*ibid.*, 11) between beaded borders. *c.* AD 130–160 (area over Building 12, unstratified, L14:02).

D107.    Form 37, Central Gaulish. The freestyle scene includes a lion (D.768 = O.1455), stag (D.860 = O.1732), bear (D.807 = O.1578), horse (D.906A = O.1911) and partly-impressed leaves (Rogers J146). All the details were used by Albucius ii, who often used the leaves as space-fillers. They occur, with the bear and horse, on a stamped bowl from London (S. & S. 1958, pl. 123, 42). *c.* AD 150–180 (Chalet 12, Building AJ, L14:10). (Not illustrated.)

D108.    Form 37, Central Gaulish. The ovolo (Rogers B157), double medallion and athlete (O.204) are on a stamped bowl of Banuus from Lezoux (Birley Collection). *c.* AD 160–190 (area over Building 12 and Alley 6, L15:01).

D109.    Form 37, Central Gaulish. The upper concavity of the scroll contains a leaf (Rogers H35?); the lower concavity has double medallion containing a bird (D.1010 = O.2316) hovering over an astragalus (Rogers R60), a horizontal column (Rogers P3), striated spindles and small rings. A bowl in the style of Paternus v (Rogers's Paternus II), with his characteristic spindles, but with a leaf apparently not attested for him, unless it is Rogers H29. A

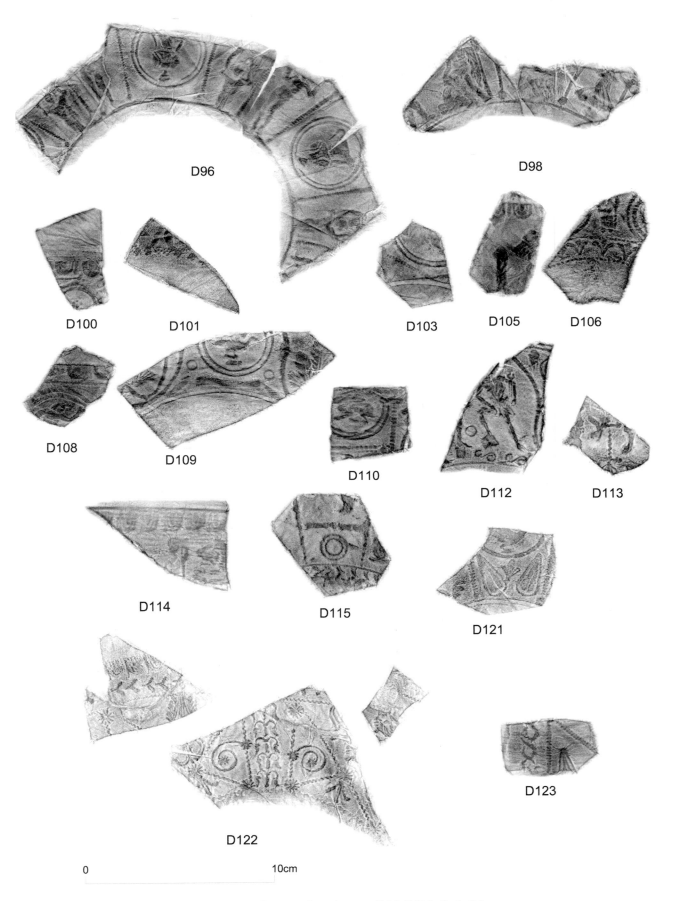

*Figure 22.05: Decorated samian nos D96–D123. Scale 1:2.*

stamped Paternus bowl from Wels, with a rim-stamp of Sextus v, has a similar, if not identical, scroll (Karnitsch 1955, Taf. 4, 8). *c.* AD 160–195 (Building 11, *contubernium* 3/4, L15:18).

D110. Form 37, Central Gaulish; a bowl in the style of Do(v)eccus i, with horizontal border of his large, square beads (Rogers A13) and vertical border of ovoid beads (Rogers A3). The upper part of one panel contains a hare (D.950a = O.2116) in a double festoon. The adjacent panel has corner astragali and a double medallion. *c.* AD 165–200 (area over Building 1 and Road 4, unstratified, M04:02).

D111. Form 37, Central Gaulish. A bowl in the style of Cinnamus ii, with leaves in the upper concavity of a scroll (Rogers H101 and 13) and an erotic group (Oswald, pl. XC, B variant) in a double medallion in the lower concavity, probably over a dog (D.934 = O.1980?). *c.* AD 150–180 (Alley 1, upper layers, M05:12). (Not illustrated.)

D112. Form 37, Central Gaulish. A bowl in the style of the Large S Potter. The lower concavity of a scroll contains a Neptune (D.14 = O.13) and Vulcan (D.39 = O.66) and the potter's characteristic S-motif. The upper concavity has a tendril and a partly-impressed acanthus (one of the series Rogers K16–35). *c.* AD 125–140 (Alley 1, lower levels, M05:16 (joining M05:12)).

D113. Form 37, Central Gaulish. The panels include: 1) a slave or satyr (D.322 = O.591). 2) A seated Apollo (D.52 = O.83). The wavy-line border has astragali (Rogers R22) across it and a trifid motif at the bottom. The arrangement of the border, but with a trifid motif at the top, appears on a bowl from Chester in the style of Pugnus ii which Rogers's calls P–14. The Apollo is on another of his bowls, from Cardurnock. *c.* AD 130–150 (Building 13, east hypocaust, M12:58).

D114. The East Gaulish (Rheinzabern) form 37 has ovolo Ricken-Fischer 1963, E18, an Amazon (*ibid.*, M238a) and a bear (*ibid.*, T2). The bowl is not assignable to a particular potter, but the very deep plain band above the decoration suggests that it may be third-century (area over Building 12, unstratified, M14:01).

D115. Form 37, Central Gaulish. A panel with astragalus borders (Rogers A10) contains a figure, separated from a small double medallion by a horizontal pillar (Rogers P3, misstamped). In the adjacent panel is a Pan standing on a mask (D.411 = O.709). The basal wreath consists of acanthi (Rogers K35). Cf. stamped bowls of Paternus v, from London (S. & S. 1958, pl. 105, 15) for the general arrangement and Carrawburgh (*ibid.*, 12) for the Pan. *c.* AD 160–195 (area over Building 12, unstratified, M14:08).

D116. Form 37, East Gaulish, with triple-bordered ovolo above a straight line. Almost certainly Argonne ware, though no precise parallel has been found. Second half of the second century (area over Building 12, unstratified, M14:16). (Not illustrated.)

D117. Form 37, with a freehand tree, as used at Rheinzabern by Ianus ii and Cerialis v (Ricken 1948, Taf. 4, 7; 7, 2; 57, 1). *c.* AD 160–190 (Chalet 12, Building AL1, M14:39). (Not illustrated.)

D118. Form 37, Central Gaulish, with a single-bordered

ovolo (Rogers B28) and wavy-line borders. The panels include: 1) a seated figure (D.527 = O.913). 2) A stag (not in D. or O.), a seated doe (D.879 = O.1752A), a leafy spray and an eight-beaded rosette (Rogers C281). The basal wreath consists of trifid motifs (S. & S. 1958, fig. 17, 1). Quintilianus i is known to have used most of the details and the guide-lines enclosing the basal wreath make the attributiom almost certain. *c.* AD 125–150 (area over Building 11 and *intervallum* road (Road 6), M16:01). (Not illustrated.)

D119. Form 37, Central Gaulish, in the style of Criciro v, with panels: 1) a hare to right and acanthus-tips (from Rogers K2) in a double medallion, over a pair of birds looking back at each other (not closely identifiable). 2) A caryatid (D.656 = O.1199). Cf. S. & S. 1958, pl. 117, 7 for the birds, pl. 117, 4 for the caryatid and pl. 118, 19 for the acanthi. *c.* AD 135–165 (under phase 1 *intervallum* road surface (Road 4), N04:15).

D120. Form 37, Central Gaulish, with panels: 1) Vulcan (D.39 = O.66). 2) A crouching lion (D.753 = O.1421) and athlete (D.403 = O.688). Both panels have striated spindles. The Vulcan and lion are on signed bowls of Arcanus from Rottenburg and Heilbronn-Böckingen, respectively (Knorr 1939, 166, 4 and 164, 1). The spindle is on a bowl probably in his style from Verulamium (Dickinson 1984, D49). The wavy-line border and rosettes are also typical of his bowls. *c.* AD 125–140 (Building 1, demolition, N05:04).

D121. Form 37, Central Gaulish, with panels: 1) an acanthus (one of the series Rogers K16–35). 2) A bird (O.2250A) in a single festoon, over a trifid motif (Rogers G93?) between almond-shaped leaves (Rogers U161). The details are all on bowls in the style of Paternus iv, a Lezoux potter who signed moulds in the nominative. The bird and festoon are on a bowl from Burgh-by-Woodbridge, the leaves on one from Watercrook and the acanthus on one from Carlisle. *c.* AD 130–160 (Building 1, demolition, N05:04).

D122. Form 37, Central Gaulish. A bowl in the style of Avitus iv, with ovolo Rogers B228 and wreath of bifid motifs (Rogers G303) over a guide-line. A panelled zone consists of alternating saltires and vertical series of anchors (Rogers G395). The saltires are generally the same, with trifid motifs at the bottom (Rogers G32), spirals at the sides, attached to the borders by nine-petalled rosettes, and eleven-petalled rosettes (Rogers G227) in the centre, but some have leaves (Rogers J10) in the top and others have a Pan-mask (D.675 = O.1214). Below the decoration is a row of beads, on a guide-line. A small, S-shaped gadroon (Rogers U154) probably occurs with a Pan-mask. Perhaps from the same mould as a bowl from Gaul (S. & S. 1958, pl. 63, II). *c.* AD 125–140 (Alley 1, dump of demolition material, N05:23; with a sherd in N14:23 (Chalet 12, Building AM2)).

D123. Form 37, Central Gaulish. A saltire has almond-shaped leaves at the sides (Rogers U161). The adjacent panel has a 'twist', impressed vertically (Rogers U103, repeated). Both are on a bowl from

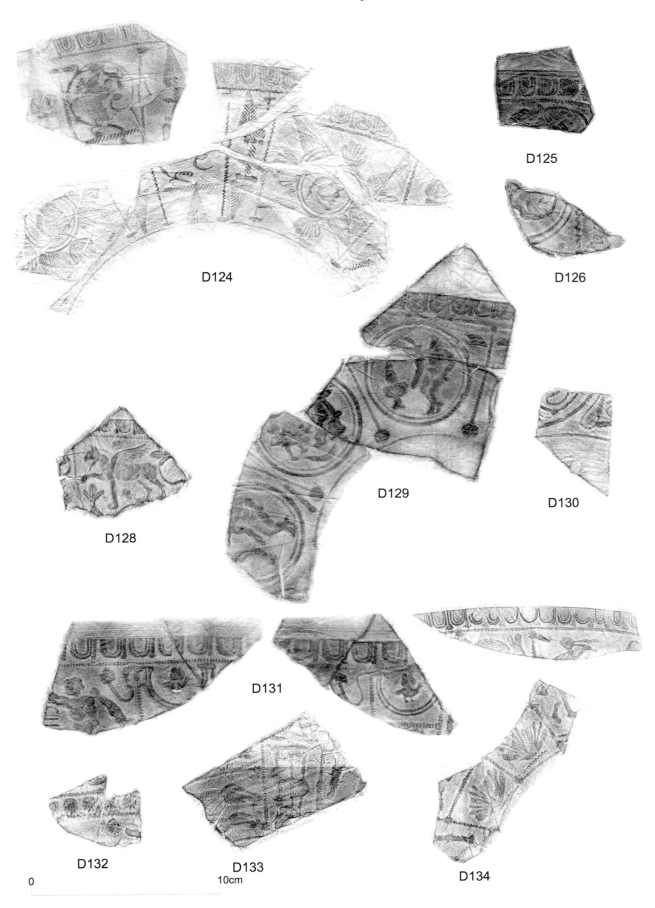

*Figure 22.06: Decorated samian nos D124–D134. Scale 1:2.*

Watercrook (Wild 1979, 287, 76) in the style of Paternus iv, who signed moulds in the nominative. *c.* AD 130–155 (Alley 1, dump of demolition material, N05:23).

D124. Form 37, Central Gaulish. A bowl in the style of X–5, with his ovolo (Rogers B31) and striated spindles. The panels contain: 1) triangular leaves (Rogers J33), joined by an astragalus. 2) A vine-scroll (Rogers M10) and the leaf again, separated by a striated spindle. 3) = 1). 4) a mask in a double medallion, surrounded by the leaves, alternating with fan-shaped motifs (Rogers G17). 5) = 1). Panels 4 and 5 are on one of X–5's bowls from London (BM M1374). Panel 4, without the mask, is on a bowl from Camelon (1970s excavations) and the mask, medallion, leaf and spindle are on a bowl from Wels (Karnitsch 1959, Taf. 32, 2). Grooved for mending. *c.* AD 125–140 (Building 3, *contubernium* 2, N07:15, 2608).

D125. Form 37, Central Gaulish, The ovolo (Rogers B47) is on a signed bowl of Criciro v from Corbridge (S. & S.1958, pl. 117, 1). No parallels have been found for the leaf in the scroll. *c.* AD 135–165 (area over Building 13, unstratified, N11:01).

D126. Form 37, Central Gaulish. One panel includes a leafy spray (Rogers H118) in a double medallion or festoon and a blob in the space below. The adjacent panel contains a column (Rogers P31). Servus iv (S. & S.'s Servus 2) used the zig-zag border (Rogers A26) and the festoon/medallion, but no other close parallels have been found. Mid- to late-Antonine (area over Building 13, unstratified, N11:01).

D127. A fragment from a Central Gaulish 'black samian' jar (form 68 etc.). The moulded decoration includes a leaf (Rogers J148) and a double medallion. Cf. Bémont 1977, pl. XXXVIII, PM314. Antonine (Building 13, room 7, N12:38). (Not illustrated.)

D128. Form 37, Central Gaulish, with another sherd in N14:11. One sherd shows a Hercules with snakes (D.464 = O.783, but the snake in the left hand has a broken tail) and an adjacent panel with a griffin (not in D. or O.), trifid motifs (Rogers G89) and leaf-tips (from Rogers J122?). The other sherd has a kilted man holding a staff which appears at the far side of the panel border. The second panel also has the trifid motif. The ovolo (Rogers B185 = B205) was used by Attianus ii and Drusus ii and occurs, together with the trifid motif, on a signed bowl of Drusus from Doncaster (Dickinson 1986a, fig. 31, 33). The leaf-tip is on his signed bowl from Asberg (Vanderhoeven 1974, Taf. 2, 14). None of the figure-types is attested for either potter, but the evidence of the motifs suggests a date *c.* AD 125–145 (area over Building 12, unstratified, N14:01).

D129. Form 37, with stamp of Clemens iii of Lezoux, CLEMENS or CLEMENTS (NT ligatured), retrograde, in the decoration (see no. S31 below). The two repeated panels include: 1) a cup (Rogers T3) and Apollo (D.55 = O.92, without mask) in a double medallion and lozenges (Rogers U30?) in the upper corners. 2) As 1), but with the medallion containing a putto(?), seated Cupid (D.259 = O.443B), leafy spray (Rogers J177) and another motif above the figures. The rosette junction-masks are

perhaps Rogers C171. The ovolo (Rogers B103) was mainly used by Advocisus, with whom Clemens may have been associated. *c.* AD 160–190 (Chalet 12, Building AM2, N14:02; with joining sherds in M14:01 (area over Building 13, unstratified) and N14:01 (area over Building 12, unstratified), 1885).

D130. Form 37, Central Gaulish, with a scroll involving striated spindles, in the manner of the Sacer i-Attianus ii group (S. & S.1958, pl. 83). Traces of a T upside-down below the decoration, as perhaps in OF.ATT retr., suggest that the bowl is by Attianus. It was made in a cracked mould. *c.* AD 125–145 (area over Alley 6, unstratified, N15:01).

D131. Form 30, with Cinnamus ii's common label-stamp, CI[NNAMI] retrograde (see no. S29 below), in a panel with an athlete (D.384 = O.652) and a corner-tendril with a polygonal leaf. The top of the adjacent panel contains a bird (O.2317) in a double festoon. The ovolo is his no. l (Rogers B223). The leaf-tendril, not common in his work, tends to appear on bowls with this ovolo and large figure-types, eg. Juhász 1935, Taf. III, 1, VIII 29 and IX, 21, from Brigetio. *c.* AD 150–180 (Chalet 12, Building AL2, N15:12; with a sherd from Building 12, chalet am, unstratified, M14:23 and a sherd from the 1988 excavations, context 8424 (*contubernium* 10, Period 2/3 occupation).

D132. Form 37, South Gaulish. The granular, orange-brown fabric and coarse cable borders suggest second-century Montans ware, though no exact parallels have been found for the decoration. The rosettes in the central wreath and in the zone below are apparently made up of repeated impressions of a ram's-horn motif. There may be a mould-stamp in the lowest of the three surviving zones. *c.* AD 115–145? (*intervallum* drain near Building 13, P12:08; joining L13:21 (Building AZ, robber trench)).

D133. Form 37, Central Gaulish, has ovolo Rogers B18 and panels: 1A) a grass-tuft (Rogers L19); 1B) bears (D.818 bis = 0.1616, over D.820 = 0.1627). 2A) a hare to left (D.950a = O.2116); 2B) a tripod (Rogers Q14). 3) A man with a staff (D.623 = 0.167). The rosette junction-masks probably consist of eight beads. Most of the details can be found on bowls in the so-called Ioenalis and Donnaucus styles at Les Martres-de-Veyre, and it is possible that the mould was made there, though the bowl itself is in Lezoux fabric. *c.* AD 125–140 (area over *intervallum* road (Road 4), unstratified, Q04:01).

D134. Form 37, South Gaulish, with sherds in Q04:01 (joining) and N05:04 (Building 1, demolition). The trident-tongued ovolo was used at La Graufesenque by Albanus iii, G. At-- Pas--, Bassinus i, Litugenus i and a potter whose name begins in Mas--.The panels include: 1A) a hare to right (D.941 = O.2056); IB) probably = 3B). 2) An erotic group (Oswald, pl. XC, A, with the female figure using a pillar as a support) and a dagger-like motif, attached to the top of the border by a rosette. 3A) A hare to left (D.949 = O.2114); 3B) a fan-shaped plant (three impressions of a smaller version of the motif Hermet 1934, pl. 14, 49) over a wavy line. 4B) = 3B. 5) = 1). The erotic group and the hares are on a

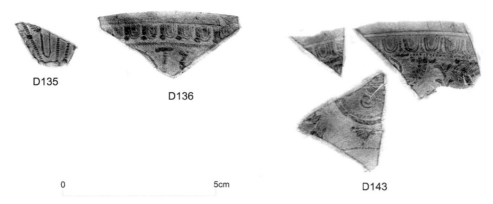

*Figure 22.07: Decorated samian nos D135–D143. Scale 1:2.*

bowl from the Bregenz Cellar hoard (Jacobs 1912, no. 11) and the hares recur on a stamped bowl of Biragillus i from Riegel (Knorr 1907, Taf. XV, 5). *c*. AD 90–110 (Rampart building (F2), unsealed rampart material, Q04:05).

D135. Form 37, from Les Martres-de-Veyre. The beaded borders and the leaves in the side quadrants of a saltire (Rogers J127) suggest that the mould was made by X–13; cf. form 30 from Brecon (S. & S. 1958, pl. 49, 588). *c*. AD 100–120 (pit in Road 4, Q04:12, probably with a sherd in the area over the East rampart, unstratified, Q05:01).

D136. Form 37, Central Gaulish, drilled for mending. The ovolo, single medallion in one panel and slave or satyr (D.374 = O.647) in the next are all on bowls from Lezoux in the style of Austrus. *c*. AD 125–140 (pit in Road 4, Q04:15).

D137. Form 37, Central Gaulish. The single-bordered ovolo (Rogers B28), with guide-line below, and small double medallion suggest the work of Quintilianus i (cf. S. & S. 1958, pl. 70, 9, from Birdoswald). *c*. AD 125–150 (pit in Road 4, Q04:15). (Not illustrated.)

D138. Form 37, Central Gaulish, by Cerialis ii or an associate, with his characteristic bud in the decoration (Rogers J178, partly impressed), together with a Hercules and lion (D.467 = O.785). *c*. AD 135–170 (area over East rampart, unstratified, Q05:02). (Not illustrated.)

D139. Form 37, Central Gaulish. The ovolo (Rogers B233) was used by potters such as Pugnus ii and X–6. The sherd may have been shaped as a counter. *c*. AD 125–150 (Building 1, officer's quarters, Q05:17). (Not illustrated.)

D140. Form 37, Central Gaulish. The ovolo (Rogers B76) and zig-zag border are on a bowl from Gloucester (unpublished) in the style of Arcanus. An animal to left is perhaps the lion D.753 = O.1421 (but with the broken tail replaced, freehand), which appears on a signed bowl from Heilbronn-Böckingen (S. & S. 1958, pl. 78, 7). The partly-impressed acanthi in the field are on a bowl in his style from Cannstatt (*ibid.*, 6). *c*. AD 125–140 (Building 1, verandah, Q05:25). (Not illustrated.)

D141. Form 37, Central Gaulish, with panels: 1) a saltire, with leaves (Rogers J50?) at the sides. 2) A slave with a basket (D.321 = O.595). 3) A sea-creature? The horizontal astragali, while not exactly paralleled, suggest a connection with potters such as Pugnus ii, Tittius or X–6. *c*. AD 125–150 (Building 1, officer's quarters, Q05:34).

D142. Form 30, Central Gaulish. An Apollo (D.52 = O.83) and ring, in a panel with a zig-zag border, are on a signed bowl of Arcanus from Rottenburg (S. & S. 1958, pl. 78, 1). *c*. AD 125–140 (area over Buildings 3 and 16, unstratified, Q08:05, 2512). (Not illustrated.)

D143. Form 37, East Gaulish (La Madeleine). The decoration includes the ovolo (Fölzer 1913, Taf. 25, 119?) and chevron festoons (*ibid.*,111), containing spirals and with series of trifid motifs between (*ibid.*, 76?) and acanthi below (*ibid.*, 74). The decoration is closed by a bead-row. *c*. AD 130–160 (Feature 2, post-Roman dereliction, Q08:11, 2595).

D144. Form 37, Central Gaulish. The Pan (D.411 = O.709), in a panel with a vertical border of squarish beads, suggests the work of Paternus v. *c*. AD 160–195 (drain east of Building 3, Period 3, Q08:18, 2591).

## The potter's stamps

Each entry gives: context number, potter (i, ii, etc., where homonyms are involved, die number, form, reading of the stamp, published example (if any), pottery of origin, discussion, date.

(a), (b) and (c) indicate:

(a) Stamp attested at the pottery in question.
(b) Potter, but not the particular stamp, attested at the pottery in question.
(c) Assigned to the pottery on the evidence of fabric, distribution and, or, form.

Ligatured letters are underlined.

S1. Advocisus 8a 37 [A]DVOCI[SI] (S. & S. 1958, pl. 169) Lezoux (a). Decorated bowls with this stamp occur elsewhere on Hadrian's Wall and at some of the Hinterland forts which were reoccupied *c*. AD 160. There are also three examples from the Wroxeter forum destruction. *c*. AD 160–190 (Cistern 1, fill, E08:29, 2305).

S2.   Aestivus 2a 31 [AIIS]TIVI:M Lezoux (b). There are several examples of this stamp in the group of late-Antonine samian recovered off Pudding Pan Rock. It was used on forms not normally made before AD 160, such as 31R and Ludowici Tg. *c.* AD 160–190 (area over Building 5 and Alley 4, unstratified, H05:01).

S3.   Aestivus 3c 31 AESTIVIM (Walke 1965, Taf. 40, 53) Lezoux (a). A stamp noted at Binchester and Haltonchesters. It comes from one of his later dies, to judge by many examples on form 31R and a few on form 79, though his occasional use of other stamps on form 27 suggests that he was at work by AD 160. *c.* AD 160–185 (rubble over west *praetentura*, H04:18, 783).

S4.   Albillus i 1b 18/31–31 ALBI[ΛΛI MA] Lezoux (b). One of Albillus's less-common stamps, without internal dating. His site record in general, including Chesters, Chesterholm, Corbridge (in a late-Antonine pottery store) and Ilkley, and his use of form 18/31R suggest a range *c.* AD 155–185 (Alley 3, F04:33, 572).

S5.   Albusa 1a 33 [Λ]LBVSΛ (Dickinson 1986b, 187, 3.11) Lezoux (a). This stamp has been found in late-Antonine groups at Lezoux, and on forms 31R and 79. There are two examples from South Shields. *c.* AD 170–200 (Chalet 12, Building AM2, M14:45, 1891).

S6.   Amando 1b 33 ΛMΛNDO Banassac (b). No other examples of this stamp have been noted so far. Apart from four stamps from London (from a different die, and perhaps all part of a single consignment), Amando is otherwise known only at Banassac. This source suggests that the Wallsend piece is Hadrianic, rather than later (levelling north of Buildings Q and R, F11:13, 1148).

S7.   Ambitotus 1a 18/31 ΛMBITOTVMΛ Lezoux (a). There are many examples of this stamp in a group of burnt samian of *c.* AD 140–150 from Castleford, mostly on form 18/31R, but also on forms 18/31 and 81 (Rush *et al* 2000, fig. 29, nos 563–75). It occurs also on the outsize variant of form 33 which was occasionally made at Lezoux in the Hadrianic and early-Antonine periods. *c.* AD 125–150 (Alley 5, F14:14, 1133).

S8.   Annius ii 4a 18/31R ΛN[NIVSF] Annius ii worked at both Les Martres-de-Veyre and Lezoux, but there is no evidence that this stamp was used at Les Martres and the Wallsend piece is certainly in Lezoux fabric. The stamp occurs in period IIC at Verulamium (*c.* AD 140–150: Hartley 1972a, S112) and at Birdoswald, where it will belong to the Hadrianic occupation. *c.* AD 130–150 (Building 7, west granary, F11:12, 956).

S9.   Asiaticus 3a 31 ASIA[TICIO] Lezoux (b). This potter's stamps appear on some of the later Antonine forms, such as 80 and Ludowici Tg/Tx. This particular stamp was used on form 79. His site record includes Catterick and South Shields. *c.* AD 160–190 (area over Building 9, unstratified, F13:04, 2643).

S10.  Atilianus i 5d 33 [Λ]TILIΛNI[M] Lezoux (b). One of Atilianus i's less-common stamps, noted twice more on form 33 and once on form 31R. His output

also includes forms 79, 79R, 80 and Ludowici Tg and stamps from one of his other dies occur in the Puddding Pan Rock wreck, *c.* AD 160–200 (Chalet 9, robbing and post-Roman dereliction, G13:03, 1012).

S11.  Aurelius ii 1a 31R [Λ]VRIIΛIM Lezoux (c). No other examples of this stamp have been noted by us, but the form of the vessel suggests mid- to late-Antonine date (Alley 7, K12:22).

S12.  Aventinus ii 1a 31 [AVENT]TINI·M (Durand-Lefebvre 1963, 36, 113) Lezoux (a). This appears on the rims of decorated bowls by early- to mid-Antonine Lezoux potters, but also on plain ware in a group of Antonine burnt samian from Aquincum, presumably destroyed in the Marcomannic Wars. *c.* AD 150–180 (*intervallum* drain near Building 13, P12:08, 1775).

S13.  Avitus iv 11a 33 ΛV[IF] Lezoux (b). This potter's decorated bowls are mainly Hadrianic, but his plain ware is common in Antonine Scotland. His output consists largely of forms 18/31 and 27, and so he is unlikely to have been at work after the middle of the second century. *c.* AD 125–150 (area over Building 2 and Alley 1, unstratified, M05:04, 29).

S14.  Banuus 1a 37 BANVI, retr. (S. & S. 1958, pl. 169) Lezoux (a). Decorated bowls with this stamp occur at forts in northern Britain reoccupied *c.* AD 160, such as Carrawburgh and Chesterholm. There is also one from the Brougham cemetery, where most of the samian is late-Antonine. *c.* AD 175–250 (Cistern 1, lower fill, E08:44, 2402 and 2393; upper fill, E08:27, 2365).

S15.  Belsus 1a 31 BELSVSƎE (Ludowici 1927, 210, a) Rheinzabern (a). A stamp noted on decorated bowls of the later second century and on a variety of plain forms, including 32 and 79. *c.* AD 175–200 (Building 8, cess pit, D12:34, 1205).

S16.  Belsus 3b 37 [BE]LSVSF, retr. (Ludowici 1927, 239, a) Rheinzabern (a). This stamp appears mainly on decorated bowls, but has also been noted on forms 31, 32, 40 and Ludowici RSc. *c.* AD 175–200 (area over Building 10, unstratified, D14:01).

S17.  Biturix 1d 81 (stamped on the collar) BITVRIX[F] Lezoux (b). The occurrence of Biturix's wares in the Rhineland suggests that he worked in the first half of the second century. This is supported by the use of this particular stamp on forms 18/31R, 27 and the Hadrianic and early-Antonine variant of form 33. *c.* AD 125–150 (Building 3, *contubernium 2*, N07:14, 2607).

S18.  Bonoxus 3c 18/31 ·:BOИOXS·F:· Lezoux (b). This is noted only on forms 18/31, 18/31R and 27, all made in the Hadrianic and early-Antonine periods. One example comes from the Saalburg Erdkastell (before *c.* AD 139: Hartley 1970, 26.15). *c.* AD 125–150 (Alley 3, F04:12, 356).

S19.  Bracisilus 4a 31 BRΛCIИLVⅠ Lavoye (b), Avocourt (b). The only dating evidence for Bracisilus comes from his forms. This particular stamp appears on forms 27, 32, 79 and 80R; another is on form 40. His use of form 27 suggests activity by the early-Antonine period, at the latest, though he was clearly still at work after AD 160. *c.* AD 140–170? (Building 7, east wall robber trench, H09:18).

S20. Cadgatis 6b 33 CADGATIS, retr., Lezoux (b). No other examples of this stamp are known to us. Cadgatis's stamps occur on Hadrian's Wall and in Antonine Scotland and one appears on the rim of a stamped, decorated bowl of Albucius ii, from Bregenz. His plain forms include 27 and 31R. *c.* AD 145–175 (area over Building 12, unstratified, L14:01, 1403).

S21. Calava 2b 18/31 [CA]ᴌAVA·F Lezoux (a). The forms on which this stamp appears include 18/31R, 27 and 31. It occurs in the Rhineland (presumably before *c.* AD 150), at Chesters and probably at Camelon. There are 11 examples from a pottery shop at Castleford destroyed by fire in the 140s (Rush *et al* 2000, fig. 29, nos 601–11). *c.* AD 125–150 (Alley 3, F04:33, 556).

S22. Calendio 2a 31 [CALEᴎD]IO Lezoux (a). Some of Calendio's stamps occur on the rims of decorated bowls by both Hadrianic and early- to mid-Antonine potters, such a Sacer i/Docilis i, the Large S Potter, Laxtucissa and Cinnamus ii. This particular stamp, used only on plain ware, appears more often on forms made before AD 160 than later, but there is one example on form 79. *c.* AD 140–170 (Building 2, *contubernium 8*, L05:25, 840).

S23. Caletus 2a 33 CAL·E[TIM] Lezoux (a). A stamp noted in groups of late-Antonine samian from Pudding Pan Rock and London (Dickinson 1986b, 187, 3.24). Examples are also noted from Bainbridge, Catterick and Malton. *c.* AD170–200 (area over Tower 1, unstratified, H03:03, 736).

S24. Camulinus 2a 31 CᴧMVᴌIᴎI Lezoux (a). A stamp of a minor Lezoux potter, noted from Chesters and South Shields and on forms 15/31, 31R and 79 or Tg. *c.* AD 150–190 (Road 1, E07:12, 2352).

S25. Carussa 3a 33 CA·:RVSSA (Dickinson 1986b, 188, 3.28) Lezoux (a). Two faint horizontal lines at the end of this stamp suggest that CARVSS<u>AF</u> may have been intended. All the evidence suggests that the die was not in use before *c.* AD 160. Examples are noted from Catterick, Chesterholm, Haltonchesters and South Shields and on forms 31R and 79. *c.* AD 160–190 (rubble west of Building 5, dereliction, E05:04, 153).

S26. Celsianus 2a 38 CELSIANI·<u>MA</u> Lezoux (a). A stamp used on some of the later Antonine forms, such as 31R, 79R and 80. *c.* AD 160–190 (Cistern 1, fill, E08:29, 2360).

S27. Cerotcus la 31 CE[ROTC]IM Lezoux (a). The record for this uncommon stamp offers no close dating evidence, but the form and fabric of the Wallsend piece are Antonine (Building BJ, G11:03, 1079).

S28–9. Cinnamus ii 5b 30 (2) [CI]NNAM[I]; CI[, retr. (Walke 1965, Taf. 39, 11) Lezoux (a). The commonest of Cinnamus's stamps on decorated ware, with many examples from both Hadrian's Wall and Antonine Scotland, though with slightly more from Scotland. *c.* AD 150–180 (area over Building 12, unstratified, L14:01, 1406; Chalet 12, Building AM, post-Roman robbing, M14:23).

S30–31. Clemens iii la 37; 33 CLEM..., retr., CLEM<u>ENTS</u> (S. & S. 1990, pl. 174, 3) Lezoux (a). This stamp is known from Benwell and Catterick. It occurs on form 79 and, sometimes, on decorated moulds which also have stamps of Priscus iii. Both potters are connected stylistically with Advocisus. *c.* AD 160–190 (Area over *Via quintana*, unstratified, G12:01, 1007; Chalet 12, Building AM2, N14:02; with joining sherds in M14:01 (area over Building 13, unstratified) and N14:01 (area over Building 12, unstratified), 1885).

S32. Cobnertus iv 4a 37 [COBNERT]VSF (Ludowici 1927, 240, a) Rheinzabern (a). This mould-stamp of one of the earlier Rheinzabern potters to export to Britain is known on decorated bowls from Benwell, Bowness-on-Solway, Haltonchesters and Stanwix. Most significantly, it occurs at the timber fort at Iza, Slovakia, destroyed in AD 170/175 (information from Dr Klara Kuzmová). It was sometimes used to stamp the rims of bowls by Reginus vi, who started his career at Heilignberg, before moving to Rheinzabern. *c.* AD 160–190 (area over Buildings Q and R, unstratified, F12:01, 1104).

S33. Conatius 3a 31 CONATIVSF (Ludowici 1927, 212, a) Rheinzabern (a). This was used on some of the later Rheinzabern forms such as 31 (Sa), 31R (Sb), 32, 32R and Ludowici Tb. The glaze is ground off under the base. Late second century or first half of third century (area over Alley 4, unstratified, F05:01, 141).

S34. Cottalus la 32 etc. COTTAL[VSFE] (Karnitsch 1960, 136) Rheinzabern (b). A stamp noted twice from Regensburg, once from the fortress, founded in the late second century, and once from the Kumpfmühl, where it may possibly read COTTALVSFEC (museum no. A2373). It is also known on form 32. Late second century or first half of third century (area over Building 10 and Road 6, unstratified, G12:15, 1183).

S35. Crucuro ii(?) Uncertain 1 18/31 ]VROᴎ·O Lezoux (c). The form and fabric of this dish are Hadrianic or early-Antonine, which would be consistent with Crucuro ii's output of forms 18/31, 18/31R and 27, among others. *c.* AD 125–150 (Building 9, *contubernium* 2, E13:13, 1134).

S36. Dagodubnus ii la 33 [DAGOD]V<u>ᴃN</u>VSF (Ludowici 1927, 213) Rheinzabern (a). This was apparently only used on cups of form 33. Examples are noted from Bainbridge and Housesteads. The forms and fabrics suggest mid- to late-Antonine date (Alley 10/Building 17 road surface, third century, E04:10, 418).

S37. Dagomarus 11a 18/31 DᴧGO[<u>MᴧRI</u>] Lezoux (c). Dagomarus worked at Les Martres-de-Veyre under Trajan and later at Lezoux. This stamp is from a die probably used only at Lezoux. It occurs in the Rhineland, in a pottery shop at Castleford destroyed in the 140s (Rush *et al* 2000, fig. 29, nos 631–2), at South Shields and in a tumulus at Helsoven, Belgium, with stamps of late-Hadrianic and early-Antonine potters (Roosens 1976, Taf. 1). *c.* AD 125–145 (Building 1, demolition/make-up, P05:08, 280, WSP281).

S38. Divicatus 3b 18/31 or 31 [DIVIC]ATVS Lezoux (a). A stamp used on forms 18/31, 27 and 38, suggesting that it was current in the Hadrianic or early-Antonine periods. Further evidence of this is its occurrence in the Rhineland, where Lezoux ware was rarely, if ever, marketed after *c.* AD 150. An example from the *vicus* at Malton is almost certainly Hadrianic. *c.* AD 140–155 (area over Building 9, unstratified, E13:28, 1482).

S39. Do(v)eccus i 11b 31 DO[VIICCVS] Lezoux (b). This was used on forms 31R and 79. It occurs at Malton and in a late-Antonine group from London (Dickinson 1986b, 189, 3.47). *c.* AD 165–200 (area over Building 14 and Road 3, unstratified, J12:05).

S40. Do(v)eccus i 11e 31R DOVIICCV⌐Lezoux (b). There are two examples of this stamp from Housesteads and another from Malton. *c.* AD 165–200 (from 'Town Hall' collection).

S41. Do(v)eccus i 13a 31 DOIICCVS (S. & S. 1958, pl. 147, 2) Lezoux (b). This occurs at Benwell (2), Haltonchesters (2) and in late-Antonine burials at the Brougham cemetery. *c.* AD 165–200 (area over Building 12, unstratified, L14:01, 1404).

S42. Falana 1a 27 ⌐ΛΚΛΛΛ retr. Lezoux (c). Stamps from this die in the Rhineland suggest that the potter was at work before the middle of the second century. One example, from the Saalburg Erdkastell (Hartley 1970, 26, 46), will be earlier than *c.* AD 139. *c.* AD 125–150 (dereliction over Alley 1, L05:29, 861).

S43. Faventinus ii 2a 31R [FAVEN]TINVS (Ludowici 1927, 214, a) Rheinzabern (a). Faventinus is not well dated, but examples of this stamp on forms 32 and Ludowici Se suggest that he may still have been at work in the third century. Late second century or first half of third century (Chalet 10, post-Roman dereliction, F15:06, 1454).

S44. Fidelis ii 2a 32 etc. [FIDII]LISFE (Ludowici 1927, 214, a) Rheinzabern (a). Stamps from this die occur at Malton (2) and an early third-century group from London (Dickinson 1986b, 189, 3.51). It was used on forms 31R and 32R. Late second century or first half of the third century (Building 16, floor, K07:08).

S45. Florus vi 2a 31R ⌐LoRV⌐ Trier (c). There is no internal dating for this stamp, but one of his others comes from the late second-century foundation of Niederbieber. Late second- or first half of the third century (from collection in Great North Museum: Hancock, Newcastle).

S46. Geamillus ii 1a 33 GIIΛM[ILLIOF] Lezoux (a). Very few stamps have been recorded for this potter and they all come from the same die. His forms include 79 and 79/80. Mid- to late-Antonine (area over *Via quintana*, unstratified, D12:01).

S47. Gemenia 1a 33 GIIMIINIA Lezoux (c). The use of this stamp on forms 79R and 80 suggests a date *c.* A.D.160–200 (Feature 2, post-Roman dereliction, Q08:11, 2569).

S48. Geminus v 1a 18/31 or 31 GE[MINI] (*ORL* B2a, 15, 7) La Madeleine (b). This stamp occurs on form 18/31R, including one from South Shields, and on unrouletted dishes which are closer to form 18/31 than to 31. *c.* AD 130–155 (Building 1, floor, M05:25).

S49–50. Genitor ii 5a 33; 31R G·E·N·I·T·O·R·F, ·G·E·N[ Lezoux (a). This occurs in a late second-century group from London (Dickinson 1986b, 189, 3.54). It appears elsewhere on form 31R. *c.* AD 160–190

(area over West rampart and gate, unstratified, D08:11, 2257; Cistern 1, rubble, E08:45, 2439).

S51. Giamillus iv 1a 31 [GI]MILLVS Rheinzabern (Ludowici 1927, 216). The potter's output seems to have consisted mainly of forms 31 and 33, though one form Ludowici Tp has been noted. The absence of any of the later Rheinzabern forms may mean that he was not at work in the third century. Mid- to late-Antonine? (Road 3, G12:02, 1008).

S52. Indercillus 2a 33 INDERCILLI Lezoux (c). An Indercillus, perhaps this potter, worked at Les Martres-de-Veyre under Trajan, but this stamp seems to have been used only at Lezoux, to judge by the associated fabrics. There are two examples from Catterick and one from Chesterholm. *c.* AD 125–140 (area over Building 3 and Alley 2, unstratified, N07:01, 2458).

S53. Iulius Numidus 4a 80 or Ludowici Tx [NVMI] DI<u>MA</u> Lezoux (a). A stamp used on forms 31R and 79. It occurs at Benwell and in a late-Antonine group from London (Dickinson 1986b, 190, 3.68). *c.* AD160–200 (area over Building 15, unstratified, J07:01).

S54. Lupinus 3a 33 (slightly burnt) LVPINIM Lezoux (a). Lupinus's stamps appear on mid- to late-Antonine forms; 3a is on form 79/80, others occur on forms 15/31R, 31R and 80. *c.* ADI55–185 (area over Building 1, unstratified, L04:01, 701).

S55. Macrinus ii 2f 27 [MAC]RINI Lezoux (b). This is one of the less-common stamps of the earlier Lezoux Macrinus, whose output consists mainly of forms 18/31 and 27. His signature is also on a form 29 mould which can scarcely be later than the Hadrianic period. His site record includes Birdoswald (from the lowest level of the Alley), Bearsden and Corbridge. *c.* AD125–150 (area over East rampart, unstratified, R05:?).

S56. Maia...? 1a 33 MΛIΛI Lezoux (c). This fairly common stamp may be illiterate, but could equally well belong to a potter whose name is Maia, or begins in Maia... The associated forms and fabrics and examples from Bainbridge and Catterick suggest mid- to late-Antonine date (area over Road 8, unstratified, F09:01, 2195).

S57. Maior i 9e or 9e' 31 M[ΛIORIM] OR M[ΛIOIIM] Vichy (Terre-Franche) (a), Lezoux (b). Later impressions of this stamp have a faint vertical stroke between O and R, as if from a crack in the die. This version appears on form 31R from Ilkley and Catterick and form 31 from Bainbridge. There is no site dating for the original impression, but it is unlikely to be earlier than AD 160, when Maior's general record is taken into account. The fabric of the Wallsend piece belongs to the Lezoux range. *c.* AD 160–200 (area over Building 1 and *intervallum* road (Road 4), unstratified, M04:01, 11).

S58. Malledo 2a 31 M[ALLEDO·F] Lezoux (a). Malledo's stamps turn up on forms made at Lezoux in the later second century, such as 31R and 80, both of which occur with Die 3a. *c.* AD160–190 (area over Building 10 and Road 9, unstratified, H15:01).

S59. Malledo 4a 33 MALLEDVF· Lezoux (a). A stamp used on forms 79, 80 and Ludowici Tx. *c.* AD 160–190 (from 'Town Hall' collection).

S60. Malluro i 3b 18/31 MALLVRO·F Lezoux (a). Much of Malluro's output consists of forms not made much after the middle of the second century, but Oswald (1931, 181) notes form 79 from Cirencester and there are other reports of single examples of forms 80 and Ludowici Tg. This presumably means that he was at work after AD160, though Die 3b, used mainly on forms 18/31 and 27 and noted on form 42, is unlikely to have survived so long and the Wallsend dish, with its shallow wall, is almost certainly Hadrianic or very early-Antonine. A graffito, Flavini, is inscribed under the base, after firing. c. AD130–140 (Alley 2, dereliction, N08:44, 2627).

S61. Marcellinus ii 2a 31R [MA]RCELLINIF. (Dickinson 1986b, 191, 3.93). Examples of this stamp occur in a kiln-dump of late-Antonine wasters at Lezoux and, twice, in the group of samian from Pudding Pan Rock. c. AD160–200 (Building S. robber trench, F11:18, 1208).

S62. Marcellus ii 3a 18/31 [MARC]KKI, retr., Les Martres-de-Veyre (c). The forms on which this stamp appears (18/31, 18/31R and 27) and the associated fabrics suggest origin at Les Martres in the Trajanic or early-Hadrianic period. c. AD100–120 (Feature 2, post-Roman dereliction, Q08:11, 2596).

S63. Marcus v 9a 31 M[ARCI·] Lezoux (b). Marcus's output includes forms 31R, 79 and 79R and his wares appear elsewhere on the Wall, at Chesters, Haltonchesters and South Shields, There are several examples from Pennine forts, including Ilkley and Bainbridge. 9a occurs at Catterick and in the Pudding Pan Rock wreck. c. AD160–200 (area over Building 8, unstratified, E10:01, 2206).

S64–5. Martius iv 1b 33 (2) MARTIM Lezoux (a). A stamp recorded from South Shields and Malton and in late-Antonine contexts at London (Dickinson 1986b, 191, 3.103) and the Brougham cemetery. c. AD160–190 (Portico AY, Period 2, H07:11, 2171; Alley 7, K12:23, 2075).

S66. Mascellio i 4b 38 or 44 MA[SCELLIO] Lezoux (a). This occurs elsewhere on the Wall, at Haltonchesters and South Shields, and is in a late-Antonine context at London (Dickinson 1986b, 192, 3.111). It was used on forms 31R and 79R. c. AD160–190 (from collection in Great North Museum: Hancock, Newcastle).

S67. Maternianus i 3a 33 MATERAIAIIAI Lezoux (a). At least 11 of the stamps noted from this die come from Pudding Pan Rock and there are three in a late-Antonine context at London (Dickinson 1986b, 192, 3.113–115). Single examples are noted from Benwell, Chesters and Housesteads. Matern(n)ian or Matern(n)iaf may have been intended, but the reading is far from clear. c. AD160–200 (Portico AY, Period 2, H07:11, 2170).

S68. Mercator ii 2f 27 MERC[AIⁱ] Lezoux (b). Only one other stamp from this die is known to us, on form 18/31 from the York colonia. Mercator ii's wares reached the Rhineland, presumably before c. AD150, and his decorated ware shows him to have been connected with the Quintilianus i group. c. AD125–150 (pit in Road 4, Q04:12, 327).

S69. Mossius ii la 31 MOSSI·MA[N] Lezoux (a). A stamp

recorded from Verulamium (in Period IID, after AD150: Hartley 1972a, fig. 82, S120) and South Shields. Other stamps from sites such as Benwell and Malton are likely to belong to the 160s or later, but his occasional use of form 27 suggests that he began work rather earlier. c. AD150–180 (rubble over west praetentura, H04:19, 810).

S70. Muxtullus 1a 33 [·MVXTVLLI·M] (Walke 1965, Taf. 43, 264) Lezoux (a). The site evidence for Muxtullus suggests that he was at work by c. AD 140, but this stamp is likely to be from one of his later dies. It is known from the Wroxeter Gutter hoard and on form 31R. In view of this, an example from South Shields is more likely to be after c. AD 160 than Hadrianic. c. AD 150–180 (pit in Assembly area, F09:23, 2260).

S71–2. Namilianus la 31R (2) NAMILIANIMA Lezoux (b). Other examples of this stamp come from Chesterholm, Malton and South Shields. c. AD160–200 (Road 3, F11:19, 1202; Great North Museum: Hancock, acc. no. 1961.3).

S73–4. Namilianus 3b 31R (2) NAM[ILIANI] Lezoux (a). There are four examples of this stamp in the late-Antonine material from Pudding Pan Rock and two from Benwell. c. AD 160–200 (area over Alley 4, unstratified, F05:01, 131; area over Via quintana, unstratified, L13:01, 1748).

S75. Nicephor ii 2a 18/31 or 31 [NIC]EPH[ORF] Lezoux (a). The occurrence of this stamp on forms 18/31, 27 and 42 and in the Rhineland is consistent with activity before the middle of the second century, but a single example on form 80 suggests that the die was still in use c. AD160, or later. c. AD140–165 (pit in Assembly area, F09:59, 2388).

S76. Paternus iii 2b 18/31 PATERNI Lezoux (b). There are five examples of this stamp from a pottery shop at Castleford destroyed by fire in the 140s (Rush et al 2000, fig. 30, nos 812–6); it is also known from Camelon. In his decorated ware this Paternus shares an ovolo with, and sometimes stamps the same moulds as, Ianuaris ii. It is possible that he is the same potter as the next, who occasionally used the same ovolo. c. AD135–150 (Alley 1, dump of demolition material, N05:23, 340; Alley 1, upper layers, N05:07, 309, and Building B, robber trench, N05:17, joining).

S77–8. Paternus v 7a 37 (2) [PA]TERNFE; ]NFE, retr. (Durand-Lefebvre 1963, 181, 562) Lezoux (a). Decorated bowls with this well-known label stamp are common on Hadrian's Wall and at Hinterland forts, but there are none from any Scottish forts with normal Antonine occupations (Hartley 1972b, 33). This, and the style of his decoration, suggest that he was not at work before AD160 or so. c. AD160–195 (area over Via quintana, unstratified, F12:01; area over Buildings 9 and 10 and Road 9, unstratified, H14:04, 1292).

S79. Paullus v 8c or 8c′ 79 P[AAAK·KI] OR P[AAAK·IⁱI] Lezoux (b). Several vessels stamped with the earlier version of Die 8c occur in the Pudding Pan Rock wreck and there are eight with the modified stamp in a late-Antonine group from London (Dickinson 1986b, 193, 3.144–51). c. AD160–200 (area over Building 12, unstratified, M14:01).

S80.  Peculiaris i 5a 27 (large) ꟼECVLIAR·F (Curle 1911, 238, 72) Lezoux (a). The earlier of Peculiaris's commoner stamps, normally used on forms not made after *c.* AD160, such as 18/31, 18/31R and 27, though two examples are noted on form 80. It occurs at Carzield and Newstead (2). *c.* AD140–170 (from 'Town Hall' collection).

S81.  Primanus iii 3b 33 PRI[MANI·M] (Juhász 1935, pl. XLVII, 229) Lezoux (b). Dating evidence for Primanus includes stamps from Benwell, Bainbridge and in late second-century groups from London and Pudding Pan Rock (from more than one die). 3b occurs in the Wroxeter Gutter (2) and on form 31R. *c.* AD160–200 (area over Building 13, unstratified, N12:01 1663).

S82.  Pugnus ii la 33 PVGNI[·Mꟲ] (Nash-Williams 1930, fig. 2, 83) Lezoux (b). This stamp occurs on plain ware in the mid- to late-Antonine Wroxeter Gutter deposit, but also appears occasionally on form 27, which suggests that it was in use before *c.* AD 160. On form 37 moulds it is associated with decoration in one of Pugnus's late styles. *c.* AD 150–180, (area over Building 5, unstratified, J05:03, 712).

S83.  Quadratus iii 1a 79/80 [QVAD]RATI· Lezoux (a). Quadratus's stamps appear on some of the later Antonine forms, such as 31R, 79, 79R and Ludowici Tg. 1a occurs on the first three and also at Malton, Newcastle and in a grave in the Brougham cemetery, together with a decorated bowl of Banuus. *c.* AD160–190 (from 'Town Hall' collection).

S84.  Reginus iv 4b 37 rim [REG]INI·MA Lezoux (b). This also appears on the rims of form 37s from Worcester and Bainesse Farm, Catterick; all three bowls have the same ovolo, used by Advocisus and his associates. Reginus's plain ware includes forms 18/31 and 27, which suggests some activity before *c.* AD160, though this stamp is unlikely to be earlier than that. *c.* AD160–180 (area over Cistern 1, unstratified, E08:20, 2295).

S85.  Reginus vi 5a 32 etc. [R]EGIꟲV[SFE] Rheinzabern (Ludowici 1927, 227e). Reginus vi worked at lttenweiler, Heiligenberg and Kräherwald before moving to Rheinzabern, where this piece was made. His career there probably falls within the range *c.* AD160–180 (area over Building 12 and Road 3, unstratified, M14:01).

S86.  Remicus lb' 33 ꟄEMICꟾ (Loeschcke 1911, Taf. LXXV, 1498–1500) La Madeleine (c). The distribution of this stamp, which read REMICF before the die broke, or became worn at the ends, is entirely in Britain and the Rhineland. It is sufficiently common in Britain to suggest origin at La Madeleine, rather than any of the other smaller East Gaulish factories. Most of the examples are on form 33, but there are a few on form 27 and one on form 31. His other die was used to stamp form 18/31. *c.* AD130–160 (area of Building 13, unstratified, L09:15, 2568).

S87.  Roppus ii la 18/31 [ROP]PV[SFE] Les Martres-de-Veyre (b). Roppus ii is probably not one of the earlier Les Martres potters, though some of his dishes are Trajanic. There are two examples of this stamp in a group of burnt samian of the 140s at Castleford (Rush *et al* 2000, fig. 30, nos 843–4). It also occurs at the Saalburg Erdkastell (before

AD139: Hartley 1970, no.56). *c.* AD110–140 (Road 8, dereliction, E09:20, 2431).

S88–9.  Sabellus 6a 18/31–31 (2) [Ꞔꟲ']BEꟗVS, Ꞔꟲ'B..[ La Madeleine (a). This stamp is particularly common in Lower Germany, but there are also several examples from Britain, including three from South Shields and one from Stanwix. It was used on forms 18/31 and 18/31R. *c.* AD130–160 (area over Building 12, unstratified, L14:01, 1555; area over Building BA, unstratified, M13:01, 1711).

S90.  Sabinus vii 1a 18/31R–31R SABINI Lezoux (a). Very few stamps are recorded for this Sabinus. 1a is known on forms 18/31R, 27 and 38 or 44 and on an unidentified form from Inveresk (Dickinson 1988, Fiche 1:B5, 2.70). The die will have been in use in the Hadrianic-Antonine period, and the form of this dish suggests early- to mid-Antonine date. See Graffiti report, no. 1 (Alley 1, dump of demolition material, N05:23, 325 and 326).

S91.  Sabinus viii 5a flat base SABI[NIOF] Lezoux (b). Sabinus viii stamped forms not made before *c.* AD160, such as 31R, 79, 79R and 80. 5a appears on form 31R and is noted from Bainbridge. *c.* AD160–190 (drain in Alley 8, F10:23, 2499).

S92.  Sacipus la 33 SꟲC[IPV.F] Lezoux (c). The four other examples of this stamp known to us are all on cups of form 33 and are all from Britain. Two stamps from another die occur on form 80. Antonine, with some activity after AD160 (area of Building 9, unstratified, G13:15, 1526).

S93.  Sanucius i 1a 31 SꟲNVCIVS[F] Lezoux (c). The record for this stamp consists of two examples on form 31R, from Benwell and Birrens, and seven others on form 31. Mid- to late-Antonine, on the evidence of the rouletted dishes (area over Building 12, unstratified, L14:01, 1552).

S94.  Saturninus i la 37 SATVRNFECIT Boucheporn (a), Chémery-Faulquemont (a), Mittelbronn (a). This bowl was presumably made at Chémery, since samian from the other two factories rarely, if ever, reached Britain. There is no site dating for it, but his activity at Chémery is likely to have been in the Trajanic or Hadrianic period. See the cursive signature no. S141 below (area over Building 5, J05:03, 713).

S95.  Saturninus ii 1b 33 SA[TVRNININIOF.] Lezoux (b). Stamps from two of this potter's other dies occur in the Pudding Pan Rock wreck and another is in a late second-century group from London (Dickinson 1986b, 195, 3.185). He is not certainly represented elsewhere on Hadrian's Wall. *c.* AD160–200 (area over Building 8, D11:08).

S96.  Senea/Senila la 33 SENII[ꟲ·M] (Dannell 1971, 315, no. 88) Lezoux (c). The potter's name is not certain, but Senea is perhaps more likely, since there seems never to be a tail to the fifth letter. His output includes forms 18/31 and 27 and decorated ware related stylistically to the Quintilianus i group. All of these could be before *c.* AD150, but 1a is in a group of burnt samian of *c.* AD170 from Tác (Hungary), which suggests that the stamp is from his latest die. *c.* AD140–170 (Building O, portico, E10:44, 2321).

S97–8.  Senilis iii 2a flat base; 31 SENIL[; SENIL[·I·M]

(Durand-Lefebvre 1963, 216, 671) Lezoux (a). The use of this stamp on forms 31R, 79, 79R and 80 suggests a range *c.* AD160–200 (area over Road 8, unstratified, E09:01, 2429; area over Building 12, unstratified, K14:01, 1290).

S99. Serullus Ia 33 SERVLLL<u>IM</u> (*sic*) Lezoux (c). This is commonest on form 33, but appears on form 31R from Piercebridge and 79 from Chesters. Mid- to late-Antonine (area over Building 10 and Alley 5, unstratified, F14:11, 1039).

S100. Sextus v 7a 33 [SE]XTVSFE Lezoux (a). Sextus v's stamps occur elsewhere on Hadrian's Wall, and in the Pudding Pan Rock wreck; 7a is noted on forms 79 and 80. *c.* AD160–200 (area over Building 11, unstratified, K15:02, 1293).

S101. Soiellus(?) Ia 31 SOI.IIᴋᴋIM (Nash-Williams 1930, fig. 3, 100) Lezoux (c). This particular stamp was used on forms 31R and 79 and occurs at Catterick. Another is in a group of late second-century samian from London. Mid- to late-Antonine (from 'Town Hall' collection).

S102. Sulpicianus Ia 31 SVLPI[CI<u>ANI</u>] Lezoux (a). All the stamps noted for Sulpicianus come from the same die. They include single examples from Haltonchesters and Newcastle and two in a group of late second-century samian from London (Dickinson 1986b, 196, 3.207–8). Mid- to late-Antonine (area over Alley 5, unstratified, G14:01).

S103. Tabus-Virtus i 1a 15/17 or 18 TABIVIꙄTABI[VI<u>RTVTI</u>Ꙅ] La Graufesenque (a). Double impressions of this stamp, which should read TABIVI<u>RTVTI</u>Ꙅ, are not uncommon. The stamp occurs in a group of samian from a ship wrecked *c.* AD 80 off Cala Culip, Spain (Nieto Prieto 1989, no. 14.1) and at the Domitianic foundations of Butzbach, Wilderspool and the Saalburg (3). However, there are also two examples on form 29, which should be earlier than AD85. The range is likely to be *c.* AD75–100, and the Wallsend dish, which seems to have been stamped when the die was worn, should fall within the later years of it (Building 4, make up material, H04:07, 487).

S104. Tintirio 4b 18/31R [T<u>INT</u>]IRI·M (de Schaetzen and Vanderhoeven 1964, pl. XIII, 32) Lezoux (c). Much of Tintirio's output belongs to the second quarter of the second century, though a single stamp on form 80 (from a different die) suggests that he was still at work after AD 160. 4b occurs in Lower Germany and on forms 18/31 and 18/31R. He also made forms 27 and 81 and there are five stamps from another die in a group of burnt samian of *c.* AD140–150 from a pottery shop at Castleford (Rush *et al* 2000, fig. 30, nos 956–70). *c.* AD140–155 (area over Building 10, unstratified, E14:01, 1125).

S105. Tituro Ia 33 TᵢTVRONIS<u>OF</u> Lezoux (a). There are two versions of this stamp. The first has no stops in the Os and the letters are sharp. Stamps from the modified die show worn letters and stops in the Os. There are three stamps from the original die in the Wroxeter Gutter, while the later version occurs at Benwell, Chesters and in a group of late second-century samian from London (Dickinson 1986b, 196, 3.211–4). *c.* AD170–190 (from 'Town Hall' collection).

S106. Titus iii 8b 18/31R or 31R TITIM Lezoux (b). Titus iii stamped form 18/31R with this die and form 31R with another. Examples of 8b occur also at Mumrills, in a group of samian of *c.* AD150–160 from Alcester (Hartley, Pengelly and Dickinson 1994, 110, S158) and in a burnt group of *c.*AD 170 from Tác (Hungary). *c.* AD 145–175 (Chalet 9, robbing and post-Roman dereliction, F13:12, 1331).

S107. Tuttabirus Ia 18/31R (slightly burnt) TVTTΛBIRV[S] Lezoux (c). Only two other examples of this stamp have been noted by us, from London and Vechten. The fabrics suggest Hadrianic or early-Antonine date (Building 2, post-Roman dereliction, P05:03, 211).

S108. Verus vi 3g 31R V[ERVꙄFE] Rheinzabern (Ludowici 1927, 232, i) Trier (b), Westerndorf (b). There is no way of telling where Verus vi began his career, but he presumably ended it at Westerndorf. The Wallsend piece is from Rheinzabern, while another stamp, from a third-century group in London, is in Trier fabric (Dickinson 1986b, 196, 3.221) and an example from Niederbieber may also have originated there. On balance, he is likely to have begun work at Rheinzabern. Late second century or first half of third century (from collection in Great North Museum: Hancock, Newcastle).

S109. Victor iv 4a 31 VICTOR·F Lezoux (a). A stamp noted in the Wroxeter Gutter (Atkinson 1942, 145) and on form 80. One of his other stamps is in a burial at Sompting, Sussex, with stamped vessels of Lezoux and Rheinzabern potters and a scarcely-worn coin of Geta as Caesar (Dannell and Hartley 1974, 312). *c.* AD170–200 (Building S, robber trench, F11:18).

UNIDENTIFIED

S110. V[ or ]Λ on form 18/31R, Central Gaulish. Hadrianic (area over North rampart, unstratified, F02:06).

S111. P[ on form 18/31 or 31, Central Gaulish. Hadrianic or early-Antonine (Building 16, L07:10).

S112. ]N<u>D</u>I on form 18/31 or 31, Central Gaulish. Hadrianic or Antonine (area over Building 12, unstratified, L14:01, 1392).

S113. Aᴋʙ[ on form 31, Central Gaulish. Antonine (area over Cistern 1, unstratified, E08:19, 2304).

S114. ]LI·M on form 31, Central Gaulish. Antonine (unstratified, 1451).

S115. CEL(L?)[ on form 31, Central Gaulish. Antonine (area over *intervallum* road (Road 5), unstratified, E04:01, 119).

S116. V[ OR ]Λ, in guide-lines in a frame with an ansate end, on form 31, Central Gaulish. Antonine (area over *intervallum* road (Road 6), unstratified, F15:01).

S117. Λ[ OR ]V on form 31, Central Gaulish. Antonine (rubble at base of plough furrow, G05:12, 164).

S118. ]CI on form 31, Central Gaulish. Antonine (area over Building 11, unstratified, K15:01, 1298).

S119. ]IM(?) on form 31, Central Gaulish. Antonine (area over Building 2 and Alley 1, unstratified, M05:04, 152).

S120. C[ on form 31, Central Gaulish. Antonine (Building 2, post-Roman dereliction, P05:03, 211).

S121. ]M on form 33 (burnt). Central Gaulish. Antonine (drain in Alley 8, F10:23, 2462).

S122. ]NIM on form 33, Central Gaulish. Antonine (area over Building 12, K14:03, 1370).

S123. \[ or ]\ on form 33, Central Gaulish. Antonine (drain in Road 1, L08:59, 2580).

S124. CΛ[ on form 33, Central Gaulish. Antonine (area over Building 12, unstratified, L14:01, 1382).

S125. ]ΛLA(?) on form 33 (heavily burnt). Central Gaulish(?). Antonine (area over Road 9, J14:01, 1417).

S126. ]M on form 33, Central Gaulish. Antonine (Alley 1, upper levels, N05:07, 289).

S127. ]IF on form 33, Central Gaulish. A hole has been bored through the centre of the base, but the footring has not been filed down. Antonine (area over Building 12 and *Via quintana*, unstratified, N14:01, 1645).

S128. ]IM on form 38 or 44(?), Central Gaulish. Antonine (area over Building 1 and *intervallum* road (Road 4), unstratified, M04:01, 737).

S129. ] ·D on form 31, Central Gaulish. Mid- to late-Antonine (area over East rampart, unstratified, Q05:02, 58).

S130. ]^M·D on form 31R, Central Gaulish. Mid- to late-Antonine (Chalet 9, Building W, D13:24, 1603).

S131. SECVNDI[ on form 31R, Central Gaulish. Mid- to late-Antonine, (Chalet 12, Building AL1, M14:38).

S132. ]CF? on form 38 or 44, Central Gaulish. Mid- to late-Antonine (area over Alley 6, unstratified, N15:01, 1675).

S133. ]IVSF on form 31, East Gaulish. Late second century or first half of third century. (Road 1, F07:03, 2334).

S134. ]\IIII[? on form 31, East Gaulish (Rheinzabern). Late second century or first half of third century (area over Road 8, unstratified, F08:01).

S135. Λ[ OR ]V, between striated borders, on form 31, East Gaulish. Late second century or first half of third century (area over Building 10 and Road 9, unstratified, H15:10, 1439).

S136. LILLVSF(?) on form 31, East Gaulish. The stamp does not correspond to any of those illustrated by Ludowici for Lillus. Late second century or first half of third century (area over Building 2 and Alley 1, unstratified, M05:04).

S137. ]SFE[? on form 32 etc., East Gaulish. Late second century or first half of third century (area over Building 1 and Alley 1, unstratified, P05:02).

S138. ]E.. on form 32 etc.. East Gaulish. Late second century or first half of third century (area over Building 10, unstratified, D14:01).

S139. C[ on form 33, East Gaulish. Late second century or first half of third century (area over Alley 6, unstratified, N15:01).

S140. ]MSFE (Building 16, floor, K07:08, WSP277) (AC).

S141. ]IM (area over Building 15, unstratified, J07:01, WSP276). (AC).

S142. ]M (area over *Via quintana*, unstratified, M13:01, WSP283). (AC).

S143. ]I[ . (Chalet 12, Building AL2, N14:37, WSP235). (AC).

S144. ]I (area over Building 2 and Alley 1, unstratified, L05:05, WSP151). (AC)

S145. C. Cin[ retr, upside down below the decoration, on form 37, from a mould inscribed in the mould before firing: C. Cincius (or Cingius) Senovirus of La Graufesenque. The potter was at work in the late first and early second centuries; another bowl with a mould-signature comes from Carrawburgh and his plain ware is known from Holt and Cannstatt. *c.* AD 85–110 (rubble between north wall of Building 19 and street drain, H05:25).

S146. fe, upside down below the decoration, on form 37, East Gaulish, from a mould inscribed before firing. Since this bowl has a mould-stamp of Saturninus i of Chémery-Faulquemont in the decoration, the signature should belong to Satto ii, but it is not certainly attributable to him. Trajanic or Hadrianic (see S94 above) (area over Building 5 and Alley 4, unstratified, J05:03, 713).

# The mortaria

*by A. Croom*
*Identifications by K. F. Hartley*

The 1975–84 and 1997–8 excavations inside the fort produced 82.967kg of mortarium sherds (1382 sherds, 4826% EVEs), approximately half of which were unstratified.

## Fabrics

Fabric descriptions of the common types can be found in Tomber and Dore 1998.

### Northern

This may include mortaria from Corbridge, Binchester and Catterick, although these have been separated where possible, as well as examples from other, unsourced local kilns. Generally the mortaria are of an orange fabric with a cream wash and multi-coloured trituration grits. The major period of production was in the second century, and those dated to the third and fourth centuries are likely to be part of the Cantley/ Catterick/Swanpool tradition. See also mortarium stamps nos 35–6, 38.
Corbridge: Fig. 22.08, nos 1–3
North-east: Fig. 22.08, nos 4–6; Fig. 22.13, nos 43, 49

### Binchester/Corbridge

This category includes the mortaria stamped by Anaus; see Mortarium stamps nos 1–13 and following discussion.
Fig. 22.13, nos 33–4, 42

### Cantley/Catterick/Swanpool

The fabrics and rim-profiles used at these production centres in the third and fourth century are very similar and cannot be distinguished macroscopically. The potters were working in a single tradition, which is likely to have been carried by potters moving from one centre to another. It is probable that many of the Wallsend examples came from Catterick.

*Colchester*
Fig. 22.08, no. 7

*Mancetter-Hartshill*
Fig. 22.08, nos 9–10; Fig. 22.21, no. 245

*Lower Nene Valley*
Fig. 22.08, no. 11; Fig. 22.21, nos 246–7

*Kent*
See mortarium stamp no. 16.

*Walton-le-Dale/Wilderspool*
See mortarium stamp no. 15.

*Little Chester*
See mortarium stamp no. 14.

*East Anglia and Norfolk*
A very small number of vessels, from a number of kilns in the area, reached the site.
Fig. 22.08, no. 12

*South of Malton*
See Monaghan 1997, 939, no. 3404.

*New Forest*
There was a single vessel in an unstratified context (G09:01), with a wavy line on the flange, dated to the third century. New Forest mortaria generally have a very restricted distribution in southern England (see Tyers 1996, fig. 123).

*Oise/Somme*
Fig. 22.08, no. 8

## Catalogue (Fig. 22.08)

1.  Corbridge, mid second-century. Feature B1, P05:03.
2.  Corbridge, Raetian type C. Optimum date 150–90. Alley10/Building 17, E04:10.
3.  Possibly Corbridge, second century. See Graffito no. 26. Road 4, N04:06.
4.  North-eastern, Antonine. Never stamped. Cistern 2, H07:03. d1.309
5.  North-eastern. Soft pinkish-brown fabric with cream slip. Three surviving rivet holes from a repair. Second century. Unstratified, G04:02.
6.  North-eastern. Orange fabric, with self-coloured slip. Late second century or later. Unstratified, F15:01.
7.  Colchester. 130–70. Building S, F12:06.
8.  Oise/Somme, probably Antonine. Building 9, G13:03.
9.  Probably Mancetter-Hartshill, 140–200. Unstratified, K14:01.
10. Mancetter-Hartshill, 220–300. Unstratified, F09:01.
11. Lower Nene Valley, slightly burnt. 230+. Unstratified, G11:01.
12. Pale grey fabric, burnt. Norfolk? 240–300. Building AP, F09:66.

## Supply to Wallsend

The mortarium assemblage from Wallsend is heavily biased towards second-century material, consisting of 52% (by weight) dated to the second century, 20% to the late second or early third centuries, 27% to the third or fourth centuries and less than 1% to the fourth century.

Of the mortaria dated to the second century, 60% as measured by EVES come from local or regional sources, and the rest from a wide range of other sites in Britain, with only a minimal amount of imported material. Colchester (21% of the mortaria dated to the second century) and Mancetter-Hartshill (13%) were the major suppliers from southern Britain, while the other sources (6%), although numerous, supplied only small quantities of vessels, presumably arriving as a minor element of other cargoes or as private possessions of soldiers or civilians coming to the northern frontier.

By the late second century the local industries were in decline, probably going out of business by the third century, and their wares make up less than 10% of the mortaria made during this period. Instead, Mancetter-Hartshill becomes the major supplier (34% of mortaria made in the late second/early third century), followed by Germany (23%; although it should be noted these were being made up until the end of the century). The importance of Germany as a supplier seems to be the result of the ease of maritime trade at the eastern end of the Wall, as German mortaria are rare in the central sector (Bidwell and Speak 1994, 210).

Amongst the mortaria dated to the third and fourth centuries, examples from Mancetter-Hartshill decrease slightly in importance, to be taken over by Lower Nene Valley, which supplied over half the mortaria. This seems to have been an important source at the eastern end of the Wall, making up 19% at Wallsend (by EVEs), 19% of all mortaria from South Shields (by vessel count) and 14% at Newcastle (by EVEs; Bidwell and Speak 1994, table 8.2; Bidwell and Croom 2002, table 15.6).

Very little stratified fourth-century material survives from the site. Of the 27 complete or incomplete Crambeck mortaria rims, only two were stratified (both of which were late fourth-century Corder 1937 type 8s). There were 15 Corder type 6 or related rims, dating to c.280+ and 12 late fourth-century types.

## The mortaria stamps (Fig. 22.09)

*by K. Hartley*

The catalogue entries include record number, original small finds number, context, location and period. The fabric examined with hand lens at X20 magnification. 'Right facing' and 'left facing' when applied to stamps indicates the relation of the stamp to the spout looking at the mortarium from the outside.

*Table 22.06: Dated mortaria from excavations inside the fort, 1975–1998 (stratified and unstratified) shown as percentages of the totals*

| Fabric | NRFRC code | Weight(%) | Sherds(%) | EVEs(%) |
|---|---|---|---|---|
| **Second century** | | | | |
| **Local products** | | | | |
| Northern | – | 12.62 | 14.80 | 9.45 |
| Binchester/Corbridge | – | 12.38 | 6.56 | 8.52 |
| Corbridge | COR WH | 9.99 | 6.17 | 7.12 |
| **Other British** | | | | |
| Colchester | COL WH | 8.69 | 6.68 | 8.43 |
| Mancetter-Hartshill | MAH WH | 5.74 | 3.73 | 5.28 |
| Verulamium | VER WH | 0.64 | 0.39 | 0.49 |
| Catterick | CTR WS | 0.42 | 0.26 | 0.40 |
| Kent | – | 0.43 | 0.39 | 0.53 |
| South Carlton | SOC WH | 0.33 | 0.51 | 0.38 |
| Walton-le-Dale | – | 0.26 | 0.13 | 0.31 |
| Unsourced | – | 0.12 | 0.39 | – |
| Upper Nene Valley | UNV WH | 0.11 | 0.13 | 0.11 |
| Little Chester | – | 0.09 | 0.13 | |
| Oxford* | OXF WH | – | – | – |
| Swanpool* | SWN WS | – | – | – |
| **Imports** | | | | |
| Oise/Somme | NOG WH 4 | 0.29 | 0.26 | 0.16 |
| **Late second to third century** | | | | |
| **Local products** | | | | |
| Corbridge | COR WH | 1.12 | 0.90 | 1.40 |
| Binchester/Corbridge | – | 0.58 | 0.13 | 0.40 |
| Northern | – | 0.45 | 0.77 | 0.96 |
| **Other British** | | | | |
| Mancetter-Hartshill | MAH WH | 6.47 | 6.43 | 7.61 |
| Lower Nene Valley | LNV WH | 2.82 | 3.21 | 2.75 |
| Colchester | COL WH | 0.70 | 1.03 | 0.69 |
| Oxford | OXF WH | 0.46 | 0.64 | 0.91 |
| Kent | – | 0.40 | 0.39 | 0.51 |
| East Anglia | – | 0.24 | 0.13 | 0.29 |
| South of Malton | – | 0.15 | 0.26 | 0.09 |
| **Imports** | | | | |
| Lower Germany | RHL WH | 5.29 | 5.14 | 5.17 |
| Oise/Somme | NOG WH 4 | 1.69 | 2.57 | 1.46 |
| **Third to fourth century** | | | | |
| **Local products** | | | | |
| Northern | – | 0.49 | 0.90 | 1.17 |
| **Other British** | | | | |
| Lower Nene Valley | LNV WH | 16.89 | 21.72 | 19.41 |
| Mancetter-Hartshill | MAH WH | 4.80 | 7.20 | 7.45 |
| Crambeck | CRA WH | 1.97 | 4.24 | 3.68 |
| Cantley/Catterick | – | 0.92 | 1.41 | 1.24 |
| Norfolk | – | 0.75 | 0.39 | 1.55 |
| Catterick | CTR WS | 0.41 | 0.51 | 0.16 |
| Oxford | OXF WH | 0.22 | 0.13 | 0.18 |
| Colchester | COL WH | 0.17 | 0.13 | 0.20 |
| South of Malton | – | 0.12 | 0.13 | 0.31 |
| Swanpool | SWN WS | 0.08 | 0.13 | 0.09 |
| New Forest | NFO WH | 0.04 | 0.13 | |
| **Imports** | | | | |
| Lower Germany | RHL WH | 0.16 | 0.13 | 0.27 |
| **Fourth century** | | | | |
| Crambeck | CRA PA | 0.43 | 0.64 | 0.67 |
| Mancetter-Hartshill | MAH WH | 0.05 | 0.13 | 0.24 |
| Totals | | 56.416kg | 778 | 4509 |

*Small quantity of non-rim sherds present in the group

Key: NRFRC = National Roman Fabric Reference Collection

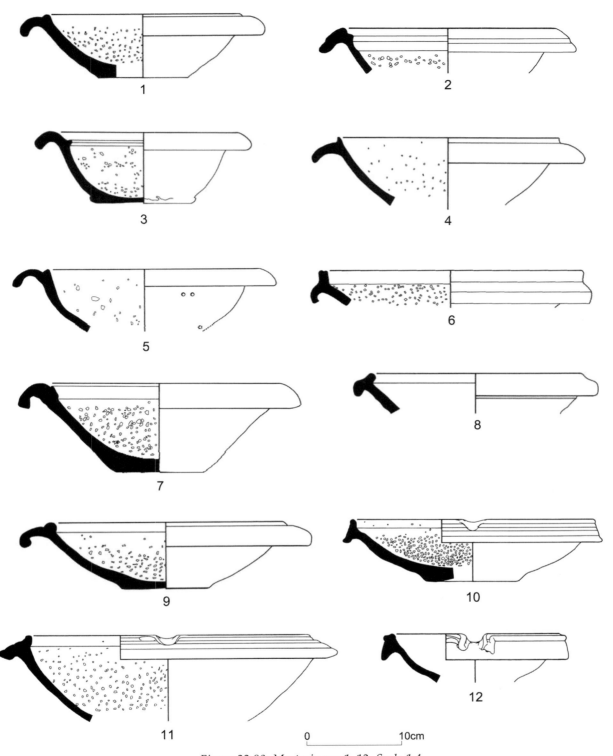

*Figure 22.08: Mortaria nos 1–12. Scale 1:4.*

1. Road 8, E09:41, 2368, WSP239 (12K).
Wt:0.020kg. Orange-brown fabric throughout except for 2mm of pale grey near underside of flange; ?cream slip. The fairly frequent, tiny to smallish, ill-sorted inclusions are mostly quartz with rare red-brown and black.

A stamp from die 1A of Anaus survives (Birley and Gillam 1948, fig. 1).

2. Area over Building 10, unstratified, E14:01, 1458, WSP241 (8K).
Wt:0.160kg. D:260mm. 16%. Pale orange-brown fabric fired almost to cream at the surface; buff-brown slip. The inclusions are fairly frequent, large to tiny and random, mostly quartz with rare brown. No trituration grit survives.

A left-facing stamp from die 1A of Anaus survives (Birley and Gillam 1948, fig. 1).

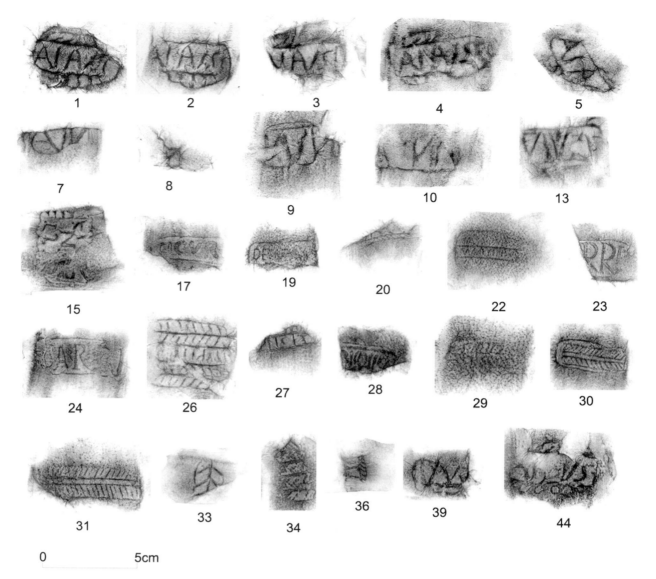

*Figure 22.09: Mortarium stamps nos 1–44. Scale 1:2.*

3. Area over Buildings 4 and 5, and Alley 3, unstratified, G04:01, 189, WSP245 (11K).

Wt:0.020kg. Flange fragment in fine-textured, powdery drab cream fabric, probably self-coloured. The fairly frequent inclusions are extremely tiny and almost all quartz with very rare orange-brown and perhaps black material.

The broken stamp is from die 1A of Anaus (Birley and Gillam 1948, fig. 1).

4. Nine joining sherds from Alley 1, dump of demolition material, N05:23, 296, WSP255; 4 sherds Alley 1, demolition material dump, lower fill, N05:19 (7K).

Wt:1.795kg. D:300mm. 94%. Orange-brown fabric throughout except for a thin trail of buff-brown in the flange and the edge of base; cream slip. The fairly frequent, random ill-sorted inclusions are mostly quartz with few black and red fragments. The trituration grit, concentrated mainly in the base is a mixture of smallish to large (up to 7mm) quartz, quartz sandstone, and red-brown sandstone; many fragments have fallen out.

The left- and right-stamps survive, both from die 1A of Anaus (Birley and Gillam 1948 1A).

5. Area over Road 4 and north fort wall; unstratified, Q04:35, WSP96 (36K).

Wt:0.178kg. D:280mm. 19%. Hard, orange-brown fabric throughout with cream slip. The fairly frequent, tiny to small inclusions are mostly quartz with very rare black material. No trituration grit survives.

Parts of the left- and right-facing stamps survive from die 1A of Anaus (Birley and Gillam 1948, fig. 1).

6. Area over Building 12, unstratified, WSP153 (40K).

Wt:0.020kg. Flange fragment in slightly powdery, very pale pinkish-brown fabric with grey core; no slip determined. The fairly frequent, ill-sorted inclusions consist mainly of quartz with rare brown material.

The broken and poorly impressed stamp is from die 1A of Anaus (Birley and Gillam 1948, fig. 1). AD120–160

7. Area over Building 1 and Alley 1, unstratified, N05:02, 62, WSP252 (13K). Other sherds which are probably from same vessel but do not join: Alley 1, dump of demolition material, N05:23; Surface over Building 1, Period 4 or later, N04:11 (four small joining flange fragments and 1 sherd not joining).
Wt:0.085kg. D:c.260mm 7% (+11%). Very hard, fine-textured, orange-brown fabric with thick blackish core and cream slip. There are moderate to fairly frequent, tiny to small inclusions, mostly quartz with some pebbly red-brown.

The broken stamp is from die 1B of Anaus (Birley and Gillam 1948, fig. 1). AD120–160. Anaus had a range of fabrics and this is the easiest one to recognize.

8. Road 4, N04:21, 511, WSP253 (10K).
Wt: 0.011kg. Flange fragment in orange-brown fabric with lighter, almost drab cream core and cream slip. The fairly frequent, ill-sorted inclusions are mostly quartz with rare black and red-brown material.

The very fragmentary stamp is probably from die 1B of Anaus (Birley and Gillam 1948, fig. 1).

9. Six joining sherds plus one other, Alley 1, upper layers, N05:07, 290, WSP254; one sherd, Alley 1, dump of demolition material, lower level, N05:23 (14K).
Wt:1.140kg. D:290mm. 8%. Very hard, fine-textured, orange-brown fabric with buff-brown core and cream slip. The fairly frequent inclusions are extremely tiny, mostly quartz with rare red-brown material. The fairly frequent trituration grit is composed entirely of milky quartz and is confined largely to the lower half of the vessel. Worn.

Two joining sherds have the incomplete, left-facing stamp of die 1B of Anaus (Birley and Gillam 1948, fig. 1).

10. Thirteen sherds, *intervallum* road (Road 4), primary surface, P04:10, 170, WSP259; one sherd with modern break, Alley 1, dump of demolition material, lowest level, N05:23 (15K).
Wt: 0.420kg. D:280mm. 13%. The fabric and trituration grit are in every way identical to no. 10 above, but the survival of parts of the two spouts leave no doubt that they are different vessels. This example has dents in the ends of the spout, a characteristic typical of Anaus.

The incompletely impressed left-facing stamp is from die 1B of Anaus (Birley and Gillam 1948, fig. 1).

Also:
10.2. Alley 1, dump of demolition material, N05:23.
Wt:0.190kg. D:290mm. 10%. No stamp surviving (eight joining sherds and one base sherd not necessarily from same vessel). The seven joining sherds are from a third mortarium in identical fabric, which can be attributed to Anaus.

11. Area over Road 9 and Alley 5, unstratified, H14:23, WSP95 (37K).
Wt:0.444kg. D:340mm. 20%. Five joining sherds making up about a quarter of a mortarium in orange-brown fabric with drab core and traces of cream slip. The fairly frequent inclusions are mostly quartz with some red-brown material. The abundant trituration grit is mostly quartz with quartz sandstone and red-brown material. Worn.

The stamp was too damaged in antiquity for identification.

One letter survives, either V or reversed N; it is likely to be a stamp of Anaus, perhaps the middle letter of die 1Bi (Birley and Gillam 1948), but certainty is not possible. North of England, possibly Binchester or Corbridge. Probably AD120–160.

12. Post-Roman rubble over drain in Road 9, H15:06, WSP98 (38K).
Wt:0.020kg. D:300mm. 6%. Flange fragment in very hard orange-brown fabric with pale grey core and cream slip. The fairly frequent, ill-sorted inclusions are mostly quartz with rare red-brown and black material.

The poorly impressed, fragmentary stamp is likely to be a stamp of Anaus, but it does not match his nearest stamps, die 1B, exactly. Probably AD120–160.

13. Alley 10/Building 17 surface, G05:06, 403, WSP246.
Wt:0.058kg. D:290mm. 6.5%. Fine-textured, orange-brown fabric with thin brownish core in flange and cream slip. The fairly frequent inclusions are mostly quartz with some red-brown; the inclusions are small to tiny with few larger.

The left-facing, incompletely impressed stamp is from die 1C of Anaus (Birley and Gillam 1948, fig. 1).

### Comments on Anaus mortaria

All of the above stamps are on different mortaria, so that in total there are at least ten stamped by Anaus with the possibility of three more, whose stamps are too fragmentary or difficult for certain attribution to him. It is no surprise that these three would be from the very difficult die 1B. Of the ten undoubtedly stamped by Anaus, six are stamped with die 1A, three with die 1B and one with die C. In total at least twelve mortaria of his are now known from Wallsend making this site along with South Shields and Benwell his major market outside the Binchester/Catterick area.

It has long been believed that Anaus had a workshop at Corbridge (Birley and Gillam 1948) and with good reason considering the number of his mortaria found there, but his distribution differs from that of other potters who can be attributed to Corbridge: not only is the number of his recorded mortaria far greater than for any other potter attributed to Corbridge, but far more of his work is found at sites outside Corbridge. There is also a markedly heavy distribution in the triangle bounded by Binchester, Bowes and Catterick – 25 compared with a total of three for seven other potters attributed to Corbridge (2 of Cudre- and 1 of Messorius Martius). His distribution leaves no reasonable doubt that he began his working life at Binchester and it seems likely that he moved to Corbridge later. His movements might well be expected to be related to the varying military occupation of these sites. The fort at Binchester was abandoned by AD125/130, and Fort 3 at Corbridge is believed to have been abandoned about the same time. If they were abandoned about the same time, he may even have had a third workshop, probably in the Catterick area where there was a thriving pottery industry.

*Table 22.07: Distribution of Anaus stamps*

| | Die A | Die B | Die C | Die D | Die E | Die F | Die G | Die H | Die I | Die J | Die ? | Total |
|---|---|---|---|---|---|---|---|---|---|---|---|---|
| Catterick | 0 | 2 | 0 | 1 | 0 | 0 | 0 | 0 | 2 | 0 | 0 | 5 |
| Piercebridge | 0 | 1 | 0 | 1 | 0 | 0 | 0 | 0 | 0 | 1 | 0 | 3 |
| Binchester | 4 | 2 | 4 | 3 | 0 | 0 | 0 | 1 | 0 | 1 | 0 | 15 |
| Bowes | 1 | 0 | 0 | 0 | 0 | 0 | 0 | 0 | 1 | 0 | 0 | 2 |
| Chester-le-Street | 1 | 0 | 0 | 0 | 0 | 0 | 0 | 0 | 0 | 0 | 0 | 1 |
| S. Shields | 3 | 9 | 0 | 0 | 0 | 0 | 0 | 0 | 0 | 0 | 0 | 12 |
| Wallsend | 7 | 4 | 1 | 0 | 0 | 0 | 0 | 0 | 0 | 0 | 0 | 12 |
| Benwell | 1 | 0 | 6 | 0 | 0 | 0 | 0 | 0 | 0 | 0 | 0 | 7 |
| Corbridge | 7 | 25 | 2 | 1 | 2 | 1 | 0 | 0 | 0 | 0 | 0 | 38 |
| Haltonchesters | 0 | 1 | 1 | 0 | 0 | 0 | 0 | 0 | 0 | 0 | 0 | 2 |
| Chesters Mus. | 1 | 4 | 0 | 0 | 0 | 0 | 0 | 0 | 0 | 1 | 0 | 6 |
| Carrawburgh | 0 | 1 | 0 | 0 | 0 | 0 | 0 | 0 | 0 | 0 | 0 | 1 |
| Housesteads | 0 | 0 | 1 | 0 | 0 | 0 | 0 | 0 | 0 | 0 | 0 | 1 |
| Birdoswald | 1 | 0 | 0 | 0 | 1 | 0 | 0 | 0 | 0 | 0 | 0 | 2 |
| Carlisle | 1 | 0 | 0 | 1 | 0 | 1 | 0 | 0 | 0 | 0 | 0 | 3 |
| Kirkby Thore | 0 | 0 | 0 | 0 | 0 | 0 | 1 | 0 | 0 | 0 | 0 | 1 |
| Lancaster | 1 | 0 | 0 | 0 | 0 | 0 | 0 | 0 | 0 | 0 | 0 | 1 |
| Brough-under-Stainmore | 1 | 0 | 0 | 0 | 0 | 0 | 0 | 0 | 0 | 0 | 0 | 1 |
| Watercrook | 0 | 0 | 1 | 0 | 0 | 0 | 0 | 0 | 0 | 0 | 0 | 1 |
| St Albans | 0 | 1 | 0 | 0 | 0 | 0 | 0 | 0 | 0 | 0 | 0 | 1 |
| Newstead | 0 | 1 | 0 | 0 | 0 | 0 | 0 | 0 | 0 | 0 | 0 | 1 |
| Cramond | 0 | 1 | 0 | 0 | 0 | 0 | 0 | 0 | 0 | 0 | 0 | 1 |
| Camelon | 0 | 2 | 0 | 0 | 0 | 0 | 0 | 0 | 0 | 0 | 0 | 2 |
| Loudon Hill | 0 | 1 | 0 | 0 | 0 | 0 | 0 | 0 | 0 | 0 | 0 | 1 |
| Risingham | 0 | 0 | 0 | 0 | 0 | 0 | 0 | 0 | 0 | 0 | 1 | 1 |
| Totals | 29 | 55 | 15 | 7 | 3 | 2 | 1 | 1 | 3 | 3 | 2 | 121 |

Notes

'Catterick' has been used to cover all the Catterick sites (including Brompton-on-Swale), except Bainesse.

Stamps in Chesters Museum are not necessarily from Chesters itself, but from sites on the Clayton estates, on or in the vicinity of Hadrian's Wall.

Dies have been given the letters used by Birley and Gillam 1948, with consecutive letters used for new dies.

One might expect the fabric of Anaus's mortaria to fall into simple straightforward groups. The orange-brown fabric with very thick bluish-black core and cream slip like no. 7 is very typical and easy to recognise; it is particularly common at Corbridge, but the remaining fabrics are not as easily defined. Further work is needed on these to link them and individual dies with the different sources. Most of his mortaria in Scotland probably came from Corbridge and one might expect this to be true of his mortaria at South Shields and on Hadrian's Wall, but an uncertain number of mortaria made by other potters, for example no. 25, at Wallsend can be attributed to potteries at Catterick.

One of his Binchester mortaria (die H) was found in an early Hadrianic context ending AD120/130 while one from South Shields is recorded from a late Hadrianic to early Antonine context (Bidwell and Speak 1994, 211, no. 7, die B). Five of his mortaria, all stamped with die B are recorded from sites in Scotland occupied in the Antonine period, indicating that this die was in use after AD140. The stamp from Risingham, now missing (die unknown) should also be Antonine. Stamps from die B are the most common at Corbridge (25 in 38). The distribution of die B suggests that it was mainly in use at Corbridge, though it would have been possible for mortaria from the Binchester/Catterick area to reach Scotland. The mortarium from Chester-le-Street should be later than AD158. A date of AD120–160 should cover the whole of his activity.

14. Area over Tower 2, unstratified, E02:11, WSP100 (44K). Wt:0.050kg. Incomplete rim-section of a very hard, apparently overfired mortarium fired to orange-brown near the surface, the rest reduced to dark grey with pale grey core; the slip is discoloured to brownish-buff. The fairly frequent inclusions are ill-sorted, though most are tiny to small-sized; they include quartz, black, brown and red-brown material. The trituration grit included quartz, brown sandstone and black material.

A fragmentary left-facing stamp survives, preserving the border and part of the F of a retrograde FECIT counterstamp used by G. Attius Marinus. This counterstamp and the namestamp which always accompanies it are essentially the same die-types which were used by G. Attius Marinus at Radlett in Hertfordshire before he opened his workshops in the Midlands. It is not possible to say how many actual dies were used throughout his midland career, but some of his stamps like this are from a die in the pristine condition of that first brought from Radlett, while many of his midland stamps are from a die or dies in which the borders especially are very degraded, never showing the fine detail visible in this example. This is a midland product and its optimum production period is, therefore, early in his midland period, within the range of AD100–120. Although none of his midland kilns have been found, there is evidence to suggest that he may have had a possibly short-lived workshop at Little Chester as well as one in the Mancetter-Hartshill potteries. Some mortaria were produced in orange-brown fabrics in the Mancetter-Hartshill potteries, especially in the early second century, but the production was minimal, whereas production in orange-brown fabrics was normal at Little Chester. This example might fit better with manufacture at Little Chester (for further details of the work of G. Attius Marinus see Hartley 1985, 126–9; Hartley 1999, 199, S21–2; and Hartley in Green (Little Chester), in preparation).

15. Building 10, *contubernium* 1/2, Period 2, E14:28, 1459, WSP242 (20K).
Wt:0.145kg. D:280mm. 14%. Softish, fine-textured, tan-coloured fabric (Munsell 5YR 6/6 'reddish-yellow'), with few black ?slag, rare orange-brown material and quartz inclusions, small to tiny and random. The plentiful, smallish to medium-sized, trituration grit is very mixed in content, mostly quartz (transparent and pinkish), black slag and possibly other black material, quartz sandstone and red-brown sandstone. There are traces of red-brown slip on the upper surface of the flange, possibly ending in a line 4mm below the top of the bead. It is almost certainly a 'Raetian' slip and only one other possible example is known of its use on a mortarium of Austinus.

Complete impressions of this partially impressed, three-line stamp read as follows: the first line ΛVST, S reversed; second line NVS retrograde; the third line, retrograde FI followed by two uncertain letters, the second apparently a lambda L. The name was clearly Austinus and the following word is no doubt intended to be some version of FECIT. Stamps from the same die have now been recorded from Middlewich, Cheshire, Wallsend; Watercrook and Walton-le-Dale (4). Mortaria stamped with the remaining eleven dies of Austinus have now been recorded from the following sites: **in Scotland** (16–19), Bar Hill; Balmuildy (2–3); Birrens; Camelon (3–4); Carzield (2); Cramond (1–2); Durisdeer; Maryport; Milton; Newstead (2); Rough Castle and Strageath; **in England** (49), Ambleside; Birdoswald (3); Cardurnock (2); Carlisle (30); Chesters; Corbridge (4); Lancaster (2); Low Borrow Bridge; Maryport; Ribchester; Stanwix; Walton-le-dale and Watercrook.

The probability that Austinus began stamping mortaria at Wilderspool was discussed in Hartley and Webster 1973, 95–97. Recent discoveries show that many of the Wilderspool potters also had a workshop at Walton-le-Dale (information kindly supplied by Dr J. Evans), and the distribution of stamps from the die used on the Wallsend mortarium suggests that it was being used there. His major and somewhat later production, was undoubtedly at Carlisle, and he is likely to have also had a workshop in the Antonine Wall area. His mortaria at sites on Hadrian's Wall and the Antonine Wall provide the key to his dating and his rim-profiles support a Hadrianic-Antonine date, perhaps within the period AD125–165, his Walton-le-Dale/Wilderspool production being c.AD125–145. The die represented here was in use early in his career, probably within the period AD125–140. The fabric of this example tends to fit better with production in the Walton-le-Dale/Wilderspool potteries; in particular, it lacks the hardness usually associated with Carlisle fabrics.

16. Area over Building 10 and Alley 5, unstratified, F14:01, 1097, WSP243 (21K).
Wt:0.039kg. D:c.240mm. 6%. Fine-textured, pinkish-brown fabric (Munsell 2.5YR 6/6 'light red') fabric with very thick yellowish-grey core (Munsell 2.5YR 7/2 'light grey'); very moderate, ill-sorted but mostly tiny inclusions including quartz, opaque grey pebbles, red-brown ?slag, opaque black and ?flint. No trituration grit survives. Slight traces of thin cream slip. The bead has been broken and turned outward to form the spout.

The fragmentary stamp, impressed along this collared mortarium reads C[......]; what may be the first and beginning of the second stroke of A can be seen following the C. No other stamp is known from the same die, but it is likely to be the work of a potter probably called Calles, who worked in Kent and whose mortaria match this in form and fabric. Calles frequently produced this unusual wall-sided type and stamped along the collar, both of which were unusual practices in Britain. The optimum date for both Calles and this example is AD150–180.

17. Building 16, floor, Period 4, N08:24, 2576, WSP256 (30K).
Wt:0.119kg. D:310mm. 13%. Hard, fine-textured cream fabric probably with self-coloured slip; very moderate, random, ill-sorted quartz and orange-brown inclusions with random patches and streaks of pale orange-brown. No trituration survives.

The stamp, probably the right-facing one, reads CICVR and is from a die which gives CICVRFE in complete impressions for Cicur(o/us) *fecit*. Only one die-type is recorded for this potter. His work can be attributed to the Mancetter-Hartshill potteries. Twenty-one of his mortaria have now been recorded from Brough, Notts; Castor; Halton Chesters; Hartshill; High Cross; Leicester (2); Lincoln (2); Papcastle; Stanground South, Cambs; Twenty Foot, nr. March; Tiddington; Upton St Leonards, Gloucester; Wall; Wallsend (3); Wappenbury and Worcester. This distribution indicates that the bulk of his mortaria went to sites in the Midlands, only five have been found in the north, four from sites on Hadrian's Wall including three from Wallsend, which has the largest number from any single site. The stamp from Halton Chesters was found in the packing underneath a floor of Period 1b. His activity is likely to have been within the period AD150–180, but his optimum date is AD150–170 because the practice of stamping could have ended around AD170+ in the Mancetter-Hartshill potteries.

18. Building 1, Period 2 demolition, Q04:02, 140, WSP262 (31K).

Wt:0.180kg. D:290mm. 21%. Two joining sherds in fine-textured pale brown fabric (Munsell 5YR 8/4, 'pink'), with slightly darker slip; moderate, ill-sorted quartz inclusions with some orange-brown and very rare black material. The few surviving trituration grits are orange-brown. The potter's stamp, CICVR[..], with second C damaged and ghostly R, is from the same die as no. 17 above. This is the third mortarium of Cicur(o/us) recorded from Wallsend and is included in the above comments. AD150–170.

19. Chalet 9, Building W, late third/early fourth century, D13:71, 1612, WSP238.
Wt:0.225kg. D:340mm. 10%. Two joining fragments from a mortarium in self-coloured, dark cream fabric merging into a thick greyish-white core with frequent, ill-sorted inclusions, mostly quartz with rare orange-brown and black material. The trituration grit consists mostly of flint with a little quartz. The potter's stamp reads from the outside DE[.]VM[.]S; DE is clearly impressed, but the remaining letters show up only on a rubbing. The name may be Decumus, but this reading cannot be regarded as certain until further stamps from the same die are found. The fabric cannot be sourced with certainty but on present knowledge the inclusions and the trituration grit would best fit the Verulamium region, though the inclusions are more ill-sorted than one would expect. The sandwich colours of the fabric would also be exceptional there, but it is difficult to find any other acceptable source for the flint trituration grit. The rim-profile and the distribution of the trituration grit would best fit a date within the period AD110–140. There is one other stamp, from Castleford (Hartley 2000, fig. 97, no. 26), which could have a similar reading, but that mortarium is probably a local product and the trituration grit and inclusions of the two mortaria are not sufficiently alike to attribute them to one source. Since the two stamps are from different dies they cannot yet be attributed to the same potter. There was also a potter called Devalus working in the Verulamium region AD60–90, but the rim-profiles recorded for him are very different, so it is not likely to be his work.

20. Area over Building 1, unstratified, L04:16, WSP97 (41K).
Wt:0.045kg. An incomplete rim sherd in very hard, sandwich fabric, fired to buff-cream at the outside and underside surface (Munsell 7.5YR8/4), with core composed largely of pale brown buff (Munsell 7.5YR 7/6) and a thin range-brown inner core; the upper surface is fired to orange-brown. Cream slip. The moderate inclusions include tiny quartz and orange-brown material, with a few larger orange-brown. One quartz trituration grit survives. The fabric has some fine streaks in it similar to those in no. 36 below.

A fine border of diagonal bars survives plus the very ends of some letters. The stamp is almost certainly from the same die as no. 36, this example showing the lower border. Only further examples will permit identification.

21. Building Row 20, Building Q, late third/early fourth century, F11:11, WSP237 (46K).
Wt:0.522kg D:270mms 42%. This worn mortarium has been considerably affected by the conditions in which it has survived. There is a brown accretion over the whole of the surface and the fractures and the surface has suffered some slight exfoliation while the fabric itself appears to have been hardened and the colour slightly altered to a yellowish-cream which is untypical for the Mancetter-Hartshill potteries where it was made. There are moderate, tiny quartz and orange-brown inclusions with rare blackish material. The trituration grit is frequent, well-sorted and probably mostly red-brown though some may be blackish, with very rare quartz.

The incompletely impressed and very poorly preserved stamp reads [....]ΛSGVS and is from a die of Lugutasgus. Mortaria of this relatively uncommon potter are now known from Alcester; Catterick; Cirencester; Corbridge; Tiddington; Wallsend; and Wasperton. His work can be attributed to the Mancetter-Hartshill potteries c.AD135–165

22. Area over Alley 6, unstratified, 1648, WSP257 (32K).
Wt:0.235kg D:360mm 15%. Fine-textured brownish-cream fabric, possibly with self-coloured slip; fairly frequent inclusions (tiny to small quartz, fewer ?slag and orange-brown and calcareous material), with fewer larger, mainly orange-brown. Two flint trituration grits survive.

The poorly impressed stamp is from the largest of the variants of a single basic die-type (Hull 1963, fig. 60, nos 6, 8 and 10) of Martinus 2, who worked at Colchester. See Hartley 1999 for further details of the die; this stamp is identical to S57, 60, 61 and 62. Martinus 2 had at least sixteen other die-types but this one with its variants is the commonest. His mortaria are now known from Braintree; Cambridge (2); Canterbury (2–3); Capel St Mary, Suffolk; Chelmsford; Colchester (up to 99); Corbridge (3–4); Gestingthorpe, Essex; Great Chesterford (3); North Ash, Kent; London/Southwark (6); Wallsend; Ware; York. Martinus 2 has the heaviest distribution outside Colchester of any of those Colchester potters who stamped names on their mortaria. He also has the heaviest distribution in north-eastern England of any of these potters and his absence from Scotland is noteworthy. The evidence as a whole suggests that his activity was within the period AD150–180.

23. Area over *Via quintana*, unstratified, M13:01, 1660 WSP251 (27K).
Wt:0.025kg D:c.270mms 9%. Flange fragment in fine-textured, cream fabric with moderate, tiny to small inclusions, mainly pinkish quartz with some opaque orange-brown material. Probably had a self-coloured surface slip. The stamp, ]RRI is from the most commonly used die of Sarrius.

24. North-south drain east of Building 1, Period 2, Q05:03, 199, WSP263 (28K).
Wt:0.455kg D:290mm 25%. Fine-textured, cream fabric with moderate, almost to fairly frequent, tiny to small inclusions, pinkish and transparent quartz with some opaque orange-brown material. Some of the self-coloured surface slip still covers a few of the trituration grits. The trituration grit is red-brown with perhaps two quartz grits mixed in. Heavily worn. The partially impressed left-facing stamp is from a die which gives SARRI with leaf stamp between AR and a central stop before the second R.

The stamps on these two mortaria are from different dies. Both mortaria are from Sarrius's workshop in the Mancetter-Hartshill potteries, which was active within the period AD135–165/70. He was the most prolific potter stamping mortaria in the second century, but he was most exceptional in having at least four workshops in the midlands, the north of England and Scotland. His Mancetter-Hartshill workshop was of major importance and the evidence suggests that it continued in production throughout his activity elsewhere at Rossington Bridge, near Doncaster (Buckland *et al* 2001), Bearsden on the Antonine Wall (Hartley 1984) and at an unlocated site in north-east England. Stamp no. 23 is from the die-type used at Mancetter, Rossington and Bearsden.

25. Area over Alley 5, unstratified, G14:01, WSP93 (35K). Wt:0.190kg D:280mm 18%.Orange-brown fabric (Munsell 5YR 6/6 'reddish-yellow'), fired to a paler colour at the surface, with traces of cream slip; moderate, ill-sorted inclusions, including quartz, quartz sandstone and orange-brown material. The trituration grit included quartz and red-brown ?sandstone.

The right-facing stamp is too battered to be readable but the dotted borders permit it to be identified as a stamp which reads SATVR on complete impressions, perhaps for Saturninus. Mortaria of this potter have now been recorded from Bainesse (4); Bowes; Catterick (5); Chesters; Corbridge; Piercebridge; and Wallsend. This distribution points to a workshop in the Catterick area. His rim-profiles would best fit a date within the period AD100–140. Saturninus 2 is not to be confused with Saturninus 1 who worked in the Verulamium region or Saturninus 3 who worked at Corbridge.

26. Area over Building 2 and Alley 1, post-Roman dereliction, M05:04, 34, WSP249; M05:04, 579; two joining sherds, Building A, north-south wall, late third/early fourth century, N05:10 (25K).
Wt:0.020kg (M05:04) Wt:0.224kg (N05:10) D:360mm 19%. Fine-textured, micaceous but slightly powdery fabric with some pink in the core and traces of a buff-cream slip; very moderate, ill-sorted and random orange-brown, quartz and slag inclusions, mostly tiny to small. A few quartz trituration grits survive.
The retrograde stamp (left-facing) is from the only known die of Valens; it has large herringbone borders above and below the name panel but all are part of one stamp. Other mortaria of his are known from Birdoswald Turret (Period 1B); Chesters (2); and Corbridge. Valens probably had his workshop at Corbridge although this example is not typical of Corbridge fabric. The find from Birdoswald Turret (Period 1B) suggests a date *c.*AD155–180 for his activity.

27. Surface over Building 1, Period 4 or later, N04:11, 178, WSP258 (2K).
Wt:0.060kg D:*c.*390mm 5%. Mortarium in greyish-cream fabric fired to greyish-buff at the surface; the frequent inclusions are mostly tiny and small, but not well-sorted quartz, with few red-brown and rare black ?slag fragments. No trituration grit survives.
The fragmentary stamp, [.]IICIT, is from the lower line of the only known die-type of Vediacus; parts of ] IA[ on the upper line also survive. Full impressions of this stamp read VIIDIACVS/IIICIT, A with diagonal dash, for 'Vediacus fecit'. His mortaria are now known from Baldock (2); Benwell; Braughing (2); Godmanchester; Great Chesterford; Great Weldon; Higham Ferrars (3); Odell,

Beds; Piddington (3); Rushden, Northants; Sandy, Beds. (2); Stanground South, Cambs; Stanwick, Northants; Stonea (2); Verulamium (4); Wallsend; Wellingborough; Wood Burcote Farm, near Towcester; and Wyboston, Beds. The only two recorded from the north are both from Hadrian's Wall. The distribution of his work indicates activity in the Upper Nene Valley, probably in Northamptonshire and his rim-profiles fit a date within the period AD140–180, perhaps not earlier than AD150. For some interesting details of his work see Hartley 1994, 18–20.

28. Alley 10/Building 17, third century, E04:10, 417, WSP240. Wt:0.085kg. D:280mm 8%. Two sherds, not necessarily joining but certainly from the same mortarium in fine-textured, micaceous, cream fabric with very smooth surface and slightly brownish-cream slip; few inclusions, most of them barely visible at X20 magnification, many probably quartz, some orange-brown with rare large orange-brown material and opaque white pebbles. Very few trituration grits survive, but they included quartz sandstone, orange-brown ?sandstone and quartz. Worn.

The broken stamp is from one of six die-types used by Vorolas; this one reads VOROLΛS retrograde when complete. Vorolas worked at South Carlton, Lincoln, where nearly 100 of his stamps have been found (Webster 1944). The fabric and profile of this example are entirely typical of his work. Other mortaria of his have now been found at Aldborough; Corbridge (2); Lincoln; Littleborough, Notts; Lutford Magna, Lincs; Templeborough; Wallsend and York. North-eastern England was, apart from the local area, the main market for potters working at South Carlton or in that vicinity, except for Crico whose work is found in Scotland. Their work is very homogeneous and there is no doubt of their Antonine date, certainly within the period AD140–180, though AD150–170 is probably the optimum date.

29. Tower 7, P04:05, 135, WSP260 (33K).
Wt:0.125kg D:280mm 13%.Self-coloured, fabric with fine-textured, cream matrix (Munsell 10YR 8/4 'very pale brown'); fairly frequent and fairly well-sorted inclusions composed of quartz and orange-brown material with few black fragments. The surface is powdery but slightly abrasive due to the heavy tempering. The trituration grit included flint and quartz.
The partially impressed herringbone stamp is from the same die as Hull 1963, fig. 60, no 33. Colchester AD140–170.

30. Building 1, verandah, Period 3, L04:20, WSP174 (42K). Wt:0.040kg. D:*c.*280mm 6%. Self-coloured mortarium in fine-textured, yellowish-cream fabric (Munsell 10YR 8/4 'very pale brown'); only rare quartz and orange-brown inclusions, barely visible at × 20 magnification. The trituration grit included flint and quartz, mostly flint on fragment.
The left-facing stamp is a nearly complete impression from a herringbone die similar to Hull 1963, fig. 60, no. 29. Impressions of this stamp appear in slightly different lengths, suggesting that more than one die was used; they are so similar that they may have been made from the same matrix and they are always treated together. Colchester, AD140–170.

31. Area over Building 1, unstratified, Q05:02, WSP94 (43K). Wt:0.170kg D:320mm 13%. Self-coloured, yellowish-cream

fabric (Munsell 10YR 7/6 'yellow'), with moderate to fairly frequent, random and very ill-sorted, flint and quartz inclusions. The trituration grit is composed of moderate to fairly frequent, vari-sized, flint and quartz, thinning out towards the bead, but with a few stragglers on top of the flange.

The herringbone stamp is the most commonly recorded of the Colchester herringbone stamps (Hull 1963, fig. 60, no. 30). AD140–170.

32. *Via principalis*, M08:09, WSP101 (45K).
Wt:0.130kg D:290mm 10%. Self-coloured, yellowish-cream fabric (Munsell 2.5Y 8/4 'yellow'), with thick pink-brown core (Munsell 5YR 7/6 'reddish-yellow'); moderate, random, very ill-sorted quartz with some opaque black material. The trituration grit is identical with that on no. 31 above except for the addition of a few soft, orange-brown fragments.

The edge of a right-facing stamp survives, which is too fragmentary for perfect identification, but it is almost certainly a herringbone stamp. This stamp is from a different vessel from all the other herringbone stamps recorded. Colchester, AD 140–170.

33. Building 1, north-south drain east of south wall, Period 2, Q05:03, 171, WSP261 (34K).
Wt:0.140kg. D:*c.*280mm. 7%. Self-coloured, fine-textured sandwich fabric, dark cream (Munsell 10YR 8/3 'very pale brown') changing to pale orange-brown (Munsell 5YR 7/8 'reddish-yellow'), with dark cream core. The fairly frequent, fairly well-sorted, tiny inclusions are mostly quartz with some orange-brown and black material. The trituration is fairly frequent and well-sorted ending neatly about 23mm from the bottom of the bead; it is well-mixed and consists of flint, quartz, red-brown (?sandstone), slag and one soft, grey-white pellet, 14mm × 1.5mm. Worn.

The broken herringbone stamp has been found on seven mortaria in Scotland and on two other sites in England, Corbridge and a site near Sandwich, Kent. The fabric and trituration grit would be atypical for Colchester and a workshop in the Canterbury area is far more likely to be the source. AD140–170.

34. Area over Building 11 and Alley 6, unstratified, L15:01, 1338, WSP248 (24K).
Wt:0.058kg D:300mm 11%. Very hard, sandwich fabric, cream at surface, light brown outer core and deep cream inner core streaked with light brown; fabric very absorbent; smooth surface. The moderate to fairly frequent inclusions include random, large opaque white material which fractures easily (non-reactive) with some quartz, and rarer small orange-brown material. The few trituration grits surviving, include quartz, greyish quartz sandstone? and red-brown slag and possibly opaque white material. There are traces of a thin reddish-brown slip on top of the flange and at the bottom of the bead; this could be a 'Raetian' slip, but it is very rarely found on mortaria in the cream range and 'Raetian' mortaria were almost never stamped in Britain, so that this option is unlikely.

At least four herringbone stamps, some overlapping, are partially impressed across the flange. These appear to be from an unknown die. The absence of flint in the trituration or on the flange makes it fairly certain that this is not from any of the workshops in East Anglia, Kent or at Wiggonholt which regularly produced mortaria with herringbone stamps.

Relatively dark slips on a cream fabric were common in the Lower Nene Valley, but herringbone stamps were rarely if ever used there. The source of this mortarium is therefore, uncertain, but the Nene Valley or Corbridge are possible sources. The rim-profile alone would tend to indicate a date in the early second century, but it is unlikely that herringbone stamps were being produced before about AD130 and most, if not all, were produced within the period AD140–170.

35. Area over Gate 3 and *intervallum* road (Road 6), unstratified, J16:01, WSP99 (39K).
Wt:0.040kg. A rim fragment, close to the spout, of a mortarium in hard, orange-brown fabric; probably self-coloured. The fairly frequent inclusions are ill-sorted quartz; no trituration grit survives.

The fragmentary left-facing trademark stamp could well be from the same die as a stamp already recorded from Wallsend (Corder 1903, 46) and South Shields (Bidwell and Speak 1994, fig. 8.2, no. 3, found in the demolition of Periods 2–3). Unfortunately both of these stamps are also fragmentary and this example would be from the unrecorded part of this stamp. This example has the same very unusual raised band under the flange as the old find from Wallsend. All of the rim-profiles suggest a date within the period AD110–140. The distribution points to a workshop in north-east England.

36. Building 1, Period 2 demolition, M04:06, 475, WSP250 (26K).
Wt:0.162kg. D:250mm 17.5%. Brownish-pink fabric fired to cream near the outer surface, with very thin cream slip. The body is slightly distorted by the presence of a large (15mm × 6mm), fragment of ?slag, but the normal inclusions are almost invisible, mostly quartz and brown slag. Only one or two quartz trituration grits survive.

The broken stamp (right-facing) reads ]TI[ with an upper border of fine diagonal bars. The stamp on no. 20, a different vessel, is probably from the same die, but no other examples are known. The fabric and provenance point to manufacture in northern England; the rim-profile should fit a date within the period AD120–170, but the use of such fine borders would best fit an Antonine date. Borders such as these are rare outside the Mancetter-Hartshill potteries and further examples will enable identification.

37. Robber trench of south wall of Building 7, F11:07, WSP234 (47K).
Wt:0.138g D:280mm 12%. A heavily worn mortarium in granular greyish-cream fabric, with the surface of the flange somewhat exfoliated; abundant quartz inclusions with rare black and red-brown material. The trituration grit is worn away except for one flint and two quartz grits. There was a cream surface slip.

The incomplete and somewhat damaged stamp is from the same die as one from Lower Warbank, Keston in Kent (unpublished). The most complete version reads [..]OMX; the × will be a space-filler and it is not clear whether or not the stamp is retrograde. The fabric used can be attributed to a workshop in the important potteries south of Verulamium, mostly between Brockley Hill and Radlett, though the inclusions are not as well-sorted as commonly in their products. The optimum date for this mortarium is AD110–140.

38. Building 10, *contubernium* 3?, Period 2, F14:44, 1626, WSP244.

Wt:0.010kg Flange fragment in hard, fine-textured, orange-brown fabric (Munsell 2.5YR 6/8, 'light red'), merging to a slightly greyer colour in core; with very moderate, random and ill-sorted inclusions, mostly quartz with some orange-brown and rare black. Cream slip.

The fragmentary stamp preserves part of a border and fragments of letters. It has not been possible to identify this stamp, but identification will be possible when further examples are found. North of England. Second century, probably before AD180.

39. Soil and rubble over end of Building 18, Period 3–4, H05:13, 817, WSP247 (23K).

Wt:0.045kg. D:*c.*250mm 7%. Orange-brown fabric (Munsell 2.5YR 6/8 'light red') with thick, well-defined darker brown core (Munsell 2.5YR 5/4 'reddish-brown'); frequent tiny inclusions, mostly quartz with few larger quartz, black slag and red-brown material. Cream slip.

The stamp, probably a left-facing one, has been impressed along the flange. The stamp cannot be identified until further examples are found. This practice of stamping along flange or collar was never common in Britain, though examples are known from some workshops at some points in the first and second centuries. One or more of these workshops using generally similar fabric to this example, was in Kent in the second half of the second century, but only the discovery of further examples will enable identification of the source. The rim-profile together with this unusual stamping suggests an optimum date of AD150–180.

*Table 22.08: Amphora from the excavations (all periods, including unstratified)*

| Fabric & principal content | Wt (kg) | Sherd (no) | EVES (%) |
|---|---|---|---|
| *Oil* | | | |
| Dressel 20 (P&W 25) | 94.7 | 87.9 | 91.9 |
| South Spanish | 0.1 | 0.5 | - |
| *Wine* | | | |
| Gauloise 4 (P&W 27) | 1.2 | 2.1 | - |
| Gauloise 12 (P&W 55) | 0.6 | 2.2 | 2.8 |
| Central Campanian | 2.4 | 5.0 | 4.7 |
| Northern Campanian | 0.5 | 1.3 | - |
| *Fish sauce?* | | | |
| Cam 186 (P&W 17) | 0.04 | 0.1 | 0.6 |
| *Uncertain* | | | |
| Biv amphora | 0.01 | 0.03 | - |
| Unsourced | 0.45 | 0.9 | - |
| Totals | 414.166 | 3293 | 2088 |

Key: P&W = Peacock and Williams 1986

# The amphorae

*by A. T. Croom*

The site produced 414kg of amphora from both stratified and unstratified contexts, making up 37.7% of all the pottery recovered from the site.

As usual on northern military sites, the assemblage is dominated by sherds from Dressel 20 amphorae, used to import olive oil for cooking and use in the bath-house. The wine amphorae, making up 10% of the assemblage by sherd count, came from both France and Italy. The flat-bottomed French amphorae were about equally split between those from southern France (Gauloise 4) and those from Normandy (Gauloise 12). They probably reached the fort during the second century and probably much of the third as well, as a Gauloise 4 amphora was recovered from Cistern 1, filled *c.*270 (Fig. 22.17, no. 114), but the quantities involved reflect the fact that much of the ration wine must have been supplied in barrels (Bidwell and Speak 1994, 216). From the middle of the third century Campanian wine began to be imported from the site, making up 3% by weight and 6% by sherd count. This is similar to the proportion found at South Shields, where the Italian amphorae make up 7% by weight (*ibid.*, table 8.9, 'black sand' and 'volcanic').

Approximately 16% (by weight) of the stratified amphorae from the site was recovered from road surfaces, although this rises to about 28% when taking into account material from contexts unassigned to specific periods. Building 16 produced the largest quantity of amphorae of any individual building (18%), almost two-thirds of which came from the base of a single Dressel 20 in pit M08:43. The other building to produce a large quantity of amphora was the hospital (10% of the amphorae by weight); nearly 60% of this came from the infilling of the latrine and 25% from the open courtyard.

## Catalogue (Fig. 22.10)

*Dressel 20*
1. Building 1, verandah, Period 3, L04:20.
See also Fig. 22.17, no. 113.

*Central Campanian*
2. Unstratified, E13:01.
3. Unstratified, H15:08.
4. Road 2, K05:07.
5. Alley 1, daub deposit, N05:23.
6. Unstratified, H15:09.
7. Unstratified, H12:29.
8. Unstratified, L05:03.

See also Fig. 22.17, no. 115

*Gauloise 4:* See Fig. 22.17, no. 114

*Biv:* see Fig. 22.17, no. 116

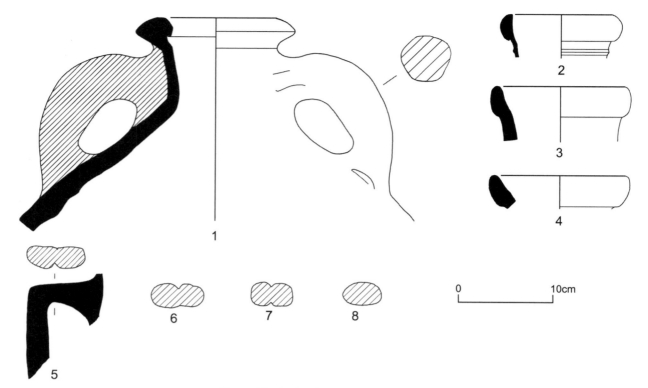

*Figure 22.10: Amphorae nos 1–8. Scale 1:4.*

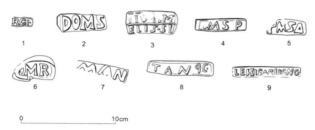

*Figure 22.11: Amphora stamps nos 1–9. Scale 1:4.*

## Amphora stamps (Fig. 22.11)

*by R. McBride*

The excavations produced 14 stamps on Dressel 20 amphorae of which 9 were legible. Catalogue entries begin with the context number, followed by the small finds number and the record number. A transcription is given with a translation if necessary along with references to parallels from the principal texts.

1. ]RGI· **ACRIGI** Callender 18, Funari 22, Rodriguez 51.
A parallel from Rome comes from a context dating 220–222. Source: La Catria 19, Guadalquivir Valley (Funari 1996, 21), (area of Building 2 and Alley 1, ploughsoil, L05:03, 590, WSP4).

2. DOMS **DOMS** Callender 552, Funari 170, Rodriguez 237.
This has been found in a context in Rome dated 145–161. Source: Alcolea (Funari 1996, 54), (area of Building 11 and Alley 6, unstratified, M15:02, 1227, WSP5).

3. LI[ ]IM/ELIS·SI **L. IUNI(US) MELISSI(US)** Callender 879, Funari 136d, Rodriguez 189.

This stamp has been dated to AD 110–190. Source: Las Delicias (Funari 1996, 46), (rubble over east rampart and *intervallum* road, Q07:07, 2571, WSP9).

4. MSP **MSP** Callender 1180, Funari 211, Rodriguez 291.
This stamp has been found in a contexts dated 145–161 and 179–180 in Rome. Source: Guadajoz (Funari 1996, 63), (area over Building 13, unstratified, N12:01, 1638, WSP6)

5. PMSA **P. M(USSDII) S(EMPRONIANI) A** Callender 1355b, Funari 155, Rodriguez 212.
Callender suggests that this stamp dates to the middle of the second century. (Funari 1996, 50), (Building 4, make up, Period 2, G04:07, 479, WSP3).

6. ]MR **QMR** Callender 1481, Funari 153, Rodriguez 209.
The first character is faint but is almost certainly Q. This stamp has been found in contexts dated to 145–161 at Rome. (Funari 1996, 49), (area over *Via principalis*, unstratified, M08:01, 2494, WSP8).

7. ]MAN **ROMAN** Callender 1541, Funari 198, Rodriguez 279.
Second half of the first century to the first half of the second century. Source: Las Delicias (Funari 1996, 60) (north-south drain east of Building 1, Period 2, Q05:28, 330, WSP2).

8. ΛΊ9C TA·
The closest parallel for this stamp is Callender 1696 which Callender suggests may date from the second half of the first century (Callender 1965, 256), (area over Building 13, unstratified, M12:01, 1696, WSP7).

9. ]LEHISAPI[..]NG

*Table 22.09: Quantity of pottery from the excavations (kg).*

|  | Stratified | Unstratified |
|---|---|---|
| Samian | 18.990 | 31.817 |
| Mortaria | 34.499 | 43.418 |
| Amphorae | 166.838 | 247.328 |
| Fine wares | 9.625 | 14.455 |
| Coarse wares | 231.320 | 300.797 |
| Total | 461.272 | 637.815 |

The obscure characters between I and N are faint but may be a ligature of NE (area over *Intervallum* road (Road 4), unstratified, Q04:01, 10, WSP1).

Illegible or incomplete:
10. VVV [ (Building 8, room, 8, mid-third century?, E10:43, WSP169)
11. ] M [ (Building 1, demolition, Period 2 demolition, M04:06, 283, WSP10).
12. ] N (area over Building 9, unstratified, E13:01, WSP159).
13. ] . V . I [ (area over Building 7, unstratified, F11:01, WSP160).
14. Illegible (Cistern 2, upper fill, late third/early fourth century, H07:03, WSP161).

## The coarse wares

### by A. T. Croom

The excavations produced a total of 1099.087kg of pottery, over half of which was unstratified. This very high proportion of unstratified material is partially the result of the destruction of most of the fourth-century levels on the site. The stratified material was fully catalogued and quantified by weight and by measuring rim percentages (EVEs), although not by sherd count, with certain assemblages of interest studied in greater detail. The unstratified amphorae, mortaria and fine wares, plus some coarse wares of interest were also fully catalogued.

### Fabrics mentioned in catalogue

See Tomber and Dore 1998 for fabrics with NRFRC code in the above table.

Pottery from two other forts in the Lower Tyne Valley have already been studied in some detail, providing the framework for work on the assemblage from Wallsend, since it it clear they all drew on the same sources of supply. The report on the pottery from South Shields included the first quantification of the mortaria and amphorae from the site, and a detailed discussion of its pottery supply, in particular the vessels in BB2 and its allied fabrics that make up a large proportion of the coarse wares during the third century (Bidwell and Speak 1994, 206–42). The report on the pottery from the fort of Newcastle expanded this discussion, with additional detailed study of local traditional wares and the well-preserved late Roman assemblages (Bidwell and Croom 2002, 139–72). The supply of pottery to the region as a whole in the late Roman period has also been investigated (Bidwell and Croom 2010). The study of pottery from the northern frontier region is continuing with the Hadrian's Wall Ceramic Database project (www.collectionsprojects.org.uk/archaeology/ceramic%20database/introduction.html), which incorporates assemblages from forts, *vici* and turrets, and hopes to provide a more regional understanding of the material recovered.

### Fine wares

#### LOWER NENE VALLEY COLOUR-COATED (LNV CC)

This is not common before the third century in northern Britain. At Wallsend it was found in the construction levels of the Period 4 barracks and the infill of the hospital latrine drain (Hodgson 2003, 244), and at South Shields it is first found in Severan contexts. It becomes the most common colour-coated ware on the site in the third century, and makes up 70% of the fine wares on the site. The industry supplied primarily beakers, but also flagons and to a lesser extent castor boxes. Many of the vessel forms have a long-life, but a few new types were introduced during the life of the industry. The funnel-necked beaker was first made near the end of the first quarter of the third century, followed in the mid or late third century by beakers based on 'Rhenish' forms (such as the funnel-necked beaker with bead rim). Colour-coated bowls in coarse ware forms generally date to *c*.360 on the northern frontier (Bidwell and Croom 2010, table 4.1).
Beaker, barbotine decoration: 87, 120–2, 268–9, 295
Beaker, funnel necked: 125–7, 129
Beaker, indented: 77–8, 100
Beaker, narrow-mouthed: 294
Beaker, plain-rimmed: 296
Beaker, rouletted decoration: 123, 299
Flagon: 84, 128
Flagon, with moulded mask: 337

#### LOWER NENE VALLEY PARCHMENT (LNV PA)

Parchment wares, often painted, seem to have been made throughout the lifetime of the industry (Perrin 1999, 108). Although made in a range of forms, flasks are the most common type found in the north. More exotic forms, such as head pots, moulded mask flagons and ring vases also occur, but only in very small numbers.
Bottle: 85, 118
Triple vase: 248

Mortaria made in Nene Valley white ware were also supplied to the fort from the late second or early third century, and the industry became the major supplier of mortaria to the site in the third and fourth centuries. A few grey ware vessels also find their way to the north, but in such low numbers it is probable they are a by-product of the transportation of the mortaria and colour-coated wares.

#### COLCHESTER?

See Anderson 1980, 33, North Gaulish fabric 2. This ware is used for rough-cast beakers. It is the most common type of second-century fine ware from the site.
Beaker: 2

#### CENTRAL GAULISH BLACK-SLIPPED (CNG BS)

This was imported from the mid second to the early third century. It is a minor fine ware at Wallsend.
Beaker: 277

#### MICA-DUSTED

This consists of a number of oxidised fabrics from different

*Table 22.10: Stratified ware by fabric type, shown as a percentage*

| Fabric | NRFRC | Wt | EVEs |
|---|---|---|---|
| **Samian** | | 6.4 | 7.5 |
| **Mortaria** | | 11.7 | 5.1 |
| **Fine wares** | | | |
| Cologne colour-coated | KOL CC | 0.1 | 0.1 |
| Moselkeramik black-slipped | MOS BS | 0.1 | 0.1 |
| Central Gaulish black-slipped | CNG BS | 0.1 | 0.1 |
| Lower Nene Valley colour-coated | LNV CC | 2.5 | 3.3 |
| Exeter group 4 | | 0.0 | 0.1 |
| Colchester colour-coated (?) | | 0.1 | 0.5 |
| Unsourced fine wares | | 0.2 | 0.7 |
| Mica-dusted | | | 0.1 |
| North Kent fine | | 0.2 | 0.7 |
| Parisian | | 0.0 | 0.1 |
| Unsourced poppyhead beakers | | 0.0 | 0.2 |
| **Coarse wares** | | | |
| Oxidised ware 1 | | 1.3 | 1.3 |
| Oxidised ware 2 | | 0.2 | 0.2 |
| Lower Tyne painted | | 0.6 | 0.5 |
| North-African style | | 0.1 | 0.1 |
| Flagon A, B, C, D, E, F, G | | 0.6 | 0.4 |
| Corbridge oxidised | COR WH | 0.1 | 0.2 |
| North Gaulish fabric 1 | NOG WH 1 | 0.2 | 0.1 |
| Buff | | 0.1 | 0.2 |
| Imported oxidised | | 0.1 | 0.1 |
| Pink grog-tempered | PNK GT | 0.1 | 0 |
| Unsourced oxidised | | 5.2 | 5.2 |
| Grey ware 1 | | 5.3 | 7.7 |
| Grey ware 2 | | 1.3 | 2.1 |
| Grey ware 3 | | 0.5 | 1.0 |
| Grey ware 4 | | 0.4 | 0.4 |
| Grey ware 6 | | 0.6 | 0.5 |
| BB1 | DOR BB 1 | 10.0 | 11.8 |
| BB2 | BB 2 | 32.2 | 25.3 |
| South-east reduced | | 13.2 | 14.6 |
| Horningsea | HOR RE | 0.6 | 0.0 |
| East Anglian grey | | 0.1 | 0.1 |
| East Yorkshire grey | | 0.1 | 0.2 |
| South Yorkshire grey | | 0.1 | 0.0 |
| Dales | DAL SH | 0.1 | 0.1 |
| Late grey gritty | | 0.1 | 0.2 |
| Calcite-gritted | CG | 1.2 | 1.5 |
| Crambeck reduced | CRA RE | 1.6 | 1.2 |
| Local traditional ware | | 0.1 | 0.1 |
| North Gaulish grey | NOG RE | 0.0 | 0.2 |
| Unsourced reduced | | 11.1 | 6.0 |
| Total | | 294.434 | 34,138 |

Fabrics represented by less than 0.1% not included in the table: Central Gaulish colour coated 2 (CNG CC 2); North Gaulish colour-coated 1; Ebor red-painted (EBO OX); highly burnished black; *Céramique à l'éponge* (EPO MA); Verulamium white (VER WH); Lower Nene Valley parchment (LNV PA); Lower Nene Valley grey; Crambeck parchment (CRA PA). Other fabrics found only in the unstratified material: Severn Valley, Crambeck red, southern shell-tempered, Savernake (SAV GT)

Key: NRFRC = National Roman Fabric Reference Collection

sources, with a slip rich in gold-mica. At Wallsend there are indented beakers and plain-rimmed bowls, but it is only a minor fine ware on the site.
Beaker: 76
Bowl: 8 (?), 206, 323

### Céramique a l'éponge (EPO MA)

This ware is rare in the region, with only a few vessels known from the northern frontier. The majority of examples in this country come from south-east England, where it is most commonly fourth-century in date (Tyers 1996, 144). Most of the few northern examples have a similar date, although there is a possible sherd from Vindolanda in a late third-century context (Bidwell 1985, 182). Wallsend has produced two vessels, both flanged bowls (Fig. 22.16, no. 112; post-Roman dereliction and ploughsoil). A single flanged bowl is known from South Shields (unpublished, context 3778, fourth-century) and one from Newcastle (Bidwell and Croom 2002, fig. 15.9, no. 99, from an Anglo-Saxon grave).
Flanged bowl: 112

## Coarse wares

### Flagon fabric

Fabric A: Dark grey fabric with orange exterior and a cream wash, found also at South Shields.
Flagon: 117, 292
There are a number of other flagon fabrics (Fabrics B to G), which occurred in small quantities. None illustrated.

### Buff ware (Exeter fabric 440)

Flagons in a buff fabric, probably imported from France. This was produced in the first century and into the early second, and is not a common ware on the site.
Flagon: 266, 287

### Ebor ware (EBO OX)

Made from c.70 to the early third century at York. A small number of vessels are known from the site. The most common type found in the northern frontier zone are the red-painted bowls, but there are also some North African-style vessels.
Dish: 319

Red-painted. See Monaghan 1997, 877–80. Date: Hadrianic-Antonine
Flanged bowl: 93

Late Ebor ware (North African style)
Date: early third century.
Casserole: 275
Head pots: 338–44
Lid: 330 (?)

### Severn Valley ware (SVW OX)

Small quantities of Severn Valley ware reached the Lower Tyne forts in the second and third centuries. At Newcastle it made up only 0.1% of the pottery assemblage (Bidwell and Croom 2002, table 15.8), and at Wallsend would be even less.
Storage jar: 304

### Locally produced grey and oxidised wares

A number of fabrics have been identified as those of locally produced wares of the second century. The main products are cooking-pots with groove or lattice decoration (particularly in grey ware), flat-rimmed carinated bowls, and plain-rimmed dishes, but also beakers, storage jars and lids. The finest oxidised fabric was often decorated with white paint (see Lower Tyne painted oxidised ware below). The forms indicate production started in the early second century and continued throughout the Antonine period.

## Grey ware 1 (GW1)

Hard mid to pale grey micaceous fabric. Very fine black and white inclusions, occasionally large. Surfaces are usually darker than the core, particularly noticeable where the surface has been chipped. This is the most common of the fabrics.
South Shields grey ware fabric 1 is the same ware (Bidwell and Speak 1994, 231).
Small jar: 3, 88
Bowl: 262
Bowl, flat-rimmed: 39, 265
Cooking-pot: 9, 10, 18–9, 54, 312
Dish, plain-rimmed: 46
Storage jar: 302

## Grey ware 2 (GW2)

Gritty grey fabric, coarser and softer than grey ware 1. Angular grey and black inclusions, and some linear black inclusions. Occasionally has grey core with paler margins. Rarely burnished, and often with a mottled surface.
Beaker, indented: 298
Bowl, flat-rimmed: 23, 40
Bowl: hemispherical: 29
Flagon, pinch-necked: 293
Cooking-pot: 50–1

## Grey ware 3 (GW3)

Micaceous grey fabric with wide buff core, and scattered, large inclusions, including sandstone. It is not as gritty as grey ware 2, but the individual inclusions can be larger.
Cooking-pot, bead-rimmed: 271

## Oxidised ware 1 (OW1)

Slightly gritty, micaceous orange fabric with medium-sized quartz and plentiful soft red inclusions. There are occasional large or very large inclusions, opaque white or fragments of sandstone. The inclusions are noticeable on the surface of the vessel, although the surfaces are often wiped.
Bowl, flat-rimmed: 22
Bowl, flat-rimmed hemispherical bowl: 47, 94
Dish, flat-rimmed: 95
Dish, flat-rimmed with groove: 111

## Oxidised ware 2 (OW2)

Probable a variant of the above, but with white inclusions more prominent than the red inclusions, and often more highly fired.
Dish, plain-rimmed: 27

## Lower Tyne painted oxidised ware (LT OW painted)

Hard orange fabric often with a grey core or interior and burnished surfaces. Small common inclusions of angular quartz and occasional small soft orange and hard grey inclusions, fragments of sandstone and some mica can be present. The painted decoration is usually cream/white, but at least one vessel also had brown paint. Decoration includes horizontal stripes, zig-zag, diagonal and herringbone lines, open circles and lines of dots. The majority of recognised examples have been found at Wallsend and South Shields, although sherds have been recorded from a number of northern sites, including Carlisle and Cramond.

Beaker: 86
Biconical strainer: 21
Bowl: 48, 259, 320, 326
Cauldron: 20
Closed form: 333

### BLACK BURNISHED WARE FABRIC 1 (DOR BB1)

The two main suppliers of coarse ware to the site during the second century were the BB1 industries and the local production sites set up by the military. In the early part of the third century, little BB1 reached the site, but from the late third century, when the supply of BB2 was in decline, BB1 again began a source of supply. Most of the BB1 from the site comes from Dorset, but there are small quantities of BB1 from other sources, such as Rossington Bridge.

Bead-rimed jar: 11, 72, 132
Bowl and dish, flat-rimmed: 24–5, 57–8, 62, 273
Bowl and dish, plain-rimmed: 191–9
Bowl, plain rimmed with groove: 41, 56
Bowl, flanged: 230–44
Cooking-pot: 12–3, 55, 66, 141–3

### BLACK BURNISHED WARE FABRIC 2 (BB2)

This ware is present in small quantities from the late second century, but becomes, with its allied industries, the major coarse ware supplier in the third century. For discussions of the dating, see Bidell and Speak 1994, Bidwell and Croom 2002, 153, 169, and Hodgson 2003, 244. By the 270s at the latest, BB1 had begun to supply pottery in some quantity again, but it appears that some BB2 continued to reach Wallsend until the final quarter of the century. The site has produced 13 examples of flanged bowls in BB2, dating to after *c*.270. The fort at Newcastle, further upriver, has also produced a number of these bowls, but surprisingly few have been found at South Shields, even though the pottery supplies for Wallsend and Newcastle must have come through its port.

Beaker: 63, 131
Bowl and dish, bead-rimmed: 207, 274
Bowl and dish, plain-rimmed: 200–2, 284
Bowl and dish, plain-rimmed with groove: 110, 203–4
Bowl and dish, rounded-rimmed: 67, 208–9, 211–29, 256–7
Bowl, flanged: 328
Cooking-pot: 6, 14, 17, 68, 144–52, 254, 313
Cooking-pot, small: 251–3
Miniature dish, plain-rimmed with groove: 98

### SOUTH EASTERN REDUCED WARES (SE RW)

Date: mostly third century.

This term is used for a number of different fabrics from several production centres that were in business at the same time as BB2, probably mainly situated in southern Essex (see Monaghan 1987; called 'fabrics allied to BB2' in Bidwell and Speak 1994, 228–31). They were imported to the northeast over the same time period as BB2, and at Wallsend are an important source of supply. Cooking-pots were made in a gritty fabric (in particular Gillam 1970 type 151 jars) and in a sandy fabric without any decoration, burnishing or slip. Storage jars were made in a slightly gritty fabric, often with a grey core, and frequently have burnished

decoration. Wide-mouthed bowls and flasks could be slipped, burnished or both, the bowls often with a black or dark grey surface and commonly wavy line decoration, and flasks with a speckled light grey surface. The ware appears alongside BB2 from the late second century, but the vessel type Gillam 151 probably only appears in the third century; at South Shields it is first seen in contexts dating after *c*.220 (Hodgson 2003, 245).

Beaker: 260
Beaker, poppy-head: 101
Bowl, wide-mouthed: 186
Bowl, S-shaped: 82, 109, 187–9
Cooking-pot: 59, 71, 80, 104–5, 153, 155–69, 172–7, 179, 261, 282
Cooking-pot with bead rim: 69, 310
Cooking-pot, Gillam 1970 type 151: 70, 92, 180–1, 314
Flagon: 291
Flask: 119
Storage jar: 15–6, 79, 135–7, 305

### HORNINGSEA (HOR RE)

Horningsea ware, always in the form of storage jars, have now been recognised at Wallsend, South Shields (Bidwell and Speak 1994, fig. 8.14, no. 162 and unpublished), Newcastle (Bidwell and Croom 2002, 153), and Benwell (McBride 2010, fig. 3, no. 2). As the jars were probably imported in small numbers at the same time as BB2 and SE RW they are likely to be mainly third-century in date on the site.

Storage jar: 134, 250, 306

### EAST ANGLIAN MICA-RICH FABRICS

Grey fabric with abundant, fine muscovite mica on the surfaces.

Platter: 44, 83

### LOCAL TRADITIONAL ('NATIVE')

This term covers a range of fabrics used for makings vessels that continued the local indigenous Iron Age traditions of pottery making (Bidwell and Croom 2002, 169–70). The fabrics are usually black, sometimes with patchy oxidised surfaces, with a range of large inclusions, and are always hand-made.

Cooking-pot: 185, 311

### DALES-TYPE

Vessels without shell-tempering, in the form of Dales ware cooking-pots. True Dales ware vessels were also present. Third-century in date.

Cooking-pot: 182–3

### EAST YORKSHIRE GREY

Date: third century

There are examples of pottery from Norton (*c*.220–80), and from Throlam (mid- or late third century to mid-fourth century) and probably also the other sites of the Holme-on-Spalding-Moor industries.

Beaker, with handle: 133
Bowl, wide-mouthed: 190
Bottle: 301
Countersunk lug-handled jar: 280
Jug: 303
Smith pot: 347

SOUTH YORKSHIRE GREY

A number of vessels are likely to come from the South Yorkshire industries, but this was never a major source of supply. There is also a bowl with internal decoration in a South Yorkshire/Lincolnshire tradition (Fig. 22.22, no. 263).
Dish: 263

LATE GRITTY GREY

Date: late third century–fourth century

Hard, mid-grey fabric with common to abundant, large quartz inclusions. Typically found as cooking-pots with everted rims that are flat-topped, cupped or double lid-seated. The vessels were both wheel-thrown, and hand-thrown with the rim finished on a slow wheel. This is one of the most important sources of pottery in the late Roman period in north-east England (for a full discussion of the ware see Croom *et al* 2008, 229–30).
Cooking-pot: 272

CALCITE-GRITTED (CG)

See Tomber and Dore 1998, 201. The National Fabric Reference Collection abbreviation HUN CG is not used in order to avoid confusion, as the ware includes non-Huntcliff-type vessels. 'Huntcliff-type' is used here to refer only to cooking-pots with an internal groove on the rim (Gillam 1970 types 162–3).

Date: small quantities from late third century, mainly fourth century

Calcite-gritted ware was originated in the pre-Roman period and continued to be made throughout the Roman period, but it was only imported to the north-east in any quantity from the late third century. In the north-east the cooking-pot is the most common form found, although some storage jars, wide-mouthed bowls and plain-rimmed bowls are known. The Huntcliff-type rim seems to appear in *c.*360, before the introduction of Crambeck parchment ware (Bidwell and Croom 2010, 29).
Cooking-pot, with Huntcliff-type rim: 108, 315
Dish, plain-rimmed: 327
Storage jar: 103

CRAMBECK REDUCED WARE (CRA RE)

The reduced ware first reaches the north in the late third century, and continues until at least the late fourth century (Bidwell 1985, 178; Bidwell and Croom 2010). It was supplied in a range of forms, such as bowls, dishes, beakers and water-carrying jars, but not cooking-pots (which seem to have been supplied by the calcite-gritted ware industries which were located in the same part of the country, but not at the same kiln sites). The conical flanged bowl with internal wavy line first appears *c.*370.

CRAMBECK RED WARE

Red fabric, often decorated with white paint, probably with a similar dating to the painted parchment ware. One example known from the site.
Bowl: 329

NORTH GAULISH GREY WARE (NOG RE).

Date: first to third century.

This ware has been found at South Shields, Wallsend and Newcastle in small quantities. The most common form is the *vase triconique*.
*Vase triconique*: 38, 81, 308

GREY WARE 4

A minor grey ware fabric. Hard grey fabric, distinctive due to the plentiful fine white quartz inclusions.
Cooking-pot: 138, 171
Bowl/dish: 205
Lid: 31–2

GREY WARE 6

Grey fabric, distinctive because of the plentiful small and common large black inclusions. A number of related fabrics, with the same common black inclusions, have been found across the eastern section of Hadrian's Wall. It has been found at a number of turrets along Hadrian's Wall, mainly between Housesteads and Rudchester, so it is possible that Corbridge could be the source for this ware. It appears to be Hadrianic and Antonine in date.
Cooking-pot: 91, 102

SOUTHERN SHELL-TEMPERED WARE. SEE BIDWELL AND SPEAK 1994, 230.
Jar: 307

*Other fabrics of interest (none illustrated)*

SAVERNAKE WARE (SAV GT)

Date: Early first century to early or mid-second century, with Lydiard Tregose kilns possibly continuing into the third or fourth centuries.

This ware usually has a limited distribution in and around Wiltshire and Bath (Tyers 1996, fig. 248), and it has not previously been identified in the north. Two sherds from jars were recovered (F11:07, G11:09, robber trench and unstratified). It is of interest that a sherd of New Forest mortaria, also of very restricted distribution, should also be found at Wallsend.

PINK GROG-TEMPERED WARE (PNK GT)

A sherd of this ware was recovered from the alley deposit (Alley 1; context N05:23). This ware is almost exclusively found in the Northamptonshire and Buckinghamshire region, but two vessels have now been found at Cramond (Ford 1991).

PARISIAN WARE

Date: late first to third century

A small number of sherds in at least three different fabrics, with stamped decoration, including roundels, rosettes and squares.

*Catalogue (Figs 22.12–26)*

*Rampart building (C11:04)*

1.  Pale orange fabric, cream to exterior. Fine fabric with very rare larger inclusions, and rare silver mica. Single handle.
2.  Colchester?
3.  GW1.
4.  Hard mid-grey fabric, with slightly paler margins, and occasional black or white inclusions. Burnished on shoulder, with vertical line rouletting on the top part and diagonal line rouletting on the lower part.
5.  Dark grey, sandy fabric, slightly micaceous. Burnished under the rim, but otherwise a sandy surface. Linear rustication.

6.      BB2.

7.      Burnished on shoulder and over rim. Fine micaceous, sandy fabric with buff core and dark grey surfaces.

8.      Soft, pale orange fabric with pale brown core. Possibly originally mica-dusted.

See also: Croom 2003, fig. 158, nos 15–9.

*Alley 1*
LOWER FILL

9.      GW1, M05:16.

10.     A second, with the rim oval in shape and body slightly flattened before firing. GW1, M05:16, M05:12.

11.     BB1, M05:16.

12.     BB1, with sooting under rim, M05:16.

13.     BB1, M05:16.

14.     BB2, M05:16.

DAUB DEPOSIT

15.     SE RW. N05:23.

16.     SE RW, N05:23.

17.     BB2. Four lines incised on top of rim. N05:23.

18.     GW1, N05:23.

19.     Zone on body left unburnished. Body slightly flattened on one side (cf. no. 10 above). GW1, N05:23, N05:19.

20.     Line of white dots, some of which have run. Lower part of body burnished. Most of vessel survives. Gillam 1970 type 174, *Cam* 302. First half of the second century to late third century or later (Bidwell and Croom 1999, 481). LT OW painted, N05:23.

21.     Originally this probably had a spout; Marsh 1978, type 46. Burnished footring. Much of vessel survives. LT OW painted, N05:23.

22.     OW1, N05:23.

23.     GW2, N05:23.

24.     BB1, N05:23.

25.     BB1, N05:23.

26.     Burnished on rim and exterior. Micaceous grey fabric, slightly sandy, with a dark grey core, white margins and mid-grey surfaces, N05:23.

27.     A second, warped in firing so that the rim is out of shape and base is not flat. OW2, N05:23, N05:24.

28.     Two surviving repair holes, on non-joining sherds; some sotting on exterior. Sandy dark grey fabric, darker towards the exterior. well-rounded quartz *c.*1mm across is the most noticeable inclusion, with less common angular grey and plentiful extremely fine micaceous inclusions, N05:23.

29.     Poor condition, battered and spalled. GW2, N05:23, N05:17.

30.     Soft orange fabric with light grey core. Concentric grooving on interior. Similar to the 'mortarium-like bowls' of the north-west, but without the groove on the flange. Cf. Birrens; Robertson 1975, fig. 63, nos 11–2. N05:23, N05:24.

31.     Darker surfaces, with uneven colouring. GW4, N05:23.

32.     GW4, N05:23.

33.     Anaus mortarium, 120–60. See mortarium stamp no. 4. N05:23, N05:19.

34.     Anaus mortarium, 120–60. See mortarium stamp no. 10, N05:23, P04:10.

See also amphora Fig. 22.10, no. 5.

UPPER FILL

35.     'Pink fabric, lighter in fracture; hard, fairly rough with moderate frequency of sub-angular grit inclusions. Traces of white external slipping. Bipartite handle' (Holbrook 1984, no. 9). Lost. M05:12.

36.     Soft orange fabric with scattered red inclusions, some large. Remains of a cream wash, M05:12.

37.     Fabric white about rim, rest mid-grey. Burnt, and body spalled. M05:12.

38.     NOG RE, M05:12.

39.     A second; warped. GW1, M05:12.

40.     Approximately one-third of the vessel survives. There is rilling on the interior towards the base, while the base is only 2mm thick in the centre. GW2, M05:12.

41.     BB1, P05:16.

42.     Anaus mortarium, 120–60. See mortarium stamp no. 9. N05:07.

43.     North-eastern, second century. P05:16.

DISTURBED UPPER FILL AND DERELICTION OVER ALLEY

44.     Fine grey fabric with darker, highly micaceous surfaces. East Anglian? Burnt white along top of rim. N05:07.

45.     White fabric with fine black inclusions and small voids and mid-grey surfaces. Same fabric as no. 90 below. N05:07.

46.     GW1, approximately one third of vessel survives, L05:29.

47.     OW1, L05:29.

48.     Not burnished. LT OW painted, with slight grey core and no evidence of paint. L05:29.

49.     Mortarium. North-east: pale orange fabric with wide grey core, with large, soft white inclusions and occasional black linear inclusions. Large red and white trituration grits. Hadrianic/Antonine. N05:07.

*Alley 3*
CLAY LAYER

50.     GW2, F04:12.

51.     GW2, F04:12.

DRIP TRENCH

52.     Hard orange fabric with dark grey core and a thick cream wash, discoloured in firing to grey on one side, F04:33.

53.     Soft, gritty orange fabric, slightly burnt near base, F04:33.

54.     GW1, F04:33.

55.     BB1, F04:33.

56.     BB1, F04:33.

57.     Slightly burnt. BB1, F04:33.

58.     BB1, F04:33.

RUBBLE OVER ALLEY

59.   SE RW, gritty fabric, K05:22.
60.   Soft orange fabric with silver mica plates and some brown inclusions. Slightly burnt on the rim, K05:22.
61.   Fine, micaceous orange fabric with red inclusions, paler orange margins and finely burnished self-slipped surfaces. The flange has been deliberately removed (50% of vessel survives), G04:15.
62.   BB1, G04:15.

## Hospital: Building 8

PERIOD 1

63.   Remains of slip on shoulder and rim. BB2, D10:20.
64.   White fabric, with thin brown wash over interior and exterior. E10:43, E10:56, E10:58.
65.   Pale orange, slightly sandy fabric with fine red and occasional black inclusions. Darker orange exterior, turning to brown on the exterior. E10:43, E10:58.
66.   Burnished decoration on the base. Although there is a complete profile, less than 15% of the vessel survives. BB1, D12:34.
67.   Bowl or dish with drooping rim and curved wall. Cf. Monaghan 1987, 5D0.2BB2, E10:76.

PERIOD 3

68.   Buried pot, found with stone lid *in situ* (see stone report, no. 35, and Fig. 25.33). BB2, D11:23.

MID THIRD CENTURY

69.   SE RW, E11:14.
70.   SE RW, E11:14.
71.   SE RW, E11:14.

See also: Croom 2003, fig. 158, nos 11–4.

## Barracks

PERIOD 2

72.   BB1, F04:07.
73.   Micaceous sandy grey fabric with pale grey core and paler margins and soft black inclusions. Sooting under rim. Cf. no. 106 below. P05:07.
74.   White fabric with plentiful fine red and black inclusions. Burnished in bands on exterior, fired to pale orange on the top of the rim, Q05:03, plus Q04:01 (unstratified).
75.   Orange fabric with fine red inclusions and paler surfaces, N07:15.

PERIOD 3

76.   Hard, micaceous orange fabric, with some sooting on the exterior. Mica-dusted, E13:23.
77.   Very dark brown on exterior. LNV CC, E13:13.
78.   Very dark brown on exterior, orange round base and on interior. LNV CC, E13:13.
79.   Approximately one third of the vessel survives. SE RW, M04:14.
80.   SE RW, M04:14.
81.   NOG RE, M05:28.
82.   Body sherd from an S-shaped bowl, with grooves and burnished tendril decoration. Wavy line is more common. SE RW, P05:04.
83.   Highly micaceous grey ware, especially visible on surfaces. East Anglian? Mid-grey core, paler margins and burnished surfaces, M05:28.

PERIOD 4

84.   Black colour coat on exterior only, thin and mottled round rim. LNV CC. E13:49,
85.   Pale brown/orange stripes. The shape of this vessel is very close to the funnel-necked beakers based on 'rhenish' forms (Perrin 1999, fig. 61, no. 173) rather than the narrow-mouthed jars more commonly made in parchment ware (Howe, Perrin and Mackreth 1980, fig. 8, nos 94–5), suggesting a date after the mid or late third century. LNV PA. M14:15, M14:01 (unstratified).
86.   Burnished in bands on neck and decorated with thin white paint. LT OW painted. M14:45.
87.   Dark brown colour coat. For dolphins on other LNV CC beakers see G. Webster 1989, 6. LNV CC. G11:10.
88.   GW1, G04:03.
89.   Fine, mid-grey fabric, burnished on exterior. Decorated with grooves and open circle stamps. Globular beakers with a similar profile but different decoration were found at Blaxton kiln site, where it was noted that the form and fabric were related to Parisian ware (Buckland and Dolby 1980, fig. 4, nos 49–50). D13:55.
90.   White fabric with fine black inclusions and small voids and mid-grey surfaces. Same fabric as no. 45 above. F12:04.
91.   GW6, Q05:28.
92.   Buried pot. SE RW, D14:10.
93.   Coarse orange fabric with large red and white inclusions. EBO OX red-painted, N15:12.
94.   Grey core and pale orange surfaces. Burnished in bands. OW1, G14:20 and G14:01 (unstratified).
95.   Roughly burnished. OW1, J15:15.
96.   Very fine, micaceous dark grey fabric with pale margins and dark surfaces, with silky finish. Barbotine leafs. Imitation Dr 36s in oxidised or colour-coated wares are much more common than examples in reduced ware. Grey ware examples may have been made in the Doncaster area, where a waster or second was found (Buckland 1986, 21, no. 23), and are also known from the Lower Nene Valley (Perrin 1999, fig. 59, no. 98), Cf. a grey ware imitation Curle 11 from South Shields (Bidwell and Speak 1994, fig. 8.8, no. 16). G11:10. Another sherd of this vessel was found unstratified in the 1997–8 excavations.
97.   Hard, mid-grey fabric, slightly sandy. F15:06.
98.   Miniature dish, with faint external groove (cf. Monaghan 1987, type 9B5.1). BB2, H05:41.

THIRD CENTURY AND LATER

99.   Dark orange fabric with remains of cream wash, E05:04.
100.  LNV CC, L05:07 and L05:03 (unstratified).
101.  SE RW poppy-headed beaker, F11:18.
102.  GW6, F11:17.
103.  CG, N05:04.
104.  Heavily sooted. SE RW, gritty fabric, overfired, J04:05.
105.  SE RW, F11:13.
106.  Highly micaceous grey fabric with dark grey core and pale grey margins. Occasional soft black inclusions. Sooting under rim. Cf. no. 73 above, N05:04.

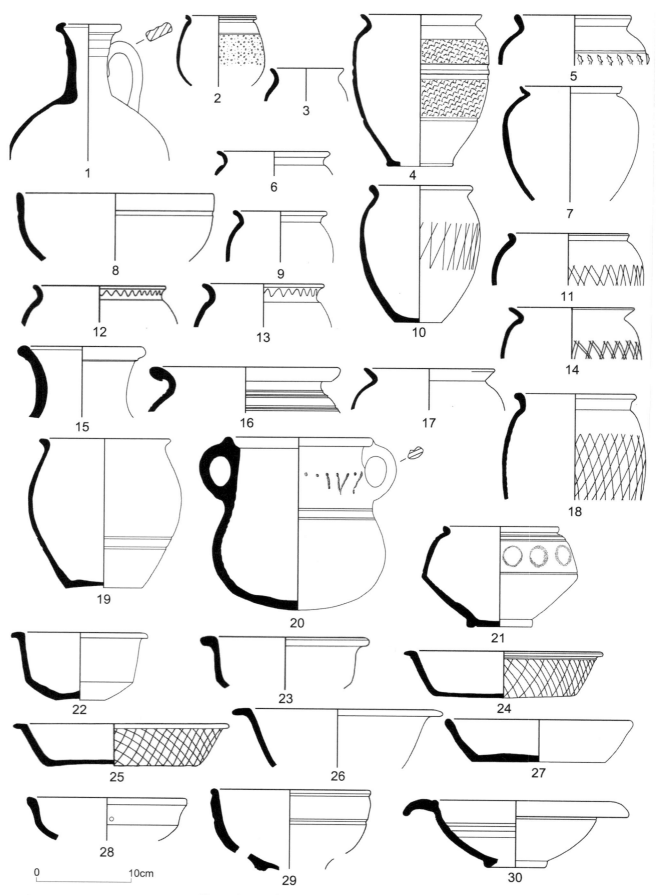

*Figure 22.12: Coarse wares nos 1–30. Scale 1:4.*

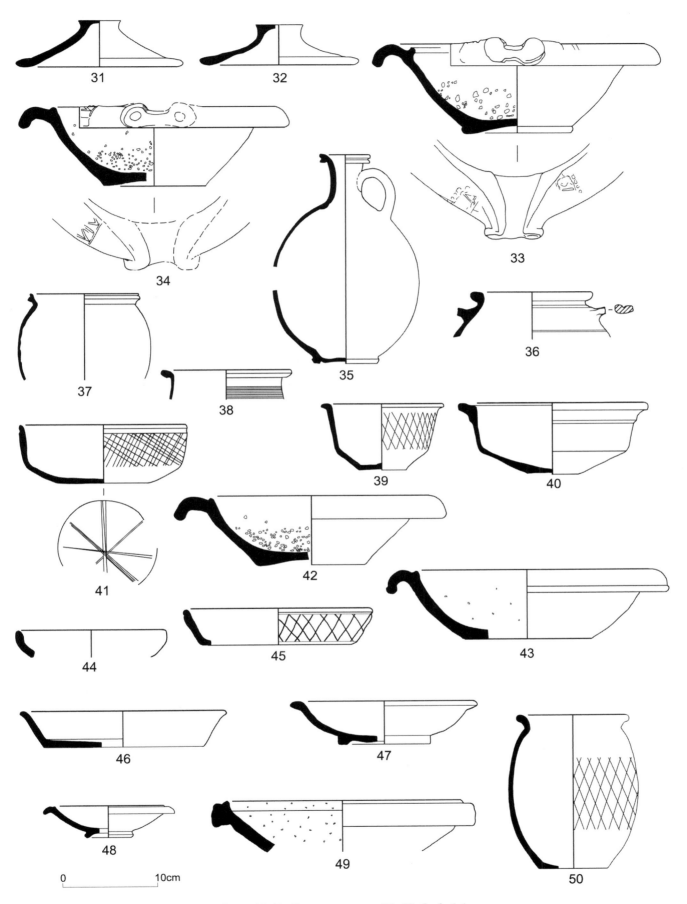

*Figure 22.13: Coarse wares nos 31–50. Scale 1:4.*

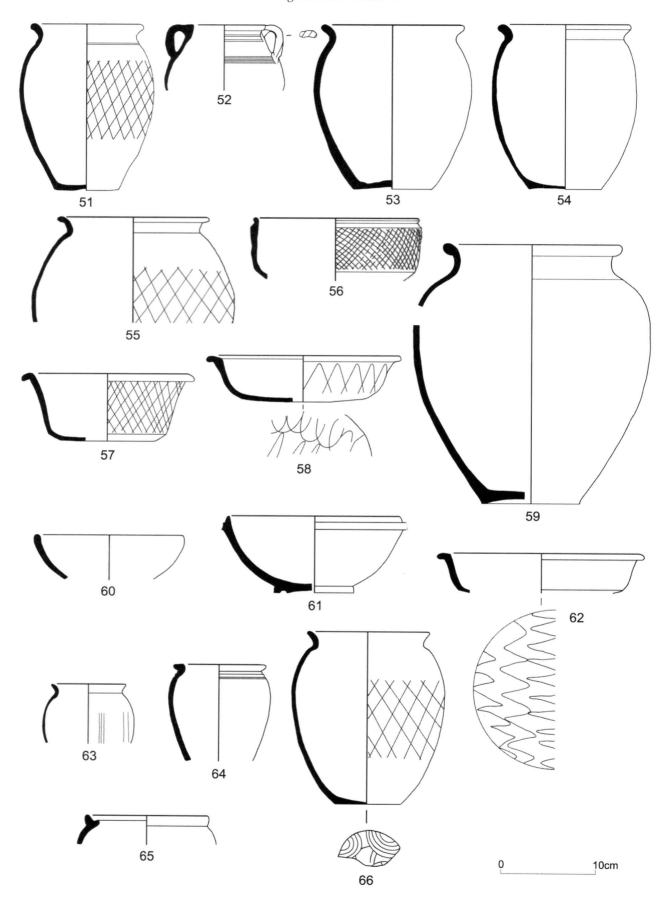

*Figure 22.14: Coarse wares nos 51–66. Scale 1:4.*

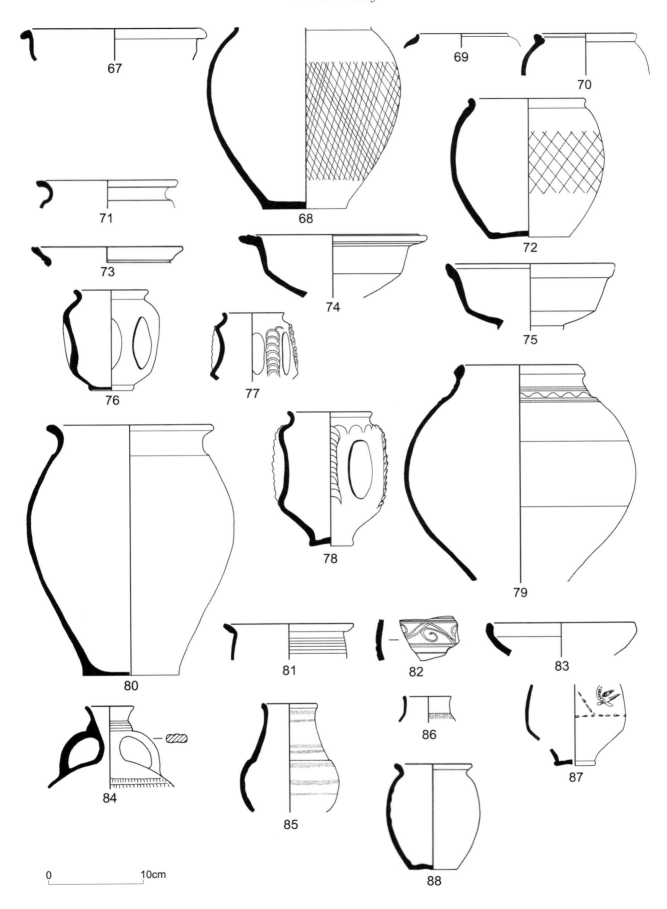

*Figure 22.15: Coarse wares nos 67–88. Scale 1:4*

107. Dark grey fabric with fine white quartz and occasional black inclusions. Slightly lighter surfaces, H04:19.
108. CG, N05:04.
109. SE RW, F11:03.
110. BB2, F11:17.
111. OW1, J04:05.
112. EPO MA. A flange fragment, from a second vessel, came from M04:01 (unstratified). P07:08.

*Cistern 1*

113. Dressel 20, E08:29.
114. Gauloise 4, E08:29.
115. Central Campanian, E08:27.
116. Biv, with thick cream wash. E08:29.
117. Almost complete vessel, flagon fabric A, without wash, E08:29.
118. Almost complete jar missing rim, LNV PA, E08:27.
119. SE RW, E08:44.
120. LNV CC, orange fabric, E08:27.
121. Approximately two-thirds of vessel surviving. LNV CC, orange fabric and black colour coat, E08:27.
122. Orange fabric, dark brown colour coat, with barbotine leaves and the tail and hindquarters of a dog. Some sooting on the lower part of the vessel. LNV CC, E08:27.
123. White fabric, tan colour-coat. LNV CC, E08:29.
124. Fine grey fabric with a few dark inclusions. Mid-grey colour coat, darker on the exterior. About quarter of the vessel survives. E08:29.
125. Approximately half of vessel surviving. LNV CC, orange fabric and black colour coat, E08:44.
126. Orange fabric, brown colour-coat. LNV CC, E08:27.
127. Black colour-coat. LNV CC, E08:44.
128. Black colour-coat, on exterior only. Probably from a small flagon (cf. Dannell *et al* 1993, fig. 16, no. 46). LNV CC, E08:27.
129. Buff fabric, black colour-coat, slightly burnt on exterior. Indented beaker with funnel mouth (*Cam* 403), cf. Colchester: Symonds and Wade 1999, fig. 5.39, no. 61. As this type is usually dated to the fourth century (Bidwell and Croom 1999, 486), this may be part of the later contamination of the cistern fill. LNV CC, E08:27.
130. Fine mid-grey fabric, paler core. Black inclusions create a speckled appearance on the non-burnished exterior. E08:27.
131. BB2, E08:29.
132. BB1, E08:29.
133. One surviving handle. East Yorkshire grey ware, E08:29.
134. HOR RE. E08:29.
135. SE RW, E08:27.
136. SE RW, E08:44.
137. SE RW, E08:27.
138. GW4, E08:29.
139. Slightly sooted under rim. Hard, slightly granular grey fabric with slightly darker surfaces. E08:29.
140. Sooted. Soft micaceous mid-grey fabric, with angular black inclusions, very fine burnishing over rim and shoulder. E08:44.
141. Heavily sooted. BB1, E08:29.
142. Heavily sooted. BB1, E08:27.

143. Sooted. BB1, E08:27.
144. Slight sooting. BB2, with oxidised surface, E08:29.
145. Sooted. BB2, E08:29.
146. BB2, E08:29.
147. Sooted. BB2, E08:29.
148. Slight sooting. BB2, E08:27.
149. Sooting on interior of, and under, rim. BB2, E08:27.
150. Sooted. BB2, E08:29.
151. Heavily sooted under the rim. BB2, E08:44.
152. BB2, E08:44.
153. Sooted. SE RW, E08:27, E08:29.
154. Sooted on exterior of rim. Micaceous grey fabric, with pink core, E08:27.
155. SE RW, E08:29.
156. SE RW, with oxidised surfaces. E08:27.
157. Sooting on body. SE RW, E08:27.
158. Sooted. SE RW, E08:29.
159. Heavy sooting on exterior and over rim. SE RW, E08:44.
160. Sooting on interior of rim and body. SE RW, E08:29.
161. Heavily sooted. SE RW, E08:44.
162. SE RW, E08:27.
163. SE RW, E08:27.
164. Heavily sooted under the rim. SE RW, E08:27.
165. Heavily sooted. SE RW, E08:27.
166. Heavily sooted. SE RW, E08:29.
167. Sooted. SE RW, E08:27.
168. SE RW, E08:27.
169. Heavily sooted. SE RW, E08:27.
170. Hard mid-grey fabric, with fine white inclusions, E08:27.
171. Slight sooting. GW4, E08:29.
172. Heavily sooted. SE RW, gritty fabric with oxidised surfaces. E08:27.
173. Sooted. SE RW, E08:29.
174. Heavy sooting on exterior, and over the rim, including all of the interior. SE RW, E08:44.
175. Sooted. SE RW, E09:44.
176. SE RW, E08:27.
177. Heavy sooting on rim and on body from below the shoulder. SE RW, E08:44.
178. Sooted on exterior of rim. Micaceous grey fabric with pink core. E08:29.
179. Slightly sooted. SE RW, E08:44.
180. SE RW, E08:29.
181. SE RW, E08:29.
182. Dales-type; black fabric with fine mixed inclusions and with pale grey margins, E08:44.
183. Heavy sooting. Dales-type; sandy brown fabric with dark grey surfaces, E08:27.
184. Sooted on interior of rim. Hard, sandy grey fabric with angular black inclusions and pale grey core. E08:29.
185. Hand-made, grey fabric with dark grey exterior and buff interior surface. Highly micaceous gritty fabric, with gold mica plates. Sooting on both surfaces of the rim, and on the body. Local traditional, E08:27.
186. SE RW, E08:29.
187. SE RW, E08:29.
188. SE RW, E08:27.
189. SE RW, E08:44.
190. East Yorkshire grey ware, E08:27.
191. Slightly sooted near base. BB1, E08:29.

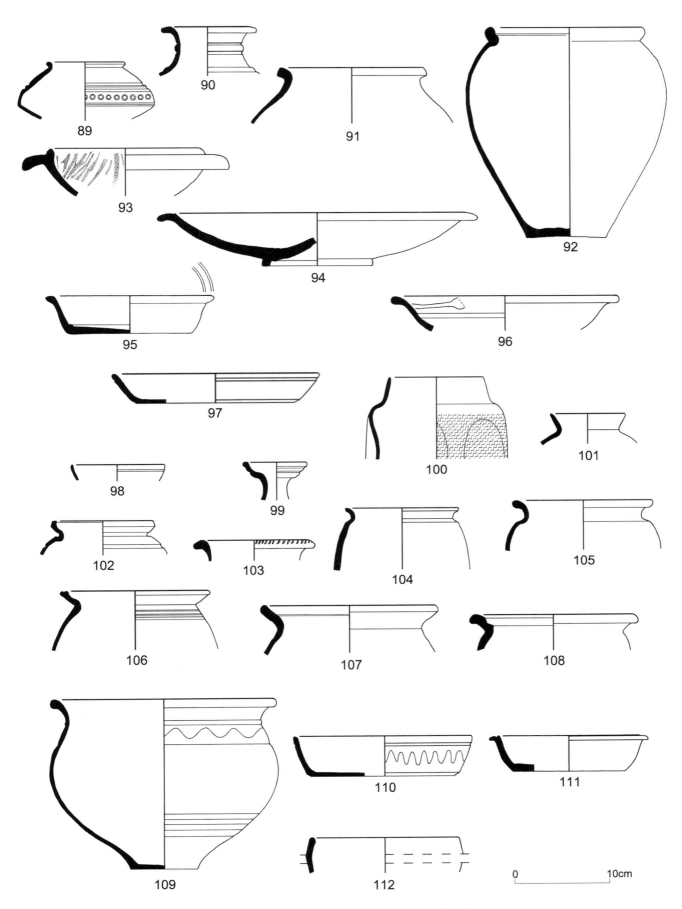

*Figure 22.16: Coarse wares nos 89–112. Scale 1:4.*

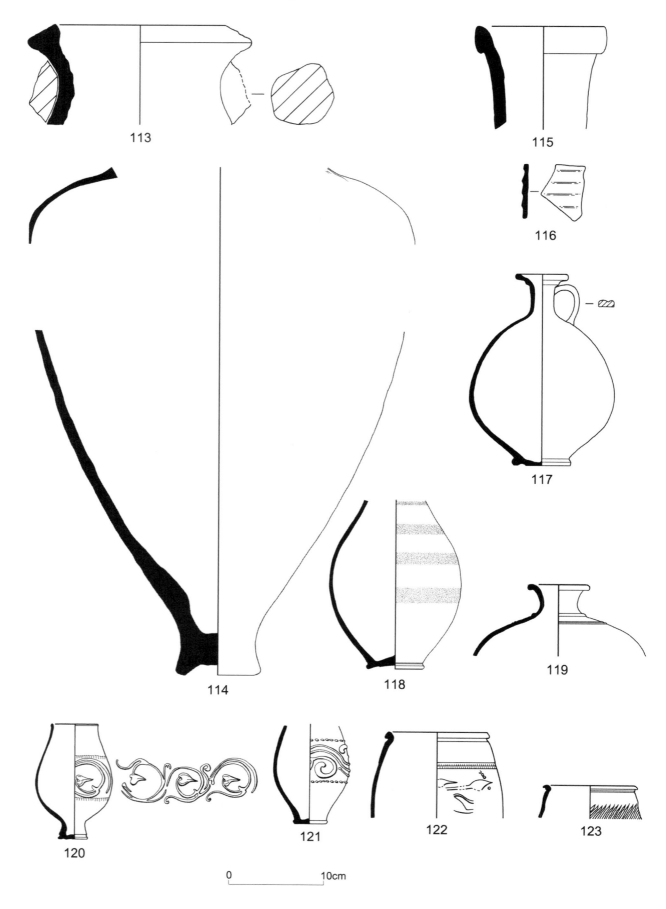

*Figure 22.17: Coarse wares nos 113–123. Scale 1:4.*

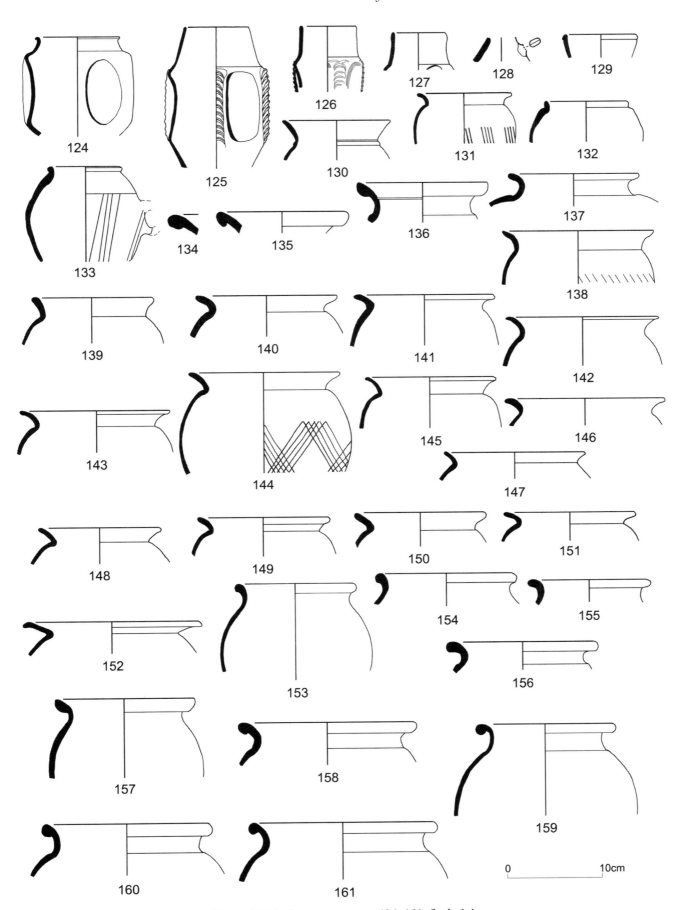

*Figure 22.18: Coarse wares nos 124–161. Scale 1:4.*

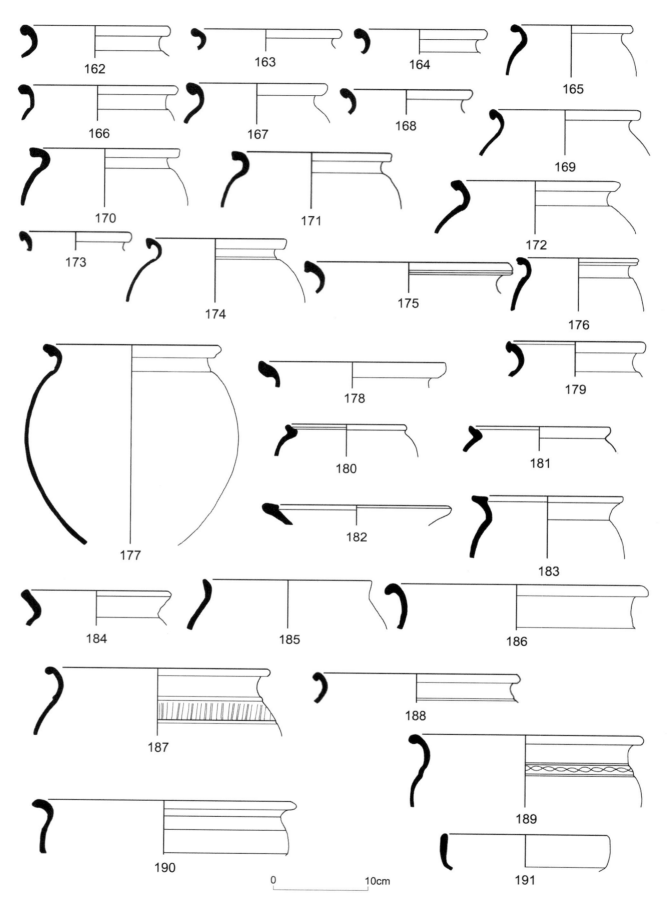

*Figure 22.19: Coarse wares nos 162–191. Scale 1:4.*

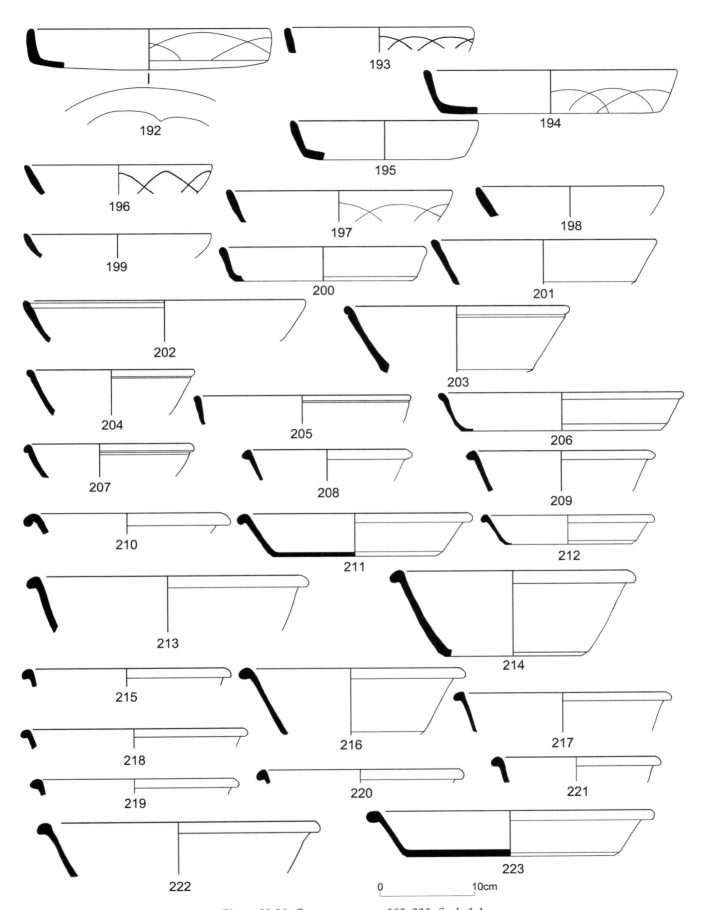

Figure 22.20: Coarse wares nos 192–223. Scale 1:4.

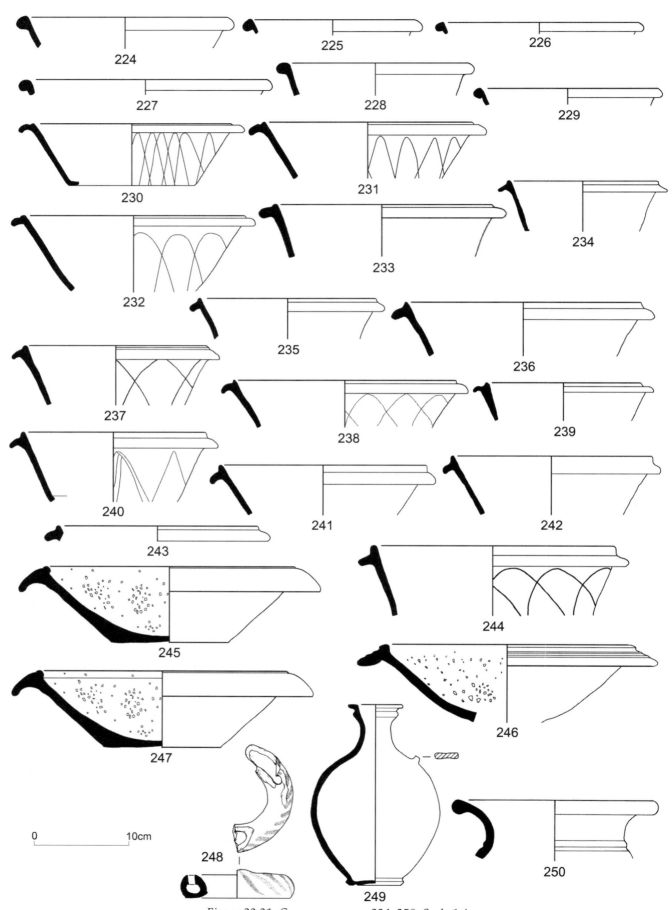

*Figure 22.21: Coarse wares nos 224–250. Scale 1:4.*

192. Heavily sooted on exterior wall and base. BB1, E08:27.
193. BB1, E08:27.
194. Heavily sooted. BB1, E08:44.
195. Slightly sooted. BB1, E08:44.
196. BB1, E08:27.
197. BB1, E08:29.
198. Sooted on top of rim. BB1, E08:27.
199. BB1, E08:29.
200. BB2, E08:27.
201. BB2, E08:29.
202. BB2, E08:27.
203. BB2, E08:29.
204. BB2, E08:44.
205. GW4, E08:29.
206. BB2, E08:27.
207. Mica-dusted. Pink fabric with cream core and orange colour coat. E08:29.
208. BB2, E08:29.
209. BB2, E08:29.
210. Hard, light grey fabric with white inclusions, E08:29.
211. About quarter of vessel surviving, with heavy sooting on base and sides. BB2, E08:27.
212. Slight sooting. BB2, E08:27.
213. Heavily sooted. BB2, E08:44.
214. Sooted. BB2, E08:27.
215. BB2, E08:29.
216. BB2, E08:27.
217. BB2, E08:29.
218. BB2, E08:29.
219. BB2, E08:29.
220. BB2, E08:29.
221. BB2, E08:29.
222. Sooted. BB2, E08:27.
223. About three-quarters of vessel surviving. BB2, E08:27, E08:29.
224. BB2, E08:29.
225. Sooted. BB2, E08:29.
226. BB2, E08:29.
227. BB2, E08:29.
228. Slight sooting under rim. BB2, E08:29.
229. BB2, E08:29.
230. Slightly sooted near base. BB1, E08:29.
231. Sooted. BB1, E08:29.
232. Sooted. BB1, E08:27.
233. BB1, E08:27.
234. Sandy dark grey fabric with brown core. E08:27.
235. BB1, E08:27.
236. BB1, E08:27.
237. BB1, E08:29.
238. Sooted. BB1, E08:27.
239. Sooted. Has traces of decoration, probably intersecting arc. BB1, E08:27.
240. Sooted. BB1, E08:27.
241. BB1, E08:27.
242. Sooted. BB1, E08:27.
243. BB1, E08:27.
244. Sooted. BB1, E08:29.
245. Mancetter-Hartshill, 140–80, E08:29.
246. Lower Nene Valley, 250–300, E08:27.
247. Lower Nene Valley, 230–400. E08:27.
248. Ring-vase with the remains of two holes, with stripes of brown paint. LNV PA, E08:27.

## Cistern 2

249. Battered rim, and missing (single) handle, but apparently thrown away in one piece. Cream fabric with fine red inclusions, occasionally up to 1mm in size, and less common fine black inclusions, J07:14.
250. HOR RE, H07:03, H07:09.
251. No sooting, but discoloured exterior. Approximately half of vessel survives. BB2, H07:03, H07:09.
252. Heavily sooted over body and rim, with white scale and some burning on interior. Approximately one third of vessel survives. BB2, H07:03, H07:09.
253. Heavily sooted on exterior up to and over the rim, with white scale and a patch of burning on the interior. See graffito no. 45. BB2, H07:09.
254. Sooted on exterior. BB2 with partially oxidised surfaces, H07:03, J07:19.
255. Hard fabric with grey core and thin orange margins and fine black inclusions. Orange interior surface, and grey and white exterior surface. Sooted on body and rim. Import? J07:19.
256. BB2, H07:09.
257. See graffiti no. 61. BB2, H07:09.

See also mortarium Fig. 22.08, no. 4.

## The rest of the fort

### PERIOD 1 AND 2
258. Hard, slightly gritty mid-grey fabric, with slightly darker surfaces. K10:28.
259. LT OW painted, thin white paint. D08:12.

### PERIOD 2 AND 3
260. Fine soapy fabric with black core, pale grey margins and dark grey interior, as used for poppy-headed beakers. The mid-grey/brown exterior surface has visible soft black inclusions. E08:64.
261. SE RW, E08:56.
262. Rouletted decoration below two grooves. GW1, with mottled exterior. K07:08.
263. Hard grey fabric, with fine black inclusions. Lincolnshire/South Yorkshire. Parallels: Dragonby: Gregory 1996, fig. 20.10, no. 933, fig. 20.25, no. 1322; Newcastle: Bidwell and Croom 2002, fig. 15.6, no. 42. K07:08.
264. Burnished on interior. Dark grey fabric with buff margins and dark grey surfaces; some possible flint inclusions up to 2mm across visible on the surface, some fine quartz and opaque white inclusions visible in the break, K07:08.
265. GW1, N11:23.

### THIRD CENTURY AND LATER
266. Buff fabric with traces of slightly paler wash. Holbrook and Bidwell 1992, 66, buff ware, type 2, Neronian to late 70s or early 80s. E08:46.
267. Soft, slightly micaceous orange fabric with worn barbotine decoration. Red exterior and brown interior colour-coat, F04:19.
268. White fabric, light brown colour coat. LNV CC, L08:52.
269. Applied teardrops over rouletting. Slightly metallic brown colour coat. Cf. Castleford: Rush *et al* 2000, fig. 70, no. 433. LNV CC. H11:33.

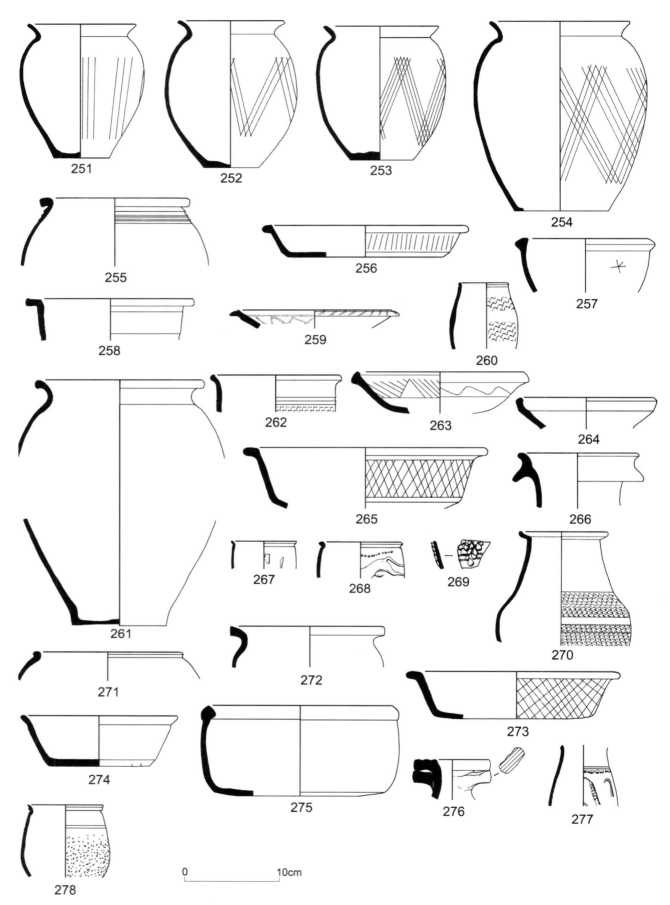

*Figure 22.22: Coarse wares nos 251–278. Scale 1:4.*

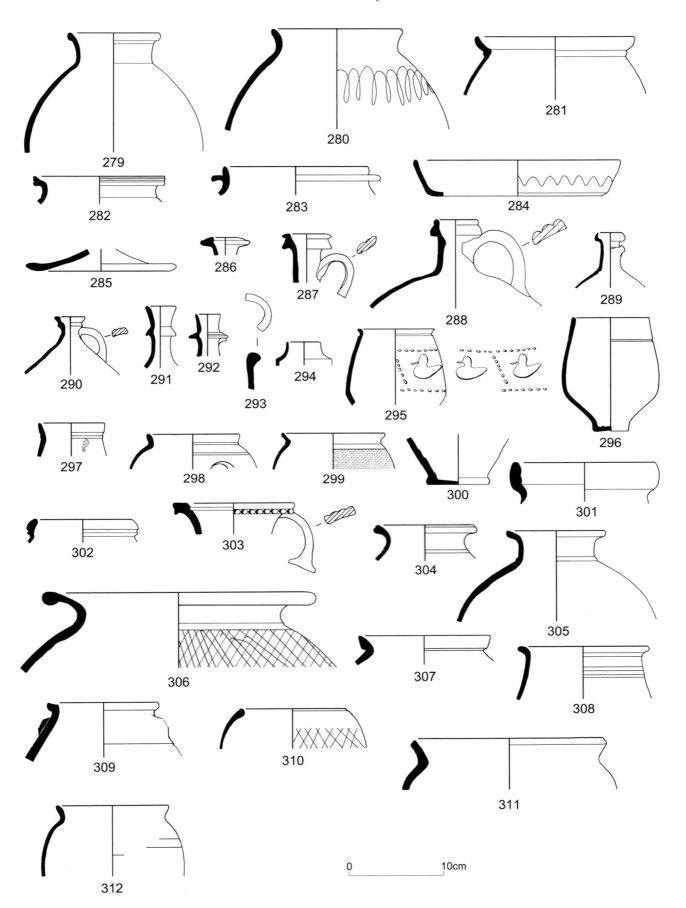

*Figure 22.23: Coarse wares nos 279–312. Scale 1:4.*

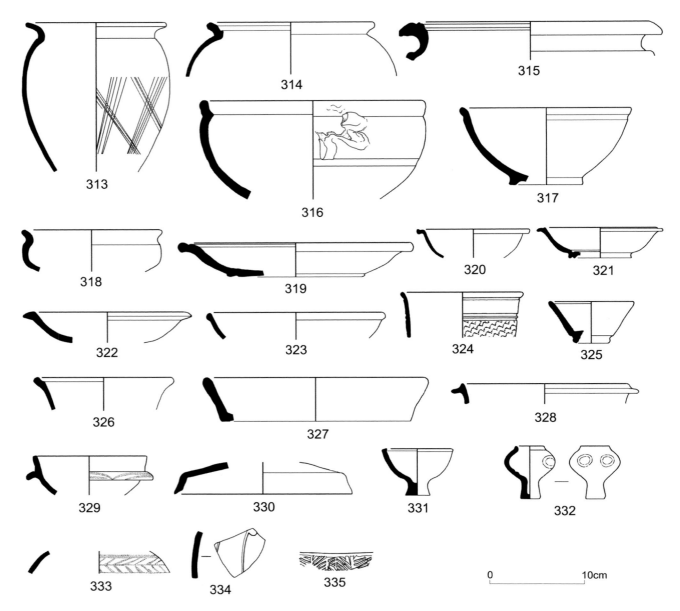

*Figure 22.24: Coarse wares nos 313–335. Scale 1:4.*

270. Hard, micaceous dark grey fabric, burnished on neck. Sooted on lower part of body. J10:25.
271. GW3, H04:24.
272. Slight sooting on the rim. Hard, gritty grey fabric with large rounded white and grey inclusions, H11:39.
273. BB1, E12:30.
274. BB2, with two grooves cut into edge of base. See graffiti no. 53. L12:02.
275. Very hard, gritty orange fabric. The base is burnt brown and both it and the walls are sooted. North African-style casserole. Cf. Swan 1992, fig. 1, no. 24. Late Ebor. N11:24, N11:29.

LATE ROMAN AND DERELICTION
276. Hard red fabric with occasional soft black inclusions, and slightly brown surfaces. K10:32.

277. CNG BS. L11:08.
278. Orange fabric, brown exterior and red interior colour coat. Q04:15.
279. Fine sandy grey fabric, burnished in irregular lines on the neck. E11:03.
280. The edge of an indentation on the body indicates this is a counter sunk lug-handled jar. East Yorkshire grey ware. G16:21.
281. Dark grey fabric with occasional large black inclusions, with paler surfaces, not burnished. E11:06.
282. SE RW, F09:07.
283. Hard grey fabric with large quartz inclusions. Mottled black and orange exterior. H10:32.
284. BB2, Q04:12, upper fill.
285. Hard grey fabric with sparse black inclusions, H05:12.

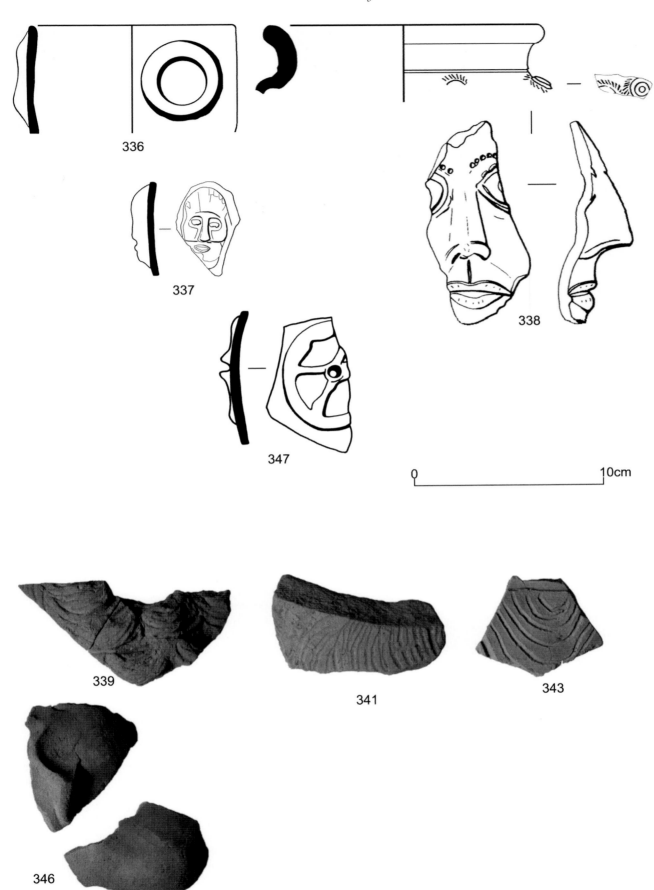

336

337

338

347

339

341

343

346

*Figure 22.25: Moulded-mask flagons, smith pot and head pots. Scale 1:2.*

**338**

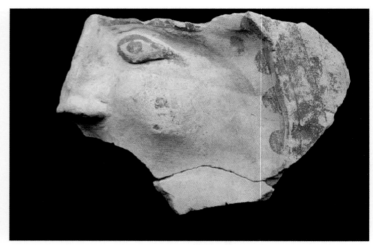

**345**

*Figure 22.26: Head pots nos 338 and 345.*

## Unstratified

286. Gritty orange fabric, with remains of thin white wash. Scar on underside of rim indicates a single handle, M05:04.
287. Buff ware. Holbrook and Bidwell 1992, 66, type 2. P05:02.
288. Fine orange fabric, slightly micaceous, paler on exterior, E10:01.
289. Soft, fine buff fabric, G14:01.
290. White fabric, slightly cream on exterior round the rim, C11:01.
291. SE RW/poppyhead beaker fabric, G12:01.
292. Flagon fabric A, E07:01.
293. Pinchneck flagon, GW2, D11:05.
294. Brown colour coat, LNV CC, J16:03.
295. Ducks are an unusual form of decoration, although a double row of ducks are known on a beaker from the Pakenham kilns (*pers. comm.* J. Plouviez). LNV CC, F11:01.
296. LNV CC, G11:01.
297. Hard, slightly gritty micaceous orange fabric, with self-coloured slip. Decorated with thick white paint, noticeably micaceous. M13:01.
298. Indented beaker. GW2, burnt, K03:02.
299. LNV CC, M14:01.
300. Soft pink fabric with wide cream core. Thick tan colour coat, easily worn away, on exterior only. A neck sherd (funnel neck?) in the same fabric but probably from a different vessel, was found in L05:07. G11:01.

301. East Yorkshire grey ware, F11:01.
302. GW1, E12:01.
303. East Yorkshire grey ware, E04:01.
304. Severn Valley, Q05:02.
305. SE RW, M07:01.
306. HOR RE, E08:13.
307. Southern shell-tempered ware, L14:01.
308. NOG RE, F12:01.
309. Pale orange fabric with fine multi-coloured inclusions and paler surfaces. Heavily covered in mortar, M12:01.
310. SE RW, N05:20.
311. Hand-made. Local traditional, L04:11.
312. Two possible burnished lines are visible within the burnishing on the shoulder (now rather patchy), with a certain burnished line below. GW1, K03:30.
313. BB2, possibly from Colchester, N05:02.
314. SE RW, E10:01.
315. CG, P05:02.
316. Wide grey core and orange surfaces. Slight ridges on interior from rough burnishing, finer burnishing on exterior below level of handle. Cf. dish version: Caerleon: Compton and Webster 2000, fig. 64, no. 587, unstratified, N05:20.
317. Slightly gritty grey fabric, very soft in places, with buff margins and traces of a darker grey surface, surviving only in patches in places, K03:21.
318. Micaceous pale grey fabric with plentiful soft black inclusions, some large. Mid-grey surfaces, M05:04.
319. EBO OX, H03:01, H03:03.
320. Burnished in bands. Very fine fabric. LT OW

painted, although there is no evidence of painted decoration on this vessel. N12:01.

321. Soft, fine orange fabric with soapy texture, G04:01.

322. Soft orange fabric, with faint ridges caused by the burnishing on the interior, L05:03.

323. Pale orange fabric, cream surfaces with mid-brown colour-coat that has been mica-dusted, F11:01.

324. Orange fabric, with very fine dark inclusions visible on the surface. Paler interior surface and burnished exterior, F14:10.

325. Oxidised, Q05:02.

326. Burnished in slightly spaced bands. LT OW painted, although there is no evidence of painted decoration on this vessel. N04:01.

327. CG, H13:10.

328. BB2, G03:05.

329. Crambeck red with white painted decoration, P05:02.

330. Hard, micaceous orange fabric with wide grey core. Heavily sooted on both exterior and interior. North African style? J14:06.

331. Hard micaceous white fabric, with some fine black inclusions and occasional large (2mm) soft white inclusions. Possibly a lid. M12:55.

332. Soapy, micaceous buff fabric with a dark grey core and the remains of a thick cream wash. There are two attachment scars on one side, suggesting this is from a triple vase of the type where the vessels touch but there is no openings in the walls. A vessel from a triple vase with a similar rim and bulbous body, although with a shorter pedestal, was found at Carlisle (May and Hope 1917, pl. 15, no. 189). F11:01.

333. Overfired sherd, with thick grey core and thin white paint. LT OW painted, N04:03.

334. Barbotine decoration with two stalks and the top of a probably ivy-shaped leaf on exterior of a closed vessel in a coarse ware fabric. White fabric with plentiful quartz inclusions, fine black inclusions and dark grey surfaces, slightly mottled on exterior, F14:01.

335. Micaceous, mid grey core, brown margins, dark grey surfaces, with roller-stamped decoration in a 'panel' style, with diagonal lines set in defined panels. At Chelmsford a similar stamp, with the diagonal lines continuing under some of the uprights, was identified as a probable Colchester product (Going 1987, fig. 48, no. 14). Roller-stamping was common at Colchester in the third century, and copied at other local kiln sites such as Mucking (*ibid.*, 31). The fort at Wallsend has produced a sherd from a second vessel in the same fabric with chevrons set in wide panels (D14:01, unstratified), while the *vicus* has produced sherds from four other roller-stamped vessels, three of which are probable Colchester products and one a Mucking product. L04:01.

## Head pots and similar (Figs 22.25–6)
### Moulded-mask flagons

336. Orange fabric with plentiful large red inclusions and micaceous surfaces, with a circular appliqué with a slightly dished top. The appliqué is in a paler version of the same fabric. The exterior surface and just over the rim has been covered in a white colour-coat, with an additional orange colour-coat over the exterior (a technique used at Swanpool). Possibly from a moulded mask flagon, in which case the applied disc could possibly represent a hair bun on the opposite side to the face, although the other known examples tend to be more elaborate (Dövener 2000, Abb. 221, 234; Howe, Perrin and Mackreth 1980, fig. 8, no. 96). F12:01.

337. Sherd with incomplete moulded mask of a male face. Brown to orange exterior colour coat, orange interior colour coat. The eyes and nose are outlined by incised lines, while the moustache and beard are recessed to leave the mouth raised. The temples are recessed, and the hair is roughly indicated by stabbed decorated. This is an example of the smaller type of mask face used on flagon rims, that fits within the height of the rim and does not rise above it (Dövener 2000, Abb. 232). Male faces are not as common as female heads. Cf. York: Monaghan 1997, fig. 333, no. 3178 (different mould). LNV CC, F12:01, WSP138.

### Head pots
#### NORTH AFRICAN STYLE

338. Three non-joining sherds, consisting of rim and body sherd with stamped bosses and part of a sculpted face. Micaceous orange fabric with noticeable plentiful multicoloured inclusions and thick buff core, grey where sherd particularly thick. The rim has parts of two stamped bosses immediately below, and the body sherd parts of two more stamped bosses. The face fragment has a sculpted nose, parts of both eyes and part of mouth. The eyebrows are depicted with incised dots and the eye defined by deep incised lines. The eyes are broken off before the pupil on both sides, but it is likely that they were stamped. There is a possible edge of a stamp, while the interior of the vessel indicates that the eyes were hollow, in a very similar way to the surviving stamped bosses. The end of the nose, the nostrils, the upper lip and septum are also marked by incised lines. There is burnishing on the forehead and part of the cheek. P05:02 (two sherds) and N05:07; 37, WSP142, WSP154 and WSP188.

#### NORTH AFRICAN STYLE – HAIR ONLY

339. Orange fabric with quartz inclusions. Sculpted, crescent-shaped curls with incised lines to represent the hair. H13:01, WSP156.

340. Three sherds, two of which join. Paler orange fabric, more yellow than no. 339 above, with quartz inclusions that are generally fine but occasionally up to 1mm across. Sculpted hair, with roughly circular, hollow curls. The incised lines to indicate the hair are quite roughly finished compared to no. 339. D14:08, 1475, WSP189.

341. Micaceous orange fabric with slightly paler surface. Incised lines representing hair. E04:07, WSP158.

342.    Micaceous orange fabric, with incised lines representing curls. Fabric as no. 341 above, but with paler body and darker exterior, so from a different vessel. N13:01, WSP155.

343.    Hard, fine fabric with red and white inclusions, orange towards interior and buff towards exterior. Curved incised lines representing hair between traces of wider grooves. D14:22, 1486, WSP210.

344.    Dark cream fabric with pale orange core and fine red inclusions. Incised lines to represent curls, and the end of a straight line edged with dots which could possibly represent the end of an eye-brow. D14:08, 1477, WSP211.

PAINTED

345.    One sherd, with a possible second, non-joining sherd. Pale orange fabric with a wide grey core towards the interior and fine quartz inclusions. The fragment includes a moulded nose, a raised applied eye, a raised eyebrow ridge and a raised hairline. The hair is painted dark brown, with semi-circles, representing curls, extending onto the cheek. The eyebrow is painted, as is the outline of the eye and iris. Burnished on cheek. The second sherd possibly shows part of the chin. F13:25 (main fragment), F13:16 (chin), 1326, WSP190.

346.    Two non-joining sherds in a fabric with plentiful fine inclusions, a grey core, white margins, and buff/pink surfaces, with burnished buff/orange exterior surface. One sherd has an applied vertical ridge of clay creating a wavy line, and other has been sculpted, possibly representing part of the chin or cheek. Probably from same source as no. 345, although not the same vessel. F11:13, WSP236.

*Smith pot?*

347.    Fine hard fabric, with fine quartz inclusions, darker grey to the interior and light grey to the exterior. Very pale grey exterior surface, with applied four-spoke wheel, with depression for the hub. Some burnished lines on the body. Probably a Yorkshire grey ware. N14:01, WSP185.

The wheel as a symbol has been found associated with a range of deities, including a native sky god, Apollo, Fortuna, and most importantly Jupiter, as well as being connected to the sun (de la Bédoyère 2002, 164–5; Kiernan 2009, 38). When found on grey ware vessels, the association seems to be with a smith god, as the wheels are found alongside smith's tools. A sherd from Malton includes tongs, two hammers, and the remains of a four-spoked wheel (Bidwell and Croom 1997, fig. 39, no. 1; four-spoked wheels seem particularly common in France: Green 1978, 19; Kiernan 2009, 12; fig. 2.1). A further two sherds with wheels with eight and nine spokes, were found at the same site in the same fabric as sherds showing smith's tools (Leach 1962, pl. VII). The exact association between a smith god and wheel is not clear, but in classical mythology the smith god Vulcan made Apollo's sun chariot with spokes of silver and a rim of gold, so the wheel may still be a solar symbol as

it appears to be when found with the other gods connected to the sky.

*Discussion*

Wallsend has produced sherds from nine different head pots from the 1975–84 excavations, and sherds from a possible tenth from the 1997–8 excavations (Croom 2003, 247). The vessel-type of head and face pots enjoyed popularity only in a number of regions round the country, including, in the north, the Yorkshire area. In York, for example, fragments from over 50 examples have been found, and 46 from the site at Piercebridge. Hadrian's Wall, however, was outside the area, and does not seem to have been an important market for the vessels. The excavations at South Shields (*c.*1900kg of pottery) have produced only three possible examples, and the fort at Newcastle one (out of *c.*92kg of pottery; Bidwell and Croom 2002, fig. 15.9, no. 105). The vessels may have been intended for some ritual use, as a number of them are clearly deities, but perhaps outside the regions where they were most popular they were simply bought for their novelty value.

It seems likely that the nine examples came from only two or three suppliers, one producing the orange sculpted head pots and the other the painted vessels. Number 338 is of particular interest, as the fabric and use of stamped bosses for hair suggests a mid or late third century date, while the strongly sculpted features and the dots for eyebrows are more typical of the early third century North African style heads. Although most of the North African type heads appear to depict females, the two sets of sherds with raised circular curls indicate that at least two vessels at Wallsend had a male hair-style. Although the number of vessels involved is small, there may have been a preference for male heads in this area; the example from Newcastle has the same type of curls, and one of the examples of a possible head-pot type vessel from South Shields was a bearded figure (Croom 1994, fig. 7.12, no. 104), while it should be noted that the moulded-mask flagon (no. 337) also depicts a male face.

Four of the sherds come from site clearance levels, and most of the rest come from the latest layers of cobble/decay on the site. There are three sherds from around building AB (nos 340, 343–4), but the fabrics of the sherds are so different they cannot come from the same vessel.

# Discussion

## *Supply to the fort*

### *Second century*

On the whole the 1975–84 excavations did not reach the Hadrianic layers of the fort, but what information there is can be supplemented by evidence from the 1997–8 excavations. The coarse wares are dominated by BB1 and local products in about equal quantities, a pattern of supply that continued throughout the Antonine period, as can be seen by the assemblages from the Rampart building (Feature 2), Alley 1 and Alley 3. BB2 and allied fabrics then begin to make an appearance, but they are not yet a major source of supply. During the second century, mortaria came overwhelmingly from local sources such as Corbridge and Binchester/Corbridge as well as from kiln sites not yet identified. Fine ware beakers are mainly imported from the Continent, from North Gaul and Cologne.

*Local production*
The local products (Grey wares 1–3; Oxidised wares 1–2 and Lower Tyne painted oxidised ware) that were such a feature of the second-century supply must have come from kiln sites in the eastern or central sector of the frontier zone, but the productions sites have not yet been located. They supplied the types of vessels required most by the army, cooking-pots and bowls in both grey and oxidised ware, but sometimes ventured other types that were usually supplied from more distant sources, as there are also small numbers of other vessels such as pinch-necked flagons, beakers and lids. The oxidised wares were produced in a slightly wider range of bowl types, more obviously tableware, and were also used to produce at least one small open lamp (Fig. 25.29). Some of the vessels were made in a fine oxidised fabric, often with a fine, burnished finish, and frequently decorated with white paint.

Grey and oxidised wares: An example of a reeded-rimmed dish found at South Shields made in grey ware 1 (Bidwell and Speak 1994, fig. 8.8, no. 2) indicates that the production of this ware started in the early second century, as this form was not made after this date. This is a form more commonly found in mica-dusted ware, but grey ware examples have been found at Gellygaer and Southwark (Marsh 1978, type 26) and an oxidised example from Corbridge (Bishop and Dore 1989, fig. 119, no. 89). Other early forms include an oxidised large dish with omphalos base (Fig. 22.16, no. 94; Marsh 1978, type 33), a carinated biconical bowl (Fig. 22.12, no. 21), and a small flanged bowl (Fig. 22.13, no. 48; Marsh 1978, type 34). There are no reeded-rimmed carinated bowls, but there are a few non-reeded examples (Fig. 22.13, no. 40; Croom 2003, fig. 158, nos 2, 4). However, the industry soon started to copy BB1 bowl forms such as the flat-rimmed bowls with low carination, and these were the most common type of bowl made (Fig. 22.12, no. 22; Fig. 22.13, no. 39, Fig. 22.16, no. 89). The quantities of pottery recovered from Period 2 show that the wares continued to be made into the Antonine period, probably going out of production when the pottery supply was switched to the BB2 industries of south-east England.

Painted ware: Most of the vessels made in this ware were bowls, ranging from large hemispherical bowls imitating Dr 37s to small segmental bowls with high flanges. Closed forms, such as beakers and flagons, were also made, but in much smaller quantities. The largest painted vessels are a carinated biconical bowl and a cauldron/bowl (Fig. 22.12, nos 20–1). Oxidised wares decorated with white paint are not common, but were perhaps briefly popular in the early second century; similar wares were made by the pottery set up to supply the fort at Little Chester near Derby during the Trajanic to early Hadrianic period. At Derby almost all the painted vessels are segmental bowls with high flanges, with only occasional other forms such as a cordoned bowl and a carinated bowl with upright rim (Brassington 1971, fig. 7; Brassington 1980, fig. 14, nos 383–5, fig. 19, no. 525). At Derby there were also a few examples of oxidised wares with both white and red-brown paint, as also known from the Lower Tyne painted ware, again on segmental bowls with high flanges (Brassington 1980, fig. 23, nos 589, 593). Another carinated bowl with upright rim, with white herringbone decoration, was found at York, where it was identified as Ebor ware, although the use of white-painted decoration on this ware is very rare, as only three such painted vessels seem to have been found (Monaghan 1997, 877; fig. 395, no. 3936).

*Third century*
It is not until the early third century that BB2 and its allied fabrics became the coarse ware supplier of choice, and the proportion of BB2 greater than the local products and BB1. At the same time, supply of fine wares was switched to the Nene Valley industries, which became the dominant fabric for beakers. Although the Lower Nene Valley also supplied some mortaria during the early third century, Mancetter-Hartshill was the more important supplier at this time, and it was not until the latter part of the century that the Lower Nene Valley became the dominant supplier.

The next major change in supply occurred in the late third century, when BB2 begins to fail and BB1 reclaims the market. During the third century small quantities of grey wares had been supplied from a number of different Yorkshire industries, but after *c.*270 Crambeck reduced ware and calcite-gritted ware began to be the most important coarse ware suppliers. Unfortunately very few undisturbed contexts from this period have survived on the site.

*Fourth century*
The post-Roman disturbance of the site means that very little fourth-century material comes from stratified contexts, but the unstratified pottery shows that occupation lasted until the late fourth century. The material comes from disturbed contexts from all periods as well as site clearance levels, but only comparatively small quantities survived. At Newcastle late third- and fourth-century Crambeck

Table 22.11: *Pottery from the Rampart building and re-instated rampart by fabric type, shown as percentages (excludes amphora)*

| Fabric type | Wt | EVEs |
|---|---|---|
| Samian | 0.5 | 1.1 |
| Mortaria | 16.5 | 4.9 |
| Fine ware: Colchester | 0.4 | 3.5 |
| Fine ware: unsourced | 0.2 | 1.5 |
| Grey ware 1 | 26.3 | 31.1 |
| Grey ware 2 | 2.1 | 3.7 |
| BB1 | 3.2 | 4.3 |
| BB2 | 0.9 | 4.6 |
| SE RW | 0.6 | 0.2 |
| Belgic | 1.6 | 1.7 |
| Native | 0.2 | 0 |
| Calcite-gritted | 0.2 | 0 |
| Unidentified oxidised | 34.7 | 32.1 |
| Unidentified reduced | 12.6 | 11.3 |
| Total | 8.927 (kg) | 1623 (%) |

Table 22.12: *Vessel types of the pottery from the rampart building and the reinstated rampart, excluding those vessels likely to date after the re-instatement of the rampart, by EVEs*

| Vessel type* | % |
|---|---|
| Flagon | 31.1 |
| Beaker | 5.6 |
| Small jar | 11.1 |
| Cooking-pot | 45.1 |
| Bowl/dish | 2.1 |
| Mortarium | 0.5 |
| Total | 1602 |

\* In this, and subsequent tables, 'flagon' includes other liquid containers such as jugs and flasks; 'beaker' includes other drinking vessels such as cups; 'small jar' includes vessels that may also have been used for drinking, such as jars that could be tankards without surviving handles, and 'storage jar' includes narrow-mouthed jars

mortaria made up 38% of all mortaria from the site by EVEs, and at South Shields 18% by vessel number but only 2.4% by EVEs at Wallsend (Bidwell and Croom 2002, table 15.6; Bidwell and Speak 1994, table 8.2). Of late-fourth century material, there were 129 rim sherds from Huntcliff-type calcite-gritted cooking-pots, 31 sherds of Crambeck painted ware and 10 Crambeck reduced ware flanged bowls with internal wavy line (Corder 1937 type 1B).

## Selected assemblages

### Possible Rampart building (Feature 2)

A large group of pottery came from an occupation deposit in a possible rampart building near the *porta quintana* (C11:04). Excavations in 1997–8 from the same, or an immediately adjacent, building produced a further assemblage very similar in nature; and although there were no visible cross-joins between the two, there were a number of sherds almost certainly from the same vessels, so the groups have been studied as one assemblage (Hodgson 2003, 162; Croom 2003, fig. 158, nos 15–9).

The material from the 1997–8 excavations included two sherds of BB2 allied fabric, which in all probability relate to the re-instatement of the rampart over the building (Hodgson 2003, 162). The pottery from C11:04 also included a few sherds of presumably intrusive later material, such as a rounded-rimmed BB2 bowl or dish and a body sherd of calcite-gritted ware. The only other BB2 consists of a few sherds from two cooking-pots (Fig. 22.12, no. 6). This very small quantity of BB2 (less than 1% of the assemblage) and a sherd of mid to late Antonine samian suggests the assemblage may date to the late 150s or 160s, when small quantities of BB2 reached Hadrian's Wall.

The assemblage consists predominantly locally produced grey wares and flagons of unknown source (c.60%), with surprisingly little BB1. Samian is under-represented, with only two sherds present in the whole assemblage. The figure for mortaria by weight is high, but is distorted by the presence of a near-complete vessel (Croom 2003, fig. 158, no. 19, dated 120–60), which is in fact the only mortarium present in the combined assemblage.

The assemblage is most noticeable because of the very low number of bowls and dishes. Sherds were found from only three bowls, two of which were represented by two sherds (2% by EVES). This is highly unusual, as bowls and dishes are usually the second most common types of vessel. There were at least four complete flagon rims, fragments of a further two, and one almost complete vessel, but as they are associated with a high number of body sherds it suggests flagons made up a large part of the original assemblage. The building excavated in 1997–8 produced clinker and hammer-scale, and therefore was probably used for iron-working, so this profile of vessel types may reflect workshop requirements rather than domestic use. It is perhaps of note that while the rubbish from the buildings included 9.334kg of pottery (including amphora sherds, all of Dressel 20), there was very little animal bone present.

### Alley 1

During excavation, an arbitrary division was made between the 'lower' and 'upper' fills of the alley deposit, although joining sherds from the same vessels between the two fills and the deposit of burnt daub indicate they are not discrete deposits. The pottery came from the central section of the alley (squares M05 and N05, with a smaller amount in P05). Square N05 produced one of the largest concentrations of pottery from any of the excavated areas in the fort (34kg stratified, 14kg unstratified).

The most interesting material from the assemblage comes from the deposit of burnt daub on the south side

Table 22.13: The vessel types in Alley 1 compared to those from the barracks (Buildings 1–5, 9–12), shown as a percentage of EVEs

| Type | Alley | Barracks |
|---|---|---|
| Flagon | 7.7 | 7.8 |
| Beaker | 3.4 | 5.6 |
| Small jar | 0.6 | 0.9 |
| Cooking-pot | 52.5 | 49.4 |
| Storage jar | 1.4 | 1.3 |
| Bowl/dish | 28.4 | 28.6 |
| Mortarium | 4.5 | 6.0 |
| Lid | 1.0 | 0.4 |
| Triple vase | 0.2 | – |
| Totals | 4866 | 5833 |

of the alley (N05:23, N05:24). This contained a number of substantially complete locally-produced second-century vessels that had not been much disturbed after deposition. There were four oxidised vessels, consisting of a handled cauldron (Fig. 22.12, no. 20), a biconical bowl (no. 21), a flat-rimmed carinated bowl imitating BB1 (no. 22) and a plain-rimmed bowl (no. 27), and most of an Anaus mortarium (Fig. 22.13, no. 33; mortarium stamp no. 4; with four sherds from the lower fill). Another substantial part of a worn Anaus mortarium came from the upper fill, with a single joining sherd from the daub deposit (Fig. 22.13, no. 42; mortarium stamp no. 9). There was also a grey ware cooking-pot (Fig. 22.12, no. 19) in the daub deposit, a sherd of which also came from the lower fill. The lower fill produced a second nearly complete grey ware cooking-pot (Fig. 22.12, no. 10), with joining sherds from the upper fill. There was one further vessel in the upper layers which was presumably part of the same group, a grey ware flat-rimmed bowl (Fig. 22.13, no. 39).

Unfortunately many of the contexts within the alley have been contaminated with later material making analysis of the assemblage difficult. The daub deposit and upper layers both contained quite large quantities of pottery dating to the third century, including sherds dating to 270+, and the upper layers also produced a sherd dating to the late fourth century. The daub deposit includes samian of early to mid Antonine date, and a Colchester mortarium dating to

Table 22.14: Vessel types from Alley 3, shown as a percentage of EVEs

| Vessel type | % |
|---|---|
| Flagon | 7.6 |
| Beaker | 0.5 |
| Cooking-pot | 57.6 |
| Honey jar | 11.4 |
| Bowl/dish | 22.8 |
| Total | 1308 |

140–200, and the upper layers samian of mid to late Antonine, and late second century to first half of the third century, although it is impossible to say if any of these come from the later contamination material. In total there were 14 sherds of Hadrianic samian, 12 of Hadrianic or Antonine date and 14 of Antonine or later date, at least suggestive of an Antonine date for the deposition of most of the assemblage.

The lower fill produced the smallest amount of pottery, approximately 90% of which was made up of cooking-pots (Fig. 22.12, nos 9–14). The pottery from the dump and the upper layers were similar to each other, and had a more varied profile, with a much larger proportion of bowls and dishes and more flagons. The quantity of amphorae in the assemblage was small, at only 7% by weight, when it makes up 38% of the pottery from the site as a whole. The profile of vessel types (Table 22.13) is very similar to the average for material found inside the barracks, indicating that this was a dump for rubbish from the nearby buildings.

*Alley 3*

The fill of the alley produced 1.152kg of pottery, much of which consisted of large parts of two locally-produced second-century cooking-pots (Fig. 22.13, no. 50; Fig. 22.14, no. 51). The original drip trench produced very little pottery (0.388kg), which was made up of a mixed range of sherds from numerous vessels. Much of the material could have been mid second-century in date, but there were also a few sherds of BB2, which first appears in small quantities in the Antonine period. Most of the alley deposit came from the re-cut drip trench (F04:33) at the eastern end of the alley. This produced 6.786kg of pottery (excluding samian), much of which consisted of fairly complete vessels that had not been disturbed much after deposition. BB1 made up 41% of the coarse wares, and was the only coarse ware fabric used for the bowls, which consisted of three bead-rimmed bowls and at least four flat-rimmed bowls and dishes (Fig. 22.14, nos 56–8). The locally-produced ware made up 29% by weight, and were almost exclusively cooking-pots. The assemblage also included the lower

Table 22.15: Vessel types from the hospital and the barracks (Periods 2 and 3 only), shown as percentages of EVEs

| Vessel type | Hospital | Barracks |
|---|---|---|
| Flagon | 9.8 | 7.8 |
| Beaker | 4.1 | 5.6 |
| Small jar | 7.9 | 0.9 |
| Cooking-pot | 52.1 | 49.4 |
| Storage jar | 2.4 | 1.3 |
| Bowl/dish | 18.4 | 27.6 |
| Mortarium | 4.9 | 6.0 |
| Lid | 0.4 | 0.4 |
| Totals | 3574 | 5833 |

half of a flagon and two honey jars (Fig. 22.14, no. 52). There was one certain Antonine samian vessel, and a few sherds of BB2 (less than 1%).

*Building 8 (stone-built hospital)*
The hospital produced one of the largest assemblages of pottery from any structure within the fort. The stone building was constructed in the Antonine period, was reduced in size in the early third century, and was finally demolished before the mid third century (Hodgson 2003 123–4). The early phase did not produce much pottery.

Room 1, with a flagged floor and hearth, had a BB2 pot buried in the floor, with a stone lid flush with the floor surface (Fig. 22.15, no. 68; Fig. 25.33). This type of deliberately buried pot is comparatively common at South Shields Roman Fort, where they are found almost entirely in barracks, suggesting that this room may have been the permanent accommodation for staff in the hospital. The hospital must also have provided accommodation for patients during treatment and recuperation, staying only on a short-term basis, but it is not known how these patients were fed, whether their *contubernia* provided cooked food for them or simply handed over their portion of the rations. A study of the animal bones has shown that the assemblage is very similar to that within the barracks although slightly more restricted in the range of species present, suggesting few luxuries were brought in (Gidney 2003, 232). The small quantities of bone recovered indicates either that the hospital was kept very clean or the occupants had less access to meat on the bone (*ibid.*, 236).

The break-down by vessel types reveals differences in the hospital assemblage and that of the barracks of similar date. In the hospital bowls and dishes form a low percentage by EVEs (the site average is 30%; see Table 22.24). Perhaps the larger sized bowls and dishes were more important for communal eating, which did not take place to the same degree in the hospital because the patients came from different *contubernia*.

An even greater contrast can be seen with the small jars or beakers (with a rim diameter of 100mm or less), which are much more common in the hospital (Fig.

22.14, no. 63). Some jars of this size, with a handle, were clearly drinking vessels, and it is possible those without handles were also drinking vessels, being similar in size to fine ware beakers. The fact that coarse ware drinking vessels were more common in the hospital possibly suggests that patients were supplied with a cheaper version of drinking vessel when in hospital. However, not all such small jars may have been used as drinking vessels, and as some are simply small versions of cooking-pots, it is also possible they were used in greater numbers in the hospital for individual portions of food, or storage of medicines or similar. Similar small jars were also present at the hospital at Housesteads Fort, with at least two published examples (Charlesworth 1976, fig. 3, nos 16, 19).

Most of the pottery from the hospital was typical of the whole site, including local grey wares, BB1, and BB2 and allied fabrics. There were three vessels of particular interest (Fig. 22.14, nos 64–5) from room 8 (all from the same context) and from the courtyard. Two of these are lid-seated vessels, of which only six certain examples are known from the whole site, with most of the sherds coming from the hospital or near to it. Almost all the stratified examples of this ware come from the hospital, with further sherds from the clearance level above; unstratified sherds are also known from above Cistern 1 and Buildings 4 and 5. The vessels are in a cream fabric with brown exterior and sometimes a yellow interior surface, and often have an elaborate rim folded back to sit on the shoulder. The third vessel, similar in size and shape, was in a different fabric, with a flat-topped rim (Fig. 22.14, no. 64). Possible parallels are known from York (Perrin 1981, fig. 33, nos 412, 414).

*Barracks*
Table 22.16 shows the break-down by vessel types of pottery from the Period 2 and 3 barracks, from the infantry barracks (Buildings 1–5) and the cavalry barracks (Buildings 9–12, including pottery from the 1997–8 excavations). The cavalry barracks have more flagons, less storage jars and slightly less cooking-pots.

*Table 22.16: Vessel types from the barracks (Periods 2 and 3) shown as a percentage of the total EVEs.*

| Vessel type | Infantry | Cavalry | Combined |
|---|---|---|---|
| Flagon | 4.8 | 10.3 | 7.8 |
| Beaker | 5.1 | 6.1 | 5.6 |
| Small jar | 1.5 | 0.4 | 0.9 |
| Cooking-pot | 53.6 | 45.9 | 49.4 |
| Storage jar | 2.9 | – | 1.3 |
| Bowl/dish | 28.4 | 28.8 | 28.6 |
| Mortarium | 3.8 | 7.8 | 6.0 |
| Lid | – | 0.7 | 0.4 |
| Totals | 2644 | 3189 | 5833 |

*Table 22.17: Vessel types from Building 13 (all periods), shown as a percentage of EVEs*

| Vessel type | % |
|---|---|
| Flagon | no rims |
| Beaker | 5.1 |
| Small jar | 0.4 |
| Cooking-pot | 39.5 |
| Storage jar | 1.1 |
| Bowl/dish | 49.2 |
| Casserole | 1.1 |
| Mortarium | 1.1 |
| Lid | 1.1 |
| Total | 1226 |

Only one buried pot deliberately built into a floor was identified from the barracks. It came from a lean-to or extension to the third-century barrack Chalet 10, Building AB (Fig. 22.16, no 92).

### Building 13 (Commanding officer's house)

The pottery from the Commanding officer's house was only 1226 by EVES, with flagons not being represented at all by rims although present as body sherds. Despite the size of the group, there seems to be a significant change in the usual proportions of cooking-pots and bowl/dishes, with the bowls and dishes making up nearly 50% of the assemblage, and cooking-pots only 40%. This could reflect less reliance on foods that made good communal meals, such as boiled meat, pottage or other stews, as a staple dish, or, more likely, the more frequent use of copper alloy vessels in a rich man's kitchen. A low proportion of ceramic cooking-pots could possibly be an indicator of a higher status building. Although there is a greater proportion of bowls and dishes, most of these are of coarse wares such as BB1 and BB2 and not more decorative tablewares or samian.

There are four separate North African-style vessels from this building; a cooking-pot and a casserole in the fill of the cistern in the courtyard (both sooted with use, N11:28, N11:29, N11:24; Fig. 22.22, no. 275), a sherd from a dish in the third room from the eastern end of the southern wing (N12:38) and a lid handle from the backfill of the west hypocaust (L12:42). This may reflect more exotic cooking techniques within the house, although sherds are known from elsewhere in the fort; stratified sherds come from the 'assembly area' and alley 3, and unstratified sherds from over Buildings 2, 4, 5 and 16. An assemblage of ten vessels was also recovered from a gully immediately outside the East gate (Croom 2003, 246–9).

### Cistern 1

The pottery from the cistern, the largest individual assemblage from the whole site, came from three main contexts. After the cistern was divided in half, the northern half was the first to be filled in, with pottery possibly from silting during use collecting in the lower layer (E08:44). The top layers of the fill, which included stone flagging and a possible water channel to the other half of the cistern (E08:27) produced a much larger quantity of the pottery. There were six examples of joining sherds or sherds obviously from the same vessel between these two contexts. The fill of the southern half of the cistern (E08:29) was very different from that found in the northern part, and indeed no joins between sherds were found between E08:44 and E08:29. However, there were cross-joins between seven vessels in E08:27 in the north and E08:29 in the south. These cross-joins, and a very distinctive bone assemblage (see animal bone report) suggest the contexts are related, and have been studied as one assemblage.

Table 22.19 shows the slight variations in dating according to the fine and coarse wares between the contexts ('late pottery' indicating pottery dating to c.270 or later). E08:27 also had more amphorae and mortaria dated to after 250 than the other two contexts. This upper layer would have been left exposed after the deliberate infilling of the cistern, and probably contains some pottery deposited later; there is certainly some contamination as it contains a single

*Table 22.18: Pottery from Cistern 1 by weight*

| Type | Wt (kg) |
| --- | --- |
| Amphorae | 9.263 |
| Mortaria | 3.364 |
| Samian | 1.169 |
| Fine wares | 2.424 |
| Coarse wares | 20.752 |
| Total | 36.972 |

*Table 22.19: The fine wares and coarse wares only from Cistern 1, shown as a percentage of the total weight*

| Context | BB2 & allied | Late pottery | All other types | Weight (kg) |
| --- | --- | --- | --- | --- |
| E08:44 | 78.7 | 0.7 | 20.6 | 4.812 |
| E08:29 | 60.1 | 1.6 | 38.3 | 9.311 |
| E08:27 | 51.6 | 5.7 | 42.7 | 9.053 |
| Combined | 60.7 | 3.0 | 36.3 | 23.176 |

*Table 22.20: Pottery from Cistern 1 (excluding amphorae) shown as a percentage*

| Type | % by weight |
| --- | --- |
| Mortaria | 12.1 |
| Samian | 4.2 |
| Fine wares | 8.7 |
| Coarse wares | 75.0 |
| Total | 27.709kg |

Note: the samian is slightly under-represented, as not all of it could be quantified

*Table 22.21: Vessel types from Cistern 1, shown as a percentage of the total minimum number (235 vessels) and EVEs*

| Vessel type | MNI | EVE |
| --- | --- | --- |
| Flagon etc | 8.1 | 3.2 |
| Beaker/small jar | 14.5 | 11.0 |
| Cooking-pot | 26.0 | 47.8 |
| Storage jar | 4.2 | 2.4 |
| Bowl/dish | 34.9 | 28.9 |
| Mortarium | 11.1 | 6.6 |
| Lid | 0.8 | 0.1 |
| Ring vase | 0.4 | – |
| Totals | 235 | 3121 |

late fourth-century Huntcliff-type rim, dating to at least a hundred years after the bulk of the assemblage.

The cistern fill produced sherds from at least 235 vessels (excluding amphorae). Table 22.21 was produced by looking at minimum numbers of vessel rather than by EVEs because it was clear there were a lot of beakers without rim sherds which would not have been represented in quantification by EVE. The minimum number was estimated by comparing form, fabric and finish, but as this can be difficult when looking at large numbers of sherds in one fabric, the quantification can only give an approximate idea of numbers for the more common vessel forms. Out of the 235 vessels, only approximately 16 were represented by substantial remains; many of the other vessels were represented by a single sherd or only a small number of pieces. Since there are also a number of residual second-century sherds, the bulk of the assemblage had clearly built up over time and had been subject to the usual mixing and sherd separation found in a typical pottery assemblage. This stands in contrast to the bone assemblage, where there was very little of the general culinary waste expected from most contexts, but evidence of a single dumping of processing waste. This suggests that while the cistern was being filled with material deliberately brought in from elsewhere, some-one took the opportunity to get rid of their processing waste at the same time. The 16 vessels were made up of seven bowls and dishes, four beakers, two mortaria, two flagons and only one cooking-pot.

The samian was very heavily biased towards bowls, with very few drinking cups, but the great majority of bowls present were coarse wares. There were a few sherds of very residual Hadrianic samian, but there were 26 sherds of late second or third century date. Of the cooking-pots *c*.40% showed evidence of sooting, many with heavy use.

The bowls and dishes are divided almost equally between BB1 and BB2 and allied fabrics, with all other fabrics only making up 5%. Flanged bowls, current from *c*.270 make up almost 20%, but it is noticeable that there is no Crambeck reduced ware and only four sherds of calcite-gritted ware, at least one of

which is intrusive, as it is a Huntcliff-type rim of the late fourth century.

## Cistern 2

The cistern produced 16.912kg of pottery, excluding samian. There were four contexts in all, with frequent joins in the pottery between H07:09 in the lower fill and H07:03 in the upper fill, but few joins between pottery in any of the other contexts. BB2 and allied fabrics made up 76% of the coarse wares in the lower fill and 63% in the upper. There were 11 samian vessels of the late second or first half of the third century, three Nene Valley ware vessels and a number of sherds of Horningsea ware, probably dating to the third century. There was one BB1 flanged bowl, three sherds of Crambeck reduced ware and two sherds of calcite-gritted ware; this late third-century material makes up only approximately 1% of the coarse wares, suggesting a date early in the final quarter of the third century for the final filling of the cistern. There was also a very leached and battered Huntcliff-type rim which must be contamination (there were also a few sherds of post-medieval pottery).

The joining sherds between contexts in the western part of the cistern suggests that much of it was filled in at the same time. The filling contains some relatively complete vessels that must have been in use close to the date of the final filling of the cistern, which was

*Table 22.23: Vessel types from Cistern 2 (excluding amphorae), shown as a percentage of EVEs*

| Vessel type | % |
| --- | --- |
| Flagon | 6.3 |
| Beaker | 7.9 |
| Cooking-pot | 52.4 |
| Storage jar | 2.5 |
| Bowl/dish | 25.9 |
| Mortarium | 4.5 |
| Lid | 0.5 |
| Total | 1827 |

*Table 22.24: Vessel types from the whole site, shown as a percentage by EVEs*

| Vessel type | % |
| --- | --- |
| Flagon | 4.4 |
| Beaker | 8.7 |
| Small jar* | 0.2 |
| Storage jar | 1.1 |
| Cooking-pot | 49.7 |
| Bowl/dish | 29.8 |
| Mortarium | 5.4 |
| Lid | 0.5 |
| Triple vase | 0.0 |
| Total | 33076 |

*under-represented as some under 'beaker'

*Table 22.22: Coarse ware bowl/dish types from Cistern 1 by EVEs, shown as a percentage*

| Rim type | BB1 | BB2 | Other | Total |
| --- | --- | --- | --- | --- |
| Plain | 20.5 | 2.0 | – | 22.5 |
| Plain with groove | – | 7.0 | 1.7 | 8.7 |
| Flat with groove | 7.7 | – | – | 7.7 |
| Rounded | – | 27.2 | – | 27.2 |
| Flanged | 18.3 | 0.7 | 0.7 | 19.7 |
| Wide-mouthed | – | 11.7 | 2.0 | 13.7 |
| Hemispherical | – | – | 0.6 | 0.6 |
| Total | | | | 820 |

not subsequently disturbed (Fig. 22.22, nos 251–4, 256). This also includes a flagon which was probably in one piece when it was discarded, probably already missing its handle and much of the rim at that time (Fig. 22.21, no. 249). Many of the vessels show evidence of sooting, which is sometimes heavy.

The assemblage consists of the equivalent of 18 vessels. Colour-coated wares were few, while cooking-pots made up half the assemblage. Flagons are over-represented, due to the presence of a complete rim.

*Buried pots*
The site records suggest five possible buried pots, but only two are certain. The most complete comes from room 1 of the hospital, set in place sometime in the first half of the third century. It is a BB2 pot with the rim deliberately removed, and was found with a stone lid *in situ* (Fig. 22.15, no. 68; Fig. 25.33). It was set into the floor over 1m from the north wall and 1m from the east wall (D11:23; see Figs 5.18 and 5.25). Originally this would have put it towards the back of the room, away from the entrance, but when the room was later remodelled this placed the pot near to the new doorway and the hearth set next to the door. It is unclear to which phase the pot belongs.

The second pot comes from Chalet 10 (officer's quarters, Building AB) and dates to after *c*.235. This is a south-eastern reduced ware cooking-pot with a complete rim surviving, although only about 75% of the vessel as a whole survives (Fig. 28, no. 92). It was placed towards one corner of the room, about 0.8m from the west wall and *c*.1.5m from the south wall, in a short-lived extension or lean-to on the west side of the building (D14:10; Fig. 16.7).

The uncertain examples include the truncated base of a large BB1 cooking-pot with acute-angle lattice, of which only about one-quarter survives, set almost in the middle of the hospital's verandah, outside room 1 (E11:45, Fig. 5.05). Another is the lower part of a BB2 cooking-pot, with unusually thick walls and a very thin base, along with body and rim sherds from other vessels. As this was found in a post-hole in Building Q of Building Row 20, it may be packing rather than a deliberately buried pot (F11:05).

The final pot is the lower part of a large south-eastern reduced ware storage jar in contubernium 8 of Building 11 (J15:18). It is not clear if it belongs to phase 2 of Building 11 or to the later Building AC (after *c*.235), but in either case it is positioned in the front stable room of the barracks, possibly in the passageway area. It is uncertain whether it was originally a complete vessel that has been truncated at a later stage, or whether only the lower part of the vessel was inserted into the floor, but in either case it would have to be securely covered to avoid the horses injuring themselves by putting a foot down it.

The exact use of these buried pots is unknown. They are not foundation offerings, as the necks are set level with the floor so that they can be easily accessed, and they are not concealed, having easily recognisable circular lids. At South Shields Roman Fort, where a number have been found in the barracks, there is usually only one per *contubernium*; as the units were occupied by up to eight men, and as they are often set out in the corridor they were not greatly secure for storing anything of value. Many are comparatively close to a doorway.

# 23. THE VESSEL GLASS AND GRAFFITI

## by D. Allen and R. S. O. Tomlin

### The vessel glass (Fig. 23.01)

*by D. Allen*

The assemblage studied comprised 130 vessel glass fragments, of which 90 are blue-green, four are pale green and 35 are colourless. Twenty-five fragments of cast window glass were also found. A total of 75 fragments were not available for study when this report was written, and the details of those pieces of interest within this group have been added later (AC).

The content is fairly typical of a site occupied from the earlier second century: most of the blue-green fragments (63 in all) are from bottles of very common first to second century type. Catalogue numbers 1, 2 and 5 similarly belong to common forms of later first-/earlier second-century tableware. Glass of the late Roman period is not well represented: only two fragments (nos 8 and 39) come from containers of the third to fourth centuries.

What is slightly surprising in an assemblage of this size is the very nice range of colourless tableware in the form of bowls, beakers or cups which is present. Twenty-one vessels have been identified (nos 18–38), and include facet and wheel-cut glass, an indented vessel, and one with pinched-out nipples, as well as a common cylindrical cup form with double base-ring. All are typical of the second and third centuries. Clearly, in common with other military garrisons, some of the better glassware from the wide variety available at that time was reaching the tables at Wallsend.

### Blue-green and pale green glass

*Jugs*

1. Area over Building 12, unstratified, K14:01, 1383, WSG11

Fragment from beneath the handle of a jug of blue-green glass. Extended tail of handle extant, decorated by pinching glass into series of ridges. Angle suggests the jug body was conical in shape.

This type of handle decoration is most characteristic of a group of long-necked jugs which was very popular in the north-western provinces during the later first and earlier second centuries. They were made with both conical and globular bodies, and the former have either a simple concave base (eg Charlesworth 1959, 52, pl. III, no. 2 from Turriff, Aberdeenshire) or a pushed-in base-ring (eg Price 1980, 66, no. 9, fig. 15 from a pit dated AD155–165 at Park Street, Towcester).

*Jars*

2. (D: *c*.50mm). *Via principalis*, N08:12, 2517, WSG1
Rim fragment of a small jar of blue-green glass. Rim folded inward and downward then outward and downward, then outward slightly, forming flaring collar.

Globular or bulbous jars of blue-green glass were made in a variety of shapes and sizes, and the smaller vessels are usually identified as ointment jars. The rim shape of this fragment most closely resembles that used on a bulbous jar type commonly found on later first- and earlier second-century sites (Price 1978, 74). Small examples have been found at Cologne (Fremersdorf 1958, 25, pl. 16), and there is a rim fragment from a context dated AD 75–85 at the Caerleon Fortress Baths (Allen 1986, 99, no. 4, fig. 40).

*Beakers/bowls*

3. (D: *c*.50mm). Alley 1, dump of demolition material, N05:23, 350, WSG95
Rim fragment of a beaker or bowl of blue-green glass. Vertical rim, fire-rounded and thickened. This fragment is not diagnostic enough to identify vessel type.

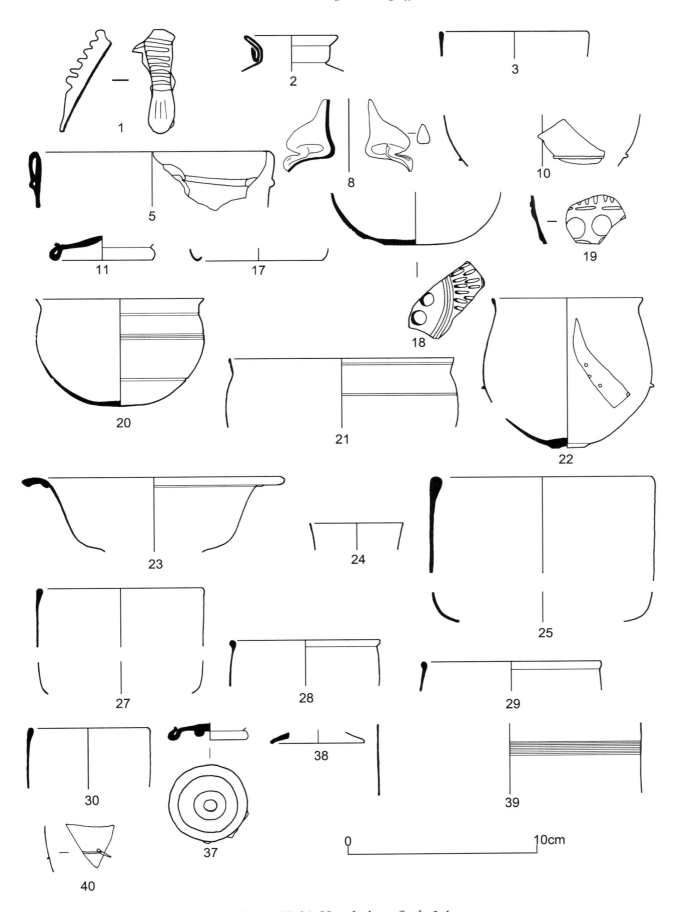

*Figure 23.01: Vessel glass. Scale 1:4.*

4. (D:80mm B:1mm). Cistern 1, filling, late third century, E08:44, WSG121
Cup of blue-green glass with slightly in-turned fire-rounded rim (AC).

5. (D: *c*.130mm). Area over *Via quintana*, unstratified, G12:01, WS6
Rim fragment of a bowl of blue-green glass; thick layer of whitish-iridescence. Rim folded outward and downward, forming hollow tube, with irregular extra ridge at edge.

Bowls with tubular rims occurred throughout much of the Roman period, but were most common during the later first and earlier second centuries. At this time a version with roughly cylindrical body, often with ribs, and an applied base-ring, became very popular (Isings 1957, 59–60, form 44a-b). An example from northern Britain is a bowl from Torwoodlee Broch, Selkirks (Charlesworth 1959, 49, fig. 7, no. 4).

## Bottles

6. The blue-green vessel glass includes the usual predominance of bottle fragments: over 60 sherds in all, including six rims, 13 handle sherds and three bases with moulded concentric circles. These vessels were used as containers for a variety of liquids, and their fragments are the commonest glass finds on first and second century sites (Charlesworth 1966) The square was the longest-lived variety, probably continuing to be made throughout the second century, and at least 18 of the Wallsend fragments can be identified as belonging to this type. A further five fragments have come from prismatic bottles (either square, hexagonal, octagonal or rectangular) and the rest are rims, handles, necks or shoulders, which are common to all bottle types.

7. (R:70mm B:7mm). *Via principalis*, E07:37, WSG120
Body sherd of blue-green bottle glass, re-used. Part of a curved edge which has been rounded down to create a smooth edge.

8. (D: *c*.22mm). Area over *Via quintana*, unstratified, N13:01, 1700, WSG16
Neck and handle fragment of a bottle of blue-green glass; many pinhead and elongated bubbles within the metal. Cylindrical neck with constriction at its base. One 'dolphin' handle adhering, with the 'head' of the 'dolphin' facing out over the shoulder, and an outer 'knife' edge.

Bottles with 'dolphin' handles were some of the later Roman vessels which replaced the first- and second-century containers discussed above. They were never as common, though, and finds are far fewer. They were usually made of colourless or pale green glass, and had cylindrical bodies. The type has been discussed by Harden with reference

to bottles from fourth century graves at Lankhills Roman Cemetery, Winchester (1979, 200, nos 20, 21 and 411, fig. 27), and he suggests that it first appeared around the middle of the third century, its period of maximum use being the later third and fourth centuries.

*Fragments of indeterminate vessel type*
9. Handle (L:25mm W:25mm). Building 1, verandah, Period 3, L04:20, WSG177
Blue-green folded handle, possibly from a small jug (AC).

10. (Max. body D:*c*.105mm). Cistern 1, filling, mid to late third century, E08:29, 2356, WSG105
Three body fragments of a vessel of blue-green glass. Vessel body thin-walled and bulbous or globular, with one self-coloured horizontal applied trail extant.

11. (D:56mm). Area over Building 7, unstratified, G11:01, WSG97
Base fragment of a vessel of blue-green glass. Pushed-in tubular base-ring.
Base rises to low central point, pontil-mark on underside.

12 - 5. Base fragments in blue-green glass, similar to no. 11 above. Not illustrated.
12. (D:55mm). Area over Road 8, unstratified, F09:01. WSG126. Pushed-in tubular base-ring (AC).
13. (D:*c*.50mm). Area over Alley 5, unstratified, G14:05, 1231, WSG104. Pushed-in tubular base-ring.
14. (D *c*.40mm). Area over Road 3 and Building 9, unstratified, H13:03, 1232, WSG73. Pushed-in solid base-ring.
15. (D:*c*.70mm). Road 8, F08:05, 2382, WSG82. Pushed-in tubular base-ring.

16. Base. Area over *Via quintana*, unstratified, M13:01, 1906, WSG173
Base ring from cup or bowl in green glass, with tubular base ring (AC).

17. (D:*c*.70mm). Area over Building 5, unstratified, J04:13, 837, WSG86
Base fragment of a vessel of pale green glass. Pushed-in open base-ring.

None of these fragments is sufficiently diagnostic for vessel types to be identified, nor can they be closely dated.

## Colourless glass
*Beakers/bowls/cups*
18. (D of body at top of fragment: *c*.90mm). Area over Building 14, unstratified, K11:01, 1734, WSG3
Fragment from the lower side of a small bowl or cup of colourless glass; now cloudy and opaque, with

iridescent surfaces. Outer surface facet- and wheel-cut: extant part shows part of a horizontal wheel-cut line, below which are two interlocking rows of vertical oval facets, then a band of three horizontal wheel-cut lines, and two of what was presumably a ring of circular facets around central base.

19. Building 13, backfill of west hypocaust, mid-third century, L12:42, 1801, WSG12
Body fragment probably of a bowl or cup of buff-colourless glass, now cloudy and opaque, with iridescent surfaces. Outer surface facet-cut: part of a row of vertical oval facets extant, with a row of horizontal oval facets beneath, then two rows of circular facets.

Both these fragments are most likely to represent hemispherical bowls, which occurred with a wide variety of facet-cut decoration during the later second and third centuries. The combination of vertical oval facets and bands of horizontal wheel-cut lines is quite common and can be paralleled elsewhere: there is one example from a pit dated AD155–165 at Park Street, Towcester (Price 1980, 63–4, fig. 14, no. 1), and another from Carbridge (Charlesworth 1959, 44, fig. 3, 6). A bowl from the Railway Station Cemetery at York also has circular facets (Harden 1962, 137, fig. 88, no. HG205.1), and a bowl from excavations at Doncaster Roman Fort bears decoration combining interlocking rows of vertical oval facets, horizontal oval facets and rows of circular facets (Doncaster Museum).

20. (D: c.90mm H as reconstructed: 59mm). Building AZ, robber trench, and unstratified, M13:07 and M13:01, 1772 and 1784, WSG13
Many fragments forming a reconstructable profile of a bowl or cup of colourless glass; surfaces very pitted and covered with flaking iridescence. Rim out-flared and ground smooth; hemispherical body, decorated with one horizontal wheel-cut line beneath the rim, another pair further down the side, and one more above the base. Base slightly flattened.

21. (D:c.120mm). Building 13, backfill of east hypocaust, Period 4, M12:54, 1851, WSG69
Rim and side fragment of a bowl of colourless glass; now slightly cloudy and opaque with flaking iridescence. Rim out-flared and ground smooth; bulbous body, with one horizontal wheel-cut line beneath rim and another further down side.

Hemispherical bowls, similar in shape to those discussed with reference to nos 18 and 19, but decorated with wheel-cut lines only, seem to belong mainly to the second century. One example came from a pit dated AD155–165 at Park Street, Towcester (Price 1980, 63–4, fig. 14, no. 2), there is another, with a base-ring, from contexts dated AD150–155/60 and AD270–5 at Verulamium (Charlesworth 1972, 206–8, fig. 77, 46), and a small, globular bowl from a late

second century burial at Ford Street, Braughing, Herts (Harden 1977, 102, pl. IX).

22. (D:c.80mm H(as reconstructed):82mm). Building 13, backfill of east hypocaust, mid-third century, M12:44, 1803, WSG15
Rim, body and base fragments of a bowl or cup of colourless glass; surfaces pitted and covered with flaking iridescence and thicker whitish weathering. Fragments do not join, but probable reconstruction is shown in drawing: rim out-flared and fire-rounded and thickened; hemispherical body decorated with pinched-out nipples; base flattened and thickened, and formed into slight base-ring, pontil mark on underside.

This reconstruction shows yet another decorative variant of the hemispherical bowl, popular during the later second and third centuries. The pinched out nipples can occur singly, as here, or in vertical rows of two or three (eg Fremersdorf 1962, 31, pls 34–5; Dappelfeld 1966, 5052, pl. 95, from Cologne). Fragments have been found at other northern sites, including Corbridge (Bulmer 1955, 131, no. 20), South Shields (Museum of Antiquities, Newcastle) and Nether Denton (Chesters Site Museum).

23. (D:c.140mm H(as reconstructed):40mm). Building Row 20, Building Q, mid-third century, F11:37, WSG14
Rim and side fragments (not joining) of a bowl of colourless glass. Rim fire-rounded and thickened, and widely flared, forming slightly overhanging flange with applied self-coloured horizontal coil beneath. Sides taper slightly downward to carination, then curve, presumably towards base-ring.

This vessel is probably related to a group of shallow bowls with flaring rims with ridge beneath which for some reason, is best known from burials in the Netherlands. Twenty-five, for example, came from a grave at Belfort in Limburg (Isings 1971, 22–4, nos 63–75, fig. 12) and there is another from a grave dated AD125–150 at Helshoeven-ander-Hoepertingen in Belgium (Janssens and Vanderhoeven 1974, 17, no. 21, fig. 8).

24. (D:c.50mm). Building 13, backfill of east hypocaust, mid-third century, M12:44, WSG106
Rim fragment probably of an indented beaker (small thin-walled fragment of an indent also extant, though not illustrated); colourless glass, surfaces pitted and iridescent. Slightly flaring rim, ground smooth.

Indented beakers of colourless glass were popular from the Flavian period to the third century. First-century examples have come from Richborough (Bushe-Fox 1926, 49, pl. 19, no. 8; Radford 1932, 85, no. 61, pl. 15), and there is one from a probable third century burial in a stone coffin at York (Harden 1962, 140, pl. 66, no. HG180).

25. (D:*c.*120mm). Area over *Via quintana,* unstratified, M13:01, 1752, WSG2
Joining rim and side fragment of a cup of colourless glass; flaking iridescent surfaces. Rim fire-rounded and thickened and turned slightly inward; body cylindrical.

26. (D(at carination):*c.*110mm). Area over Building 13, unstratified, M12:02, 1766, WSG65
Lower body fragment of a cup of colourless glass; flaking iridescent surfaces. Lower part of cylindrical body extant.

27. (D:*c.*65mm). Building 13, backfill of east hypocaust, mid-third century, M12:17, 1782, WSG103.
Rim and side fragments of a cup of colourless glass; surfaces iridescent, some pieces white and opaque. Rim fire-rounded and thickened and turned slightly inward; body cylindrical.

28. (D:*c.*80mm). Building 13, room 7, mid-third century, N12:08, 1763 and 1765, WSG05.
Two joining rim fragments of a cup of colourless glass now white and opaque, surfaces iridescent. Rim fire-rounded and thickened and turned slightly outward, body apparently cylindrical.

29. (D:*c.*95mm). Area over Building 13, unstratified, M12:01, 1692, WSG79
Rim fragment of a cup of colourless glass; surfaces iridescent. Rim fire-rounded and thickened and turned slightly inward.

30. (D:*c.*95mm). Area over Building 12, unstratified, L14:01, 1783, WSG4.
Rim fragment of a cup of colourless glass; surfaces dulled and swirled. Rim fire-rounded and thickened and turned slightly inward; body cylindrical.

31. Bowl (D:120mm B:2mm). Building 13, probably from fill of east hypocaust, M12:55, WSG205
Colourless out-turned bowl rim with circles between horizontal rice-grain facets. (AC)

32. Cup (D:100cm B:1mm). Chalet 9, Building W, late third/early fourth century, D13:70, 1608, WSG92
Colourless rim and body sherds of cylindrical cup with slightly in-turned fire-rounded rim. One sherd from the outer base ring. (AC)

33. Cup (D:*c.*70mm B:0.5mm). Building 13, probably from fill of east hypocaust, M12:55, WSG204
Colourless cup with fire-rounded rim. (AC)

34. Cup (D:100mm B:1mm). Area over Building 2, ploughsoil, L05:03, WSG232
Colourless cup with fire-rounded rim, slightly in-turned. (AC)

35. Cup (B:2mm). Unstratified, WSG50
Colourless body sherd with staggered rows of vertical rice-grain facets. (AC)

36. Cup (B(min):0.5mm). Area over Alley 4, unstratified, E05:01, WSG137
Colourless small body sherd from near base with vertical rib. (AC)

37. (D(base):42mm). Rerouted *Via principalis,* Roman/post-Roman, E08:13, 2290, WSG77
Base of a cup of colourless glass. Pushed-in solid base-ring with inner concentric applied coil base-ring (D:18mm). Broken body walls appear to have been chipped away to enable re-use of base as counter or gaming piece.
   This simple cup form, with its fire-rounded rim, cylindrical body and double base-ring, was very common during the second half of the second and first half of the third centuries, particularly *c.*AD160–230. Fourteen fragments, for example, were found in a drain deposit of this date at the Legionary Fortress Baths at Caerleon (Allen 1986, 113, nos 69–73, fig. 43), and at least another 25 have come from the fortress and *vicus* there (National Museum of Wales). Bulmer recorded 30–40 at Corbridge (1955, 128), and more have been found since, and about 50 have been recovered from Verulamium (Verulamium Museum).
   The reworking of the base-ring of a broken cup into a simple disc, presumably to be used as a counter or gaming piece, was also quite a common device. There are two examples using this same double base-ring form from York (Yorkshire Museum), and another using a single base-ring from Fishbourne (Harden and Price 1971, 355, no. 77, fig. 141).

38. (D:*c.*50mm). Alley 3, Period 3, F04:33, 558, WSG89
Fragment from the foot of a vessel, probably a beaker or goblet, of colourless glass. Pad foot, blown separately from vessel body and applied beneath; edge ground smooth. This is most likely to be from some form of goblet, or perhaps a flask, with beaded stem and blown foot (eg Isings 1957, 103, form 86 or 110, form 93). Its date is probably later second- or third-century.

*Bottle/flask*
39. (D of body:*c.*140mm). Area over Building 2 and Alley 1, post-Roman, M05:04, 24, WSG9
Body fragment of a bottle or flask of colourless glass. Cylindrical body, with part of a band of five horizontal wheel-cut lines extant.
   The blue-green bottles of the first two centuries AD were replaced during the later second, third and fourth centuries by a variety of colourless containers, most of them with cylindrical bodies, often decorated with bands of wheel-cut lines (eg Isings 1957, forms 100, 102, 126 and 127). Fragment no. 39 may have

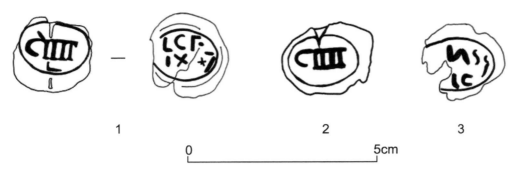

*Figure 23.02: Lead sealings. Scale 1:1.*

come from any of these, although its relatively large diameter perhaps suggests a bottle with one or two angular, ribbed handles.

*Indeterminate*
40. Chalet 12, Building AM2, (mid-)late third century, M14:11, 1858, WSG81
Body fragment of colourless glass; dulled and opaque. Start and overlapping end of applied self-coloured trail extant. This fragment is not sufficiently diagnostic to allow close identification.

41. Body sherd (B:1mm). Chalet 9, Building W, late third/early fourth century, D13:70, WSG213
Colourless body sherd probably from near rim with a raised horizontal trail.(AC)

### Window glass
42. Twenty-five fragments of window glass were found, all of the blue-green, matt/glossy variety in use to about 300 (Boon 1966a). Eight have the characteristic rounded 'thumb' edge produced by casting in a shallow tray.

## Lead sealings and graffiti
*by R. S. O. Tomlin*

### Lead sealings (Fig. 23.02)
1. Lead sealing (L:24mm W:20mm). Yard south of Building 13, Period 1–2, N13:03, 1795, WSIM43
Published: *RIBII* 2411.109
Oval leaden sealing damaged by thin cord or wire which it enclosed, and subsequently by corrosion. Impressed die reads:
Obv    CIIII L
Rev    LCF / C(ohors) (quarta) L(ingonum)

This is the first recorded sealing of *Cohors IV Lingonum*, which is attested as the third- and fourth-century garrison of Wallsend (*RIBI* 1299, 1300, 1301; *Not. Dig. Occ.* 40.33). Its location in Britain during the second century, and the second-century garrison of

Wallsend are not known. A leaden sealing in itself is not conclusive evidence of the location of a unit. The letters *LCF* on the reverse are presumably the initials of the issuing officer, *L(ucius) C(...) F(...)*. The second line is unfortunately corroded; after *LX* there seems to be a star (sometimes found on sealings) rather than *X* (for *L(egio) XX*), followed by a centurial sign.

2. Lead sealing (L:25mm W:20mm B:4mm). *Via principalis*, L08:66, 2587, WSIM41
Oval leaden sealing. Impressed die reads:
Obv: CIIII

Another sealing of *Cohors IV Lingonum.*

3. Lead sealing (L:21mm W:20mm). East-west drain north of wall of Building 1, Period 2, P05:18, 519, WSIM40
Published: *RIBII* 2411.292
Major fragment of an oval leaden sealing. It was pierced by a thin cord or wire which has left a groove on the reverse; the obverse has been stamped with a lettered die which seems to read: MS7 / [.]LC

The reading is difficult because the die was unevenly impressed on a surface since corroded. The die cannot be paralleled, but in form resembles the centurial marks impressed on the *reverse* of some cohortal sealings found at Brough-under-Stainmore (Richmond 1936, 117–9, nos 17–21).

### Graffiti (Fig. 23.03)
Graffiti are in capitals, unless otherwise stated, and were all made after the vessel was fired. They are almost all personal names, presumably of members of the second-century garrison.

*Samian*
1.    Alley 1, dump of demolition material, N05:23, 325 and 326, WSIM5, *RIBII* 2501.215. See samian report no. S90. Base sherd (form 18/31R–31R) scratched underneath: [...]Ç(*or* G)RΛT[...]

    Probably *Grat[us].*

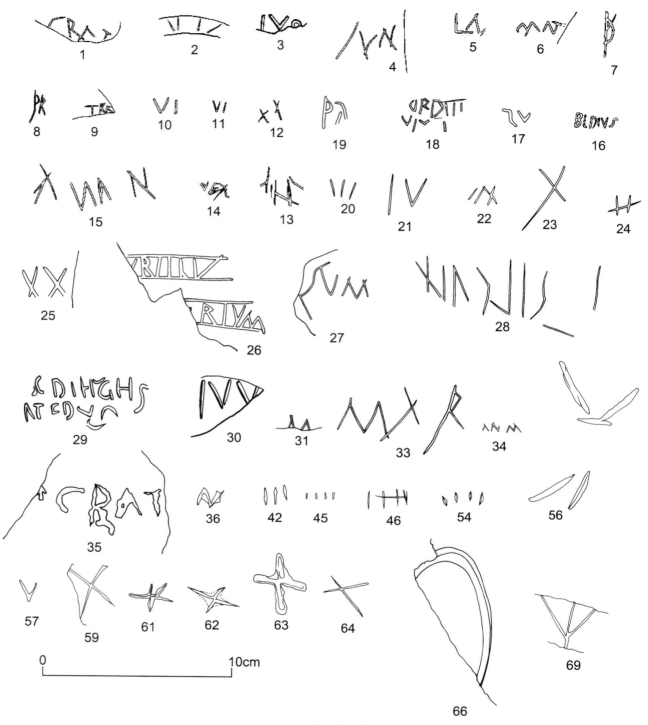

*Figure 23.03: Graffiti. Scale 1:2.*

2. Area over Building 11, unstratified, K15:01, 1373, WSIM16
   Part of a footring (form 31R?), incised underneath: IM[...].

3. Area over Building 13 and *Via quintana*, unstratified, H13:01, 1237, WSIM15, *RIBII* 2501.253
   Base sherd (form 18/31), scratched underneath: IVÇ(*or* S)[...].

*S* is less likely than *C*. Probably *Iuc[undus]*

4. Area over Building 10 and Alley 5, unstratified, E14:03, 1078, WSIM8, *RIBII* 2501.274
   Base sherd (form 31), scratched underneath: [...]IVN.

Probably complete, and thus an abbreviated *Iun(ius)*.

5. Area over Building 1 and Alley 1, unstratified, P05:02, 134, WSIM2
   Base sherd (form 31), scratched underneath: [...]LΛ.[...].

The angle of *L* to the footring suggests that it is the first letter, and thus that the next letter is *A* not *M*. The third letter might be *M* but there are other possibilities.

6. Area over Building 14, unstratified, K10:01, 1973, WSIM21, *RIBII* 2501.354
   Base sherd (form 31), scratched underneath: MΛT[...].

Probably *Mat[ernus]* or, less likely, *Mat[urus]*; but many other less common names cannot be excluded.

7. Chalet 9, dereliction, post-Roman, G13:03, 1519, WSIM31
   Base sherd (form 31), scratched underneath with an elongated letter: P̣[...]

8. Debris over Cistern 1, late Roman/post-Roman, E08:13, 2593, *RIBII* 2501.438
   Base sherd; scratched underneath at the very centre with elongated letters: PR

Apparently complete, and thus presumably an abbreviated personal name: the choice is wide (*Primus, Priscus, Probus, Proculus* etc).

9. Area over Buildings 4 and 5 and Alley 3, unstratified, G04:01, 161, WSIM35, *RIBII* 2501.549 and 2501.802
   Base sherd (form 31R?) scratched underneath: TRE̢[...].

10. Road 8, F09:08, 2437, WSIM24, 2007.3043
    Rim sherd (form 33) scratched on outer wall: VI[...].

*Vi[ctor]* or *Vi[talis]* are the most likely, but there are many other possibilities.

11. Building 8, entranceway, Period 4, E11:22, 1145, WSIM11
    Rim sherd (form 31R), scratched on the outer wall: VI[...].

See no 10 above.

12. *Via principalis*, L08:60, 2558, WSIM26
    Base sherd (form 27) roughly scratched underneath: XX

Probably not a numeral, but a double star or cross, for identification.

13. Area over East rampart, unstratified, C11:10, 1171, WSIM14
    Wall sherd (form 31R), scratched underneath: [...].M[...].
14. Building 1, floor, Period 2, M05:25, 909, WSIM30
    Base sherd, scratched underneath: [...]N (*or* V)ER[...].

The *R* is cursive.

*Coarse ware*

15. Drain in rerouted *Via principalis*, late third/early fourth century, E08:05, 2306, WSIM25, *RIBII* 2503.96
    Four conjoining sherds from the shoulder of a BB2 cooking pot: ΛMΛ N

The first *A* could be called cursive; the first stroke is made with two strokes, or else one of them is a vertical third stroke. The graffito seems to be complete, but its meaning is obscure.

16. North wall of fort, Q04:03, 238, WSIM4, *RIBII* 2503.211
    Sherd of a BB2 cooking pot, scratched just below the rim: BLDIVS.

The graffito seems to be complete, and is presumably a blundered personal name, perhaps *Bl(an)di(n)us*.

17. Area over Building 2 and Alley 1, post-Roman dereliction, M05:04, 136, WSIM32
    Rim sherd of a BB1 bowl, inscribed just below the rim in cursive: LV[...].
18. Alley 2, M07:07, 2632, WSIM33
    Base sherd of a large grey pot, with an abraded graffito underneath. The letters are also irregular, and the reading is uncertain: ORDITI̢ / V̢[...].
19. Soil over north-south drain east of Building 3, Period 3–4, Q07:10, 2631, WSIM53
    Rim sherd of a grey jar, inscribed below the rim: PR[...].

The *R* is cursive, but the *P* resembles the capital form. This *P*, which is standard in fourth-century New Roman Cursive, is sometimes found in earlier cursive texts, as here. Many names could be restored (see above, no. 8).

20. Building 8, entranceway, Period 4, E11:22, 1153, WSIM13, *RIBII* 2503.51
    Rim sherd of a grey ware jar, with three vertical strokes incised on the rim: III, '3'.
21. Building 13, dereliction, N12:13, 1852, WSIM20, *RIBII* 2503.55
    Rim of a BB2 pot, incised on the inner face of the rim: [...?]IV.

The graffito may well be complete, and thus another numeral, '4'. ΛI[...] could be read the other way round, but not ΛII[...] (for *Ae[...]*); however, personal names beginning ΛI[...] are not common.

22. Chalet 9, dereliction, post-Roman, F13:16, 1108, WSIM9, drawing as *RIBII* 2503.73, but see also *RIBII* 2503.63
    Rim sherd of a BB2 bowl, incised on the rim: IIX, '8'.

This seems to be the sequence of strokes, and would imply that the graffito was made (and meant to be read) from the outside of the vessel. The reading XII, '12', should thus be excluded.

23. Building 1, demolition, Period 2, N05:04, 207, WSIM3, *RIBII* 2503.67

Wall sherd of a large closed vessel in oxidized ware, shallowly incised: X.

A numeral, '10', or perhaps a mark of identification.

24. Area over Building 8, unstratified, E11:11, 1152, WSIM12, *RIBII* 2503.82
    Rim sherd of a BB2 bowl, incised on the rim: XX, '20'.

A diagonal stroke was first incised, and then two vertical strokes. This sequence would exclude the reading 'H'.

25. Area over Building 13, unstratified, N11:01, 1684, WSIM52
    Rim sherd of BB2 pot, deeply incised on the rim: [...] XX, '(at least) 20'.

26. West rampart (F2), N04:06, 25, WSIM50, *RIBII* 2497.4
    Sherd preserving about one-third, rim and base included, of a pinkish-cream mortarium of Hadrianic date, found sealed in clay rampart material. Underneath is incised in crude capitals between pairs of layout lines: [.]VRIILI / [...]RIVM, perhaps *[A]ureli* / *[morta]rium*, 'mortarium of Aurelius'.

The last vertical stroke in line 1 (read as *I*) is followed by a more shallowly incised diagonal stroke, but *V* makes no sense. *Aureli* seems to be the only name which can be restored here, and its occurrence on a Hadrianic sherd in a Hadrianic context is noteworthy. *Aurelius* is comparatively rare until the accession of Marcus Aurelius (AD 161), but thereafter one would not expect to find it used, as here, without *praenomen* or *cognomen*. *Mortario* ('as a mortarium') occurs as a graffito, but scratched before firing, on the side of a samian mortarium from Corbridge (Haverfield 1913, 270, no. 8).

27. Wall of post-Roman building, unstratified, N05:02, 137, WSIM54, *RIBII* 2503.4
    Sherd of a pink flagon with white slip, incised in neat cursive letters on the shoulder: [..]LSVM, perhaps *[mu]lsum*, 'honey-sweetened wine'.

For wine and honey (separately) in the Roman military diet, see Davies 1971, 131.

28. Dereliction over Alley 1, L05:29, 888, WSIM7, *RIBII* 2494.122
    Amphora sherd, faintly inscribed downwards with a fine point in elongated letters: [...]NΛLIIS .[...], *[...]nales* .[...].

A number of personal names end in *...nalis*, but the plural is puzzling. Brothers can be excluded, since the names are all *cognomina*; they tend to theophoric (*Neptunalis, Saturnalis*, etc), so a group of worshippers or other religious reference is possible. A more likely restoration, however, in this military context is *[contuber]nales*, 'messmates'.

*Tile*

29. Fired clay support (L:120mm+ W:80mm B:74mm). Building AP, late third century, F09:66, 2481, WSIM36, *RIBII* 2491.142
    Fragment of a fired clay support inscribed before firing with a stylus or similar implement. A two-line graffito reads: [c2]CDIIFGH.[...] / .ΛTCDVF[...].

Line 1 is presumably an alphabet, *[ab]cdefgh[i... (etc)]*, and line 2 perhaps an attempt by a second hand to copy it. For other examples of alphabets and other 'writing practice' on bricks and tiles before firing, see McWhirr 1979, 239.

### *Additional graffiti*
*by A. T. Croom*
Further examples of graffiti were found during the cataloguing of the pottery.

*Amphora*
30. Alley 8, upper surface, H09:14, WSIM56
    Dr 20, probably from the handle, but a small sherd, inscribed: I V [
    Start of another diagonal stroke after the V.

*Samian*
31. Area outside East rampart, unstratified, C08:04, WSIM44
    Inscribed on exterior surface of the base of a form 18/31, inside the foot-ring: M

32. Road 3, M14:28, WSIM89
    M inscribed on exterior surface of samian bowl.

*Coarse wares*
33. Cistern 2, upper fill, late third/early fourth century, H07:03, WSIM66
    Almost complete BB2 bowl. Inscribed in large letters on wall of bowl: MAR
34. Rubble over Building 8 (B3), late third century, D12:09, WSIM61
    Along the inner top edge of everted rim from jar, unknown fabric, inscribed: ]AN M[
35. Alley 1, dump of demolition material, N05:23, WSIM49
    Body sherd on wall of storage jar of unknown grey ware, inscribed: ] CRAT [
    There is the end of a diagonal stroke before the C
36. Building 13, dereliction, N12:13, WSIM82
    N inscribed on rim of BB2 bowl/dish. Small sherd, so could originally have been more letters.
37. Black earth (B2), H05:21, WSIM92
    Incomplete N or M inscribed on exterior of a samian cup, form 33, just above the mid-body groove.
38. Building 14, drain in north wall, Period 1 or 2, H08:12, WSIM70
    Body sherd of mortarium, inscribed: ]IVS.

NUMBERS AND PATTERNS
### 39–65. Numerals or ownership marks
Lines inscribed on rim of BB2 bowl/dishes:

39. One+ lines. Area over Building 4 and Alley 3, unstratified, H04:13, WSIM76
40. Three lines, deeply cut, on top of rim. Area over Buildings 7 and 8, unstratified, F10:12, WSIM38
41. Three lines, on outer edge. Building 8, cess-pit fill, mid third century?, D12:34, WSIM62
42. Three lines, on top surface. Area over Building 11 and Alley 6, unstratified, L15:15, WSIM78
43. Three lines. Building 8, drain in courtyard, mid-third century?, E11:14, WSIM64
44. Two lines +, on outer edge. North-east drain east of south wall of Building 1, Period 2, Q05:03, WSIM84
45. Four lines, on outer edge. Cistern 2, lower fill, Period late third/early fourth century, H07:09, WSIM58
46. Four+ lines (last line either badly inscribed I or very narrow V). Building Row 20, Building R, mid-third century, G11:17, WSIM72

Lines inscribed on end of mortarium flange
47. Three+ lines. Area over Building 7, unstratified, F11:01, WSIM68

Lines inscribed on top edge of jar rims (cooking pots, unless otherwise stated)
48. Two lines. South-eastern reduced ware, G151-type. Alley 10/Building 17, disturbed rubble inside building, G04:16, WSIM73.
49. Two lines. Small vessel; BB2. Building 8, room 2, D12:45, WSIM63
50. Two+ lines. Small vessel; south-eastern reduced ware. Building 8, drain in courtyard, mid-third century?, E11:14, WSIM65
51. Two+ lines. BB2. Area over *Via quintana*, unstratified, G12:01, WSIM75
52. Three lines. Poppyhead beaker. Drain in Road 3, G11:07, WSIM74

Lines inscribed on base of BB2 bowl/dish
53. Two lines on edge of base. Building 13, west baths, late third century, L12:02, WSIM77.

Lines inscribed on base of cooking pot
54. Four lines on edge of base. South-eastern reduced ware. Cistern 1 filling, mid to late third century, E08:29, WSIM60.

V inscribed on wall of samian bowl
55. Inverted V, below carination of form 18/31. Alley 1, dump of demolition material, N05:23, WSIM90

V inscribed on rim of Dr 20 amphora
56. Complete rim. V on one side, with a slightly slanted V almost opposite it. Area over Building 12, unstratified, M14:01, WSIM46

V inscribed on rim of BB2 bowl
57. V inscribed on the rim of the bowl. Rubble at base of plough furrow, H05:04, WSIM87

X inscribed on samian bowl
58. Small X, on interior of body, near rim. Gate 2, floor, Period 3–4?, D08:40, WSIM88

X inscribed on rim of BB2 cooking pot
59. On inner surface, deeply cut. Building 14, drain in south wall, Period 1 or 2, H12:09, WSIM86

X inscribed on exterior surface of base of BB2 bowl/dish
60. Area over Building 7, unstratified, G11:01, WSIM39
61. With extra diagonal line between north and east arms. Cistern 2, lower fill, H07:09, WSIM85

X inscribed on mortarium base
62. Local fabric; deeply cut over edge of the base. Area over Building 10, Alley 5 and *intervallum* road (Road 6), unstratified, F14:01, F15:01, WSIM67

X inscribed on Dr 20 amphora
63. Handle. Area over *Via quintana*, unstratified, N13:01, WSIM47
64. Handle. Road 8, F08:10, WSIM48
65. On body just above the handle; possibly accidental. Building 1, verandah, Period 3, L04:20, WSIM57

66–69. Patterns
66. Area over Building 12, unstratified, M14:01, WSIM83
Dr 20 amphora body sherd. *Ante-cocturam*, large loop or oval.

67. Building 4, make-up material, Period 2, G04:07, 479, WSIM37
Handle of Dr 20 amphora. Three lines converging to a point, crossed by a horizontal line, deeply incised.

68. Chalet 12, Building AL2, (mid-)late third century, N14:37, WSIM71
Series of connected triangles and lines, inscribed within foot-ring on base of samian bowl.

69. Area over Building 10 and *intervallum* road (Road 6), unstratified, F15:01, WSIM45
Three lines converging downwards to a point. Body sherd of BB2 bowl/dish near base.

*Bone counters*
See bone report for counters nos 42 (four vertical lines and motif), 50 (LVI), 52 (M) and 54 (four oblique strokes).

*Throwing stones*
See Fig. 25.34. no. 61 (marked I), no. 130 (IV), no. 54 (V), nos 88, 121 (I+), nos 72, 94 (X), no. 59 (XX).

# 24. THE COINS

## by P. J. Casey and R. Brickstock

The coins from Wallsend discussed here consist exclusively of those recovered from the excavations, excluding those coins from the Museum collection which have, in the past, been ascribed to the Fort but the bulk of which are clearly donations and acquisitions which have nothing to do with the site or with Roman Britain in general (the full catalogue is available in the Museum archive). A number of museums, especially those with seaport connections like Wallsend and across the river South Shields, contain similar collections of exotica and special care needs to be exercised by archaeologists in drawing conclusions from items not otherwise found in controlled excavation contexts (Casey 1984). In the circumstances it is impossible to winnow out the items which are genuine finds from the Fort since these will consist of coins which are as common in the areas in which exotic items might have been acquired as the more easily recognized intrusive element. No large-scale distortion of the pattern of coinage on the site is imposed by the adoption of a cautious strategy of exclusion of suspect items. For post-Roman coinage up to 1900 see p210.

In presenting the coins in a graphical form (Fig. 24.01) well-established procedures have been followed the methodology of which has been explained on a number of occasions (Casey 1986). However in the case of Wallsend the very lowest limit of the integrity of the method is reached. The total identifiable coins used in the computation, 215 items (excluding pre-

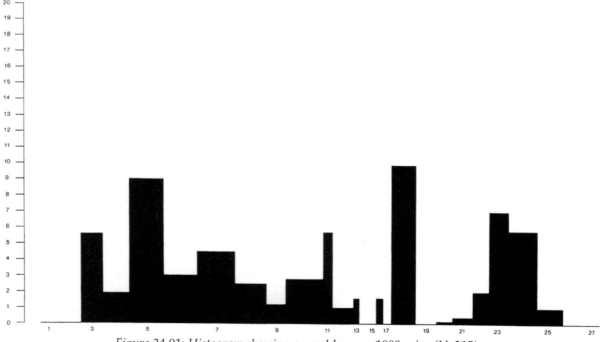

*Figure 24.01: Histogram showing annual loss per 1000 coins (N=215).*

*Table 24.01: Breakdown of illegible coins.*

| Period | No. of coins | % illegible |
|--------|--------------|-------------|
| C1–2   | 40           | 34          |
| C2–3   | 18           | 18          |
| C3–4   | 21           | 42          |

Claudian issues), is barely acceptable for statistical purposes and inherent mathematical problems arise which create visual distortions that may deceive the interpreter of the resulting histogram. The problem resides in the apparently heavy representation of coins in very short reigns often when the reality consists of a single item occurring in the site record. This is further compounded when the item falls into a period when coins are not normally abundant. In the case of Wallsend attention is drawn to the graphical over-representation of the coins of Period 11 (Elagabalus, 218–22), Period 13 (Maximus Thrax, 235–8) and Period 16 (Trajan Decius, 299–51).

To deal with the main features of the coin display, before elaborating on individual aspects, we may note that the overall balance of the coinage is that of the first, second and third centuries as compared to the fourth century which is, in statistical terms, more lightly represented. The weighting of coinage towards the earlier periods is also evident if we consider the contribution of the coins which are too corroded to attribute to individual rulers or periods and which have, consequently, not been used in the computation of the site histogram:

This overall early weighting is normal for sites on, and associated with, Hadrian's Wall. Discussion of the reasons for this has advanced the view that the relative lack of fourth-century material does not necessarily represent a diminution of garrison forces but may equally be the result of payments being made in goods and services to fourth century soldiers under the *annona militaris* system (Casey 1974). A comparison with Housesteads shows that the pattern is repeated. Here a computation of the value of the fourth-century issues, with a due weighting for the effect of the *annona*, gives an exact parallel between the third- and fourth-century coinage ratios at Corbridge, a site which displays a characteristically civilian pattern in these periods and one which a population decline might be discounted (Casey 1974, 50). Late sites in the hinterland of the wall, notably Piercebridge, and the Saxon Shore forts in the south, have better representation of fourth-century coinage, in absolute terms, a component of which is silver issued as part of the imperial donative system. The near absence of fourth-century silver from the Wall (there is a single *siliqua* from Wallsend), might suggest that Wall garrisons did not receive major donatives, the conversion of which, into small denomination currency, would have provided the flow of coin so notably absent from Hadrian's Wall deposits. If this

is so we may have evidence of two classes of *limitanei* possibly to be distinguished as *castellani*, the inferior regiments, and *riparienses*, named from the highly trained river patrol troops on the Rhine/Danube frontier, for the superior. This suggestion is, at the present stage, very speculative.

A notable feature of the Wallsend coin distribution is the relatively low frequency of issues of Period 18 (258–73). This period, which encompasses the *floruit* of the Gallic Empire, saw the collapse of imperial silver currency, with the precious metal content of the double-*denarius* (the so-called *antoninianus*) falling to a low of two percent. This coinage, representing a phase of hyperinflation, is extremely abundant and normally achieves loss rates of up to twenty coins per annum per thousand in site statistical presentations. An element of the coinage of this period consists of copies of the official issues. In reality these copies were almost certainly produced and circulated in Period 19 when reformed coins of Aurelian fail to appear in British contexts, presumably because of an imperial supply problem. If we take this view of events the 45% of the Period 18 coin finds relate to the years 273–86. Whatever the manner in which the material is statistically manipulated the relative dearth of Period 18 deposits indicates a situation which is abnormal and may be ascribed, perhaps, to a diminution in garrison strength. This situation persists in the reign of Carausius (286–93) whose coinage, together with that of Allectus (293–6), is seriously under-represented. [However, the coins from the 1997–8 excavations do not show the low frequency of period 18 issues: see Brickstock 2003, 201].

The pattern for the fourth century, in the light of the points made above, is consistent with other northern sites but with a slightly heavier weight of coinage in Period 24 (348–64) than is normal. The reformed heavy issues of the period, together with copies produced after 354, usually constitute not more than one fifth of the volume of coinage of the preceding Period 23 (330–48). In the case of Wallsend the heavier weight of genuine coins and copies (40% and 60% respectively) is unusual but may represent a freak in the data collection as easily as a real problem of antiquity, but an increase in site activity, or a reinforcement of the garrison cannot be ruled out since it is just at this time that the coins from the hinterland fort of Piercebridge show a re-activation of the fort after several decades of abandonment. There may be a phase of interest in the area by Constantius II after his recovery of the West from Magentius.

The low scores from the coinage of the House of Valentinian (Period 25) and the House of Theodosius (Periods 26 and 27) are normal for the area and a possible explanation for this phenomenon have been offered above. It should not be overlooked that degradation of the site in modern times may have contributed to the pattern since the latest coin issues

*Table 24.02: Condition of the coins*

|            | Unworn | Slightly worn | Worn    | Very worn | Extremely worn |
|------------|--------|---------------|---------|-----------|----------------|
| Vespasian  |        |               | 4 (44)  | 2 (22)    | 3 (33)         |
| Domitian   |        |               |         | 2 (50)    | 2 (50)         |
| Trajan     |        | 6 (24)        | 8 (32)  | 2 (8)     | 9 (36)         |
| Hadrian    |        | 4 (36)        | 5 (45)  | 1 (9)     | 1 (9)          |
| Pius       | 1(5)   | 7 (36)        | 4 (21)  | 7 (36)    |                |
| Aurelius   |        | 1 (13)        | 3 (38)  | 4 (50)    |                |

(Figures in parenthesis are the percentages of coins in each category for each reign)

*Table 24.03: Coins by period*

| Period      | Chronological spread of dated coins                                                                 |
|-------------|-----------------------------------------------------------------------------------------------------|
| 1           | Republic, 69–79, 100, 101–1, 208, 200–c.250                                                          |
| 2           | 81–96, 84–5, 96–8?, 98–103, 98–117, 117–38, 134–8?, 161–2, 229, 249–51, 255–8?, 330–5, 351+         |
| 3           | 96–7, 98–117, 117–38, 119, 134–8, 198–211                                                            |
| 3–4         | 69–79, 98–117, 119, 152–5, 180–92, 193–6, 268–70                                                     |
| 4 or later  | Republic, 69–79, 98–117, 103–17, 270–3, 273+, 321–4, 332–3, 350–1, 367–75                            |
| Mid C3      | 76, 103–11, 121–2, 161–2, 218–22                                                                     |
| Late C3/C4  | 80–1, 121–2, 138–61, 141–61, 153–5, 160–92, 180–3, 190–1, 211, 218–22, 258–73?, 273+, C3/C4          |
| Dereliction | 70–3, 98–117, 125–8, 145–6, c. 164–9, 194+, 202–10, c. 202–35, 219, 346–8                            |

would reside in the uppermost levels of the site. The fact that the fort and its garrison appear in the *Notitia Dignitatum* suggests that the lack of latest period coinage, which is normally lightly represented even in strong coin lists, is partly a function of the generally poor numismatic record for the site in general.

Interpretation of the coinage in terms of occupation patterns and the dating of individual stratigraphic contexts is bedeviled by the problem of residually. This fact of archaeological life operates in two ways in archaeological numismatic contexts. At the simplest level coins, once lost, are subject to random re-disposition as physical adaptations and alterations to the site take place over time. More complex is the residually of coins within the active coin pool of which they formed a component. An analysis of the wear characteristics of the uncorroded coins of the first and second centuries at Wallsend is instructive.

Although wear can represent a long circulation it can equally represent an intensive but short circulation so that the absolute time values cannot be ascribed. However, the overall trend, and the evidence of hoards, points to the circulation of early coinage into the third century, probably up to the late 250s when the early ages denominations lost all value during the inflation of the base silver coinage Period 18.

In terms of the physical condition the categories of wear and tear are distinguished as follows:

| | |
|---|---|
| Unworn | A virtually uncirculated coin |
| Slightly worn | The highest relief attenuated by wear |
| Worn | The relief abraded but all details of legends visible |
| Very worn | Considerable abrasion, legends indistinct |
| Extremely worn | Almost complete erosion of details and legend. |

Since almost no small change currency was supplied to Britain in the third century the prolific earlier issues made up the deficit. A relative decline in third-century deposits cannot, therefore, be interpreted as evidence of attenuated occupation.

## Period dating

In terms of numismatic dating phases the stratified coins from the established phase scheme are as follows:

### Garrison and coinage

The garrison evidence from Wallsend suggests that it was held by a *cohors quingenaria equitata* in the reign of Hadrian, a regular 500-strong infantry cohort in the later second century and a *cohors quingenaria equitata* again in the third century. If we make a few assumptions, perhaps unwarranted, we can achieve an overall view of the economic potential of the site in terms of army pay in the period from *c.*126

to the mid-third century. The assumptions are that the original unit served until the Antonine period, that a gap occurs between *c*.138 and *c*.170, that the replacement unit is a *cohors quingenaria peditata* which serves until the Severan period and that the *Cohors IIII Lingonum Equitata* thereafter constitutes the garrison.

Even if this scheme is defective in detail it permits a broad canvas on which the monetary situation may be painted. Pay and nominal unit strengths in the following calculations are based on the figures established by Watson (Watson 1973).

*Table 24.04: The potential site money pool at Wallsend*

| Unit | | Annual pay | Occupation (years) | Total pay(denarii) |
|---|---|---|---|---|
| Cohors Equitata | 500- | Cavalry 150 Infantry 100 | 13 | 717,600 |
| Cohors Peditata | 550- | Infantry 100 | 23 | 1,104,00 |
| Cohors Equitata | 500- | a Cavalry 225 Infantry 150 b Cavalry 337 Infantry 225 | 57 | 4,841,304 |
| Total site money pool | | | | 6,662,904 |
| Value of coin recovered | | | | 71.8 |
| Percentage of pool recovered | | | | 0.00107 |

(NB. Two calculations are needed to express the pay of the latest garrison necessitated by the two pay rises awarded by Septimius Serverus and by Caracalla. Calculation of the recovered coinage includes pre-Claudian coins and illegible items. Counterfeits are counted as genuine.)

## **Catalogue** (Key at end)

**No　Ruler**

1　L. ANTES GRAGV?　　　　　　　　**Denom:** DEN　　　**Obv** Helmeted head of Roma r., behind ?GRAG

　　**Date:** 136 BC?　**Mint:** RM　**cat:** CRAW238/1
　　**diam:** 17.5 mm　**wt:** 2.4 g　**wear:** VW/VW　　　**Rev** Jupiter in quadriga r. [L. AES below, ROMA in exergue]

2　C. POSTUMI AT or TA　　　　　　**Denom:**　　　　**Obv** Bust of Diana r. etc.

　　**Date:** 74 BC　**Mint:**　　**cat:** CRAW394/1a
　　**diam:** 17.0 mm　**wt:** 2.2 g　**wear:** W/W　　　**Rev** Hound running r., spear beneath. In ex. C. POSTUMI A

3　M. ANTONIUS　　　　　　　　　　**Denom:** DEN　　　**Obv** Ship r. ANT AVG Below, [III VIR RPC]

　　**Date:** 32-31 BC　**Mint:**　　**cat:** CRAW544/24
　　**diam:** 18.0 mm　**wt:** 1.9 g　**wear:** VW/VW　　　**Rev** Three standards LEG X

4　REPUBLICAN　　　　　　　　　　**Denom:** DEN　　　**Obv** -

　　**Date:** C1/2 BC　**Mint:**　　**cat:** -
　　**diam:** 18.5 mm　**wt:** 2.8 g　**wear:** C/C　　　**Rev** -

5　VESPASIAN　　　　　　　　　　　**Denom:** DEN　　　**Obv** -

　　**Date:** 69-79　**Mint:**　　**cat:** -
　　**diam:** 18.5 mm　**wt:** 1.7 g　**wear:** C/C　　　**Rev** -

6　VESPASIAN?　　　　　　　　　　**Denom:** AS　　　**Obv** -

　　**Date:** 69-79　**Mint:**　　**cat:** -
　　**diam:** 26.0 mm　**wt:** 3.7 g　**wear:** C/C　　　**Rev** - [SC]

7　VESPASIAN　　　　　　　　　　　**Denom:** AS　　　**Obv** IMP CAESAR VESPAS[...]

　　**Date:** 69-79　**Mint:**　　**cat:** -
　　**diam:** 27.0 mm　**wt:** 10.7 g　**wear:** C/C　　　**Rev** ?[IVDEA CAPTA] SC

8　VESPASIAN　　　　　　　　　　　**Denom:** DP　　　**Obv** -

　　**Date:** 69-79　**Mint:**　　**cat:** -
　　**diam:** 27.5 mm　**wt:** 7.5 g　**wear:** C/C　　　**Rev** - [SC]

9　VESPASIAN　　　　　　　　　　　**Denom:** SEST　　　**Obv** .....AVG P[M....]

　　**Date:** 69-79　**Mint:**　　**cat:** -
　　**diam:** 33.0 mm　**wt:** 20.3 g　**wear:** VW/EW　　　**Rev** - [SC]

10　VESPASIAN　　　　　　　　　　**Denom:** AS　　　**Obv** -

　　**Date:** 69-79　**Mint:**　　**cat:** -
　　**diam:** 27.5 mm　**wt:** 7.3 g　**wear:** W/W　　　**Rev** - [SC]

| No | SF no | REC no | Context | Description |
|---|---|---|---|---|
| 1 | 2535 | WSC202 | M08:26 | Building 16, clay floor, Period 1 |
| 2 | 2532 | WSC016 | M08:26 | Building 16, clay floor, Period 1 |
| 3 | 156 | WSC212 | P04:02 | North *intervallum* road, third century |
| 4 | 1561 | WSC300 | K15:12 | Building 11, *contubernium* 6, Period 1 |
| 5 | 2526 | WSC070 | M08:26 | Building 16, clay floor, Period 1 |
| 6 | 1121 | WSC199 | E13:01 | Area over Building 9, unstratified |
| 7 | 1583 | WSC125 | K13:11 | Area over *Via quintana*, unstratified |
| 8 | 228 | WSC196 | M04:03 | Building 1, Period 3-4 |
| 9 | 165 | WSC090 | N04:07 | Surface over Building 1, Period 4 or later |
| 10 | 1212 | WSC037 | D12:45 | Building 8, room 2 floor, Period 2-3 |

| No | Ruler | | | | | | |
|---|---|---|---|---|---|---|---|
| 11 | VESPASIAN | | | **Denom:** | AS | **Obv** | - |
| | **Date:** 69-79 | **Mint:** | | **cat:** | - | | |
| | **diam:** 25.0 mm | **wt:** | 4.2 g | **wear:** | VW/EW | **Rev** | - [SC] |
| 12 | VESPASIAN | | | **Denom:** | AS | **Obv** | - |
| | **Date:** 69-79 | **Mint:** | | **cat:** | - | | |
| | **diam:** 28.0 mm | **wt:** | 5.0 g | **wear:** | EW/C | **Rev** | - |
| 13 | VESPASIAN | | | **Denom:** | DEN | **Obv** | [IMP CAES] VESP [AVG PM...] |
| | **Date:** 70-73 | **Mint:** RM | | **cat:** | 37/49 | | |
| | **diam:** 16.0 mm | **wt:** | 1.6 g | **wear:** | W/SW | **Rev** | [TRI POT] Vesta |
| 14 | VESPASIAN | | | **Denom:** | DP | **Obv** | - |
| | **Date:** 71-79 | **Mint:** | | **cat:** | as 475 | | |
| | **diam:** 25.5 mm | **wt:** | 6.3 g | **wear:** | VW/VW | **Rev** | - [SC] |
| 15 | VESPASIAN | | | **Denom:** | AS | **Obv** | [...]VESPASIAN AVG COS IIII |
| | **Date:** 72-73 | **Mint:** | | **cat:** | - | | |
| | **diam:** 27.0 mm | **wt:** | 8.4 g | **wear:** | VW/C | **Rev** | - [SC] |
| 16 | TITUS and DIVUS VESPASIAN | | | **Denom:** | SEST | **Obv** | [IMP T CAES DIVI VESP F AVG PM TRP PP COS VIII SC] |
| | **Date:** 80-81 | **Mint:** | | **cat:** | TITUS 143/4 | | |
| | **diam:** 33.5 mm | **wt:** | 20.4 g | **wear:** | C/C | **Rev** | [DIVO AVG VESP(AS) SPQR] |
| 17 | TITUS under VESPASIAN | | | **Denom:** | AS | **Obv** | [T. CAE]S IMP AVG[F TRP COS VI CENSOR] |
| | **Date:** 77-78 | **Mint:** LG | | **cat:** | Vespasian 786 | | |
| | **diam:** 28.0 mm | **wt:** | 8.0 g | **wear:** | W/W | **Rev** | - SC |
| 18 | DOMITIAN under VESPASIAN | | | **Denom:** | DEN | **Obv** | [CAESAR AVGF] DOMITIANVS |
| | **Date:** 76 | **Mint:** RM | | **cat:** | Vespasian 238 | | |
| | **diam:** 18.5 mm | **wt:** | 1.6 g | **wear:** | W/W | **Rev** | COS IIII Pegasus walking r. |
| 19 | DOMITIAN | | | **Denom:** | SEST | **Obv** | - |
| | **Date:** 81-96 | **Mint:** | | **cat:** | - | | |
| | **diam:** 34.5 mm | **wt:** | 23.1 g | **wear:** | EW/EW | **Rev** | - [SC] |
| 20 | DOMITIAN | | | **Denom:** | DP | **Obv** | - |
| | **Date:** 81-96 | **Mint:** | | **cat:** | - | | |
| | **diam:** 27.0 mm | **wt:** | 8.7 g | **wear:** | C/C | **Rev** | - [SC] |

| No | SF no | REC no | Context | Description |
|---|---|---|---|---|
| 11 | 790 | WSC076 | H04:19 | Rubble over west *praetentura* |
| 12 | 1193 | WSC204 | F11:19 | Road 3 |
| 13 | 2599 | WSC012 | P07:10 | Building 3, abandonment/post-Roman dereliction |
| 14 | | WSC157 | C35:32 | Unstratified |
| 15 | 1336 | WSC086 | F13:16 | Chalet 9, post-Roman |
| 16 | 373 | WSC129 | G04:19 | Rubble in Building 17 |
| 17 | 1864 | WSC200 | L12:14 | Yard south of Building 13, Period 1-2 |
| 18 | 1142 | WSC033 | D11:27 | Building 8, make-up layer for room 1, mid-third century? |
| 19 | 2565 | WSC100 | L09:14 | Area over Building 13 and Alley 7, unstratified |
| 20 | 1553 | WSC150 | E13:23 | Building 9, *contubernium* 1, Period 2 |

| No | Ruler | | | | | | |
|----|-------|--|--|--|--|--|--|
| 21 | DOMITIAN | | | **Denom:** | AS | **Obv** | - |
| | **Date:** 81-96 | **Mint:** | | **cat:** | - | | |
| | **diam:** 27.5 mm | **wt:** | 7.0 g | **wear:** | C/C | **Rev** | - [SC] |

| 22 | DOMITIAN | | | **Denom:** | AS | **Obv** | IMP CAES DOMITIAN AVG GERM COS [X or XI] |
|----|----------|--|--|-----------|----|---------|----|
| | **Date:** 84-85 | **Mint:** RM | | **cat:** | as 250a | | |
| | **diam:** 27.5 mm | **wt:** | 7.0 g | **wear:** | VW/VW | **Rev** | [SALVTI AVGVST(I)] SC Altar |

| 23 | DOMITIAN | | | **Denom:** | AS | **Obv** | IMP CAES DOMIT AVG GERM COS XII CENS PER[PP] |
|----|----------|--|--|-----------|----|---------|----|
| | **Date:** 86 | **Mint:** | | **cat:** | 335 | | |
| | **diam:** 27.0 mm | **wt:** | 7.2 g | **wear:** | VW/EW | **Rev** | MONE[TA AVGVSTI] SC |

| 24 | DOMITIAN | | | **Denom:** | DEN | **Obv** | [IMP CAES DOMIT AVG GERM PM TRP...] |
|----|----------|--|--|-----------|-----|---------|----|
| | **Date:** 90-96 | **Mint:** | | **cat:** | as 148 | | |
| | **diam:** 17.5 mm | **wt:** | 1.0 g | **wear:** | VW/VW | **Rev** | [TRP...COS] XV [...] |

| 25 | FLAVIAN | | | **Denom:** | AS | **Obv** | - |
|----|---------|--|--|-----------|----|---------|----|
| | **Date:** 69-96 | **Mint:** | | **cat:** | - | | |
| | **diam:** 27.0 mm | **wt:** | 9.8 g | **wear:** | C/C | **Rev** | - [SC] |

| 26 | NERVA | | | **Denom:** | DEN | **Obv** | IMP NERVA CAES AVG PM TRP COS [II or III PP] |
|----|-------|--|--|-----------|-----|---------|----|
| | **Date:** 96-97 | **Mint:** | | **cat:** | 9/20 | | |
| | **diam:** 17.5 mm | **wt:** | 2.3 g | **wear:** | UW/UW | **Rev** | [SALVS] PVBLICA |

| 27 | NERVA? | | | **Denom:** | AS | **Obv** | - |
|----|--------|--|--|-----------|----|---------|----|
| | **Date:** 96-98? | **Mint:** | | **cat:** | - | | |
| | **diam:** 27.5 mm | **wt:** | 7.4 g | **wear:** | EW/EW | **Rev** | - [SC] |

| 28 | NERVA | | | **Denom:** | DEN | **Obv** | IMP NERVA CAES [AVG GERM PM TRP II] |
|----|-------|--|--|-----------|-----|---------|----|
| | **Date:** 98 | **Mint:** | | **cat:** | 47 | | |
| | **diam:** 17.0 mm | **wt:** | 1.6 g | **wear:** | W/W | **Rev** | IMP II COS IIII PP |

| 29 | TRAJAN | | | **Denom:** | AUREUS | **Obv** | IMP CAES NERVA TRAIA-N AVG GERM Head laureate |
|----|--------|--|--|-----------|--------|---------|----|
| | **Date:** 100 | **Mint:** RM | | **cat:** | RIC 34 | | |
| | **diam:** 7.3 mm | **wt:** | 19.5 g | **wear:** | SW/SW | **Rev** | PM TRP COS III PP Fortuna standing, holding rudder on prow and cornucopia |

| 30 | TRAJAN | | | **Denom:** | SEST | **Obv** | IMP CAES NERVA TRAIAN AVG G[ERM PM] |
|----|--------|--|--|-----------|------|---------|----|
| | **Date:** 98-103 | **Mint:** | | **cat:** | as 430 | | |
| | **diam:** 34.0 mm | **wt:** | 22.9 g | **wear:** | VW/EW | **Rev** | [TR POT COS IIII] SC Concordia |

| No | SF no | REC no | Context | Description |
|----|-------|--------|---------|-------------|
| 21 | 1430 | WSC194 | H14:30 | Area over Building 9 and Alley 5, unstratified |
| 22 | 2583 | WSC083 | M07:12 | Building 16, wall foundation, Period 1 |
| 23 | 2601 | WSC094 | | Unstratified |
| 24 | 1523 | WSC072 | K15:11 | Area over Building 11, unstratified |
| 25 | 2209 | WSC093 | E09:01 | Area over Road 8, unstratified |
| 26 | 2604 | WSC141 | M18:33 | Building 16, pit, Period 3 |
| 27 | 195 | WSC123 | N05:04 | Building 1, Period 2 demolition |
| 28 | 175 | WSC035 | Q05:02 | Area over Building 1, unstratified |
| 29 | 2525 | WSC044 | M08:26 | Building 16, clay floor, Period 1 |
| 30 | 2397 | WSC097 | E10:74 | Building 8, room 8, Period 2 |

| No | Ruler | | | | | Denom: | | Obv | |
|---|---|---|---|---|---|---|---|---|---|
| 31 | TRAJAN | | | | | Denom: | SEST | Obv | - |
| | Date: | 98-117 | Mint: | | | cat: | - | | |
| | diam: | 34.5 mm | wt: | 19.1 g | | wear: | C/C | Rev | - |
| 32 | TRAJAN | | | | | Denom: | AS | Obv | - |
| | Date: | 98-117 | Mint: | | | cat: | - | | |
| | diam: | 25.0 mm | wt: | 7.9 g | | wear: | C/C | Rev | - [SC] |
| 33 | TRAJAN | | | | | Denom: | SEST | Obv | - |
| | Date: | 98-117 | Mint: | | | cat: | - | | |
| | diam: | 31.0 mm | wt: | 9.0 g | | wear: | C/C | Rev | - [SC] |
| 34 | TRAJAN | | | | | Denom: | SEST | Obv | - |
| | Date: | 98-117 | Mint: | | | cat: | - | | |
| | diam: | 33.5 mm | wt: | 18.7 g | | wear: | EW/C | Rev | - [SC] |
| 35 | TRAJAN | | | | | Denom: | SEST | Obv | - |
| | Date: | 98-117 | Mint: | | | cat: | - | | |
| | diam: | 30.0 mm | wt: | 12.9 g | | wear: | EW/EW | Rev | - [SC] |
| 36 | TRAJAN | | | | | Denom: | SEST | Obv | - |
| | Date: | 98-117 | Mint: | | | cat: | - | | |
| | diam: | 32.5 mm | wt: | 21.5 g | | wear: | C/C | Rev | - |
| 37 | TRAJAN | | | | | Denom: | SEST | Obv | - |
| | Date: | 98-117 | Mint: | | | cat: | - | | |
| | diam: | 33.0 mm | wt: | 17.4 g | | wear: | EW/EW | Rev | - [SC] |
| 38 | TRAJAN | | | | | Denom: | SEST | Obv | - |
| | Date: | 98-117 | Mint: | | | cat: | - | | |
| | diam: | 34.0 mm | wt: | 15.9 g | | wear: | EW/EW | Rev | - [SC] |
| 39 | TRAJAN | | | | | Denom: | AS | Obv | - |
| | Date: | 98-117 | Mint: | | | cat: | - | | |
| | diam: | 26.5 mm | wt: | 7.9 g | | wear: | C/C | Rev | - [SC] |
| 40 | TRAJAN | | | | | Denom: | DP | Obv | - |
| | Date: | 98-117 | Mint: | | | cat: | - | | |
| | diam: | 26.5 mm | wt: | 8.6 g | | wear: | C/C | Rev | - [SC] |

| No | SF no | REC no | Context | Description |
|---|---|---|---|---|
| 31 | 2544 | WSC016 | P07:07 | Building 3, abandonment/post-Roman dereliction |
| 32 | 2182 | WSC082 | F09:01 | Area over Road 8, unstratified |
| 33 | 792 | WSC107 | H14:19 | Rubble over west *praetentura* |
| 34 | 697 | WSC208 | L04:03 | Area over Building 1, unstratified |
| 35 | 2621 | WSC098 | | Unstratified |
| 36 | 1268 | WSC137 | J15:01 | Area over Building 11, unstratified |
| 37 | 2201 | WSC099 | E08:01 | Area over Cistern 1, unstratified |
| 38 | 2250 | WSC096 | F08:10 | Road 8 |
| 39 | 329 | WSC079 | M05:15 | Building 1, officer's quarter's demolition/make-up, Period 3 |
| 40 | 1524 | WSC145 | L15:20 | Building 11, *contubernium* 3/4, Period 2 |

**No  Ruler**

| | | | | | | | |
|---|---|---|---|---|---|---|---|
| 41 | TRAJAN | | | **Denom:** | SEST | **Obv** | - |
| | **Date:** 98-117 | **Mint:** | | **cat:** | - | | |
| | **diam:** 32.0 mm | **wt:** | 20.1 g | **wear:** | C/C | **Rev** | - [SC] |

| | | | | | | | |
|---|---|---|---|---|---|---|---|
| 42 | TRAJAN? | | | **Denom:** | AS | **Obv** | - |
| | **Date:** 98-117 | **Mint:** | | **cat:** | - | | |
| | **diam:** 26.5 mm | **wt:** | 6.6 g | **wear:** | C/C | **Rev** | - |

| | | | | | | | |
|---|---|---|---|---|---|---|---|
| 43 | TRAJAN | | | **Denom:** | DP | **Obv** | - |
| | **Date:** 98-117 | **Mint:** | | **cat:** | - | | |
| | **diam:** 26.0 mm | **wt:** | 6.9 g | **wear:** | C/C | **Rev** | - [SC] |

| | | | | | | | |
|---|---|---|---|---|---|---|---|
| 44 | TRAJAN | | | **Denom:** | AS | **Obv** | - |
| | **Date:** 98-117 | **Mint:** | | **cat:** | - | | |
| | **diam:** 29.0 mm | **wt:** | 15.6 g | **wear:** | ?W/C | **Rev** | - [SC] |

| | | | | | | | |
|---|---|---|---|---|---|---|---|
| 45 | TRAJAN | | | **Denom:** | SEST | **Obv** | [IMP CAES NERVAE] TRAIANO AVG [GER DAC] PM TRP [COSVPP] |
| | **Date:** 101-11 | **Mint:** | | **cat:** | 497 | | |
| | **diam:** 33.0 mm | **wt:** | 29.4 g | **wear:** | ?SW/SW | **Rev** | [SPQR OPTI]MO PRINCIPI SC Aequitas |

| | | | | | | | |
|---|---|---|---|---|---|---|---|
| 46 | TRAJAN | | | **Denom:** | DEN | **Obv** | IMP TRAIANO AVG GER DAC PM TRP |
| | **Date:** 103-11 | **Mint:** | | **cat:** | 118 | | |
| | **diam:** 19.0 mm | **wt:** | 2.8 g | **wear:** | C/SW | **Rev** | COS V PP SPQR OPTIMO PRINCIPI |

| | | | | | | | |
|---|---|---|---|---|---|---|---|
| 47 | TRAJAN | | | **Denom:** | SEST | **Obv** | [IMP CAES NERVAE TRAIAN]O AVG [GER DAC PM TRP COS V PP] |
| | **Date:** 103-11 | **Mint:** | | **cat:** | as 527 | | |
| | **diam:** 33.0 mm | **wt:** | 18.8 g | **wear:** | W/?W | **Rev** | [SPQR OPTIMO PRINCIPI] SC |

| | | | | | | | |
|---|---|---|---|---|---|---|---|
| 48 | TRAJAN | | | **Denom:** | DEN | **Obv** | [IMP TRAIANO] AVG GER DAC [PM TRP COS V PP] |
| | **Date:** 103-11 | **Mint:** | | **cat:** | 172 | | |
| | **diam:** 19.5 mm | **wt:** | 2.2 g | **wear:** | SW/W | **Rev** | SPQR [OPTIMO PRI]NCIPI |

| | | | | | | | |
|---|---|---|---|---|---|---|---|
| 49 | TRAJAN | | | **Denom:** | SEST | **Obv** | [.....]AVG GER DAC[...] |
| | **Date:** 103-11 | **Mint:** | | **cat:** | as 500 | | |
| | **diam:** 34.0 mm | **wt:** | 23.6 g | **wear:** | EW/EW | **Rev** | - [Fortuna SC] |

| | | | | | | | |
|---|---|---|---|---|---|---|---|
| 50 | TRAJAN | | | **Denom:** | DP | **Obv** | [IMP CAES NERVAE TRAIAN]O AVG GER DAC [PM TRP C]OS V PP |
| | **Date:** 103-11 | **Mint:** | | **cat:** | as 481 | | |
| | **diam:** 26.5 mm | **wt:** | 9.7 g | **wear:** | W/C | **Rev** | - SC |

| No | SF no | REC no | Context | Description |
|---|---|---|---|---|
| 41 | 234 | WSC158 | N05:13 | Clay puddling pit, Period 3 demolition |
| 42 | 1329 | WSC084 | J15:01 | Area over Building 11, unstratified |
| 43 | 912 | WSC151 | M05:29 | Building 1, *contubernium* 7 hearth, Period 2 |
| 44 | 754 | WSC193 | L04:03 | Area over Building 1, unstratified |
| 45 | 2178 | WSC132 | J07:20 | Building 15, Period 1 |
| 46 | 1924 | WSC073 | J12:01 | Area over Building 14 and *Via quintana*, unstratified |
| 47 | 1921 | WSC115 | K11:01 | Area over Building 14, unstratified |
| 48 | 1397 | WSC034 | L14:01 | Area over Building 12, unstratified |
| 49 | 1203 | WSC205 | D12:34 | Building 8, latrine fill, mid-third century? |
| 50 | 1541 | WSC152 | K14:01 | Area over Building 12, unstratified |

| No | Ruler | | | | | | | Obv / Rev | |
|----|-------|--|--|--|--|--|--|-----------|---|

**No  Ruler**

**51  TRAJAN**

| | | | | **Denom:** | AS | | **Obv** | [IMP CAES NERVAE] TRAIANO AVG GER DAC PM [TRP COSV PP] |
|--|--|--|--|--|--|--|--|--|

**Date:** 103-11   **Mint:**   **cat:** 561   **Obv** [IMP CAES NERVAE] TRAIANO AVG GER DAC PM [TRP COSV PP]
**diam:** 27.5 mm   **wt:** 10.7 g   **wear:** VW/VW   **Rev** SPQR OPTIMO PRINCIPI SC

**52  TRAJAN**   **Denom:** DP   **Obv** [IMP CAES NERVAE TRAIANO AVG GER DAC PM TRP COSV PP]
**Date:** 103-11   **Mint:**   **cat:** 502
**diam:** 26.5 mm   **wt:** 10.0 g   **wear:** SW/SW   **Rev** SPQR OPTIMO PRINCIPI] SC

**53  TRAJAN**   **Denom:** SEST   **Obv** [IMP CAES NERVAE TRIANO AV]G GER DAC PM T[RP COS V PP]
**Date:** 103-11   **Mint:**   **cat:** 564
**diam:** 32.0 mm   **wt:** 22.5 g   **wear:** VW/EW   **Rev** [SPQR OPTIMO PRINCIPI] SC in exergue

**54  TRAJAN**   **Denom:** DEN   **Obv** [IMP TRAIA]NO [AVG] GER DAC PM TRP
**Date:** 103-11   **Mint:**   **cat:** 96
**diam:** 18.0 mm   **wt:** 2.1 g   **wear:** W/W   **Rev** [COS V PP] SPQR OPTIMO PRINC, DAC CAP in exergue

**55  TRAJAN**   **Denom:** DP   **Obv** [IMP CAES NERVAE TRAIAN]O AVG G[ER....]
**Date:** 103-17   **Mint:**   **cat:** as 462
**diam:** 18.0 mm   **wt:** 10.8 g   **wear:** C/C   **Rev** - [SC]

**56  TRAJAN**   **Denom:** SEST   **Obv** [IMP CAES NER...] TRAIANO [AVG...]
**Date:** 103-17   **Mint:**   **cat:** as 459
**diam:** 34.0 mm   **wt:** 20.0 g   **wear:** C/C   **Rev** - SC

**57  TRAJAN**   **Denom:** DP   **Obv** -
**Date:** 103-17   **Mint:**   **cat:** as 505
**diam:** 25.0 mm   **wt:** 8.3 g   **wear:** ?SW/C   **Rev** ?Pax - [SC]

**58  TRAJAN**   **Denom:** SEST   **Obv** [IMP....TRAI]ANO AVG GER [....]
**Date:** 103-17   **Mint:**   **cat:** as 459 etc.
**diam:** 33.5 mm   **wt:** 21.2 g   **wear:** C/C   **Rev** - [SC]

**59  TRAJAN**   **Denom:** SEST   **Obv** IMPCAES NERVAE TRAIANO AVG GER DAC PM TRP COSVI PP
**Date:** 112-14   **Mint:** RM   **cat:** 610
**diam:** 34.5 mm   **wt:** 24.6 g   **wear:** W/W   **Rev** SPQR OPTIMO PRINCIPI SC, in exergue ARABADQ

**60  TRAJAN**   **Denom:** DP   **Obv** [IMP CAES NERVAE TRAIANO AVG GER DAC PM TRP COS VI PP]
**Date:** 112-14   **Mint:**   **cat:** 626
**diam:** 25.5 mm   **wt:** 8.8 g   **wear:** C/C   **Rev** [FELICITAS AVGVST] SC

| No | SF no | REC no | Context | Description |
|----|-------|--------|---------|-------------|
| 51 | 1729 | WSC117 | L12:01 | Area over Building 13 and *Via quintana*, unstratified |
| 52 | 2324 | WSC147 | G09:30 | Building 7, west granary |
| 53 | 983 | WSC030 | G12:01 | Area over *Via quintana*, unstratified |
| 54 | 960 | WSC025 | E14:01 | Area over Building 10, unstratified |
| 55 | 2332 | WSC156 | F07:03 | *Via principalis*, Period 4 |
| 56 | 1747 | WSC116 | P12:08 | *Intervallum* road drain by Building 13 |
| 57 | 1463 | WSC153 | E14:24 | Building 10, *contubernium* 2, Period 2 |
| 58 | 2246 | WSC041 | E09:18 | Road 8 |
| 59 | 1744 | WSC134 | P11:01 | Area over Building 13, unstratified |
| 60 | | WSC155 | | Unstratified |

**No  Ruler**
61  TRAJAN                                    **Denom:**  SEST              **Obv**  IMPCAESNER
                                                                                    TRAIANOOPTIMOAVGGERDACP
   **Date:**  114-17      **Mint:**           **cat:**    642                       ARTHICOPM[TRPCOSVI]PP
   **diam:**  34.0 mm     **wt:**  22.2 g     **wear:**   W/W               **Rev**  [ARMENIA ET M]ES0POTAMIA [IN
                                                                                    POTESTATEM REDACTAE] SC

62  TRAJAN                                    **Denom:**  SEST              **Obv**  IMPCAES NER TRAIANO
                                                                                    OPTIMO AVGGERPARTHICO
   **Date:**  114-17      **Mint:**           **cat:**    663                       PMTRP COSVIPP
   **diam:**  33.0 mm     **wt:**  20.1 g     **wear:**   SW/SW             **Rev**  PROVIDENTIA AVGVSTI SPQR SC

63  TRAJAN                                    **Denom:**  DEN               **Obv**  IMP CAES NER TRAIAN OPTIM
                                                                                    AVG GERM DAC
   **Date:**  114-17      **Mint:**           **cat:**    332               **Rev**  PARTHICO PM TRP COS VI PP
   **diam:**  18.0 mm     **wt:**  2.6 g      **wear:**   SW/SW                      SPQR

64  TRAJAN                                    **Denom:**  SEST              **Obv**  [IMP CAES(NER) TRAIANO
                                                                                    OPTIMO AVG GERDAC PMTRP
   **Date:**  114-17      **Mint:**           **cat:**    651/2                     COSVIPP]
   **diam:**  33.5 mm     **wt:**  20.1 g     **wear:**   EW/EW             **Rev**  FORT [RED] in exergue,
                                                                                    [SENATVS POPVLVSQVE
                                                                                    ROMANVS] SC

65  TRAJAN/HADRIAN?                           **Denom:**  SEST              **Obv**  -
   **Date:**  c. 98-117   **Mint:**           **cat:**    -
   **diam:**  34.5 mm     **wt:**  17.8 g     **wear:**   C/C               **Rev**  - [SC]

66  HADRIAN                                   **Denom:**  SEST              **Obv**  -
   **Date:**  117-38      **Mint:**           **cat:**    -
   **diam:**  33.0 mm     **wt:**  23.2 g     **wear:**   VW/VW             **Rev**  - [SC]

67  HADRIAN                                   **Denom:**  DEN               **Obv**  [...HADRIANVS...]
   **Date:**  117-38      **Mint:**           **cat:**    as 270
   **diam:**  17.5 mm     **wt:**  1.4 g      **wear:**   SW/SW             **Rev**  ?Salus, seated l.

68  HADRIAN                                   **Denom:**  SEST              **Obv**  -
   **Date:**  117-38      **Mint:**           **cat:**    as 610
   **diam:**  30.0 mm     **wt:**  21.6 g     **wear:**   C/C               **Rev**  - [SC]

69  HADRIAN                                   **Denom:**  AS                **Obv**  [IMP CAESAR TRAIAN(VS)
                                                                                    HADRI]ANVS AVG
   **Date:**  119         **Mint:**           **cat:**    577               **Rev**  [PONT MAX TR POT] COS III SC
   **diam:**  26.5 mm     **wt:**  9.0 g      **wear:**   C/?W

70  HADRIAN                                   **Denom:**  SEST              **Obv**  IMP CAESAR TRAIANVS
                                                                                    HADRIANVS [AVG]
   **Date:**  119         **Mint:**           **cat:**    563b              **Rev**  PONT MAX [TR POT] COS III SC
   **diam:**  34.5 mm     **wt:**  22.3 g     **wear:**   W/W

| No | SF no | REC no | Context | Description |
|----|-------|--------|---------|-------------|
| 61 | 1423 | WSC136 | L14:01 | Area over Building 12, unstratified |
| 62 | 425 | WSC101 | P05:16 | Alley 1, upper levels |
| 63 | 367 | WSC024 | | Unstratified |
| 64 | 1 | WSC127 | Q04:01 | Area over *intervallum* road (Road 4), unstratified |
| 65 | 2358 | WSC110 | F07:03 | *Via principalis*, Period 4 |
| 66 | 27 | WSC089 | M05:05 | Area over Building 2 and Alley 1, unstratified |
| 67 | 924 | WSC074 | M05:28 | Building 1, clay floor, Period 2 |
| 68 | 2378 | WSC111 | E07:11 | Drain in road near Cistern 1, Period 3 |
| 69 | 278 | WSC124 | Q05:05 | Building 2, north-south drain east of east wall, Period 3 |
| 70 | 2602 | WSC046 | Q08:15 | Building 3, officer's quarters, Period 3-4 |

| No | Ruler | | | Denom: | | Obv | |
|----|-------|--|--|--------|--|-----|--|
| 71 | HADRIAN | | | Denom: | DP | Obv | [IMP CAESAR TRAIAN(VS) HADRIANVS AVG PM TRP COS III] |
| | Date: 119-21 | Mint: RM | cat: 605 | | | | |
| | diam: 25.5 mm | wt: 9.3 g | wear: W/W | | | Rev | [VIR]TVTI [AVGVSTI] SC |

| | | | | | | | |
|----|-------|--|--|--------|--|-----|--|
| 72 | HADRIAN | | | Denom: | SEST | Obv | [IMP CAESAR TRAIA]N [HADRIANVS AVG] |
| | Date: 121-22 | Mint: | cat: 612a | | | | |
| | diam: 33.0 mm | wt: 20.2 g | wear: C/W | | | Rev | [PM TRP COS I]II SC |

| | | | | | | | |
|----|-------|--|--|--------|--|-----|--|
| 73 | HADRIAN | | | Denom: | QUAD | Obv | IMP CAES[AR TR]AIAN HADRIANVS AVG |
| | Date: 121-22 | Mint: RM | cat: 623a | | | | |
| | diam: 17.5 mm | wt: 2.6 g | wear: SW/SW | | | Rev | [PM TR]P COS II[I] SC Rostrum tridens, r. |

| | | | | | | | |
|----|-------|--|--|--------|--|-----|--|
| 74 | HADRIAN | | | Denom: | AS | Obv | [HADRI]ANVS AVG[VSTVS] |
| | Date: 125-28 | Mint: RM | cat: 664 | | | | |
| | diam: 27.0 mm | wt: 9.2 g | wear: W/W | | | Rev | Minerva [COS III] SC |

| | | | | | | | |
|----|-------|--|--|--------|--|-----|--|
| 75 | HADRIAN | | | Denom: | SEST | Obv | [HADRIANVS AVG…] |
| | Date: 125-38 | Mint: | cat: as 631 | | | | |
| | diam: 33.0 mm | wt: 21.9 g | wear: SW/C | | | Rev | - [SC] |

| | | | | | | | |
|----|-------|--|--|--------|--|-----|--|
| 76 | HADRIAN | | | Denom: | SEST | Obv | [HADRIA]NVS AVG COS [....] |
| | Date: 134-38 | Mint: RM | cat: as 745 | | | | |
| | diam: 32.0 mm | wt: 21.8 g | wear: ?SW/C | | | Rev | - [SC] |

| | | | | | | | |
|----|-------|--|--|--------|--|-----|--|
| 77 | HADRIAN | | | Denom: | AS | Obv | [HADRIA]NVS AVGVSTVS PP |
| | Date: 134-38 | Mint: RM | cat: 975 | | | | |
| | diam: 27.0 mm | wt: 7.2 g | wear: VW/EW | | | Rev | [COS III] SC |

| | | | | | | | |
|----|-------|--|--|--------|--|-----|--|
| 78 | HADRIAN | | | Denom: | DP | Obv | HADRIANVS AVGVSTVS PP |
| | Date: 134-38? | Mint: | cat: 974 | | | | |
| | diam: 28.5 mm | wt: 10.0 g | wear: SW/?SW | | | Rev | HILARITAS PR COS III SC |

| | | | | | | | |
|----|-------|--|--|--------|--|-----|--|
| 79 | ANTONINUS PIUS | | | Denom: | AS | Obv | - |
| | Date: 138-61 | Mint: | cat: - | | | | |
| | diam: 27.5 mm | wt: 6.8 g | wear: C/C | | | Rev | - [SC] |

| | | | | | | | |
|----|-------|--|--|--------|--|-----|--|
| 80 | ANTONINUS PIUS | | | Denom: | AS | Obv | - |
| | Date: 138-61 | Mint: | cat: | | | | |
| | diam: 25.5 mm | wt: 10.2 g | wear: W/C | | | Rev | - [SC] |

| No | SF no | REC no | Context | Description |
|----|-------|--------|---------|-------------|
| 71 | 1396 | WSC144 | | Unstratified |
| 72 | 2249 | WSC114 | E10:47 | Building O, east wall, late third century |
| 73 | 1206 | WSC048 | D12:34 | Building 8, latrine fill, mid-third century? |
| 74 | 33 | WSC119 | M05:04 | Area over Building 2 and Alley 1, post-Roman dereliction |
| 75 | 1702 | WSC045 | K11:01 | Area over Building 14, unstratified |
| 76 | 2081 | WSC091 | K11:36 | Building 14, crosshall, Period 3 |
| 77 | 75 | WSC047 | P05:02 | Area over Building 1 and Alley 1, unstratified |
| 78 | 430 | WSC195 | N05:25 | Building 1, south wall foundation, Period 2 |
| 79 | 1302 | WSC209 | K14:01 | Area over Building 12, unstratified |
| 80 | 1234 | WSC210 | H14:04 | Area over Building 9 and Alley 5, unstratified |

**No  Ruler**

81  ANTONINUS PIUS                                 **Denom:** AS              **Obv**  -
    **Date:** 138-61      **Mint:**              **cat:** as 519b
    **diam:** 23.5 mm   **wt:** 5.2 g     **wear:** C/C             **Rev**  - [SC]

82  ANTONINUS PIUS                                 **Denom:** AS              **Obv**  -
    **Date:** 138-61      **Mint:**              **cat:** -
    **diam:** 26.0 mm   **wt:** 6.1 g     **wear:** VW/VW         **Rev**  - [SC]

83  ANTONINUS PIUS                                 **Denom:** AS              **Obv**  -
    **Date:** 138-61      **Mint:**              **cat:** -
    **diam:** 25.5 mm   **wt:** 4.1 g     **wear:** C/C             **Rev**  - [SC]

84  ANTONINUS PIUS                                 **Denom:** SEST            **Obv**  -
    **Date:** 138-61      **Mint:**              **cat:** -
    **diam:** 32.5 mm   **wt:** 22.0 g    **wear:** C/C             **Rev**  -

85  ANTONINUS PIUS                                 **Denom:** DEN             **Obv** [IMP T] AEL CAES HADR ANTONINVS
    **Date:** 139          **Mint:** RM          **cat:** 26
    **diam:** 18.5 mm   **wt:** 2.4 g     **wear:** SW/SW         **Rev** AVG PIVS PM TRP COS II

86  ANTONINUS PIUS                                 **Denom:** DP              **Obv** ANTONINVS AVG [PIVS...]
    **Date:** 139-61      **Mint:**              **cat:** as 551
    **diam:** 26.5 mm   **wt:** 9.5 g     **wear:** W/W            **Rev** LIBERT[AS....] SC

87  ANTONINUS PIUS                                 **Denom:** SEST            **Obv** ANTONINVS AVG PI-VS P[P TRP COS III]
    **Date:** 140-44      **Mint:**              **cat:** 597
    **diam:** 32.5 mm   **wt:** 21.3 g    **wear:** ?W/VW          **Rev** [ANNONA AV]G SC

88  ANTONINUS PIUS                                 **Denom:** AS              **Obv** ANTONINVS AVG [PIVS PP TRP COS III]
    **Date:** 140-44      **Mint:** RM          **cat:** 675
    **diam:** 26.5 mm   **wt:** 9.9 g     **wear:** SW/SW         **Rev** [A]N[NONA AVG] SC

89  ANTONINUS PIUS                                 **Denom:** SEST            **Obv** [ANTONINVS A]VG PI[-VS ...]
    **Date:** 140-60      **Mint:**              **cat:** as 610
    **diam:** 33.5 mm   **wt:** 24.2 g    **wear:** C/C             **Rev**  - SC

90  ANTONINUS PIUS                                 **Denom:** SEST            **Obv** ANTONINVS AVG PI-VS [PP T]RP COS IIII
    **Date:** 145-61      **Mint:**              **cat:** 779
    **diam:** 31.0 mm   **wt:** 25.7 g    **wear:** SW/W           **Rev** SC Minerva adv. r.

| No | SF no | REC no | Context | Description |
|----|-------|--------|---------|-------------|
| 81 | 2214 | WSC078 | F09:04 | Area over Road 8, unstratified |
| 82 | 23 | WSC206 | P04:01 | Area over *intervallum* road (Road 4), unstratified |
| 83 | 2243 | WSC077 | E07:04 | Area over Road 1, unstratified |
| 84 | 1178 | WSC108 | G11:10 | Building Row 20, Building R, late third/early fourth century |
| 85 | 1994 | WSC344 | K08:01 | Area over Building AO, unstratified |
| 86 | 1375 | WSC146 | G13:03 | Chalet 9, post-Roman |
| 87 | 1147 | WSC039 | F11:15 | Area over Buildings 7 and 8 and Road 3, unstratified |
| 88 | 1927 | WSC092 | K11:01 | Area over Building 14, unstratified |
| 89 | 1069 | WSC197 | G11:03 | Building BJ, post-Roman |
| 90 | 2226 | WSC011 | L10:05 | Alley 7 |

**No  Ruler**

**91  ANTONINUS PIUS**

| | | | **Denom:** | SEST | **Obv** | ANTONINVS AVG PIVS PP TRP XI[III] |
| **Date:** | 150-51 | **Mint:** | **cat:** | 867 | | |
| **diam:** | 32.5 mm | **wt:** | 19.6 g | **wear:** VW/W | **Rev** | [LIBERALI]TAS, VI on vexillum [COS IIII] SC |

**92  ANTONINUS PIUS**

| | | | **Denom:** | DP | **Obv** | ANTONINVS AVG [PIVS PP TRP XVI..] |
| **Date:** | 152-55 | **Mint:** | **cat:** | as 908 | | |
| **diam:** | 25.5 mm | **wt:** | 10.9 g | **wear:** W/VW | **Rev** | LIBERT[AS COS] IIII SC |

**93  ANTONINUS PIUS**

| | | | **Denom:** | DP | **Obv** | ANTONINVS [AVG PI]-VS PP TRP XVII |
| **Date:** | 153-54 | **Mint:** RM | **cat:** | 920 | | |
| **diam:** | 24.5 mm | **wt:** | 8.4 g | **wear:** SW/SW | **Rev** | L[IBERTAS COS] IIII SC |

**94  ANTONINUS PIUS**

| | | | **Denom:** | SEST | **Obv** | [ANTONINVS AVG PIVS PP TRP XVII or XVIII] |
| **Date:** | 153-55 | **Mint:** RM | **cat:** | 916/928 | | |
| **diam:** | 29.5 mm | **wt:** | 16.4 g | **wear:** VW/VW | **Rev** | [LIBERTAS COS IIII] SC |

**95  ANTONINUS PIUS**

| | | | **Denom:** | DEN | **Obv** | ANTONINVS AVG PIVS PP TRP XVIII |
| **Date:** | 154-55 | **Mint:** RM | **cat:** | 238 | | |
| **diam:** | 17.5 mm | **wt:** | 2.0 g | **wear:** SW/W | **Rev** | COS IIII |

**96  ANTONINUS PIUS**

| | | | **Denom:** | AS | **Obv** | [ANTONINVS AVG PIVS PP TRP XVIII] |
| **Date:** | 154-55 | **Mint:** | **cat:** | 934 | | |
| **diam:** | 25.0 mm | **wt:** | 8.8 g | **wear:** W/W | **Rev** | BRITANN[IA COS IIII] SC |

**97  ANTONINUS PIUS**

| | | | **Denom:** | DP | **Obv** | [ANTONINVS AVG PIVS PP TRP XVIII or XIX] |
| **Date:** | 154-56 | **Mint:** | **cat:** | 933/950 | | |
| **diam:** | 26.5 mm | **wt:** | 7.0 g | **wear:** SW/W | **Rev** | [LIBER]TAS COS [IIII] SC |

**98  FAUSTINA I, POSTH.**

| | | | **Denom:** | DP | **Obv** | DIVA FAVS[TINA] |
| **Date:** | 141-61 | **Mint:** | **cat:** | A. Pius 1163b | | |
| **diam:** | 26.5 mm | **wt:** | 11.7 g | **wear:** VW/VW | **Rev** | AETERNITAS SC |

**99  FAUSTINA I, POSTH.**

| | | | **Denom:** | AS | **Obv** | DIVA FAVSTINA |
| **Date:** | 141-61 | **Mint:** | **cat:** | as A. Pius 1154 | | |
| **diam:** | 26.0 mm | **wt:** | 7.1 g | **wear:** SW/C | **Rev** | - SC |

**100  FAUSTINA I, POSTH.**

| | | | **Denom:** | DP | **Obv** | DIVA [FAVS]TINA |
| **Date:** | 141-61 | **Mint:** | **cat:** | as A. Pius 1164 | | |
| **diam:** | 26.0 mm | **wt:** | 10.5 g | **wear:** SW/W | **Rev** | [AETER]NITAS SC |

| No | SF no | REC no | Context | Description |
|---|---|---|---|---|
| 91 | 1920 | WSC020 | L11:01 | Area over Building 13, unstratified |
| 92 | 438 | WSC029 | G04:10 | Building 17, Period 3-4 |
| 93 | 1122 | WSC023 | F14:24 | Chalet 9, post-Roman |
| 94 | 1465 | WSC095 | D13:06 | Chalet 9, Building W, late third/fourth century |
| 95 | 1356 | WSC036 | K14:03 | Area over Building 12, unstratified |
| 96 | 1629 | WSC085 | N14:01 | Area over Building 12, and *Via quintana*, unstratified |
| 97 | 2597 | WSC148 | P07:09 | Area over Building 3, unstratified |
| 98 | 2491 | WSC015 | L09:14 | Area over Building 13 and Alley 7, unstratified |
| 99 | 1389 | WSC118 | H14:38 | Chalet 9, post-Roman |
| 100 | 1175 | WSC130 | F11:13 | Levelling north of Buildings Q and R, late third/fourth century |

*Segedunum. Volume 2*

| No | Ruler | | | Denom: | | Obv | |
|---|---|---|---|---|---|---|---|

**No  Ruler**

**101  FAUSTINA II [A. PIUS]**

| | | | | Denom: | DP | Obv | [FAVSTINA AVG....] |
|---|---|---|---|---|---|---|---|
| Date: | 145-46 | Mint: | | cat: | as A. Pius 1408 | | |
| diam: | 24.0 mm | wt: | 8.4 g | wear: | W/VW | Rev | ?[VENVS] SC |

**102  MARCUS AURELIUS, CAESAR**

| | | | | Denom: | AS | Obv | [AVRE]LIVS [CAE]SAR [AVG P]II FIL |
|---|---|---|---|---|---|---|---|
| Date: | 145-61 | Mint: | | cat: | as A. Pius 1342 | | |
| diam: | 27.0 mm | wt: | 11.8 g | wear: | UW/UW | Rev | [TR POT...] COS II SC |

**103  MARCUS AURELIUS**

| | | | | Denom: | DEN | Obv | [IMP.]M AVREL ANTO[NINVS AVG] |
|---|---|---|---|---|---|---|---|
| Date: | 161-62 | Mint: | | cat: | as 2 | | |
| diam: | 16.5 mm | wt: | 1.5 g | wear: | SW/W | Rev | CON[CORD AVG TRP XV(I)] in exergue COS III |

**104  MARCUS AURELIUS**

| | | | | Denom: | AS | Obv | IMP CAES M AVREL ANTONINVS AVG |
|---|---|---|---|---|---|---|---|
| Date: | 161-62 | Mint: | | cat: | obv. as 819 | | |
| diam: | 25.5 mm | wt: | 9.5 g | wear: | W/W | Rev | SC inside laurel wreath [type as Hunterian Hadrian 572] |

**105  MARCUS AURELIUS**

| | | | | Denom: | DP | Obv | - |
|---|---|---|---|---|---|---|---|
| Date: | 161-80 | Mint: | | cat: | - | | |
| diam: | 24.0 mm | wt: | 7.6 g | wear: | ?SW/C | Rev | - [SC] |

**106  MARCUS AURELIUS**

| | | | | Denom: | DP | Obv | [M.ANT]ONINVS [AVG...] |
|---|---|---|---|---|---|---|---|
| Date: | 174-80 | Mint: | | cat: | as 1133 | | |
| diam: | 24.5 mm | wt: | 8.0 g | wear: | VW/VW | Rev | [Annona etc.] - [SC] |

**107  FAUSTINA II (M. AURELIUS)**

| | | | | Denom: | AS | Obv | FAVSTINA AVGVSTA |
|---|---|---|---|---|---|---|---|
| Date: | 161-75 | Mint: | | cat: | 1639 M. Aurelius | | |
| diam: | 25.0 mm | wt: | 13.1 g | wear: | W/VW | Rev | FECVNDITAS SC |

**108  FAUSTINA II (M. AURELIUS)**

| | | | | Denom: | SEST | Obv | - |
|---|---|---|---|---|---|---|---|
| Date: | 161-75 | Mint: | | cat: | - | | |
| diam: | 30.0 mm | wt: | 19.5 g | wear: | C/C | Rev | - [SC] |

**109  LUCILLA**

| | | | | Denom: | SEST | Obv | [LVCIL]LA [....] |
|---|---|---|---|---|---|---|---|
| Date: | c. 164-69 | Mint: | | cat: | - | | |
| diam: | 32.0 mm | wt: | 20.5 g | wear: | C/C | Rev | - [SC] |

**110  LUCILLA**

| | | | | Denom: | SEST | Obv | [LVCI]L[LA....] |
|---|---|---|---|---|---|---|---|
| Date: | c. 164-69 | Mint: | | cat: | 1750/1 M. Aurelius | | |
| diam: | 31.5 mm | wt: | 17.3 g | wear: | C/VW | Rev | [IVNO REGINA] SC |

| No | SF no | REC no | Context | Description |
|---|---|---|---|---|
| 101 | 2239 | WSC149 | E08:13 | Rerouted *Via principalis*, Roman/post-Roman |
| 102 | 1585 | WSC038 | J14:05 | Area over Building 12 and Road 9, unstratified |
| 103 | 1204 | WSC224 | G11:17 | Building Row 20, Building R, mid-third century |
| 104 | 2592 | WSC013 | Q08:18 | North-south drain east of Building 3, Period 2 |
| 105 | 2225 | WSC154 | D08:01 | Area over West rampart, unstratified |
| 106 | 1249 | WSC225 | H15:08 | Area over Building 10 and Road 9, unstratified |
| 107 | 1528 | WSC088 | K14:18 | Area over Building 12, unstratified |
| 108 | 30 | WSC065 | M05:04 | Area over Building 12 and Alley 1, unstratified |
| 109 | 2223 | WSC113 | | Unstratified |
| 110 | 1971 | WSC133 | | Unstratified |

| No | Ruler | | | Denom: | | | Obv | |
|---|---|---|---|---|---|---|---|---|
| 111 | LUCILLA | | | Denom: | SEST | | Obv | LVCILLAE AVG ANTO[NINI AVG F] |
| | Date: | c. 164-69 | Mint: | cat: | 1756 M. Aurelius | | Rev | [PIETAS] SC |
| | diam: | 30.5 mm | wt: | 17.8 g | wear: | W/VW | | |
| 112 | LUCILLA | | | Denom: | SEST | | Obv | LVCILLA AVGVSTA |
| | Date: | c. 164-69 | Mint: | cat: | 1740 M. Aurelius | | Rev | HILARITAS SC |
| | diam: | 30.0 mm | wt: | 19.9 g | wear: | W/W | | |
| 113 | COMMODUS | | | Denom: | SEST | | Obv | - |
| | Date: | 180-92 | Mint: | cat: | - | | Rev | - [SC] |
| | diam: | 30.0 mm | wt: | 18.4 g | wear: | C/C | | |
| 114 | COMMODUS | | | Denom: | DEN | | Obv | [M.COM]M ANT P FEL AVG BRIT PP] |
| | Date: | 190-91 | Mint: | cat: | 224 | | Rev | ROM FEL PM TRP XVI COS VI |
| | diam: | 17.5 mm | wt: | 2.3 g | wear: | SW/SW | | |
| 115 | CRISPINA | | | Denom: | AS | | Obv | [CRI]SPIN[A AVGVSTA] |
| | Date: | 180-83 | Mint: | cat: | as 680 Commodus | | Rev | - SC |
| | diam: | 24.0 mm | wt: | 8.9 g | wear: | VW/VW | | |
| 116 | SEPTIMIUS SEVERUS | | | Denom: | DEN | | Obv | L SEPT SEV [PERT..]AVG IM[P II..] |
| | Date: | 194-97 | Mint: | cat: | as 461 | | Rev | [VICTOR AVG] |
| | diam: | 17.0 mm | wt: | 1.6 g | wear: | UW/W | | |
| 117 | SEPTIMIUS SEVERUS | | | Denom: | DEN | | Obv | SEVERVS AVG PART MAX |
| | Date: | 200-01 | Mint: RM | cat: | 167a | | Rev | RESTITVTOR VRBIS |
| | diam: | 18.5 mm | wt: | 2.4 g | wear: | UW/SW | | |
| 118 | SEPTIMIUS SEVERUS | | | Denom: | DEN | | Obv | [SEVE]RVS [PIVS AVG] |
| | Date: | 202-10 | Mint: | cat: | 266 | | Rev | IN[DVLGENTIA] AVGG in exergue: IN CARTH |
| | diam: | 17.0 mm | wt: | 1.0 g | wear: | SW/SW | | |
| 119 | 'SEPTIMIUS SEVERUS' | | | Denom: | DENpl | | Obv | L SEPT SEV[....] |
| | Date: | 194+ | Mint: | cat: | c. as 39 | | Rev | - Virtus |
| | diam: | 16.5 mm | wt: | 2.5 g | wear: | SW/SW | | |
| 120 | 'SEPTIMIUS SEVERUS' | | | Denom: | DENpl | | Obv | - |
| | Date: | 194+ | Mint: | cat: | c. as 58 | | Rev | [.....]COS II P[P] Victory adv. l. |
| | diam: | 16.5 mm | wt: | 1.7 g | wear: | W/SW | | |

| No | SF no | REC no | Context | Description |
|---|---|---|---|---|
| 111 | 1124 | WSC026 | F11:01 | Area over Building 7, unstratified |
| 112 | 2548 | WSC014 | P07:07 | Building 3, abandonment/post-Roman |
| 113 | 774 | WSC160 | H05:13 | Soil and rubble over Building 18 |
| 114 | 825 | WSC342 | J05:15 | Fill of plough furrow |
| 115 | 1606 | WSC087 | D13:71 | Chalet 9, Building W, late third/early fourth century |
| 116 | 2267 | WSC346 | F08:10 | Road 8 |
| 117 | 1069 | WSC159 | G11:03 | Building BJ, post-Roman |
| 118 | 257 | WSC142 | E05:04 | Rubble over west *praetentura* |
| 119 | 2240 | WSC009 | E08:13 | Rerouted *Via principalis,* Roman/post-Roman |
| 120 | 1313 | WSC198 | K15:01 | Area over Building 11, unstratified |

| No | Ruler | | | Denom: | | Obv | |
|---|---|---|---|---|---|---|---|

**No　Ruler**

**121　'SEPTIMIUS SEVERUS'**　　Denom: DENpl　Obv [IMP CAE L SEP SEV PERT] AVG [COS II]

　Date: 194+　Mint:　cat: c. of 380

　diam: 18.5 mm　wt: 2.1 g　wear: UW/UW　Rev [FORT]VNA REDVX

**122　JULIA DOMNA**　　Denom: SEST　Obv [IVL]IA DO-[MNA AVG]

　Date: 193-96　Mint: RM　cat: Severus 843

　diam: 28.5 mm　wt: 17.1 g　wear: W/W　Rev [VESTA] SC

**123　JULIA DOMNA**　　Denom: DEN　Obv IVLIA AVGVSTA

　Date: 196-211　Mint:　cat: 553

　diam: 15.0 mm　wt: 2.4 g　wear: UW/C　Rev FORTVNAE FELICI

**124　CARACALLA**　　Denom: DEN　Obv -

　Date: 198-211　Mint:　cat: -

　diam: 18.0 mm　wt: 1.8 g　wear: SW/C　Rev -

**125　CARACALLA**　　Denom: DEN　Obv ANTONINVS PIVS AVG

　Date: 208　Mint: RM　cat: as 105

　diam: 19.5 mm　wt: 3.2 g　wear: SW/SW　Rev PONTIF TRP [X]I COS III

**126　CARACALLA**　　Denom: DEN　Obv ANTONINVS-PIVS AVG BRIT

　Date: 211　Mint: RM　cat: 191

　diam: 18.5 mm　wt: 2.9 g　wear: UW/UW　Rev PONTIF TRP-XIIII COS III

**127　CARACALLA**　　Denom: DEN　Obv ANTONINVS PIVS AVG GERM

　Date: 215　Mint:　cat: 268?

　diam: 18.5 mm　wt: 1.7 g　wear: UW/SW　Rev PM TRP X[VI]II CO[S IIII PP] ?Pax

**128　CARACALLA/GETA CAESAR**　　Denom: DEN　Obv -

　Date: 198-211　Mint:　cat: -

　diam: 18.0 mm　wt: 1.1 g　wear: C/C　Rev -

**129　ELAGABALUS**　　Denom: DEN　Obv IMP [ANTONINVS AVG]

　Date: 218-22　Mint:　cat: 88/91

　diam: 19.0 mm　wt: 1.7 g　wear: SW/SW　Rev [IN]VICTVS SACERDO[S AVG]

**130　ELAGABALUS**　　Denom: DEN　Obv [IMP ANTO]ININVS PIVS AVG

　Date: 218-22　Mint: RM　cat: 106

　diam: 17.5 mm　wt: 0.6 g　wear: SW/SW　Rev [LIBER]TAS AVG

| No | SF no | REC no | Context | Description |
|---|---|---|---|---|
| 121 | 1522 | WSC139 | L14:-- | Area over Building 12, unstratified |
| 122 | 801 | WSC128 | H05:12 | Rubble over west *praetentura* |
| 123 | 2252 | WSC052 | F08:10 | Road 8 |
| 124 | 264 | WSC203 | M05:11 | Building 2, *contubernium* 5 clay floor, Period 3 or later |
| 125 | 1805 | WSC066 | L12:44 | Building 13, room 4 floor, Period 1 |
| 126 | 2372 | WSC340 | E08:44 | Cistern 1, lower fill, late third century |
| 127 | 2007 | WSC222 | K08:04 | Area over Road 1, unstratified |
| 128 | 2213 | WSC063 | F09:11 | Area over Road 8, unstratified |
| 129 | 1779 | WSC061 | L12:16 | Building 13, west hypocaust backfill, mid-third century |
| 130 | 2364 | WSC211 | E08:27 | Cistern 1, upper fill, late third century |

| No | Ruler | | | | | | | | |
|----|-------|---|---|---|---|---|---|---|---|
| 131 | 'ELAGABALUS' | | | Denom: | DENpl | Obv | IMP ANTO[NINVS P]IVS AVG | | |
| | Date: '219' | Mint: | | cat: | c. of 17 | | | | |
| | diam: 19.5 mm | wt: | 1.9 g | wear: | SW/SW | Rev | PM [TRP II CO]S II PP | | |
| 132 | 'ELAGABALUS' | | | Denom: | DENpl | Obv | [IMP] ANTONINVS PIVS AVG | | |
| | Date: 218+ | Mint: | | cat: | c. of 146 | | | | |
| | diam: 19.5 mm | wt: | 1.8 g | wear: | SW/W | Rev | SVMMVS SACERDOS AVG | | |
| 133 | 'ELAGABALUS' | | | Denom: | DENpl | Obv | [IM]P ANTON[INVS PIVS AVG] | | |
| | Date: 218-22 | Mint: | | cat: | c. of 146 | | | | |
| | diam: 17.5 mm | wt: | 0.8 g | wear: | SW/SW | Rev | [SVMMV]S SACERDOS AVG | | |
| 134 | SEVERUS ALEXANDER | | | Denom: | DEN | Obv | IMP CM AVR SEV [ALEXAND AVG] | | |
| | Date: 222-28 | Mint: | | cat: | 180 | | | | |
| | diam: 19.5 mm | wt: | 1.4 g | wear: | SW/SW | Rev | VICTORIA AVG | | |
| 135 | SEVERUS ALEXANDER | | | Denom: | DEN | Obv | IMP SEV ALE-XAND AVG | | |
| | Date: 229 | Mint: | | cat: | 92 | | | | |
| | diam: 19.0 mm | wt: | 2.1 g | wear: | UW/UW | Rev | PM TRP VIII COS III PP | | |
| 136 | 'SEVERUS ALEXANDER' | | | Denom: | DENpl | Obv | IM[P CM AVR SEV] ALEXAN[D AVG] | | |
| | Date: '227' | Mint: | | cat: | c. of 70 | | | | |
| | diam: 21.0 mm | wt: | 3.7 g | wear: | SW/UW | Rev | [PM TR]P VI COS II PP | | |
| 137 | MAXIMUS under MAXIMINUS I | | | Denom: | SEST | Obv | MAXIMVS CAES [GERM] | | |
| | Date: 236-38 | Mint: | | cat: | 13 | | | | |
| | diam: 28.5 mm | wt: | 16.8 g | wear: | VW/VW | Rev | PRINCIPI IVVENTVTIS SC | | |
| 138 | HERENNIA ETRUSCILLA | | | Denom: | ANT | Obv | HER ETRVSCILLA AVG | | |
| | Date: 249-51 | Mint: | | cat: | Trajan Decius 59b | | | | |
| | diam: 21.0 mm | wt: | 2.0 g | wear: | SW/SW | Rev | PVDICITIA AVG | | |
| 139 | GALLIENUS? | | | Denom: | ANT | Obv | [IMP... GALLIENVS..AVG] | | |
| | Date: 255-58? | Mint: | | cat: | as 119 | | | | |
| | diam: 17.0 mm | wt: | 0.9 g | wear: | C/C | Rev | PM [TRP...COS..] | | |
| 140 | GALLIENUS | | | Denom: | ANT | Obv | [GALLIEN]VS AVG | | |
| | Date: 258-68 | Mint: | | cat: | as 208 | | | | |
| | diam: 18.0 mm | wt: | 1.5 g | wear: | SW/SW | Rev | [IOVI CO]NSERVA | | |

| No | SF no | REC no | Context | Description |
|----|-------|--------|---------|-------------|
| 131 | 882 | WSC143 | K04:04 | Latest surviving *Via praetoria* surface |
| 132 | 2603 | WSC018 | M10:14 | Building 13, robbing |
| 133 | 1265 | WSC138 | J14:03 | Road 9 |
| 134 | 692 | WSC008 | K04:02 | Area over Building 4 and Road 2, unstratified |
| 135 | 2028 | WSC343 | K08:07 | Building AO, Period 2 |
| 136 | 1749 | WSC140 | M12:01 | Area over Building 13, unstratified |
| 137 | 2218 | WSC131 | F09:05 | Area over Road 8, unstratified |
| 138 | 910 | WSC031 | L04:25 | Building 1, demolition material, Period 2 |
| 139 | 2405 | WSC075 | F08:35 | *Via principalis,* Period 2 |
| 140 | 1303 | WSC053 | K13:01 | Area over *Via quintana*, unstratified |

| No | Ruler | | | Denom: | ANT | Obv | [...GALLIENVS...] |
|----|-------|--|--|--------|-----|-----|------------------|
| 141 | GALLIENUS | | | | | | |
| | Date: 258-68 | Mint: | | cat: | - | Rev | - |
| | diam: 17.0 mm | wt: | 1.9 g | wear: | SW/C | | |

| No | Ruler | | | Denom: | ANT | Obv | [GALLIE]NVS AVG |
|----|-------|--|--|--------|-----|-----|------------------|
| 142 | GALLIENUS | | | | | | |
| | Date: 258-68 | Mint: | | cat: | 233 | Rev | LIBERTA[S AVG] |
| | diam: 19.0 mm | wt: | 2.7 g | wear: | SW/SW | | |

| No | Ruler | | | Denom: | ANT | Obv | GALLIENVS AVG for IMP G... |
|----|-------|--|--|--------|-----|-----|------------------|
| 143 | GALLIENUS | | | | | | |
| | Date: 258-68 | Mint: RM | | cat: | 180var. | Rev | DIANAE CONS AVG |
| | diam: 21.5 mm | wt: | 2.9 g | wear: | UW/UW | | |

| No | Ruler | | | Denom: | ANT | Obv | [...GALLIENV]S AVG |
|----|-------|--|--|--------|-----|-----|------------------|
| 144 | GALLIENUS? | | | | | | |
| | Date: 258-68? | Mint: | | cat: | - | Rev | - |
| | diam: 20.0 mm | wt: | 2.1 g | wear: | SW/C | | |

| No | Ruler | | | Denom: | ANT | Obv | [GALLIENVS AVG] |
|----|-------|--|--|--------|-----|-----|------------------|
| 145 | 'GALLIENUS' | | | | | | |
| | Date: 258+ | Mint: | | cat: | c. of 179 | Rev | [DIANAE CONS AVG] |
| | diam: 17.0 mm | wt: | 1.0 g | wear: | C/SW | | |

| No | Ruler | | | Denom: | ANT | Obv | - |
|----|-------|--|--|--------|-----|-----|------------------|
| 146 | 'GALLIENUS' | | | | | | |
| | Date: 260+ | Mint: | | cat: | c. as 193 | Rev | - |
| | diam: 18.5 mm | wt: | 3.3 g | wear: | SW/SW | | |

| No | Ruler | | | Denom: | ANT | Obv | [IMP] CLAVDIVS [PFAVG] |
|----|-------|--|--|--------|-----|-----|------------------|
| 147 | CLAUDIUS II | | | | | | |
| | Date: 268-70 | Mint: ME | | cat: | 171 | Rev | VI[CTORIA A]VG |
| | diam: 17.5 mm | wt: | 3.8 g | wear: | UW/SW | | |

| No | Ruler | | | Denom: | ANT | Obv | [IMP..CLAVDIVS AVG] |
|----|-------|--|--|--------|-----|-----|------------------|
| 148 | CLAUDIUS II | | | | | | |
| | Date: 268-70 | Mint: | | cat: | as 94 | Rev | [PROVIDE]NT[..AVG] |
| | diam: 18.0 mm | wt: | 1.8 g | wear: | SW/SW | | |

| No | Ruler | | | Denom: | ANT | Obv | [IMP(C) CLAV]DIVS A[VG] |
|----|-------|--|--|--------|-----|-----|------------------|
| 149 | CLAUDIUS II | | | | | | |
| | Date: 268-70 | Mint: | | cat: | c. as 62 | Rev | [LI]BLRT [AVG] sic |
| | diam: 18.5 mm | wt: | 1.6 g | wear: | SW/UW | | |

| No | Ruler | | | Denom: | ANT | Obv | [...CLAVDI]VS AVG |
|----|-------|--|--|--------|-----|-----|------------------|
| 150 | CLAUDIUS II? | | | | | | |
| | Date: 268-70 | Mint: | | cat: | - | Rev | - |
| | diam: 17.5 mm | wt: | 1.7 g | wear: | SW/C | | |

| No | SF no | REC no | Context | Description |
|-----|-------|--------|---------|-------------|
| 141 | 1727 | WSC172 | K12:02 | Alley 7 |
| 142 | 1263 | WSC054 | J16:01 | Area over Gate 3 and Road 6, unstratified |
| 143 | 2019 | WSC007 | K08:11 | Building AO |
| 144 | 1723 | WSC170 | K12:02 | Alley 7 |
| 145 | 1221 | WSC027 | C12:05 | Road surface within *Porta quintana* |
| 146 | 2450 | WSC103 | G09:14 | East granary flagged floor |
| 147 | 1530 | WSC345 | K14:03 | Area over Building 12, unstratified |
| 148 | 718 | WSC186 | L03:48 | North gate |
| 149 | 1929 | WSC010 | J11:01 | Area over Building 14, unstratified |
| 150 | 776 | WSC181 | H05:13 | Soil and rubble over Building 18 |

| No | Ruler | | | | | | | | |
|----|-------|---|---|---|---|---|---|---|---|
| 151 | 'P0STUMUS' | | | | Denom: | ANT | | Obv | [IMP]C PO[STVMVS PFAVG] |
| | Date: | 258+ | Mint: | | cat: | c. of 77 | | | |
| | diam: | 19.0 mm | wt: | 1.8 g | wear: | UW/UW | | Rev | [ORIE]NS AVG |
| 152 | VICTORINUS | | | | Denom: | ANT | | Obv | IMPC VICTORINVS PFAVG |
| | Date: | 268-70 | Mint: | | cat: | as 61 | | | |
| | diam: | 18.5 mm | wt: | 2.0 g | wear: | SW/C | | Rev | - |
| 153 | VICTORINUS/TETRICUS I | | | | Denom: | ANT | | Obv | - |
| | Date: | 268-73 | Mint: | | cat: | - | | | |
| | diam: | 18.0 mm | wt: | 1.8 g | wear: | C/C | | Rev | - |
| 154 | 'VICTORINUS/TETRICUS I' | | | | Denom: | ANT | | Obv | - |
| | Date: | 273+ | Mint: | | cat: | c. of - | | | |
| | diam: | 15.0 mm | wt: | 1.6 g | wear: | C/C | | Rev | - |
| 155 | 'VICTORINUS/TETRICUS I' | | | | Denom: | ANT | | Obv | - |
| | Date: | 273+ | Mint: | | cat: | c. as - | | | |
| | diam: | 14.5 mm | wt: | 2.4 g | wear: | SW/NSU | | Rev | - |
| 156 | 'VICTORINUS/TETRICUS I' | | | | Denom: | ANT | | Obv | - |
| | Date: | 273+ | Mint: | | cat: | c. as E676 | | | |
| | diam: | 15.5 mm | wt: | 1.5 g | wear: | W/W | | Rev | [INVICTVS] |
| 157 | 'TETRICUS I' | | | | Denom: | ANT | | Obv | [IMPC TETRICVS PFAVG] |
| | Date: | 273+ | Mint: | | cat: | c. as E779 | | | |
| | diam: | 16.5 mm | wt: | 1.5 g | wear: | SW/SW | | Rev | [SALVS AVGG] |
| 158 | 'TETRICUS I' | | | | Denom: | ANT | | Obv | - |
| | Date: | 273+ | Mint: | | cat: | c. as - | | | |
| | diam: | 13.0 mm | wt: | 0.7 g | wear: | C/C | | Rev | - |
| 159 | TETRICUS II | | | | Denom: | ANT | | Obv | - |
| | Date: | 270-73 | Mint: | | cat: | as E769 | | | |
| | diam: | 17.0 mm | wt: | 1.6 g | wear: | C/C | | Rev | [SPES....] |
| 160 | TETRICUS II | | | | Denom: | ANT | | Obv | - |
| | Date: | 270-73 | Mint: | | cat: | as 254 | | | |
| | diam: | 17.5 mm | wt: | 1.6 g | wear: | UW/UW | | Rev | [PIETAS AV]GG |

| No | SF no | REC no | Context | Description |
|----|-------|--------|---------|-------------|
| 151 | 1051 | WSC180 | D12:11 | *Via quintana* |
| 152 | 2005 | WSC055 | | Unstratified |
| 153 | 1040 | WSC161 | D12:11 | *Via quintana* |
| 154 | 1319 | WSC105 | J16:01 | Area over Gate 3 and Road 6, unstratified |
| 155 | 985 | WSC058 | E12:01 | Area over Building 8 and *Via quintana*, unstratified |
| 156 | 992 | WSC057 | D12:08 | Make-up layer over Building 8, Building N, late third century |
| 157 | 1966 | WSC060 | J10:01 | Area over Building 14, unstratified |
| 158 | 2040 | WSC182 | L09:01 | Area over Building 13 and Alley 7, unstratified |
| 159 | 2369 | WSC197 | | Unstratified |
| 160 | 2021 | WSC104 | K08:12 | *Via principalis*, Period 4 |

| No | Ruler | | | | | | |
|----|-------|--|--|--|--|--|--|
| 161 | TETRICUS II | | | Denom: | ANT | Obv | C PIV ES[V TETRICVS CAES] |
| | Date: 272-73 | Mint: | | cat: | E769 | | |
| | diam: 20.0 mm | wt: | 1.6 g | wear: | SW/SW | Rev | [SPES PVBLICA] |
| 162 | RADIATE | | | Denom: | ANT | Obv | - |
| | Date: 258-68? | Mint: | | cat: | - | | |
| | diam: 18.5 mm | wt: | 0.8 g | wear: | C/C | Rev | - |
| 163 | RADIATE? | | | Denom: | ANT | Obv | - |
| | Date: 258-73? | Mint: | | cat: | - | | |
| | diam: 18.0 mm | wt: | 1.1 g | wear: | C/C | Rev | - |
| 164 | RADIATE? | | | Denom: | ANT | Obv | - |
| | Date: 258-73? | Mint: | | cat: | - | | |
| | diam: 16.0 mm | wt: | 1.3 g | wear: | UW/C | Rev | - |
| 165 | RADIATE COPY | | | Denom: | ANT | Obv | - |
| | Date: 273+ | Mint: | | cat: | c. as - | | |
| | diam: 17.0 mm | wt: | 1.0 g | wear: | C/C | Rev | ..A...RI... |
| 166 | RADIATE COPY | | | Denom: | ANT | Obv | - |
| | Date: 273+ | Mint: | | cat: | c. as - | | |
| | diam: 11.0 mm | wt: | 0.3 g | wear: | SW/SW | Rev | - |
| 167 | RADIATE COPY | | | Denom: | ANT | Obv | - |
| | Date: 273+ | Mint: | | cat: | c. as - | | |
| | diam: 8.0 mm | wt: | 0.3 g | wear: | C/C | Rev | - |
| 168 | RADIATE COPY | | | Denom: | ANT | Obv | - |
| | Date: 273+ | Mint: | | cat: | c. as - | | |
| | diam: 14.5 mm | wt: | 1.6 g | wear: | C/C | Rev | - |
| 169 | RADIATE COPY | | | Denom: | ANT | Obv | - |
| | Date: 273+ | Mint: | | cat: | c. as - | | |
| | diam: 17.0 mm | wt: | 1.2 g | wear: | C/C | Rev | - |
| 170 | RADIATE COPY | | | Denom: | ANT | Obv | - |
| | Date: 273+ | Mint: | | cat: | c. as - | | |
| | diam: 17.5 mm | wt: | 2.0 g | wear: | SW/SW | Rev | - |

| No | SF no | REC no | Context | Description |
|----|-------|--------|---------|-------------|
| 161 | 1712 | WSC032 | K12:01 | Area over Building 14 and *Via quintana*, unstratified |
| 162 | 1090 | WSC183 | G11:06 | Area over Building 7, unstratified |
| 163 | 989 | WSC056 | D12:08 | Make-up layer over Building 8, Building N, late third century |
| 164 | 1395 | WSC184 | L14:01 | Area over Building 12, unstratified |
| 165 | 2278 | WSC059 | F08:10 | Road 8 |
| 166 | 1713 | WSC171 | L12:01 | Area over Building 13 and *Via quintana*, unstratified |
| 167 | 2001 | WSC173 | spoil tip | Unstratified |
| 168 | 2063 | WSC185 | G08:02 | *Via principalis*, Period 4 |
| 169 | 990 | WSC187 | D12:08 | Make-up layer over Building 8, Building N, late third century |
| 170 | 1976 | WSC102 | | Unstratified |

| No | Ruler | | | | | | | | |
|---|---|---|---|---|---|---|---|---|---|
| 171 | CARAUSIUS | | | | **Denom:** | AUREL | **Obv** | [IMP..CARAVSIVS..AVG] | |
| | **Date:** 286-93 | **Mint:** | | | **cat:** | as 118 | | | |
| | **diam:** 21.5 mm | **wt:** | 2.3 g | | **wear:** | C/UW | **Rev** | P[AX AVG] | |
| 172 | DIOCLETIAN | | | | **Denom:** | FOLL | **Obv** | IMPC DIOCLETIANVS PF AVG | |
| | **Date:** c. 301 | **Mint:** TR | | | **cat:** | as 6TR502 | | | |
| | **diam:** 29.0 mm | **wt:** | 6.1 g | | **wear:** | SW/SW | **Rev** | GENIO POPV-LI ROMANI | |
| 173 | MAXIMINUS | | | | **Denom:** | FOLL | **Obv** | IMP MAXIMINVS PFAVG | |
| | **Date:** 310-12 | **Mint:** LN P | | | **cat:** | 6LN209b | | | |
| | **diam:** 22.5 mm | **wt:** | 3.9 g | | **wear:** | SW/SW | **Rev** | GENIO POP ROM | |
| 174 | CONSTANTINE I | | | | **Denom:** | | **Obv** | [CONSTAN]-TINVS AVG | |
| | **Date:** 323-24 | **Mint:** LG P | | | **cat:** | 7LG214 | | | |
| | **diam:** 19.0 mm | **wt:** | 1.6 g | | **wear:** | SW/SW | **Rev** | [SARMATIA-DEVICTA] | |
| 175 | CONSTANTINE I | | | | **Denom:** | | **Obv** | [VRB]S [ROMA] | |
| | **Date:** 330-35 | **Mint:** | | | **cat:** | as 7TR522 | | | |
| | **diam:** 16.5 mm | **wt:** | 1.1 g | | **wear:** | W/SW | **Rev** | Wolf and Twins | |
| 176 | CONSTANTINE I | | | | **Denom:** | | **Obv** | [VRBS] ROMA | |
| | **Date:** 332-33 | **Mint:** TR S | | | **cat:** | 7TR547 | | | |
| | **diam:** 17.5 mm | **wt:** | 2.0 g | | **wear:** | W/SW | **Rev** | Wolf and Twins | |
| 177 | CONSTANTINE I | | | | **Denom:** | | **Obv** | [CONSTAN]-TIN[OPOLIS] | |
| | **Date:** 330-35 | **Mint:** | | | **cat:** | as 7TR523 | | | |
| | **diam:** 18.0 mm | **wt:** | 1.1 g | | **wear:** | SW/SW | **Rev** | Victory on prow | |
| 178 | CONSTANTINE I | | | | **Denom:** | | **Obv** | CONSTANTINOPOLIS | |
| | **Date:** 332-33 | **Mint:** TR S | | | **cat:** | 7TR548 | | | |
| | **diam:** 17.0 mm | **wt:** | 2.0 g | | **wear:** | SW/SW | **Rev** | Victory on prow | |
| 179 | 'CONSTANTINE I' | | | | **Denom:** | | **Obv** | [VRBS] R[OMA] | |
| | **Date:** 341-46 | **Mint:** TR P | | | **cat:** | c. of 7TR522 | | | |
| | **diam:** 15.5 mm | **wt:** | 1.1 g | | **wear:** | C/C | **Rev** | Wolf and Twins | |
| 180 | 'CONSTANTINE I' | | | | **Denom:** | | **Obv** | [CONSTANTINOPOLIS] | |
| | **Date:** 341-46 | **Mint:** | | | **cat:** | c. as 7TR523 | | | |
| | **diam:** 13.5 mm | **wt:** | 1.0 g | | **wear:** | C/C | **Rev** | Victory on prow | |

| No | SF no | REC no | Context | Description |
|---|---|---|---|---|
| 171 | 1815 | WSC214 | K12:02 | Area over Building 14 and Road 3, unstratified |
| 172 | 1256 | WSC357 | J15:03 | Area over Building 11, unstratified |
| 173 | 1386 | WSC028 | J16:01 | Area over Gate 3 and Road 6, unstratified |
| 174 | 593 | WSC218 | H05:01 | Area over Building 5 and Alley 4, unstratified |
| 175 | 2157 | WSC162 | G08:04 | *Via principalis,* Period 2 |
| 176 | 2269 | WSC043 | F08:16 | Area over Road 8, unstratified |
| 177 | 2273 | WSC215 | F08:10 | Road 8 |
| 178 | 1260 | WSC217 | J16:01 | Area over Gate 3 and Road 6, unstratified |
| 179 | 2403 | WSC216 | F08:19 | Building AO, south wall robber trench |
| 180 | 1405 | WSC219 | L14:01 | Area over Building 12, unstratified |

**No  Ruler**

**181  CRISPUS CAESAR**

| | | | **Denom:** | | **Obv** | CRISPVS-NOB CAES |
|---|---|---|---|---|---|---|
| **Date:** | 321 | **Mint:** | LG P | **cat:** | 7LG133 | | |
| **diam:** | 18.0 mm | **wt:** | 3.1 g | **wear:** | UW/UW | **Rev** | BEATA TRANQVILLITAS VO/TIS/XX |

**182  CRISPUS CAESAR**

| | | | **Denom:** | | **Obv** | CRISPVS - [N]O[BILC] |
|---|---|---|---|---|---|---|
| **Date:** | 321-24 | **Mint:** | | **cat:** | 7LN212 | | |
| **diam:** | 18.5 mm | **wt:** | 1.9 g | **wear:** | UW/C | **Rev** | [BEATA TRANQVILLITAS] VOT/IS/XX |

**183  CONSTANTINE II, CAESAR**

| | | | **Denom:** | | **Obv** | CONSTANTINVS IVN NOBC |
|---|---|---|---|---|---|---|
| **Date:** | 323-24 | **Mint:** | | **cat:** | as 7TR434 | | |
| **diam:** | 18.0 mm | **wt:** | 1.6 g | **wear:** | UW/UW | **Rev** | CAESARVM NOSTRORVM VOT/X |

**184  CONSTANTINE II, CAESAR**

| | | | **Denom:** | | **Obv** | CONSTANTINVS IVN NOBC |
|---|---|---|---|---|---|---|
| **Date:** | 326-28 | **Mint:** | | **cat:** | as 7TE157 | | |
| **diam:** | 18.0 mm | **wt:** | 0.9 g | **wear:** | SW/SW | **Rev** | PROVIDEN-TIAE CAESS mm: SM[TSA?] |

**185  CONSTANTINE II, CAESAR**

| | | | **Denom:** | | **Obv** | CONSTANTINVS IVN NOBC |
|---|---|---|---|---|---|---|
| **Date:** | 330-35 | **Mint:** | | **cat:** | as 7TR520 | | |
| **diam:** | 16.5 mm | **wt:** | 1.5 g | **wear:** | SW/SW | **Rev** | GLOR-IA EXERC-ITVS 2 stds |

**186  CONSTANTIUS II, CAESAR**

| | | | **Denom:** | | **Obv** | FL IVL CONSTANTIVS NOBC |
|---|---|---|---|---|---|---|
| **Date:** | 330-35 | **Mint:** | | **cat:** | as 7TR521 | | |
| **diam:** | 16.0 mm | **wt:** | 0.9 g | **wear:** | W/W | **Rev** | GLOR-IA EXERC-ITVS 2 stds |

**187  CONSTANTIUS II, CAESAR**

| | | | **Denom:** | | **Obv** | [FL IVL C]ONSTANTIVS NOBC |
|---|---|---|---|---|---|---|
| **Date:** | 330-35 | **Mint:** | | **cat:** | as 7TR239 | | |
| **diam:** | 16.5 mm | **wt:** | 0.7 g | **wear:** | SW/SW | **Rev** | [GLOR-IA EXERC]-ITVS 2 stds |

**188  CONSTANTIUS II, CAESAR**

| | | | **Denom:** | | **Obv** | FL IVL CONSTANTIVS NOBC |
|---|---|---|---|---|---|---|
| **Date:** | 332-33 | **Mint:** | TR S | **cat:** | 7TR540 | | |
| **diam:** | 16.0 mm | **wt:** | 1.7 g | **wear:** | UW/UW | **Rev** | GLOR-IA EX[ERC-ITVS] 2 stds |

**189  CONSTANTIUS II, CAESAR**

| | | | **Denom:** | | **Obv** | [FL IVL] CONSTANTIVS [NOBC] |
|---|---|---|---|---|---|---|
| **Date:** | 335-37 | **Mint:** | | **cat:** | as 7TR592 | | |
| **diam:** | 16.0 mm | **wt:** | 0.9 g | **wear:** | W/SW | **Rev** | [GLOR-IA E]XERC-ITVS 1 std |

**190  HELENA/THEODORA**

| | | | **Denom:** | | **Obv** | - |
|---|---|---|---|---|---|---|
| **Date:** | 337-41 | **Mint:** | | **cat:** | - | | |
| **diam:** | 14.0 mm | **wt:** | 1.4 g | **wear:** | SW/C | **Rev** | - |

| No | SF no | REC no | Context | Description |
|---|---|---|---|---|
| 181 | 1255 | WSC005 | | Unstratified |
| 182 | 987 | WSC227 | G15:19 | Chalet 10, Building X, Period 4 |
| 183 | 1415 | WSC233 | L14:01 | Area over Building 12, unstratified |
| 184 | 2427 | WSC213 | C08:07 | Midden material west of fort, pit C08:10/D08:71 |
| 185 | 2010 | WSC232 | K07:03 | Area over Building 16 and Road 2, unstratified |
| 186 | 1223 | WSC228 | C12:04 | Road surface in *Porta quintana* |
| 187 | 1042 | WSC229 | E12:11 | Road 3 |
| 188 | 2461 | WSC192 | N08:02 | Building 16, partition, Period 4 |
| 189 | 1970 | WSC207 | L09:01 | Area over Building 13 and Alley 7, unstratified |
| 190 | 1977 | WSC223 | | Unstratified |

**No Ruler**

191 CONSTANS      **Denom:**      **Obv** [CONSTAN]-S PF AVG
**Date:** 346-48    **Mint:**    **cat:** as 8TR185
**diam:** 14.0 mm    **wt:** 0.8 g    **wear:** SW/C      **Rev** [VICTORIAE DDAVGGQNN]

192 CONSTANS      **Denom:**      **Obv** CONSTAN-S PF AVG
**Date:** 346-48    **Mint:** TR    **cat:** 8TR185
**diam:** 14.5 mm    **wt:** 0.8 g    **wear:** SW/W      **Rev** VICTORIAE DDAVGGQNN

193 CONSTANS      **Denom:**      **Obv** CONSTAN-S PF [AVG]
**Date:** 346-48    **Mint:**    **cat:** as 8TR185
**diam:** 14.5 mm    **wt:** 1.1 g    **wear:** SW/W      **Rev** [VICTORIAE DDAVGGQNN]

194 CONSTANS      **Denom:**      **Obv** [DN CONSTANS PFAVG]
**Date:** 346-48    **Mint:**    **cat:** -
**diam:** 14.5 mm    **wt:** 1.1 g    **wear:** SW/C      **Rev** [VICTORIAE DDAVGGQNN]

195 CONSTANS      **Denom:**      **Obv** [CONSTAN]-S PF AVG
**Date:** 346-48    **Mint:** TR P    **cat:** 8TR195
**diam:** 14.5 mm    **wt:** 1.3 g    **wear:** UW/SW      **Rev** [VICTORIAE DDAVGGQNN]

196 CONSTANS      **Denom:**      **Obv** CONSTAN-S PF AVG
**Date:** 346-48    **Mint:** TR    **cat:** 8TR185
**diam:** 15.5 mm    **wt:** 0.9 g    **wear:** SW/SW      **Rev** VICTORIAE DDAVGGQNN

197 CONSTANS      **Denom:**      **Obv** [CONSTAN]-S PFAVG
**Date:** 346-48    **Mint:**    **cat:** as 8TR186
**diam:** 15.5 mm    **wt:** 1.0 g    **wear:** SW/UW      **Rev** [VICTORIAEDD]AVGGQ[NN]

198 CONSTANS      **Denom:**      **Obv** CONSTAN-S PF AVG
**Date:** 346-48    **Mint:** TR S    **cat:** 8TR195
**diam:** 16.0 mm    **wt:** 1.2 g    **wear:** SW/SW      **Rev** VICTORIAE DDAVGGQNN

199 CONSTANS      **Denom:**      **Obv** DN CONSTA-NS PF AVG
**Date:** 348-50    **Mint:** LG    **cat:** 8LG74
**diam:** 23.5 mm    **wt:** 3.9 g    **wear:** SW/SW      **Rev** FEL TEMP [REPARATIO] Galley-phoenix

200 CONSTANS      **Denom:**      **Obv** [DN CONSTA-]NS [PF] AVG
**Date:** 348-50    **Mint:** LG P    **cat:** 8LG86
**diam:** 19.5 mm    **wt:** 2.8 g    **wear:** C/SW      **Rev** [FEL REMP RE]PAR-[AT]IO Hut

| No | SF no | REC no | Context | Description |
|---|---|---|---|---|
| 191 | 2470 | WSC240 | Q08:04 | Area over Building 16, unstratified |
| 192 | 704 | WSC242 | K05:09 | Area over Road 2, unstratified |
| 193 | 998 | WSC239 | D12:11 | *Via quintana* |
| 194 | 1320 | WSC238 | J15:01 | Area over Building 11, unstratified |
| 195 | 1045 | WSC286 | D11:02 | Area over Building 8 and Road 5, unstratified |
| 196 | 598 | WSC241 | L05:03 | Area over Building 2, unstratified |
| 197 | 1726 | WSC237 | K11:01 | Area over Building 14, unstratified |
| 198 | 1114 | WSC287 | F12:01 | Area over *Via quintana*, unstratified |
| 199 | 1044 | WSC163 | D12:11 | *Via quintana* |
| 200 | 1289 | WSC021 | J16:01 | Area over Gate 3 and Road 6, unstratified |

| No | Ruler | | | Denom: | | Obv | |
|----|-------|---|---|--------|---|-----|---|

**No Ruler**

**201 CONSTANTIUS II**
| | | | | **Denom:** | | **Obv** | [CONSTANTI]-VS PF AVG |
| **Date:** 337-40 | **Mint:** LG | **cat:** 8LG22 | | | | | |
| **diam:** 14.0 mm | **wt:** 1.1 g | **wear:** UW/UW | | | | **Rev** | GLORI-A EXER-[CITVS] 1 std |

**202 CONSTANTIUS II**
| | | | | **Denom:** | | **Obv** | DN CONSTAN-TIVS PF AVG |
| **Date:** 353-55 | **Mint:** TR P | **cat:** 8TR359 | | | | | |
| **diam:** 17.0 mm | **wt:** 1.5 g | **wear:** W/C | | | | **Rev** | [FEL TEMP] REPARATIO FH3 |

**203 CONSTANTIUS II**
| | | | | **Denom:** | | **Obv** | DN CONSTAN-TIVS PF AVG |
| **Date:** 353-55 | **Mint:** LG P | **cat:** 8LG190 | | | | | |
| **diam:** 18.0 mm | **wt:** 1.7 g | **wear:** UW/UW | | | | **Rev** | FEL TEMP REPARATIO FH3 |

**204 CONSTANTIUS II**
| | | | | **Denom:** SILIQ | | **Obv** | DN CONSTAN-TIVS PF AVG |
| **Date:** 355-61 | **Mint:** AR S | **cat:** 8AR261/291 | | | | | |
| **diam:** 18.0 mm | **wt:** 1.7 g | **wear:** W/W | | | | **Rev** | VOTIS/XXX/MVLTIS/XXXX |

**205 'CONSTANTIUS II'**
| | | | | **Denom:** | | **Obv** | [DN CONSTANTIVS PFAVG] |
| **Date:** 353+ | **Mint:** | **cat:** c. as 8TR359 | | | | | |
| **diam:** 9.0 mm | **wt:** 0.4 g | **wear:** C/UW | | | | **Rev** | [FEL TEMP REPARATIO] FH3 |

**206 'CONSTANTIUS II'**
| | | | | **Denom:** | | **Obv** | [DN CONSTANTIVS PFAVG] |
| **Date:** 353+ | **Mint:** | **cat:** c. as 8TR359 | | | | | |
| **diam:** 16.0 mm | **wt:** 1.0 g | **wear:** SW/C | | | | **Rev** | [FEL TEMP REPARATIO] FH3 |

**207 'CONSTANTIUS II'**
| | | | | **Denom:** | | **Obv** | [DN CONSTANTIVS] PF AVG |
| **Date:** 353+ | **Mint:** | **cat:** c. as 8TR359 | | | | | |
| **diam:** 16.0 mm | **wt:** 1.7 g | **wear:** W/W | | | | **Rev** | [FEL TEMP RE]PARAT[IO] FH3 |

**208 'CONSTANTIUS II'**
| | | | | **Denom:** | | **Obv** | [DN CONSTAN-]TIVS [PF] AVG |
| **Date:** 353+ | **Mint:** | **cat:** c. as 8TR359 | | | | | |
| **diam:** 15.5 mm | **wt:** 1.4 g | **wear:** C/W | | | | **Rev** | [FEL TEMP REPAR]ATIO FH3 (conceivably intended as FH2) |

**209 'CONSTANTIUS II'**
| | | | | **Denom:** | | **Obv** | [DN CONSTANTIVS PFAVG] |
| **Date:** 353+ | **Mint:** | **cat:** c. as 8TR359 | | | | | |
| **diam:** 8.0 mm | **wt:** 0.2 g | **wear:** UW/UW | | | | **Rev** | [FEL TEMP REPARATIO] FH3 |

**210 'CONSTANTIUS II'**
| | | | | **Denom:** | | **Obv** | [DN CONSTANTIVS PFAVG] |
| **Date:** 353+ | **Mint:** | **cat:** c. as 8TR359 | | | | | |
| **diam:** 8.0 mm | **wt:** 0.2 g | **wear:** SW/W | | | | **Rev** | [FEL TEMP REPARATIO] FH3 |

| No | SF no | REC no | Context | Description |
|-----|-------|--------|---------|-------------|
| 201 | 2045 | WSC042 | | Unstratified |
| 202 | 1967 | WSC234 | J10:01 | Area over Building 14, unstratified |
| 203 | 1374 | WSC004 | G13:03 | Chalet 9, post-Roman |
| 204 | 2190 | WSC017 | F08:01 | Area over Road 8, unstratified |
| 205 | 2001 | WSC174 | spoil tip | Unstratified |
| 206 | 1402 | WSC273 | L15:01 | Area over Building 11, unstratified |
| 207 | 2484 | WSC230 | G11:51 | Drain immediately west of Building 7 |
| 208 | 2020 | WSC188 | K08:11 | Building AO |
| 209 | 2001 | WSC175 | spoil tip | Unstratified |
| 210 | 2001 | WSC176 | spoil tip | Unstratified |

| No | Ruler | | | | | | | |
|----|-------|---|---|---|---|---|---|---|
| 211 | 'CONSTANTIUS II' | | | **Denom:** | | **Obv** | [DN CONSTANTIVS PFAVG] | |
| | **Date:** 353+ | **Mint:** | | **cat:** | c. as 8TR359 | | | |
| | **diam:** 9.5 mm | **wt:** | 0.5 g | **wear:** | SW/?SW | **Rev** | [FEL TEMP REPARATIO] FH3 | |
| 212 | 'CONSTANTIUS II' | | | **Denom:** | | **Obv** | [DN CONSTANTIVS PF AVG] | |
| | **Date:** 353+ | **Mint:** | | **cat:** | c. as 8TR359 | | | |
| | **diam:** 15.5 mm | **wt:** | 1.6 g | **wear:** | C/SW | **Rev** | [FEL TEMP] REPARATIO FH3 | |
| 213 | 'CONSTANTIUS II' | | | **Denom:** | | **Obv** | [DN CONSTANTIVS PFAVG] | |
| | **Date:** 353+ | **Mint:** | | **cat:** | c. as 8TR359 | | | |
| | **diam:** 9.5 mm | **wt:** | 0.4 g | **wear:** | W/W | **Rev** | [FEL TEMP REPARATIO] FH3 | |
| 214 | CONSTANTIUS II/CONSTANS | | | **Denom:** | | **Obv** | [DN FL CONST...AVG] | |
| | **Date:** 337-40 | **Mint:** | RM | **cat:** | as 8RM9 | | | |
| | **diam:** 13.5 mm | **wt:** | 1.0 g | **wear:** | SW/SW | **Rev** | [SECVRITAS REIP] | |
| 215 | CONSTANTIUS II/CONSTANS | | | **Denom:** | | **Obv** | - | |
| | **Date:** 346-48 | **Mint:** | | **cat:** | - | | | |
| | **diam:** 15.0 mm | **wt:** | 1.0 g | **wear:** | C/C | **Rev** | [VICTORIAE DDAVGGQNN] | |
| 216 | CONSTANTIUS II/CONSTANS | | | **Denom:** | | **Obv** | CONSTA[... PF AVG] | |
| | **Date:** 346-48 | **Mint:** | TR S | **cat:** | 8TR183/5 | | | |
| | **diam:** 15.5 mm | **wt:** | 1.2 g | **wear:** | SW/SW | **Rev** | VICTORIAE DDAVGGQNN | |
| 217 | CONSTANTIUS II/CONSTANS | | | **Denom:** | | **Obv** | - | |
| | **Date:** 346-48 | **Mint:** | | **cat:** | - | | | |
| | **diam:** 15.0 mm | **wt:** | 1.3 g | **wear:** | C/SW | **Rev** | [VICTORIAED]D[AVGGQNN] | |
| 218 | HOUSE OF CONSTANTINE | | | **Denom:** | | **Obv** | - | |
| | **Date:** 335-41 | **Mint:** | | **cat:** | as 7TR586 | | | |
| | **diam:** 15.5 mm | **wt:** | 0.9 g | **wear:** | C/C | **Rev** | [GLORIA EXERCITUS]? 1 std | |
| 219 | 'HOUSE OF CONSTANTINE' | | | **Denom:** | | **Obv** | - | |
| | **Date:** 341-46 | **Mint:** | | **cat:** | c. as 7TR518 | | | |
| | **diam:** 14.0 mm | **wt:** | 1.1 g | **wear:** | SW/C | **Rev** | [GLORIA EXERCITUS] 2 stds | |
| 220 | MAGNENTIUS | | | **Denom:** | | **Obv** | IM CAE MAGN-[ENTIVS AVG] | |
| | **Date:** 350-51 | **Mint:** | TR | **cat:** | 8TR264 | | | |
| | **diam:** 21.5 mm | **wt:** | 3.4 g | **wear:** | W/SW | **Rev** | [FELICITAS REIPVBLICE] | |

| No | SF no | REC no | Context | Description |
|----|-------|--------|---------|-------------|
| 211 | 2001 | WSC177 | spoil tip | Unstratified |
| 212 | 977 | WSC281 | D11:01 | Area over Building 8, unstratified |
| 213 | 2001 | WSC178 | spoil tip | Unstratified |
| 214 | 1933 | WSC236 | J12:01 | Area over Building 14 and *Via quintana*, unstratified |
| 215 | 2057 | WSC235 | H08:01 | Area over Building AO, unstratified |
| 216 | 2274 | WSC019 | F08:10 | Road 8 |
| 217 | 1554 | WSC231 | E14:09 | Chalet 10, post-Roman dereliction |
| 218 | 1316 | WSC226 | J16:01 | Area over Gate 3 and Road 6, unstratified |
| 219 | 2199 | WSC303 | F08:01 | Area over Road 8, unstratified |
| 220 | 1683 | WSC022 | N13:01 | Area over *Via quintana*, unstratified |

| No | Ruler | | | | | | | | |
|----|-------|--|--|--|--|--|--|--|--|

**221 MAGNENTIUS**
Date: 350-51    Mint: LG P    Denom:    cat: 8LG112
diam: 21.0 mm    wt: 3.4 g    wear: UW/UW
Obv: DN MAGNEN-TIVS PF AVG
Rev: FELICITAS REIPVBLICE

**222 MAGNENTIUS**
Date: 353    Mint:    Denom:    cat: as 8AM39
diam: 25.0 mm    wt: 5.8 g    wear: ?SW/SW
Obv: [DN MAGNEN]-TIVS PFAVG
Rev: [SALVS DDNN AVG ET CAES]

**223 'MAGNENTIUS'**
Date: 351+    Mint:    Denom:    cat: c. as 8LG123
diam: 16.5 mm    wt: 1.4 g    wear: SW/?SW
Obv: [DN MAGNEN-TIVS PFAVG]
Rev: [VICTORIA]E DDN[N AVG ET CAE]

**224 'MAGNENTIUS'**
Date: 351+    Mint:    Denom:    cat: c. as 8LG126
diam: 15.0 mm    wt: 1.1 g    wear: UW/UW
Obv: DN MAGNEN-TIVS P[F AVG]
Rev: VICTORIA[E DDNN AVG ET CAE] VOT/V/MVLT/X, mm: RS[LG]

**225 'MAGNENTIUS'**
Date: 351+    Mint:    Denom:    cat: c. as 8AM5
diam: 18.0 mm    wt: 3.0 g    wear: UW/UW
Obv: [DN M]ABN[EN-TIVS PFAVG]
Rev: [VICTORIAE] DDNN A[VG ET CAE] VOT/V/MVLT/X

**226 VALENTINIAN I**
Date: 364-75    Mint:    Denom:    cat: as CK525
diam: 18.0 mm    wt: 2.0 g    wear: W/W
Obv: DN VAL[ENT]INI-[ANVS PFAVG]
Rev: SECVRITAS REIPVBLICAE

**227 VALENS**
Date: 364-75    Mint: AR II    Denom:    cat: as CK483
diam: 19.0 mm    wt: 2.0 g    wear: SW/SW
Obv: DN VALEN-S PFAVG
Rev: SECVRITAS REIPVBLICAE

**228 VALENS**
Date: 367-75    Mint: AQ P    Denom:    cat: CK1012
diam: 17.5 mm    wt: 2.0 g    wear: W/W
Obv: DN VALEN-S PF AVG
Rev: [GLORIA RO-]MANORVM

**229 ILLEGIBLE**
Date: C2BC-AD    Mint:    Denom: DEN    cat: -
diam: 16.0 mm    wt: 1.2 g    wear: C/C
Obv: -
Rev: -

**230 ILLEGIBLE**
Date: C1st    Mint:    Denom: AS    cat: -
diam: 26.5 mm    wt: 4.9 g    wear: C/C
Obv: -
Rev: - [SC]

| No | SF no | REC no | Context | Description |
|-----|-------|--------|---------|-------------|
| 221 | 830 | WSC191 | K05:07 | Rubble over west *praetentura* |
| 222 | 1753 | WSC221 | | Unstratified |
| 223 | 1285 | WSC189 | J13:05 | Road 9 drain fill |
| 224 | 2154 | WSC003 | G08:04 | *Via principalis*, Period 2 |
| 225 | 2181 | WSC201 | F08:01 | Area over Road 8, unstratified |
| 226 | 2490 | WSC040 | F08:51 | Building AO, south wall robber trench |
| 227 | 1878 | WSC220 | M13:12 | Building BA, robber trench |
| 228 | 835 | WSC006 | J05:07 | Rubble over west *praetentura* |
| 229 | 2524 | WSC064 | M08:26 | Building 16, clay floor, Period 1 |
| 230 | 2412 | WSC122 | E10:76 | Building 8, room 8, Period 2 |

| No | Ruler | | | | | | | |
|---|---|---|---|---|---|---|---|---|
| 231 | ILLEGIBLE | | | | Denom: | AS | Obv | - |
| | Date: | C1st | Mint: | | cat: | - | | |
| | diam: | 25.5 mm | wt: | 8.0 g | wear: | C/C | Rev | - [SC] |
| 232 | ILLEGIBLE | | | | Denom: | SEST | Obv | - |
| | Date: | c. 69-138 | Mint: | | cat: | - | | |
| | diam: | 34.0 mm | wt: | 21.1 g | wear: | C/C | Rev | - [SC] |
| 233 | ILLEGIBLE | | | | Denom: | DEN | Obv | - |
| | Date: | C1-2nd | Mint: | | cat: | - | | |
| | diam: | 17.5 mm | wt: | 1.8 g | wear: | C/C | Rev | - |
| 234 | ILLEGIBLE | | | | Denom: | AS | Obv | - |
| | Date: | C1/2nd | Mint: | | cat: | - | | |
| | diam: | 27.0 mm | wt: | 8.6 g | wear: | C/C | Rev | - |
| 235 | ILLEGIBLE | | | | Denom: | SEST | Obv | - |
| | Date: | C1/2nd | Mint: | | cat: | - | | |
| | diam: | 30.0 mm | wt: | 15.4 g | wear: | C/C | Rev | - [SC] |
| 236 | ILLEGIBLE FRAGMENT | | | | Denom: | [AE] | Obv | - |
| | Date: | C1/2nd | Mint: | | cat: | - | | |
| | diam: | 14.5 mm | wt: | 0.8 g | wear: | C/C | Rev | - |
| 237 | ILLEGIBLE | | | | Denom: | AS | Obv | - |
| | Date: | C1/2nd | Mint: | | cat: | - | | |
| | diam: | 25.5 mm | wt: | 6.5 g | wear: | C/C | Rev | - [SC] |
| 238 | ILLEGIBLE | | | | Denom: | AS | Obv | - |
| | Date: | C1/2nd | Mint: | | cat: | - | | |
| | diam: | 25.5 mm | wt: | 4.3 g | wear: | C/C | Rev | - [SC] |
| 239 | ILLEGIBLE | | | | Denom: | SEST | Obv | - |
| | Date: | C1/2nd | Mint: | | cat: | - | | |
| | diam: | 30.0 mm | wt: | 12.4 g | wear: | C/C | Rev | - [SC] |
| 240 | ILLEGIBLE | | | | Denom: | AS | Obv | - |
| | Date: | C1/2nd | Mint: | | cat: | - | | |
| | diam: | 24.0 mm | wt: | 5.8 g | wear: | C/C | Rev | - [SC] |

| No | SF no | REC no | Context | Description |
|---|---|---|---|---|
| 231 | 1167 | WSC121 | F11:04 | Rubble east of Building 8 (B3), late third/early fourth century |
| 232 | 2480 | WSC112 | M09:01 | Area over Building 13, unstratified |
| 233 | 2534 | WSC067 | M08:26 | Building 16, clay floor, Period 1 |
| 234 | 1197 | WSC280 | G11:13 | Building Row 20, Building R, late third/early fourth century |
| 235 | 831 | WSC109 | J04:13 | Area over Building 4, unstratified |
| 236 | 2268 | WSC307 | F08:16 | Area over Road 8, unstratified |
| 237 | 1282 | WSC080 | F14:01 | Area over Building 10 and Alley 5, unstratified |
| 238 | 245 | WSC120 | P05:05 | Building 1, south wall, Period 2 |
| 239 | 2367 | WSC306 | E08:44 | Cistern 1, lower fill, late third century |
| 240 | 508 | WSC293 | E04:31 | Alley 3, Period 3 |

| No | Ruler | | | | | | | | |
|----|-------|---|---|---|---|---|---|---|---|
| 241 | ILLEGIBLE | | | | Denom: | DEN | | Obv | - |
| | **Date:** | C1/2nd | **Mint:** | | cat: | - | | | |
| | **diam:** | 16.0 mm | **wt:** | 2.1 g | wear: | C/C | | Rev | - |
| 242 | ILLEGIBLE | | | | Denom: | DEN | | Obv | - |
| | **Date:** | C1/2nd | **Mint:** | | cat: | - | | | |
| | **diam:** | 17.0 mm | **wt:** | 1.1 g | wear: | C/C | | Rev | - |
| 243 | ILLEGIBLE | | | | Denom: | DP | | Obv | - |
| | **Date:** | C1/2nd | **Mint:** | | cat: | - | | | |
| | **diam:** | 25.0 mm | **wt:** | 4.1 g | wear: | C/C | | Rev | - [SC] |
| 244 | ILLEGIBLE FRAGMENTS | | | | Denom: | DEN | | Obv | - |
| | **Date:** | C1/2nd | **Mint:** | | cat: | - | | | |
| | **diam:** | 14.5 mm | **wt:** | 0.5 g | wear: | C/C | | Rev | - |
| 245 | ILLEGIBLE | | | | Denom: | DP/AS | | Obv | - |
| | **Date:** | C1/2nd | **Mint:** | | cat: | - | | | |
| | **diam:** | 27.0 mm | **wt:** | 7.4 g | wear: | C/C | | Rev | - [SC] |
| 246 | ILLEGIBLE | | | | Denom: | AS | | Obv | - |
| | **Date:** | C1/2nd | **Mint:** | | cat: | - | | | |
| | **diam:** | 18.0 mm | **wt:** | 8.3 g | wear: | C/C | | Rev | - [SC] |
| 247 | ILLEGIBLE | | | | Denom: | DEN | | Obv | - |
| | **Date:** | C1/2nd | **Mint:** | | cat: | - | | | |
| | **diam:** | 17.0 mm | **wt:** | 2.4 g | wear: | C/C | | Rev | - |
| 248 | ILLEGIBLE | | | | Denom: | [AE] | | Obv | - |
| | **Date:** | C1/2nd? | **Mint:** | | cat: | - | | | |
| | **diam:** | 20.0 mm | **wt:** | 2.1 g | wear: | C/C | | Rev | - |
| 249 | ILLEGIBLE FRAGMENT | | | | Denom: | DEN | | Obv | .....LT... |
| | **Date:** | C1/3rd | **Mint:** | | cat: | - | | | |
| | **diam:** | 11.0 mm | **wt:** | 0.3 g | wear: | UW/SW | | Rev | .....BL... |
| 250 | ILLEGIBLE | | | | Denom: | DP/AS | | Obv | - |
| | **Date:** | C2nd | **Mint:** | | cat: | - | | | |
| | **diam:** | 27.0 mm | **wt:** | 10.0 g | wear: | C/C | | Rev | - |

| No | SF no | REC no | Context | Description |
|----|-------|--------|---------|-------------|
| 241 | 2537 | WSC071 | M08:26 | Building 16, clay floor, Period 1 |
| 242 | 2528 | WSC068 | M08:26 | Building 16, clay floor, Period 1 |
| 243 | 2453 | WSC285 | L07:01 | Area over Building 16, unstratified |
| 244 | 2538 | WSC302 | M08:26 | Building 16, clay floor, Period 1 |
| 245 | 507 | WSC305 | M04:10 | Building 1, *contubernium* 5 clay floor, Period 2 |
| 246 | 2507 | WSC081 | L08:47 | Building 16, floor, Period 4 |
| 247 | 2497 | WSC069 | Q07:07 | Rubble over East rampart and *intervallum* road |
| 248 | 1736 | WSC304 | L13:15 | Building AZ, Period 4 |
| 249 | 1024 | WSC312 | D12:02 | Rubble over Building 8 and *intervallum* road, late third/early fourth century |
| 250 | 595 | WSC308 | H02:03 | Area over Tower 1, unstratified |

| No | Ruler | | | | | | | |
|---|---|---|---|---|---|---|---|---|
| 251 | ILLEGIBLE FRAGMENT | | | | Denom: | DEN | Obv | - |
| | Date: C2nd | Mint: | | | cat: | - | | |
| | diam: 13.5 mm | wt: | 0.3 g | | wear: | C/C | Rev | - |
| 252 | ILLEGIBLE | | | | Denom: | SEST | Obv | - |
| | Date: C2, late | Mint: | | | cat: | - | | |
| | diam: 31.0 mm | wt: | 14.3 g | | wear: | C/C | Rev | - |
| 253 | ILLEGIBLE | | | | Denom: | | Obv | - |
| | Date: C2/3rd | Mint: | | | cat: | - | | |
| | diam: 17.5 mm | wt: | 1.1 g | | wear: | C/C | Rev | - |
| 254 | ILLEGIBLE | | | | Denom: | [AE] | Obv | - |
| | Date: C2/3rd | Mint: | | | cat: | - | | |
| | diam: 20.0 mm | wt: | 2.7 g | | wear: | C/C | Rev | - |
| 255 | ILLEGIBLE | | | | Denom: | DEN | Obv | - |
| | Date: C2/3rd | Mint: | | | cat: | - | | |
| | diam: 19.0 mm | wt: | 3.2 g | | wear: | C/C | Rev | - |
| 256 | ILLEGIBLE | | | | Denom: | | Obv | - |
| | Date: C2/3rd | Mint: | | | cat: | - | | |
| | diam: 18.5 mm | wt: | 2.0 g | | wear: | C/C | Rev | - |
| 257 | ILLEGIBLE | | | | Denom: | DEN | Obv | - |
| | Date: C2/3rd | Mint: | | | cat: | - | | |
| | diam: 16.5 mm | wt: | 1.7 g | | wear: | C/C | Rev | - |
| 258 | ILLEGIBLE | | | | Denom: | DENpl | Obv | - |
| | Date: c. 200-35 | Mint: | | | cat: | - | | |
| | diam: 19.5 mm | wt: | 0.8 g | | wear: | C/C | Rev | - |
| 259 | ILLEGIBLE | | | | Denom: | DENpl | Obv | - |
| | Date: c. 200-35 | Mint: | | | cat: | - | | |
| | diam: 18.0 mm | wt: | 1.2 g | | wear: | C/C | Rev | - |
| 260 | ILLEGIBLE FRAGMENT | | | | Denom: | DENpl | Obv | - |
| | Date: c. 200-35 | Mint: | | | cat: | c. of - | | |
| | diam: 15.0 mm | wt: | 0.9 g | | wear: | C/C | Rev | - |

| No | SF no | REC no | Context | Description |
|---|---|---|---|---|
| 251 | 2540 | WSC301 | M08:26 | Building 16, clay floor, Period 1 |
| 252 | 1461 | WSC135 | D13:06 | Chalet 9, Building W, late third/fourth century |
| 253 | 1719 | WSC294 | K11:01 | Area over Building 14, unstratified |
| 254 | 1847 | WSC296 | N12:13 | Building 13, dereliction |
| 255 | 1708 | WSC062 | L12:01 | Area over Building 13 and *Via quintana*, unstratified |
| 256 | 1720 | WSC295 | K12:02 | Alley 7 |
| 257 | 1549 | WSC292 | L15:07 | Building 11 |
| 258 | 699 | WSC283 | H02:03 | Area over Tower 1, unstratified |
| 259 | 1567 | WSC277 | H13:01 | Area over Building 9 and *Via quintana*, unstratified |
| 260 | 1224 | WSC278 | H14:02 | Area over Building 9 and Alley 5, unstratified |

| No | Ruler | | | | | | | | |
|---|---|---|---|---|---|---|---|---|---|

**261 ILLEGIBLE**  
**Date:** c. 200-53 **Mint:** **Denom:** ANT?  **Obv** -  
**diam:** 17.0 mm **wt:** 0.6 g **cat:** - **wear:** C/C **Rev** -

**262 ILLEGIBLE [SEVERAN+]**  
**Date:** c. 202-35 **Mint:** **Denom:** DENpl  **Obv** -  
**diam:** 18.5 mm **wt:** 1.4 g **cat:** c. as Severus 261 **wear:** C/UW **Rev** FELIC[ITAS.....]

**263 ILLEGIBLE COPY**  
**Date:** c. 220-35 **Mint:** **Denom:** DENpl  **Obv** -  
**diam:** 18.0 mm **wt:** 1.1 g **cat:** c.of - **wear:** C/C **Rev** -

**264 ILLEGIBLE**  
**Date:** C3/4th **Mint:** **Denom:**  **Obv** -  
**diam:** 14.5 mm **wt:** 0.8 g **cat:** - **wear:** C/C **Rev** -

**265 ILLEGIBLE**  
**Date:** C3/4th **Mint:** **Denom:**  **Obv** -  
**diam:** 14.0 mm **wt:** 0.5 g **cat:** - **wear:** C/C **Rev** -

**266 ILLEGIBLE**  
**Date:** C3/4th **Mint:** **Denom:**  **Obv** -  
**diam:** 11.5 mm **wt:** 0.4 g **cat:** - **wear:** C/C **Rev** -

**267 ILLEGIBLE**  
**Date:** C3/4th **Mint:** **Denom:** [AE]  **Obv** -  
**diam:** 19.0 mm **wt:** 1.8 g **cat:** - **wear:** C/C **Rev** -

**268 ILLEGIBLE COPY**  
**Date:** C3/4th **Mint:** **Denom:**  **Obv** -  
**diam:** 12.0 mm **wt:** 1.2 g **cat:** - **wear:** C/C **Rev** -

**269 ILLEGIBLE**  
**Date:** C3/4th **Mint:** **Denom:** [AE]  **Obv** -  
**diam:** 17.5 mm **wt:** 1.3 g **cat:** - **wear:** C/C **Rev** -

**270 ILLEGIBLE COPY**  
**Date:** C3/4th **Mint:** **Denom:**  **Obv** -  
**diam:** 5.5 mm **wt:** 0.3 g **cat:** c. as - **wear:** C/C **Rev** -

| No | SF no | REC no | Context | Description |
|---|---|---|---|---|
| 261 | 2527 | WSC275 | M08:26 | Building 16, clay floor, Period 1 |
| 262 | 879 | WSC310 | K04:04 | Latest surviving *Via praetoria* surface |
| 263 | 1091 | WSC315 | G11:01 | Area over Building 7, unstratified |
| 264 | 991 | WSC316 | D12:08 | Make-up layer over Building 8, Building N, late third century |
| 265 | 2042 | WSC319 | J08:01 | Area over Building AO, unstratified |
| 266 | 1715 | WSC322 | L12:01 | Area over Building 13 and *Via quintana*, unstratified |
| 267 | 1694 | WSC297 | N14:11 | Area over Building 12 and Road 3, unstratified |
| 268 | 1721 | WSC323 | K12:02 | Alley 7 |
| 269 | 1942 | WSC276 | H12:01 | Area over *Via quintana*, unstratified |
| 270 | 1731 | WSC314 | K12:02 | Alley 7 |

**No Ruler**

271 ILLEGIBLE

| | | | | | Denom: | | **Obv** | - |
|---|---|---|---|---|---|---|---|---|
| **Date:** | C3/4th | **Mint:** | | | cat: | - | | |
| **diam:** | 16.0 mm | **wt:** | 0.8 g | | wear: | C/C | **Rev** | - |

272 ILLEGIBLE

| | | | | | Denom: | | **Obv** | - |
|---|---|---|---|---|---|---|---|---|
| **Date:** | C3/4th | **Mint:** | | | cat: | - | | |
| **diam:** | 15.5 mm | **wt:** | 1.3 g | | wear: | C/C | **Rev** | - |

273 ILLEGIBLE

| | | | | | Denom: | | **Obv** | - |
|---|---|---|---|---|---|---|---|---|
| **Date:** | C3/4th | **Mint:** | | | cat: | - | | |
| **diam:** | 16.0 mm | **wt:** | 1.2 g | | wear: | C/C | **Rev** | - |

274 ILLEGIBLE COPY

| | | | | | Denom: | | **Obv** | - |
|---|---|---|---|---|---|---|---|---|
| **Date:** | C3/4th | **Mint:** | | | cat: | - | | |
| **diam:** | 11.0 mm | **wt:** | 0.5 g | | wear: | C/C | **Rev** | - |

275 ILLEGIBLE

| | | | | | Denom: | | **Obv** | - |
|---|---|---|---|---|---|---|---|---|
| **Date:** | C3/4th | **Mint:** | | | cat: | - | | |
| **diam:** | 16.5 mm | **wt:** | 1.3 g | | wear: | C/C | **Rev** | - |

276 ILLEGIBLE COPY

| | | | | | Denom: | | **Obv** | - |
|---|---|---|---|---|---|---|---|---|
| **Date:** | C3/4th | **Mint:** | | | cat: | - | | |
| **diam:** | 13.0 mm | **wt:** | 1.0 g | | wear: | C/C | **Rev** | - |

277 ILLEGIBLE FRAGMENTS

| | | | | | Denom: | | **Obv** | - |
|---|---|---|---|---|---|---|---|---|
| **Date:** | C3/4th | **Mint:** | | | cat: | - | | |
| **diam:** | 12.0 mm | **wt:** | 0.4 g | | wear: | C/C | **Rev** | - |

278 ILLEGIBLE

| | | | | | Denom: | | **Obv** | - |
|---|---|---|---|---|---|---|---|---|
| **Date:** | C3/4th | **Mint:** | | | cat: | - | | |
| **diam:** | 14.5 mm | **wt:** | 1.1 g | | wear: | C/C | **Rev** | - |

279 ILLEGIBLE

| | | | | | Denom: | | **Obv** | - |
|---|---|---|---|---|---|---|---|---|
| **Date:** | C3/4th | **Mint:** | | | cat: | - | | |
| **diam:** | 17.5 mm | **wt:** | 1.7 g | | wear: | C/C | **Rev** | - |

280 ILLEGIBLE

| | | | | | Denom: | | **Obv** | - |
|---|---|---|---|---|---|---|---|---|
| **Date:** | C3/4th | **Mint:** | | | cat: | - | | |
| **diam:** | 17.5 mm | **wt:** | 1.3 g | | wear: | C/C | **Rev** | - |

| No | SF no | REC no | Context | Description |
|---|---|---|---|---|
| 271 | 594 | WSC289 | H05:01 | Area over Building 5 and Alley 4, unstratified |
| 272 | 184 | WSC290 | F04:01 | Area over Building 5 and Alley 3, unstratified |
| 273 | 997 | WSC281 | D12:11 | *Via quintana* |
| 274 | 999 | WSC291 | D12:11 | *Via quintana* |
| 275 | 1334 | WSC309 | H13:06 | Area over Building 9 and Road 9, unstratified |
| 276 | 655 | WSC284 | M05:01 | Area over Buildings 1 and 2 and Alley 5, unstratified |
| 277 | 1834 | WSC298 | N11:25 | Building 13, courtyard, Period 3-4 |
| 278 | 1733 | WSC313 | K11:01 | Area over Building 14, unstratified |
| 279 | 953 | WSC318 | E10:01 | Area over Building 8, unstratified |
| 280 | 745 | WSC321 | L04:01 | Area over Building 1 and *intervallum* road (Road 4), unstratified |

| No | Ruler | | | | | | | | |
|----|-------|--|--|--|--|--|--|--|--|
| 281 | ILLEGIBLE | | | | Denom: | | | Obv | - |
| | Date: | C3/4th | Mint: | | cat: | - | | | |
| | diam: | 13.0 mm | wt: | 0.5 g | wear: | C/C | | Rev | - |
| 282 | ILLEGIBLE | | | | Denom: | | | Obv | - |
| | Date: | C3/4th? | Mint: | | cat: | - | | | |
| | diam: | 17.5 mm | wt: | 1.7 g | wear: | C/C | | Rev | - |
| 283 | ILLEGIBLE FRAGMENT | | | | Denom: | | | Obv | - |
| | Date: | C3/4th? | Mint: | | cat: | - | | | |
| | diam: | 12.5 mm | wt: | 0.2 g | wear: | C/C | | Rev | - |
| 284 | ILLEGIBLE | | | | Denom: | | | Obv | - |
| | Date: | C3/4th? | Mint: | | cat: | - | | | |
| | diam: | 15.5 mm | wt: | 0.9 g | wear: | C/C | | Rev | - |
| 285 | ILLEGIBLE FRAGMENT | | | | Denom: | [AE] | | Obv | - |
| | Date: | - | Mint: | | cat: | - | | | |
| | diam: | 16.5 mm | wt: | 0.6 g | wear: | C/C | | Rev | - |
| 286 | ILLEGIBLE COPY | | | | Denom: | | | Obv | - |
| | Date: | - | Mint: | | cat: | - | | | |
| | diam: | 11.0 mm | wt: | 0.4 g | wear: | C/C | | Rev | - |
| 287 | ILLEGIBLE | | | | Denom: | | | Obv | - |
| | Date: | - | Mint: | | cat: | - | | | |
| | diam: | 24.0 mm | wt: | 4.0 g | wear: | C/C | | Rev | - |
| 288 | ILLEGIBLE, DISINTEGRATED | | | | Denom: | | | Obv | - |
| | Date: | - | Mint: | | cat: | - | | | |
| | diam: | 0.0 mm | wt: | 0.0 g | wear: | C/C | | Rev | - |

| No | SF no | REC no | Context | Description |
|----|-------|--------|---------|-------------|
| 281 | 1444 | WSC320 | D13:01 | Area over Building 9, unstratified |
| 282 | 1056 | WSC311 | D13:01 | Area over Building 9, unstratified |
| 283 | 1546 | WSC279 | L15:01 | Area over Building 11 and Alley 6, unstratified |
| 284 | 1174 | WSC282 | E12:30 | Road 3 |
| 285 | 639 | WSC299 | J05:03 | Area over Building 5 and Alley 4, unstratified |
| 286 | 1068 | WSC288 | D13:01 | Area over Building 9, unstratified |
| 287 | 370 | WSC317 | G04:15 | Wall tumble over Alley 3 |
| 288 | 2536 | lost | M08:26 | Building 16, clay floor, Period 1 |

**Extra coins found after catalogue was completed**

| No | Ruler | | | | | | | | |
|----|-------|--|--|--|--|--|--|--|--|
| 289 | M. AURELIUS/COMMODUS? | | | **Denom:** | DUP | **Obv** | - |
| | **Date:** 160-92 | **Mint:** RM | | **cat:** | - | | |
| | **diam:** 25.0 mm | **wt:** 7.8 g | | **wear:** | C/C | **Rev** | - [SC] |
| 290 | SEVERUS ALEXANDER | | | **Denom:** | DEN | **Obv** | IMP CM AVR SEV ALEXAND AVG |
| | **Date:** 222-8 | **Mint:** RM | | **cat:** | RIC 127 | | |
| | **diam:** 18.0 mm | **wt:** 1.9 g | | **wear:** | SW/SW | **Rev** | AEQVIT[TAS] AVG |
| 291 | CONSTANTINE | | | **Denom:** | | **Obv** | IMP CON[SATN]-TINVS MAX AVG |
| | **Date:** 319 | **Mint:** TR S | | **cat:** | RIC 7 TR 221 | | |
| | **diam:** 18.0 mm | **wt:** 2.9 g | | **wear:** | SW/SW | **Rev** | VICTORIAE [LAETAE] PRINC PERP [VOT/PR] * / .STR |
| 292 | ILLEGIBLE | | | **Denom:** | DEN | **Obv** | - |
| | **Date:** | **Mint:** | | **cat:** | - | | |
| | **diam:** | **wt:** | | **wear:** | | **Rev** | - |
| 293 | ILLEGIBLE | | | **Denom:** | SEST | **Obv** | - |
| | **Date:** C1/C2 | **Mint:** | | **cat:** | - | | |
| | **diam:** 32mm | **wt:** | | **wear:** | | **Rev** | - |
| 294 | ILLEGIBLE | | | **Denom:** | | **Obv** | - |
| | **Date:** C4? | **Mint:** | | **cat:** | - | | |
| | **diam:** 13mm | **wt:** | | **wear:** | | **Rev** | - |
| 295 | LOST | | | **Denom:** | | **Obv** | - |
| | **Date:** '309-337' | **Mint:** | | **cat:** | - | | |
| | **diam:** | **wt:** | | **wear:** | | **Rev** | - |

| No | SF no | REC no | Context | Description |
|----|-------|--------|---------|-------------|
| 289 | 1889 | WSC126 | N14:22 | Chalet 12, Building AM2, (mid)-late third century |
| 290 | 1899 | WSC1 | M12:61 | Building 13, east hypocaust, Period 4 |
| 291 | - | WSC2 | | Unstratified |
| 292 | 2533 | lost | M08:26 | Building 16, clay floor, Period 1 |
| 293 | 187 | WSC356 | F04:01 | Area over Building 5 and Alley 3, unstratified |
| 294 | - | WSC355 | F08:10 | Road 8 |
| 295 | 2068 | lost | G09:02 | The site records provide the provisional date |

**Key to Catalogue:**

*Denomination* (prefaced by 'denon'):
ANT: *Antoninanus*, DENpl: plated counterfeit *denarius*, AS: As, DP: *Dupondius*, AUREL: 'Aurelianus', FOLL: '*Follis*', DEN: *Denarius*, SEST: *Sestertius*

*Mint*:
AQ: Aquileia, AR: Arles, LG: Lyons, LN: London, RM: Rome, TR: Trier
The mint is followed, where appropriate, by *officina* letter, *e.g.* P, I, or A, denoting Primo, 1st or Alpha, *e.g.* TR, P.

*Catalogue references(s)* (cat):
Catalogue references are to RIC unless otherwise stated:
For abbreviations see page 230

A copy or counterfeit of a particular ruler or issuer is denoted by single quotation marks, *e.g.* 'CLAUDIUS II', and by the use of a lower case 'c' in the catalogue reference, *e.g.* '*c*. of 261' = 'a copy of RIC 261'. The use of the word 'of' indicates that a precise catalogue reference has been obtained; while, for both regular issues and copies, 'as' is used to denote an incompletely catalogued coin.

*Diameter (*diam*)*:
Flan diameter is given in millimetres (mm).

*Weigh (*wt*)*:
Weight is given in grams (g).

*Condition (*wear*)*:
The wear is denoted by the following abbreviations:

| | | |
|---|---|---|
| UW | Unworn | The coin shows virtually no signs of wear. |
| SW | Slightly worn | Some abrasion of the highest relief elements of the coin-type is visible (*e.g.* on the brow of the bust-portrait). |
| W | Worn | Considerable abrasion of the higher relief of the coin. |
| VW | Very worn | Much of the detail is flattened, and the legends are severely abraded. |
| EW | Extremely worn | The type and legend are almost flattened or entirely removed. |
| C | Corroded | The poor state of preservation precludes an assessment of wear. |
| NSU | Not struck up | The coin was badly struck, so that the type would have appeared in only very low relief or not at all: an accurate assessment of wear is therefore impractical. |

These are combined to give both the obverse and reverse, *e.g.* C/SW, UW/UW.

# 25. THE SMALL FINDS

*by L. Allason-Jones*
*with contributions by R. Brickstock, A. T. Croom, W. B. Griffiths,*
*M. Henig, J. Tipper, C. Waddington and R. G. Willis*

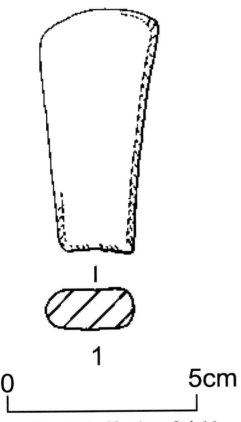

*Figure 25.01: Silver ingot. Scale 1:1.*

## Silver (Fig. 25.01)

1.   Ingot (L:32mm W:12mm, T:5mm). Road 8, F08:10, 2276, WSAR1, 2001.1846
     Wedge-shaped ingot of silver debased with copper. XRF also shows some lead and gold content.

## Copper alloy (Figs 25.02–16)

1.   Bow Brooch (L:58mm W of head:28.5mm W of bow:3mm L of catchplate turnover:24mm). Gate 2, floor, late third century, D08:14, 2326, WSCA102, 2001.1142
     Bow brooch with narrow rectangular-sectioned bow decorated with a row of notches along one edge of a groove. This motif is repeated in a series of six lines down the head. The head is a curved bar covering the spring, with a short projection at the top curving with the spring cross-bar to hold it in position. The ends of the head are bent back and pierced by the iron spring pin. The spring has six coils on one side of the missing pin and six on the other. The tip of the pin survives, corroded into the catchplate turnover. The catchplate has a large openwork motif and a lightly incised line. The foot is decorated with a double groove. Riha 1979, Group 4.2, first century AD.

2.   Brooch fragment (L:22mm W:5.5mm). Alley 1, lowest level, M05:16, 331, WSCA249, 2001.1289
     Fragment of a brooch bow with a central groove and a hollow back.

3.   Trumpet Brooch (L:44mm W across head:13mm). Chalet 9, Building W, Period 4, D13:28, 1558, WSCA42, 2001.1082
     Simple trumpet brooch with a small undecorated head. The decoration at the waist is merely a series of transverse grooves and ribs which are confined to the front of the bow. The lower bow is semicircular in section with two marginal grooves running to the cylindrical foot which is decorated with incised lines. The catchplate and pin are missing. Collingwood and Richmond 1969, Type Riii. See Snape 1993, Group 4.1 for local parallels. Early second century.

4.   Trumpet Brooch (L:56mm W across head:17mm L of catchplate turnover:17mm). Clay puddling pit, Period 3 demolition, N05:15, 213, WSCA32, 2001.1072
     Trumpet brooch in very good condition but lacking its hinged pin. The head is undecorated and the bow moulding, consisting of a plain globular centre between two milled bands each confined between two ribs, is limited to the front of the bow. A third milled band runs around the end of the bow above a globular foot, separated from it by a wide groove and rib. The hinge and stop piece survive as well as the long

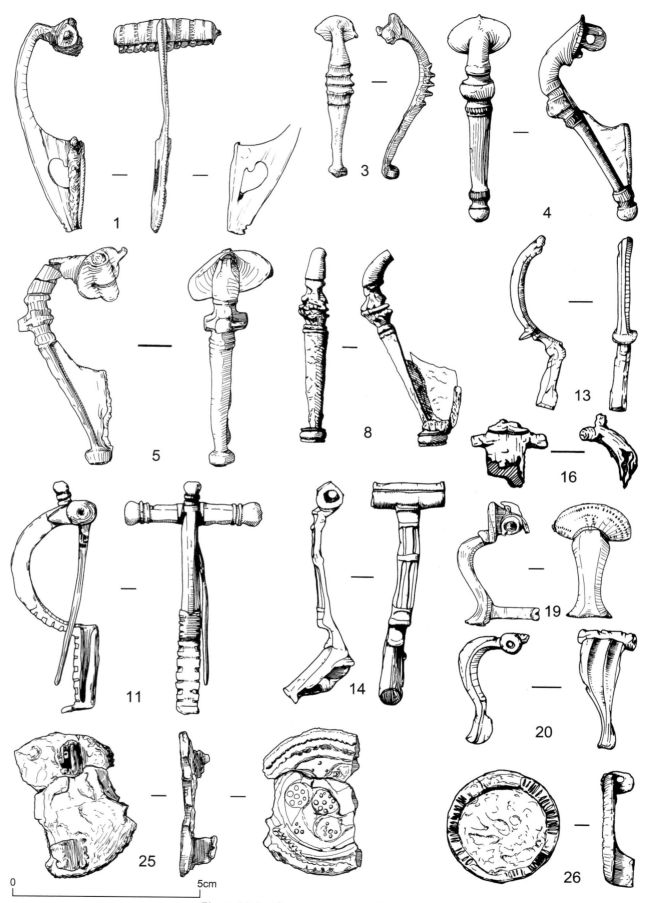

*Figure 25.02: Copper alloy nos 1–26. Scale 1:1.*

catchplate which is decorated with a single incised line down the side of the turnover. Collingwood and Richmond 1969, Type Riii. See Snape 1993, Group 4.1 for local parallels. Early second century.

5. Trumpet Brooch (L:62mm W across head:24mm). Area of Building 9, no details, E13:27, 1467, WSCA33, 2001.1073
Trumpet brooch with a plain head. The acanthus leaf motif encircles the waist but is very stylized with a rib-and-groove motif above and below. The lower bow is triangular in section above a cylindrical foot decorated with two shallow grooves. The catchplate turnover has snapped off and the pin is missing. A tubular hinge runs across the back of the head which also has an unpierced stop piece projecting from the top. Collingwood and Richmond 1969, Type Riii. See Snape 1993, Group 4.1 for local parallels. Early second century.

6. Trumpet Brooch (L:38mm W across waist:7mm). Area over Cistern 1, unstratified, E08:01, 2202, WSCA229, 2001.1269
Fragment of a much corroded trumpet brooch. A band of knobs runs around the waist with the more prominent to the front. Above the waist the bow is circular in section and narrows to the distorted head. Possibly rejected before completion. Collingwood and Richmond 1969, Type Riii. See Snape 1993, Group 4.1 for local parallels. Early second century.

7. Trumpet Brooch (L:55mm). Area of Gate 1 and Road 4, modern, K03:02, 703, WSCA218, 2001.1258
Fragment of a large trumpet brooch missing its head and spring. The lower bow is triangular in section and the disc foot is riveted into position. Snape 1993, Group 4.1.

8. Trumpet Brooch (L:54mm L of catchplate:27mm). Unstratified, WSCA259, 2001.1299
Incomplete trumpet brooch lacking its head. The bow is very thin with a short band of acanthus motifs around the waist between two sets of ribs. The catchplate is very long and wide in comparison with the proportions of the rest of the brooch. The convex face of the lower bow has incised marginal lines and ends in a cylindrical foot with a milled band set between two ribs. The base of the foot has a deep dimple. Collingwood and Richmond 1969, Type Rii. Snape 1993, Group 4.1. Early second century.

9. Trumpet Brooch (L:21mm). Drain west of Building 5, E05:22, 510, WSCA408, 2001.1448
Head of a very corroded trumpet brooch with the spring and part of the head loop surviving. There are no traces of decoration.

10. Trumpet Brooch (L:50mm). Road surface associated with the north-west shacks (B2), dereliction, E05:04, 210, WSCA217, 2001.1257
Triangular-sectioned lower bow of a trumpet brooch. The foot has a milled band between two ribs.

11. Crossbow Brooch (L:62.5mm W across arms:36mm L of pin:51mm L of catchplate:22mm). *Via principalis*, L08:56, 2542, WSCA30, 2001.1070
Complete crossbow (P-shaped) brooch with hexagonal-sectioned arms ending in globular terminals on double disc necks. The central terminal is much smaller than those on the arms, although the same shape. Two flanges emerge from the head to flank the triangular-sectioned bow. The front of the tubular, side entry catchplate is deeply chip-carved along both edges, the motifs carrying on well up the bow. There is a short frontal projection at the foot. The hinged pin is complete and held in place by an iron pin. Keller (1971) Type I; *c.*290–320AD. Cf. Jobst 1975, Taf. 30–2, nos 226–39; Riha 1979, Type 6.5. See Snape 1993, Group 8.8 for local parallels.

12. Crossbow Brooch (approx. surviving L:50mm). Area over Road 3, unstratified, J13:08, 1345, WSCA133, 2001.1173
Incomplete crossbow or P-shaped brooch in two pieces. The bow is narrow and of semicircular section. The terminals are plain knobs. Collingwood and Richmond 1969, Group T. Late third century. See Snape 1993, Group 8.8 for local parallels.

13. Crossbow Brooch (L:47mm W of bow:3mm L of catchplate:18mm). Building 3 abandonment/post-Roman, P07:07, 2493, WSCA121, 2001.1161
Lower part of a crossbow brooch with a very thin facetted bow separated from the foot by a splayed flange. The expanded foot is tubular with a back opening. The surface is heavily tinned. Collingwood and Richmond 1969, Group T. See Snape 1993, Group 8.8 for local parallels. Late third century.

14. Bow Brooch (L:60mm W across head:19mm W across bow:5mm L of catchplate:19mm). Area over Building AO, unstratified, J08:01, 1978, WSCA103, 2001.1143
Bow brooch with a distorted long strip bow decorated with two longitudinal grooves filled with gilding. A wide groove separates the bow from the cylindrical head and another separates the bow from the long, facetted, tubular catchplate with a side entry. The foot has a short frontal projection. The head has a row of shallow dots in front of the spring opening. The spring and pin are both missing. The whole surface is silvered and the gilding applied to the grooves afterwards – the original effect must have been striking. Riha 1979, Group 5.5. Late first–second century.

15. Bow Brooch (W of head:18mm). Area over Building BA, unstratified, M13:01, 1738, WSCA166, 2001.1206
Head of a small bow brooch with a fragment of the hinged pin surviving. The cross bar is tubular with a thick wide projection at the top. What survives of the bow suggests a wide strip with marginal and median ribs.

16. Bow Brooch (L:19mm W of arms:20mm). Building 16, robber trench, M08:29, 2563, WSCA160, 2001.1200
Fragment of a brooch with a wide strip bow and short arms. A crested flange projects from the head. The pin has been hinged from a cylindrical spring-case. Riha 1979, Group 4.4. First century.

17. Bow Brooch (W of head:23mm L of pin:46mm). Area over Building 14, unstratified, K11:01, 1930, WSCA101, 2001.1141
Head of a divided bow brooch with a cylindrical spring-case and a crested flange. Both bows have central ribs and there is a small boss between these ribs. The spring has five coils on one side of the tapering pin and seven on the other. The whole brooch has been heavily gilded. Similar brooches are known from Housesteads (Birley and Charlton 1934, pl. XXIX, no. 3) and Vindolanda (Bidwell 1985, no. 5, 119). See

Snape 1993, Group 8.2 for local parallels. Early third century.

18. Head-stud Brooch (D of stud:7mm). Road surface associated with the north-west shacks (B2), dereliction, E05:04, 240, WSCA286, 2001.1326
Circular ring-and-boss vestigial head-stud from a brooch similar to above with a fragment of the lower bow. No trace of enamel survives.

19. Knee Brooch (L:32mm W across head:20mm). Building 3, abandonment/post-Roman, P7:10, 2578, WSCA31, 2001.1071
Knee brooch with a faceted angular bow which tapers to a flared foot. The head is fan-shaped and separated from the bow by a ridge. A design of stamped squares decorates the head. The hinge tube is cast in one with the brooch and holds a spring of three coils on either side of the pin. The loop of the spring fits into a groove along the hinge tube. This hinge is of copper alloy. The catchplate is a long rectangular bar which projects at right angles from the foot and is hooked at the end. This is an example of the knee brooch which was common on the German *limes* in the late second century. Cf. Vindolanda: Bidwell 1985, fig. 39, no. 8. See also Almgren 1923, nos 246–7; Böhme 1972, Type 19–20; Ettlinger 1973, Type 53; Jobst 1975, Type 13; Riha 1979, Type 3.12. See Snape 1993, Group 5.1 for local parallels.

20. Knee Brooch (L:31mm W across head:15.5mm). Building 2, post-Roman dereliction, P05:03, 194, WSCA151, 2001.1191
Developed knee brooch with a tubular head. The sharply tapering bow is decorated with three deep channels between high ridges. The pin spring and catchplate are missing. See Snape 1993, Group 5.1 for local parallels.

21. Knee Brooch (L:30mm W across head:19mm). Area over *intervallum* road (Road 5), unstratified, E04:01, 18, WSCA75, 2001.1115
Distorted knee brooch with a tubular head and a narrow bow leading to a well splayed foot. The pin and spring are missing and the long catchplate is lacking its hooked end. Although knee brooches are known in the north of England (see Snape 1993, Group 5.1), those with tubular heads would appear to have been less popular than the fan-head type as above. Late second century.

22. Knee Brooch (L:24mm). Area over Building 9, unstratified, E13:01, 1118, WSCA201, 2001.1241
Small knee brooch lacking foot plate, spring and pin.

23. Knee Brooch (L:14mm). Area over Building 12 and Road 9, unstratified, J14:01, 1344, WSCA409, 2001.1449
Small fragment of the bow and flange of a knee brooch.

24. Knee Brooch (W:5mm). Area over Building 9, unstratified, E13:01, 1136, WSCA410, 2001.1450
Fragment of the bow of a knee brooch.

25. Disc Brooch (D:40mm). Area over Building 12 and Alley 6, unstratified, L15:01, 1287, WSCA47, 2001.1087
Large copper alloy disc brooch with a silver repoussé plate attached to the face by lead-tin alloy. The plate is damaged but appears to display the typical triskele design with groups of raised dots confined within a double pellet border. The pin is missing. This type of plate brooch is common throughout Britain but was

particularly popular in the north of Britain from the mid first century AD. See Allason-Jones and Miket 1984, no. 3.148 for local parallels.

26. Disc Brooch (D:30mm L of catchplate:9mm). Building 16, hearth, Period 1?, K07:21, 2041, WSCA169, 2001.1209
Disc brooch of copper alloy with a silver repoussé plate attached to the face by lead-tin alloy. All that remains of the plate is the pelleted border. Part of the catchplate and double-lugged hinge survive.

27. Disc Brooch (D:24mm). Building 2, *contubernium* 5, Period 3 or later, M05:11, 273, WSCA411, 2001.1451
Several fragments of a gilded silver disc still attached to the copper alloy backing plate of a disc brooch by lead-tin alloy. The disc has a repoussé design showing a pelleted border although the central design is unclear.

28. Disc Brooch (D:26mm). Area over Building AM, unstratified, N14:01, 1641, WSCA41, 2001.1081
Circular disc brooch with a concentric rib to hold a now missing glass inset which would have been keyed into position by a small reserved metal ring. In the channel between the rib and the raised edge of the brooch there is a series of stamped S-shaped motifs. The face is gilded. The catchplate and part of the pin are missing and the spring pin is made of iron held between two hinge lugs. See Allason-Jones and Miket 1984, no. 3.138, for local parallels. These brooches and their oval counterparts are particularly common in the military sector: Snape 1993, Group 15.2. Third-fourth century.

29. Plate Brooch (W:26mm H:20mm Total T:6mm). Area over *intervallum* road (Road 5), unstratified, E04:01, 18, WSE2, 2001.1617
Crescent-shaped plate brooch with two concentric bands of enamel; the inner band of red, the outer band of black or very dark blue. Part of the catchplate survives as well as the double lugged hinge with fragments of a coiled spring with an iron hinge pin. Crescentic brooches are known (see Riha's (1979) Type 7.5), but the closest parallel to this example is a pendant from Wiesbaden (Oldenstein 1976, Taf. 45, no. 449).

30. Plate Brooch (L:41mm). Building 10, *contubernium* 3?, Period 2, F14:44, 1310, WSE1, 2001.1616
Circular plate brooch with four openwork *peltae* arranged around a raised flat boss which contains a disc of red enamel which has been made separately and riveted into position. The *peltae* and the brooch itself have raised edges and the resultant sunken field is filled with blue enamel. The catchplate and hinge survive behind two of the lugs. This brooch has parallels from Canterbury (Smith 1880, pl. XXI), Knaith Park, Lincolnshire (in private hands), Turret 18B (Allason-Jones 1988, 198–9, no.1) and South Shields (Allason-Jones 1983, no. 190). Examination of the brooches suggests the possibility that they may have been products from the same mould. Late second century.

31. Plate Brooch (D:29mm). Building 8, abandonment, mid-third century?, E11:37, 1158, WSE11, 2001.1626
Disc brooch with a concentric, reserved rib separating an outer ring of blue enamel from an inner ring of white. In the centre there is a waisted knob with a

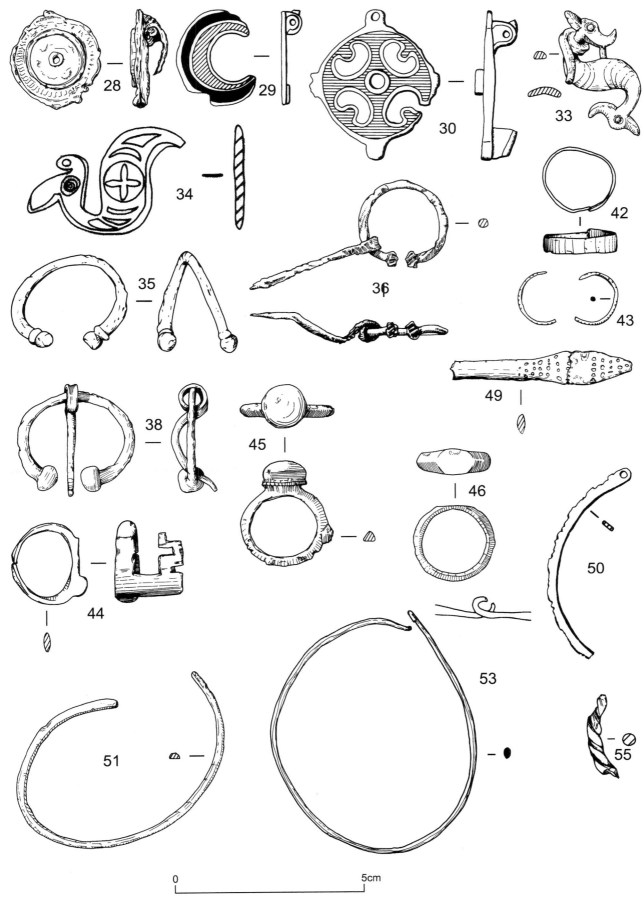

0          5cm

*Figure 25.03: Copper alloy nos 28–55. Scale 1:1.*

small central projection. The catchplate and hinge are both missing and the disc is incomplete. Cf. Coventina's Well: Allason-Jones and McKay 1985, no. 45; Riha 1979, Type 7.14. Late second century.

32.   Plate Brooch (D:33mm). Area over Building 12, unstratified, K14:03, 1353, WSE10, 2001.1625
      Fragment of a disc brooch with concentric ribs creating ring fields. The outer field contains green enamel whilst the second ring has small reserved metal dots emerging from blue enamel. Cf. Coventina's Well: Allason-Jones and McKay 1985, no. 42. Second century.

33.   Dragonesque Brooch (L:38mm, Max.W:16mm). Building 16, floor, Period 4, L07:02, 2026, WSCA99, 2001.1139
      Complete dragonesque brooch. The body is hollowed at the back whilst the convex front is decorated with incised curved lines. The heads are thin and lively with deeply stamped circles for the eyes. One head has a short bar running from the chin to the body and has the incomplete pin wrapped around its neck. This piece has all the essentials of the true dragonesque brooch except for the enamelling. A large example from South Shields (Allason-Jones and Miket 1984, no. 3.131), which also lacks enamel, was described by Collingwood (1930) as an imitation of the true dragonesque brooch, influenced by examples from Corbridge and Victoria Cave, Settle. The same cannot be said of this example from Wallsend. The form is North British, occurring predominantly in military contexts north of the Severn-Humber line, developing into the elaborately enamelled form by the second century. This brooch may be earlier in the series if the enamelling is seen as a degeneration. See Feachem 1951, 32–44.

34.   Dragonesque Brooch. Unstratified, 1358, lost.
      The site notebook describes it as being recessed for enamel inlay.

35.   Penannular Brooch (D:30mm T of shank:3mm). Gateway 1, no details, K02:02, 772, WSCA86, 2001.1126
      Penannular brooch with a circular-sectioned shank. The globular terminals sit on disc necks. The brooch is distorted and missing its pin. Fowler 1960, Type A3. First to third century.

36.   Penannular Brooch (D:29.5mm L of pin (including hinge) :36mm). Building 8, west wall, Period 2, D11:09, 1146, WSCA34, 2001.1074
      Penannular brooch with oval-sectioned shank and milled knobbed terminals. The pin has been formed by rolling a copper alloy sheet, flattening it and curling one end around the brooch shank. Fowler 1960, Type A2. First – fourth century.

37.   Penannular brooch (L:28mm). Chalet 9, Building W, late third/early fourth century, D13:06, 1476, WSCA209, 2001.1249
      Terminal of an oval-sectioned penannular brooch decorated with bands of nicks on the shank and incised lines at the ends. Fowler 1960, Type E. See Allason-Jones and Miket 1984, no. 3.117 for local parallels. Third – fourth century.

38.   Penannular Brooch (D:32mm L of pin:31mm). Soil over north-south drain east of Building 3, Period 3–4, Q07:10, 2594, WSCA125, 2001.1165
      Penannular brooch in four fragments. The shank is circular in section enlarging to the globular terminals.

The pin is formed of oval-sectioned wire flattened at the end and tightly curled. Fowler 1960, Type A1. First century BC– third century AD.

39.   Curved Rod (L:29mm T:5mm). Chalet 9, Building W, late third/early fourth century, D13:06, 1489, WSCA412, 2001.1452
      Fragment of a curved rod which tapers from the surviving terminal. Part of a plain penannular brooch?

40.   Brooch Pin (L:35mm). Area over Building 16, unstratified, K07:03, 1985, WSCA238, 2001.1278
      Short, tapering, circular-sectioned brooch pin with one end coiled twice to provide a spring.

41.   Brooch Catchplate (L:25mm). Area over Building 12, unstratified, K14:01, 1304, WSCA200, 2001.1240
      Catchplate from a crossbow brooch?

42.   Ear-ring (D:19mm W:0.5mm T:4.5mm). Building 10, *contubernium* 7, Period 2, G15:20, 978, WSCA94, 2001.1134
      Penannular ring which is undecorated but tinned or silvered. Ear-ring of Allason-Jones 1989a, Type 1.

43.   Ear-ring (Int. diam:12.5mm W:0.75mm T:1mm). Gateway 2, no details, C07:07, 2399, WSCA112, 2001.1152
      Penannular ring of oval section with oblique nicks along one face. The ends are overlapped and taper sharply. Ear-ring of Allason-Jones 1989a, Type 2e.

44.   Finger Ring (D of ring:22mm L of key:18mm). Area over Building 13, unstratified, N12:01, 1631, WSCA28, 2001.1068
      Finger ring with projecting key. The shank is triangular-sectioned, expanding to the shoulder. The tubular key shaft projects from a flat rectangular area which is chip-carved. The ward is also chip-carved. See Colchester: Crummy 1983, no. 2195, for a similar key still in position in the lock of a small chest. See also Verulamium: Goodburn and Grew 1984, no. 163.

45.   Finger Ring (int. diam:17mm W:3mm D of boss:11mm). Area over Building 15, unstratified, J07:01, 1997, WSCA39, 2001.1079
      Finger ring with triangular-sectioned shank. A circular boss projects from a disc to give the impression of a stone inset into a cupped bezel.

46.   Finger Ring (int. diam:16.5mm W:2mm Centre plate:9 × 7mm). Area over Building 14, unstratified, K10:01, 1965, WSCA45, 2001.1085
      Finger ring of oval section expanding to triangular-sectioned shoulders and a flat oval centre plate.

47.   Finger Ring (int. diam:17mm W:1.75mm T:3mm). Area over Building 14, unstratified, H10:01, 1964, WSCA240, 2001.1280
      Two fragments of a finger ring of semi-oval section with pelleted decoration around the outer face.

48.   Finger Ring (int. diam:15mm W:1mm T:3mm). Area over Building AO, unstratified, K08:01, 1989, WSCA252, 2001.1292
      Fragment of a strip finger ring with the outer face decorated with transverse ridges. Cf. Crummy 1983, no. 1770; Charlesworth 1961, pl. II, nos 1 and 2.

49.   Bracelet (L:60mm). Area over Building 9, unstratified, D13:01, 1075, WSCA48, 2001.1088
      Fragment of a strip bracelet with a snake's head terminal decorated with incised dots. Cf. Jewry Wall, Leicester: Kenyon 1948, Type E, decorated with dots and grooves; Verulamium Theatre: Kenyon 1934, fig.

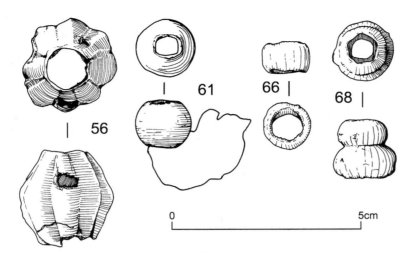

*Figure 25.04: Copper alloy nos 56–68. Scale 1:1.*

12, nos 2 and 5, late fourth and late second centuries respectively. Allason-Jones and Miket 1984, Type 6, no. 3.243.

50. Bracelet (int. diam:48mm W:3mm T:1mm). Area over Building 16, unstratified, K07:01, 1982, WSCA161, 2001.1201
Fragment of a strip bracelet with groups of ridge and-groove motifs along the outer edge. The surviving terminal is flattened and pierced by a circular hole. Wheeler and Wheeler 1932, Type Q, no. 58; Allason-Jones and Miket 1984, Type 13, nos 3.265–9.

51. Bracelet (W:2mm T:3mm). Area over Road 3, unstratified, H13:10, 1254, WSCA71, 2001.1111
Oval-sectioned wire tapering to one terminal and curved to an open circle. Bracelet?

52. Bracelet (L:23mm T:1.5mm). Gateway 3, no details, J16:20, 1364, WSCA269, 2001.1309
Fragment of a sliding knot expanding bracelet. Allason-Jones and Miket 1984, Type 8, nos 3.249–50.

53. Bracelet (W:1.5mm T:2.5mm). Building R, mid-third century?, G11:16, 1194, WSCA214, 2001.1254
Fragmentary, thin strip bracelet of elliptical section. Hooked terminals.

54. Bracelet (W:10mm T:1.5mm). Area of Building 4, unstratified, J04:13, 834, WSCA250, 2001.1290
Wide strip curved to form a bracelet with two longitudinal bands of notches on the ridge-and-grooved upper face. Cf. Verulamium: Waugh and Goodburn 1972, fig. 32, nos 30 and 31.

55. Bracelet (T:3.25mm). Building AO, south wall robber trench, F08:19, 2400, WSCA345, 2001.1385
Fragment of a bracelet made from two strands of wire twisted together. Allason-Jones and Miket 1984, Type 13, nos 265–9.
See also no. 379.

56. Collar (H:2mm D:25mm). Area over *intervallum* road (Road 5), unstratified. E04:01, 115, WSCA68, 2001.1108
Fluted collar resembling a melon bead with a small hole pierced through the side.

57. Bead or collar (L:24mm W:11.5mm). Area of Building 13 and Road 3, unstratified, L12:01, 1701, WSCA183, 2001.1223
Fragment of a large barrel-shaped bead or collar with deep vertical grooves.

58. Bead or collar (L:36mm W:16mm). Chalet 9, post-Roman dereliction, F13:16, 1325, WSCA179, 2001.1219
Fragment of a large barrel-shaped bead or collar with vertical grooves.

59. Bead (D:17mm H:11.5mm). Building 14, courtyard, Period 1 or 2, J10:56, 2180, lost
Globular bead. Cf. Allason-Jones and Miket 1984, no. 3.754.

60. Bead (D:10mm T:3.5mm D of hole:5.5mm). Road associated with the north-west shacks (B2), Period 3–4, H05:12, 791, WSCA225, 2001.1265
Small disc bead with traces of leather inside the hole.

61. Bead (D:15mm H:12mm). Area over Building 12, unstratified, L14:44, 1800, WSCA17, 2001.1057
Barrel bead in molten copper alloy waste, attached to no. 179. See also the metalworking report.

62. Bead (D:10 H:5mm). Road 3, E12:30, 1177, WSCA405, 2001.1445
Barrel bead.

63. Bead (D:12mm H:7mm). Area over Building 12, unstratified, L14:01, 1418, WSCA226, 2001.1266
Barrel bead.

64. Bead (D:15mm H:8mm). Road 1, unstratified, L08:06, 2008, WSCA235, 2001.1275
Fragment of a barrel bead.

65. Bead (D:12mm H:7.5mm). Area over Building 11 and Alley 6, unstratified, L15:01, 1281, WSCA162, 2001.1202
Drum-shaped bead or collar.

66. Bead (H:12mm H:8mm). Area of Building 10 and Road 6, modern, F15:07, 1455, WSCA57, 2001.1097
Drum-shaped bead.

67. Collar (L:23mm W:12mm). Chalet 9, post-Roman dereliction, G13:03, 1498, WSCA380, 2001.1420
Collar of semicircular section.

68. Collar (L:16mm Min.D:13mm, Max.D:16mm). Area over Building 12, unstratified, L14:01, 1422, WSCA89, 2001.1129
Collar consisting of one small drum on top of a larger drum.

69. Collar (D:12mm). Area over Building 11, unstratified, J15:01, 1252, WSCA206, 2001.1246
Distorted collar with three incised longitudinal lines on the outer face.

73

0 10cm

*Figure 25.05: Copper alloy no. 73. Scale 1:2.*

70. Collar (D:13mm T:4mm). Chalet 9, post-Roman dereliction, H13:08, 1501, WSCA470, 2001.1510
    Penannular collar.

71. Collar (D:13mm H:7mm). Chalet 9, dereliction, G13:03, 1380, WSCA407, 2001.1447
    Fragment of a collar.

72. Collar (D:15mm H:12mm). Road 3, unstratified, J13:08, 1366, WSCA395, 2001.1435
    Collar in several fragments.

73. Statuette (H:150mm). Building 13, room 7, Period 4, N12:38, 1659, WSCA136, 2001.1176
    Cast statuette of a female figure wearing a *chiton* with extra drapery wrapped around her right thigh and left shoulder. She holds a large cornucopia in her left hand, the horn of which rests on her left shoulder. Her right leg is slightly flexed. The attribute held in her right hand is missing. She wears a head-dress over a curled hair style which is parted in the centre and ends in a rough bun at the nape of the neck. A circular brooch, pelleted around a central boss, is worn at her right shoulder. There is a break across the neck of the statuette and the metal of the head and top of the cornucopia differs from the rest of the body, suggesting that they were added separately. The back is plain and roughly finished giving the impression that it was not intended to be seen. The execution is rough and angular with the details of the dress added after removal from the mould, implying provincial workmanship on the classical theme of Fortuna, although the goddess Spes may offer an alternative identification. The statuette is complete bar the tip of the cornucopia and the attribute in the right hand.

74. Miniature Axe (L:30mm W of head:16mm Max T:4mm). Area over Building 12, unstratified, M12:01, 1672, WSCA44, 2001.1084
    Miniature axe with a wide cutting blade and a narrower hammer. The circular-sectioned shank may be complete or may have continued as a pin. For a discussion on miniature axes and axe-hammers and their part in Roman religion, see Green 1978, 32–3.

75. Amulet (L:89mm Max W:19mm Max T:14mm). Building 11, *contubernium* 3/4, Period 2, L15:23, 1533, WSCA43, 2001.1083
    Curved amulet, hollowed at the back with a central circular hole. One end is shaped to represent a phallus, the other a hand clenched over a projecting thumb, a symbol used to ward off the Evil Eye. The amulet has been made in two sections and welded together; this would have meant it was too weak for use as a handle. This form of amulet is common in bone: Verulamium: Green 1976, pl. XXVIa; Wroxeter: Bushe-Fox 1912, pl. X, fig. 1, no. 7; Chester-le-Street: Young 1933, 120; Colchester: Crummy 1983, 139; but some are known in bronze: Newstead: Curle 1911, pl. LXXVII, nos 2 and 3.

76. Candlestick (H:69mm D of base:40mm D of rim:33mm). Building 8 abandonment/Building N make-up layer, mid-late third century, E12:03, 986, WSCA1 2001.1041
    Lathe-turned candlestick with a hollow flared lip and base and a bulging shank. Bands of incised lines decorate all three elements. There is a possible patch repair or fault in the metal on one side. A similar candlestick, now in Vienna, has a matching saucer base and has been dated to 'about the birth of Christ' (Mutz 1972, pl. 462). This example is likely to have been of some age when it reached Wallsend.

77. Hanging Lamp (H:26mm Total surv. L:85mm). Road 5, dereliction, E04:07, 150, WSCA85, 2001.1125
    Hanging lamp with a flanged counterpoise decorated to resemble a vine leaf. The filling hole is circular and surrounded by two concentric grooves. Both wick arms have broken off. A fine length of copper alloy wire runs through a circular hole in the counterpoise

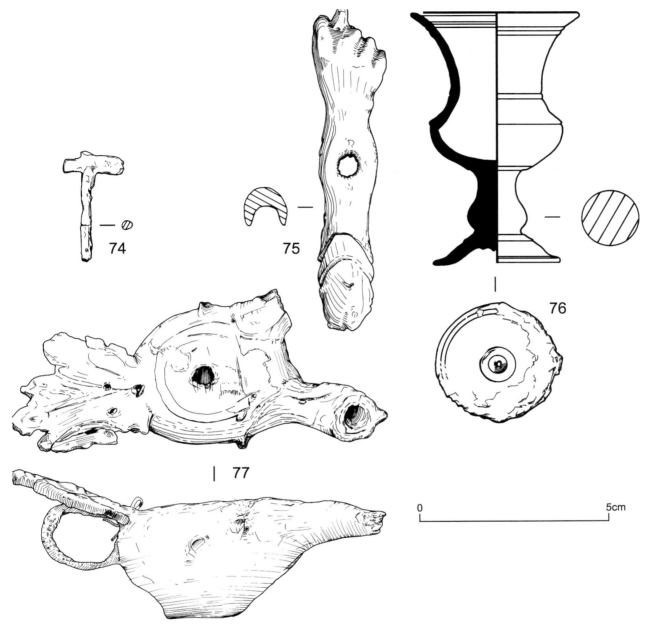

*Figure 25.06: Copper alloy nos 74–77. Scale 1:1.*

and emerges underneath leaving a loop. The handle is a strip emerging from under the counterpoise and meeting the body halfway down. Two perforated lugs emerge from the side of the body to take a hanging chain. The base is missing. Similar oil lamps with single wick holes are illustrated by Mutz (1972, nos 408, 409 and 412).

78.  Ramshead Skillet (D of bowl:180mm H of bowl:48mm D of flanged boss:62mm L of handle:129mm T of shank:23mm). Chalet 9, Building W, late third/early fourth century, D13:34, 1559, WSCA147, 2001.1187
Very corroded, circular skillet with a flat, in-turned rim. In the centre of the bowl there is a large boss with concentrically ribbed flange which has been attached separately. A wide ring base surrounds a dimpled washer in the centre of the base. The separate handle is a hollow tube with a flared end designed

to clip over the rim of the bowl. The other end of the handle is fashioned to represent a stylized ram's head. Two short ribs run back along the handle from the ram's collar flanking a wide band delineated by two rows of stamped dots. Such skillets are common finds throughout the Roman Empire and were manufactured in Italy in the first century AD. See den Boesterd 1956, nos 68–70. For a discussion of the method of manufacture see Mutz 1972, no. 140, and Strong and Brown 1976, 33.

79.  Bucket (H:126mm D of base:124mm D of rim:17 × 130mm W of neck ring:10mm T of walls:1mm). Building 12, robbing *contubernium* 9/officer's quarters, Period 3, M14:61, 1895, WSCA148, 2001.1188
Vessel with a circular flat base. The thin walls belly out to curved shoulders. The rim is straight with a slightly thickened edge. The vessel is distorted so that

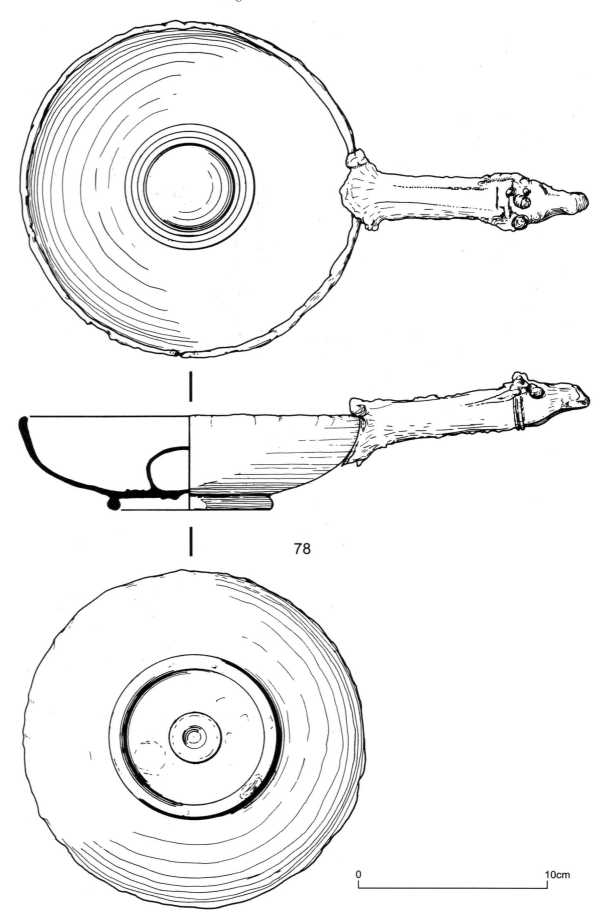

78

0                                    10cm

*Figure 25.07: Copper alloy no. 78. Scale 1:2.*

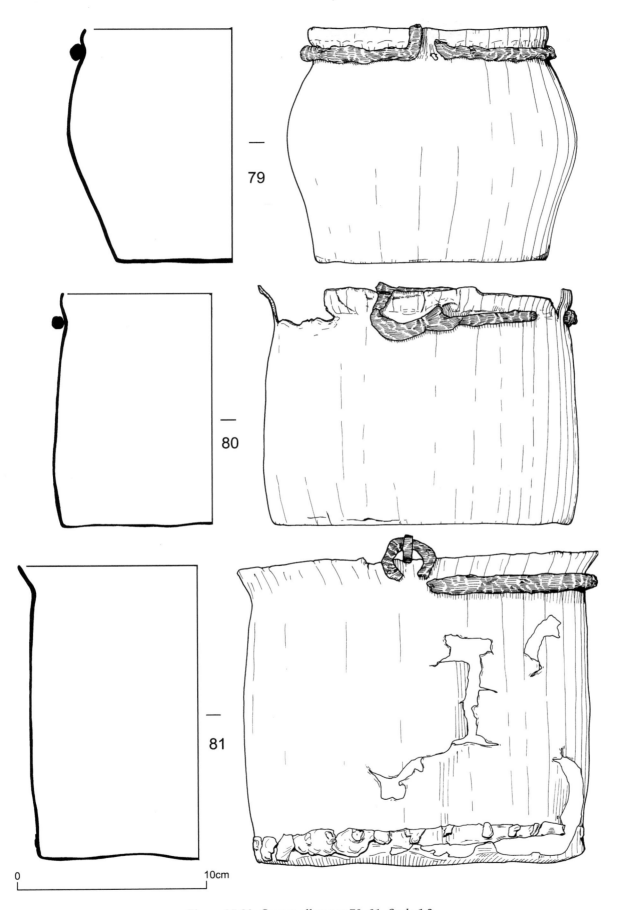

*Figure 25.08: Copper alloy nos 79–81. Scale 1:2.*

the rim is now oval in shape. An iron ring of oval section fits tightly around the neck. Pieces of the iron handle are attached by corrosion to the fragmentary ring, but neither of the escutcheon loops survive. Radnóti (1938) illustrates a similar vessel from Vajta in Pannonia dated to the third century (pl. XXXVIII, no. 4, 123–4).

80. Bucket (H:128mm D of base:147mm D of rim:170mm W of neck ring:8mm section of handle: 12 × 8mm T of walls:1mm). Building 12, robbing *contubernium* 9/officer's quarters, Period 3, M14:61, 1894, WSCA150, 2001.1190
Vessel with a circular flat base similar to above. The thin walls are straight, curling out at the rim which is thickened at the edge. An oval-sectioned iron ring fits around the neck of the vessel with fragments of the iron handle resting on the rim. Neither of the escutcheon loops survives.

81. Bucket (H:168mm D of base:165mm D of rim:192mm W of iron ring:9mm T of walls:0.75mm). Building 12, robbing *contubernium* 9/officer's quarters, Period 3, M14:61, 1893, WSCA149, 2001.1189
Vessel, similar to above, with a circular flat base and straight sides which curve out at the neck. The edge of the rim is slightly thickened. Fragments of an oval-sectioned iron ring survive around the neck but no trace of a handle or escutcheon loops survive.

The three buckets were found in a group, no. 79 sitting in no. 80 which in turn was resting in its larger parallel, no. 81. There are parallels to all three vessels in Pannonia (Radnóti 1938, pl. XXXV, nos 1–5, 116) where the straight-sided buckets are more common than the curved form (as no. 79). All are known from first- and second-century contexts surviving into the third century. From complete examples it can be seen that the iron neck rings are bent to form looped escutcheons in two places, onto which are hooked the ends of the iron handle.

82. Escutcheon (L:85mm W:50mm). Unstratified, 1956, lost
Large bucket or bowl escutcheon with a long triangular body and oval loop. The back is hollow and the face convex. Cf. Verulamium: Waugh and Goodburn 1972, no. 132.

83. Escutcheon (L:62mm H:20mm). Alley 5, F14:38, 1311, WSCA67, 2001.1107
Solid bucket or bowl escutcheon in the form of a three-dimensional duck with a long triangular body and extended neck. There has been no attempt at modelling feathers but small dots indicate the eyes. There is a thin layer of lead on the base and traces of a possible shank or rivet. Examples are known from Romano-British sites, such as Ashby-de-Launde: Green 1976, pl. XXIIb, Barton: Eggers 1966, Abb.18, no. 41, and from Continental sites, such as Nauheim and Sacjrau: Henry 1936, 209–246. They also appear on Longley's (1975) Type 5 hanging bowls which had a long period of production from the fourth to the seventh centuries.

84. Tripod support (H:29mm). East *intervallum* road (Road 7), Q05:04, 174, WSCA123, 2001.1163

Support from a tripod or lamp shaped to represent a horse's hoof and fetlock.

85. Tankard handle (L:66mm Max W:19mm H:37mm D of discs:21mm). Area over Building 11, unstratified, K15:01, 1300, WSCA35, 2001.1075
Tankard handle with a V-sectioned strip shank with a central rib fitting into two disc terminals held together by a thin rod. Both discs have square loops projecting from the back. The handle is further decorated by two incised marginal lines. A close parallel dating to the third century is known from Okstrow Broch, Orkney: MacGregor, M., 1976, no. 291. See also Corcoran 1952, Class V.

86. Jug handle (L:32mm). Building 8 abandonment or Building N, mid/late third century?, E12:04, 1151, WSCA297, 2001.1337
Top of a jug handle with thumb-stop and wide flanges. Cf. den Boesterd 1956, pls X, XI, XII: second-third century.

87. Bowl (D:23mm L:30mm D:63mm T:0.5mm). Building 1, floor, Period 2, M05:28, 923, WSCA95, 2001.1135
Fragment of a bowl with a short out-turned rim. There are traces of tinning on the outer face which also has three scored parallel lines under the rim.

88. Bowl (D:16mm). Area over *Via principalis* (Road 1), unstratified, M08:01, 2622, WSCA173, 2001.1511
Fragment of the rim of a bowl. (AC)

89. Lid (D:18mm T:5mm). Area of Building 4, no details, J04:11, 654, WSCA301, 2001.1341
Small disc lid with raised lip on both faces.

90. Seal box lid (D:24mm T:1mm). Area over Alley 4, unstratified, F05:02, 275, WSE6, 2001.1621
Circular seal box lid with a leaf design of reserved metal contained within a raised border. The resultant fields contain red and blue enamel. Cf. Jewry Wall, Leicester: Kenyon 1948, fig. 84; also Bateson 1981, fig. 7c.

91. Plate (L:12mm T:1.75mm). Area over Building 15, unstratified, J07:01, 1999, WSCA329, 2001.1369
Fragment of a rectangular plate with raised edges. The face is divided into cells by ribs which may have held enamel.

92. Mirror (D of original mirror:90mm T:1mm). Area over Building 7, unstratified, G11:01, 961, WSCA270, 2001.1310
Fragment of a disc mirror which has been tinned on both faces. One face is highly polished whilst the other has lightly scored concentric circles. Cf. Corbridge: Lloyd-Morgan 1977, pl. XVIII, 335–8; Lloyd-Morgan 1981.

93. Bell (H:46mm). Area over Building 7, unstratified, G11:01, 950, WSCA131, 2001.1171
Incomplete bell with a long body and square mouth. The lozenge-shaped loop is pierced by a circular hole. Cf. Leicester: Kenyon 1948, fig. 87, no. 7.

94. Key (L:47mm W of head:22mm D of tube:5.5mm). Building 16, floor, Period 4, L07:02, 2024, WSCA152, 2001.1192
Very short tubular key with a ward projecting at right-angles at the end. The ward is damaged but appears to consist of two tangs. At the top a wide, three-ribbed, rectangular-sectioned panel leads to a flattened oval head pierced by a grooved circular hole (D:6mm). The head is set at right angles to the ward.

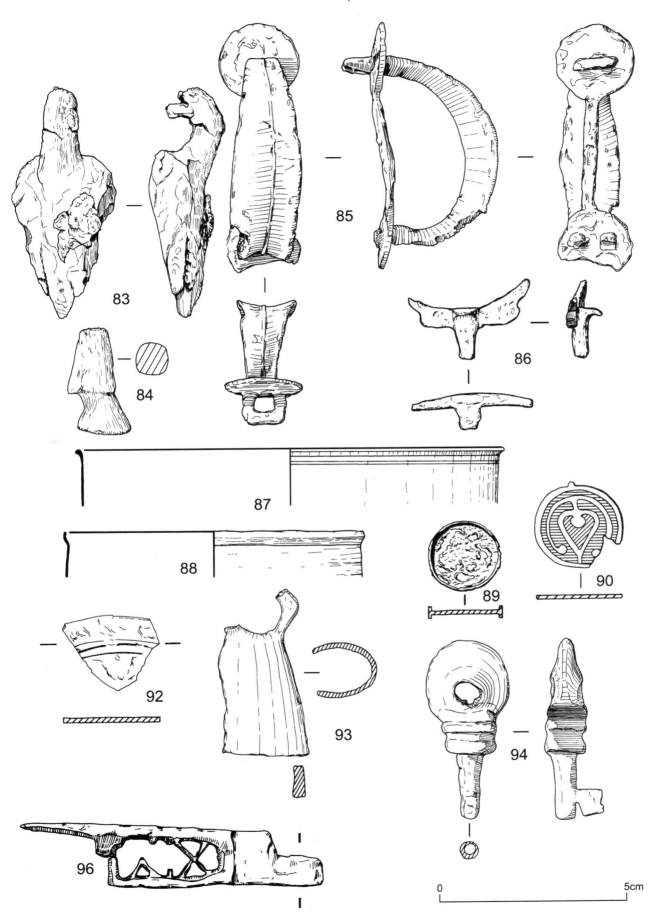

*Figure 25.09: Copper alloy nos 83–96 Scale 1:1.*

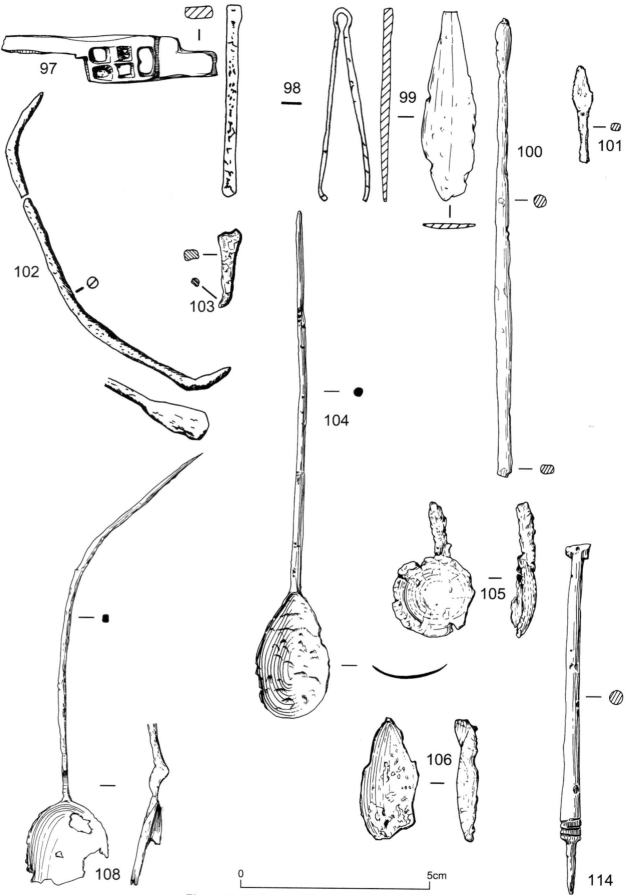

*Figure 25.10: Copper alloy nos 97–114. Scale 1:1.*

95. Key handle (L:42mm). Building 3, abandonment/ post-Roman, P07:08, 2556, WSCA159, 2001.1199
Incomplete key handle with deep baluster-moulded neck and openwork head which appears to be of the common *fleur-de-lis* type which has been dated to post AD 150 (*ORL* 8, Taf. 12, no. 51). Part of the iron key shank survives in the base of the handle.

96. Lock bolt (L:80mm W:16mm T:9mm). Area over Building 9, unstratified, F13:04, 1036, WSCA40, 2001.1080
Tumbler lock bolt of rectangular section. The eight triangular cut-outs are arranged in two rectangular patterns of four. See diagram of use in Smith 1922, fig. 44.

97. Lock bolt (L:57mm W:13mm B:6mm). Unstratified, WSCA76, 2001.1116
Tumbler lock of rectangular section. The cut-outs are arranged in two lines of three squares. See also the iron example below, no. 33.

98. Tweezers (L:51mm W of arms: 5mm T of arms:1mm). Building 13, room 7, Period 4, N12:37, 1883, lost
Pair of tweezers with straight arms curving only at the tips.

99. Medical instrument (L:51mm W:14mm T:1mm). Rampart building north of *Porta quintana*, Period 2–3, C11:04, 1196, WSCA261, 2001.1301
Flat, leaf-shaped blade from a medical instrument. Cf. South Shields: Allason-Jones and Miket 1984, no. 3.455. See also Kunzl 1982, pls 9; 20, no. 5; 43, nos 6 and 7; 69, no. 1; 79, no. 5.

100. Medical instrument (L:125mm T:4mm). Rampart building north of *Porta quintana*, Period 2–3, 1199, WSCA77, 2001.1117
Fragment of a medical instrument with an octagonal-sectioned shank and a bulbous probe. See Allason-Jones and Miket 1984, nos 3.451, 3.453, and 3.456 for local parallels. See Milne 1907, 53, for the use of such probes.

101. Medical instrument (L:26mm T:1.5mm). North gate, east tower, Period 1–2, L03:32, 886, WSCA55, 2001.1095
Small, leaf-shaped terminal from a medical instrument. One face is slightly concave. Cf. Milne 1907, pl. XIV, no. 5.

102. Medical instrument (L:120mm W of head:8.5mm). Alley 7, K12:02, 1816, lost
Distorted, tapering, circular-sectioned shank with a rounded spatulate terminal.

103. Medical instrument (L:20mm). Chalet 9, Building ET, Period 4, G13:14, 1575, WSCA267, 2001.1307
Terminal of a medical instrument with an angled circular head which has broken where a small hole pierces through the neck. Cf. Chesters: Chesters Museum Acc. No. 6011.817 (1072).

104. Spoon (L:140mm W of bowl:20mm). Lower fill of pit cut into primary phase of Road 4, Q04:15, 498, WSCA2, 2001.1042
Spoon with a pear-shaped bowl and a long tapering handle leading straight from the bowl. Cf. Verulamium: Waugh and Goodburn 1972, fig. 35, no. 74: AD 135–45.

105. Spoon bowl (D:22mm). Building 1, *contubernium* 2–4 cleaning, Period 2?, N04:18, 515, WSCA247, 2001.1287
Deep, circular spoon bowl with incised concentric circles around the edge on the inner face. Tinned on all surfaces. Cf. Verulamium: Goodburn and Grew 1984, fig. 15, no. 121: undated but an unillustrated example came from a context dated to 145–155.

106. Spoon bowl (L:32mm). Area over Building 1, unstratified, L04:11, 884, WSCA245, 2001.1285
Pear-shaped spoon bowl. Tinned.

107. Spoon bowl (W:20mm). Building 16, floor, Period 4, L08:47, 2508, WSCA340, 2001.1380.
Incomplete bowl near the junction with the handle. Very poor condition.

108. Spoon (L:123mm W of bowl:22mm). Rampart building north of *Porta quintana*, Period 2–3, C11:04, 1201, WSCA56, 2001.1096
Incomplete, very distorted spoon with an oval bowl and a tapering, rectangular-sectioned handle which is set slightly higher than the bow.

109. Spoon bowl (L:31mm W:26mm). Gateway 2, no details, D07:02, 2222, WSCA319, 2001.1359
Distorted, lute-shaped spoon bowl broken at the neck.

110. Spoon bowl (W:27mm). Building 16, floor, Period 4, P08:05, 2504, WSCA288, 2001.1328
Fragment of a lute-shaped spoon bowl with a thickened edge.

111. Spoon? (L:64mm approx W of bowl:34mm). Area over Building 16, unstratified, K07:03, 1986, lost
Fragmentary oval plate, slightly concave with a tapering curled strip projecting from one edge.

112. Spoon handle (L:67mm). Drain from tank south of Building 14, late third/early fourth century, J12:34, 2164, WSCA242, 2001.1282
Tapering handle of a spoon broken at the keel.

113. Spoon handle (L:36mm Max T:3mm). *Via principalis*, L08:57, 2555, WSCA135, 2001.1175
Fragment of a spoon handle broken at the keel. The handle emerges from the keel as square-sectioned but continues as circular-sectioned after a double rib motif. Tinned. Cf. South Shields: Allason-Jones and Miket 1984, no. 3.327.

114. Stylus (L:94mm W:5mm W of head:6.5mm L of point:14mm). Cistern 1 filling, mid to late third century, E08:29, 2312, WSCA3, 2001.1043
Stylus with a circular-sectioned shank tapering to a short rectangular eraser with bevelled faces. The long pointed tip is separated from the shank by three deep grooves. Analysis has shown the metal to be a high tin bronze with some lead.
See also no. 380.

115. Stylus? (L:89mm W of head:9mm). Road 8, F08:10, 2272, WSCA104, 2001.1144
Tapering, circular-sectioned rod with a long, wedge-shaped head decorated with incised cross-hatching. Possibly a stylus although the head appears to have been rounded at the end.

116. Pin (L:24mm D of head:24mm T of shank:3mm). Unstratified, 2003, WSCA115, 2001.1155
Incomplete pin with a circular-sectioned shank and an onion-shaped head on a disc neck.

117. Pin (L:84mm). Fill of drain in Road 9, J14:06, 1343, WSCA59, 2001.1099
Circular-sectioned pin with the end hooked. The head is square-sectioned and decorated with several transverse grooves.

118. Pin (L:112mm T:3.5mm). Building 5, drain fill, Period

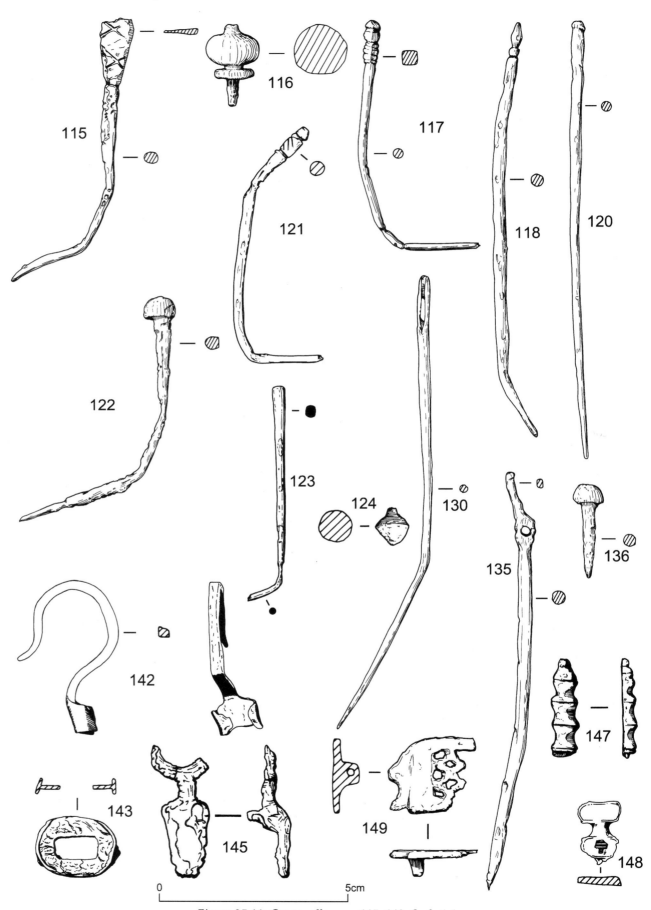

*Figure 25.11: Copper alloy nos 115–149. Scale 1:1.*

2, E05:38, 1491, WSCA78, 2001.1118
Circular-sectioned pin broken across the baluster-moulded head.

119. Pin (L:80mm T:2.5mm). Chalet 12, Building AL2, (mid)-late third century, M15:21, 1862, lost
Incomplete pin with a globular head on a baluster-moulded neck and a circular-sectioned shank.

120. Pin (L:120mm T:3mm). Building BJ, foundation, post-Roman, G11:12, 1164, WSCA153, 2001.1193
Circular-sectioned pin with a domed head.

121. Pin (L:90mm). Area over Building 12, unstratified, M14:01, 1649, WSCA80, 2001.1120
Circular-sectioned pin with a lathe-turned head.

122. Pin (L:82mm). Area over Buildings 1 and 2 and Alley 1, unstratified, N05:01, 7, WSCA51, 2001.1091
Very battered pin of circular section with a globular head.

123. Pin (L:61mm T:4mm). *Via principalis*, L08:50, 2523, WSCA418, 2001.1458
Circular-sectioned pin with a globular head.

124. Pin (D:8.5mm). Building 16, 'kiln', Period 1–2, M07:14, 2606, WSCA348, 2001.1388
Conical head of a pin with a circular-sectioned shank.

125. Pin (D:7mm). Road 3, F10:32, 2330, WSCA351, 2001.1391
Conical head of a pin.

126. Pin (L:61mm W:5mm T:4mm). Area over Building 16 and *Via principalis*, unstratified, N08:01, 2473, WSCA363, 2001.1403
Incomplete pin of oval section thickening to a rounded head.

127. Pin? (L:20mm). Building 13, backfill of east hypocaust, Period 4, M12:54, 1843, WSCA184, 2001.1224
Possible pin with a globular head and a wide shank with two longitudinal grooves.

128. Pin (L:83mm). Rerouted *Via principalis* (Road 1), Roman/post-Roman, E08:13, 2285, WSCA227, 2001.1267
Circular-sectioned pin. The head is too corroded for the form to be identified.

129. Pin (L:13mm D of head:7mm). *Via principalis*, L09:17, 2566, WSCA291, 2001.1331
Pin with circular-sectioned shank and a globular head.

130. Needle (L:120mm). *Via principalis*, L08:59, 2585, WSCA128, 2001.1168
Long needle of oval section with a countersunk rectangular eye.

131. Rod (L:40mm T:2mm). Building 1, verandah, Period 3, P05:13, 244, WSCA419, 2001.1459
Tapering, circular-sectioned rod; shank of pin or needle.

132. Rod (L:47mm T:2mm). Area over Building 1, unstratified, L04:01, 726, WSCA420, 2001.1460
Tapering, circular-sectioned rod; shank of pin or needle.

133. Rod (L:55mm T:3.5mm). Area over Building BB, unstratified, N13:01, 1657, WSCA421, 2001.1461
Rod of circular section with one pointed end.

134. Rod (L:75mm). Area over Building 12 and *Via praetoria*, unstratified, J14:01, 1261, WSCA208, 2001.1248
Curved rod with one end flattened and pierced to take a small copper alloy ring. The other end expands slightly and is broken across a hole. Balance? Cf. Chesters Museum Acc. No. 602.818(1073).

135. Rod (L:113mm). Building 2, *contubernium* 8 demolition material, Period 3 or later, L05:25, 843, WSCA154, 2001.1194
Thick rod of circular section flattened near one end to enclose a circular hole and with a square-sectioned head. Balance arm?

136. Nail (L:25mm D of head:7mm). Area over Road 8, unstratified, F09:04, 2215, WSCA119, 2001.1159
Nail with a globular head and a short tapering shank.

NAILS WITH DISC HEADS

137. Nail (L:12mm D:17mm). Building 2, *contubernium* 5, Period 3 or later, M05:11, 294, WSCA423, 2001.1463

138. Nail (L:25mm D:14mm). Road 4, G03:04, 624, WSCA379, 2001.1419

139. Nail (L:25mm D:11mm). Area over east fort wall, unstratified, R05:01, 633, WSCA215, 2001.1255

140. Nail (L:19mm D:22mm). Area over Building 9, unstratified, F13:01, 1080, WSCA422, 2001.1462

141. Nail (D:13mm). Area over Road 9, unstratified, J14:05, 1385, WSCA398, 2001.1438

142. *Dolabra* sheath (L:42mm). Road 3, no details, J13:18, 1346, WSCA37, 2001.1077
Square-sectioned hook with a flanged end from a *dolabra* sheath: Collingwood and Richmond 1969, fig. 108h.

143. Knife guard (L:21mm T:4mm hole:12 × 6mm). Area over Building 10 and *intervallum* road (Road 6), unstratified, F15:01, 1453, WSCA195, 2001.1235
Oval dagger or knife-guard with raised edges and a rectangular hole to take the tang. Cf. Corbridge: Bishop and Dore 1989, fig. 84, no. 147.

144. Binding (L:79mm W:7mm). Road surface (B2), Period 3–4, K07:14, 2049, WSCA239, 2001.1279
Fragment of U-sectioned shield or scabbard binding which follows a slight curve.

145. Scabbard runner (L:35mm W:12mm). Building 11, *contubernium* 3/4, Period 2, L15:18, 1593, WSCA272, 2001.1312
Fragment of the looped end of a scabbard runner with a plain chamfered face. Traces of gilding survive. Cf. Niederbieber: Oldenstein 1976, Taf. 13, nos 55, 56; Feldberg; South Shields: Allason-Jones and Miket 1984, no. 3.646.

146. Belt-plate (L:72mm W:33mm). Building 12 demolition, Period 3, M14:54, 1880, lost
Rectangular belt-plate with chamfered edges and a peltate projection from one end. The back is hollow with two disc-headed shanks. The open centre has lost its bar. Late second century.

147. Belt-plate bar (L:27mm W:7mm T:3mm). Building 2, *contubernium* 8, Period 3 or later, L05:44, 911, WSCA330, 2001.1370
Centre bar for an open belt-plate as no. 146 above. The bar is flat at the back with four transverse grooved ribs across the front. The surviving end terminates in a short spigot. For enamelled examples see Henry 1933, figs 38 and 39.

148. Belt-plate bar (L:17mm). Area over Building 1, unstratified, L04:11, 883, WSE12, 2001.1627
Fragment of the centre bar of an open belt-plate. One oval and one rectangular panel survives, both filled with blue enamel. Cf. Vimose, Brough-in-

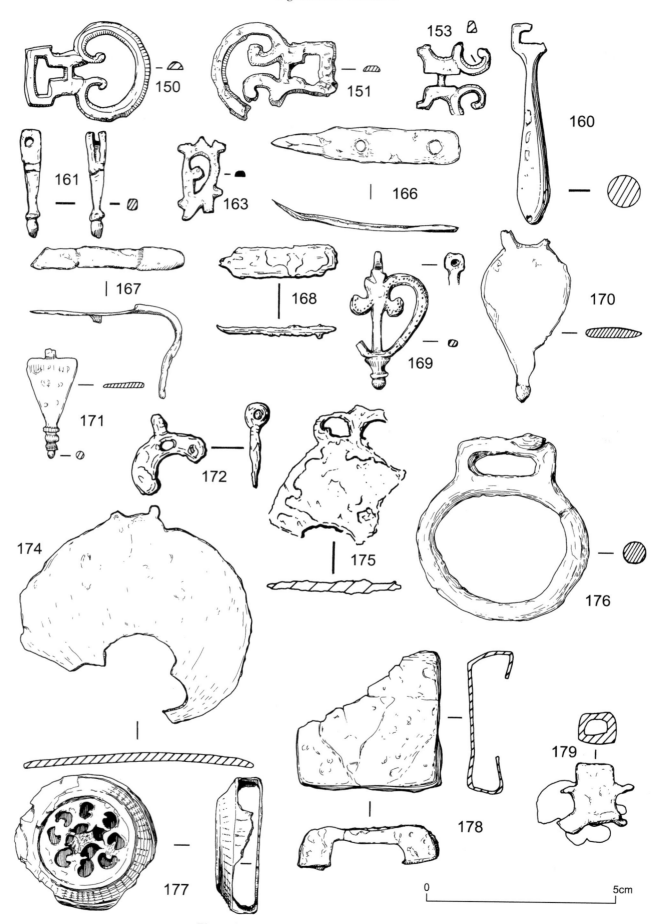

*Figure 25.12: Copper alloy nos 150–179. Scale 1:1.*

Westmorland, Felixstowe, and South Shields: Henry 1933, fig. 38, no. 4; fig. 39, nos 2, 3 and 5.

149. Belt-plate (L:25mm W:20mm). Chalet 12, Building AH, Period 4, L14:07, 44, WSCA260, 2001.1300
Fragment of a belt-plate with the centre filled with fretted openwork. The surviving end is peltate with a loop projecting from the back. Cf. Great Chesters: Allason-Jones 1996a, fig. 10, no. 38; Osterburken: Oldenstein 1976, Taf. 62, no. 791.

150. Buckle (L:32mm Max W:27mm T:3mm). Building 1, *contubernium* 1–3 demolition, Period 2, N05:32, 567, WSCA83, 2001.1123
Buckle with an oval loop of triangular section with two projections curling into the void. The T-shaped hinge plate is thicker than the loop.

151. Buckle (L:33mm Max W:26mm T:2.5mm). Building Row 20, Building R, mid-third century, G11:18, 1222, WSCA69, 2001.1109
Buckle with an incomplete oval loop of semi-oval section with two projections curling into the void. The hinge plate is rectangular with a T-shaped hole cut to take the missing hinge pin.

152. Buckle (L:32mm W:28mm T:2.5mm). Area over Building 11 and Alley 6, unstratified, L15:15, 1517, WSCA122, 2001.1162
Buckle with an oval loop of semi-oval section. Part of the tongue survives *in situ.*

153. Buckle (L:19mm). Building 1, demolition/make-up, Period 3–4?, M05:09, 419, WSCA204, 2001.1244
Fragment of a buckle of square section consisting of part of the hinge loop and two projections curling into the centre. Tinned.

154. Buckle (W:15mm). Western rampart (F2), P04:04, 31, WSCA424, 2001.1464
Fragment of a buckle consisting of a T-shaped hinge loop set in a trapezoidal plate. The shank is semi-oval in section.

155. Buckle (W:20mm). Building 11, *contubernium* 4, Period 1, L15:29, 1618, WSCA417, 2001.1457
Fragment of an oval buckle with a projection into the centre.

156. Buckle (L:13mm). Area over Building 5, unstratified, J05:01, 600, WSCA425, 2001.1465
Fragments of the trapezoidal hinge loop plate of a buckle.

157. Buckle (W:10mm). Rampart building north of *Porta quintana*, Period 2–3, C11:04, 1169, WSCA391, 2001.1431
Hinge fragment from a buckle. Traces of an iron hinge pin survive.

158. Buckle (no measurements possible). Area over Building 12, unstratified, K14:03, 1347, WSCA377, 2001.1417
Buckle in many fragments.

159. Buckle hinge (W:21mm). Chalet 12, AF, Period 4 or later, M15:12, 1620, WSCA426, 2001.1466
Trapezoidal hinge loop from a buckle.

160. Strap-end (L:55mm Max W:9mm). Building 8, entrance, Period 4, D11:21, 1010, WSCA65, 2001.1105
Heavy strap-end with a long bulbous body and a squared loop. Cf. Pfünz: Oldenstein 1976, Taf. 37, no. 327. Mid third century.

161. Strap-end (L:29mm Max W:6mm Max T:5mm). Area over Building 1, unstratified, P05:02, 114, WSCA60, 2001.1100
Tapered strap-end with a knobbed terminal. The wider end is cleft and pierced by a rivet hole. Cf. Zugmantel: Oldenstein 1976, Taf. 36, nos. 311, 312.

162. Strap-end (L:36mm T:7mm). Building 13, south corridor, Period 3 or 4, L11:25, 1821, WSCA182, 2001.1222
Elongated bulbous end of a strap-end.

163. Strap-end (L:32mm B:2mm). Area of Building 2, post-Roman?, N05:16, 236, WSCA275, 2001.1315
Fragment of an elongated openwork strap-end. Cf. Niederbieber: Oldenstein 1976, Taf. 41, nos 390, 393, 395, 396; Zugmantel: Oldenstein 1976, Taf. 41, nos 391, 394, 397. Second–third century.

164. Hinge (L:21mm W:15mm D of stud head:7mm). *Via quintana* (Road 3), K14:15, 1590, WSCA210, 2001.1250
Rectangular hinge formed by folding a sheet and securing it with a disc-headed stud.

165. Hinge (L:19mm B:5mm). Area over Building 9, unstratified, E13:01, 1066, WSCA296, 2001.1336.
Similar to above.

166. Cuirass hook (L:49mm W:9mm T:1mm). Area over *Via principalis*, unstratified, L08:01, 1972, WSCA124, 2001.1164
Incomplete girdle plate tie-hook from *lorica segmentata* of Robinson's (1975) Corbridge Auxiliary Cavalry Type B. Neither of the two circular holes retains its rivet and only part of the hook survives. First-second century.

167. See no. 181

168. Cuirass hook (L:33mm W:9mm B:2mm). Area of Building 2, post-Roman?, N05:16, 130, WSCA281, 2001.1321
Rectangular sheet with rivet shank surviving at one end. The other narrows to a broken terminal, curving upwards.

169. Pendant (L:37mm W:20mm T:1.5mm). Road north of Building 17, third century, G04:09, 372, WSCA36, 2001.1076
Heart-shaped openwork armour or harness pendant. Cf. Stockstadt: *ORL* 33, Taf. VII, no. 41.

170. Pendant (L:47mm W:24mm T:2mm). Road associated with the north-west shacks (B2), Period 3–4, H04:19, 789, WSCA81, 2001.1121
Flat, pear-shaped pendant with knobbed terminal and a large loop. An example decorated with incised circles is known from Wiesbaden: Oldenstein 1976, Taf. 30, no. 197.

171. Pendant (L:30mm). Building BJ, post-Roman, G11:03, 1086, WSCA52, 2001.1092
Heart-shaped pendant with the strap hook missing. The terminal has a thick triple ribbed knob. Cf. Pfünz: Oldenstein 1976, Taf. 30, no. 200.

172. Pendant (D:21mm). Area over Building 8 and *Via quintana*, unstratified, E12:01, 1116, WSCA190, 2001.1230
Crescentic pendant with a convex face and a hollow back, pierced by a rectangular hole. The broken loop sits at right angles to the body, Cf. Pfünz, Wiesbaden and Munningen: Oldenstein 1976, Taf. 45, nos 448, 449 (enamelled) and 450 (enamelled).

173. Fitting (L:32mm T:1.5mm). Unstratified, WSCA156, 2001.1196
Narrow rectangular fitting with the remains of two shanks projecting from the back.

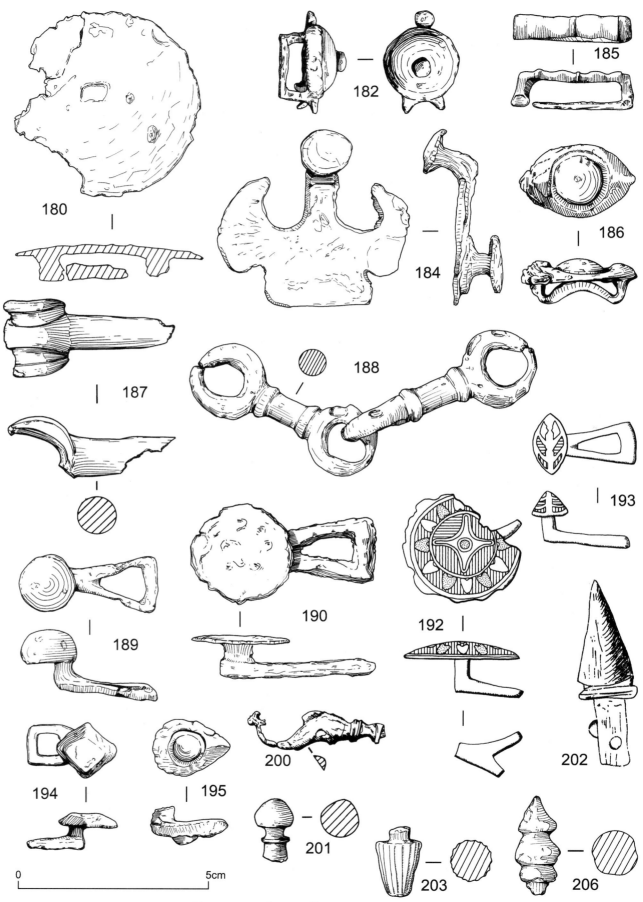

*Figure 25.13: Copper alloy nos 180–206. Scale 1:1.*

174. Fitting (L:61mm W:62mm). Area over *Via quintana*, unstratified, J13:01, 1321, WSCA222, 2001.1262
Large, incomplete peltate harness fitting.

175. Fitting (T:1.5mm). Area over Building 12, unstratified, K14:01, 1538, WSCA207, 2001.1247
Fragment of a circular harness fitting with peltate openwork projecting from one edge.

176. Terret (W:45mm Total L:50mm W of loop:25mm T:6mm). Area over Building 2, ploughsoil, L05:03, 601, WSCA84, 2001.1124
Oval terret ring with a rectangular loop projecting from the edge. Published examples are known from Verulamium: Waugh and Goodburn 1972, no. 126, and Richborough: Bush-Fox 1949, pl. XXXVI, no. 124. There is also an unpublished terret of similar type from Chesters (Chesters Museum Acc. No. 726.1439).

177. Harness lead (D:36mm T:11mm). Alley 1, post-Roman dereliction, M05:14, 580, WSCA98, 2001.1138
Hollow, circular harness lead which has had four rectangular trace holes. The domed upper face has a central decoration of eight deep *peltae* containing red enamel. A concentric rib separates the *peltae* from grooves which radiate to the edge. An undecorated example is known from Chesters (Chesters Museum Acc. No. 886.369 (1093)), and some decorated examples are known from the German *Limes*: see Oldenstein 1976, Tafs 22–4. Early third century.

178. Harness lead (L:40mm W:40mm B:12mm). Building 12, drain in officer's quarters, Period 1, J14:22, 1409, WSCA279, 2001.1319
Incomplete square harness lead.

179. Harness lead (L:19mm W:20mm). Area over Building 12, unstratified, L14:44, 1800, WSCA17, 2001.1057
Fragment from a four-armed harness lead, broken up and partially melted down, along with a bead (no. 61). See also metalworking report.

180. Disc stud (D:49mm T of head:1.5mm). Area over Building 16, unstratified, L07:01, 1993, WSCA107, 2001.1147
Large disc stud with a slightly convex face. A rectangular loop in poor condition projects from the back. Probably horse harness decoration.

181. Junction loop fastener (L:41mm W:7mm T:1mm). Building 1, officer's quarters, Period 3, N05:12, 270, WSCA134, 2001.1174
Incomplete, plain junction loop fastener. Cf. Wroxeter: Webster 2002, fig. 4.12, no. 56 (undated).

182. Harness mount (L:28mm Max W:19mm, Total H:17mm). Building 11, *contubernium* 3/4, Period 2, L15:23, 1535, WSCA61, 2001.1101
Circular boss with two rectangular loops across the hollow back. A knob projects from the centre of the boss whilst a broken loop and a knob project from the flanged border. Harness fitting.

183. Harness mount (L:32mm Max W:23mm Total T:9mm). Area over Building 12, unstratified, L14:01, 1411, lost Y-shaped mount, hollow at the back and convex on the face. A disc-headed shank projects from behind each arm whilst strips projecting from the edges of the stem of the 'Y' curl back to form a collar or socket. Harness fitting.

184. Harness mount (L:48mm). Clay puddling pit, Period 3 demolition, N05:14, 265, WSCA127, 2001.1167
Incomplete, harness mount terminating in a wide

disc-headed stud. A second stud projects from the back. The end is squared off and the surviving side is winged. Cf. Zugmantel: Oldenstein 1976, nos 880–1.

185. Harness slide (L:32mm W:11mm B:6mm). Unstratified, WSCA88, 2001.1128
Thin rectangular fitting, with a loop on the back the length of the fitting. Possibly associated with no. 188, as both have similar patina. (AC)

186. Harness slide (L:32mm W:19mm H:13mm). Area over Building 11, unstratified, K15:01, 1497, WSCA38, 2001.1078
Lentoid mount with a central circular boss. A rectangular loop runs the length of the stud at the back. M. MacGregor (1976, 134) links such studs with button-and-loop fasteners and cites a parallel from Middlebie, Dumfriesshire (*ibid.*, fig. 8, no. 1).

187. Bridle fragment (L:44mm D of socket:9mm W of loop:19.5mm). Area over Road 8, unstratified, F08:01, 2197, WSCA171, 2001.1211
Incomplete tubular socket with deep flanges and a median rib. A plain tube projects at right angles to the socket and appears to contain traces of a lead-tin alloy. Part of a bridle: cf. Llyn Cerrig: Fox 1958, pl. 5b.

188. Bit (L:58mm) W(loop):22mm D(shaft):6mm). Unstratified, WSCA87, 2001.1127
Centre- and side-link from a three-link horse-bit of native tradition, used from the first century BC through to the mid or late first century AD (Jope 2000, pls 276–9). Possibly associated with no. 185. (AC)

189. Button-and-loop fastener (L:35mm D of button: 15mm W of loop:16mm). Cistern 2, lower fill, late third/early fourth century, J07:19, 2172, WSCA100, 2001.1140
Button-and loop fastener with a triangular loop attached to the top lip of a hollow circular boss button. Wild 1970a, Class IV. Second century.

190. Button-and-loop fastener (L:47mm D of button:25mm W of loop:17.5mm). Area over Alley 5, unstratified, F05:01, 84, WSCA29, 2001.1069
Button-and-loop fastener with a triangular loop and a disc button. Wild 1970a, Class Vc; Gillam 1958, Type C. Second century AD.

191. Button-and-loop fastener (no measurements possible). Area over Building 11, unstratified, K15:01, 1299, WSCA427, 2001.1467
Very fragmentary button-and-loop fastener which appears to have had a triangular loop and a disc button, similar to above.

192. Button-and-loop fastener (D:33mm L:32mm). Building 1, verandah, Period 2, M04:29, 937, WSE5, 2001.1620
Slightly domed disc head with raised rib creating two concentric circles. The outer circle has petals in a light-coloured enamel, the inner circle has a central dot and a diamond in pale enamel created by four oval cells of discoloured enamel. Incomplete triangular attachment loop.

193. Button-and-loop fastener (L:27mm W of button:16mm W of loop:11mm). Area of Building 10 and Road 9, no details, H15:05, 1236, WSE9, 2001.1624
Button-and-loop fastener with a triangular loop and a lentoid button, the angled face of which is decorated with triangles of blue and yellow champlevé enamel. This does not correspond with any of Wild's 1970a class numbers.

194. Button-and-loop fastener (L:24mm W of button:15mm W of loop:11mm). Area over *intervallum* road (Road 4), unstratified, P04:01, 50, WSCA62, 2001.1102
Small button-and-loop fastener with a squared loop and a lozenge-shaped button which has a raised centre. This does not correspond with any of Wild's 1970a class numbers.

195. Button-and-loop fastener (L:20mm W:16mm). Alley 5, G14:04, 1274, WSCA92, 2001.1132
Tear-drop or petal button of a button-and-loop fastener of Wild's (1970a) Class III and Gillam's (1958) Type B. Late first century to second century.

196. Button-and-loop fastener (Button: 12 × 9mm). Area over Building 14 and *Via quintana*, unstratified, J12:01, 1932, lost.
Rectangular button of a button-and-loop fastener with deep transverse rib-and-groove decoration.

197. Button-and-loop fastener (L:45mm). Chalet 9, Building ET, Period 4, G13:14, 1566, WSCA211, 2001.1251
Stem and fragment of a triangular loop of a button-and-loop fastener.

198. Fastener (D:14mm L:19mm). Area of Tower 2, unstratified, E02:11, 748, WSCA199, 2001.1239
Ring and shank from a fastening.

199. Terminal (L:17mm). Building 16, floor, Period 1–2, L07:13, 2103, WSCA175, 2001.1215
Decorated terminal from an openwork mount. The extreme end is onion-shaped and sits on a splayed base with curled sides. A rectangular-sectioned shank projects from the back. Cf. South Shields: Allason-Jones and Miket 1984, no. 3.780.

200. Appliqué (L:36mm). Area over Building 9, Alley 5 and Road 9, unstratified, H14:04, 1226, WSCA295, 2001.1335
Small, stylized dolphin, moulded on the front but flat at the back. The snout is attached to a ridge suggesting that the dolphin was one of a pair of confronting dolphins, similar to those on helmet handles of the second and third centuries (see Allason-Jones and Miket 1984, nos 3.410–412; and 2564 below). The lack of a shank and its size suggests that this example was used as appliqué. Cf. Weißenburg: *ORL* 72, Taf. VI, no. 21.

201. Dumb-bell button (L:16mm W:9.5mm). Area over Building AO, unstratified, G08:01, 2053, WSCA232, 2001.1272
Incomplete dumb-bell button with a wide groove and collar and a globular end. Such buttons are common finds on forts in the Hadrian's Wall area and have been related to the button-and-loop fasteners discussed above, by Gillam in his theory of the inter-Wall school of metalworking (1958). MacGregor (M., 1976) has suggested a late first- to possibly third-century date for production.

202. Plumb-bob (L:51mm D:15.5mm W of shank:9.5mm T of shank:3mm). Chalet 12, Building AL1, Period 4, M14:39, 1778, lost.
Long, solid conical plumb-bob with a deep groove around the circumference. A rectangular-sectioned shank is pierced by a circular hole.

203. Weight (H:19mm Max D:12mm). Building 1, *contubernium* 5 floor or demolition material, Period 2, M04:11, 512, WSCA73, 2001.1113
Conical steelyard weight decorated with longitudinal grooves. Cf. South Shields: Allason-Jones and Miket 1984, nos 3.475, 3.476.

204. Weight (H:10mm D:13mm). Area over Buildings 4 and 5 and Alley 3, unstratified, G04:01, 56, WSCA428, 2001.1468
Part of a circular weight with tapering sides.

205. Weight? (L:21mm T:9mm). Road surface associated with the north-west shacks (B2), Period 3–4, H05:13, 777, WSCA256, 2001.1296
Solid cone with a collar and a short shank. Steelyard weight or helmet knob.

206. Terminal (L:27mm T:11.5mm). *Via principalis*, E07:02, 2313, WSCA110, 2001.1150
Baluster-moulded terminal ending in a cone. An oval-sectioned iron rod projects from the end.

207. Terminal (L:16mm T:12mm). *Via principalis*, L08:50, 2519, WSCA170, 2001.1210
Cupped terminal on a circular-sectioned shank.

208. Terminal (L:24mm T:10mm T of shank: 5mm). Building 3, *contubernium* 3, Period 2, N07:15, 2609, WSCA114, 2001.1154
Baluster-moulded terminal on a wide, circular-sectioned shank.

209. Terminal (L:8mm). Area of Building 11 and Alley 6, no details, L15:03, 1507, WSCA400, 2001.1440
Tiny acorn terminal.

210. Terminal (L:20mm). Area east of Building 10, post-Roman, H15:06, 1441, WSCA198, 2001.1238
Roughly fashioned conical terminal of a square-sectioned curved rod.

211. Knob (D:20mm H:30mm). Area over Road 6, unstratified, M16:08, 1740, lost
Globular knob with a flaring shank. Both knob and shank are globular and decorated all over with horizontal grooves.

212. Helmet knob (H:14mm D:9mm). Area of Alley 1, post-Roman dereliction, M05:04, 39, WSCA253, 2001.1293
Conical helmet knob with a flared border.

213. Handle (L:49mm). Area over Building 13, unstratified, M09:01, 2564, WSCA230, 2001.1270
Part of a handle, probably from a helmet, which has been in the form of a pair of confronting dolphins. Only one dolphin survives, very stylized with a short narrow body and fin and a very long wide tail. There is little modelling except for the tail which provides the attachment loop. See Allason-Jones and Miket 1984, nos 3.410–412. See also no. 200 above.

214. Handle (L:75mm T:4mm). Road 4, P04:04, 28, WSCA82, 2001.1122
Handle, possibly from a helmet. The lozenge section expands slightly to long bulbous terminals, one of which is missing.

215. Handle (L:84mm T:8mm). Clay puddling pit, Period 3 demolition, N05:13, 231, WSCA106, 2001.1146
Handle of circular section tapering to both missing terminals.

216. Handle (L of handle:65mm L of loops:35mm T of handle:4.5mm). Alley 10/Building 17, disturbed surface inside building, third century, G04:16, 369, WSCA74, 2001.1114
Handle of oval section tapering to knobbed terminals. A double-spiked loop encloses each terminal suggesting that this is a furniture or box handle rather than a helmet handle.

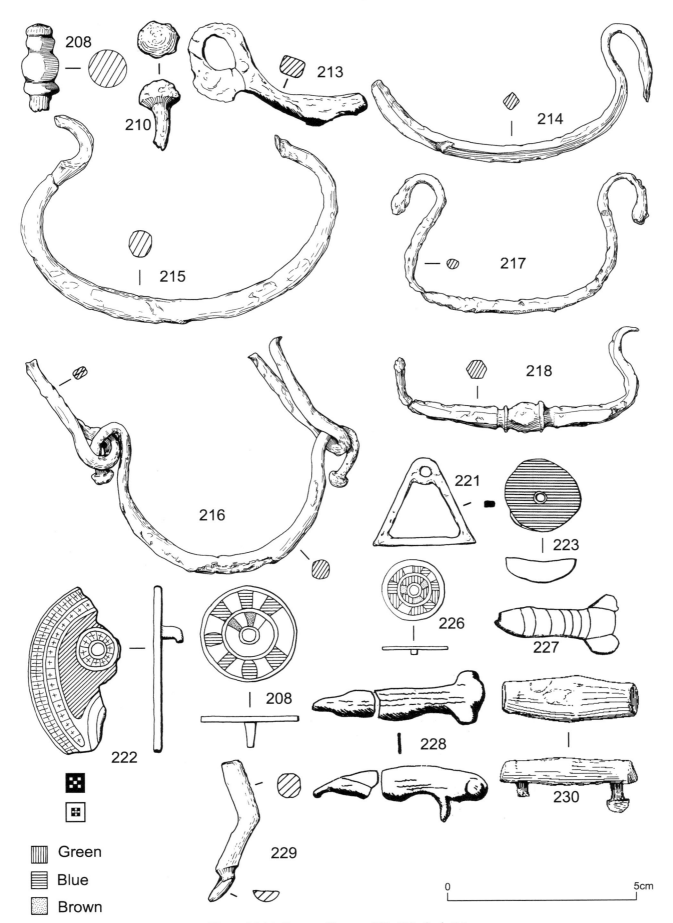

*Figure 25.14: Copper alloy nos 208–230. Scale 1:1.*

217. Handle (L:66mm). Road 3, F11:19, 1184, WSCA126, 2001.1166

    Handle of oval section tapering to knobbed terminals. The shank of the handle is straight, not curved as in the examples above.

218. Handle (L:65mm Max T:8mm). Area over Alley 5, unstratified, G14:01, 1041, WSCA79, 2001.1119

    Handle of hexagonal section with central bead-and-reel motif. Both terminals are missing. Cf. South Shields: Allason-Jones and Miket 1984, no. 3.413.

219. Handle terminal (D:6mm). Area over *intervallum* road, unstratified, N04:01, 21, WSCA246, 2001.1286

    Curved, oval-sectioned rod ending in a rounded knob. The terminal of a small handle?

220. Chape (No measurements possible). Building 9, *contubernium* 2, Period 2, F13:36, 1570, WSCA213, 2001.1253

    Several fragments of a triangular openwork chape, probably of a similar type to Allason-Jones and Miket 1984, no 3.396.

221. Chape (W:27mm H:24mm T:1.5mm). Area over Building 14, unstratified, K10:01, 1963, WSCA177, 2001.1217

    Open triangle with a circular hole at the apex. The inner angles are rounded. Back plate from a scabbard chape.

222. Stud (L:45mm). Area over Building 11, unstratified, K15:01, 1323, WSE3, 2001.1618

    Incomplete stud with turned back edges. One short shank projects from the back. The face has a complicated design with a central area of red enamel surrounded by, as well as containing, panels of white and blue millefiori enamel. The panels alternate with the white and blue in turn being the dominant colour, but each panel has a central dot of red. The back is covered with a cement made from carbonaceous sandstone with some quartz and some calcite but this appears to be secondary, the piece probably having decorated leather originally. Although incomplete, there are indications that the stud was not the usual circular shape but was in the shape of a curled leaf. Late second century AD.

223. Mount (D:20mm T:6mm). Building 4, make-up material, Period 2, J04:25, 940, WSE8, 2001.1623

    Circular mount with a convex back. The concave face is decorated with swirls of blue and green (or white) enamel. There is a circular hole in the centre.

224. Stud (D:26mm T:7mm). Chalet 9, make up layer, Period 4, G13:19, 1576, WSE7, 2001.1622

    Circular stud with its face divided by two concentric circular ribs. The central circle contains blue enamel whilst the surrounding ring is divided into wedge-shaped panels containing alternating colours, one of which is orange, an unusual colour on metalwork in the north of England. The panels in the outer ring contain alternately blue and black enamel. A short, square-sectioned shank projects from the back. This type of stud is common in the northern military zone: see Allason-Jones and Miket 1984, no. 3.5; and Bateson 1981, 53.

225. Stud (D:31mm H:8mm). Area over Building 13, unstratified, M12:01, 1682, lost

    Disc-headed stud with three concentric cells separated by reserved metal ribs. None of the cells now contain enamel. A single squat shank projects from the back.

226. Stud (D:16mm). Area over Building 14, unstratified, J11:01, 1928, WSE4, 2001.1619

    Small, disc-headed stud with the face divided by two concentric circular ribs. The central circle contains transparent turquoise enamel; the surrounding ring contains wedged panels of alternately opaque brown and light blue transparent enamel, and the outer ring contains wedged panels of alternately transparent turquoise and opaque dark green enamel. This use of transparent enamel suggests a recycling of vessel glass. The square-sectioned shank at the back is broken. The edge of the stud is decorated with nicks. Cf. Corbridge: Bishop and Dore 1989, fig. 86, no. 18. An example from Verulamium is dated to 150–155/60 (Waugh and Goodburn 1972, fig. 37, no. 96).

227. Mount (L:29mm W:14mm H:9mm). Area over Road 6, unstratified, M16:08, 1739, lost

    Mount in the form of a stylised phallus with traces of niello in the grooves. Two shanks with hammered ends project from the back. Several studs with transverse grooves from Corbridge have shown traces of niello (Allason-Jones 1989b) but this is the only phallic stud which has shown such traces so far in the Hadrian's Wall zone. See also Allason-Jones and Miket 1984, no. 3.588.

228. Mount (L:40mm W:15mm). *Intervallum road* (Road 6), primary level, M16:20, 1854, lost

    Stylised phallic stud with longitudinal rather than transverse grooving. Two shanks project from the back.

229. Terminal (L:43mm W:7mm). Area over Building 14 and *Via quintana*, unstratified, K12:01, 1690, WSCA251, 2001.1291

    Oval-sectioned rod bent to an angle. One end is broken whilst the other has an oval terminal with an incised line emerging from a groove, possibly intended to be phallic.

230. Stud (L:36mm W:12mm H:10mm). Chalet 12, Building AJ, robber trench, L14:20, 1424, WSCA63, 2001.1103

    Angular, barrel-shaped stud of semicircular section. Two disc-headed shanks project from the hollow back and the face is decorated by three transverse incised grooves.

231. Stud (L:20mm W:8mm). Building 9, *contubernium* 2, Period 2, E13:41, 1572, WSCA429, 2001.1469

    Long rectangular mount with an oval projection from the surviving end. A single shank projects from the hollow back and the face is convex. A set of six similar belt fittings is known from Verulamium: Waugh and Goodburn 1972, fig. 33, no. 43: AD130–150.

232. Mount loop (W:27mm H:29mm). Chalet 10, Building AB, Period 4, D14:12, 1483, WSCA90, 2001.1130

    Semi-oval loop of rectangular section with a splayed spigot projecting from the base. Oldenstein (1976, Taf. 85) shows these being used as backing loops for plain bronze mounts but they were also used on openwork *balteus* mounts (Allason-Jones 1985a, fig. 2).

233. Openwork mount (L:17mm T:1mm). Structure in north-east corner of Building AO, L08:13, 2055, WSCA334, 2001.1374

    Small fragment of an openwork mount.

234. Openwork mount (L:21mm T:5mm). Building 3, *contubernium* 2, Period 2, N07:15, 2614, WSCA336, 2001.1376

Small fragment of an openwork mount.

235. Mount (L:34mm W:30mm T:1mm). Road surface associated with the north-west shacks (B2), Period 3–4, H05:13, 775, WSCA137, 2001.1177
Fragment of a plate with raised edges. The face is divided into rectangles by ribs but there is no trace of enamelling. A short shank projects from the back.

236. Mount (L:24mm W:12mm Total H:8mm). Area over Building 14, unstratified, K11:01, 1922, WSCA105, 2001.1145
Rectangular mount heavily moulded with transverse ribs across the convex front. The back is hollow with a single projecting shank.

237. Mount (L:20mm W:3mm B8:mm). Road surface associated with the north-west shacks (B2), dereliction, E05:04, 183, WSCA257, 2001.1297
Very narrow rectangular plate, with one surviving disc-headed shank projecting from the back.

238. Mount (L:31mm W:32mm). Chalet 12, Building AM2, mid-late third century, M14:11, 1856, lost
Openwork peltate mount with a shank at the upper end bent down to form a hook. At the base a large rectangle has been roughly cut out. The edge of the mount is chamfered. Cf. Oldenstein 1976, nos 646–649. Early third century.

239. Mount (L:19mm W:18mm). Unstratified, 1797, WSCA189, 2001.1229
Three fragments of a peltate mount similar to above with a single stumpy shank projecting from the back.

240. Lunate mounts (W:17.5mm). Building 9, *contubernium* 2, Period 2, F13:36, 1571, WSCA202–3, 2001.1242–1243
Two tiny lunate mounts with convex faces and hollow backs. Two square-sectioned shanks project from each. Cf. Richborough: Cunliffe 1968, pl. XXXIII, no. 134; Newstead: Curle 1911, pl. XCII, no. 3; Pfünz: Oldenstein 1976, Taf. 45, no. 448.

241. Mount (T:1.5mm). Area over Building 12, unstratified, K14:03, 1539, WSCA386, 2001.1426
Fragment of a peltate mount.

242. Mount (H:13mm W:21.5mm Max T:3mm). *Via praetoria* (Road 2), J07:08, 2052, WSCA180, 2001.1220
Peltate mount with one wing solid whilst the other forms an open sleeve.

243. Fitting (L:32mm W:17mm). Area over Building 10 and Alley 5, unstratified, F14:01, 1067, WSCA244, 2001.1284
Incomplete fitting consisting of a curved strip with a loop projecting from the back.

244. Mount (L:35mm). Building 12, *contubernium* 6, Period 3?, L14:26, 1525, WSCA97, 2001.1137
Curved mount of roughly rectangular shape with two cross bars.

245. Mount (L:53mm W:33mm). Area over *intervallum* road (Road 4), unstratified, P04:01, 46, WSCA224, 2001.1264
Badly corroded, rectangular mount with splayed ends and a convex face. Two disc-headed shanks project from the back. Traces of organic matter, such as grass, were found but no trace of leather or textile. Cf. Saalburg: Jacobi 1897, Taf. LIII, 1 and 3; Zugmantel: Oldenstein 1976, Taf. 59, no. 733.

246. Mount (L:12mm). Area over Building 12, unstratified, L14:01, 1398, WSCA205, 2001.1245
Fragment of a mount similar to above.

247. Mount (L:37mm W:15mm B:4mm). Building 12 demo-lition, Period 3, M14:63, 1902, WSCA273, 2001.1313
Incomplete oval mount with slightly thicker terminal at one end. Two shanks project from the back.

248. Mount (D:19mm B:22mm). Unstratified, 1898, WSCA258, 2001.1298
Domed fitting with two attachment loops surviving, and the remains of a third.

249. Fitting (L:30mm W:12.5mm H:9mm). *Via quintana* (Road 3), M14:41, 1860, WSCA178, 2001.1218
Undecorated rectangular fitting with two shanks projecting from the back. Apparently an unfinished product.

250. Stud (D:30mm H:13mm). Building 3, abandonment/ post-Roman, P07:10, 2598, WSCA172, 2001.1212
Disc stud with a central dimpled cone surrounded by deep concentric grooves. The appearance is like the face of a bell-shaped stud (see below). A disc-headed shank projects from the back.

251. Stud (D:26mm). Area over Building 14, unstratified, H11:01, 2058, WSCA241, 2001.1281
Incomplete stud distorted by heat (casting waste?). The head consists of a circular rib surrounded by a wide flange with a circular-sectioned shank projecting form the back.

252. Stud or bolt (L:39mm D of head:19.5mm T of head:5mm shank:8.5mm × 4mm). Area over *Via principalis*, unstratified, L08:01, 2468, WSCA72, 2001.1112
Stud or bolt with a thick disc head, the edge of which is decorated with two incised lines. The face is also decorated with incised concentric circles. The shank is rectangular in section and is pierced by a 3.5mm hole at the end.

253. Disc stud (D: 26mm H:18mm). Area over Building 10 and Alley 5, unstratified, E14:01, 1132, WSCA53, 2001.1093
Disc stud with decorative notching around the edge. A wide rectangular-sectioned shank projects from the back and is broken across the pierced end. Cf. South Shields: Allason-Jones and Miket 1984, no. 3.885; Straubing, Saalburg, and Oberdorf: Oldenstein 1976, Taf. 50, nos 564, 567, and 568 respectively.

254. Disc stud (D:17mm H:8mm). *Via praetoria* (Road 2), K07:05, 2039, WSCA266, 2001.1306
Small disc-headed stud with a circular-sectioned shank. The head is decorated with notches round the edge but is much smaller than is normal with this type.

255. Disc stud (D:20mm Shank W:8mm B:1mm). West rampart, Period 1, D10:25, 2308, WSCA365, 2001.1405.
Stud with a slightly domed disc head and the remains of a wide rectangular-sectioned shank projecting from the back.

256. Disc stud (D:13mm H:10mm). Building 13, pit in room 8, mid-third century, N12:25, 1842, lost
Disc stud with a raised border set close to but not on the rim. A single shank projects from the back.

257. Disc stud (D:17mm T of shank:6mm). Area over Building 12, unstratified, L14:01, 1412, WSCA403, 2001.1443
Very corroded stud with a disc head and a circular-sectioned shank.

258. Disc stud (D:28mm). Area over Building 10 and Alley 5, unstratified, F14:01, 1283, WSCA382, 2001.1422
Disc stud, slightly domed with a short, square-sectioned shank.

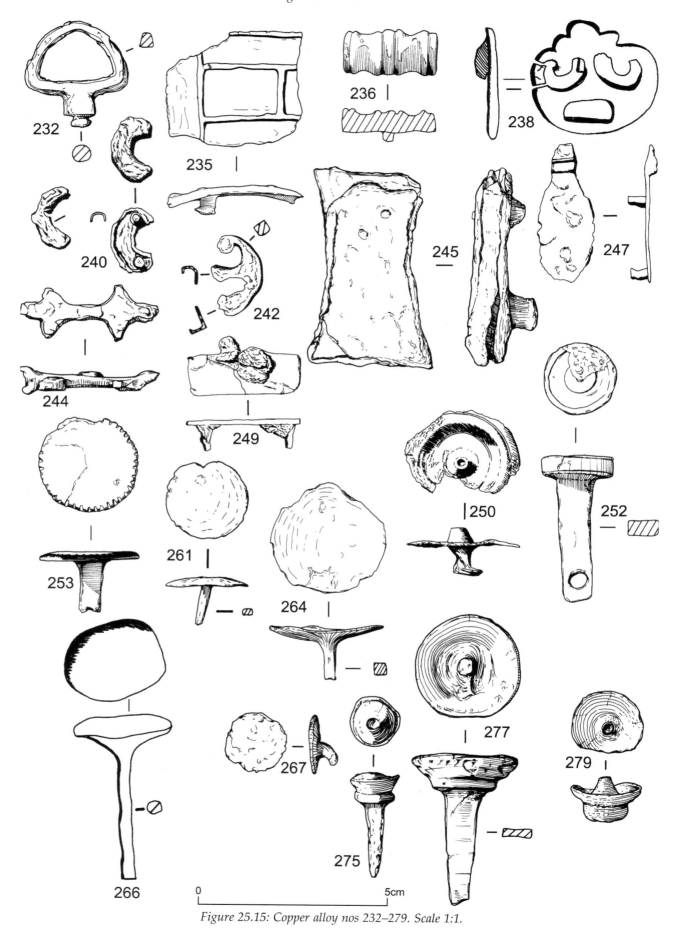

*Figure 25.15: Copper alloy nos 232–279. Scale 1:1.*

259. Disc stud (D:25mm T:0.5mm). Building 2, *contubernium* 6, Period 3, M05:13, 424, WSCA431, 2001.1471
Disc stud covered in iron corrosion. X-rays show no sign of a shank or rivet.

260. Disc stud (D:21mm). Area of Gateway 3 and Road 6, modern, G16:19, 1073, WSCA416, 2001.1456
Disc stud covered with iron corrosion. The face has a marginal groove.

## Disc studs with square-sectioned shanks

261. Disc stud (D:22mm). Area over Building 12, unstratified, L14:01, 1420, WSCA66, 2001.1106

262. Disc stud (D:29mm). Area over *intervallum* road (Road 5), unstratified, E04:01, 160, WSCA192, 2001.1232

263. Disc stud (D:34mm). Building L, demolition, Period 4, G04:03, 328, WSCA430, 2001.1470

264. Disc stud (D:30mm). Building 1, north wall foundation, Period 2, M04:04, 362, WSCA50, 2001.1090

265. Disc stud (D:17mm W of shank:7mm T:3mm). Gateway 1, robber trench, L03:43, 871, WSCA280, 2001.1320
Stud with a slightly domed disc head and a wide rectangular-sectioned shank.

266. Disc stud (D:24mm H:35mm). Building 13, stoking room, Period 4, M12:37, 1810, lost
Stud with a distorted disc head and a very long, oval-sectioned shank with a hammered end. There are traces of lead on the underside of the head.

267. Disc stud (D:16mm). Road 8, F08:10, 2258, WSCA117, 2001.1157
Disc-headed stud with a rectangular-sectioned shank moulded to a right angle.

268. Disc stud (D:14mm H:10mm T of shank:4mm). Building 1, phase 1 demolition, Period 3–4, M04:03, 214, WSCA197, 2001.1237
Disc stud with a thick, short, tapering shank.

## 269–75. Bell-shaped studs with square-sectioned iron shanks. Type 1 (Allason-Jones 1985b)

269. (H:14mm D:27mm). Area over Alley 4, unstratified, F05:01, 125, WSCA219, 2001.1259
Traces of gilding survive on the face.

270. (H:12mm D:26mm). Road 8, F09:07, 2220, WSCA46, 2001.1086

271. (H:23.5rnm, H:14mm). Area over Road 8, unstratified, F08:01, 2196, WSCA108, 2001.1148
Wide shallow skirt separated from the waist by a rib.

272. (D: 31mm). Road surface associated with the north-west shacks (B2), dereliction, J05:16, 839, WSCA278, 2001.1318

273. (H: 17mm). Building 2, *contubernium* 8 demolition material, Period 3 or later, L05:25, 860, WSCA54, 2001.1094

274. (H: 16mm). Area over Building 10 and *intervallum* road (Road 6), unstratified, F15:01, 1053, WSCA91, 2001.1131

275. (H:26mm). Area over *intervallum* road (Road 6), unstratified, L16:01, 1340, WSCA113, 2001.1153

## 276–8. Bell-shaped studs, with shank cast in one with the head. Type 2 (Allason-Jones 1985b)

276. (H:25mm D:10.5mm W of shank:8mm T:5mm). Area over Building 16 and *Via principalis*, unstratified, N08:01, 2474, WSCA228, 2001.1268

277. (H:41mm D:28mm). Unstratified, WSCA402, 2001.1442.

278. (H: 29mm). Area of Building 9, modern, E13:16, 1135, WSCA109, 2001.1149

279. Bell-shaped stud (H:12mm, D:18mm). Building 14, crosshall, Period 2?, K11:39, 2080, WSCA234, 2001.1274
Very small bell-shaped stud with a short curved skirt. A narrow dimpled cone projects from the face. The top is broken so it cannot be assigned to a type.

## 280–2. Domed studs filled with lead-tin alloy

280. (D:18mm H:7mm). Area over Building 14, unstratified, J11:01, 1937, WSCA164, 2001.1204
No trace of the iron shank survives.

281. (D:26mm H:10mm). Drain north of Building AZ, robber trench, L12:18, 1741, WSCA174, 2001.1214
A rectangular-sectioned iron shank.

282. (no measurements possible). M16:08, 1855, WSCA165, 2001.1205

283. Stud (D of head:15mm H:12mm D of rove:12mm). *Via principalis*, E07:35, 2415, WSCA231, 2001.1271
Hollow, domed stud with a tapering shank which ends in a disc rove.

284. Stud (D:10mm H:9mm). Area over Building 10 and *intervallum* road (Road 6), unstratified, F15:01, 1352, WSCA223, 2001.1263
Small, dome-headed stud with a circular-sectioned shank.

285. Stud (D:17mm). Gate 1, modern, L03:03, 678, WSCA415, 2001.1455
Hollow, domed stud head. No shank survives.

286. Stud (D:17mm). Building 2, *contubernium* 5, Period 3 or later, M05:11, 276, WSCA404, 2001.1444
Domed head of a stud. No shank survives.

287. Stud (D:6mm). *Via quintana* (Road 3), K14:15, 1588, WSCA473–7, 2001.1513–1517
Six tiny studs, each with a domed head and a disc rove held 1.5mm apart.

288. Stud (D:34mm). Chalet 9, post-Roman dereliction, F13:16, 1573, WSCA221, 2001.1261
Circular stud with convex face and an oval-sectioned shank.

289. Stud (D:19mm). Area over Building 11 and Alley 6, unstratified, L15:15, 1521, WSCA432, 2001.1472
Stud with a domed head and a disc rove with fragments of wood held between the two. Cf. Buch and Saalburg: Oldenstein 1976, Taf. 46, nos 486 and 487 respectively.

290. Stud (D:11mm). Building 14, crosshall, Period 1 or 2, H11:51, 2148, WSCA233, 2001.1273
Hollow, domed stud head. The circular-sectioned shank passes through the head.

291. Stud (H:15mm D:24mm). Building 14, drain in west wall, Period 1 or 2, H11:34, 2073, WSCA120, 2001.1160
Hollow, domed stud with a short, circular-sectioned shank and a disc rove.

292. Stud (L: 20mm). Area over Building 14 and Alley 3, unstratified, H04:01, 670, WSCA433, 2001.1473
Fragment of a stud with a rectangular-sectioned shank with a hole pierced through the rounded end.

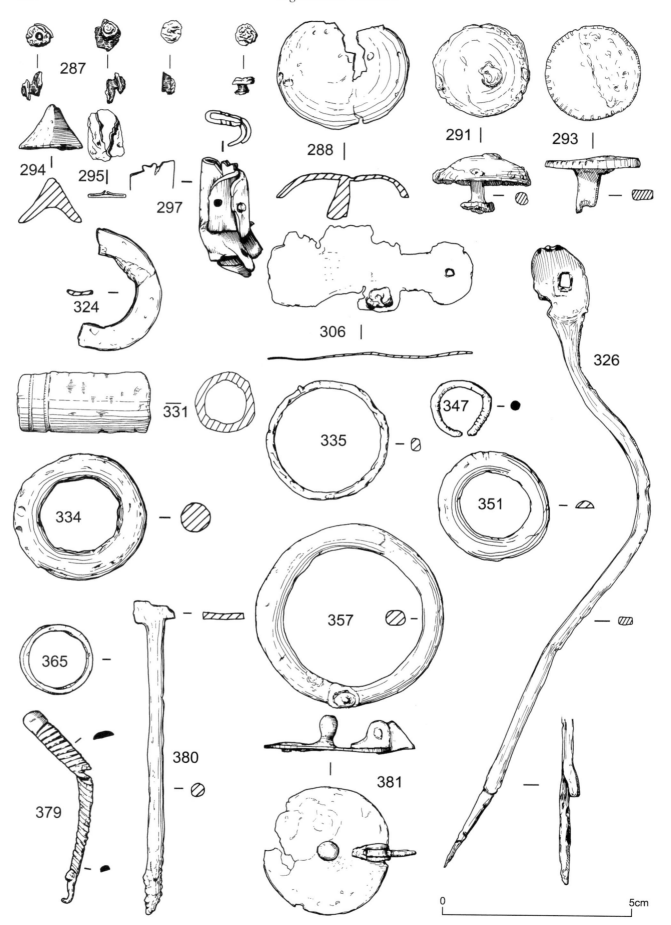

*Figure 25.16: Copper alloy nos 287–381. Scale 1:1.*

293. Disc stud (D:25mm H:15mm). Building 3, contubernium 1/2 partition, Period 3–4, N07:06, 2589, WSCA116, 2001.1156
Disc stud with notched edge and rectangular-sectioned shank pierced by a circular hole at the rounded end. Cf. South Shields: Allason-Jones and Miket 1984, 3.885.

294. Boss (H:12mm D:17mm). Area over Building 8 and *Via quintana*, unstratified, D12:01, 1019, WSCA220, 2001.1260
Hollow conical boss.

295. Clip (L:14mm W:9mm B:4mm). Fill of *intervallum* drain (Road 7) outside Building 13, P12:08, 1780, WSCA5, 2001.1045

296. Strip (L:19mm W:7mm T:0.5mm). Area over Alley 1, ploughsoil, N05:03, 185, WSCA248, 2001.1288
Rectangular strip with decorative cut-outs along one edge and pierced by two large rivet holes.

297. Sheet (L:33mm W:15mm B:1mm). Building BA, Period 4, M13:10, WSCA21, 2001.1061
Folded rectangular sheet with decorative cut-outs along one edge and pierced by four rivet holes at the corners. One rivet survives.

298. Strip (L:26mm W:12mm). Tower 2, no details, E02:15, 905, WSCA387, 2001.1427
Strip of curved section pierced by two roughly, circular holes.

299. Strip (L:40mm W:5mm T:1.5mm). Rubble over Building 8 and nearby roads (B3), late third/early fourth century, E12:08, 1166, WSCA138, 2001.1178
Strip expanding to the broken ends. One end has split across a circular hole.

300. Strips (T:0.5mm). Building Row 20, Building Q, mid-third century, F11:36, 1195, WSCA434, 2001.1474
Several large strips of copper alloy, one with an edge folded over. Possible fragment of armour.

301. Strip (L:3mm T:1mm). Area over Building 13, unstratified, N12:01, 1671, WSCA435, 2001.1475
Fragments of a strip of slightly curled section with one straight edge.

302. Strip (L:31mm W:15mm T:2mm). Chalet 9, Building ET, Period 4, G13:14, 1563, WSCA191, 2001.1231
Rectangular strip with a central grooved rib. The surviving end is stepped and pierced by a circular hole.

303. Strip (L:19mm T:3mm). Alley 10/Building 17, road surface, late third/early fourth century, J05:20, 906, WSCA436, 2001.1476
Triangular strip with a thick projection at the apex. The base has broken across a circular hole.

304. Strip (L:20mm). Area over Building 13 and Alley 7, unstratified, L09:01, 2482, WSCA283, 2001.1323
Curled strip.

305. Plate (L:26mm W:10mm T:0.5mm). Drain from tank south of Building 14, late third/early fourth century, J12:34, 2168, WSCA310, 2001.1350
Rectangular plate pierced at the corners by small circular holes.

306. Plate (L:54mm W:24mm B:0.5mm). Building 13, courtyard, Period 3–4, N11:34, 1897, WSCA20, 2001.1060
Thin sheet with remains of small rivets, probably a fitting from a box.

307. Plate (T:1mm hole:7x7mm). Building 9, *contubernium* 6, Period 2, G13:24, 1586, WSCA406, 2001.1446
Fragment of an irregularly shaped plate with a square hole cut through.

308. Sheet (L:60mm W:29mm T:0.75mm). Chalet 12, Building AM2, mid/late third century, M14:11, 1853, lost
Incomplete, rectangular sheet with at least five circular rivet holes, one of which still contains a disc-headed rivet.

309. Sheet (Total L:65mm W:9mm T:0.5mm). Area of Building 14, no details, H11:26, 2000, WSCA265, 2001.1305
Several fragments of rectangular sheet.

310. Sheet (L:19mm W:22mm T:0.5mm). Building 14, pit, fourth century?, H09:34, 2149, WSCA305, 2001.1345
Triangular sheet with two corners cut off.

311. Sheet (L:25mm). Drain from tank south of Building 14, late third/early fourth century, J12:34, 2167, WSCA326, 2001.1366
Fragment of a rectangular sheet with a marginal repoussé rib. Pierced by at least one circular hole.

312. Sheet (L:20mm B:0.25mm). *Via principalis*, J08:19, 2151, WSCA328, 2001.1368
Several thin sheets pierced by random holes.

313. Sheet (L:14mm T:1mm). *Via praetoria*, B07:03, 1988, WSCA93, 2001.1133
Incomplete sheet, pierced by one small circular hole. Several oblique ribs run across the face.

314. Sheet (L:46mm T:0.25mm). Area over Road 9, unstratified, E09:01, 2351, WSCA337, 2001.1377
Fragment of a thin sheet folded in half. A repoussé rib runs close to one edge.

315–20. DISCS

315. (T:1mm). Area over Gate 1, unstratified, L03:01, 631, WSCA438, 2001.1478. Incomplete.

316. (D:28mm). Building 1, south wall foundation, Period 2, N05:25, 437, WSCA437, 2001.1477. Incomplete. From the iron corrosion on one face it appears that this formed the facing disc from an iron stud.

317. (D:34mm T:1mm holes:1mm). Area of Building 16, no details, K07:04, 2009, WSCA185, 2001.1225. Much corroded disc which has been lathe-turned – the turning lines and chuck hole are still clear. Both faces are polished although there is no trace of tinning. Three tiny holes are pierced at the very edge.

318. (D:19mm T:0.5mm). Area over Building 14, unstratified, J11:01, 1938, WSC167, lost

319. (D:33.5mm T:1mm). Area over Building 14, unstratified, J09:01, 1951, WSCA181, 2001.1221. Slightly curved in section.

320. (D:33mm T:1mm). Area over Building 16 and *Via praetoria*, unstratified, K07:01, 1996, WSCA254, 2001.1294. Incomplete.

321–4. WASHERS

321. (D:15mm T:1mm). Area over *intervallum* road (Road 4), unstratified, P04:01, 15, WSCA414, 2001.1454.

322. (D:35mm W:8.5mm). Unstratified, 2620, WSCA188, 2001.1228. Curved.

323. (D:25mm W:7mm). Building 14, pit, fourth century?, H09:34, 2149, WSCA307, 2001.1348. Curved.

324. (D:28mm T:0.75mm). Building Row 20, Building

AX, mid-third century, H11:57, 2445, WSCA338, 2001.1378. Incomplete.

325. Hook (L:14mm). Area over Building 11 and Alley 6, unstratified, L15:01, 1280, WSCA381, 2001.1421
Fragment of a hook of oval section.

326. Rod (L:172mm W:14mm hole:4mm). Rubble over Building 8 (B3), late third/early fourth century, D11:02, 1061, WSCA70, 2001.1110
Rectangular sectioned shank ending in an oval plate which is pierced by a square hole.

327. Shank (L:18mm W:12mm). Unstratified, 2166, WSCA243, 2001.1283
Incomplete, rectangular-sectioned shank ending in an oval plate which is pierced by a rough circular hole.

328. Rod (L:18mm W:6mm T:2.5mm). Building 11, *contubernium* 3/4, Period 2, L15:19, 1617, WSCA271, 2001.1311
Rectangular-sectioned rod which has broken across a transverse hole. The other end splays out curling around a central knob.

329. Rod (L:33mm). Rubble over east rampart and *intervallum* road, Q07:07, 2572, WSCA361, 2001.1401
Rectangular-sectioned rod thickening from a point to a hooked end.

330. Rod (Total W:20mm W of rod:3.5mm T:3mm). Area over Buildings H and Z, unstratified, L13:01, 1882, WSCA167, 2001.1207
Oval-sectioned rod bent to form a ring with the ends overlapped at an angle.

331. Tube (L:34mm D:17mm T:3mm). Area over Building 1, unstratified, P05:02, 45, WSCA49, 2001.1089
Tube with thick sides decorated with two incised bands.

332. Tube (L:19mm W:9mm). Area over Building 10 and Alley 6, unstratified, M15:01,1607, WSCA452, 2001.1492
Tube of lentoid section with one end nipped close.

333–76. RINGS
## Circular or oval section

333. (D:40mm T:3mm). Area over *intervallum* road (Road 6), unstratified, L16:01, 1259, WSCA370, 2001.1410. Incomplete.

334. (D:34mm W:7mm T:5.5mm). Building 3, abandonment/post-Roman, N07:08, 2552, WSCA343, 2001.1383

335. (D:34mm T:4mm). Road surface associated with the north-west shacks (B2), late third/early fourth century, J04:05, 807, WSCA129, 2001.1169.

336. (D:30mm W:3.5mm T:2.5mm). Area over *intervallum* road (Road 6), unstratified, L16:01, 1257, WSCA392, 2001.1432. Hexagonal section, worn on one side.

337. (D:27mm W:5mm T:5mm). Area over Building 13, unstratified, N12:01, 1665, WSCA299, 2001.1339. Incomplete.

338. (D:24mm W:3mm T:2mm). Area over Building 2, ploughsoil, L05:03, 680, WSCA457, 2001.1497.

339. (D:23mm T:3mm). Levelling east of Building Row 20, Building R, late third/fourth century, G12:19, 1220, WSCA461, 2001.1501.

340. (D:21.5mm W:1.25mm T:4mm). *Via principalis*, M08:09, 2501, WSCA284, 2001.1324

341. (D:21mm T:4mm). Area over Road 8, unstratified, F08:01, 2455, WSCA362, 2001.1402. Incomplete.

342. (D:20mm T:2.5mm). Area over Building 10 and Road

9, unstratified, H15:01, 1266, WSCA462, 2001.1502.

343. (D:20mm). Building 4, make-up layer, Period 2, G04:07, 485, WSCA455, 2001.1495.

344. (D:19mm W:2mm T:3mm). Area over Building 14 and *Via quintana*, unstratified, K12:01, 1926, WSCA353, 2001.1393. Incomplete.

345. (D:18mm W:2mm T:3mm). Area over *Via principalis*, unstratified, G08:01, 2066, WSCA255, 2001.1295. Incomplete.

346. (D:17mm W:1.5mm T:2mm). *Via principalis*, L08:57, 2551, WSCA341, 2001.1381. Incomplete.

347. (D:16mm T:2mm). Area over Building 12, unstratified, L14:01, 1531, WSCA371, 2001.1411.

348. (L: 23mm T: 4mm). Building 4, officer's quarters, Period 2, F03:22, 901, WSCA478, 2001.1518.

349. (T:3mm). Area of Alley 5, no details, H14:21, 1271, WSCA463, 2001.1503. Incomplete.

## Semi-circular section
350. (D:28mm), Building 18, *contubernium* 1, Period 3–4, F05:15, 432, WSCA130, 2001.1170.

351. (D:28mm W:6mm T:2mm). Area over Buildings H and Z, unstratified, L13:01, 1750, WSCA132, 2001.1172. Worn in one section.

352. (D:27mm W:3mm T:4.5mm). Building 1, floor, Period 2, M05:28, 922, WSCA456, 2001.1496.

353. (D:21mm W:3mmT:4mm). Gate 2, post-Roman, D08:17, 2411, WSCA356, 2001.1396. Penannular.

354. (D:20mm W:2.5mm T:3mm). Area over Building 13, unstratified, N12:01, 1653, WSCA467, 2001.1507.

355. (D:18.5mm W:2mm T:3.5mm). Area over Building 14, unstratified, J11:01, 1934, WSCA168, 2001.1208. Very corroded.

356. (D:11mm T:5mm). Area over Building 11, unstratified, J15:01, 1272, WSCA389, 2001.1429. Penannular, with two grooves.

## Square or rectangular section
357. (D:48mm W:5mm T:4.5mm). Area over Building 12, unstratified, K14:03, 1384, WSCA465, 2001.1505. Repair on one side.

358. (D:27mm W:4mm). Building 11, *contubernium* 4, Period 2, L15:33, 1540, WSCA375, 2001.1415.

359. (D:23mm W:2.5mm). Area over Building 11, unstratified, K15:01, 1372, WSCA464, 2001.1504.

360. (D:22mm W:2.5mmT:2mm). Building 18, *contubernium* 1, Period 3–4, F05:15, 431, WSCA458, 2001.1498.

361. (D:21mm W:3.5mm T:3mm). Building Row 20, Building R, late third/early fourth century, G11:25, 2418, WSCA354, 2001.1394.

362. (D:21mm W:2.5mm T:3mm). Area over Building 11, unstratified, K15:02, 1295, WSCA399, 2001.1439.

363. (D:20mm W:3mm). Area of Alley 5, no details, G14:07, 1598, WSCA466, 2001.1506.

364. (D:20mm W:2.5mm T:2mm). Area over Building 11, unstratified, J15:01, 1264, WSCA372, 2001.1412.

365. (D:19mm W:1.5mm T:2.5mm). Gate 2 floor, Period 3–4?, D08:40, 2380, WSCA342, 2001.1382.

366. (D:19mm T:3mm W:3mm). Road 8, F08:10, 2310, WSCA237, 2001.1277.

367. (D:18mm T:2mm). Area over *intervallum* road (Road 6), unstratified, L16:01, 1258, WSCA469, 2001.1509. Incomplete.

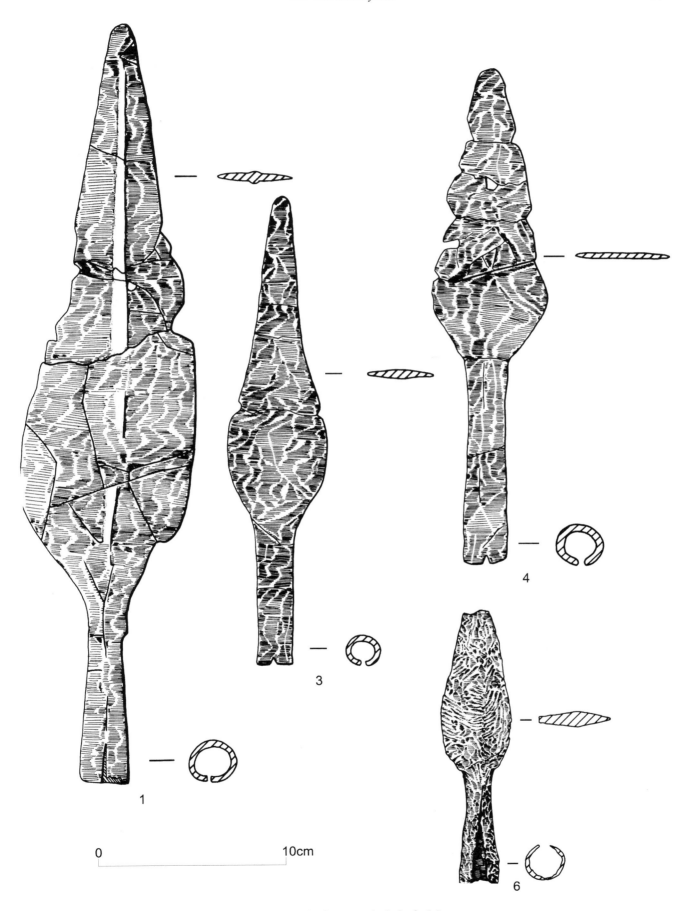

*Figure 25.17: Iron nos 1–6. Scale 1:2.*

368.  (W:3mm T:2mm). Building 2, *contubernium* 5, Period 3 or later, M05:11, 295, WSCA454, 2001.1494. Incomplete.

## Diamond section

369.  (D:26mm W:5mm T:3mm). *Via principalis*, L08:57, 2547, WSCA339, 2001.1379.
370.  (D:23mm W:4mm T:2.5mm). Area over Building 8 and *Via quintana*, unstratified, D12:01, 1033, WSCA459, 2001.1499.
371.  (D:23mm). Area south of Building 5, Roman/post-Roman, H05:13, 591, WSCA472, 2001.1512.

## Unclear

372.  (D:23mm). Building 12, *contubernium* 5, Period 3?, M14:42, WSCA22.
373.  (D:20mm T:3mm). Rampart building north of *Porta quintana*, Period 2–3, C11:04, 1093, WSCA460, 2001.1500. Incomplete.
374.  (D:20mm). Area over Road 2, unstratified, K04:02, WSCA373. Thin.
375.  (D:16mm T:2.25mm). Building AW robber trench, H11:71, 2612, WSCA350, 2001.1390.
376.  (D:8mm). Area over Building 1, ploughsoil, Q05:02, 116, WSCA453, 2001.1493. Incomplete.

377.  Block (W:30mm T:5mm). Area over Building AO, unstratified, K08:01, 2031, WSCA333, 2001.1373
      Part of a hexagonal block thickening to the edges.
378.  Shank (L:36mm D of head:14.5mm). Road 8, F08:10, 2263, WSCA187, 2001.1227
      Short, circular shank with a waisted rod ending in a disc. The casting lines have not been filed down. The piece may have been rejected on being taken from the mould because of a gash across the top of the disc.
379.  Bracelet (L:52mm W:5mm B:2mm). West *intervallum* road, D12:10, 1046, WSCA262, 2001.1302.
      Terminal of bracelet with D-shaped cross section and incised decoration on the upper surface (AC).
380.  Stylus (L:89mm D:4mm). Area over Building 5 and Alley 4, unstratified, H05:01, 1246, WSCA193, 2001.1233
      Stylus with a circular-section shank and incomplete eraser, with traces of groove decoration. The pointed end if corroded, but has traces of groove decoration (AC).
381.  Lid (D:33mm Total H:8.5mm). Area over *Via principalis*, unstratified, L08:01, 1984, WSCA176, 2001.1216
      Plain, circular disc with a hinge projecting from the back at one edge. An iron hinge pin holds a fragment of the vessel. From the centre of the lid projects a knob with a globular end.

# Iron (Figs 25.17–20)

1.  Spearhead (L:410mm, D of socket:26mm Max. W of blade:93mm, L of entry:249mm). Building 1, officer's quarters, Period 3, N05:05, 196, WSFE19, 2001.1949
    Very large spearhead with a leaf-shaped blade, low shoulders and straight edges. A central rib runs down both faces. The split socket is very short in proportion to the blade, and is also very narrow, containing fragments of mineral-replaced wood. Scott 1980, Type 5, 337.
2.  Spearhead (L:155mm W:60mm B:10mm). Area over Alley 5, unstratified, G14:03, WSFE143, 2001.2040

Incomplete fragment of spearhead blade with a central rib running down each face. (AC)

3.  Spearhead (L:270mm, D of socket:24mm Max. W of blade:63mm, L of entry:132mm). Road/surface (B1), N05:16, 346, WSFE10, 2001.1940
    Leaf-shaped spearhead with low shoulders and straight edges. The faces are flat and the socket split. Scott 1980, Type 5, 337.
4.  Spearhead (L:255mm, D of socket:18mm, L of entry:140mm). Building 5, Period 1?, G04:20, 534, WSFE12, 2001.1942
    Leaf-shaped spearhead with an elongated point, flat faces and a split socket. Scott 1980, Type 9, 339: the largest group of these weapons comes from Chesters and Scott has suggested that, as the blades have no cutting edge, they were used for parade or practice.
5.  Spearhead (W(blade):55mm D(socket):23mm). Area over Building 5 and Alley 4, unstratified, H05:01, 311, WSFE337, 2001.2215
    Very fragmentary spearhead.
6.  Spearhead (L:148mm, D of socket: 20mm). Building 2, *contubernium* 5, Period 3 or later, M05:11, 300 (duplicate), WSFE47, 2001.1972
    Leaf-shaped spearhead with the tip missing. The socket is split.
7.  Spearhead (L:130mm, Max. W of blade: 62mm). Building 11, *contubernium* 3/4, Period 2, L15:18, 1602, WSFE326, 2001.2206
    Leaf-shaped spearhead missing top of the blade, with angular low shoulders. Missing much of split socket. Scott 1980, Type 4, 335.
8.  Spearhead (L:145mm, D of socket:12mm Max. W of blade:38mm). Area over Building 12, unstratified, L14:01, 1557, WSFE5, 2001.1936
    Short, leaf-shaped spearhead lacking the tip. The faces are flat and the socket split.
9.  Spearhead (L:138mm, Max. W of blade:21mm D of socket:18mm). Building 3, east wall, Q07:04, 2449, WSFE2, 2001.1933
    Incomplete spearhead with a long narrow blade with no obvious shoulders. The socket is split and contains mineral-replaced wood. The midline of the blade is thick but there is no obvious midrib. Brailsford 1962, Group B; Scott 1980, Type 6, 337; Manning 1985, Group III, 166–7.
10. Spearhead (L(surviving):16mm and 70mm D(socket):15mm). Building 9, *contubernium* 2, Period 2, E13:41, FE357, 2001.2233
    Two non-joining fragments of incomplete leaf-shaped spearhead missing tip. Split socket.
11. Spearhead (L(surviving):100mm: D(socket):15mm W:4mm). Chalet 9, Building W, late third/early fourth century, D13:34, WSFE336, 2001.2214
    Incomplete leaf-shaped spearhead.
12. Spearhead (L:133mm B:3mm). Building 8, room 8, Period 2, E10:76, 2407, WSFE146, 2001.2043
    Incomplete leaf-shaped spearhead missing tip and most of socket.
13. Conical ferrule (L:122mm, Max.D:25mm). Building AO, south wall robber trench, F08:19, 2391, WSFE221, 2001.2115
    Long conical ferrule. See Manning 1985, 141 for a discussion of function.
14  Ferrule (D(max):20mm). Road/surface (B1), N05:16, 322, WSFE253, 2001. 2147

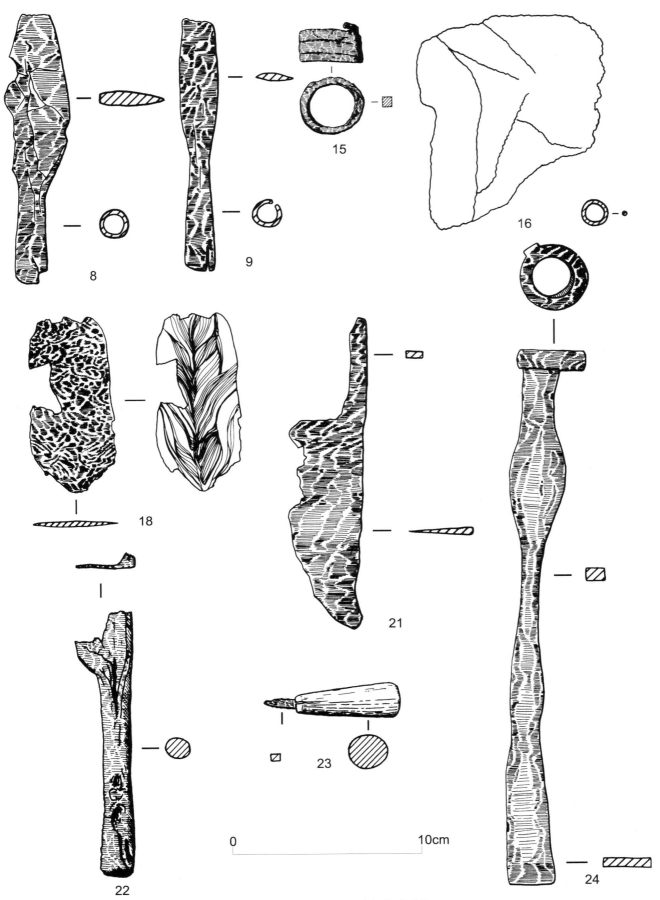

*Figure 25.18: Iron nos 8–24. Scale 1:2.*

Fragmentary.

15. Spiral ferrule (D(int):22mm B(rod):4mm L:20mm). Building 1, make-up, Period 2, L05:46, WSFE31, 2001.1961
Rectangular-sectioned rod, twisted round three times to form a ferrule for a spear or tool. Iron Age or Roman. (AC)

16. Ring-mail (L:105mm W:105mm B:30mm Loop D:7mm B:1.5mm). Building 1, *contubernium* 1–4, Period 2, N05:32, 565, WSFE333, 2001.2211
Fragment of a ring-mail shirt, folded over at one end. This is a large piece of ring-mail, which is usually found in smaller fragments. (AC)

17. Ring-mail (D:7mm B:1.5mm). Road associated with north-west shacks (B2), late third/early fourth century, J04:05, 826, WSFE155, 2001.2052
Single loop.

18. Pattern-welded dagger (L:96mm W:46mm B:4mm). Chalet 12, Building AL1, Period 4, M14:39, WSFE358, 2001.2234
Small fragment of a pattern-welded blade, with a single line of herring-bone pattern. Third-century. Cf. Künzing: Bishop and Coulston 2006, 164. (AC)

19. Knife (L:163mm, W:33mm). Building 7, no details, G08:11, 2204, WSFE83, 2001.2002
Incomplete knife with a straight back and a long rectangular-sectioned tang set at the midpoint. The edge also appears to be straight. Manning 1985, Type 15, 115–16.

20. Knife (L:77mm W:24mm B:5mm). Area over Building 11, unstratified, K15:10, WSFE84, 2001.2003
Incomplete knife with a straight back and a rectangular-sectioned tang set at the mid-point.

21. Knife (L:170mm W:40mm B:4mm). Alley 8, H09:16, WSFE20, 2001.1950
Knife with large triangular blade, curving up slightly at the tip. Rectangular cross-sectioned tang.

22. Handle (L:145mm D:12mm W(blade):30mm). Building 18, *contubernium* 1, floor, Period 3–4, F05:39, 492, WSFE334, 2001.2212
Roughly circular section handle, with terminal created by folding over the end expanding into blade. There is a solid ridge on the outer, vertical edge, but the expanded side is only approximately 1.5mm thick. (AC)

23. Awl (L(overall):72mm L(handle): 54mm D:(max, handle):18mm D:5mm). Building 16, Period 3, L07:10, 2034, WSFE378, 2005.3701
Polished circular-sectioned handle of red deer antler which tapers towards a short circular-sectioned iron rod. The rod tapers to a point, apparently intentionally, and can be identified as an awl. See Manning 1985, 39–41.

24. Paring chisel (L:267mm, W of blade:25mm, D of collar:38mm). Building 4, officer's quarters, Period 2, F04:25, 559, WSFE15, 2001.1945
Paring chisel of rectangular section tapering slightly to the blade which is chamfered on both faces. The other end bulges before narrowing to fit into a circular iron collar. Possibly there has been a wooden handle with the collar set at the top, slipping down as the handle rotted. Manning 1985, Type 3, fig. 4.

25. Chisel (L:65mm, W of blade:36mm). Chalet 9, post-Roman, G14:13, 1511, WSFE76, 2001.1996
Fragment of a former chisel with a flat blade and a socketed shank set high over the blade. Manning 1985, fig. 4, no. 4. (AC)

26. Chisel (L:91mm D:10mm). Alley 7, K12:23, WSFE28, 2001.1958
Circular-sectioned shank, tapering to a point at one end and to a flat blade at the other. Cf. Manning 1985, pl. 11, no. B43. (AC)

27. Adze-hammer (L:220mm, W of blade:71mm, Socket:22 × 19mm). Chalet 12, Building AG, Period 4, K14:26, 1605, WSFE14, 2001.1944
Complete adze-hammer with a splayed cutting blade set at an angle to the expanded socket and with a very short counter balance. The junction of the blade and oval socket is sharply undercut. The collar is short. See Manning 1985, 17–18 for discussion and parallels.

28. Lift-key (L:174mm, W across head:37mm). Building 14, courtyard, late third/early fourth century, J09:05, 2004, WSFE27, 2001.1957
T-shaped lift-key with a rectangular-sectioned shank which ends in a tightly curled loop. The two teeth taper away from the head. Cf. Manning 1985, fig. 25, no. 1.

29. Lift-key (L:overall of all pieces 114mm W:40mm B:7mm). Building 5, officer's quarters, Period 2, E04:25, WSFE368, 2001.2244
Incomplete.

30. Lift-key (L:86mm W:11mm B:9mm head W:44mm). Chalet 9, Building W, late third/early fourth century, D13:34, WSFE377
L-shaped lift-key with a rectangular-sectioned shank which ends in a curled loop. The head has three teeth. Cf. Manning 1985, fig. 25, no. 3. (AC)

31. Slide-key (L:62mm W: 30mm B:(shank):4mm (foot)17mm). Area of Building 4, no details, G04:25, 387, WSFE263, 2001.2155
L-shaped slide-key in poor condition, probably with a straight bit (Manning 1985, Type 2). Drawn from X-ray. (AC)

32. Slide-key (L77mm W:30mm). Building 1, verandah, Period 3, N05:18, 553, WSFE375, 2001.2251
Identified from X-ray; now disintegrated. (AC)

33. Lock bolt (L:56mm W:13mm T:6mm). Area over Building 11, unstratified, J15:05, 1496, lost
Rectangular-sectioned tumbler-lock bolt for use with a slide key. The end is countersunk and the body of bolt has four rectangular shaft holes. Such bolts are unusual in iron but common in copper alloy; see above, copper alloy nos 96–7.

34. Padlock (D of ring:84mm, presumed width of box:50mm). Building 11, *contubernium* 3/4, Period 2, L15:19, 1604, WSFE11, 2001.1941
Padlock consisting of an iron ring and box-lock. It is very corroded and incomplete but X-rays suggest that the box holds three or four levers. Cf. Saalburg: Jacobi 1897, 477, Fig. 76, no. 21; also Herrmann 1969, Abb. 9, no. 2.

35. Shackle (D(internal):50mm W:6mm B:6mm). Building 16, floor, Period 1–2, L07:13, WSFE330, 2001.2208
One arm of a shackle with hinge loop at one end, and an incomplete oval loop at the other. Beyond the loop, the arm ends in a point. The size suggests a wrist shackle. See Manning 1985, figs 22–3. (AC)

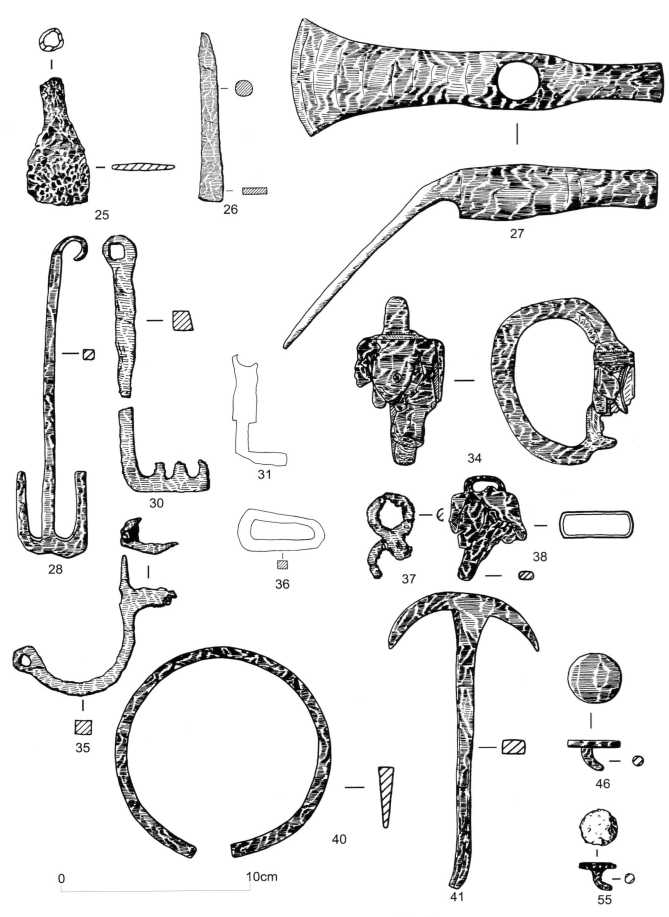

*Figure 25.19: Iron nos 25–55. Scale 1:2.*

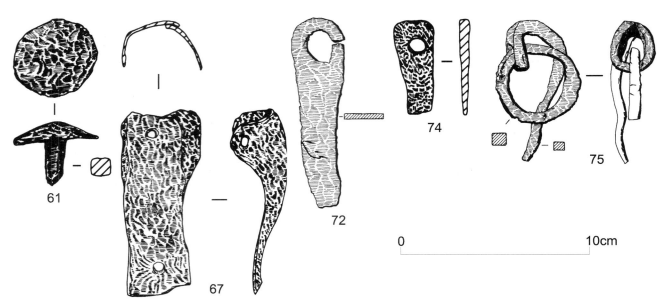

*Figure 25.20: Iron nos 61–75. Scale 1:2.*

36. Chain link (L:45mm W:20mm B:4mm). Building 9, *contubernium* 1, Period 2, E13:42, WSFE362, 2001.2238
    Slightly tapering oval chain link. Square-sectioned. Drawn from X-ray. (AC)

37. Chain link (L:45mm D:25mm B:5mm). Building 11, *contubernium* 4, Period 1, L15:29, WSFE363, 2001.2239
    Two incomplete figure-of-eight chain links. Only one link illustrated.

38. Bell (Surviving L of bell:56mm L of clapper:47mm, Max.W:42mm, Max.T:16mm). Building 5, Period 1?, G04:20, WSFE6, 2001.1937
    Incomplete bell of rounded rectangular section with a rectangular handle. Inside, a double-sided clapper, shaped like a double-spiked loop, hangs from a ring.

39. Martingale? (L:34mm). Road 5, D07:28, 2325, WSFE3, 2001.1934
    Curved strip of iron with a narrower thinner strip projecting into the inner edge of the curve. Part of a martingale? Cf. copper alloy example from South Shields: Allason-Jones and Miket 1984, no. 3.665–6.

40. Hub linings (D:111mm H:38mm T:3–6mm). Area of Building 4, no details, G04:25, 389, WSFE7, 2001.1938
    Two hub linings shaped like collars, one annular, the other penannular. The bands thicken towards one edge. See Manning 1985, 72, H35–8.

41. Clamp (L:160mm W across head:80mm T across head:21mm). Building 1, demolition material, Period 2, N05:04, 198, WSFE8, 2001.1939
    T-shaped clamp. The head is curved back from the rectangular-sectioned tapering shank. See Manning 1985, 132.

42. Clamp (L:55mm W:45mm). Building 9, *contubernium* 4, Period 2, F13:44, WSFE22, 2001.1952
    Incomplete T-shaped clamp with slightly curved arms.

43–56. Disc-headed studs with copper alloy sheet
Disc-headed iron studs with rectangular shanks. A circular sheet of copper alloy is fixed on top of each head. These have been found at a number of other fort sites in the area.

43. (D:28mm). Building 1, *contubernium* 1–4, Period 2, N05:32, 561, WSFE351, 2001.2227

44. (D:28mm). Area over Building 12, unstratified, K14:01, 1562, WSFE352, 2001.2228

45. (D:27mm). Building 9, *contubernium* 3, Period 2, F13:50, 1581, WSFE17, 2001.1947

46. (D:27mm). Building 9, *contubernium* 3, Period 2, F13:50, 1582, WSFE16, 2001.1946

47. (D:25mm). Alley 1, upper layer, M05:12, 355, WSFE353, 2001.2229

48. (D:25mm). Alley 1, upper layer, M05:12, 358, WSCA163, 2001.1203

49. (D:25mm). Area of Alley 5 and Road 9, unstratified, H14:30, 1428, WSCA492, 2001.1532

50. (D:25mm). Chalet 9, Building ET, Period 4, G13:14, 1565, WSFE347, 2001.2223

51. (D:c.25mm). Road associated with north-west shacks (B2), dereliction, E05:04, 251, WSCA491, 2001.1531

52. (D:24mm). Alley 5, post-Roman debris, F14:13, 1120, WSFE344, 2001.2221

53. (D:23mm). Building 9, *contubernium* 1, Period 2, E13:24, 1140, WSCA488, 2001.1528

54. (D:22mm). Building 1, *contubernium* 2–4 cleaning, Period 2?, N04:20, 509, WSFE350, 2001.2226

55. (D:21mm). Building 1, demolition/make-up, Period 3, P05:08, 288, WSFE18, 2001.1948

56. (D:20mm). Area over Building 10 and Alley 5, unstratified, E14:01, 1367, WSFE354, 2001.2230

57–60. Disc headed stud without copper alloy sheet

57. (D:22mm). Building 1, *contubernium* 5, Period 2, M04:10, 521, WSFE128, 2001.2032

58. (D:20mm). Area over Buildings 4 and 5 and Alley 3, unstratified, G04:21, 786, WSFE154, 2001.2051

59. (D:23mm). Building 1, sub-phase 1 demolition material, Period 2, L04:25, 930, WSFE308, 2001.2191

60. (D:23mm). Building 1, floor, Period 2, M04:09, 525, WSFE343, 2001.2220. With 28mm long incomplete shank, bent into L-shape.

61. Stud (D:45mm, H:33mm). Area over West rampart,

unstratified, C09:01, 2224, WSFE332, 2001.2210
Large stud with a convex disc head and a short tapering shank.

62. Stud (D:39mm). Tower 7 demolition material, N04:18, WSFE66, 2001.1987
Large stud with a convex disc head. No surviving shank. (AC)

63. Stud (D of head:17mm H:14mm). Area over Building 13, unstratified, N12:01, 1650, WSFE324, 2001.2204
Stud with a slightly convex disc-head. Only part of the circular sectioned shank remains.

64. Stud (D:14mm H:11mm). Building 14, post hole, fourth century?, H09:34, WSFE373, 2001.2249
Disc-headed stud with a convex face. The shank is square in section.

65. Plate (L:51mm). Building 16, floor, Period 3, L07:10, 2036, WSFE64, 2001.1985
Fragment of iron plate pierced by two disc-headed rivets.

66. Strip (L:113mm. Max. W: 32mm). Building 1, contubernium 1–4, Period 2, P05:17, 533, WSFE13, 2001.1943
Large blade or hinge section of triangular shape. No obvious cutting edge or rivet holes.

67. Strip (L:110mm, W of shank:36mm). Building 16, Period 3, K07:18, 2046, WSFE81, 2001.2000
Wide strip expanding to a T-shape with rounded ends to the arms, both of which are pierced by a square hole (4 × 4 mm). A circular hole is pierced in the centre of the strip at the top and bottom (D:5mm). The arms curve inwards to form a sheath. Manning (1976, nos 198–9) in his discussion of similar items says, 'bindings of this type were made for a particular purpose and with the loss of the wood to which they were normally attached, their function must remain uncertain'.

68. Double spiked loop (L:86mm W: 41mm). Building 2, contubernium 5, Period 3 or later, M05:11, 300, WSFE21, 2001.1951
Large double spiked loop.

69. Double spiked loop (L:53mm W:22mm B:8mm). Road associated with north-west shacks (B2), Period 3–4, H04:19, WSFE366, 2001.2242
Small example.

70. Curved bar (L:103mm W(max):30mm T(max):17mm). Building 8, room 6, Period 2, F10:15, 2404, WSFE219, 2001.2113
Rectangular-sectioned bar tapering in width and section to a hooked end.

71. Sheet (L:115mm, Max.W:51mm). Chalet 9, post-Roman dereliction, G13:03, 1510, WSFE325, 2001.2205
Sheet with one edge curled over.

72. Escutcheon (L:102mm W:28mm B:7mm). Area over Building 12, unstratified, L14:01, WSFE24, 2001.1954
Incomplete bar expanding towards a D-shaped loop terminal. Possibly escutcheon from a bucket.

73. Escutcheon (L:67mm W:25mm B:5mm). Road associated with north-west shacks (B2), Period 3–4, H04:19, WSFE365, 2001.2241
Incomplete example, pierced by 7mm diameter hole below remains of loop terminal.

74. Strip (L:60mm W(max):21mm T:7mm). Building 3, abandonment/post-Roman dereliction, P07:07, 2624, WSFE216, 2001.2110

Rectangular-sectioned strip snapped off at one end and expanding to the other which is pierced by a large circular hole (D:8mm). Possibly part of a box-hinge (cf. Schönberger 1967, Abb. 7, nos 1–7).

75. Loop (L:78mm B:6mm D(loop):45mm B:5mm). Building Row 20, Building AX(N) south wall, G11:38, WSFE43
Loop with square cross-section hanging from spike with circular attachment loop. (AC)

| No. | Site details |
| --- | --- |
| 32 | Building 1, demolition material, Period 2, N05:04, 81, WSFE292, 2001.2178 |
| 12 | Chalet 12, Building AL2, Period 4, M14:04, 377, WSFE99, 2001.2013 |
| 17 | Building 2, contubernium 8, Period 3 or later, L05:44, 913, WSFE283, 2001.2172 |
| 9 | Area over Buildings 1, 2 and Alley 1, ploughsoil, N05:03, 129, WSFE4, 2001.1935 |
| 6 | Area over Building 2, ploughsoil, L05:03, 610, WSFE130, 2001.2034 |
| 4 | Clay puddling pit, Period 3 demolition, N05:14, 249, WSFE202, 2001.2096 |

76. Hobnails (D of nail heads:6mm). Area over Building 2 and Alley 1, unstratified, M05:01, 1490, WSFE82, 2001.2386
Fragment of leather boot sole with three rows of square-sectioned dome-headed hobnails in position.

Hobnails were found in the following contexts. The number indicates the quantity found.

One or two hobnails were found in a further nine contexts. A total of 92 hobnails were found, with the find-spots well spread over the site indicating casual loss. This limited number of hobnails is also reflected in the remarkably limited number of iron nails found on the site, probably accounted for by the soil conditions which have led to poor preservation of the iron in general.

77. Nail (L:96mm W:7mm T:7mm). Area over Building 13, unstratified, L10:01, 2625, WSFE220, 2001.2114
Nail with square-sectioned shank bent through a right angle with fragments of wood over the sides and end. Of the 207 nails found, the majority had disc heads, with two globular heads and one spatulate. With the exception of two large masonry nails the rest were all of a size suitable for carpentry.

## Lead (Figs 25.21–22)

1. Portable shrine (H:75mm, W:36mm). Unstratified, from modern pipe trench, F14:38, 1307, WSL4, 2001.2265. Published: Allason-Jones 1984.
Portable shrine in the form of a cupboard with a rounded back. The two rectangular doors each have projecting spigots at two corners which fit into looped hinges at each front corner of the cupboard. The doors have raised decoration on both faces: on one face lattice work with pellets at the angles is contained in a pellet border, on

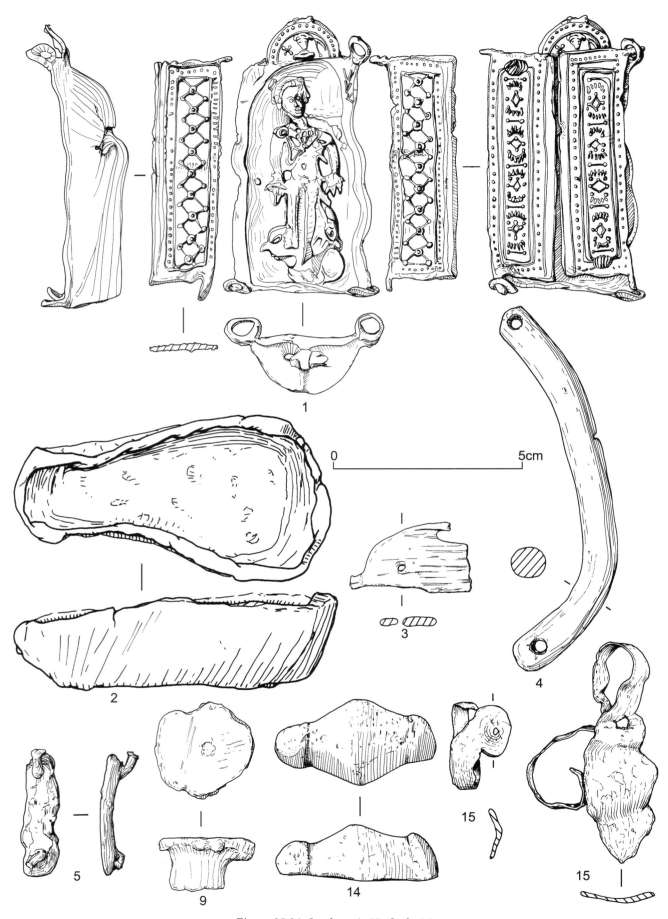

*Figure 25.21: Lead no. 1–15. Scale 1:1*

the other a more complex rib-and-pellet border contains panels of diamond shapes and stylized shells. The pattern over-runs the border at one end of each door. There is no obvious way of fastening the doors.

Above the doors there is a semicircular projecting pediment with a male bust in relief wearing a crown of rays. He is flanked by the whip and wheel symbols of the sun god. This scene is contained within a border of raised pellets between two ribs. A fragment of a hanging loop survives. In the upper section of each hanging edge there is a branch motif in relief.

The cupboard itself contains the figure of a nude male wearing what appears to be a winged head-dress or helmet over his curly hair; a cloak is secured over his right shoulder by a disc brooch. He is holding an unidentifiable object in his right hand and his left hand is splayed. Around his feet are curled the figures of a dolphin and a bridled seahorse. The scene has been made by pressing a lead sheet into a mould, creating a 'cardboard cut-out' effect but with shallow relief. The figure is hollow at the back and has been positioned by slotting a tab through a hole in the floor of the cupboard.

The object has the appearance of a portable shrine, copying in miniature the larger domestic shrines discussed by Boon (1983) and, in particular, a wooden shrine from Herculaneum. Smaller shrines in the form of temples with pedimented doors made from stone are also known, such as at Luxembourg (Boon 1983, pl. vi), and Titelberg (Ésperandieu 1913, no. 4193). The pipeclay shrines holding Venus figurines made in the Samian factories of Gaul may also be comparable (Reinach 1921, 131, fig. 64).

There is some difficulty in identifying which deity the shrine is venerating. The cupboard has the symbols of the sun god but the winged helmet and possible purse of the main figure suggest Mercury. The dolphin and the seahorse add further confusion by implying a sea deity. The cupboard and doors are of better workmanship than the figure, which may suggest that the shrines were mass-produced, the worshipper asking for the deity of choice whose figure was then slotted into position. If this is so then the attributes shown on the pediment of the cupboard need have no direct relevance to the god venerated inside. However, the bust of the sun god with the whip and wheel symbols may be a reference to Jupiter and thus to Mercury's role as messenger of the sun god. Amongst his various roles as god of profit, patron of thieves and protector of cattle and herds, Mercury/Hermes was also the patron and protector of travellers and conductor of souls to the Underworld (Lindgren 1980, 38ff). It is possible that the seahorse and dolphin indicate his specific role as protector of those travelling on water or across the River Styx. The seahorse may particularly refer to travellers on the sea as the motif occurs on statuettes or reliefs of Neptune whilst the dolphin is more commonly used in the context of rivers and would appear to have a connection with well worship and in turn with the cult of the dead.

The use of lead is unusual as the lead figurines and reliefs known from Roman Britain are few in number and poor in quality. Two lead openwork reliefs from Gorsium in Hungary have points of similarity with the Wallsend shrine as they each depict a deity standing on a rock in an archway, one representing Venus, the other Minerva, but these appear to be mounts rather than free-standing shrines (Bánki 1972, nos 29, 30). Lead was more commonly used in the production of coffins, tanks and caskets, and

the decoration on the doors of the Wallsend shrine is very similar to the motifs used on fourth-century lead coffins (Toller 1977). However, three more exact British parallels are known to the Wallsend shrine. A shrine with a figurine of Minerva was found in a late Roman/early medieval context at Dorchester (Henig 1993a, fig. 72). A cupboard, lacking its doors but with a figure of Venus, was found in the 1984 excavations at Wroxeter *macellum* from one of a series of pits containing early to mid third-century pottery and a few third- or fourth-century small finds (Lloyd-Morgan 2000, fig. 4.31; 137). The 1976 *vicus* excavations at Vindolanda also produced a fragment of a door stratified in a floor level of mid to late fourth-century date (Vindolanda Museum Ref. No. 2033). These parallels may suggest that the shrines were more common than might at first be thought and to imply a fourth-century date. They also support the theory that the cupboards were mass-produced and the deity added on request.

On excavation, the shrine was associated with barracks dated to the fourth century (Allason-Jones 1984, 232), which have now been re-dated to the third century. The trench in fact cut through both the Period 2 *contubernium* 4 of Building 10 and the alley between the Period 4 chalets AA and Z. (AC)

2. Lamp (L:84mm Max.W:44mm H:22mm). Area over western rampart, unstratified, C11:02, 980, WSL16, 2001.2277
Small lamp or lamp-holder of very angular appearance with a nipped nozzle. Open lamps of this type are common in iron and pottery but less common in lead. For a general discussion of open lamps see Manning 1985, 98–9.

3. Appliqué (L:32mm T:1.5mm). Area over Building 10, unstratified, D14:01, 1468, WSL58, 2001.2319
Lead alloy appliqué in the form of a stylized dolphin. The eye is a pierced circular hole.

4. Rod (L:100mm T: 8.5mm W:9mm), Building 16, kiln, Periods 1–2, M08:14, 2506, WSL40, 2001.2301
Curved rod of oval section with an oval hole cut through both ends. A deep notch has been cut across the outer face. Handle?

5. Rod (L:32mm Max.D:14mm Min.D:8mm Weight:30gm). Chalet 10, Building X, Period 4, G15:11, 1434, WSL28, 2001.2289
Long rod of cylindrical section tapering to one end.

6. Cramp (L: 46mm). Area over Alley 4, unstratified, E05:01, 133, WSL19, 2001.2280
Lead cramp of the type used for mending pottery. A fourth-century cooking pot from South Shields (MA acc. no. 1956.128.118.A) shows how soft lead was placed across the break on the inner and outer faces of the pot forming a double bridge and forced into holes drilled on either side of the break to join the bridges and keep them in position.

7. Cramp (L: 24mm). Road associated with north-west shacks (B2), Period 3–4, H04:19, 804, WSL20, 2001.2281
Lead pottery cramp of the same type as above.

8. Plug (D:9 × 5mm). Area over Building 1, ploughsoil, Q05:02, 108, WSL23, 2001.2284
Small circular plug.

9. Plug (D:26mm). Building 8, room 1, Period 3, D11:28,

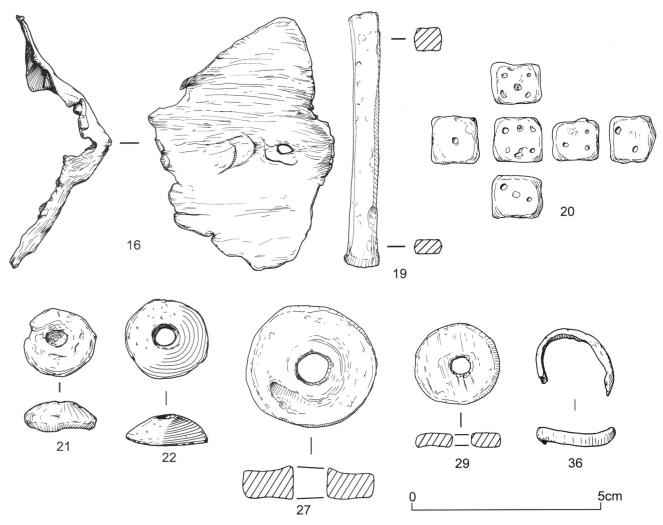

*Figure 25.22: Lead nos 16–36. Scale 1:1.*

1192, WSL18, 2001.2279
Disc-headed plug.

10. Plug (L:34mm W of head:18mm). Area over Building AO, unstratified, G08:01, 2152, WSL17, 2001.2278
Plug shaped like a nail and made from one sheet of rolled lead with a wedge-shaped head.

11. Plug (L:22mm W:18mm B:13mm). Area over Building 10 and Alley 5, unstratified, E14:01, 1138, WSL82, 2001.2342
Plug with roughly triangular head.

12. Plug (L:50mm W:38mm B:30mm). Building 11, *contubernium* 4, Period 1, L15:25, WSL123, 2001.2376
Roughly oval plug with a flat base and widening to the top. The remains of an iron ?nail projects from the top.

13. Plug (L:40mm W:35mm B:45mm). Building 11, *contubernium* 4, Period 1, L15:25, WSL122, 2001.2375
Second example from same context.

14. Block (L:43mm W:25mm H:13mm Weight 70gm). Area over Buildings 4 and 5 and Alley 3, unstratified, G04:01, 148, WSL38, 2001.2299
Lozenge-shaped block with globular ends, flat on the back with a deep convex face.

15. Strip (L:*c*.420mm). Alley 1, upper layers, M05:12, 357, WSL37, 2001.2298
Long, distorted strip expanding to both ends and pierced by two holes (D:4 × 4mm and 8 × 8mm)

16. Sheet (L: 83mm T: 1mm Hole: 3 × 3mm). Road 8, F08:10, 2277, WSL62, 2001.2323
Fragment of sheet of roughly triangular shape with a square hole punched through near one edge. Traces of a square-headed iron nail survive in the hole.

17. Sheet (L:50mm). Road 8, F08:05, 2255, WSL63, 2001.2324
Oval sheet folded into four.

18. Sheet (L:62mm Max.W:51mm). Building 5, *contubernium* 1, Period 2, G05:23, 568, WSL32, 2001.2293
Sheet of trapezoidal shape.

19. Ingot (L:69mm W:9mm T:7mm). Area over Building 1, unstratified, L04:01, 730, WSL34, 2001.2295
Rectangular-sectioned strip snapped off at one end. Ingot?

20. Die (L:13mm W:13mm B:13mm). Area over Building 10 and Alley 5, unstratified, F14:01, 1284, WSL5, 2001.2266
Square lead die with incised dots for numerals.

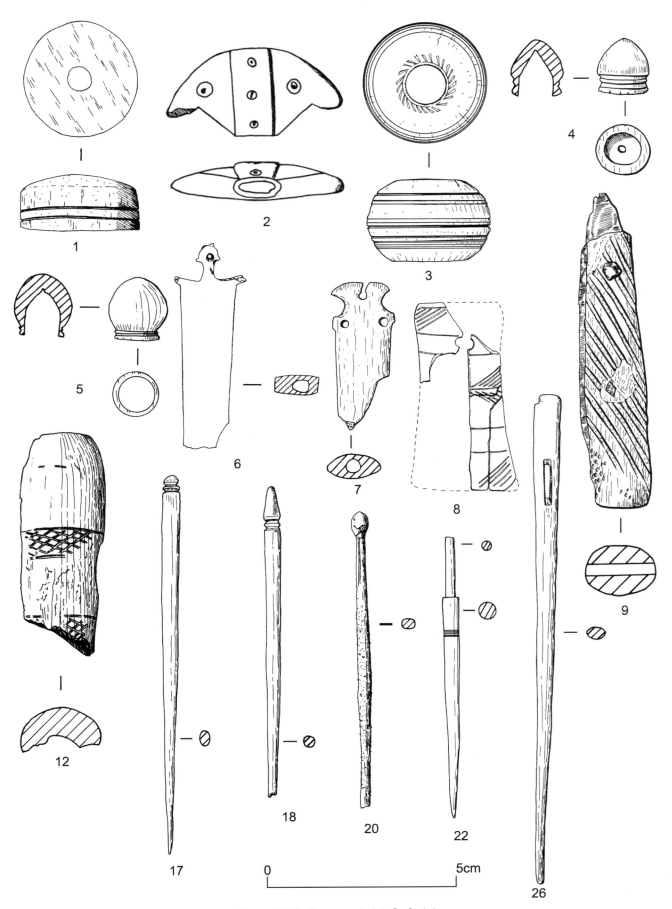

*Figure 25.23: Bone nos 1–26. Scale 1:1.*

21. Block (D:18.5mm H:8mm). Road associated with north-west shacks (B2), Period 3–4, H04:19, 794, WSL30, 2001.2291
Bun-shaped block. Counter?

22. Weight (D:23mm H:6mm). Road associated with north-west shacks (B2), late third/early fourth century, J04:05, 805, WSL1, 2001.2262
Domed circular weight.

### 23–35. DISCS

#### Discs with central circular hole

23. (D:30mm T: 4mm). Building 2, *contubernium* 6, Period 3 or later, L05:34, 890, WSL57, 2001.2318

24. (D:28mm T:6mm Weight:25gm, hole:5mm). Area over Building 10 and *intervallum* road (Road 6), unstratified, G15:01, 1449, WSL29, 2001.2290

25. (D:26mm T:4.5mm Hole:6mm). Building 8, drain, Period 4, E11:38, 1143, WSL55, 2001.2316. Made in a mould.

26. (D:25mm Hole:5mm T:4mm). Road 3, K13:18, 2076, WSL54, 2001.2315

27. (D:34mm T:7mm). Area of Building 9, no details, E13:27, 1466, WSL3, 2001.2264

28. (L:29mm W:26mm B:2mm D(hole):4mm). Cistern 3, mid-third century, L08:08, 2011, WSL53, 2001.2314. Slightly irregular.

29. (D:24mm T:4mm D(hole):5mm). Area over Building 11 and Alley 6, unstratified, M15:01, 1670, WSL2, 2001.2263

#### Disc with central square hole

30. (D:28mm T:5mm Hole:5mm Weight:20gm). Rubble over Building 8 and *intervallum* road (B2), late third/early fourth century, D11:02, 1081, WSL22, 2001.2283

#### Unpierced discs

31. (D: 52mm T: 5mm). Building 3, officer's quarters, Period 3–4, P08:14, 2545, WSL64, 2001.2325. Rough disc with irregular scratches on both faces.

32. (D:31mm T: 4mm). Area over Building 5 and Alley 3, unstratified, F04:01, 1618, WSL36, 2001.2297

33. (D: 26mm). Building 7, west granary, G09:29, 2270, WSL67, 2001.2328. One convex face.

34. (D:24mm T:2mm). Alley 7, L09:13, 2030, WSL50, 2001.2311. With iron corrosion adhering.

35. (D: 15mm T: 3mm). Area over Building 12, unstratified, K14:01, 1324, WSL6, 2001.2267

36. Ring (Ext.D:21mm W:2mm T:3.5mm). Area over Building 10 and Alley 5, unstratified, F14:01, 994, WSL25, 2001.2286
Fragment of a ring of semi-oval section.

## Antler and bone (Figs 25.23–25)

1. Pommel (D:32mm H:14mm hole D:7mm). Road 8, F08:10, 2247, WSB83, 2005.3693
Bun-shaped bone dagger pommel with two incised lines around the base. The central hole shows no signs of wear.

2. Pierced plate (L:*c*.24mm W:*c*.46mm B:*c*.7mm). Area over Building 12, unstratified, L14:01, 1362, lost
Pierced plate decorated with dot and ring. A similar example found in a late fourth-century context at Ravenglass is described as a toggle or buckle (Potter 1979, fig. 27, no. 52). (AC)

3. Ball (H:21mm D:32mm). Area over Building 13, unstratified, N10:01, 1633, WSB2, 2001.662
Bone ball pierced by a 12mm diameter central hole which has a series of small vertical nicks cut around its edge at both ends. One end is further decorated by a frame of incised oblique lines around the hole. The surface of the ball has three bands of four lathe-turned lines. Dagger pommel?

4. Knob (H:14mm D:15mm). Building 1, *contubernia* 1–4, sub-phase 1 demolition material, Period 2, N05:32, 563, WSB5, 2001.665
Highly polished, hollow, domed bone knob with a heavily ridged collar. The inner wall shows signs of the knob having been screwed into position. A similar knob from Gross-Gerau is described as having been used as the tip of a dagger pommel (Simon 1965, 38–99, Abb. 7, 7–8). Examples are also known in bronze: e.g. Wiesbaden: *ORL* B31, Taf. 10, nos 4, 5.

5. Knob (H:16mm D:15mm). Area over North rampart, unstratified, M03:01, 751, WSB3, 2001.663
Highly polished, hollow, onion-shaped bone knob with a heavily ridged collar. As with No. 3 above this shows signs of having been screwed into position.

6. Handle (L:55mm W:18mm T:6.5mm). Chalet 9, post-Roman dereliction, F13:12, 1117, WSB50, 2005.3660
Finely worked and highly polished bone handle of rectangular section tapering to the socketed end. The decoratively shaped terminal is pierced by a 2mm diameter hole. This is a particularly fine piece and may have been the handle from a medical instrument rather than a domestic knife. There are no traces of iron or bronze in the socket.

7. Handle (L:40mm W:17mm T:7mm). Area over *Via quintana*, unstratified, F12:01, 1027, WSB6, 2001.666
Finely worked and highly polished bone handle of elliptical section with a circular socket. The terminal is pierced by three small holes arranged in a triangle. As with no. 6 above this may have been the handle of a medical instrument.

8. Handle (L:41mm). Tower 7, P04:05, 132, WSB28, 2005.3638
Fragment of a two-piece bone knife handle of elliptical section. The terminal is splayed and the face decorated by groups of incised oblique and horizontal lines. Two bronze rivets have held the two plates together.

9. Handle (L:76mm W:17mm B:14mm). Drain immediately north of forehall, Period 1, L08:38, WSB7, 2001.667
Two-piece bone knife handle decorated with incised diagonal lines held in place by two iron rivets. Remains of iron blade surviving.

10. Handle (L:87mm W:23mm T:17mm). Area over Building 10 and *intervallum* road (Road 6), unstratified, F15:01, 1059, WSB49, 2005.3659
Two-piece handle of red deer antler with the iron tang and blade of a clasp knife still *in situ*. Three iron rivets hold the handle in position. The end is rounded and the handle retains the natural curve and exterior surface of the antler. Possibly post-Roman.

11. Handle (L:61mm T:16mm). Building 1, verandah

demolition material, Period 3, Q05:25, 255, WSB29, 2005.3639
Tubular antler handle with a smoothed surface and a fragment of the iron knife blade *in situ*.

12. Toggle (L:61mm W:22mm). Area over Building 11 and Alley 6, unstratified, L15:01, 1400, WSB56, 2005.3666
Fragment of a toggle made from a long bone. The terminal is rounded and the face is decorated with two bands of incised cross hatching enclosed in line borders. There is the remains of a slot on one face. Possible native bridle fitting.

### 13–25. PINS

#### Shallow conical heads. Crummy 1979, Type 1.

13. (L:76mm T:6mm). Area over Building 10 and Alley 5, unstratified, E14:01, 1083, WSB45, 2005.3655
14. (L:77mm D:6mm). Area over Building 11 and Alley 6, unstratified, L15:01, 1413, WSB57, 2005.3667. Highly polished.
15. (L:64mm D:7mm). Chalet 12, Building AM1, mid-third century, M14:46, 1888, WSB18, 2001.678

#### Pointed conical heads. Allason-Jones and Miket 1984, Type H.

16. (L:124mm W:6.5mm T:6mm). Building 13, south corridor, Period 2, L11:29, 1839, WSB72. Oval-sectioned.

#### Ridge-and-groove decorated head. Crummy 1979, Type 2; Allason-Jones and Miket 1984, Type E.

17. (L:102mm T:4.5mm). Building 1, *contubernia* 1–4, subphase 1 demolition material, Period 2, N05:32, 562, WSB9, 2001.669
18. (L:83mm). Building Row 20, Building R, late third/early fourth century, G11:10, 1127, WSB10, 2001.670. Highly polished.

#### Spherical head. Crummy 1979, Type 3; Allason-Jones and Miket 1984, Type A.

19. (L:47mm W of Head:6.5mm). Post-Roman rubble over Road 9, H14:24, 1244, WSB52, 2005.3662. Incomplete.
20. (L:80mm D of head:5mm). Building 13, over west bath, late third century, L12:02, 1717, WSB69, 2005.3679. Roughly facetted, oval-sectioned shank tapering to both ends.

#### Other

21. (L:44mm T:3mm) Area over Road 3, unstratified, J13:08, 1361, lost
Incomplete, small bone pin tapering to both ends with a very small flat oval head. The oval-sectioned shank has been roughly shaped.
22. Pin (L:76mm T:4mm L of spigot:16mm). Area over Building 12 and Road 3, unstratified, N14:11, 1689, WSB15, 2001.675
Highly polished bone pin with a tapering, circular-sectioned shank decorated with a band of four incised grooves. The head is shaped into a long spigot and probably held a bead of glass or jet; cf. Allason-Jones and Miket 1984, Type G.

23. Pin rough-out (L:42mm T:4.5mm). *Via quintana* drain, E12:18, 1043, WSB44
Roughly fashioned tapering bone rod.
24. Pin rough-out (L:112mm W:21mm). Building Row 20, levelling north of Buildings Q and R, late third/fourth century, G11:14, WSB99
Roughly fashioned fragment of long bone.
25. Rod (L:41mm B:45mm). Area over Building 12, unstratified, K14:01, 1391, WSB55, 2005.3665
Short length of rod tapering to both ends.

### 26–30. NEEDLES

26. Needle (L:133mm Max.W:7mm). Building 13, room 7, mid-third century, N12:08, 1759, WSB11, 2001.671
Large bone needle with a spatulate head. The rectangular eye has been cut well down the shank. cf. Allason-Jones and Miket 1984, nos 2.263–270.
27. Needle (L:27mm T:3.5mm). Building 16, post hole, Period 1, K07:26, 2047, WSB77, 2005.3687
Pointed head of a needle of circular section with rectangular eye.
28. Needle (L:61mm W:4mm). Area over Building BB, unstratified, N13:01, 1693, WSB66, 2005.3673
Incomplete bone needle of circular section with a blunt head and a rectangular eye.
29. Needle (L:65mm D:4 × 3mm). Area over Building 12, unstratified, L14:01, 1542, WSB59, 2005.3669. Oval section, snapped across eye.
30. Needle (L:31mm D:3mm). Building 13, backfill of east hypocaust, Period 4, M12:67, 1901, WSB19, 2001.679. Snapped across eye. Dyed green.

31. Spindlewhorl (D:47mm B:10mm). Building 12, officer's quarters, Period 1, N14:38, 1887, WSB16, 2001.676
Antler spindlewhorl.
32. Bobbin (L:110mm W:22mm). Chalet 12, AM, Period 4 or later, M14:23, WSB100
Sheep's metacarpal perforated in the middle for use as a bobbin.
33. Bobbin (L:92mm). Building 5, drain fill, Period 2, E05:38, 552, WSB34, 2005.3644
Sheep's metacarpal perforated in the middle for use as a bobbin. This is a native implement of Iron Age origin which may have been used only in Britain (Wild 1970b, 34 and 130). They are becoming increasingly common finds on northern forts, e.g. South Shields and Chesters (Allason-Jones and Miket 1984, 2.24) and recent excavations at Corbridge (Bishop and Dore 1989), Housesteads and Piercebridge, so far unpublished.
34. Weaving Comb (L:37mm W:37mm T:9mm). Area over Building 10 and Road 15, unstratified, H15:10, 1437, WSB58, 2005.3668
The oval terminal and part of the shank of a bone weaving comb with a deeply incised X stretching across the width. Although this type of implement is traditionally referred to as a weaving comb there has been a suggestion that they were intended for dressing skins (Roth 1918, 129ff). Hodder and Hedges 1977, Type ShG.
35. Comb (L:142mm L of teeth:11mm W:13mm). Area over Building 8, unstratified, E10:01, 1112, WSB8, 2001.668

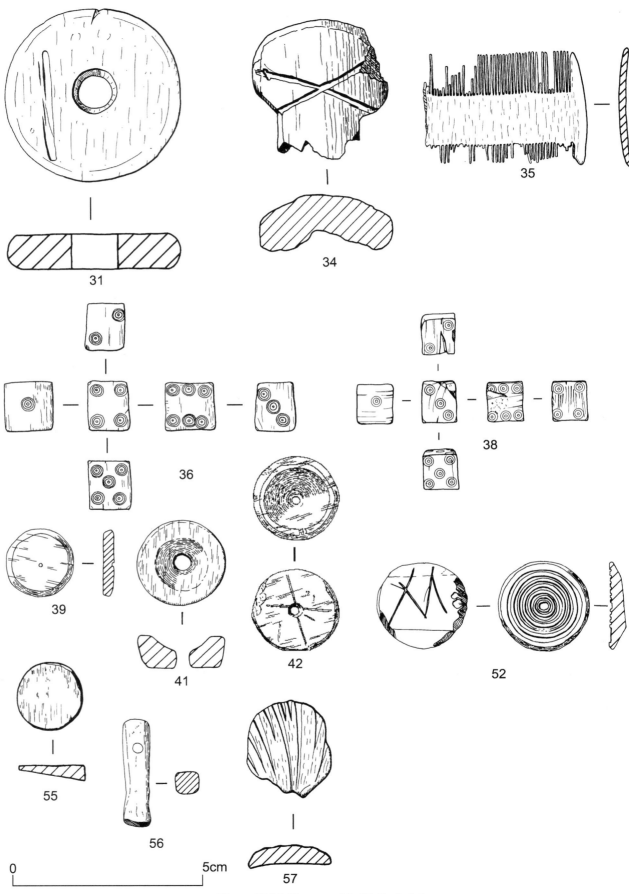

*Figure 25.24: Bone nos 31–57. Scale 1:1.*

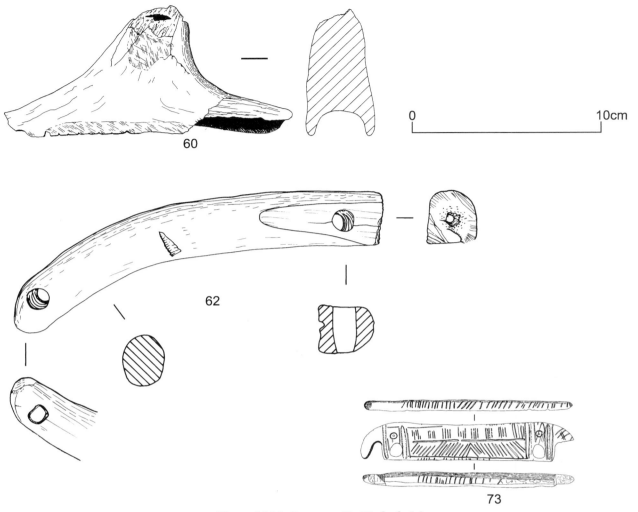

*Figure 25.25: Bone nos 60–73. Scale 1:2.*

Incomplete, single piece bone comb with two rows of fine teeth. The surviving end is plain and rounded.

<sub>36–8.</sub> Dice

Bone dice, with the numbers indicated by stamped double dot and ring motifs. The numbers on the opposing sides add up to seven. It is difficult to see how Roman dice were used in dice-throwing games as they are rarely pure cubes; no. 36 in particular is shaped so that it invariably lands on six. Although Roman dice are not as noticeably rectangular as the parallelepiped examples from the Scottish Iron Age, the discussions on the use of the latter should be borne in mind: Wheeler (1943, 310–11) suggested that they were used as dominoes whilst O'Riordain (1940, 156) reasoned that the dice were not thrown but placed and covered by one person while the other player guessed the number shown uppermost. These suggestions are among those discussed by Clarke (1970, 214ff).

36. (L:13mm T:10.5mm W:11mm). Building 10, *contubernium* 2, Period 2, E14:24, 1464, WSB12, 2001.672. Small rectangular die.

37. (L:14mm W:11mm T:13mm). Alley 5, post-Roman debris, F14:13, 1084, WSB46, 2005.3656

38. (L:11mm W:9mm T:9mm). Area over Building 9, unstratified, D13:01, 1137, WSB13, 2001.673

<sub>39–55.</sub> Counters

Counters made from ungulate long bone are common finds on military and civilian sites in the Hadrian's Wall area but, unfortunately, few complete sets have survived to suggest whether the game involved was *ludus duodecim scriptorum, ludus latrunculorum,* or *tabula.* See MacGregor, A., 1976; Austin 1935; Bell 1960.

Greep 1995, type 1; Kenyon 1948, Type C.

39. (D:18mm T:2.5mm). Building 3, *contubernium* 2, Period 2, N07:15, 2610, WSB90, 2005.3700.

40. (D:18mm T:3mm). Area over Building 10 and Alley 5, unstratified, F14:01, 1095, WSB48, 2005.3658. Very worn bone counter with a central incised dot.

Greep 1995, Type 2; Kenyon 1948, Type A.

41. (D:23mm T:7mm). Area over *Via quintana*, unstratified, D12:01, 1030, WSB43, 2005.3653. Central 5mm

diameter central hole. The edge of both faces is bevelled.

42. (D:23mm T:3mm). Building 14, room D, Period 1 or 2, J12:31, 2147, WSB81, 2005.3691. Central hole. The edge of the upper face is bevelled with a group of four short vertical scratches. On the reverse a motif has been roughly scratched before the hole was drilled.

43. (D:22mm T:4mm). Area over Building 12, unstratified, L14:28, 1547, WSB61, 2005.3671.

44. (D:21mm T:3.5mm). Building 14, room D, Period 1 or 2, J12:31, 2146, WSB80, 2005.3690.

45. (D:19mm T:3mm). Area over Building 10, unstratified, D14:01, 967, WSB40, 2005.3650.

46. (D:19mm T:3mm). Area over Building 13, unstratified, M12:01, 1661, WSB64, 2005.3674.

47. (D:19mm T:3mm). Area over Building 12 and Alley 6, unstratified, J14:01, 1350, WSB54, 2005.3664. The dished face has worn to a perforation.

48. (D:19mm T:2.5mm). *Via principalis*, E08:14, 2323, WSB84, 2005.3694.

49. (D:18mm T:3mm). Area over Road 8, unstratified, F09:09, 2212, WSB82, 2005.3692.

50. (D:18mm T:2mm). Road 3, F11:19, 1185, WSB51, 2005.3661. LVI is lightly scratched on the reverse.

51. (D:16mm T:3mm). Building 14, room A, Period 2?, H11:04, 2083, WSB78, 2005.3688.

## Greep 1995, Type 3, Kenyon 1948, Type B.

52. (D:24mm T:3.5mm). Building 14, room D, Period 2?, J12:26, 2082, WSB79, 2005.3689. On the reverse the letter M has been firmly scratched.

53. (D:19mm T:1.5mm). Area over Building 14 and Alley 8, unstratified, H10:01, 1949, WSB94, 2005.3704.

54. (D:18mm T:1.5mm). Area over Building 13, unstratified, N12:01, 1642, WSB63, 2005.3673. Very worn. The reverse has four lightly incised oblique strokes.

## Other

55. (D:18mm T:3mm). Chalet 12, Building AM2, (mid-) late third century, M14:11, 1857, WSB75. Flat, plain surfaces.

56. Peg (L:28mm T:8mm). Building 5, *contubernium* 1, Period 2, G05:23, 557, WSB62
   Phalanx of a large bird? pierced by a 2mm diameter hole near one end. Part of a musical instrument?

57. Shell (L:26mm T:5mm). Latest surviving *Via praetoria* surface, K04:04, 893, WSB1, 2001.661
   Fragment of a long bone which has been carved to represent a cockle shell. The back has been roughly hollowed and the piece is pierced by a 2mm diameter hole at the 'hinge'. A similar example from Intercisa has an extra hole pierced at the edge (Vago 1971, pl. LXII). Examples are also known in bronze, eg. Faimingen: Oldenstein 1976, Taf. 57, nos 700–703; and Xanten: Steiner 1911, Taf. XII, No. 16.

58. Ring. Building 13, room 3, Period 2, L11:11, 1705, WSB68
   Annular antler ring in three pieces.

59. Antler Ring (D:33mm T:16mm). Building 1, verandah demolition material, Period 3, N05:18, 279, WSB33, 2005.3643

Thick slice cut across a red deer antler tine. The core has been hollowed out but the outer, surface is untouched.

60. Antler implement (L:155mm). Area over Building 1, ploughsoil, Q05:02, 95, WSB24, 2005.3634
   Fragment of red deer antler which has been cut to leave the joint between the beam and a tine. The long edge has been carefully sliced down the beam and smoothed with a series of nicks cut across at regular intervals. This appears to be an implement in its own right rather than an off-cut.

61. Antler (L:140mm). Area over Building 12, unstratified, L14:01, 1543, WSB60, 2005.3670
   Curved length of red deer antler pierced by a 17mm diameter hole at one end. This is not a netting needle as the unperforated terminal is thickened and blunt, yet the hole is not large enough to take a hammer shaft.

62. Antler (L:200mm W:29mm T:25mm). Area over Building 12, unstratified, L14:01, 1410, WSB4, 2001.664
   Length of curved antler tine with one rounded and one blunt end, both of which are pierced by a 12mm diameter hole. The blunt end has been shaved to a squared section before the hole was cut. Tent block?

63. Tine (L:207mm). Area over Building 12, unstratified, L14:01, 1818, WSB22, 2001.682
   Very large red deer tine which is untrimmed at the base and has, not been polished. Towards the tip the surface has been trimmed flat and is pierced by a large oval hole across which the tine has broken.

### Antler and bone waste

64. (L:72mm). Building 2, north wall, Period 2, M05:06, 415, WSB30, 2005.3640. Smoothed tine of red deer antler which has been sawn.

65. (L:75mm). Area over *Via quintana*, unstratified, D12:01, 1026, WSB42, 2005.3652. Tine of red deer antler which has been broken at both ends. The surface is worn or worked smooth and there is a series of horizontal nicks around the base.

66. (L:92mm). Rubble over Road 5, D07:10, 2584, WSB89, 2005.3699. Tine of red deer antler tine carefully sawn.

67. (L:175mm). Unstratified, WSB97, 2005.3712. Tine of red deer antler which has been sawn.

68. (L:48mm Max.D:20mm). Building 13, room 8, mid-third century, N12:09, 1863, WSB73, 2005.3683. Trimmed point of a red deer tine with the tip sawn off.

69. (L:42mm). Road associated with north-west shacks (B2), late third/early fourth century, G05:18, 482, WSB31, 2005.3641. Fragment of ungulate bone with score marks across the surface.

70. (T:7mm). Area over Building 3 and Alley 2, unstratified, N07:01, 2460, WSB87, 2005.3697. Slice cut across an ungulate long bone.

71. (L:90mm). Post-Roman dereliction over East rampart, Q07:07 or Q08:11, WSB101. End of ungulate long bone with the original surface trimmed away.

72. Building 13, pit in room 7, mid-late fourth century, N12:28, WSB103. Waste ends of an ungulate long bone.

73. Bone plate (L:115mm W:21mm T:7mm). Road 1, phase

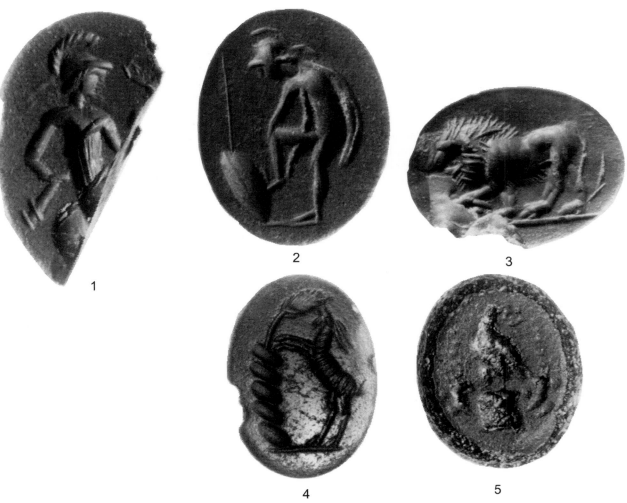

*Figure 25.26: Intaglios. Scale 4:1. Photos by R. Wilkins © Institute of Archaeology, University of Oxford.*

2, F07:08, 2396, WSB86, 2005.3696

Bone plate with hooked ends both pierced by a 6mm diameter circular hole. One face is flat and undecorated with no trace of wear, the other face is convex and decorated by a complex series of incised oblique and vertical lines. A dot-and-ring motif at each end give the terminals a slightly zoomorphic appearance. Both edges are decorated by oblique lines and there are traces of wear between the holes and the lower edge. This piece bears a strong resemblance to the ninth- and tenth-century comb and comb covers discussed by MacGregor (1978, fig. 29); however, the publication of finds from a cave in Settle has produced a further two examples of similar plates. Both are undecorated and smaller in size, and one has polishing along the lower edge. They are likely to come from Victoria Cave, where material dating from the second to fourth centuries has been found, but no certain post-Roman material (Dearne and Lord 1998, fig. 31, nos 117–8).

## The intaglios (Fig. 25.26)

*by M. Henig*

Descriptions are of the actual gem; left and right would be reversed in a sealing (impression) from which the devices would often have been viewed.

1.  Red jasper intaglio (surviving H:18mm surviving W:10mm B:3mm). Building 16, floor, Period 1 construction, L08:28, 2044, WSINT1, 2001.1926

Red jasper intaglio, shape F1. The stone is broken diagonally across. The subject is *Dea Roma*, helmeted and wearing a chiton, seated in profile to the right (though the corselet on which she was presumably resting was on the missing portion of the gem). She has her right hand to her sword (*parazonium*), which is envisaged as hanging from a baldric, and in her left hand a little figure of Victory of which only the arm of the image holding out a wreath remains. On the ground beneath Roma is her shield.

The gem should be compared with a cornelian intaglio from a sewer in the fortress of York (Henig 1976, 8, no. 10 = Henig 1978, no. app. 85) and a fragmentary nicolo from a similar drain at Caerleon (Zienkiewicz 1986, 135, no. 42), both of them ascribed on grounds both of stratigraphy and style to the second century. Stylistically the best parallel from Britain is an onyx from Silchester, Hampshire where the goddess holds a *patera* rather than a *victoriola* (Henig 1978, no. 249). A tentative first-century dating was given to this stone because it seems the type represents a pre-Hadrianic cult image (Vermeule 1959, 68) but, if so, it is clear that it continued to be a popular image on later gems and the iconography by itself cannot be used as a reliable indication of when it was cut. The patterned treatment of helmet and chiton of Roma on the Wallsend intaglio is typical of Antonine glyptic art (Henig 1988, 149–51).

2.    Red jasper intaglio (16mm by 13mm by 3mm). Building 16, occupation, Period 3, K08:33, 2096, WSINT2, 2001.1927

Red jasper intaglio, shape F1. Complete but upper face somewhat worn. The subject is a youth, nude apart from his helmet and cloak (*chlamys*) in profile to the left, bending his back and raising one leg in order to put on a greave. In front of him is a spear and shield. There is a short ground line.

There is no doubt the intaglio depicts Achilles, the premier Greek hero of the Trojan war, arming himself and preparing for battle after hearing of the death of his friend, Patroclus. Two gems from an auxiliary fort at Loughor, West Glamorgan complete the scene with a column on which was an urn containing the ashes of Petroclus (Henig 1997, 395, nos 1 and 2) while a gem from Melain in France depicts Thetis, provider of Vulcan's wonderful armour, standing in front of her son (Guiraud 1988, 137, no. 439).

Material and style suggest, again, a second-century date. Images of a youth holding a sword (Theseus) and a youth holding a spear and helmet (Achilles) seem to have been popular at this time and I suggested long ago (Henig 1970) that these types would have had a special significance for the Roman soldier who was himself as the heir to the classical tradition of military prowess; indeed examples of these types from Corbridge and Caerleon are suggestive. Professor Kleinbrink (Maaskant-Kleibrink 1978, 238, no. 608 and see no. 843) rightly attributed the same significance to the image-type represented here, and this surmise is strengthened by the findings of specimens in forts at Loughor and now at Wallsend.

3.    Jasper intaglio (14mm by 11.5mm by 2mm). Area over Building 5, unstratified, J05:03, 651, WSINT3, 2001.1928

Mottled red-orange jasper intaglio, Shape F1. Chipped front left side of the gem. The subject is a lion walking to the left. Ground line. Damage to the front of the stone, noted above, makes it impossible to establish whether the animal held an animal head in its jaws. Its boldly patterned mane and the hair on its underside, likewise carefully executed, assign it to the patterned style of the second century.

For the type note Henig 1978, no. 629 (nicolo from Chesters), no. app. 173 (yellow jasper from Wroxeter); Henig 1993b, 206, no. 489 (onyx from a Trajanic/Hadrianic context at Caernarfon [Segontium]): Maaskant-Kleibrink 1986, no. 128 (yellow jasper from River Waal at Nijmegen).

The lion, so familiar from tombstones, was probably a *memento mori* (see Henig 1977, 3556–7), although it should be recalled Leo was a sign of the zodiac. In any case the image would have been thought to protect the wearer.

4.    Cornelian intaglio (14mm by 10mm by 2mm). Rubble over Building 8 and *intervallum* road (B2), late third/early fourth century, E12:08, 1186, WSINT4, 2001.1929

Orange with a few dark inclusions. Chipped on left side and some wear on front face.

A goat standing on its hind legs to the left, browses from a palm which grows from a rocky cliff represented by five superimposed stones. Ground line. The style of cutting and the texture of the cutting of the goat's patterned coat and the tree is typically Antonine.

For the same type as here, see Henig 1978, no. 609 (Caerleon): Philp and Henig 1985, 464, no. 5 (drain in *Classis Britannica* fort at Dover). Closely related are intaglios which show the goat browsing from deciduous tree (generally no rocky cliff); for example Henig 1978, nos 610–12, especially no. 611 from High House milecastle, Cumbria and 612 from Charterhouse on Mendip: Zienkienwicz 1986, no. 77 from Caerleon. Other intaglios depict goats browsing from trees being watched by herdsmen as Henig 1978, nos 497–502 (no. 498 from Chester; 499 from Newstead): Henig 1980, 179, no. 2 (from Strageath).

The device evokes the prosperity of the countryside. Such themes, which relate to the idealisation of Rome's traditional rustic roots, are common on gems including gems from military sites. In the practicalities of daily life soldiers were, of course, concerned with prosperity. In addition one is justified in speculating whether the connection was made between the goat and the capricorn, the sign of the zodiac which was also the emblem of *Legio II Augusta*.

5.    Nicolo-glass intaglio (14mm by 11mm (upper face 11mm by 9mm) by 3mm). Area over Building 11, unstratified, K15:01, 1369, WSINT5, 2001.1930

Device moulded rather than cut. Shape F2. Some chemical leaching of glass and underside chipped, but the intaglio is in good condition. The subject is an eagle standing on an altar. The bird stands to the left but looks over its shoulder to the right; it has a wreath in its beak. On either side of the altar is a *cornucopia* with a legionary standard issuing from the mouth of each.

There are several gemstones depicting an eagle between standards from military sites in Britain (Henig 1978, no. 705 from Hod Hill, no. 706 from Caerleon, no. 708 from Hod Hill and a recent discovery from excavations at Birdoswald). In addition we should note nicolo-glass intaglio from Newstead showing two eagles with a standard between them (Henig 1978, no. app. 187).

*Cornucopiae* add another element evoking prosperity. In this regard we may note a cornelian from Holditch, Staffordshire showing an eagle and a *cornucopia* (Henig 1978, no. 694) and another from Caerleon showing and eagle and a *cornucopia* with a trophy between them (Zienkiewicz 1986, no. 80). Although not from a military context but rather a betrothal ring for a young girl, a gem from a grave at Puckeridge, Hertfordshire depicting three eagles, two of them perched on *cornucopiae* and a third on a *cantharus*, all of them associated with the *dextrarum iunctio* show the power of the symbol (Henig 1978, no. app. 36). Close parallels to the Wallsend intaglio are provided by two gems in Vienna which, like it, show a standard issuing from a *cornucopia* on either side of an eagle (Zwierlein-Diehl 1991, nos 1932, 1933).

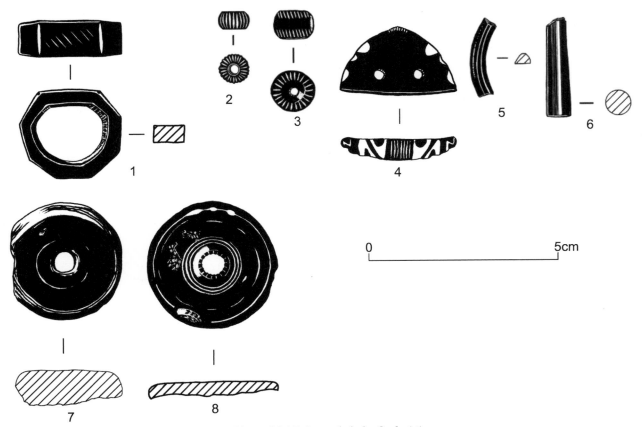

*Figure 25.27: Jet and shale. Scale 1:1.*

6. Intaglio (L:16mm). Building Row 20, Building T, late third/early fourth century, G11:13, 1207, lost

The site finds book records an intaglio of unknown material depicting Mars standing holding a spear in his left hand and his right hand on a shield resting on the ground. (AC)

## Discussion

Although this is only a small group of gems, it does suggest the range of particular preoccupations of the Roman soldier, his loyalty to Rome (*Dea Roma*) and to his unit (eagle and standards), his desire to emulate the prowess of the great heroes of the mythical past (Achilles), his need for amulets against sudden death (the lion) and his hopes for prosperity (the goat). Although close dating is not available, the intaglios all fall within a period of about eighty years from the foundation of the fort even if, of course, some were actually lost later.

## Jet and shale (Fig. 25.27)

1. Jet finger ring (Ext. D: 27mm). Area over Building 2 and Alley 1, post-Roman dereliction, M05:04, 107, WSJ4, 2001.2256

Jet finger ring of rectangular section with eight external facets, the largest of which forms the main panel. Comparable rings of third-century date from Cologne have inscriptions on their main panels (Hagen 1937, Taf. 19, Abb.1, A6). See also Allason-Jones 1996b, no. 173.

2. Jet bead (D: 9.5mm H: 6mm). Road 8, F08:05, 2340, WSJ1, 2001.2253

Finely carved small jet melon bead. For discussion see Allason-Jones 1996b, 28. Cf. South Shields: Allason-Jones and Miket 1984, 7.35.

3. Jet bead (D:11.5mm H:8mm). Area over Road 3, unstratified, K13:01, 1770, WSJ7, 2001.2259

Globular jet bead decorated with incised lines top and bottom but with a plain band around the middle.

4. Jet bead (W:31mm H:18mm T:5.5mm). Area over Building 1 and Road 4, unstratified, M04:01, 83, WSJ6, 2001.2258

Jet bead of semi-oval shape with the decoration of incised grooves, both oblique and transverse, confined to the curved edge. Pierced by two circular holes (D:3mm). Similar beads, which appear to have been used mostly as armlet beads, are known wherever Roman jet objects have been found. This example, however, is unusual in its central group of closely grouped incised lines. See Allason-Jones 1996b, 27–8.

5. Shale fragment (W: 4mm D(int): 34mm). Area over Building 12, unstratified, L14:01, 1394, WSJ2, 2001.2254

Curved fragment of shale, possibly from a pendant or bracelet. The section is damaged but was probably oval.

6. Jet pin or spindle (L:28.5mm D:6.5mm). Building 13, room 7, mid-third century, N12:08, 1760, WSJ8, 2001.2260

Tapering rod of circular section with a blunt head. Pin or spindle?

7. Shale spindlewhorl (D: 35mm). Area over Road 3,

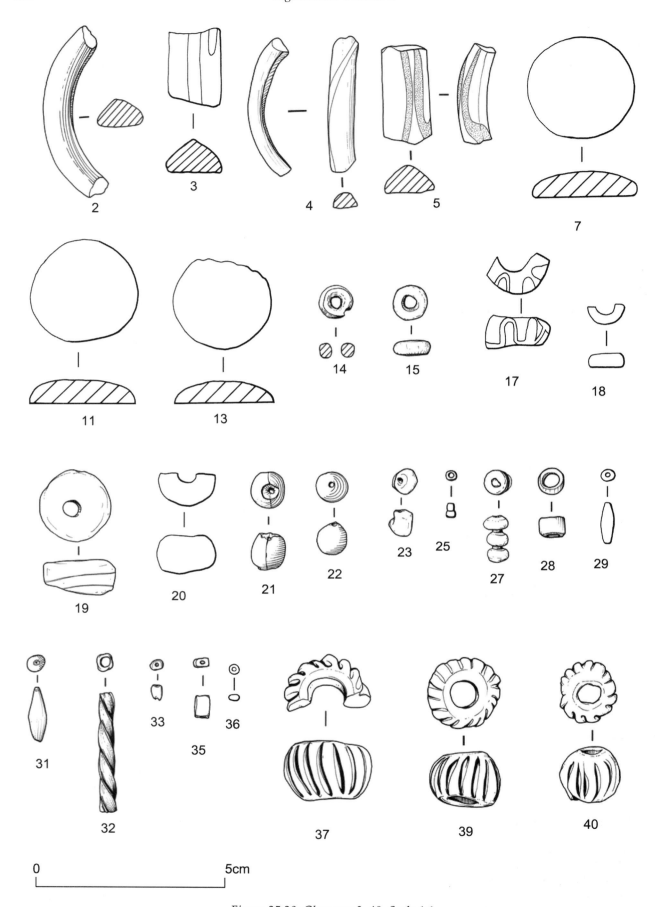

*Figure 25.28: Glass nos 2–40. Scale 1:1*

unstratified, N13:01, 1655, WSJ5, 2001.2257
Incomplete shale spindlewhorl with an incised marginal line on the surviving face. Three incised concentric circles surround the 5.5mm central hole, the edges of which show wear lines.

8. Cannel coal spindlewhorl (D: 32mm D of hole:6mm). Area over Building 7, unstratified, G10:01, 2069, WSJ3, 2001.2255
Incomplete spindle whorl of cannel coal. The whorl is circular with a flat top and curved sides with a single incised line around the hole and one at the edge. Several incised lines appear to run around the sides but the whorl is cracking along natural planes so some of the lines may be natural.

9. Shale block (L:75mm W:35mm B:30mm). Road 8, F09:58, 2350, WSJ9, 2001.2261
Unworked block of shale.

## Glass (Fig. 25.28)

1. Armlet (W:8mm, T:11mm). Alley 1, dereliction, L05:29, WSG114, 2001.1760
Fragment of an ice-blue translucent armlet with a central cable of mid-blue and white.

2. Armlet (W:11mm T:7mm). Rampart building north of *Porta quintana*, Period 2–3, C11:04, 1191, WSG20, 2001.1666
Fragment of an opaque, bluey-white armlet of semi-circular section. Kilbride-Jones 1938, Type 3A. This is the commonest form of glass bracelet to be found in the Hadrian's Wall area and had a long period of manufacture from the first to the fourth centuries, being most popular in the first and second centuries. For lists of parallels and dating evidence see Kilbride-Jones 1938 and Allason-Jones and Miket 1984.

3. Armlet (W:9mm, T:13mm). Building 16, floor, Period 1–2, L07:13, 2098, WSG141, 2001.1787
Fragment of an opaque white armlet of triangular section with marvered yellow lines. Kilbride-Jones 1938, Type 3D, dated to the first half of the second century and largely confined to Scotland.

4. Armlet (W:7mm T:5mm). Area over Building 4 and Alley 3, unstratified, H04:01, 618, WSG26, 2001.1672
Fragment of an uncoloured translucent armlet of hemispherical section with a single white opaque marvered line. Kilbride-Jones 1938, Type 3F. On the evidence of the Traprain Lawe examples Kilbride-Jones suggested that the manufacture of Type 3F bracelets may not have started before the beginning of the second century.

5. Armlet (W:13mm T:7mm int. diam.:65mm). Area over Building 11 and Alley 6, unstratified, L15:17, 1504, WSG34, 2001.1680
Fragment of an uncoloured translucent armlet of triangular section with opaque yellow marvering. Kilbride-Jones 1938, Type 3G.

6. Inset (D:11mm H:6mm). Building L, demolition, Period 4, G04:03, 232, WSG152, 2001.1798
Domed, circular, opaque white inset for a finger ring or brooch.

7–10. **BUN-SHAPED COUNTERS**
7. (D:28mm). Building 3, officer's quarters, abandonment/

post-Roman, P08:13, 2577, WSG189, 2001.1835. Opaque black.

8. (D:19mm H:6mm). Building 13, post-Roman, M12:33, 1769, WSG31, 2001.1677. Opaque black.

9. (D:15mm). Road associated with north-west shacks (B2), Period 3–4, G05:12, 480, WSG21, 2001.1667. Opaque white.

10. (D:14mm). Area over Tower 2, unstratified, E02:11, 744, WSG155, 2001.1801. Opaque white.

11–13. **COUNTERS WITH CONVEX UPPER FACE**
11. (D:29mm). Building 14, room C make-up, Period 2?, J12:37, 2208, WSG19, 2001.1665. Opaque dark red.

12. (D:29mm B:6mm). Building 14, crosshall, Period 3, J11:26, 2094, WSG196, 2001.1842. Opaque black.

13. (D:25.5mm B:5.5mm). Building 14, crosshall, Period 3, J11:31, 2094, WSG18, 2001.1664. Dark green.

14–16. **OPAQUE YELLOW GLASS BEADS**
Annular beads of opaque yellow glass. Guido 1978, Class 8, 250 BC to AD 50.
14. (D:9.5mm T:2.5mm). Chalet 12, Building AM2, (mid)-late third century, M14:12, 1783, WSG202, 2001.683

15. (D: 10mm T: 4mm). Chalet 9, post-Roman, G13:03, 1238, WSG41, 2001.1687

16. (D: 9mm, T: 3mm). Chalet 9, post-Roman, D12:18, 1058, lost.

17. Bead (D:17mm T:8mm). Chalet 9, post-Roman, G14:16, 1239, WSG143, 2001.1789
Cobalt blue translucent annular bead with white opaque marvered trails. Guido 1978, Group 5A. This type had a long period of popularity, the earliest known examples in England dating to third–fourth centuries BC, and continuing into the sixth and seventh centuries AD (Guido 1978, 62–4, Schedules 128ff).

18. Bead (D:10mm T:4mm). Rubble over Building 8 (B2), late third century, D12:09, 1009, WSG158, 2001.1804
Half an annular dark blue translucent glass bead. Guido 1978, Group 6ivb. Guido suggests that the presence of such beads on a Roman site is usually indicative of a native element. Examples have been found in contexts dating from sixth-fifth centuries BC to the eighth century AD.

19. Bead (D:19mm T:9mm). Area over North rampart, unstratified, M03:01, 767, WSG22, 2001.1668
Large annular bead of an uncoloured greyish translucent glass. The bead is wedge-shaped in section and may have been made from waste glass. Guido 1978, Group 7, 69.

20. Bead (D:16mm T:11mm). Area over Alley 5, unstratified, G14:01, 1060, WSG145, 2001.1791
Half of a large globular translucent blue glass bead. This is a common type, although this example is unusually large, and almost undateable. Guido 1978, 9, Group 7i.

21. Bead (D:9mm T:9mm). Area over Building 2, ploughsoil, L05:03, 666, WSG25, 2001.1671
Globular, pale blue translucent glass bead. Guido 1978, 69, Group 7i.

22. Bead (D:8mm T:8mm). Area over Building 11, unstratified, K15:01, 1342, WSG40, 2001.1686

Globular, uncoloured translucent glass bead. Guido 1978, 69, Group 7ii.

23. Bead (D:6.5mm L:7mm). Area over Building 12 and *Via quintana*, unstratified, N14:01, 1825, WSG32, 2001.1678
Globular bead of uncoloured translucent glass.

24. Bead (D:8mm T:6mm). Area over Building 2 and Alley 1, unstratified, M05:01, 619, WSG144, 2001.1790
Globular, sky-blue opaque glass bead. Guido 1978, Group 7v, 70; note particularly the comments on dating.

25. Bead (L:4mm T:3mm). Area over Building 2, ploughsoil, L05:03, 613, WSG154, 2001.1800
Fragment of a white glass segmented bead apparently with white metal foil enclosed instead of the more common gold foil. Such beads are usually found in Britain in late contexts and were imported from the Near East and Egypt. See Boon 1966b, Boon 1977, and Guido 1978, 93.

26. Bead (L:4mm). Building 2, *contubernium* 5, Period 3 or later, M05:11, 272, WSG157, 2001.1803
Fragment of a segmented white glass bead enclosing gold foil. See above.

27. Bead (L:13mm T:6.5mm). Drain in Road 3, G11:07, 2409, WSG29, 2001.1675
Segmented bead of green opaque glass. This type is not as common in the Hadrian's Wall region as the gold foil type. Guido 1978, 91 ff.

28. Bead (L:5mm D:6mm). Building L, demolition, Period 4, G04:03, 146, WSG27, 2001.1673
Tubular bead of opaque green glass. Examples of this type are known in England from the first century at Santon Downham but did not reach maximum popularity until after the third century.

29. Bead (L:11mm Max. T:3.5mm). Area over Building 12, unstratified, L14:01, 1288, WSG146, 2001.1792
Biconical green opaque bead. This type of bead is well known in the north of England but green examples are less common than blue. Guido 1978, 97–98; third to fourth centuries.

30. Bead (L:9mm). Area over Building 11, unstratified, J15:05, 1495, WSG142, 2001.1788
Small biconical blue opaque bead. Guido 1978, 98. This type of bead was largely confined to the south and midlands during the second and early third century but is known from sites on Hadrian's Wall in late third- and fourth-century contexts.

31. Bead (L:15mm). Area over Building 11 and Alley 6, unstratified, L15:01, 1544, WSG36, 2001.1682
Biconical opaque cobalt blue bead. See above.

32. Bead (L:52mm T:4mm). Area over Buildings 7 and 8, unstratified, F10:01, 2189, WSG33, 2001.1679
Long translucent green twisted cylinder bead of square section.

33. Bead (L:4mm, T:3mm). Building 13, M12:55, 1833, WSG30, 2001.1676
Small, royal-blue, opaque cylinder bead of circular section. See Guido 1978, 94–5 and 207–8.

34. Bead (L:5.5mm D:4mm). Building 14, courtyard, late third/early fourth century, J09:21, 2145, WSG24, 2001.1670
Cylindrical opaque green bead. Guido 1978, 95 and 208–12.

35. Bead (L:6mm W:4mm T:2mm). Building 14, robber trench, H08:04, 2161, WSG23, 2001.1669

Translucent, dark green cylinder bead of rectangular section. Guido 1978, 96 and 212–5.

36. Bead (D:3mm). Area over Buildings 1, 2 and Alley 1, unstratified, N05:03, 127, WSG160, 2001.1806
Very small globular bead which is now iridescent blue with a patch of green but was possibly white originally.

### 37–45. MELON BEADS

Guido (1978, 100) has suggested that most blue or green glass melon beads can be found in Flavian or Antonine contexts, apparently dying out in the late second century and not reappearing until post-Roman times.

37. (D:23mm H:15mm). Road 9, post-Roman, H15:06, 1481, WSG35, 2001.1681. Dark blue glass.

38. (D:22mm H:17mm). Area over Road 9, unstratified, H14:49, 1235, WSG28, 2001.1674. Blue frit.

39. (D:19mm H:15mm). Area over Building 10 and Road 9, unstratified, H15:01, 1433, WSG42, 2001.1688. Blue frit.

40. (D:17mm H:14mm). Area over Building 1 and Alley 1, unstratified, P05:02, 109, WSG38, 2001.1684. Blue frit.

41. (D:16mm H:14mm). Chalet 12, Building AF, Period 4, L15:12, 779, WSG37, 2001.1683. Pale green frit.

42. (D:14mm H:11.5mm). Building AO, Period 4?, J07:15, 2176, WSG159, 2001.1805. Blue frit.

43. (D:12mm H:9mm). Building N, late third century, E11:06, 1028, WSG201, 2001.1453. Pale green frit.

44. (H:15mm). West rampart (F2), Q04:16, 408, WSG161, 2001.1807. Bright blue frit.

45. (H:11mm). Building 9, *contubernium* 8, Period 2, G14:17, 1597, WSG163, 2001.1809. Blue frit.

## Pottery (Fig. 25.29)

*For the abbreviations used to describe the pottery fabrics, please see* Chapter 22.

1. Statuette (L:95mm W:48mm). Soil over north-south drain east of Building 3, Period 3–4, Q07:10, 2590, WSP143, 2001.2456
Incomplete front section of a pipeclay *dea nutrix* statuette showing the goddess seated in a high-sided basketwork chair with a high plinth, suckling two infants. Such figurines were mass-produced in the Allier district of Gaul in the second century in moulds. Although common finds in the south-east of Britain they are less commonly found in the military north than the comparable Venus figurines. Examples are known from Binchester, Chesterholm, Corbridge, Piercebridge, South Shields: see Green 1978. For a general discussion see Jenkins 1957.

2. Statuette (D(base): 38mm). West of Building C, Period 3–4, F05:08, 448, WSP197, 2001.2510
Fragment of the domed base of a pipeclay statuette of Venus of which only the back of the feet survive. Whilst the clay was still plastic a 'V' was deeply incised just above the dome. These figurines were manufactured in the samian factories of Gaul from the mid first century AD until the centre of manufacture

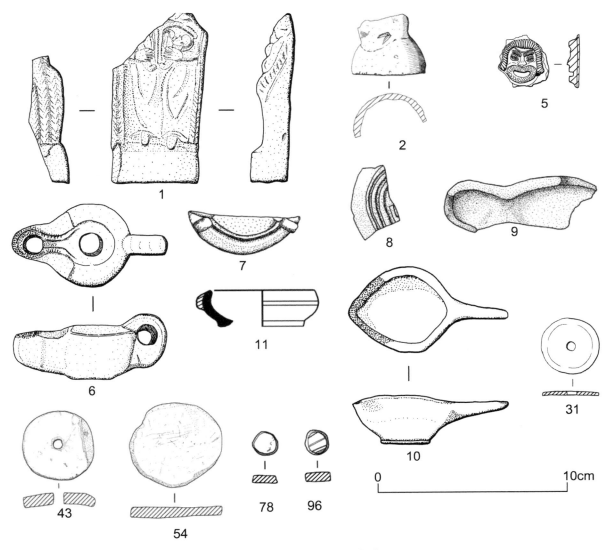

*Figure 25.29: Pottery. Scale 1:2.*

moved to Cologne at the end of the century. See Jenkins 1958.

3.   Statuette (L:37mm). Area over Building 8, unstratified, E10:01, WSP92, 2001.2405
     Fragment of a pipeclay figurine. Two strands of hair drape the shoulder, suggesting that this is from a Venus figurine.

4.   Statuette (H: 26mm, W: 22mm, T: 11mm). Area of Building B and K, post-Roman, L05:07, 828, WSP196, 2001.2509
     Foot from a pipeclay figurine.

5.   Lamp (L of mask:24mm T of lamp wall:1.5mm). Area of Building 13, unstratified, M11:02, 1768, WSP216, 2001.2528
     Fragment from the discus of a mould made *firmalampe* of brown fabric showing a slave mask in relief. The mask has a ridged 'page-boy' hairstyle, pronounced eyebrows, a hooked nose and a gaping mouth with herring-bone motifs around the lips. There is a thumbprint on the back of the mask. Late first or early second century. North Italian: cf. Bailey 1975–96, 288, Q185.

6.   Lamp (L: 82mm H: 26mm, Oil hole: 12mm, Wick hole: 10mm, Handle hole: 9mm). Building 8, room 8, Period 2, E10:74, 2398, WSP171, 2001.2484
     Complete pottery lamp of buff fabric with a light brown colour coat. The single wick hole is well sooted and the oil hole is countersunk. The only decoration is two shallow ribs across the sloping shoulders. Donald Bailey has suggested (*pers. comm.*) that this *firmalampe* was made in Holland or Germany although a French origin cannot be ruled out. Loeschcke 1919, Type X; Evelein 1928, Type B.

7.   Lamp (D(of *discus*):37mm). Building 8, room 1, mid-third century?, D11:15, WSP152, 2001.2465
     Fragment of the *discus* and rim of a *firmalampe* with two lugs on the rim. Grey fabric, red on interior surface. (AC)

8.   Lamp (H:20mm). Building 10, *contubernium* 3/4/5, Period 2, F15:20, WSP149, 2001.2462
     Two joining wall sherds of a *firmalampe* in a pale orange fabric with scattered fine inclusions and occasional large (1mm) red inclusions. The surfaces are slightly paler in colour, and the upper part of the exterior wall

has been burnished. The base has two concentric rings and part of one letter of a name-stamp. (AC)

9.  Lamp (L:90mm H:25mm). Area over Building 2 and Alley 1, unstratified, M05:01, WSP147, 2001.2460. Incomplete open lamp in a gritty, micaceous orange fabric with a grey core and occasional large (1mm) black inclusions. There is sooting on the both nozzle and the rim of the side wall. Open lamps are usually first- or second-century in date. (AC)

10. Lamp (L: 82mm, H: 25mm). Alley10/Building 17, disturbed surface inside building, third century, G04:16, 402, WSP187, 2001.2500
    Small, pear-shaped ladle or open lamp. There are traces of burning on the lip of the fine pink-beige fabric. A short tapering handle projects on a line with the rim diametrically opposite the lip. The base is wire drawn.

11. Lamp (H:18mm). Area over Building 2 and Alley 1, post-Roman dereliction, M05:04, WSP267, 2001.2579
    Fragment of a small, wheel-thrown bowl with part of an applied handle. Probably small open lamp as no. 10 above. Locally produced oxidised ware fabric 1. Loeschcke 1919, Type XII. Cf. Eckardt 2002, fig. 107, no. 768. (AC).

12. Lamp (L: 40mm, W: 26mm, H. of handle: 11mm). West of Building C, Period 3–4, F05:08, 435, WSP193, 2001.2506
    Base and handle of a very small clay lamp. There is no indication that there was ever a receptacle for oil and this was probably a toy or votive model. Cf. Bailey 1975–96, Q62, Q145, Q601.

13. Number not used.

### 14–50. Perforated pottery discs

As has been discussed in Allason-Jones and Miket 1984, 337–8, there is doubt as to whether all pottery discs with central holes should be identified as spindlewhorls as has invariably been the case in the past. The majority of the Wallsend examples are particularly unlikely to have been spindlewhorls as they are roughly made, vary considerably in thickness and several of the holes are off-centre. It is more probable that they were used as gaming tallies although the larger ones could have been used as lids.

## Grey or black colour

14. (D:46mm T:4mm). Building 2, *contubernium* 5, Period 3 or later, M05:11, 301, WSP227, 2001.2539. South-eastern reduced ware cooking pot body sherd from near shoulder, so highly curved.

15. (D:42mm, T:6mm). Rubble over east rampart and *intervallum* road, Q07:07, 2498, WSP220, 2001.2531. BB1 bowl/dish base sherd.

16. (D:41mm T:5mm). Road surface (B2), Period 3–4, H05:14, 778, WSP114, 2001.2427. Possibly from a BB2 bowl/dish.

17. (D:39mm T:7mm). Area over Building 13 and Alley 7, unstratified, L09:01, 2060, WSP113, 2001.2426. Unknown reduced ware, cooking pot body sherd with lattice decoration.

18. (D:38mm T:6mm). Debris over Cistern 1, Roman/post-Roman, E08:13, 2266, WSP221, 2001.2532. BB2 bowl/dish body sherd.

19. (D:37mm T:9mm). Area over Road 8, unstratified, E09:13, 2238, WSP108, 2001.2421. Unknown reduced ware, probably a cooking pot.

20. (D:37mm T:9mm). Gate 2, floor, late third century, D07:07, 2328, WSP107, 2001.2420. Unknown reduced ware, burnt. Possibly from the base of a cooking pot.

21. (D:37mm T:7mm). Area over Building 7, unstratified, F11:01, 1157, WSP229, 2001.2541. BB2 bowl/dish body sherd.

22. (D:36mm T:6mm). Building Row 20, Building Q, late third/early fourth century, F11:11, 1195, WSP106, 2001.2419. BB2.

23. (D:36mm T:5mm). Area over Building 9, unstratified, D13:01, 1480, WSP228, 2001.2540. BB2 bowl/dish.

24. (D:36mm T:5mm). Area over rampart by Gate 2, unstratified, D08:01, 2228, WSP219, 2001.2530. Unknown reduced ware cooking pot body sherd.

25. (D:35mm T:6mm). Road 9 drain fill, J14:06, 1378, WSP103, 2001.2416. Unknown reduced ware cooking pot body sherd, with lattice decoration.

26. (D:34mm T:8mm). Area over Building 12, unstratified, K14:03, 1625, WSP115, 2001.2428. NVCC beaker base, black colour coat.

27. (D:34mm T:5mm). Area over Building 2 and Alley 1, post-Roman, M05:04, 41, WSP226, 2001.2538. BB2 bowl/dish base sherd.

28. (D:33mm T:6mm). Area of Building 11 and Alley 6, no details, L15:03, 1550, WSP225, 2001.2537. Unknown reduced ware.

29. (D:31mm T:4mm). Area over Building 10 and *intervallum* road (Road 6), unstratified, G15:01, 1452, WSP231, 2001.2543. BB2 cooking pot body sherd. Unfinished, with hole drilled on one side only.

30. (D:30mm T:7mm). Area over Building 11 and Alley 6, unstratified, L15:17, 1556, WSP222, 2001.2533. Grey ware cooking pot body sherd.

31. (D:30mm T:2.5mm). Area over Building 11 and Alley 6, unstratified, L15:01, 1393, WSP141, 2001.2454. NVCC beaker base sherd, black colour coat.

32. (D:29mm T:6mm). Alley10/Building 17, disturbed surface inside building, third century, G04:16, 411, WSP105, 2001.2418. Unknown reduced ware, probably a cooking pot.

33. (D:25mm T:6mm). Building 1, Period 2 demolition, Q04:02, 102, WSP224, 2001.2536. BB2 bowl/dish.

## White

34. (D:42mm T:6.5mm). Area over Building 12, unstratified, L14:01, 1276, WSP206, 2001.2518. White ware flagon body sherd.

## Orange (samian, unless otherwise stated)

35. (D:49mm B:5mm). Area over Building 10 and *intervallum* road (Road 6), unstratified, F15:01, 1054, WSP181, 2001.2494. Base of North Gaulish fabric 2 fine ware beaker, orange fabric and brown colour coat.

36. (D:42mm T:8.5mm). Area over Road 8, unstratified, F08:01, 2183, WSP205, 2001.2517. CG

37. (D:41mm T:8mm). Area over Building 12 and Road 3, unstratified, N14:11, 1704, WSP109, 2001.2422. CG

38. (R:*c*.20mm). Area over Building 2, unstratified, L05:01, 617, lost. Incomplete.
39. (D:39mm T:7mm). Area over Building AO, unstratified, L08:01, WSP167, 2001.2480.
40. (D:38mm T:5mm). Area over Building 11, unstratified, J15:05, 1520, WSP230, 2001.2542. CG Dr. 33
41. (D:36mm T:5mm). Area over Buildings 7 and 8, unstratified, F10:12, 2235, WSP213, 2001.2525. EG
42. (D:36mm T:8mm). Cistern 1, lower fill, late third century, E08:44, 2370, WSP207, 2001.2519. EG
43. (D:36mm T:5.5mm). Area over Building 2 and Alley 1, unstratified, M05:01, 665, WSP139, 2001.2452. CG Dr. 18/31 body sherd.
44. (D:35mm T:9mm). Building AO, Period 4?, J07:15, 2160, WSP215, 2001.2527.
45. (D:34mm T:7mm). Area over *intervallum* road (Road 4), unstratified, P04:01, 16, WSP104, 2001.2417. South-eastern reduced ware cooking pot body sherd.
46. (D:33mm T:6mm). Area over Building 1, unstratified, L04:15, 891, WSP208, 2001.2520. CG
47. (D:32mm B:9mm). Chalet 12, Building AL2, (mid)-late third century, M15:21, 1892, WSP168, 2001.2481.
48. (D:30mm T:6mm). Area over *Via quintana*, unstratified, G12:01, 1168, WSP111, 2001.2422. CG Dr. 31 or 18/31.
49. (D:26mm T:5mm). Area over Building 4 and *Via praetoria*, unstratified, K04:01, 768, WSP199, 2001.2512. EG
50. (D:16mm T:6mm). Area over Building BA, unstratified, M13:01, 1686, WSP110, 2001.2423. CG

51–97. Discs

It was a common practice for discs to be cut from sherds of pottery and such discs are usually identified as gaming counters. However, some of the discs in this assemblage are larger than would be required for gaming counters and it is probable that some were used as lids, bungs, or weights.

## Amphora (Dressel 20)
51. (D:110mm B:18mm). Building 9, *contubernium* 2, Period 2, E13:13, WSP265, 2001.2577.
52. (D:105mm B:25mm). Timber Building 2, Period 1, E10:77, WSP264, 2001.2576.
53. (D:55mm). Area over Building 4, unstratified, J04:01, WSP266, 2001.2578.

## Grey or black in colour
54. (D:48mm T:7mm). Building 8, courtyard, Period 4, E10:11, 1156, WSP118, 2001.2431. BB2 bowl/dish base sherd.
55. (D:45mm T:9mm). Building 8, room 8 cess-pit fill, mid-third century?, E10:43, WSP170, 2001.2483. BB2 bowl/dish base sherd.
56. (D:43mm T:5mm). Yard south of Building 13, Period 1–2, N13:03, 1846, WSP223, 2001.2534. BB2 bowl/dish base sherd.
57. (D:40mm T:5mm). Road 9, post-Roman, H15:06, 1448, WSP127, 2001.2440. South-eastern reduced ware cooking pot body sherd.
58. (D:37mm T:6–8mm). Building 1, Period 2 demolition, N05:04, WSP150, 2001.2463. BB2 bowl/dish base.
59. (D:35mm T:6mm). Rubble over Building 8 (B3),

mid-third century or later, E10:53, 2316, WSP119, 2001.2432. BB2 bowl/dish base sherd.
60. (D:34mm T:6mm). Area over Building 10, unstratified, D14:01, 1082, WSP122, 2001.2435. Unknown reduced ware.
61. (D:33mm T:8mm). Area over Buildings 7 and 8, unstratified, F10:12, 2256, WSP117, 2001.2430. BB2 cooking pot base.
62. (D:33mm T:8mm). Area of Building 1 and Road 4, no details, M04:24, WSP148, 2001.2461. BB2 bowl/dish base sherd.
63. (D:32mm T:6mm). Road 3, E12:30, 1182, WSP121, 2001.2434. BB2, possibly a cooking pot.
64. (D:32mm T:4mm). Area over Building 1, unstratified, L04:03, WSP91, 2001.2404. NVCC beaker base, brown colour coat.
65. (D:31mm T:5mm). Building 8 abandonment/make-up layer for Building N, mid/late third century?, E12:03, 1029, WSP120, 2001.2433. BB2 bowl/dish body sherd.
66. (D:30mm T:6mm). Building 11, *contubernium* 3/4, Period 2, L15:23, 1624, WSP130, 2001.2443. BB2 bowl/dish body sherd.
67. (D:29mm T:6mm). Area over Building AO, unstratified, K08:01, WSP145, 2001.2458. BB2 bowl/dish base sherd.
68. (D:28mm T:6mm). Rubble over west *praetentura*, Period 4, 824, WSP125, 2001.2438. BB2 bowl/dish, probably a base sherd.
69. (D:25mm T:5mm). Area over Building 10 and *intervallum* road (Road 6), unstratified, F15:01, 1055, WSP129, 2001.2442. BB2 body sherd.
70. (D:25mm T:5mm). Area over Building 10 and Alley 5, unstratified, F14:01, 1421, WSP124, 2001.2437. BB2 bowl/dish, with hole started from both side. Unfinished pierced disc?
71. (D:24mm T:5mm). Building 2, *contubernium* 8, demolition rubble, Period 3 or later, L05:25, WSP146, 2001.2459. Unknown grey ware beaker base.
72. (D:21mm T:5mm). Building 1, Period 2 demolition, Q04:02, 89, WSP131, 2001.2444. BB2 bowl/dish body sherd.
73. (D:21mm T:4mm). Unstratified, L15:??, WSP144, 2001.2457. Unknown reduced ware.
74. (D:19mm T:5.5mm). Area over Building 2, ploughsoil, L05:03, 608, WSP123, 2001.2436. BB2, possibly cooking pot.
75. (D:19mm T:6mm). Area over Building 2, ploughsoil, L05:03, 609, WSP128, 2001.2441. South-eastern reduced ware cooking pot body sherd.
76. (D:16mm T:6mm). Area over Building 2, ploughsoil, L05:03, 607, WSP126, 2001.2439. BB2 cooking pot.
77. (D:16mm B:5mm). Area over Building 1, ploughsoil, Q05:02, 63, WSP135, 2001.2448. Burnt samian.
78. (D:13mm T:4.5mm). Building 8, room 1, mid-third century?, D11:15, 1049, WSP116, 2001.2429. BB2 cooking pot body sherd.

## Orange (samian, unless otherwise stated)
79. (D:44mm T:6mm). Area over Building 12, unstratified, K14:03, 1537, WSP182, 2001.2495. CG.
80. (D:42mm T:7mm). Area over Building 9, unstratified, H13:06, 1253, WSP184, 2001.2497. CG, late Antonine.
81. (D:33mm T:8mm). Chalet 10, Building X, Period 4, G15:16, 962, WSP132, 2001.2445. EG, late Antonine.

82.  (D:33mm B:9mm). Area over Building 13 and *Via quintana*, unstratified, L12:01, 1676, WSP209, 2001.2521. Decorated body sherd.
83.  (D:32mm B:12mm). Area over Building 1, unstratified, L04:11, WSP275, 2001.2586.
84.  (D:31mm). Road 8, F08:10, 2254, WSP214, 2001.2526. CG Dr.18/31, Antonine.
85.  (D:30mm). Clay puddling pit, Period 3 demolition, N05:14, WSP272, 2001.2583.
86.  (D:20mm B:7mm). Area over Buildings 4, 5 and Alley 3, unstratified, G04:02, WSP278, 2001.2589.
87.  (D:20mm B:6mm). Area over Road 9, unstratified, J14:05, WSP274, 2001.2585.
88.  (D:24mm T:11mm). Area over Cistern 1, unstratified, E08:08, 2230, WSP183, 2001.2496. EG, late Antonine-third century.
89.  (D:19mm T:5.5mm). Alley 4, F05:47, 483, WSP140, 2001.2453. CG with ovolo border filling half the face.
90.  (D:19mm B:5mm). Area over Building AO, unstratified, K08:01, WSP273, 2001.2584.
91.  (D:18mm T:5mm). Area over Building 13, unstratified, M12:01, 1662, lost.
92.  (D:17mm T:5mm). Area over Building 2, ploughsoil, L05:03, 625, WSP112, 2001.2425 CG or EG.
93.  (D:16mm T:6mm). Building 14, crosshall, Period 1 or 2, K11:55, 2162, WSP203, 2001.2515. Unknown oxidised ware, polished after manufacture.
94.  (D:16mm T:5mm). Area over Building 2, ploughsoil, L05:03, 606, WSP134, 2001.2447. Slip removed completely on one face.
95.  (D:15mm B:5mm). Unstratified, WSP204, 2001.2516.
96.  (D:13mm T:5mm). Area over Building 2, ploughsoil, L05:03, 605, WSP212, 2001.2524. CG. Slip removed almost completely on one face.
97.  (D:13mm T:6mm). Building 8, room 1 wall, Period 2, D11:11, 993, WSP133, 2001.2446.

## Tile (Fig. 25.30)

1.  Disc (D: 53mm T: 15mm). Wall of medieval or modern building, N05:02, 192, WST21
     Roughly circular disc cut from the top end of a *tegula* roof tile, utilising the nail hole. Net sinker or loom weight.

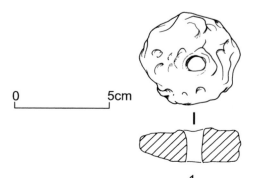

0                    5cm

1

*Figure 25.30: Tile. Scale 1:2.*

## Stone (Figs 25.31–3)

1.  Palette (L:101mm W:63mm T:9mm). Building 18, *contubernium* 1, floor, Period 3–4, F05:39, 486, WSS266, 2001.3122
     Rectangular slate palette which narrows slightly to one end. Three edges are bevelled; the evidence from the Continent suggests that the bevelled edges were to enable the palettes to slide into grooved metal frames. See Allason-Jones and Miket 1984, no. 12.68.
2.  Palette (L:81mm, W:62mm, T:16mm). Area over Building 7, unstratified, E11:17, 1111, WSS68, 2001.2925
     Rectangular slate palette with rounded edges on three sides. The fourth edge has been deliberately cut across.
3.  Palette (L:75mm W:68mm). Building 3, abandonment/post-Roman dereliction, P07:07, WSS85, 2001.2942
     Incomplete rectangular palette bevelled on three edges.
4.  Slate Palette (D:77mm T:3mm). Building 2, *contubernium* 8 wall, Period 3, L05:54, 947, WSS82, 2001.2939
     Half of an oval slate palette which tapers slightly to the rounded edge.

5–13. WHETSTONES WITH AN OVAL CROSS-SECTION
Fine-grained sandstone unless otherwise stated.

5.   (L:103mm W:53mm T:18mm). Chalet 10, Building X, Period 4, H15:10, 1429, WSS295, 2001.3151. Greywacke. With rounded end.
6.   (L:71mm W:42mm T:27mm). Area of Building 2, no details, L05:20, 889, WSS73, 2001.2930. Incomplete. Flat end.
7.   (L:65mm W:35mm T:24mm). Area over Building 10, post-Roman, D14:08, 1478, WSS276, 2001.3132. Micaceous sandstone. Incomplete, with rounded end.
8.   (L:48mm W:33mm T:20mm). Chalet 9, post-Roman dereliction, G13:03, 1240, WSS250, 2001.3106. Carboniferous. Very coarse stone. Incomplete.
9.   (L:95mm W:31mm T:24mm). Area over Gate 3 and *intervallum* road (Road 6), unstratified, J16:01, 1322, WSS277, 2001.3133. Carboniferous. Incomplete, with a tapering, squared end.
10.  (L:79mm W:27mm T:16mm). Alley 3 eaves drip trench, Period 3, F04:33, 578, WSS269, 2001.3125. Greywacke. Incomplete, with rounded end.
11.  (L:49mm W:24mm T:11mm). Area over Building 3 and Alley 2, unstratified, N07:01, 2465, WSS285, 2001.3141. Lentoid section, with squared end.
12.  (L:83mm W:22mm T:13mm). Building 7, west granary make-up layers, F11:12, 957, WSS274, 2001.3130. Iron-rich sandstone. Slightly curved, with rounded ends.
13.  (L:81mm W:20mm, T:14mm). Area over Building 13, unstratified, N10:01, 2471, WSS74, 2001.2931. Incomplete, rounded at one end.

14–30. WHETSTONES WITH A SQUARE OR RECTANGULAR CROSS-SECTION
Fine-grained sandstone unless otherwise stated.

14.  (L:170mm W:52mm T:26mm). Building 1 foundations, officer's quarters, Period 3, Q05:17, 297, WSS71, 2001.2928. Squared end.
15.  (L:120mm W:49mm T:18mm). West rampart, mid-third century, D08:12, 2408, WSS65, 2001.2922. Rounded end.

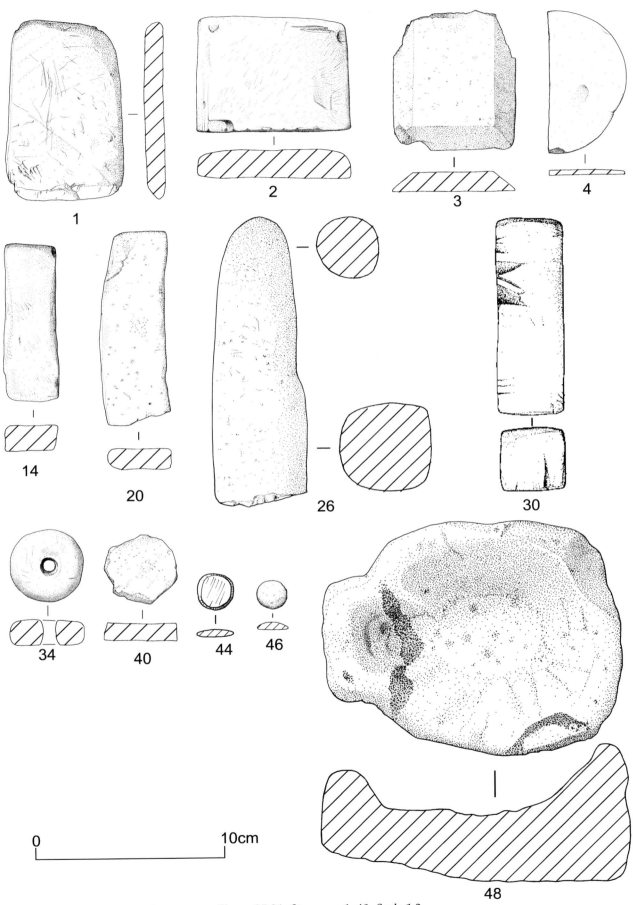

*Figure 25.31: Stone nos 1–48. Scale 1:2.*

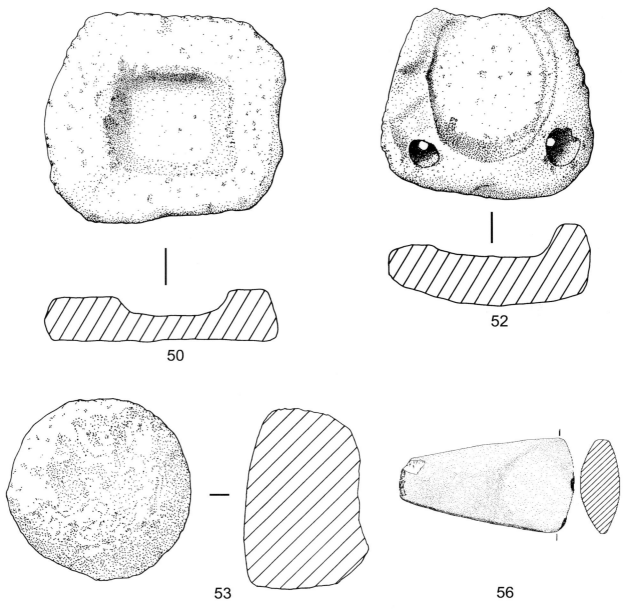

*Figure 25.32: Stone nos 50–56. Scale 1:2.*

16. (L:56mm W:39mm T:17.5mm). Rampart building north of *Porta quintana*, Period 2–3, C11:04, 1216, WSS284, 2001.3140. Incomplete.

17. (L:150mm W:36mm T:18mm). Building 16, floor, Period 1–2, K07:08, 2114, WSS69, 2001.2926. Fine-grained whin. Very worn in one area.

18. (L:55mm W:35mm T:35mm). Road 3, F11:19, 1217, WSS70, 2001.227. Incomplete, with rounded ends and edges. One very smooth face.

19. (L:63mm W:35mm T:16mm). Road 8, F09:07, 2354, WSS281, 2001.3137. Incomplete, with squared end.

20. (L:108mm W:34mm T:11mm). Building 1, *contubernia* 2–4, Period 2?, N04:18, 529, WSS279, 2001.3135. Incomplete. Curved.

21. (L:32mm W:32mm B:20mm). Area over Building 1 and *intervallum* road (Road 4), unstratified, M04:01, 13, WSS292, 2001.3148. Incomplete, squared end. Burnt.

22. (L:81mm W:31mm B:20mm). West *intervallum* road, E04:23, WSS87, 2001.2944. Incomplete, upper face tapering to meet lower face at end.

23. (L:61mm W:29mm T:16mm). Building 1, officer's quarters, Period 2, Q05:34, 528, WSS275, 2001.3131. Incomplete.

24. (L:95mm W:25mm B:19mm). Building 3, *contubernium* 2, Period 2, N07:15, 2633, WSS86, 2001.2943. Squared ends.

25. (L:59mm W:25mm B:15mm). Chalet 12, Building AL2, (mid-)late third century, M15:21, 1861, WSS294, 2001.3150. Incomplete.

26. (L:78mm W:24mm T:24mm). Area over Building 4 and *Via praetoria*, unstratified, K04:01, 725. WSS67, 2001.2924. Tapering to circular cross-section at one end.

27. (L:60mm W:23mm T:16mm). Building 13, room 7, Period 4, N12:37, 1886, WSS271, 2001.3127. Very flat

*Figure 25.33: Stone lid (no. 35) used with cooking pot (coarse ware pottery cat. no. 68).*

faces and crisp edges. A broad rib runs along two sides. Incomplete.

28. (L:120mm T :22mm W :37mm). Area east of Building 10, post-Roman rubble, H15:06, 1446, SS289, 2001.3145. Coarse sandstone. Incomplete, with squared end.

29. (L:80mm W:21mm T:15mm). Area over Building 11, unstratified, K15:01, WSS290, 2001.3146. Very fine-grained sandstone. With oblique ends which show saw marks.

30. (L:52mm W:18mm T:17mm). Area over Building 10 and Alley 5, unstratified, F14:01, 1470, WSS106, 2001.2963. Short, with squared ends. Showing signs of heavy use.

31–2. FLAT SANDSTONE WHETSTONES

31. (L:78mm W:60mm T:23mm). Clay puddling pit, Period 3 demolition, N05:13, 271, WSS66, 2001.2926. Incomplete. Highly polished on one face.

32. (L:109mm Max W:59mm T:24.5mm). Building 18, *contubernium* 1, Period 3–4, F05:15, 440, WSS278, 2001.3134. Large, flat fine-grained sandstone whetstone with curved edges.

33. Pierced disc (D:120mm B:15mm). Unstratified, WSS49, 2001.2906
Large flat disc with small central hole.

34. Spindlewhorl (D:42mm T:19mm). Chalet 12, Building AM2, (mid-)late third century, M14:11, 1859, WSS81, 2001.2938
Circular micaceous sandstone spindlewhorl or loom-

weight with a 7mm diameter central hole. Slightly burnt.

35. Pot lid (D:148mm). Building 8, room 1, Period 3, D11:23, WSS108, 2001.2965
Roughly shaped sandstone disc, found *in situ* over a BB2 cooking pot (Fig. 22.15, no. 68) set into the floor of a room in Building 8.

36–7. POT LIDS

Roughly worked sandstone discs. Possibly used as pot lids.

36. (D:127mm, T:20mm). Road associated with north-west shacks (B2), Period 3–4, H04:19, 802, WSS265, 2001.3121.

37. (D:140mm B:40mm). Building 16, Period 3 occupation, K08:33, 2097, WSS51, 2001.2908.

38–46. DISCS

The smaller examples, especially those which are bun-shaped, were probably used as counters.

38. (D:62mm B:20mm). Building 14, robber trench, K11:30, 1908, WSS53, 2001.2910. Sandstone.

39. (D:57mm B:8mm). Cistern 2, upper fill, late third/early fourth century, J07:14, WSS84, 2001.2941. Sandstone.

40. (D:36mm T:9mm). Lower fill of north-south drain in Alley 9, F10:23, 232, WSS75, 2001.2932. Roughly shaped disc of pink micaceous sandstone.

41. (D:33mm T:6mm). Area over Alley 5, post-Roman, G14:08, 1314, WSS79, 2001.2936. Micaceous sandstone. Flat.

42. (D:25mm T:2mm) Road 8, F08:10, 2446, WSS282, 2001.3138. Sandstone.
43. (D:22mm B:6mm). Area over Building 2 and Alley 1, unstratified, M05:01, 12, WSS301, 2001.2449. Soft white stone.
44. (D:19mm T:3mm). Area over Building 8, unstratified, E11:01, 1103, WSS80, 2001.2937. Sandstone. Flat with a rounded edge.
45. (D:18mm B:5mm). Road 8, F09:06, 2219, WSS107, 2001.2964. Natural pebble, possibly used as counter.
46. (D:15mm T:4mm). Rampart building north of *Porta quintana*, Period 2–3, C11:04, 1085, WSS262, 2001.3118. Fragment of pebble, possibly used as counter.

47. Disc (D:85mm B:35mm). Area over Road 8, unstratified, E09:01, 2205, WSS52, 2001.2909
   Sandstone disc, tapering slightly to edges, with circular hollow on upper surface.
48. Lamp (L:165mm W:130mm B:65mm). Building 16, floor, Period 4, N08:24, 2559, WSS58, 2001.2915
   Roughly circular sandstone lamp, with nozzle on one side. Burnt.
49. Lamp? (L:170mm W:80mm B:11mm; recess L:90mm W:50mm B:20mm). Area of Road 3, modern, K13:02, 1387, WSS54
   Tall, roughly rectangular-shaped block of sandstone, with a lamp-shaped recess pecked out of one surface. Slightly shallower at nozzle end, but with no sign of burning. Unstratified, so could be post-Roman.

50–52. RECESSED STONES
Stone with hollow recesses on side, that might have been used as moulds. Some possibly post-Roman.
50. (L:120mm W:110mm B:25mm; recess L:60mm W:55mm B:10mm). Soil over north-south drain east of Building 3, Period 3–4, Q07:10, 2617, WSS56, 2001.2913
   Shallow rectangle of sandstone, with heavy signs of burning on lower surface. Upper surface has a finely worked shallow rectangular recess.
51. (L:120mm W:120mm B:70mm). Area over Building 16, unstratified, Q08:01, 2483, WSS57, 2001.2914
   Incomplete sandstone block, with one corner of shallow square or rectangular recess. Some signs of burning.
52. (L(complete):135mm (surviving):100mm W:111mm H:40mm). Levelling between Buildings Q and R, late third/early fourth century, F11:18, 1180, WSS55, 2001.2912
   Sandstone block with shallow oval recess, tapering to one end. There are two depressions in the wide end, as if to take location pins. Originally in one piece, one end now lost.

53. Sandstone block (H: 62mm, D: 98mm). Area over Building 1 and *intervallum* road (Road 4), unstratified, M04:01, 14, WSS264, 2001.3120
   Bun-shaped sandstone block posibly used as a pounder.
54. Bead (D:16mm B:6mm). *Intervallum* road, mid to late third century?, D14:12, 1493, WSS302, 2001.2450
   Roughly made stone bead in a soft white stone.
55. Crinoid ossicle. (D:13mm B:5mm). Building 16, floor, Period 4, L07:20, 2043, WSS258, 2001.3114

Large example, pierced. The site has produced four pierced examples and 11 non-pierced. Fossil *crinoid ossicles* are commonly found on Roman sites in the north. This may be a natural distribution but the form lends itself easily to bead manufacture and the numbers found suggest that the fossils were used in such a way. See Allason-Jones and Miket 1984, 12.3–10.
56. Stone axe (L:97mm W:53mm B:21mm). Area over Buildings 7 and 8, unstratified, F11:01, 1109, WSS109
   *C. Waddington writes:* A fine ground and polished stone axe. It has evidence of limited utilisation along the blade edge, although some of this may be due to post-depositional damage such as ploughing. There are also some flakes detached from the distal butt end which could also be the result of plough damage rather than purposive use. It seems likely, therefore, that the axe may have been originally discarded in a pristine condition which suggests that it have been a votive rather than a functional item. Ground and polished stone axes are diagnostic tools of the Neolithic period with types such as this common, but not exclusive to, Early Neolithic contexts. This is a relatively small specimen.

## 'Ballista' balls (Figs 25.34–35)
*by W. B. Griffiths*
Rounded stones slightly larger than a cricket ball, but with one or two flattened sides (usually on opposite sides of the stone) are not uncommon finds on military sites across the Roman Empire. Wallsend has yielded up the largest number of such worked stones of any site in Roman Britain (a total of 136 from the Daniels' excavations alone, with more from the excavations both within and surrounding the fort in the 1990s (Griffiths 2003, 230).

### Recording
The stones were weighed and measured. The diameter was taken parallel to the flattened side(s) if present. The measurements for each stone are given in the catalogue below, where they are ordered by their overall diameter. The diameters recorded range from 55–126mm (for complete examples). The weight range from 159–1485g, again for complete examples.
   The catalogue is subdivided according to the basic form of the stone. Some stones clearly exhibited the classic shape of two flattened sides, and some only clearly showed one flattened side. Other examples which could not be so readily classified are recorded in a third group, which includes stones which are only roughly rounded, the shape created from a faceting of several faces, some being so rough that they effectively represented a cube. Some stones are exceptionally well rounded, with no obviously flat face.
   The subdivision need indicate nothing more than different hands being involved in the manufacture of the stones; with the more roughly shaped, faceted

stones indicating less experienced hands at work, or at least less application to the task in hand. It might reasonably be inferred that this was not a task for specialists. A group of three stones (14, 15, and 21, all found together, context M07:15), reused in a Period 3 flagged floor in Building 3, all appear to have been made by the same hand.

## Catalogue

Each entry has diameter, weight, context number, site small finds number and current record number.

### Stones with two sides

|  |  |  |  |
|---|---|---|---|
| 1. | D:126mm | Wt:1485g | Unstratified, WSS207. |
| 2. | D:113mm | Wt:1326g | *Intervallum road* (Road 6), secondary level, M16:16, 1827, WSS209. |
| 3. | D:113mm | Wt:1201g | *Intervallum road* (Road 6), secondary level, M16:16, 1831, WSS210. |
| 4. | D:108mm | Wt:1285g | Unstratified, WSS176. |
| 5. | D:107mm | Wt:1096g | Unstratified, WSS211. |
| 6. | D:106mm | Wt:1122g | Building 3, *contubernium* 2, Period 2, N07:15, 1635/8, WSS190. |
| 7. | D:106mm | Wt:1013g | Building 4, *contubernium* 9, Period 2, K04:21, 943, WSS233. |
| 8. | D:104mm | Wt:900g | Unstratified, WSS223. |
| 9. | D:101mm | Wt: 880g | Area over Road 4, unstratified, G03:05, 724, WSS199. |
| 10. | D:101mm | Wt:799g | Building 3, *contubernium* 2, Period 2, N07:15, 2635/15, WSS191. |
| 11. | D:100mm | Wt:1320g | Unstratified, WSS229. |
| 12. | D:98mm | Wt:1067g | Building 9, *contubernium* 1 partition, Period 1, E13:38, 1594, WSS142. |
| 13. | D:98mm | Wt:816g | Building 3, *contubernium* 2, Period 2, N07:15, 2635/18, WSS175. |
| 14. | D:97mm | Wt:886g | Building 3, *contubernium* 2 floor, Period 2, M07:15, 2634/2, WSS183. |
| 15. | D:96mm | Wt:826g | Building 3, *contubernium* 2 floor, Period 2, M07:15, 2634/1, WSS184. |
| 16. | D:96mm | Wt:811g | Unstratified, WSS245. |
| 17. | D:96mm | Wt:772g | Area of Building 4, no details, F03:13, 894, WSS222. |
| 18. | D:94mm | Wt:780g | Building 4, *contubernium* 9, Period 2, K04:21, 942, WSS239. |
| 19. | D:93mm | Wt:871g | Building 4, *contubernium* 9, Period 2, K04:21, 942, WSS240. |
| 20. | D:92mm | Wt: 760g | Area of Road 5, no details, E04:17, 477, WSS159. |
| 21. | D:92mm | Wt:635g | Building 3, *contubernium* 2 floor, Period 2, M07:15, 2634/3, WSS182. |
| 22. | D:90mm | Wt:673g | Building 1, *contubernium* 1–3 demolition, Period 2, N05:32, 574, WSS128. |
| 23. | D:90mm | Wt:N/A | Building 4, *contubernium* 9, Period 2, K04:21, 942, WSS242. |
| 24. | D:89mm | Wt:679g | Area of Tower 2, unstratified, ?E02:11, 785, WSS157. |
| 25. | D:88mm | Wt:763g | *Intervallum road* (Road 6), secondary level, M16:16, 1830, WSS138. |
| 26. | D:88mm | Wt:701g | Road 5, E03:08, 932, WSS204. |
| 27. | D:88mm | Wt:468g | Unstratified, WSS141. |
| 28. | D:87mm | Wt:695g | Building 3, *contubernium* 2, Period 2, N07:15, 2635/14, WSS188. |
| 29. | D:87mm | Wt:403g | Building 3, *contubernium* 2, Period 2, N07:15, 2635/3, WSS187. |
| 30. | D:87mm | Wt: 339g | Area over Building 11, unstratified, J15:01, 1267, WSS160. |
| 31. | D:86mm | Wt:613g | Building 3, *contubernium* 2, Period 2, N07:15, 2635/19, WSS194. |
| 32. | D:86mm | Wt:606g | Road associated with the north-west shacks (B2), late third/early fourth century, J04:05, 803, WSS155. |
| 33. | D:86mm | Wt:603g | Assembly area, F09:54, 2447, WSS139. |
| 34. | D:85mm | Wt:605g | Layer west of Building C, Period 3-4, F05:08, 433, WSS126. |
| 35. | D:84mm | Wt:547g | Unstratified, WSS212. |
| 36. | D:83mm | Wt:880g | Building 9, *contubernium* 5/6 partition, Period 2, G13:35, 1580, WSS164. |
| 37. | D:83mm | Wt:583g | Building 3, *contubernium* 2, Period 2, N07:15, 635/6, WSS179. |
| 38. | D:82mm | Wt:684g | Building 4, partition between *contubernium* 2 and 3, Period 2, G04:31, 463, WSS135. |
| 39. | D:82mm | Wt:617g | Road 1, E07:12, 2355, WSS201. |
| 40. | D:82mm | Wt:582g | Building 3, *contubernium* 2, Period 2, N07:15, 2635/7, WSS185. |
| 41. | D:82mm | Wt:533g | Unstratified, WSS200. |

| 42. | D:81mm | Wt:682g | Building 4, partition between *contubernium* 2 and 3, Period 2, G04:31, 465, WSS134. |
| 43. | D:81mm | Wt:622g | Area over Building 11, unstratified, K15:02, 1294, WSS143. |
| 44. | D:81mm | Wt:518g | Area over Building 13 and Alley 7, unstratified, L09:01, WSS196. |
| 45. | D:80mm | Wt:625g | Building 4, partition between *contubernium* 2 and 3, Period 2, G04:31, 473, WSS118. |
| 46. | D:79mm | Wt:617g | Unstratified, WSS202. |
| 47. | D:78mm | Wt:643g | Unstratified, WSS238. |
| 48. | D:76mm | Wt:505g | Area of Building 12 and Road 3, no details, N14:12,1879, WSS213. |
| 49. | D:76mm | Wt:444g | Unstratified, WSS236. |
| 50. | D:75mm | Wt:413g | Unstratified, WSS101. |
| 51: | D:74mm | Wt:446g | Area over Building 12, unstratified, N14:01, 1667, WSS88. |
| 52. | D:73mm | Wt:515g | Building 4, partition between *contubernium* 2 and 3, Period 2, G04:31, 464, WSS123. |
| 53. | D:73mm | Wt:438g | Unstratified, WSS140. |
| 54. | D:71mm | Wt:513g | Building 4, make-up material, Period 2, G04:07, 143, WSS95. Inscribed 'V': *RIB II* 2451.5. |
| 55. | D:69mm | Wt:364g | Area over Building 10, unstratified, E14:01, WSS121. |
| 56. | D:68mm | Wt:526g | Building 3, *contubernium* 2, Period 2, N07:15, 2635/2, WSS168. |
| 57. | D:68mm | Wt:416g | Building 4, gully, Period 2, J04:18, 809, WSS153. |
| 58. | D:67mm | Wt:315g | Building 4, partition between *contubernium* 2 and 3, Period 2, G04:31, 468, WSS225. |
| 59. | D:66mm | Wt:280g | Building 4, partition between *contubernium* 2 and 3, Period 2, G04:31, 462, WSS89. Inscribed 'XX': *RIB II* 2451.10. |
| 60. | D:64mm | Wt:397g | Building 1, *contubernium* 1-4 demolition, Period 2, N05:29, WSS91. |
| 61. | D:64mm | Wt:292g | Unstratified, 1910, WSS94. Inscribed 'I': *RIB II* 2451.3. |
| 62. | D:61mm | Wt:229g | Area over Gate 1, unstratified, K03:01,746, WSS154. |
| 63. | D:55mm | Wt:241g | Rubble over west *praetentura*, Period 4, J05:07, 823, WSS148. |
| 64. | D:51mm | Wt:116g | Building 4, partition between *contubernium* 2 and 3, Period 2, G04:31, 469, WSS247. |

### Stones with only one side

| 65. | D:114mm | Wt:1220g | Unstratified, WSS228. |
| 66. | D:109mm | Wt:1028g | Building 10, *contubernium* 6, Period 2, G14:31,1601, WSS178. |
| 67. | D:105mm | Wt:1341g | Building 3, *contubernium* 2, Period 2, N07:15, 2635/13, WSS206. |
| 68. | D:105mm | Wt:1058g | Building 3, *contubernium* 2, Period 2, N07:15, 2635/10, WSS174. |
| 69. | D:102mm | Wt:899g | Alley 3, H04:26, 811, WSS173. |
| 70. | D:96mm | Wt:895g | Building 3, *contubernium* 2, Period 2, N07:15, 2635/9, WSS189. |
| 71. | D:96mm | Wt:822g | Building 9, *contubernium* 1, Period 1, E13:34, 1596, WSS166. |
| 72. | D:93mm | Wt:819g | Building 4, partition between *contubernium* 2 and 3, Period 2, G04:31, 459, WSS224. Inscribed 'X': *RIB II* 2451.9. |
| 73. | D:88mm | Wt:790g | Road 9, post-Roman, H14:24, 1245, WSS162. |
| 74. | D:88mm | Wt:706g | Building 3, *contubernium* 2, Period 2, N07:15, 2635/11, WSS192. |
| 75. | D:88mm | Wt:617g | North-south drain east of south wall of Building 1, Period 2, Q05:28, WSS235. |
| 76. | D:87mm | Wt:726g | Building 4, make-up material, Period 2, G04:07, 399, WSS129. |
| 77. | D:87mm | Wt:671g | Unstratified, WSS124. |
| 78. | D:84mm | Wt:560g | Building 3, *contubernium* 2, Period 2, N07:15, 2635/1, WSS172. |
| 79. | D:83mm | Wt:620g | Building H, demolition, Period 4, J05:07, 827, WSS215. |
| 80. | D:82mm | Wt:662g | *Intervallum road* (Road 6), M16:20,1876, WSS152. |
| 81. | D:82mm | Wt:527g | Assembly area, late surface, D09:11, 2318, WSS205. |
| 82. | D:82mm | Wt:515g | North rampart (F2), Period 1, G02:06, 684, WSS170. |
| 83. | D:81mm | Wt:577g | Area over North rampart, unstratified, M03:01, 752, WSS156. |
| 84. | D:78mm | Wt:529g | Unstratified, 1229, WSS127. |
| 85. | D:78mm | Wt:512g | Unstratified, WSS125. |
| 86. | D:77mm | Wt:568g | Alley10/Building 17, disturbed surface inside building, third century, F04:19, 426, WSS116. |

| | | | |
|---|---|---|---|
| 87. | D:77mm | Wt:558g | Building 10, *contubernium* 5/6 partition, Period 2, G14:29, 1599, WSS131. |
| 88. | D:76mm | Wt:480g | Building 4, make-up material, Period 2, G04:07, 401, WSS226. Inscribed 'I+': *RIB II* 2451.7. |
| 89. | D:75mm | Wt:472g | Building 1, north wall foundation, Period 2, Q05:32, 476, WSS119. |
| 90. | D:74mm | Wt:532g | Area over Building 8, unstratified, E10:01, 982, WSS112. |
| 91. | D:73mm | Wt:479g | Unstratified, WSS93. |
| 92. | D:72mm | Wt:391g | Unstratified, 428, WSS234. |
| 93. | D:72mm | Wt:376g | Road associated with the north-west shacks (B2), late third/early fourth century, J04:05, 813, WSS167. |
| 94. | D:70mm | Wt:390g | Building 4, partition between *contubernium* 2 and 3, Period 2, G04:31, 471, WSS244. Inscribed 'X': *RIB II* 2451.8. |
| 95. | D:69mm | Wt:326g | Unstratified, WSS195. |
| 96. | D:67mm | Wt:309g | Area over Building 5, unstratified, J05:03,728, WSS149. |
| 97. | D:67mm | Wt:289g | Building 4, make-up material, Period 2, G04:07,143, WSS96. |
| 98. | D:67mm | Wt:279g | Road 5, E04:17, 477, WSS115. |
| 99. | D:66mm | Wt:351g | Unstratified, WSS98. |
| 100. | D:58mm | Wt:258g | Building 1, *contubernium* 1-4, Period 2, N05:29, 549, WSS97. |

*Other: faceted, very well rounded and cubes*

| | | | |
|---|---|---|---|
| 101. | D:100mm | Wt:847g | *Via quintana* (Road 3), F13:24, 1600, WSS165. Unfinished. |
| 102. | D:100mm | Wt:100g | Building 1, verandah, Period 3-4?, L04:20, WSS221. Faceted. |
| 103. | D:96mm | Wt:935g | Unstratified, WSS133. Faceted. |
| 104. | D:96mm | Wt:769g | Unstratified, WSS203. Faceted. |
| 105. | D:95mm | Wt:890g | Unstratified, WSS132. Faceted. |
| 106. | D:93mm | Wt:898g | *Intervallum road* (Road 6), secondary level, M16:16, 1828, WSS208. Rough shape. |
| 107. | D:92mm | Wt: 816g | Cobbles near Cistern 1, Period 3 demolition, E08:57, 2406, WSS217. Faceted. |
| 108. | D:92mm | Wt:745g | *Intervallum road* (Road 6), primary level, M16:20, 1874, WSS216. Faceted. |
| 109. | D:92mm | Wt:707g | *Intervallum road* (Road 6), primary level, M16:20, 1870, WSS144. Rough cube. |
| 110. | D:90mm | Wt:868g | *Intervallum road* (Road 6), primary level, M16:20, 1871, WSS150. Faceted. |
| 111. | D:89mm | Wt:656g | Chalet 9, post-Roman, H13:08, 1512, WSS158. Faceted. |
| 112. | D:84mm | Wt:630g | Building 4, partition between *contubernium* 2 and 3, Period 2, G04:31, 467, WSS99. |
| 113. | D:83mm | Wt:523g | Building 9, *contubernium* 1 partition, Period 1, E13:38, 1595, WSS161. Pecked, rounded. |
| 114. | D:83mm | Wt:458g | Building 3, *contubernium* 2, Period 2, N07:15, 2635/5, WSS193. Faceted. |
| 115. | D:82mm | Wt:898g | Building 3, *contubernium* 2, Period 2, N07:15, 2635/17, WSS186. Almost a cube. |
| 116. | D:82mm | Wt:592g | Building 3, *contubernium* 2, Period 2, N07:15, 2635/16, WSS171. Right angles. |
| 117. | D:81mm | Wt:657g | Building 12 demolition, Period 3, M14:63,1919, WSS110. Roughout. |
| 118. | D:79mm | Wt:629g | Building 3, *contubernium* 2, Period 2, N07:15, 2635/12, WSS177. Faceted. |
| 119. | D:79mm | Wt:518g | *Intervallum road* (Road 6), primary level, M16:20,1873, WSS218. Rough cube. |
| 120. | D:78mm | Wt:526g | Alley 1, upper layers, P05:16, 414, WSS111. Faceted. |
| 121. | D:78mm | Wt:486g | Building 4, partition between *contubernium* 2 and 3, Period 2, G04:31, 458, WSS230. Inscribed 'I+': *RIB II* 2451.6 |
| 122. | D:77mm | Wt:660g | *Intervallum road* (Road 6), primary level, M16:20, 1872, WSS137. Elongated cube. |
| 123. | D:77mm | Wt:502g | Building 4, partition between *contubernium* 2 and 3, Period 2, G04:31, 470, WSS103. Well rounded. |
| 124. | D:76mm | Wt:534g | Unstratified, WSS102. Rounded cube. |
| 125. | D:74mm | Wt:385g | Building H, demolition, Period 4, J05:07, 822, WSS169. Faceted. |
| 126. | D:73mm | Wt:483g | Building 4, make-up material, Period 2, G04:07, 400, WSS100. Round. |

| 127. | D:72mm | Wt:451g | Road associated with the north-west shacks (B2), late third/early fourth century, J04:05, 806, WSS163. Faceted. |
| 128. | D:71mm | Wt:466g | Building 4, partition between *contubernium* 2 and 3, Period 2, G04:31, 460, WSS90. Well rounded. |
| 129. | D:71mm | Wt:383g | Unstratified, WSS145. Cube. |
| 130. | D:70mm | Wt:403g | Building 4, make-up material, Period 2, G04:07, 143, WSS96. Inscribed 'IV': *RIB II* 2451.4. Well rounded. |
| 131. | D:70mm | Wt:377g | Unstratified, WSS219. Well rounded. |
| 132. | D:67mm | Wt:352g | Building 8, entrance, Period 4, E11:22, 1155, WSS113. Faceted. |
| 133. | D:65mm | Wt:415g | Building 4, partition between *contubernium* 2 and 3, Period 2, G04:31, 466, WSS130. Ball. |
| 134. | D:64mm | Wt:398g | Unstratified, WSS122. Faceted. |
| 135. | D:63mm | Wt:339g | Building 4, partition between *contubernium* 2 and 3, Period 2, G04:31, 472, WSS92. Faceted. |
| 136. | D:57mm | Wt:159g | Assembly area, E09:48, 2433, WSS198. Faceted. |

## Purpose

Various suggestions have been put forward for the use of these stones, ranging from game balls to stoppers for amphorae (Corder 1933, 38, who found one *in situ* in the neck of an amphora in a civilian context at York). However, the vast majority of examples known from this country are found at military sites. Generally they are regarded as having been missiles for artillery pieces but they may perhaps also have been used for throwing by hand (Baatz 1983, Griffiths 1992, 1994c). The flattened sides of the stones can be interpreted as making it easier to stack the stones ready for use, which would suit either interpretation.

The traditional interpretation that they were for artillery pieces deserves some consideration. Generally, missiles of this size would be for smaller 'field' pieces, Ballistae, two-armed stone-throwers. Some of the celebrated larger machines were capable of firing stones in excess of 26kg (one talent: Vitruvius, *De Architectura* X, 11, 3). However, these were more likely to be deployed in sieges, to attack defended circuits; they would have been of only limited use in defending a fort.

There has been much debate as to the likely presence of artillery at auxiliary forts. The traditional view is that only the legions were issued with artillery (*c*.55 pieces to a legion, giving us 165 pieces in Britannia: Marsden 1969, 179). However there are alternative views, including suggestions that every tower on Hadrian's Wall could have deployed such an item (Donaldson 1988, 127). The presence of stone balls at Wallsend cannot in itself be used to argue for the provision of artillery at the site, as they may have been used as a hand-launched missile; instead we must turn to the rarely found items from artillery pieces (no examples of which have yet been recovered from Wallsend). For example, the discovery of two fragments from two separate artillery pieces at Elginhaugh (Allason-Jones 2007, 405), a similarly extensively excavated fort in Flavian Scotland, could indicate that auxiliary units may have been issued with artillery. However, Elginhaugh was occupied during and after an extensive campaign that included legionary units, so special pleading could be made for a legionary presence, or at least supply chain, at some point. The only conclusion that can be reached on the basis of present evidence is that stone balls such as these could have been used for artillery pieces, but cannot be used in themselves to argue for its presence.

It is clear that the Roman army was trained in throwing stones by hand (Vegetius, *Epitoma Rei Militaris*, II:23; Arrian, *Tactica*, XLIII:1) and stones of a similar size and weight would be more effective than simply gathering random stones for such use: 'a high rate of accurate fire' would not 'be achieved with stones of uncertain weight' (Baatz 1983, 136). There is no firm evidence to support the use of the hand-thrown stone by the Roman army in battle, although there is evidence, both literary (eg Aeneas Tacticus, XXII:12 and XXXVIII:6–7) and sculptural (Arch of Constantine), that stones were thrown by hand in the defence of towns, and it is possible that this could be applied to forts. Indeed, experiments from the reconstructed gateway at South Shields Roman Fort showed that such stones could provide a withering rate of fire, with a range that covered the 'kill-zone' of the 25 metres from the outer ditch to the fort wall (Griffiths 1992).

Regardless of their exact purpose (and it may be that in fact they had a duality of purpose, hand-throwing and artillery), it seems likely that the stones were prepared for the defence of the fort. An alternative possibility is that they could have been held ready to take to the field with artillery as is indicated by Arrian (*Tactica*, XLI, 1), who, apparently, credits auxiliary units with firing artillery on campaign. However, this interpretation is disputed (Campbell 1986, 127), and as stated above, auxiliary units are generally regarded as not being equipped with artillery.

## Distribution within the fort

The stones were found throughout much of the fort,

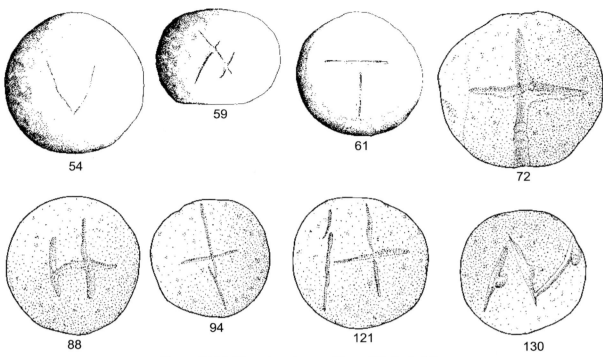

*Figure 25.34: Throwing stones with graffiti. Scale 1:2.*

*Table 25.01: Numbers of stones by location type*

| Stratified | |
|---|---|
| Infantry barracks | 52 |
| Roads and alleys | 25 |
| Cavalry barracks | 7 |
| Defences | 2 |
| Other | 2 |
| Timber buildings | 3 |
| Hospital | 1 |
| Total | 92 |
| Unstratified | |
| Over infantry barracks | 2 |
| Over roads and alleys | 4 |
| Over cavalry barracks | 5 |
| Over defences | 2 |
| Over hospital | 1 |
| No details | 30 |
| Total | 44 |
| Total | 136 |

as can be seen on Fig. 25.35 showing their distribution by site grid. There was almost no detailed excavation of the defences, explaining why few were found in the areas they might perhaps most readily be anticipated.

Many of the stones were scattered finds. However, there were some concentrations, in particular two in the northern range of the fort (26 stones in Building 4 and 21 in Building 3). Twenty-one of the stones from Building 4 were recovered from two contexts G04:07 and G04:31. The former contained six stones

(two inscribed; see below) and is described as a probable make-up level below the flooring in *contubernium* 2, while the majority of stones (including four inscribed examples) are from the partition slot between *contubernia* 2 and 3. This phase of the building is identified as Period 2, the later second-century rebuilding of the fort, which included the reconstruction of the timber barracks in stone (Hodgson 2003, 5). A possible interpretation therefore is that they were identified as no longer required, and became a convenient source of building rubble/ packing material in the construction of the barrack. Eighteen of the stones from Building 3 were recovered from context N07:15, described as a soil layer under the flagged floor of room 2 (contexts N07:14, M07:15), which produced three more stones. Again the contexts are dated to Period 2.

In all cases we can consider that the stones were no longer required as ammunition, and simply used as rubble/packing. The question is, why should this be so? If we interpret them as artillery ammunition then one could simply argue that there was no longer artillery kept at the fort. However, if they are regarded as being used for hand-throwing then their re-use is more problematic, although of course it may simply be that they became mixed up with other rubble, or in the case of the partition slot they were conveniently to hand for the builders.

## Inscriptions

Eight of the stones (*RIB II* 2451.3–10) were inscribed

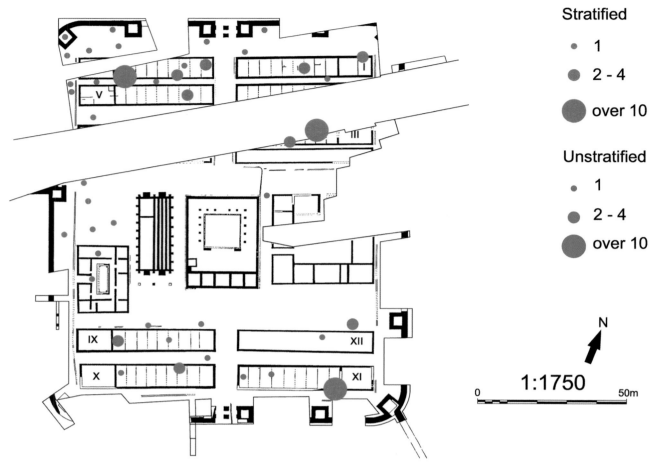

Stratified

• 1

● 2 - 4

⬤ over 10

Unstratified

• 1

● 2 - 4

⬤ over 10

N

1:1750

0                    50m

*Figure 25.35: Distribution of throwing stones.*

with what appear, for the most part, to be numerals. There is no clear evidence to suggest a purpose of these numbers. Possibilities include a mason's or maker's mark, a tally mark, or markings for some form of game. Only two other stone balls from Britain have been recovered with inscriptions, *RIB II* 2451.1 from Caerleon, inscribed with an M and *RIB II* 2451.2 from Corbridge, now lost. There is some uncertainty as to the exact interpretation of the inscription of the Corbridge example. In all cases that the markings take the style of a graffito as opposed to a formal inscription. All the stones apart from no. 61 (*RIB II* 2451.3), which was unstratified, were found in the construction levels of *contubernium* 2 in Building 4 in Period 2.

### Conclusions

The combination of the inscribed examples, and sheer quantity of stones, makes this assemblage distinctive, but need not signify activity out of the ordinary. Wallsend remains one of the most comprehensively excavated forts in the Roman world, and it may be that excavations of a similar scale could yield similar numbers (indeed excavations of the Antonine fort at

Bar Hill have yielded 110 examples: MacDonald and Park 1906, 21, 32, 89; see also Marchant 1991, 90–98 for a catalogue of examples from other sites in Britain).

## Quern stones (Figs 25.36–37)
*by R. G. Willis*

Of the 63 quern stones found during the 1975–1984 excavations, only 20 were stratified. This, and the fact that broken querns are frequently used as building stone (18 fragments come from road surfaces), means that it difficult to say much concerning their development as most are likely to be chronologically removed from their original context of use. This widespread problem has led to rather simplistic statements concerning the development of milling stones, based on subjective interpretations of lesser or greater 'primitiveness', and there is a great need for an intensive study of their context of production, use and exchange. Basic questions still remain unresolved, such as whether differences in form can be related to functional variation rather than chronological development, how far raw material choice was governed by intended use and whether every hand quern was designed to grind grain. For example, the traditional potters on the island of Iz, in Dalmatia, use hand querns predominantly to grind calcite temper, and rarely for grinding grain (Carlton 1988). For the present analysis the traditional broad classifications have been adhered to as in most other recent studies (*e.g.* Welfare 1985), simply to provide a comparative basis for all further research.

With the invaluable help of Dr B. R. Turner, in the Geology Department of the University of Newcastle upon Tyne, an exploratory thin sectioning programme was initiated, in an attempt to source the raw material used for quern production. The hand specimen analysis had suggested that all of the non-lava stones were almost certainly made from local Northumbrian sandstone sources. After the initial thin-sectioning and examining of a few stones, it seemed very unlikely that the microscopic approach would provide any higher resolution in distinguishing between these sources, and so the project was terminated. Similarly, no more precise sourcing of the lava stones was achieved other than their origin in the continental quarries of Mayen, although without an extensive thin-sectioning programme, their exact provenance is by no means certain. For instance, some may have a source in France (A. Welfare *pers. comm.*).

### The beehive stones

This category is formulated purely on the morphology of the upperstones, which are relatively thick (*c.*100–200 mm) in relation to their diameter (*c.*300–400 mm). The upperstone is often nearly hemispherical externally, usually with a wide hopper leading into the feed pipe. Upperstones with a flatter, 'bun-shaped' profile are also included in this category. The grinding face of the lower stones can be conical or shaped like the segments of a sphere, following the shape of the upperstone, or can, as in the case of some of the Wallsend beehives, be practically flat. The upperstone was usually turned by means of a horizontal handle, projecting radially from a socket in the side, or from a groove on top.

Only two of the Wallsend stones have 'typical' beehive profiles (nos 1 and 3), the former having an almost hemispherical cross section with a flattish top, and a flat grinding face. The rest seem to have either a conical profile (*e.g.* no. 2), or a low, flat 'bun-shaped' appearance (no. 9). Generally the hoppers are small in diameter (90–100 mm), and taper into rather narrow feedpipes (20–50 mm). Six of the stones have horizontal handle sockets (*e.g.* no. 1) which are usual for this type of quern, although two of these are a steep angle (nos 2 and 7) which is unusual. The grinding surfaces are generally flat and all are ungrooved.

On the whole the design and the dressing of the stones is simple. There are two exceptions however. First, no. 4 has an unusual socket drilled into the side of the feedpipe, the purpose of which is unclear, although it must be related to the spindle/rynd arrangement in some way. In the lowest portion of the feedpipe are the remains of a metal cylinder, which may have served to protect the feedpipe from wear, or alternatively, may have performed the role of the spindle itself. Second, no. 9 has two well preserved handle sockets, one of which is flush with the grinding surface. There is also a possible rynd chase high in the feedpipe.

Quern stones of these type are usually assigned to a pre-Roman, 'native' tradition in the North of England, and it is at least likely that at least some of these stones from Wallsend are products of a previous Iron Age tradition. However, they are found quite predictably on Roman military sites (*e.g.* Vindolanda, and Randylands milecastle 54), the stones from Randylands indicating that these querns were still in use in the later second century (Curwen 1937). Although only four out of the 12 stones of this series occurred in dated contexts, the evidence from Wallsend indicates the possible use of the stones into the third century. Stones like no. 9, although essentially an extension of a local tradition, do show advanced features, and an economy in size that could have made them competitive to the German imports, unless of course the types had two completely different functions.

The fact that these stones appear in third-century contexts at Wallsend show that they may be the products of an industry that survived well into the Roman period. The exact context of production, whether it was solely native or an adaptation, still remains unknown however, and an excavation into the location of quarry sits would surely be productive. One should perhaps look into the Fell sandstone outcrops of Northumberland, which were exploited for raw material with which to make millstones well into the nineteenth century (Jobey 1986). Current survey work in the area has unearthed hand-mill quarries which could be of Roman date (D. Cowley *pers. comm.*).

### The continental lava stones

It is generally accepted that a new type of milling stone, as far as we know made from raw material extracted from volcanic sources near Mayen in the Eifel Hills in Germany, was introduced to northern Britain with the Roman army (Peacock 1980). Fragments of 31 of these stones were found at Wallsend. However, preservation of these stones on the site is very bad, fragments rarely representing more than 20% of the original stone, due to their brittleness in post-depositional contexts. This often makes the identification of upper and lowerstones very difficult, and greatly restricts the amount of information that can be extracted in general. These new milling stones are distinguished from previous types not only by the

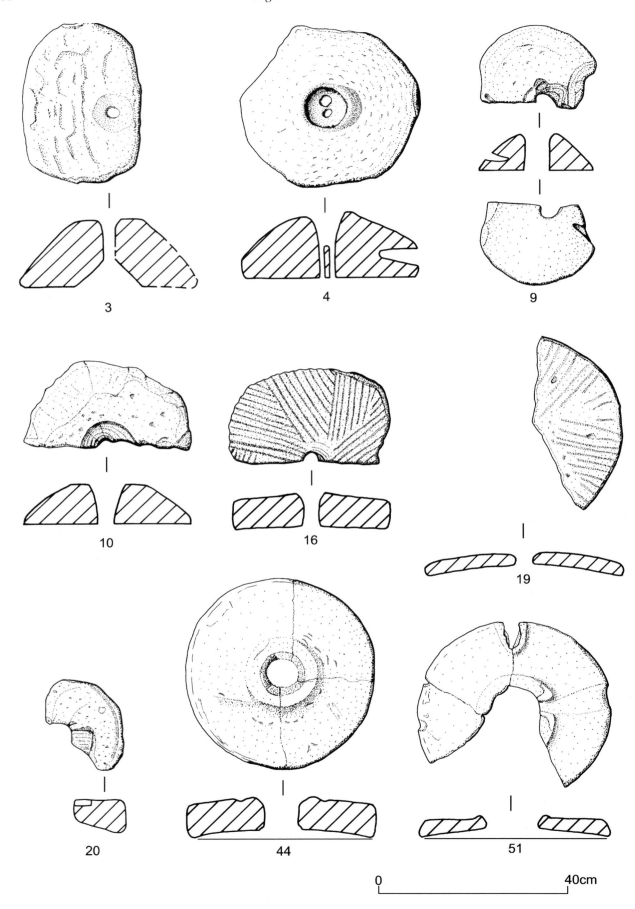

*Figure 25.36: Querns nos 3–51. Scale 1:8*

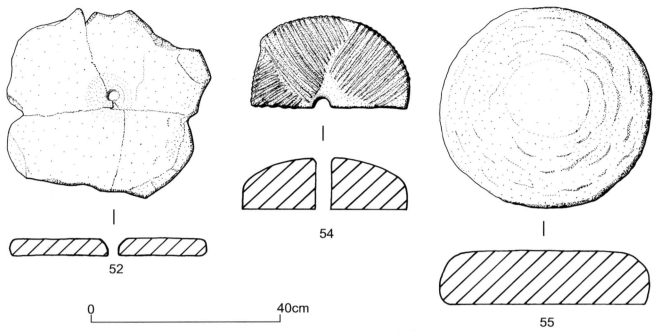

Figure 25.37: Querns nos 52–55. Scale 1:8.

exotic raw material, but also by new morphological features and new kinds of dressing.

A major development was in the extensive use of the rynd and spindle, almost certainly allowing greater control over the grinding process as a whole. Unfortunately only two of the stones from Wallsend have remains of rynd chases (nos 20 and 27), from which we can try to reconstruct the arrangement. The rynds each consisted of a piece of iron with a wedge at each end, which fitted into notches on opposite sides of the feedpipe, and which were probably fixed with molten lead. In the middle was an eye through which the spindle fitted, thus taking the weight of the upperstone, and acting as a pivot at the same time. It is probably that adjustments to the gap between the two stones were made to suite the job in hand. These could either have been made where the spindle connected to the rynd, or by simply altering the length of the spindle. Unfortunately finds of spindle and rynds are unusual, the examples from Newstead (Curle 1911) and Vindolanda (Welfare 1985) being rare instances.

Similarly, little evidence remains of the handle arrangements employed, only two stones revealing such information. First, no. 34 has a distinct channel cut into the rim, for an iron hoop handle. A groove running laterally across the top surface of the upperstone may be connected to this handle arrangement. Second, no. 39 has the remnants of a vertical handle socket, which appears to be rectangular in shape, although only a small portion is preserved, and which appears to perforate the stone entirely. Practically all the stones have grooved grinding faces, the striae usually being set out in a 'harp' pattern (e.g. no. 27). The sides (or rim) as well as the upper surface are commonly dressed with parallel grooves which probably do not have a functional role, unlike those of the grinding face which may serve to direct the ground substance through the grinding space.

Dating of these as always is a problem, only 17 of them being from stratified contexts. Of these five can be dated to the late third/early fourth century and one stone from Period 1. This sequence at least gives a general indication of the time span during which this type of quern was used. Certainly the evidence from Wallsend does nothing to counter the idea that these querns were introduced to Northern Britain by the military. Though how far these new stones 'excelled' other types, and created a 'revolution in diet' (Welfare 1985, 156), is unclear, and some experimental work in this area would be informative. Certainly the vesicles in the lava give material a texture that helps retain good grinding properties as the rock wears. Probably their most important asset was their lightness and mobility, which must have been a considerable advantage in a military context. It is clear that the stones were produced to a more or less standardised design and exported to Britain in large numbers.

### The Romano-British milling stones

Although the mechanism is not very clear, it seems that a new form of quern or milling stone, essentially the product of a local industry, was gradually produced in competition with the continental Mayen types. In fact the local industries had probably never stopped production completely, as the number of traditional beehive types found in the second- and third-century military contexts in northern Britain, bears witness. The existence of local industries, capable of competing with the Mayen imports is not surprising when one considers the plentiful supply of raw material suitable for quern production in the area. Even in the Iron Age, quern quarries had quite sizeable distributional networks in some parts of Britain (Hayes *et al* 1980).

Due to the raw material used for the manufacture (locally derived sandstone), this group of stones are far better preserved than the Mayen types. The upperstones are generally flat, and a lot thicker than the volcanic continental stones. The profiles are commonly rectilinear (*e.g.* no. 44). A pronounced collar around the feedpipe is also a common feature (*e.g.* nos 44, 51, 56), as it is among this group of stones at Vindolanda (Welfare 1985). Both upper and lowerstones show 'continental' characteristics, such as the harp style grooving found on numerous grinding faces, on both upper and lowerstones (*e.g.* nos 49 and 54). Equally some stones have a very simple design, with no special features or dressing.

There is very little evidence for the handle arrangements employed to turn these stones. Only the upperstone no. 51 has a slot in the upper surface to take the horizontal handle. There is also a channel that traverses the entire upper surface of the stone, which is best interpreted as a slot for a lateral handle which could be attached directly to the spindle. Out of 8 upperstones, 5 have clear remains of rynd chases (nos 44, 48, 49, 51 and 56). This compares favourably with the Mayen stones which are far more fragmentary. The chases are rectangular in plan, and in the case of stone no. 48, the remnants of the rynd are still visible. Two of the lowerstones (nos 45 and 54) have unusual 'stepped' spindle perforations, the purpose of which is unclear.

Six out of the 14 stones in this group are lowerstones, which is a comparatively large proportion. However this may be misleading, as lowerstones usually do not show the characteristics of upperstones that allow them to be more easily classified. In fact the dating of the stones as a whole is fairly tight, although re-use remains a problem. All of the six stones from dateable contexts are assigned to the mid or late third-century contexts. This would seem to fit in well with the emergence in the later Roman period (late third and fourth centuries), of a revitalised local industry.

## Conclusion

Unfortunately the stratification of the quern stones from Wallsend does not allow a detailed analysis of chronological change. In addition, the largest group of stones, the Mayen lava querns, were the most badly preserved, which obviously limited the analysis. Also, one suspects that there is a differential transform operating here, in that the larger, more robust beehive and Romano-British stones were more suited to re-use as building material than were the more brittle Mayen lava stones. Exactly how far this distorts our view of the evidence is unclear, but its effect must be considerable. Our knowledge would be greatly increased by research into quarry production in Northumberland, by further attempts to source the locally and continentally produced stone more precisely by an extensive thin-sectioning programme, and a greater involvement in experimental work.

## Catalogue

The descriptions of each individual stone in the catalogue have been kept as concise as possible. Special features are described where relevant, and measurements of complete dimensions given where possible.

### Beehive stones

1. Upperstone (D:*c.*340mm B(max):180mm). Area over Building 4 and Road 4, unstratified, G03:05, 681, WSQ59
Hemispherical exterior with flat top. Lateral handle socket. Flat grinding surface.

2. Upperstone (D:*c.*400mm B(max):190mm). Area over Building 9, unstratified, F13:01, 973, WSQ57
Conical shaped upperstone, with remains of steep angled handle socket. Grinding surface slightly convex.

3. Upperstone (D:*c.*400mm B(max):182mm). Building 8, make-up for room 1, mid-third century?, D11:15, 1037, WSQ61
Large fragment of tall beehive upperstone. Spindle socket separate from feedpipe. Flat grinding surface.

4. Upperstone (D:*c.*380mm B(max):150mm). Unstratified, 1327, WSQ1
Well preserved, bun-shaped upperstone. Curious socket in feedpipe. Metal cylinder preserved in lower portion of feedpipe. Flat grinding surface. Lateral handle socket.

5. Upperstone (D:*c.*360mm B(max):130cm). Unstratified, 1348, WSQ50
Large fragment of bun-shaped upperstone. Very simple design. No handle or spindle/rynd arrangement evident.

6. Upperstone (D:*c.*280 mm B(max):120cm). Area over Alley 5 and Road 9, unstratified, H14:30, 1431, WSQ21
Conical shaped upperstone. Grinding face badly damaged. Evidence of rynd chase but mechanism unclear. No evidence of handle.

7. Upperstone (D:*c.*320mm B(max):100cm). Building 13, entrance in west range, Period 1, L11:45, 1911, WSQ45
Fragment of bun-shaped upperstone, with wide hopper, flat grinding surface, and an angled lateral handle socket.

8. Upperstone (D:*c.*380mm B(max):160cm). West granary make-up layers, G10:12, 2232, WSQ60
Bun-shaped upperstone. Lateral handle socket. Grinding surface slightly convex.

9. Upperstone (D:*c.*320mm B(max):110cm). Surface round Cistern 1, Period 3, E08:57, 2414, WSQ37
Large fragment of bun-shaped upperstone. Rynd chase, high in feedpipe. Two lateral handle sockets,

one flush with flat grinding surface. Profile is asymmetrical.

10. Upperstone (D:*c.*360 mm B(max):110cm). Chalet 12, Building AH, Period 4, L14:07, 2648, WSQ24
    Simple bun-shaped upperstone. Flat grinding surface, with protruding collar to feedpipe.

11. Upperstone (D:*c.*370mm B(max):140cm). Chalet 12, Building AJ, Period 4, L14:09, 2649, WSQ56
    Simple bun-shaped upperstone, with very narrow feedpipe.

12. Upperstone (D:*c.*380mm B(max):110cm). Area over Road 5, dereliction/modern, E04:07, 2651, WSQ23
    Fragment of bun-shaped upperstone. Faint circular groove in feedpipe may indicate rynd chase.

## The continental lava stones

13. Lowerstone (D:*c.*450mm B(max):50cm). Building 2, post-Roman dereliction, P05:03, 222, WSQ26
    Small fragment of probable lowerstone. Grooved grinding surface.

14. Upperstone (D:*c.*400mm B(max):85cm). Area over Road 5, dereliction/modern, E04:07, 223, WSQ10
    Small fragment of upperstone. Harp style grooving on grinding surface. Upper surface has circular groove delineating hopper.

15. Lowerstone (D:*c.*450mm B(max):65cm). Road surface associated with the north-west shacks (B2), dereliction, E05:04, 224, WSQ29
    Fragment of lowerstone. Rim and grinding surface are grooved.

16. Lowerstone (D:unknown B(max):90cm). Building 18, *contubernium* 1, Period 3–4, F05:07, 225, WSQ32
    Half or totally perforated lowerstone. Grinding surface grooved in harp style. Rim badly damaged so no diameter measurement possible.

17. Upperstone (D:*c.*400 mm B(max):65cm). Unstratified, WSQ2
    Fragment of upperstone. Grooving on all three surfaces.

18. Fragment (B(max):90cm). Unstratified, 770, WSQ34
    Badly damaged fragment. Only has one surface which is grooved.

19. Lowerstone (D:*c.*400mm B(max):40cm). Area over Building 8 and *intervallum* road, unstratified, D11:01, 972, WSQ19
    Large fragment of very thin lowerstone. No features apart from faint traces of grooving on the grinding surface.

20. Upperstone (D:unknown B(max):80cm). Road 3, E12:11, 1050, WSQ11
    Large fragment of upperstone. Upper surface grooved. Has fan-shaped rynd chase. Rim badly damaged, so diameter unknown.

21. Fragment (measurements not possible). Area over Building 9, unstratified, E13:01, 1087, WSQ17
    Tiny fragment of grooved surface from a quern.

22. Fragment (measurements not possible). Building 8, entrance, Period 4, E11:22, 1141, WSQ8
    Only the raw material and one dressed surface identify this fragment as part of a quern stone, probably a thick lowerstone.

23. Upperstone (D:*c.*400mm B(max):110mm). Unstratified, 1149, WSQ35
    Very small fragment of extremely thick upperstone.

Circular groove delineates hopper. Grinding surface heavily grooved.

24. Fragment (B(max): 80mm). Area over Building 9, unstratified, E13:01, 1160, WSQ33
    Badly damaged fragment, probably a lowerstone. One surface grooved.

25. Upperstone (D:*c.*400mm B(max):40mm). Building Row 20, levelling north of Buildings Q and R, late third/early fourth century, F11:13, 1162, WSQ25
    Small fragment of upperstone. Rim is grooved, but all other surfaces are plain.

26. Lowerstone (D:*c.*450mm B(max):30mm). Rubble over Building 8, *Via quintana* and road to the east (B3), late third/early fourth century, E12:08, 1173, WSQ16
    Thin fragment of lowerstone. Surfaces ungrooved. Grinding surfaces worn smooth at edge.

27. Upperstone (B(max):30mm). Unstratified, 1176, WSQ13
    Large fragment of upperstone. Both upper and lower surfaces are grooved. Circular groove on upper surface, surrounds hopper. Well defined rynd chase.

28. Quern (no measurements possible). Building Row 20, levelling west of Building Q, late third/fourth century, F12:10, 1187, WSQ4
    Very small fragment of grooved surface of quern, Badly damaged.

29. Lowerstone (B(max):35mm). Road 3, F11:19, 1211, WSQ63
    The totally perforated spindle socket, probably of a lowerstone, but difficult to tell. Upper surface looks worn.

30. Upperstone (D:*c.*450mm B(max):50–10mm). Area over Building 11, unstratified, K15:01, 1301, WSQ46
    Fragment of thin, flat upperstone. Grinding surface grooved in harp style. The profile is asymmetrical.

31. Upperstone (D:*c.*400mm B(max):*c.*50mm). Area over Building 11 and Alley 6, unstratified, L15:01, 1408, WSQ28
    Fragment of upperstone. Grooved grinding surface. Circular groove in upper surface.

32. Fragment (no measurements). Unstratified, 1513, WSQ5
    Badly damaged fragment. One surface has harp style grooving.

33. Lowerstone (D:*c.*400mm B(max):*c.*40mm). *Intervallum road* (Road 6), primary level, M16:20, 1869, WSQ18
    Small fragment of lowerstone. Grinding surface faintly grooved, while underside is very roughly dressed.

34. Upperstone (D:*c.*400mm B(max):*c.*60mm). *Via principalis*, H08:17, 2065, WSQ42
    Fragment of fairly thick upperstone. Groove in rim for iron hoop handle. Lateral groove in upper surface may be connected with this handle arrangement. Grinding surface roughly dressed and ungrooved.

35. Upperstone (D:*c.*400mm B(max):*c.*35/40mm). Road 3, J13:02, 2158, WSQ52
    Two fragments make up part of a flat, simply designed upperstone. Only feature preserved is a small part of the feedpipe.

36. Upperstone (D:*c.*400mm B(max):*c.*100mm). *Via principalis*, E07:02, 2311, WSQ48
    Fragment of very thick upperstone. Has a well defined hopper, and the grinding surface is grooved in the harp style.

37. Upperstone (D:*c*.450mm B(max):*c*.60–10mm). Rerouted *Via principalis,* late third/early fourth century, E08:24, 2345, WSQ39
Fragment of upperstone. Faint hopper is outlined, the stone becomes extremely thin towards the feedpipe.

38. Upperstone (D:*c*.400mm B(max):*c*.45mm). Road 5, D08:32, 2348, WSQ3
Small fragment of probable, flat upperstone, but may be lowerstone. One side is grooved the other plain but worn.

39. Upperstone (D:*c*.450mm B(max):*c*.60–15mm). Building AP, posthole, late third century, F09:66, 2394, WSQ44
Small fragment of upperstone. Grooved on both surfaces, though grinding surface is worn. Has vertical handle socket, rectangular in shape, perforates stone totally. Circular groove in upper surface. Stone becomes very thin near feedpipe.

40. Upperstone (D:c.400mm B:*c*.70–20mm). Building 3, abandonment or post-Roman dereliction, P07:08, 2505, WSQ40
Approximately 30% of an upperstone, with very wide and gently sloping hopper, tapering to narrow feedpipe. Ungrooved.

41. Fragment (D:*c*.400mm B(max):*c*.80mm). *Via principalis,* L08:50, 2550, WSQ6
Very small fragment of an upper or lower stone with a flat, grooved grinding surface.

42. Upperstone (D:*c*.400mm B(max):*c*.70–25mm). Road 3, G11:71, 2636, WSQ7
Small fragment of upperstone. Grooved grinding surface, with circular groove in upper surface. Profile tapers to the feedpipe.

43. Lowerstone (D:*c*.450mm B(max):*c*.90mm). Building 14, robber trench for unfinished building, Period 1, K11:45, 2646, WSQ47
Extremely thick fragment of lowerstone. Grinding surface grooved.

44. Upperstone (D:*c*.350mm B(max):40/20mm). Area over Building 5 and Alley 3, unstratified, F04:01, 2647, WSQ12
Half of simply designed upperstone. Grinding surface worn smooth. No other features.

## The Romano-British milling stones

45. Upperstone (D:*c*.400mm B(max):*c*.80mm). Area over Building 2 and Alley 1, unstratified, M05:01, 495, WSQ14
Whole upperstone, in three fragments. Fairly thick and flat, with a collar round the top of wide feedpipe, and a rynd chase open to the grinding face.

46. Upperstone (D:*c*.400mm B(max):60mm). Area over Building 10 and Road 9, unstratified, H15:10, 1435, WSQ49
Small fragment, with a pronounced collar around the hopper. Small portion of rynd chaser survives.

47. Lowerstone (D:*c*.400mm B(max):*c*.120mm). Building 5, *contubernium* 1, Period 2, G05:23, 497, WSQ58
Totally perforated, thick lowerstone. Grinding face is gently conical. Spindle socket is 'stepped'.

48. Lowerstone (D:*c*.450mm B(max):45mm). Area over Building 2, ploughsoil, L05:03, 671, WSQ54
Fragment of flat lowerstone. No features.

49. Upperstone (D:*c*.350mm B(max):*c*.100mm). Rubble between Building 18 and street drain, H05:25, 921, WSQ22
Fragment of upperstone made from Penrith sandstone. Very thick for its diameter. Grinding face gently inclined.

50. Upperstone (D:*c*.350mm B(max):*c*.60mm). Building Row 20, levelling between Buildings Q and R, late third/early fourth century, F11:18, 1179, WSQ41
Fragment of upperstone, remarkable for having remains of rynd still in rectangular shaped rynd chase. Gently sloping, well worn grinding face.

51. Upperstone (D:*c*.350mm B(max):*c*.80mm). Area over *Via quintana,* unstratified, K13:01, 1359, WSQ36
Smallish flat upperstone. Spacious hopper leading into feedpipe, with rynd chase. Grinding surface grooved in harp pattern.

52. Upperstone (D:*c*.400mm B(max):*c*.50–20mm). Chalet 9, Building W, late third/early fourth century, D13:11, 1492, WSQ38
Small, fairly light upperstone. Becomes very thin towards feedpipe. Slight groove around rim may indicate iron hoop handle.

53. Upperstone (D:*c*.400mm B(max):*c*.40mm). Chalet 9, Building W, late third/early fourth century, D13:39 and D13:47, 1578 and 1579, WSQ20
Three fragments of upperstone. Flat on top with conical grinding face. Very wide hopper and feedpipe, with remains of rynd chase. Other features are a collar around the hopper, a horizontal handle slot, and a channel running across the whole diameter of the upper surface, probably connected to the handle arrangement.

54. Upperstone (D:*c*.400mm B(max):*c*.35mm). Area of Building 12 and Road 3, no details, N14:09, 1877, WSQ15
Wide, flat upperstone. Roughly dressed. Grinding surface worn. Condition is bad: the stone is incomplete, consisting of four fragments.

55. Lowerstone (D:*c*.400mm B(max):*c*.50mm). Road 8, F09:07, 2210, WSQ53
Fragment of flat lowerstone. Grinding surface grooved in harp pattern, while the underside is roughly dressed.

56. Lowerstone (D:*c*.420mm B(max):*c*.110mm). Area over Road 1, unstratified, E07:03, 2233, WSQ31
Lowerstone with sub-ovoid profile. Harp grooving on grinding face. Has stepped spindle socket similar to no. 47 above.

57. Lowerstone (D:*c*.420mm B(max):*c*.110mm). *Via principalis,* F08:27, 2369, WSQ62
Large complete lowerstone. Flat grinding face, with spindle socket. Curved underside is roughly dressed.

58. Upperstone (B: *c*.60–50mm). Building 16, robber trench, P08:27, 2600, WSQ43
Small fragment of upperstone, with very pronounced collar round hopper. Circular groove in grinding surface surrounds feedpipe, possibly as fitting for rynd.

59. Upperstone (no measurements possible). Alley 10/ Building 17, disturbed surface inside building, third century, G05:17, 2645, WSQ9
Small fragment of probable upperstone. Has very worn harp grooving on one face.

60. Lowerstone (D:*c*.350mm B(max):*c*.50–25mm). Area over Buildings B and K, post-Roman, L05:07, 2650,

WSQ51

Thin, flat probable lowerstone of simple design. Totally perforated by spindle socket. One side of stone may have been reshaped. Profile is asymmetrical.

## Other

61. Lowerstone (D:*c.*250mm B(max):*c.*40mm). Alley 4, G05:07, 478, WSQ27
    Very small rim fragment of lowerstone. No other features.

62. Saddle quern (no measurements possible). Unstratified, 1912, WSQ55
    Smallish, asymmetrical stone with one smooth surface. Cannot possibly identify as a rotary quern stone; could possibly be part of a saddle quern.

63. Upperstone (no measurements possible). Surface round Cistern 1, Period 2 or 3, E08:64, 2443, WSQ30
    What could be a fragment of a very small bun-shaped upperstone, but too badly damaged for exact identification.

## The finds in context

*by A. T. Croom*

Just over 1400 finds of interest from the excavations have been reported upon in this volume, coming from over 24 different buildings and major features. As the Hadrianic layers were not extensively explored and the late Roman occupation layers were largely destroyed by later use of the site, the assemblage dates mainly to the period between the third quarter of the second century and the late third century. Due to the later activity on the site, the post-Roman features and layers are very rich in Roman finds, with almost half of all the small finds and the pottery from the excavations coming from site clearance and later features. Whilst this has made looking at distribution patterns difficult, it has been possible to look at the site assemblage as a whole for a number of different categories.

### Military equipment

In total there were 38 items of military equipment (including weapons other than throwing stones) and a further 34 that could be either military equipment or horse harness. To these figures can be added objects found during the 1997–8 excavations, providing an overall total of 55 items of military equipment and 42 either military equipment or horse harness.

### Belt and baldric fittings

Almost half of the material identified as being possible military equipment was made up of the decorative fittings, buckles and fasteners that could belong to either soldiers' equipment or horse harness. Those fittings that were clearly belt or baldric fittings were of types with a long life, the designs being introduced first in the Antonine period but continuing until the late third century. There were no obvious fourth-century fittings.

### Armour

There are two pieces from legionary armour, an incomplete vertical fastener or tie hook (Fig. 25.12, no. 166, unstratified; Thomas 2003, category Gi or Hi), and a vertical fastener (Fig. 25.12, no. 168, post-Roman?; *ibid.*, category Gii). Small quantities of legionary armour have also been found at South Shields, where it is assumed they relate to the presence of the Sixth Legion during the construction of the fort, and the few items from Wallsend probably also come from its builders rather than reflecting the equipment of the auxiliary soldiers (Allason-Jones and Miket 1984, 3.689, 3.691, 3.696, 3.705; Bidwell and Speak 1994, 19; Bishop 2002, 91). There was only one large fragment of ring-mail (Fig. 25.18, no. 16, Antonine in date), and no examples of scale mail.

### Weapons

There were 12 spearheads in total, but only three ferrules. One of the spearheads was too large for practical use, while the rest show a range of blade shape and socket diameter, with the smaller ones, mounted on slender shafts, more likely to be javelins for throwing rather than spears for thrusting. The earliest example, from underneath the Antonine stone barracks, was a large spearhead with elongated point (Fig. 25.17, no. 4). Five were found in or above the cavalry barracks, six from the infantry barracks, and one from the hospital. This example, and one from Building 9, came from make-up levels for floors, while three others came from floors. Some of these may have been deliberately included during building work as a form of foundation deposit.

The size of the fragment of pattern-welded blade (Fig. 25.18, no. 18) suggests that it comes from a dagger rather than a sword. The technique of pattern-welding produces a blade with a visible design of black lines against the silver of the metal, in this case a herring-bone pattern up the centre of the blade. Due to the work involved, it would have been a relatively expensive weapon that must have belonged to an officer. The fragment was found in a mid-third century occupation layer, in the officer's house of Building 12.

### 'Native'

The fort has produced a relatively large number of 'native' objects. Although agricultural use of the site before the construction of the fort indicates that there was a pre-Roman settlement in the area that has not yet been located, only one of the artefacts dates to before the occupation of the fort site (Hodgson 2003, 13). The other 10 items are all long-lived types that continued to be made in the Roman period or whose manufacture started during the Roman period.

The pre-Roman object is part of a three-link horse bit of a type used up to the mid or late first century (Fig. 25.13, no. 188). There are also a number of

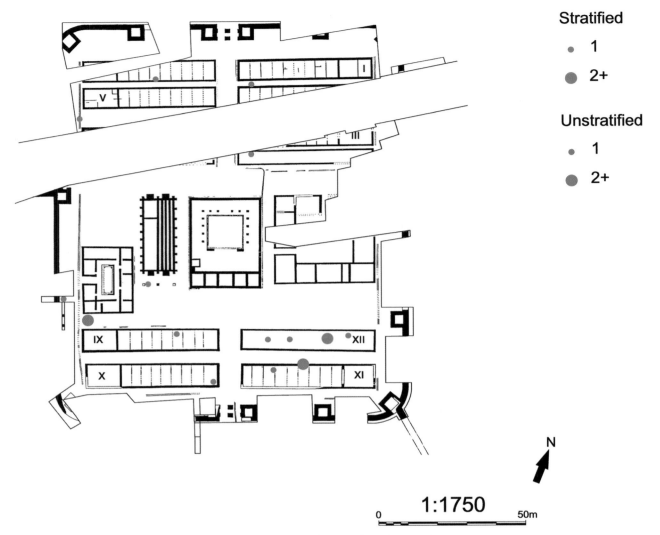

*Figure 25.38: Distribution of 'native' artefacts.*

opaque yellow beads which are traditionally said to go out of production by AD 50 (glass small finds, nos 14–6), but there is some evidence that these may have continued in use into the second century (Price 1985, 213, nos 52–3).

Other items that could be pre-Roman or Roman in date are horse harness fittings such as the copper alloy bridle fragment (Fig. 25.13, no. 187) and the two bone toggles (Fig. 25.23, no. 12; Croom 2003, fig. 147, no. 76, from Building Row 20). Domestic material includes a long-handled 'weaving' comb (Fig. 25.24, no. 34), and a tankard handle of a type made from the late first century through most of the Roman period (Fig. 25.09, no. 85; Jope 2000, 130–1). There are two further beads, one dark blue and the other blue with a white trail, which belong to long-lived classes that began production in the Iron Age, the dark blue in particular being described as a type often indicative of a native element (Fig. 25.28, nos 17–8). There were also a number of hand-made vessels in local traditional ware from inside the fort (see Chapter

22).The section of Hadrian's Wall excavated near the fort has also produced an enamelled pin (SF no. E501, unpublished), and the *vicus* another example of a long-handled comb (SF no. WSB519, unpublished).

Three of the 'native' items relate to horse harness. These may have belonged to irregular cavalry troops stationed in the fort in the third century (Hodgson 2003, 150–1), but may equally have belonged to the members of the regular auxiliary cavalry, as there are some suggestions that they may have been particularly attracted to native-style equipment. It has been suggested of the torc found in the cavalry fort at Benwell, for example, that Roman cavalrymen liked to wear them as personal ornaments (Cessford 1995, 235). Figure 25.38 shows the distribution of glass beads, armlets, 'weaving' combs, horse equipment, pierced metatarsals and the tankard handle; it should also be noted that three of the four spearheads with ridged blades (another pre-Roman tradition) also came from in or above the area of the cavalry barracks.

Unlike the local traditional ware vessels, the native

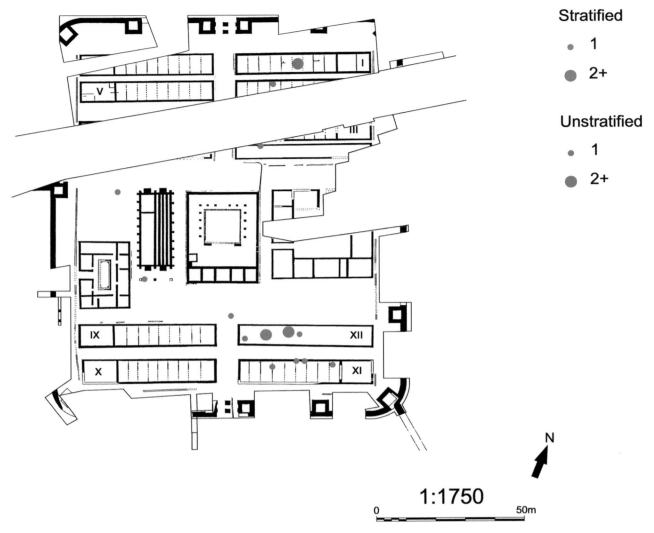

Stratified

· 1

● 2+

Unstratified

· 1

● 2+

1:1750

0                    50m

N

*Figure 25.39: Distribution of horse harness.*

objects are concentrated in the southern third of the fort. The one exception is an unstratified bridle piece from above the assembly area. Two beads came from close to the *Porta quintana*, an area that has produced a number of jewellery items, and are perhaps related to a possible market there, although one of the beads is an example of the yellow bead that probably went out of use in the second century and the suggested market was later in date. The other items come from the four cavalry barracks or the disturbed layers above them, apart from one bone toggle from Building Row 20 (Croom 2003, fig. 147, no. 76).

### Horse harness

There are 16 probable pieces of horse harness, of which only five were stratified. Of the 16, one is a terret from a vehicle, one is a pre-Roman bit and one has been partially recycled for its metal, leaving 12 items of horse harness likely to have used by the cavalry. Of the 12 that could be given a location, seven came from

in or over the cavalry barracks (plus another four from the 1997–8 excavations: Hodgson 2003, 72, table 4). Three others came from in or near Building 1 in the *praetentura* which had been converted into a stable (one from a possible floor inside the building, one from the dereliction over Alley 1 and one from the demolition material used to backfill the clay puddling pit). The remaining two came from above Building 16 and one from above road 8.

Another possible piece of harness is an incomplete fitting that could be a bridle cheek-piece (Fig. 25.12, no. 174), and another that could be a fitting or slide (Fig. 25.12, no. 175). There are also other fittings that are known to have dual uses, such as the button-and-loop fasteners that were used on both horse harness and as belt attachment for dagger and sword scabbards (Fig. 25.13, nos 189–97; Croom 2003, 211) and the buckles with rectangular or splayed attachment loops that were also used as belt buckles (Fig. 25.12, nos 150–3, 156, 159; Bishop and Coulston 2006, fig. 124; Croom 1995, fig. 3, no. 9). Enamel studs similar to no. 226, phallic studs with niello decoration such as no. 227 and small lunate mounts similar to no. 240 have all been found on the headstall found buried with a horse at Beuingen, the Netherlands (Zwart 1998, fig. 3), but it is uncertain if they were only used on harness. Peltate mounts (cf. Fig. 25.15, no. 238) were certainly used as both harness and belt decoration (Aurrecoechea Fernández 1996, figs 15–6).

The assemblage includes only one of the junction-loop fasteners typical of an assemblage of second century equestrian equipment (Fig. 25.13, no. 181), and it is likely most of the fittings belong to the new fashions that developed in the very late second century but which were most common in the third century, and possibly later; little is known of fourth-century horse harness.

## Medical implements

There were seven possible medical implements (Fig. 25.10, nos 99–103; Fig. 25.23, nos 6–7). None were found in the Hospital, although a bone handle possibly from a medical implement was found unstratified just to the east of the building, and a leaf-shaped blade and a probe were found in the same context in the possible building in the rampart by the *Porta quintana* to the west of the Hospital.

## Female presence

There are at least 63 (and possibly 72) objects used primarily or exclusively by women that have been identified from excavations inside the fort (both 1975–84 and 1997–8), although only 25 were stratified. The categories of objects identified are as follows:

*Hairpins.* Only bone examples were included, as while there is clear evidence that bone pins were used in the hair, there is some suggestion that metal pins may also have been used for fastening clothes and may not, therefore, have been used only by women (Philpott 1991, 151). Women would have owned a number of hairpins in a range of materials at any one time, with groups of up to 16 pins known from burials. However, while the evidence of pins apparently worn at burial suggests that while up to seven could be used at any one time, one or two pins were more typical.

*Bracelets and ear-rings.* These were worn only by women until the very late Roman period (Swift 2003, 50).

*Beads.* Beads were used to make necklaces and bracelets and to decorate ear-rings, all of which were worn almost exclusively by women. Melon beads have been excluded because of their possible use on horse harness.

*Mirrors.* The mirror, being associated with the vanity of facial appearance, was seen as being a typical female item in the Roman world.

*Spindlewhorls.* Large numbers of pierced discs cut from pottery sherds are frequently found on Roman sites, but the numbers involve suggest it is likely that they have uses other than as spindlewhorls (42 pottery examples and five in other materials have been found inside the fort; if these are all spindlewhorls women were losing them at a higher rate than their hairpins). The only examples to be included here are those that have been professionally made, in this case decorated shale.

*Brooches.* Pairs of trumpet brooches were certainly worn by women to fasten their tunics, the brooches sometimes connected by a decorative chain similar to a necklace. It can be argued that men would not want to wear a brooch that was so closely associated with both a purely female style of dress and a female style of jewellery.

The assemblage is made up of 26 beads (three jet, the rest glass), 19 bracelets (one jet, five glass and the rest copper alloy), 12 bone hair pins, two copper alloy ear-rings, one fragment of jet hair pin or spindle, two shale spindlewhorls and one fragment of mirror. There are also nine trumpet brooches.

The items come from all over the fort, with only one noticeable concentration round the *Porta quintana*. These are mainly bracelet fragments from fourth-century road surfaces, and it may well represent the loss of a single collection of bracelets, scattered and damaged (1997–8 excavations; Croom 2003, 215). The objects, where they can be dated, range from the second century through to the fourth century, but the earlier material is often residual in later contexts and only a small number of items can be allocated to occupation phases.

One of the few places where this can be done is in the Commanding Officer's house (Building 13), which also has the largest number of stratified 'female' items from any single building, although this is a not very impressive three. The building produced two bone pins (bone report nos 16, 20) and a fragment of jet pin or spindle (jet report no. 6). These came from an occupation layer in a corridor, a floor in room 3 and the fill of a depression over the baths. This is the one building inside the fort where there were certainly women as part of the Commanding Officer's family and household, and yet the numbers are still low. Other items come from both the infantry and cavalry barracks, but the numbers are small, and not many are associated with occupation layers. Although the assemblage includes a number of small items such as beads easy to overlook when lost and not always worth the trouble of retrieving, which are therefore more common in the archaeological record, the total number of female items from the site (at least

63) compares well with the number of items of the certainly male items of military equipment (between 55 and 97).

## Lighting

The fort has produced 12 items of equipment using for lighting, consisting of 10 lamps and one candlestick. The military were one of the major users of lamps in Britain, but they were never as popular here as on the Continent, and their use was already in decline by 100 (Eckardt 2002, 153). For most of the soldiers the open fire in the *contubernia* may have provided all the light necessary. Iron open lamps or iron or wooden candlesticks may have also been used, although none are represented in the assemblage from the site. Artificial lighting would have been most important in those rooms without open fires, such as high-status rooms with underfloor heating, and within the Commanding Officer's house where Mediterranean-style lighting must have been used. The copper alloy hanging lamp (Fig. 25.06, no. 77), for use with a lamp-stand, would certainly have belonged to an officer.

There are fragments from five *firmalampen*, closed lamps for burning oil (although one of these fragments is a decorative mask cut from the *discus* of a lamp that may have reached the site as an amulet or similar rather than as a complete lamp). A matching pair was found in the hospital, the earliest of which was found in a layer under the stone building (mid Antonine or later). There were also five open lamps, for burning oil or, more frequently, animal fat. This type of lamps tends to be less delicate than the oil lamps, and the assemblage includes one in stone and one in lead, as well as examples in pottery. The exceptions are two very small pottery lamps based on miniature bowls, one certainly the product of local kilns and the other likely to be so as well (Fig. 25.29, nos 10–1). The complete example has a pinched-out spout and an applied straight handle, a form unusual in pottery and more typical of lead lamps. There is a possible parallel from York (Perrin 1990, fig. 127, no. 1434), and a larger version from the Antonine kiln at Roxby (Rigby and Stead 1976, fig. 68, no. 66).

## Ritual

The unit at Wallsend seems to have had a tradition of burying complete items during the construction of their barracks. This is not a practise common in all forts and seems to reflect cultural differences retained by individual units within the army. Such items could be gifts to bring good luck or prosperity to new buildings (or to buildings that had changed use), or to protect the building and its occupants from evil, such as the envy of other people, or as offerings to appease local guardian spirits or deities. The most costly offering

at Wallsend would have been the complete ring-mail suit found buried in a pit dug before the construction of the Period 4 Barrack 12 (Croom 2003, 217, no. 53). In this case, the ring-mail was found under the position of the central *contubernium* of the barrack, but other possible offerings are more commonly found in the officer's quarters. Three stacked copper alloy cooking pots came from the Antonine decurion's quarters of Building 12 (Fig. 25.08, nos 79–81), while a complete ramshead *patera* was found in the make-up layers of the third-century decurion's quarters of Building 11 (Fig. 25.07, no. 78). The very large spearhead, presumably originally of ceremonial use during its active life, was buried whole within the flagged floor of the officer's quarters in Building 1, although it is unclear whether this was during the construction of the floor or as a later insertion.

It is not clear if the miniature axe (Fig. 25.06, no. 74) is a complete votive object (Kiernan 2009, type 1c) or part of an incomplete pin (*ibid.*, 120; Cool 1990b, group 18C, fourth-century type). Both types of artefacts are more common from religious sites than military, and it may be significant that it came from the area near the finds-spot of the Fortuna statuette in the Commanding Officer's house, although it is unfortunately unstratified.

## Religion

Altar and statue fragments recovered from the general area of the fort reflect the official worship of two of the three major state gods, Jupiter Best and Greatest and Minerva, the goddess of war (Snape and Bidwell 1994, 24–5). Minerva was represented in a large statue found outside the fort, but the head of a more modest statue of her was also found re-used inside the fort (Fig. 21.02). Both deities appealed to the military, as did Fortuna, represented by a copper alloy statue in the Commanding Officer's house (Fig. 25.05, no. 73), Mars, depicted on an intaglio and Dea Roma, holding both a sword and a figure of Victory, also on an intaglio (Fig 25.26, no. 1; cat. no. 6).

Two dedication slabs and a fragment of a statue indicate that there was a temple dedicated to Mercury to the west of the fort (*CSIR* 1.1, nos 202–4). It is possible that he is also the god represented in the small portable shrine used for more private worship (Fig. 25.21, no. 1). He was one of the most popular gods within Britain, but as the god of trade, profit and commerce, and protector of travellers (and thieves), was usually more popular with civilians than the military.

The pipeclay figurines also represent domestic worship, being comparatively cheap, mass-produced statues that could set up in small wall-mounted shrines within houses or barracks. Approximately eight such figurines are known from Wallsend, three representing a nursing mother goddess (*dea nutrix*), three Venus and two unknown human or animal figurines. Five of them come from the *vicus* south of the fort, and only three from inside the fort. One of those from inside the fort, from a possible midden east of Building 3, is a nursing mother (Fig. 25.29, no. 1). The subject matter perhaps makes it more likely that this was originally owned by a woman.

### Copper alloy vessels

The fort as a whole has produced evidence of ten copper alloy vessels, of which nine can be given a location. Some are utilitarian kitchen vessels (such as the buckets with iron handles found in the decurion's quarters of Building 12) and others are tablewares. Copper alloy vessels would have been more expensive than pottery equivalents and probably also more expensive than glass vessels (which often imitated the more desirable metal versions: Fleming 1997, 12), and of the six vessels found in barracks it is noticeable that all four complete vessels (deliberately buried) were found in an officer's quarters. Of the three remaining vessels, one came from the hospital and two were unstratified, but from near Building 16 which has produced gold and silver coins and intaglios. The three buckets buried together date to Period 2, while the rest date to contexts of the second half of the third century and probably later.

### Survivals

The assemblages include a number of first-century items that were in use for some time before they were deposited on the site. The copper alloy candlestick could have been approximately 200 years old when it was deposited, and would have been still functional at the time (Fig. 25.06, no. 76). The ramshead *patera* would have been at least 125 years old when it was deliberately buried as an offering, its age perhaps making it more precious as a gift (Fig. 25.07, no. 78). There were also two first-century brooches, one found in a post-Roman robber trench (Fig. 25.02, no. 16) and one in an undated context within the interior of one of the fort gateways (Fig. 25.02, no. 1). This second brooch has been dated to *c*.50–70 and is of a type with a restricted distribution in the south-west (cf. Mackreth 1993, fig. 23, no. 4; Mackreth 1994, fig. 75, nos 5–6; also an unpublished example from Princesshay, Exeter).

### Curiosities

Amongst the collection of flints from the site there were two barbed and tanged arrowheads, one leaf-shaped arrowhead and one polished stone axe, all in good condition (Fig. 25.32, no. 56). Only one of these is stratified (from the fill of a drain near Building 1), but it is possible rather than being disturbed accidentally from pre-Roman layers, they may have been curiosities picked up and kept by soldiers within the fort. Stone axes in particular have been found from a number of

Roman sites, and it is thought they may have been kept for superstitious or religious reasons (Adkins and Adkins 1985). Some other objects seem to have been brought to the fort as curiosities, such as the crinoid ossicles that may have been collected near Holy Island about 80km further up the coast (*pers. comm.* S. Humphries), and a roughly worked piece of whale-bone found in the *vicus* (unpublished, WSB513) which must also have been picked up from the beach.

## Buildings and their associated finds

The quantity of finds varied considerably between buildings, sometimes reflecting the area actually excavated, and sometimes reflecting the original barren nature of the building itself.

### Barrack: Building 1

The very large spearhead (Fig. 25.17, no. 1) was found in the floor of the officer's quarters. It was too large to be of much practical use, as its disproportionate weight at the end of the shaft would make such a spear very difficult to control or use effectively after a very short length of time. Its size makes it impossible for it to have been accidentally left on the floor, and it may have been a ritual deposit of some type, either as the floor was being laid or on its abandonment. The building produced nine throwing stones built into floors and walls (see also Building 3).

### Barrack: Building 2

The building was only partially excavated. There was another spearhead on a floor (Fig. 25.17, no. 6), but it was not a large example, and it may have no significance.

### Barrack: Building 3

The most distinctive element of the finds from this building was the number of throwing stones incorporated into the foundations of the Antonine building. There were originally 18 stones under the floor of *contubernium* 2 and a further three in the floor itself. The stones must have been manufactured during the Hadrianic period and although by their very nature are long-lived weapons, by the Antonine period they were no longer needed and were reduced to being treated as building material.

### Barrack: Building 9 and Chalet range 9

There was an incomplete spearhead in a floor level in *contubernium* 2, and another in the make-up for a new surface in room W (p.164, nos 10, 11). The same make-up layer also included an offering of a complete bronze skillet (Fig. 25.07, no. 78).

### Barrack: Building 11

This building had a spearhead in the floor of *contubernium* 3/4 (iron cat. no. 7). The same layer also contained a fragment of a padlock. These are sometimes found connected to chains and are also known to have been used on shackles.

*Barrack: Building 12 and Chalet range 12*
An adze-hammer was found in constructional(?) material in phase 1 of the building (Fig. 25.19, no. 27). It may have been accidentally buried during construction work, although as it is 220mm long and its original wooden handle would have made it even bulkier, it is possible that it was a deliberate offering. An offering of three buckets was certainly made at the officer's quarters (Fig. 25.08, nos 79–81). An incomplete spearhead was incorporated in a construction layer of chalet AJ (Croom 2003, fig. 144, no. 57).

*Workshop: Building 16*
This building has been identified as a workshop, but it contained an interesting amount of non-industrial material. There were two intaglios (the only building in the fort to have more than one), two brooches and a fragment of a glass armlet. There were parts of two spoons and a key, as well as the hoard of 12 silver and one gold coin. It is possible much of this material, if not simply random background clutter, may have been present for recycling or repair, but the only item of military equipment was a fragment of a belt mount or fitting, and more items might be expected if metal items were being made or repaired in the building. Tools included a small iron awl, a bone needle and a whetstone, all of which would also be used in domestic surroundings. There was only a single piece of copper alloy casting waste (no. 3). This building also contained an iron shackle, possibly for use on an animal, but just as likely to be used on a human. Shackles seem to have used principally for transporting people, and in particular slaves, and may also have been used in military situations when dealing with British prisoners.

*Hospital: Building 8*
The building produced 23 small finds, of which four related to the military use of the site. These consisted of a spearhead in the clay floor of large room 8 (Small finds report, iron no. 12), a strap-end in the entrance (Fig. 25.12, no. 160), a fragment of ring-mail found in construction material (Croom 2003, 219, no. 53.3) and a throwing stone, probably re-used as building material (cat. no. 132). The only possible medical implement from the whole building was recovered from a Period 2 occupation layer in room 3 (Croom 2003, 215, no. 34.2).

The building had an interesting selection of lighting equipment. There was a complete lamp with heavy sooting round the nozzle found in a possible 'natural' layer under room 8 of the stone building, associated with Antonine samian (Fig. 25.29, no. 6). A second complete but broken lamp, which had had its filling hole enlarged but which showed no signs of use, was found in the Period 2 occupation/demolition layers of room 5 during the 1997–8 excavations (Croom 2003, fig. 149, no. 90). The two lamps were of exactly the same fabric and form, and must originally have been associated.

There was a fragment of a third pottery lamp found in room 1, but as this came from a phase 4 make-up layer it may have been brought in with building material from elsewhere. There was also a complete copper alloy candlestick in the soil above the flagstones of room 3 relating to the abandonment of the building (Fig. 25.06, no. 76). Artificial lighting was used for both religious purposes, such as purification and as votive offerings to deities, and for funerary purposes, such as pre-burial rituals and as grave goods (Eckardt 2002, 95,115). Religious rituals were no doubt carried out in the hospital as part of the medical care, and there would also inevitably be corpses to deal with. However, while there were clearly uses for lamps in the building, one of the complete lamps showed no evidence of ever having been used. The symbolic importance of lamps may have made this lamp a suitable termination offering, if it was associated with the demolition of the building.

*Commanding Officer's house: Building 13*
The 29 small finds recovered from the building are typical for a domestic assemblage, incorporating items from the toilette, recreation and household work. Under the category of personal adornment there are two or three hairpins and a pair of tweezers; there are two counters from a game, and tools such as a needle and a whetstone, and a possible spindle fragment. Furnishings are represented by a stud from a box, a decorative copper alloy plate probably also from a box, and a couple of studs that might have decorated either a box or a door. The only military items are part of a belt strap end, a throwing stone and a lead sealing. There are two items that are loosely connected to ritual, one of which is an appliqué theatrical mask cut from a pottery oil-lamp brought from North Italy (Fig. 25.29, no. 5). It may have been kept simply as a pretty object, or it might have had greater significance, perhaps as an amulet, to its owner. The other artefact is a statuette of provincial manufacture, probably intended for a shrine since it was not designed to be seen from the back, although of a larger size than most religious statuettes (Fig. 25.05, no. 73).

There is nothing amongst this assemblage that reflects the high status of the family living in the building, and parallels for almost all the items can be found in the accommodation of the ordinary soldiers. The statuette, although not a common site find, is not of a particularly high quality. However, lack of high quality objects is not unexpected, as there would be more slaves than family members within the household, and many of the items that would have indicated the family's status, such as expensive textiles and silver dinner services, are unlikely to enter the archaeological record.

### Headquarter's building: Building 14

This building had eight counters in stratified layers and another unstratified example that may also have come from it. The eight represents the largest number of counters from any single building inside the fort, all but one of which were professionally made out of bone or glass. Three came from room d, presumably from the same set, one from room a, three from the crosshall, and one from the floor(?) of the strongroom. The *principia* at South Shields Roman Fort has also produced a large number of counters, with 12 examples in bone, pottery and stone (Croom 1994, fig. 7.5, nos 72–3, nos 75, 75/B183, 75/B184; fig. 7.15, no. 123, no.123/S6; 198, no. 107/P119; 200, nos 108/P71, 108/P76, 108/P98). Pottery discs come in a large range of sizes, so the term 'counter' has been reserved for those under approximately 33mm in diameter, this being the maximum size of professionally made bone examples and are therefore considered suitable for use for board games, although such discs did not have to be used purely as counters on a board. Their presence in the *principia* is therefore of interest, but as some of the counters from both sites come from construction layers, they may in fact not have anything to do with the use of the building.

## The post-Roman finds

### Early medieval

*Pottery (Fig. 25.40)*
by J. Tipper
A single sherd of decorated handmade early Anglo-Saxon 'pagan' pottery was recovered from an unstratified context over the site of the *principia* (Building 14, context J09:01).

#### FABRIC AND FORM
Wt: 92.4g. D(max):875mm B(max):14.28mm. The fabric is a fine sandy matrix, with some coarse sub-rounded quartz inclusions <2mm. The sherd is dark grey in colour and has a smoothed, but not burnished, finish. The exterior surface of the sherd is in good condition; the interior is pitted and has been abraded. A linear groove on the interior was probably created during manufacture of the vessel. The sherd is from the shoulder region of a globular jar, probably a sub-biconical urn. There are no indications to suggest a bossed design. It is difficult to estimate the size of the vessel from the single sherd.

#### DECORATIVE SCHEME
The sherd has elaborate stamped and incised decoration; a three-line (narrow) pendant triangle filled with a vertical row of stamps. Outside the pendant is a zone of incised decoration, which is unclear due to the small size of the sherd, but might possibly be a three-line chevron enclosed within two single lines. A single stamp has been used, with a rectangular grid motif (criss-crossed), which is most similar to motif C2a using Briscoe's typology (Briscoe 1983).

#### COMPARATIVE DECORATIVE SCHEMES
The decoration found on the sherd falls within a strong tradition of pottery production and decoration, and finds most similar parallels from the cremation cemeteries north and south of the River Humber, e.g. Sancton, Heworth and Elkington. The use of stamped pendant triangle decoration is very typical of the sixth century and designs of this kind were extensively used by several of the more prolific workshops, notably Illington-Lackord and Sancton-Baston (Myres 1977, 52–6).

The design is similar to some from the Sancton-Baston 'workshop', first identified by Myres (Myres and Southern 1973; Myres 1977, 59–60; figs 347–8) and later analysed by Arnold (1983). Arnold, however, doubted whether 'potter' or 'workshop' were appropriate terms and suggested that the symbols may have had a totemic significance relating to family affiliation (Arnold 1983, 27). The most characteristic feature of the Sancton-Baston pottery is the interlocking stamp-filled pendant triangles. The main pendant triangle nearly always carries two stamps, a concentric circle or rosette and the other a criss-crossed grid rectangle, which is very similar to that from Wallsend. The most complex designs are found on vessels at Sancton, Yorkshire, simpler designs from Norfolk, Nottinghamshire, Lincolnshire and Leicestershire. None illustrated in Myres' corpus, however, have narrow pendant triangles with a single line of stamps (Myres 1977).

#### SIGNIFICANCE OF THE SHERD
The importance of a single unstratified sherd is difficult to assess and it is difficult to discuss its original provenance. One might normally expect a

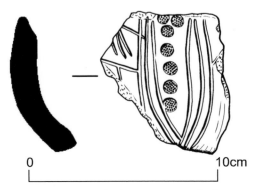

*Figure 25.40: Anglo-Saxon pottery. Scale 1:2.*

0                                    10cm

highly decorated vessel in a funerary context, rather than in domestic use. Such a vessel might occur as an accessory vessel within an inhumation or as a cremation urn. The practice of inferring burials from stray objects, in this case a single sherd of unstratified pottery, is however unsatisfactory (Miket 1980, 290). The generalised pattern of cremations and furnished inhumations between Deira and Bernicia is striking. There are no large cremation cemeteries to the north of the Yorkshire Wolds and no mixed cremation and inhumation cemeteries north of Hob Hill, Saltburn. There is a total lack of cremations north of the Tees (Cramp 1988, 72). The Wallsend sherd is, therefore, more likely to come from an accessory vessel within an inhumation grave than from a cremation burial.

There are few examples of decorated pottery from excavations within the region with which to compare the Wallsend sherd. The sixth-century inhumation cemetery at Norton-on-Tees contained eighteen vessels, including three used as cremation urns, but none of which were decorated (Sherlock 1992, 54–5). Hob Hill, Saltburn, is a mixed cremation and inhumation cemetery, dating to the sixth century and excavated early in the century (Gallagher 1987). The total number of graves is unknown and, unfortunately, only a small proportion of the pottery is preserved (Gallagher 1987, 19–21). The remaining pottery does, however, show strong links to Deira and the south; a *Buckelurne* from Hob Hill is comparable with vessels from Heworth and Sancton (Gallagher 1987, 19).

Of particular relevance to this discussion is the evidence of occasional and isolated early Anglo-Saxon burials inside other Roman forts in north-east England. Sixth-century burials have been found within the fort at Aldborough (Cramp 1983, 267). A female inhumation burial was found within the *praetorium* at Binchester, which contained a brooch, beads and sherds of a vessel dating to the mid-sixth century (Coggins 1979, 236; Miket 1980, 297). At Catterick the fort buildings were in decay by the time sixth-century Anglian burials were inserted in the ruins (Cramp 1983, 267). An early sixth-century burial at Corbridge occupied a central position within the fort; a scabbard strap mount and a small pot were found at one site and two Group II cruciform brooches and a string of glass beads at another site in Corbridge (Miket 1980, 293; Cramp 1983, 268).

On comparison with this evidence it does not seem implausible that an isolated burial, or burials, were placed within the fort at Wallsend but which has been disturbed at a later point, as evidenced by the unstratified sherd of early Anglo-Saxon pottery.

ACKNOWLEDGEMENTS
I am grateful to Catherine Hills who kindly read and commented upon this report and to Matthew Buckley for his help in producing an impression and cast of the stamp.

## Small finds (Fig. 25.41)
*by L. Allason-Jones*

1. Fitting (L:29mm B:2mm). Unstratified, WSCA926 Fragment of an openwork handle mount from a wooden bucket. Martin 1976, type IIIA, sixth-century. Cf. Bael-Bernerring, *ibid.*, Grab 33, no. 16b; Krefeld-Gellep: Pirling 1974, Taf. 50, no. 1b. This is a Continental type of handle mount which in this country is found almost exclusively in Kent (Cook 2004, 30, 43). Other type IIIA mounts are known from Gilton, Kent and West Stow, Suffolk (*ibid.*, no. 106; West 1985, fig. 268, no. 4). (AC)

2. Copper alloy strap end (L:37mm W:15mm T:1mm). G03:04, 620, WSCA155, 2001.1195
Incomplete strap end tapering to a trilobate end. The back in plain but the front is intricately decorated with a central rosette inside a wreath surrounded by a series of open squares within a ribbed border. A hole is pierced at the top where there is also some iron corrosion. Eight- or ninth-century in date and possibly of Northumbrian manufacture. Hawkes and Dunning 1961, Type VA. See also four silver strap ends of similar appearance from Lilla Howe in North Yorkshire: Watkin and Mann 1981, 155–7.

3. See the copper alloy escutcheon (Fig. 25.09, no. 83, possibly fourth to seventh century).

## Medieval

4. Copper alloy buckle (W:26mm T:4mm). F08:01, 2198, WSCA118, 2001.1158
Incomplete oval buckle with expanded decoration on one face on either side of the pin rest. The shank is semi-oval in section. *c.*1250–1400.

5. Copper alloy pin (L:30mm T of head:1.5mm). F11:67, 2216, CA927
Very small brass pin with a globular head formed by twisting wire around the end. Although such pins were found on Roman forts in the area, evidence suggest that they are medieval and post medieval in date. Egan and Pritchard 1991, 299.

## Post-medieval

### Glass
*by A. T. Croom*
There were a number of seventeenth-century beakers with chequered spiral trail decoration, in pale green glass (cf. Haslam 1993, fig. 71, nos 665–7).

6. (D:80mm B:1mm). L15:01, WSG209
Out-turned rim and single line of trail surviving.

7. (D:70mm B:1mm). G04:01, WSG182
Two lines of trail surviving.

8. (B:1.5mm). L14:01, 1432, WSG207
Two lines of trail surviving.

9. (B:1mm). E14:01, WSG208
Two lines of trail surviving.

## Coins
*by R. Brickstock (RB)*

| 10. Elizabeth I | 1d | 1538–1601 | F08:02, 2229, WSC243 |
| 11. Charles I | ½ groat | 1625–49 | L05:03, 907, WSC335 |
| 12. Charles I/II | | 1625–85 | K11:01, 1718, WSC244. Scottish |
| 13. Charles I/II | | 1625–85 | M05:01, 599, WSC254. Scottish |
| 14. Charles I/II | | 1625–85 | M04:01, 3, WSC246. Scottish |
| 15. Charles I/II | | 1625–85 | M11:01, 1685, WSC245. Scottish |
| 16. Unknown | | 1639 | G10:01, 2071, lost: site record provides provisional date |
| 17. Charles II | 2d | 1663 | N13:01, 1654, WSC169. Scottish. Stewart 243 |
| 18. William III | ½ d | 1694–1701 | K03:07, 682, WSC252 |
| 19. Illegible | | C17th | F09:01, 2186, WSC251 |
| 20. George II | ½ d | 1750 | G13:02, 297, WSC336 |
| 21. George III | ½ d | 1760–1820 | K04:03, 689, WSC268 |
| 22. Danish | | 1771 | F09:01, 2184, WSC257 |
| 23. George III | ½ d | 1775 | P13:01, 1777, WSC269. Peck 908 |
| 24. George III | ½ d | 1775 | E11:17, 1139, WSC262. Peck 908 |
| 25. George III | ½ d | 1799 | L09:01, 1968, WSC263. Peck 1235 |
| 26. George III | ½ d | 1806 | N12:01, 1632, WSC352 |
| 27. George III | ½ d | 1807 | L09:01, 1969, WSC261.  Peck 1378 |
| 28. Victoria | ½ d | 1860s | M07:09, 2557, WSC265. As Peck 1754 |
| 29. Victoria | 6d | 1899 | Unstratified, 1286, WSC274 |

Key: Peck = Peck 1964; Stewart = Stewart 1955

## Tokens

30.  Q08:03, 2451, WSC258
Token for 1¼ d. James I/Charles I, 1603–49. As Peck 308. (RB)

31.  Token (D: 24mm T: 2mm). Unstratified, 1228, WSL56, 2001.2317
Circular token with a raised anchor on one face and a wheel shape on the other. This type of token is commonly found along the north-east coast of Britain and is known as a sailor's token although its exact use is unknown. (LA-J)

32.  Unstratified, 938, WSC260
'Rowland Shipyard Newcastle on Tyne 1d'. (RB)

## Cloth sealing

33.  Lead cloth sealing (L:31mm D:24mm B:3mm). L03:11, 773, WSIM42
Cloth sealing of two-part type, poorly stamped with image of a ship within a beaded circle.

## Small finds

34.  Pewter buckle (L:53mm W:36mm B(max):4mm). F11:66, 2211, WSL126, 2001.2379
Rectangular buckle with a drilled frame for a separate spindle. There are traces of fine vertical line decoration on the front. (AC)

35.  Copper alloy buckle (L:100mm). F11:01, 952, WSCA481
Fragment of rectangular shoe buckle with openwork interlace (c.1720–1790s). (AC)

36.  Copper alloy button (D:28mm B:9mm). Unstratified, 1076, WSCA393, 2001.1433
Flat engraved button (eighteenth century or later). There were a number of other examples. (AC)

37.  Bone button (D:23mm). G05:02, 17, 2001.680, WSB20
Deeply concave button with four circular holes, dyed green. Eighteenth-century or later.

## Bone buttons with single hole

Buttons with a single hole had a copper alloy attachment loop fed through the central hole, and often also had a decorative copper alloy cover over the front. Eighteenth-century or later.

38.  (D:19mm T:1.5mm). L05:03, 685, WSB36

39.  (D:12mm T:2mm). E05:01, 121, WSB27

40.  Glass bead (D:19mm T:8mm). H13:03, 723, lost
Globular, cobalt blue translucent bead.

41.  Glass bead (L:11mm T:11mm). N05:01, 101, WSG39, 2001.1685
Spherical black bead. Probably post-Roman, although the type is known in the Roman period.

42.  Glass bead (D:9mm T:6.5mm). H16:05, 1270, WSG156, 2001.1802
Globular white opaque bead with the walls of the hole dragged to one side.

43.  Wig curler (L: 30mm, T: 9mm). E02:11, 763, 2001.2508
Incomplete pipe-clay wig curler, seventeenth- to eighteenth-century.

44.  Bone handle (L:37mm T:7mm). E10:01, 966, WSB39, 2005.3649
Fragment of a two-piece bone knife handle of originally oval section. Traces of iron survive on the inner face and the outer face is decorated by incised double lines.

45.  Handle (L:90mm Max.W:21mm Max T:5mm). M09:01, 2476, WSB88, 2005.3698
One section of a two-piece antler knife handle with a convex face which has been roughly trimmed but retains some of the natural surface of the antler. The end is rounded and slightly wider and thicker than the rest of the handle. The handle has been fixed to the iron knife tang by three iron rivets, two placed on the centre line and the third very close to one edge at the end.

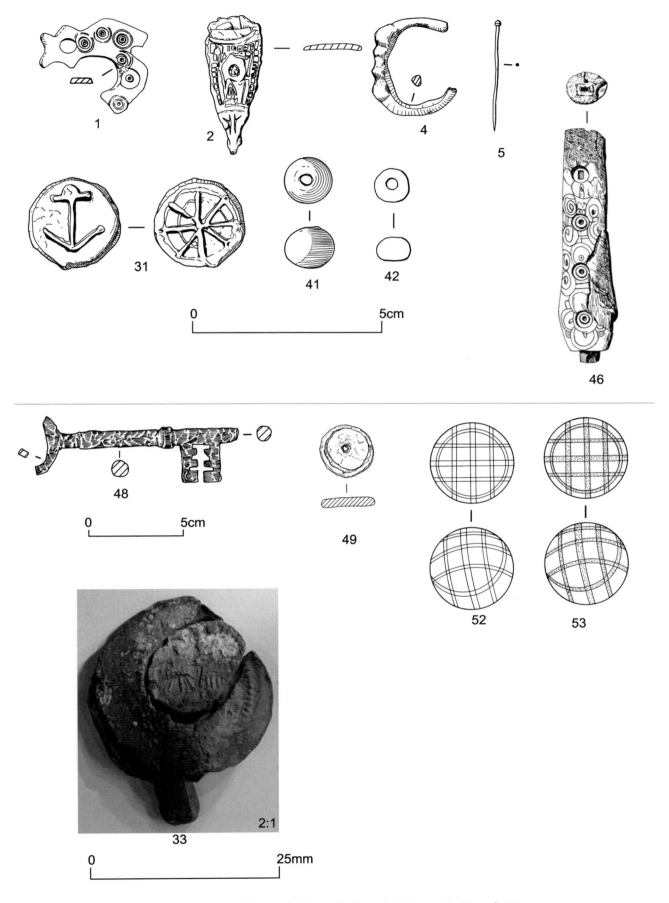

Figure 25.41: Post-Roman finds nos 1–46, scale 1:1; nos 48–53, scale 1:2.

46.   Bone handle (L:64mm W:15mm T:1mm). M14:01, 1644, WSB17, 2001.677

One-piece handle formed from a long bone with traces of the iron knife tang surviving in the socket. The face is decorated all over by a series of complex motifs each centred round a sunken circular area with a deeper centre which possibly housed an inset. A short projection from the terminal suggests that a secondary material was attached.

Cf. Newcastle: Vaughan 1987, fig. 31, no. 199, nineteenth-century context.

47.   Bone spoon (L:116mm W:13mm). R05:09, 657, WSB35, 2005.3645

Long, thin bone spoon with a triangular-sectioned handle. The bowl is incomplete but appears to have been shallow and spatulate. The terminal is shaped to a point.

48.   Iron key (L:109mm D:8mm). J13:03, WSFE331, 2001.2209

Post-medieval key with symmetrical bits. (AC)

49.   Lead disc (D: 29mm T: 4mm). Unstratified, 586, WSL39, 2001.2300

Disc with a central circular hole and an incised marginal line. This would appear to be a post-medieval dress weight or button.

50.   Block (L: 34mm W: 45mm). F10:13, 2293, WSL51, 2001.2312

A block of lead which has been pressed into a four-cornered shape, connecting four sheets of a hard dark brown and black material 4mm thick.

51.   Whetstone? (L:153mm W:50mm B:50mm) L03:10, 656, WSS272, 2001.3128

Large square-sectioned whetstone, incomplete, tapering to one end. Pecked surfaces. (AC)

52.   Pottery ball (D: 40mm). E13:01, 1018, WSP172, 2001.2485

White ball with a clear glaze over a design of dark blue lines crossing in three directions. Such balls were common products of potteries in the nineteenth century and were made in matching pairs, used in sets of six, with a smaller plain ball as the jack in the game of carpet bowls. Similar bowls are known from the Garrison Pottery in Sunderland where they are dated 1830–1865 (Baker 1984, 66, fig. 89, *pers. comm.* N. Dolan).

53.   Pottery ball (D: 32mm). E12:01, 1016, WSP173, 2001.2486

Small white pottery carpet bowl similar to above, with a design in dark blue of sets of three lines crisscrossed in three directions.

54.   Pot lid (D:80mm). N12:01, 1658, WSP186

Complete lid with blue under-glaze transfer print with a picture of two bears against trees and mountains, surrounded by an interlace pattern. The legend reads 'Genuine Russian bears grease for increasing the growth of hair'. 1870s. Cf. Dale 1987, types B31, B38.

## Discussion

Whilst there are only a few finds from the early medieval period from the site, they do indicate some activity in the area at this period. There is the fragment of sixth-century pottery perhaps from an inhumation burial, a possible sixth-century bead from the outside the east gate (unpublished, WSG610) and a possible sixth or seventh-century annular loom-weight from near the Branch Wall (unpublished, WSP518). There is also the fragment of sixth-century bucket mount, but as this was a chance find from the site, and as the type has a British distribution based in Kent, it is possible this is a fragment that has been brought to the site in modern times. There is less material from the eighth to tenth centuries: a single strap end of the eighth or ninth century. By the Norman period the settlement had moved away from the river and was now about 1km inland. This is reflected by the very small quantity of pottery and other finds from this period on the fort site, and it is not until the seventeenth century that the quantity of pottery, glass and coins suggest heavier use of the site. In 1709 a visitor recorded that 'the old inhabitants thereabouts still tell you of vast quantities of stones that have in their remembrance been dug out of it and carried away to build houses' (Whitworth 2000, 47). In 1732 the site is described as having been ploughed, and by 1778 the first mine-shafts had been sunk (Snape and Bidwell 1994, 15). The presence of the collieries led to buildings both near and on top of fort itself, although it was not until the late nineteenth century that the site was comprehensively covered by terraced housing built for workers in the riverside shipyards.

# 26. METALWORKING AND ENVIRONMENTAL EVIDENCE

## by L. Allason-Jones and L. J. Gidney

## Metalworking debris

### Ironworking

It appears from the small quantities recovered that only samples of slag and furnace lining were kept, much of which was unstratified and so cannot certainly be identified as Roman.

### Copper alloy metalworking waste

by L. Allason-Jones
*Recycling*
1. Area of Building 12, unstratified, L14:44, 1800, WSCA17, 2001.1057
   A bead and a fragment of horse harness, broken and partially remelted (see Copper alloy cat. no. 61).
2. Area over Building 8, unstratified, E10:13, 2264, WSCA264
   Including fragment of plating.

*Sprue caps*
3. (L:29mm). Building 16, floor, Period 1, M08:26, 2530, WSCA111, 2001.1151
4. Debris over Cistern 1, Roman/post-Roman, E08:13, 2307, WSCA315

*Casting waste*
5. Unsealed rubble over west *praetentura*, E05:04, 237, WSCA141
6. Area over Building 14 and Alley 7, unstratified, K11:01, 1709, WSCA318
7. Area of Building 14 and Road 3, no details, K12:03, 1722, WSCA313
8. North *intervallum* road, phase 3 surface, P04:02, 154, WSCA142
9. Building 2, north wall robber trench, Period 2, N05:17, 364, WSCA918

*Moulds*
There were three recessed stones that might have been used as moulds (see stone report nos 50–2), the most interesting of which has possible location pins as if used for a two-piece mould (Fig. 25.32, no. 52).

The evidence for copper alloy working was spread across the site, and showed no concentration in any one area or type of building. There was only one piece (no. 3) from Building 16, identified as a workshop.

## The animal bones (Figs 26.01–08)
*by L. J. Gidney*

### Introduction

The preservation of the bone was generally mediocre, and the assemblage is biased in favour of the larger, more visible and robust bone fragments. An assessment of the complete surviving assemblage provided a quite restricted species list, with the majority of bones coming from the domestic animals, cattle, sheep/goat and pig. Cattle bone was present in the greatest number of contexts, while goat was present as well as sheep, which included a polled variant. Horse and red deer were also present, but were not numerous; the red deer elements included meat-bearing bones besides lower limb bones and antler. Roe deer bones were also present, indicating hunted game. The dog bones all appear to be disarticulated fragments with no suggestions of whole bodies. Small mammals were indicated by a single tooth, and shell-fish were sparse.

Detailed study was made of the bones from two deposits of interest, from Cistern 1 and Building 13. The assessment of the assemblage of animal bones identified the late third-century fills of Cistern 1 as being of particular interest. The quantity of bone recovered from this single feature was large in comparison with the majority of features on this site. The assemblage was tightly dated to the late third century and appears to have accumulated over a relatively short time span. The assessment highlighted the fact that there appeared to be an unusual degree of selectivity in the skeletal elements

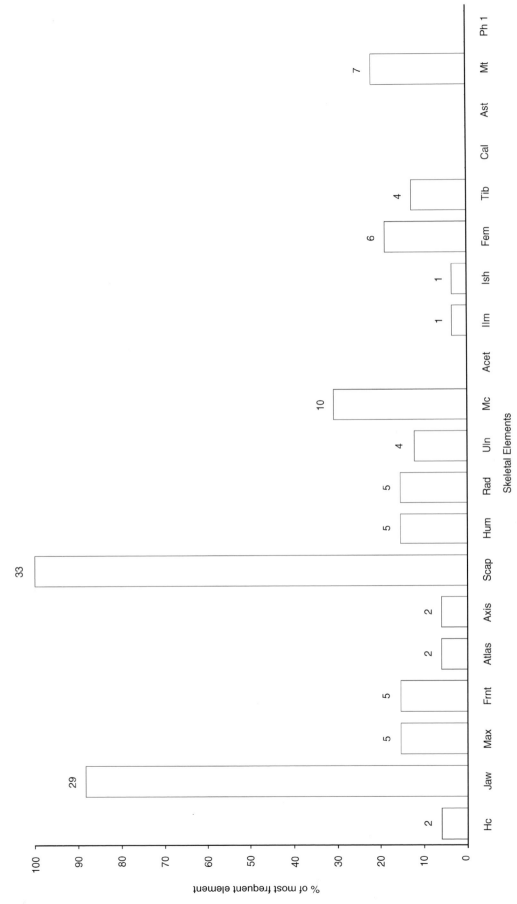

*Figure 26.01: Skeletal elements of cattle bones from Cistern 1, context E08:27*

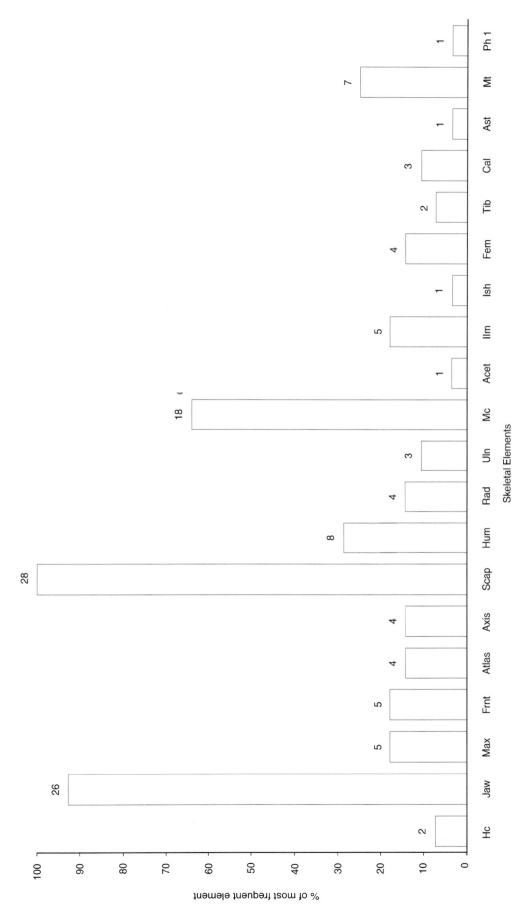

*Figure 26.02: Skeletal elements of cattle bones from Cistern 1, context E09:29*

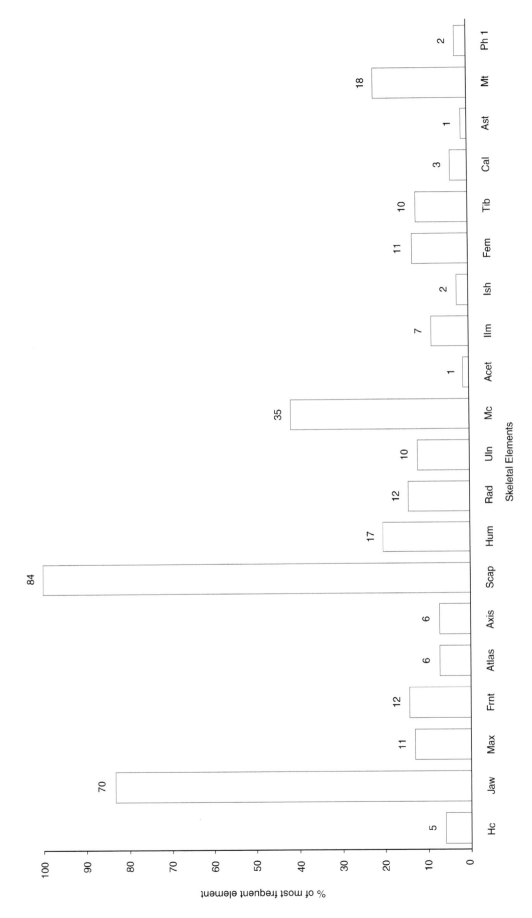

*Figure 26.03: Skeletal elements of cattle bones from Cistern 1, all contexts*

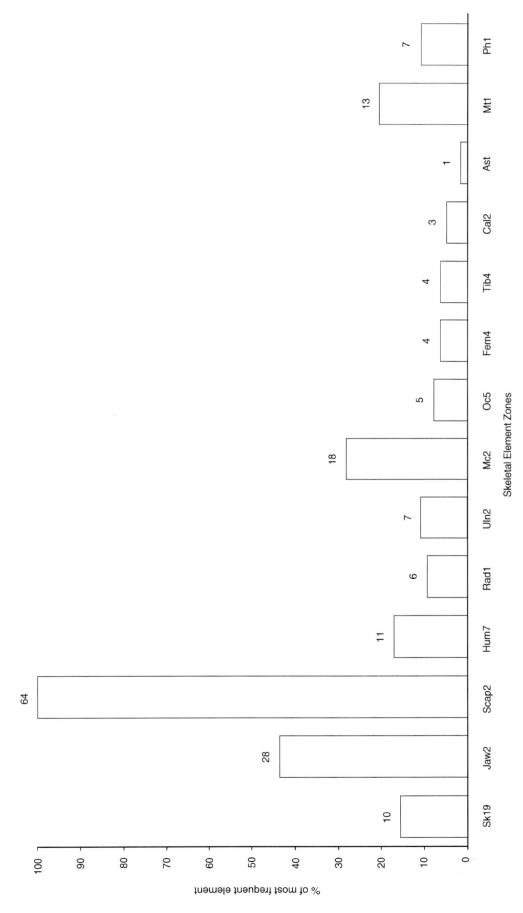

*Figure 26.04: Skeletal element zones of cattle bones from Cistern 1, all contexts*

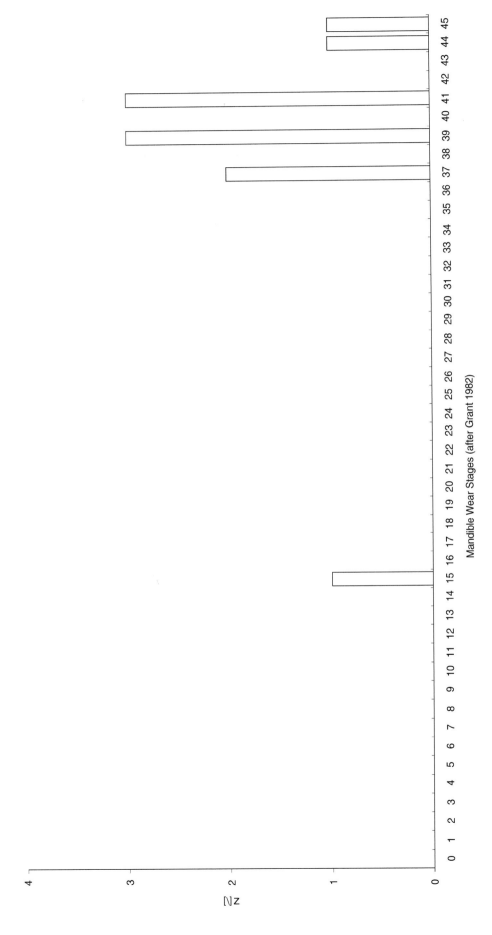

*Figure 26.05: Mandible wear of cattle bones from Cistern 1, all contexts*

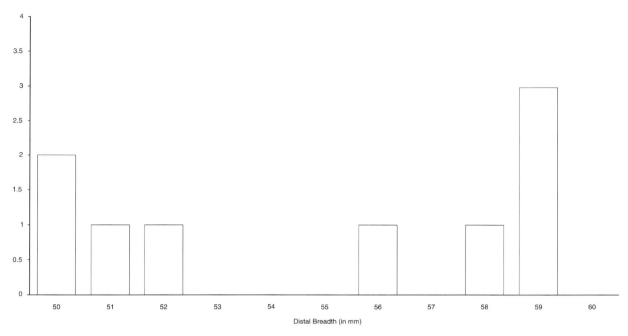

*Figure 26.06: Distal breadth of cattle metacarpals from Cistern 1*

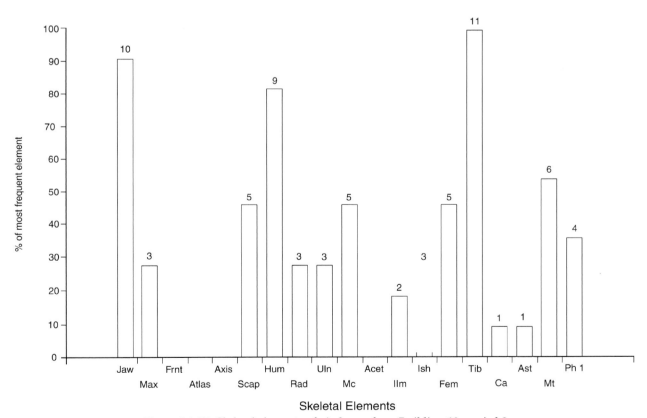

**Skeletal Elements**

*Figure 26.07: Skeletal elements of pig bones from Building 13, period 3*

of cattle deposited. The immediate impression gained was that preservation of the bones was marginally better for this feature than the general run of finds.

The majority of the bird bones recovered were associated with the commanding officer's house (Building 13). The presence of bird bones on this site indicates both a more benign burial environment and refuse originating from a higher status establishment. Work previously done on the animal bone assemblage from the commanding officer's house at South

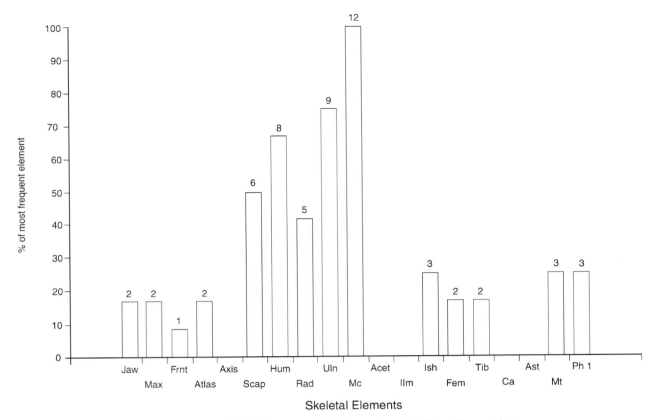

*Figure 26.08: Skeletal elements of pig bones from Building 13, period 4*

Shields (Stokes 1992) has already indicated that the provisioning of a commanding officer's house included items which appear not to have been generally available to the troops. It therefore was deemed appropriate to target this group, both for information on supply of foodstuffs to the residence of the senior officer and for data to compare with an equivalent house at, for example, South Shields.

## Methodology

All fragments of cattle, sheep/goat or pig bone with a 'zone', *sensu* Rackham (1986), or tooth were catalogued, with information on element, epiphysial fusion, tooth-wear and metrical data, where appropriate. All fragments of other species were recorded.

## Cistern 1

Detailed recording of this group revealed that the standard of preservation was not as good as originally thought; the condition was superficially good but leaching of the mineral content has caused brittleness and surface flaking. The bones are not robust and the extra handling caused by repacking after the assessment and handling for recording has led to a large number of fresh breaks. This disintegration does reinforce the interpretation that the assemblage

*Table 26.01: Fragment counts for the species present in Cistern 1*

|  | Context | | | | |
|---|---|---|---|---|---|
|  | E08:27 | E08:29 | E08:37 | E08:44 | Total |
| Cattle | 130 | 150 | – | 73 | 353 |
| Sheep/goat | 10 | 7 | – | 2 | 19 |
| Sheep | – | 1 | – | – | 1 |
| Pig | 3 | 12 | 1 | – | 16 |
| Horse | 1 | 2 | – | 1 | 4 |
| Dog | 2 | 1 | – | 2 | 5 |
| Red deer | – | 1 | – | – | 1 |
| Large ungulate | 6 | 11 | – | 1 | 18 |
| Small ungulate | – | – | – | 1 | 1 |
| Totals | 152 | 185 | 1 | 80 | 418 |

has not been disturbed between the initial deposition and the excavation.

It can be seen from Table 26.1 that only two contexts within the cistern fills produced abundant finds of animal bones, with a smaller quantity from a third context. Each of the two larger contexts presumably represents a single episode of rubbish dumping from one source. The volume of bone is large but much of the bulk is provided by individual, largely complete, scapulae and lower jaws.

## Species

Table 26.01 shows that the overwhelming majority,

*c*.90%, of the identified animal bones deposited in the cistern were cattle or cattle-sized bones. Sheep/goat bones contribute a further 5% of the assemblage. Pig, horse, dog and red deer bones are also present but not in significant numbers.

CATTLE

The representation of the skeletal elements of cattle has been previously noted as one of the points of particular interest about this group. Figures 26.01–03 illustrate the frequency of fragments of 20 skeletal elements, chosen as being the most commonly found and representing the whole carcase. To equate with the paired elements, the number of first phalanges has been divided by four while the number of atlas and axis has been doubled.

For context E08:27, Figure 26.01 shows striking peaks of scapula and lower jaw fragments but some surprising absences that cannot be attributed to differential preservation. The calcaneum, astragalus and first phalanx are all extremely dense bones that survive well but are totally absent from the context, together with parts of the pelvis: the acetabulum. The number of maxilla fragments is extremely low compared to the abundance of lower jaw. The other skull and neck bones are also sparse, suggesting processing of the jaw bones separately from the remainder of the head and neck prior to deposition. Context E08:29 in Figure 26.02 has the same abundance of scapula fragments. The lower jaw is still the second most abundant element but the metacarpal is noticeably more abundant than in Figure 26.01. The maxilla and other skull bones are again under-represented in comparison with the lower jaw. Of the elements not seen in E08:27, none are also absent from E08:29. The information from all three contexts is summed together in Figure 26.03 to show an overall pattern of a superabundance of scapula and lower jaw fragments and a disproportionally high number of metacarpal compared to metatarsal fragments. All remaining elements are represented. Such a pattern is indicative of human selectivity in the disposal of carcase elements in this feature.

What is not immediately apparent from this method of analysis is the paucity of vertebrae and rib fragments. For convenience, these are normally recorded under the "Large Ungulate" category. It can be seen from Table 26.01 how few fragments were designated in this section.

Appendix 1 lists the counts of zones for each cattle element, while Figure 26.04 illustrates the frequencies of the most numerous zone for 14 of the elements considered in Figures 26.01–03. Because there are fewer individual zones than fragments, all the cistern fills are considered together in Figure 26.04. The skull and pelvis are treated as single units for the zone counts. Figure 26.04 should give an indication of the minimum number of individual elements present for

cattle and show which elements are over-represented in the fragment counts because of excessive breakage.

The zone frequencies in Figure 26.04 mirror the trends seen from the fragment frequencies in Figure 26.03. The predominance of scapula fragments is still striking. Lower jaw remains the second most common element but the zone frequencies suggest that breakage has enhanced the representation of lower jaw in the fragment counts. The frequency of metacarpal fragments is much reduced for the zone counts, approaching parity with the humerus, but still more abundant than the metatarsus. The remaining elements suggest a similar, low, level of utilisation and discard of undifferentiated parts of the carcase.

Consideration of the zones present for the scapula in Appendix 1, shows that there are surprisingly low numbers of zone 5, the posterior of neck with foramen, compared to zones 1–3 of the glenoid. This is unlikely to be caused by differential preservation as zone 5 is a dense area of bone, unlike zones 4, 6 and 7 which are usually poorly represented. Unfortunately recent cracking and breakage, together with flaking surfaces, has obscured details of the original butchery patterns of this bone. Certainly no evidence was seen for the classic hole in the scapula blade which is normally associated with smoking the shoulder blade meat. Trimming of the glenoid was regularly seen, resulting in lower numbers of zone 1 compared to zones 2 and 3. A proportion of the scapulae appear to have been deposited as more or less complete bones but the impression gained was that many scapulae consisted primarily of the detached glenoid segment with the origin of the spine. The cut marks indicate that the spine was routinely sliced off, hence the low numbers of zone 4.

The lower jaw bones also show evidence for a systematic pattern of dismemberment. The commonly found zones are 1–3 from the front part of the jaw with the incisors and zone 7 at the back of the molar tooth row. Very sparse are zones 4 and 5, the articulation of the jaw with the skull. It seems that the jaw was chopped off leaving the articulation of the jaw embedded in the muscle attached to the skull. These fragments must have been deposited elsewhere on the site, as skull fragments are generally rare in the cistern. Most common is zone 9 on the maxilla, suggesting that some lower jaws may have been dumped with part of the corresponding upper tooth row. It was not possible to match any lower tooth rows with the few upper tooth rows.

Some clear evidence was observed for the longitudinal splitting of long bones through the articular ends for marrow extraction (Stokes 1996, 40). This is reflected in the zone counts by, for example, the higher number of zone 7 on the distal humerus, the medial condyle, compared to the lateral zone 8, and also the proximal radius with zone 1, the medial condyle, compared to the lateral zone 2. Similar

*Table 26.02: Tooth wear data for cattle bones in Cistern 1 (teeth in approximate order of eruption)*

| Cattle | U | S/W | H/W | |
|---|---|---|---|---|
| M1 | 5–6m | – | 1 | 31 |
| M2 | 15–18m | – | 6 | 31 |
| P2 | 24–30m | – | 10 | 1 |
| P3 | 18–30m | 1 | 7 | 11 |
| M3 | 24–30m | 1 | 4 | 24 |
| P4 | 28–36m | 6 | 8 | 14 |
| *Sheep/goat* | U | S/W | H/W | |
| M1 | 3–5m | – | – | 1 |
| M2 | 9–12m | – | 2 | – |
| P2 | 21–24m | 1 | – | – |
| P3 | 21–24m | – | – | – |
| M3 | 18–24m | – | 1 | – |
| P4 | 21–24m | – | – | – |
| *Pig* | | U | S/W | H/W |
| M1 | 4–6m | – | 1 | 3 |
| M2 | 7–13m | 1 | 2 | – |
| P2 | 12–16m | – | – | – |
| P3 | 12–16m | – | 2 | 2 |
| P4 | 12–16m | – | 3 | – |
| M3 | 17–22m | 3 | 1 | – |

Key: m = months, U = unerupted/deciduous, S/W = slight wear, H/W = heavy ware
Ages after Silver 1969

butchery was also seen on some metapodials but, particularly for the metacarpal, most of the fragments with corresponding zones appear to have been dumped together.

The bones had been extensively modified, principally by chopping with a heavy cleaver, before disposal. Clear chop marks were observed on 162 identified fragments, 39% of the assemblage. This excludes unidentified fragments and identified fragments where flaking surfaces have obscured such evidence. There is no doubt that these bones had been deliberately selected and dismembered. Two frontal bones demonstrated that considerable effort was expended in removing the horns. One metacarpal and one metatarsal showed signs of burning midshaft. This practice is widespread on Roman sites, particularly in Carlisle (Stallibrass 1991 and 1993). The author believes this process to have served the dual function of liquefying the marrow and making the bone brittle so it could be snapped easily to pour the marrow out, and has carried out experimental work with Mr P. Stokes to demonstrate the hypothesis is plausible.

The cattle supplied to the fort whose bones were finally dumped in the cistern appear to have been mainly mature animals. The tooth wear data in Table 26.02 show a complete absence of young calves with the first molar unerupted and only one first-year beast with molar 1 coming into wear. More numerous are late shedding deciduous teeth and permanent teeth coming into wear, probably from second- to third-year animals, but most common are permanent teeth

in full wear from third-year and older animals. This is further illustrated by the Mandible Wear Scores in Figure 26.05 from the jaws with complete tooth rows surviving. Only one younger, second year, animal with molar 2 coming into wear is present at MWS 15. The remaining ten jaws span MWS 37–45. These have all molars present and in wear. By analogy with my own reference collection of Dexter cattle mandibles, those jaws at MWS 44–45 represent animals at least 10 years old and probably several years older. Breakage of the jaws has obscured the incidence of congenital absence of premolar 2 but one example was noted, as well as an example of malocclusion on molar 3.

Tooth wear data is spares for the pigs but Table 26.02 suggests the presence of mainly second-year animals with permanent teeth coming into wear. There appear to be no very young or aged pigs represented by teeth.

The epiphysial data in Table 26.03 complement the tooth wear data in showing that the majority of the bones are from adult animals with fused epiphysial ends. Only one unfused scapula is present and was noted as deriving from a calf. The few remaining unfused epiphyses are from the later fusing elements and probably correspond with the limited cull of second- to third-year animals postulated from the teeth.

Only four bones were sufficiently complete to be used for estimates of withers height, using the factors of Zalkin (1960) where the sex of the animal is not known. Three metacarpals indicate withers heights of 1.02m, 1.11m and 1.14m, while two

*Table 26.03: Cattle epiphyses in approximate order of fusion, from Cistern 1*

|  | F | JF | U |
|---|---|---|---|
| **By 18 months** |  |  |  |
| Scap. tub. | 34 | - | 1 |
| Acet. symph. | 1 | - | - |
| Prox. rad. | 7 | - | - |
| Dist. hum. | 13 | - | - |
| Prox. ph. 2 | 3 | - | - |
| Prox. ph. 1 | 7 | - | - |
| **By 2-3 years** |  |  |  |
| Dist. tib. | 2 | - | 1 |
| Dist. mc. | 18 | - | - |
| Dist. mt. | 7 | - | 1 |
| **By 3.5-4 years** |  |  |  |
| Prox. cal. | 1 | - | 1 |
| Prox. fem. | 3 | - | - |
| Dist. rad. | 2 | - | 1 |
| Prox. hum. | - | - | 1 |
| Prox. tib. | 4 | - | 1 |
| Dist. fem. | 2 | 1 | - |
| P & D uln. | - | - | - |
| **By > 5 years** |  |  |  |
| Ant. Vert. ep. | - | - | 3 |
| Post. Vert. ep. | - | - | 4 |

Key: F = fused, JF = just fused, U = unfused
Ages of fusion after Silver 1969

metatarsals indicate heights of 1.08m and 1.14m. The distal metacarpal was the only element to provide a reasonable sample of metrical data. The nine bones in Figure 26.06 appear to fall into two groups. The smaller range from 50 to 53mm and may be female while the larger range from 56 to 59 mm and may be male. The single cattle skull with horn cores attached appeared feminine.

OTHER SPECIES
Bones from animals other than cattle appear to be incidental refuse included in the cistern fill. Of these, sheep bones are the most common. One skull with feminine horn cores had been split sagitally and a further two bones had been chopped. Two fused and two unfused bones were seen and one lower jaw with all permanent molars present but little wear on molar 3, so probably aged about two years at death. Further evidence for the culinary source of this deposit lies in the chop marks seen one pig bone, one horse bone and the red deer bone.

Two of the dog bones were sufficiently complete for withers height to be estimated using the factors given by Harcourt (1974, 154). Both bones are probably from one animal with a height of about 28 to 30cm. Dogs obtained access to some of the bones before they were tipped into the cistern as canid gnaw marks were observed on six cattle bones and four sheep bones.

*Summary*
The late third-century fills of the cistern have produced a most unusual, specialised deposit of cattle bone. There is evidence for considerable human selectivity, suggesting that much of this refuse derives from specialised processing involving principally the scapula and lower jaw of cattle, with some marrow extraction from other major limb bones, particularly the metacarpal. The low numbers of skull fragments suggest that primary slaughter waste was not included in this deposit, likewise the low numbers of ribs and vertebrae suggest that general food preparation and consumption waste has not been dumped here. A small proportion of general culinary waste may be indicated by the inclusion of bones from species other than cattle.

Some possible reasons for the utilisation of bone marrow have been discussed by Stokes (1996). For large deposits of highly fragmented limb bones, the "soup kitchen" hypothesis postulated for Zwammerdam (van Mensch 1979) has been discredited and, in any case, this assemblage is not of a comparable scale. The soup suggestion may, however, be relevant to the lower jaws from the cistern. These have been broken in such a way as to open the marrow cavity. Sadly, there are no surviving recipe collections from Roman Britain. However, in more recent historical periods ox cheek soup frequently figures in recipe collections, often with the admonition to first break the bones (Raffald 1970, 5). Finds of cattle scapulae with the glenoid trimmed and a hole in the blade are frequently encountered on Roman sites and are generally interpreted as evidence for brined and smoked shoulder beef. Clear evidence for the meat hook holes in the blade was missing for the scapulae from the cistern but a similar product may be envisaged, perhaps boiled salt shoulder beef rather like a modern ham with the glenoid used to hold the joint for carving. A minimum of 49 scapulae and 23 lower jaws would have provided a substantial amount of food, without taking into account the meat and marrow attached to the remaining bones and any vegetative waste for which the evidence has not survived. This is not catering by barrack block but rather by garrison, suggesting a special meal for a special event. Saturnalia or some other comparable religious or military festival may have coincided with the decommissioning of the cistern which became the fortuitous repository of this unusual assemblage.

## Building 13

*Species*
Detailed recording of this group revealed that the standard of preservation was generally better than the average of the assessed contexts. This is reflected in the presence of bones from small and juvenile animals. It can be seen from Table 26.04 that Period 2

produced the richest group both in terms of numbers of identifiable bones and species diversity. The Period 3/4 group has fewer identified bones and a noticeable absence of some species present in Period 2, in particular goat, horse, red deer and hare. While the numbers of fragments are small, Table 26.05 indicates some further, interesting differences between the phases. Cattle bones are most abundant in Period 2, decline in proportion in Period 3/4 but increase again from the mid-third century, though not to the level of frequency seen for Period 2. The sheep/goat bones remain proportionally constant in all three phases, but from the mid-third century+ the sheep/goat bones are more numerous than those of cattle. Pig bones are the most abundant finds in all three phases but the proportion fluctuates in relation to the cattle bones, with pig bones peaking in the mid-third century+ which has the lowest proportion of cattle bones.

This contrasts strongly with the findings of

Stokes (1992) for the commanding officer's house at South Shields. The methodology used is not totally compatible with the present system but data thought to be equivalent are presented in Table 26.05. The chronological decline of cattle bones at Wallsend contrasts with a substantial increase in the proportion of cattle bones between Periods 7 and 8 (late third and fourth centuries) at South Shields. Sheep bones are considerably more abundant in Period 7 at South Shields than any of the Wallsend phases, but decline in Period 8 to a similar proportion to that encountered at Wallsend. Pig bones at South Shields do not approach the abundance found at Wallsend but do not vary so dramatically between the two phases as the cattle and sheep. These data suggest that the choice of the Wallsend household lay between cattle and pig meats, with a standard supply of sheep meat. Conversely the South Shields household appears to have chosen between cattle and sheep meats, with pig meat as a standard supply.

The changes between Periods 2 and 3/4 at Wallsend may suggest a change in the tastes of the people occupying the house or a change in housecleaning routines, removing more of the larger cattle and deer bones but not the smaller pig bones.

### CATTLE

Only Period 3 produced sufficient cattle bones for any analyses. All parts of the body are represented with similar numbers of bones from the feet, fore and hind-quarters but far fewer from the head, including loose teeth. As can be seen from Table 26.06, the surviving bones are predominantly from adult animals, only a quarter of the epiphysial ends found were unfused. There were noted three bones from infant, bobby, calves and one bone from an older, veal, calf. No calf bones were seen in Period 3/4 but the equally small group from the mid-third century+ produced three bones, all from the forequarter of a veal calf.

### SHEEP/GOAT

Both sheep and goat are present. Goat is represented by two joining halves of one horned female skull found in N11:29 and N11:31. Sheep is indicated by a polled female skull from M12:44. A further metatarsal

*Table 26.04: Fragment count for the species present in Building 13*

|  | Periods |  |  |
| --- | --- | --- | --- |
|  | 2 | 3/4 | mid C3+ |
| Cattle | 49 | 15 | 9 |
| Sheep/goat | 20 | 11 | 2 |
| Sheep | – | 1 | – |
| Goat | 3 | – | – |
| Pig | 86 | 71 | 21 |
| Horse | 2 | – | 1 |
| Dog | 2 | 5 | – |
| Red deer | 3 | – | 1 |
| Roe deer | 6 | 1 | – |
| Hare | 3 | – | – |
| Large ungulate | 17 | 2 | 1 |
| Small ungulate | 13 | 10 | 5 |
| Domestic fowl | 17 | 7 | 1 |
| Goose | 6 | 11 | – |
| Black grouse | 1 | – | – |
| Mussel | 2 | 1 | – |
| Fish sp. | 1 |  |  |
| Totals | 231 | 136 | 41 |

*Table 26.05: Relative proportions of domestic species present in Building 13, Wallsend and the Commanding officer's house, South Shields, shown as percentages*

|  | Building 13 |  |  | C.O.'s house |  |
| --- | --- | --- | --- | --- | --- |
|  | Periods |  |  | Periods |  |
|  | 2 | 3/4 | mid C3+ | 7 | 8 |
| Cattle and large ungulate | 5 | 15 | 26 | 46 | 65 |
| Sheep/goat and small ungulate | 19 | 20 | 18 | 31 | 15 |
| Pig | 46 | 65 | 55 | 23 | 20 |
| Totals | 188 | 110 | 38 | 214 | 240 |

*Table 26.06: Cattle epiphyses in approximate order of fusion, from Building 13*

| | F | JF | U |
|---|---|---|---|
| *By 18 months* | | | |
| Scap. tub. | 1 | - | - |
| Acet. symph. | - | - | - |
| Prox. rad. | 2 | - | 1 |
| Dist. hum. | 1 | - | - |
| Prox. ph. 2 | 2 | - | 1 |
| Prox. ph. 1 | 3 | - | - |
| *By 2-3 years* | | | |
| Dist. tib. | - | - | 1 |
| Dist. mc. | 3 | - | 1 |
| Dist. mt. | 3 | - | - |
| *By 3.5-4 years* | | | |
| Prox. cal. | - | - | - |
| Prox. fem. | 1 | - | 1 |
| Dist. rad. | 1 | - | - |
| Prox. hum. | - | - | - |
| Prox. tib. | 1 | - | - |
| Dist. fem. | - | - | 1 |
| P & D uln. | - | - | - |
| *By > 5 years* | | | |
| Ant. Vert. ep. | 5 | 1 | 4 |
| Post. Vert. ep. | 5 | 2 | 4 |

Key
F = fused, JF = just fused, U = unfused
Ages of fusion after Silver 1969

*Table 26.07: Sheep/goat epiphyses in approximate order of fusion, from Building 13*

| | Period 2 | | | | Period 3/4 | |
|---|---|---|---|---|---|---|
| | F | JF | U | F | JF | U |
| *By 1 year* | | | | | | |
| Dist. hum. | 1 | – | – | – | – | – |
| Prox. rad. | 1 | – | – | – | – | – |
| Scap. tub. | – | – | – | – | – | – |
| Acet. symph. | – | – | – | – | – | – |
| *By 1–2 years* | | | | | | |
| Prox. ph. 2 | – | – | – | – | – | – |
| Prox. ph. 1 | – | – | – | – | – | – |
| Dist. tib. | – | – | 1 | – | – | 1 |
| Dist. mc. | – | – | 1 | – | – | – |
| Dist. mt. | 1 | – | – | – | – | – |
| *By 2.5–3.5 years* | | | | | | |
| Prox. fem. | – | – | – | – | – | 1 |
| Prox. cal. | – | – | – | – | – | – |
| Dist. fem. | – | – | – | – | – | 2 |
| Prox. tib. | – | – | – | – | – | 2 |
| Dist. rad. | – | – | – | – | – | – |
| Prox. hum. | – | – | – | – | – | – |
| P & D uln. | 1 | – | 1 | – | – | 1 |
| *By > 5 years* | | | | | | |
| Ant. Vert. ep. | 2 | – | 1 | – | – | 1 |
| Post. Vert. ep. | 2 | – | 3 | – | – | 1 |

Key: F = fused, JF = just fused, U = unfused
Ages of fusion after Silver 1969

from M12:37 falls within the goat side of the range established by Rowley-Conwy (1998, 252) for the plot of Greatest Length against Distal Breadth. The remaining bones in the sheep/goat category appeared to be sheep rather than goat. In general all parts of the body are represented in Period 2, with the exception of the small toe bones that are easily missed during excavation. Period 2 also has roughly equal numbers of fused and unfused epiphyses in Table 26.07, while the mid-third century+ has only unfused ends. This apparent difference may simply be a product of small sample size. Three bones from young lambs and one further bone from an infant lamb were seen in Period 2. These tiny bones give an indication of the season of these deposits. Even unimproved cattle can calve all year round, pigs can farrow twice a year but sheep lamb once in the spring.

PIG

It is appreciated that the sample size is very small. Nonetheless Figures 26.07 and 26.08 suggest a meaningful change in body part representation between Periods 2 and 3/4. In Period 2, Figure 26.07 shows that bones of the head, forequarter and hindquarter occur in similar proportions. In Period

3, Figure 26.08 shows that bones of the forequarter are most common. The elements of the head and hindquarter occur in similar proportions but at roughly half the abundance of the forequarter.

As can be seen from Table 26.08, the majority of the pig bones were from immature animals with unfused epiphysial ends. Period 3/4 appears to have more slightly older animals, with fused bones, from the trotters. This is deceptive as a large proportion of the unfused bones in Period 3/4 are from piglets. Period 3/4 produced 26 piglet bones compared to 9 from Period 2. Many of these were probably deposited in articulation but it is not now possible to reconstruct how much of a body was deposited where. These tiny bones are not easy to recover by hand and these deposits would have benefited from whole earth samples to recover the full assemblage. Assuming these bones all derive from culinary waste from the consumption of sucking pig, the piglets appear to have ranged in size from perinatal to several weeks old, in comparison with the wild boar piglets in the reference collection of the Biological Laboratory. One piglet bone from Period 3/4 had been nibbled by a rodent, the only evidence from this assemblage for the presence of commensal species.

*Table 26.08: Pig epiphyses in approximate order of fusion, from Building 13*

| | Period 2 | | | Period 3/4 | | | Mid C3+ | | |
|---|---|---|---|---|---|---|---|---|---|
| | F | JF | U | F | JF | U | F | JF | U |
| **By 1 year** | | | | | | | | | |
| Acet. symph. | – | – | 1 | – | – | 1 | – | – | 2 |
| Scap. tub. | – | – | 1 | – | – | 3 | 1 | – | – |
| Prox. rad. | 1 | – | – | 1 | – | 3 | – | – | – |
| Dist. hum. | 2 | 1 | 3 | – | – | 2 | – | – | – |
| Prox. ph. 2 | – | – | – | – | – | 1 | – | – | – |
| **By 2-2.5 years** | | | | | | | | | |
| Prox. ph. 1 | 2 | – | 2 | 3 | – | – | – | – | – |
| Dist. mc. | – | – | 5 | 2 | 1 | 9 | – | – | 7 |
| Dist. tib. | – | – | 4 | – | – | 1 | – | – | – |
| Dist. mt. | – | – | 4 | 1 | – | 1 | – | – | – |
| Prox. cal. | – | – | 1 | – | – | – | – | – | – |
| **By 2.5-3.5 years** | | | | | | | | | |
| P & D uln. | – | – | 3 | – | – | 7 | – | – | – |
| Prox. tib. | – | – | 1 | – | – | 1 | – | – | – |
| Prox. hum. | – | – | 2 | – | – | 2 | – | – | – |
| Dist. rad. | – | – | 1 | – | – | 2 | – | – | 1 |
| P & D fem. | – | – | 4 | – | – | – | – | – | – |
| **By > 5 years** | | | | | | | | | |
| Ant. Vert. ep. | – | – | 2 | – | – | 1 | – | – | – |
| Post. Vert. ep. | – | – | 2 | – | – | – | – | – | – |

Key: F = fused, JF = just fused, U = unfused
Ages of fusion after Silver 1969

## HORSE

Remains of horse were sparse with two elements from Period 2 and one from the mid-third century+. Those from Period 2 are a tooth and a metapodial. That from the mid-third century+ is also a metapodial but appears to be an offcut from the manufacture of an artefact. The shaft has been neatly chopped all round to detach the distal, fused, articulation from the shaft. The blows were carefully angled from the distal end and are dissimilar to the butchery marks generally encountered.

## DOG

Dog bones were encountered in Periods 2 and 3/4. Period 3/4 produced one intact, fused, tibia from which an estimated height of 25cm was calculated using the factor of Harcourt (1974, 154). The mid-third century+ produced three bones, with unfused epiphyses, from one immature animal from contexts M12:17 and M12:42 (backfill of the eastern hypocaust). These would appear to indicate a disturbed burial. Stokes (1992) identified only two dog bones, one from each phase, from the commanding officer's house at South Shields. These were also from fairly small, lap-sized, animals.

## RED AND ROE DEER

Red deer bones were not numerous but the presence of two lower limb bones and a jaw in Period 2 does imply the supply of a carcase to the residence. A further lower limb bone was recovered from the mid-third century+ and an antler fragment from a post-Roman context. Roe deer bones were most numerous in Period 2 and comprise five lower limb bones and a jaw, with a further lower limb bone from Period 3/4. For the small size of the assemblage, deer bones are more common at Wallsend than at South Shields, though the latter site produced more antler.

## HARE

Three hare bones were found in Period 2. Hare was present only in period 7 (late third or early fourth century) of the commanding officer's house at South Shields and the remains were not numerous.

## BIRDS

Domestic fowl and goose bones were found, overall, in similar numbers. Period 2 produced more fowl than goose bones with the reverse in Period 3/4. Black grouse, represented by one bone in Period 2, is the only wild species present. This is a game bird highly esteemed for the table and consonant with the status of the commanding officer.

## MOLLUSCA AND FISH

Shellfish were remarkably sparse with only mussel shells recovered from Periods 3/4 and the mid-third century+. This contrasts with South Shields where six types of marine mollusc shell were identified from the commanding officer's house. The generally inhospitable soils at Wallsend have militated against the general survival of fish bone. However the exceptional preservational conditions associated with the commanding officer's house have led to the recovery of tiny fragments of fish bone from Periods 2 and 3/4. While these cannot be identified, their presence does indicate that fish was procured for consumption.

*Summary*
It is appreciated that the assemblage under discussion is extremely small and subject to inherent bias. Nonetheless, the deposits associated with the commanding officer's house are notable for the better condition of the bones which has led to the survival of bones from small and juvenile animals. This in turn has led to an enhanced species list which is dominated by pig rather than cattle, with goat attested as well as sheep. Hunting, particularly in Period 2, is indicated by bones of both red and roe deer, hare and black grouse.

# Appendix: Count of 'zones' in cattle bones from Cistern 1

|  | 'Zone' | E08:27 | E08:29 | E08:44 | Total |
|---|---|---|---|---|---|
| Skl. | 1 | – | – | – | 0 |
|  | 2 | – | – | – | 0 |
|  | 3 | 1 | 2 | 1 | 4 |
|  | 4 | – | – | – | 0 |
|  | 5 | 4 | 3 | 1 | 8 |
|  | 6 | – | – | – | 0 |
|  | 7 | – | – | – | 0 |
|  | 8 | – | 3 | 1 | 4 |
|  | 9 | 2 | 7 | 1 | 10 |
|  | 0 | 1 | 2 | – | 3 |
| Jaw | 1 | 5 | 5 | 4 | 14 |
|  | 2 | 14 | 7 | 7 | 28 |
|  | 3 | 5 | 5 | 5 | 15 |
|  | 4 | 1 | 3 | – | 4 |
|  | 5 | – | 2 | 2 | 4 |
|  | 6 | 2 | 3 | 1 | 6 |
|  | 7 | 6 | 6 | 4 | 16 |
|  | 8 | 1 | 1 | 1 | 3 |
| Scap. | 1 | 17 | 9 | 8 | 34 |
|  | 2 | 27 | 21 | 16 | 64 |
|  | 3 | 24 | 19 | 13 | 56 |
|  | 4 | 2 | 3 | 1 | 6 |
|  | 5 | 7 | 8 | 6 | 21 |
|  | 6 | – | – | – | 0 |
|  | 7 | – | 1 | – | 1 |

|  | 'Zone' | E08:27 | E08:29 | E08:44 | Total |
|---|---|---|---|---|---|
| Hum. | 1 | – | – | – | 0 |
|  | 2 | – | – | – | 0 |
|  | 3 | – | – | – | 0 |
|  | 4 | – | – | – | 0 |
|  | 5 | – | – | 1 | 1 |
|  | 6 | 2 | 2 | 1 | 5 |
|  | 7 | 3 | 7 | 1 | 11 |
|  | 8 | 3 | 4 | 1 | 8 |
|  | 9 | 4 | 1 | 3 | 8 |
| Rad. | 1 | 2 | 2 | 2 | 6 |
|  | 2 | 1 | 1 | 1 | 3 |
|  | 3 | 1 | 2 | – | 3 |
|  | 4 | 1 | 1 | – | 2 |
|  | 5 | – | 1 | – | 1 |
|  | 6 | 1 | – | 1 | 2 |
| Uln. | 1 | – | – | – | 0 |
|  | 2 | 4 | 2 | 1 | 7 |
|  | 3 | 4 | 2 | 1 | 7 |
|  | 4 | – | – | – | 0 |
| Car. R | | – | 1 | – | 1 |
| Car. I | | – | – | – | 0 |
| Car. U | | – | – | – | 0 |
| Car. 2+3 | | – | – | – | 0 |
| Car. 4 | | – | – | – | 0 |
| Mc. | 1 | 4 | 7 | 5 | 16 |
|  | 2 | 5 | 8 | 5 | 18 |
|  | 3 | 4 | 8 | 2 | 14 |
|  | 4 | 5 | 9 | 2 | 16 |
|  | 5 | 4 | 10 | 2 | 16 |
| Oc. | 1 | – | – | – | 0 |
|  | 2 | – | 2 | – | 2 |
|  | 3 | – | 2 | 1 | 3 |
|  | 4 | – | 1 | – | 1 |
|  | 5 | – | 5 | – | 5 |
|  | 6 | – | – | – | 0 |
|  | 7 | – | 1 | – | 1 |
|  | 8 | – | – | – | 0 |
|  | 9 | 1 | 3 | 1 | 4 |
|  | 0 | 1 | – | – | 1 |
| Fem. | 1 | 1 | 1 | – | 2 |
|  | 2 | – | – | – | 0 |
|  | 3 | 2 | – | – | 2 |
|  | 4 | 2 | 2 | – | 4 |
|  | 5 | 1 | 1 | – | 2 |
|  | 6 | 1 | – | 1 | 2 |
|  | 7 | – | – | 1 | 1 |

|      | 'Zone' | E08:27 | E08:29 | E08:44 | Total |
|------|--------|--------|--------|--------|-------|
| Pat. |        | –      | –      | –      | 0     |
| Tib. | 1      | 2      | –      | –      | 2     |
|      | 2      | 1      | 1      | –      | 2     |
|      | 3      | 2      | –      | –      | 2     |
|      | 4      | 1      | –      | 3      | 4     |
|      | 5      | 1      | –      | 1      | 2     |
|      | 6      | 1      | –      | 1      | 2     |
|      | 7      | 1      | 1      | 1      | 3     |
| Mal. |        | –      | –      | –      | 0     |
| Cal. | 1      | –      | 1      | –      | 1     |
|      | 2      | –      | 3      | –      | 3     |
|      | 3      | –      | 1      | –      | 1     |

|       | 'Zone' | E08:27 | E08:29 | E08:44 | Total |
|-------|--------|--------|--------|--------|-------|
| Ast.  |        | –      | 1      | –      | 1     |
| Cq.   |        | –      | –      | –      | 0     |
| Mt.   | 1      | 5      | 6      | 2      | 13    |
|       | 2      | 4      | 5      | 2      | 11    |
|       | 3      | 2      | 3      | –      | 5     |
|       | 4      | 2      | 4      | 1      | 7     |
|       | 5      | 2      | 4      | 2      | 8     |
| Ph. 1 | 1      | –      | 6      | 1      | 7     |
|       | 2      | –      | 6      | 1      | 7     |
| Ph. 2 |        | –      | 2      | –      | 2     |
| Ph. 3 |        | –      | 1      | –      | 1     |

# BIBLIOGRAPHY

## Abbreviations

| | |
|---|---|
| *AE* | *L'Année épigraphique.* |
| *Cam* | Hawkes, C. F. C. and Hull, M. R., 1947 *Camulodunum*, Oxford |
| *CIL* | *Corpus Inscriptionum Latinarum.* |
| CK | Hill, P. V. and Kent, J. P. C., 1960 *Late Roman Bronze Coinage, part 1*, London |
| CR | Crawford, M., 1974 *Roman Republican Coinage, Vols 1–2*, London |
| *CSIR* 1.1 | Phillips, E. J., 1977 *Corpus Signorum Imperii Romani, Great Britain, Volume I, Fascicule 1: Corbridge, Hadrian's Wall East of the North Tyne*, Oxford |
| *CSIR* 1.4 | Keppie, L. J. F. and Arnold, B. J., 1984 *Corpus Signorum Imperii Romani, Great Britain, Volume I, Fascicule 4: Scotland*, Oxford |
| *CSIR* 1.6 | Coulston, J. C. and Phillips, E. J., 1988 *Corpus Signorum Imperii Romani, Great Britain, Volume I, Fascicule 6: Hadrian's Wall West of the North Tyne, and Carlisle*, Oxford |
| D. | Figure-type in Déchelette, J., 1904 *Les Vases Céramiques Ornés de la Gaule Romaine*, Paris |
| HK | Carson, R. A. G. and Kent, J. P. C., 1960 *Late Roman Bronze Coinage, part 2*, London |
| *ILS* | *Inscriptiones Latinae Selectae.* H. Dessau, Berlin, 1892–1916. |
| *ND* | *Notitia Dignitatum* (ed.) O. Seeck, Berlin, 1876 (repr. Frankfurt 1962). |
| *ND Occ.* | *Notitia Dignitatum omnium in partibus Occidentis.* |
| *ND Or.* | *Notitia Dignitatum omnium in partibus Orientis.* |
| O. | Figure-type in Oswald, F., 1936–7 *Index of Figure-types on Terra Sigillata ("Samian Ware")*, Liverpool |
| ORL | *Der obergermanisch-raetische Limes des Römerreiches* |
| *RIBI* | Collingwood, R. G. and Wright, R. P., 1965 *The Roman Inscriptions of Britain. Volume I: Inscriptions on Stone*. Oxford. |
| *RIBII* | Frere, S. and Tomlin, R., (eds) 1990–5 *Roman Inscriptions of Britain* II, Stroud |
| RIC | Mattingly, H., Sydenham, E., Webb, P. H., Sutherland, C. H. V. and Carson, R. A. G., 1926–84 *The Roman Imperial Coinage, vols 1–10*, London |
| Ricken-Fischer | Ricken, H. and Fischer, C., 1963 *Die Bilderschüsseln der römischen Töpfer von Rheinzabern, Textband*, Bonn |
| Rogers | Rogers, G. B., 1974 *Poteries Sigillées de la Gaule Centrale. I: les Motifs non figures*, *Gallia* Supplement **28**, Paris |
| S. & S. 1958 | Stanfield, J. A. and Simpson, G., 1958 *Central Gaulish Potters*, London |

Adkins, L. and Adkins, R. A., 1985 'Neolithic axes from Roman sites in Britain', *Oxford Journal of Archaeology* **4(1)**, 69–76

Allason-Jones, L., 1983 Small finds in Miket, R., *The Roman Fort at South Shields: Excavations of the Defences 1977–8*, Newcastle upon Tyne, 108–42

Allason-Jones, L., 1984 A lead shrine from Wallsend, *Britannia* **15**, 231–2

Allason-Jones, L., 1985a An eagle mount from Carlisle, *Transactions of the Cumberland & Westmorland Antiquarian & Archaeological Society* n. ser. **85**, 262–6

Allason-Jones, L., 1985b Bell-shaped studs? in Bishop, M. C., (ed.), *The Production and Distribution of Roman Military Equipment*, British Archaeological Report **S275**, Oxford, 95–105

Allason-Jones, L., 1988 Small finds from turrets on Hadrians Wall, in Coulston, J. C., (ed.), *Military Equipment and the Identity of Roman Soldiers: proceedings of the Fourth Roman Military Equipment Conference*, British Archaeological Report **S394**, 197–233

Allason-Jones, L., 1989a *Earrings in Roman Britain*, British Archaeological Report **201**, Oxford

Allason-Jones, L., 1989b Niello studs, *Arma* **1**, 10–11

Allason-Jones, L., 1996a Roman military and domestic artefacts from Great Chesters, *Archaeologia Aeliana* 5 ser **24**, 187–214

Allason-Jones, L., 1996b *Roman Jet in the Yorkshire Museum*, York

Allason-Jones, L., 2007 Small objects, in Hanson, W. S., *Elginhaugh: A Flavian Fort and its Annex – Volume 2*, Britannia Monograph **23**, 396–443, London

Allason-Jones, L. and Miket, R. F., 1984 *Catalogue of Small Finds from South Shields Roman Fort*, Newcastle upon Tyne

Allason-Jones, L. and McKay, B., 1985 *Coventina's Well*, Chesters

Allen, D. A., 1986 The glass vessels, in Zienkiewicz 1986, 98–116

Almgren, O., 1923 *Studien über nordeuropäische Fibelformen*, Leipzig

Anderson, A. C., 1980 *A Guide to Roman Fine Wares*, Vorda Research Series **1**, Highworth

Archaeological Practice, The, 2006 *52 Carville Road, Wallsend, North Tyneside: Archaeological Evaluation*, unpublished report for Paragon Care Group

Arnold, C. J., 1983 The Sancton-Baston potter, *Scottish Archaeological Review* **2.1**, 17–28

Atkinson, D., 1942 *Report on Excavations at Wroxeter, 1923–1927*, Oxford

Aurrecoechea Fernández, J., 1996 Bronze studs from Roman Spain, *Journal of Roman Military Equipment Studies* **7**, 97–146

Austin, R. G., 1935 Roman board games, *Greece and Rome* **IV** (1934), 23–34, 76–83

Baatz, D., 1973 *Kastell Hesselbach und andere Forschungen am Odenwaldlimes*, Limesforschungen **12**, Berlin

Baatz, D., 1983 Town walls and defensive weapons, in Maloney, J. and Hobley, B., *Roman Urban Defences in the West*, Council for British Archaeology Research Report **51**, 136–40, London

Bailey, D. M., 1975–96 *A Catalogue of the Lamps in the British Museum*, London

Baker, J. (ed.), 1984 *Sunderland Pottery*, Newcastle upon Tyne

Bánki, Z., 1972 *Az István Király Múzeum Gyűjteménye. Római Kori Figurális Bronz, Ezüst és Ólom Tárgyak*, Székesfehérvár

Bateson, J. D., 1981 *Enamel-working in Iron Age, Roman and Sub-Roman Britain*, British Archaeological Report **93**, Oxford

Bédoyère, G. de la, 2002 *Gods with Thunderbolts: Religion in Roman Britain*, Stroud

Bell, R. C., 1960 *Board and Table Games from Many Civilizations*, Oxford

Bémont, C., 1977 *Moules de Gobelets Ornés de la Gaule Centrale au Musée des Antiquités Nationales*, Gallia Suppl. **33**, Paris

Bidwell, P., 1985 *The Roman Fort of Vindolanda*, London

Bidwell, P. T., 1997 *Roman Forts in Britain*, London

Bidwell, P. T. (ed.), 1999 *Hadrians Wall 1989–1999: A Summary of Recent Excavations and Research prepared for the Twelfth Pilgrimage of Hadrians Wall, 14–21 August 1999*, Kendal

Bidwell, P., 2005 The dating of Crambeck parchment ware, *Journal of Roman Pottery Studies* **12**, 15–21

Bidwell, P. T. and Croom, A. T., 1997 The coarse wares, in Wenham, L. P and Heywood, B., *The 1968 to 1970 Excavations in the Vicus at Malton, North Yorkshire*, Yorkshire Archaeological Report **3**, 61–103

Bidwell, P. and Croom, A. T., 1999 The *Camulodunum/Colchester* type series, in Symonds and Wade 1999, 468–87

Bidwell, P. T. and Croom, A. T., 2002 The Roman pottery, in Snape, M. and Bidwell, P., *Excavations at Castle Garth, Newcastle upon Tyne, 1976–92 and 1995–6: the excavation of the Roman Fort*, Archaeologia Aeliana 5 ser. **31**, 139–72

Bidwell, P. T. and Croom, A. T., 2010 The supply and use of pottery on Hadrians Wall in the fourth century AD, in Collins, R. and Allason-Jones, L., *Finds from the Frontier: Material Culture in the 4th–5th Centuries*, Council for British Archaeology Research Report **162**, 20–36, York

Bidwell, P. T. and Hodgson, N., 2009 *The Roman Army in Northern England*, Newcastle upon Tyne

Bidwell, P.T., Miket, R. and Ford, B., 1988 The reconstruction of a gate at the Roman fort of South Shields, in Bidwell, P. T., Miket, R. and Ford, B. (eds), *Portae cum turribus: Studies of Roman Fort Gates*, British Archaeological Report **206**, 155–231, Oxford

Bidwell, P. T., Snape, M. and Croom, A. T., 1999 *Hardknott Roman Fort, Cumbria, including an account of the excavations by the late Dorothy Charlesworth*, Kendal

Bidwell, P. T. and Speak, S., 1994 *Excavations of South Shields Roman Fort volume I*, Society of Antiquaries of Newcastle upon Tyne Monograph **4**, Newcastle

Bidwell, P. T. and Snape, M. E., 2002 The history and setting of the Roman fort at Newcastle upon Tyne, *Archaeologia Aeliana* 5 ser. **31**, 251–83

Birley, A. and Birley, A., 2010 A Dolichenum at Vindolanda, *Archaeologia Aeliana* 5 ser. **39**, 25–51

Birley, E. and Charlton, J., 1934 Third report on excavations at Housesteads, *Archaeologia Aeliana* 4 ser. **11**, 185–205

Birley, E. and Gillam, J. P., 1948 Mortarium stamps from Corbridge 1906–1938, *Archaeologia Aeliana* 4 ser. **26**, 172–201

Birley, R., Blake, J. and Birley, A. R., 1998 *Interim Report on the 1997 Excavations on the Praetorium Site, Vindolanda*, Roman Army Museum Publications for the Vindolanda Trust, Carvoran

Birley, R., Birley, A. and Blake, J., 1999 *The Excavations at Vindolanda. The Praetorium Site: Interim Report*, Roman

Army Museum Publications for the Vindolanda Trust, Carvoran

Bishop, M. C., 2002 *Lorica Segmentata, Volume I*, Journal of Roman Military Studies Monograph **1**

Bishop, M. C. and Coulston, J. C. N., 2006 *Roman Military Equipment from the Punic Wars to the fall of Rome* (2nd edn), Oxford

Bishop, M. C. and Dore, J. N., 1989 *Corbridge: Excavations of the Roman Fort and Town 1947–1980*, Historic Buildings & Monuments Commision Archaeological Report **8**, London

Boersterd, M. H. P. den, 1956 *Description of the Collections in the Rijksmuseum G. M. Kam at Nijmegen V: The Bronze Vessels*, Nijmegen

Böhme, A., 1972 Die Fibeln der Kastelle Saalburg und Zugmantel *Saalburg-Jahrbuch* **29**, 5–122

Boon, G. C., 1966a Roman window glass from Wales, *Journal of Glass Studies* **8**, 41–5

Boon, G. C., 1966b Gilt glass beads from Caerleon and elsewhere, *Bulletin of the Board of Celtic Studies* **22**(1), 104–9

Boon, G. C., 1977 Gold-in-glass beads from the ancient world, *Britannia* **8**, 193–207

Boon, G. C., 1983 Some Romano-British domestic shrines and their inhabitants, in Hartley, B. and Wacher, J. (eds), *Rome and her Northern provinces*, 33–55, Gloucester

Bosanquet, R. C., 1904 Excavations on the line of the Roman Wall in Northumberland. 1. The Roman camp at Housesteads, *Archaeologia Aeliana* 2 ser. **25**, 193–300

Brailsford, J. W., 1962 *Hod Hill I: Antiquities in the Durden Collection*, London

Braithwaite, G., 2007 *Faces from the Past: a Study of Roman Face Pots from Italy and the Western provinces of the Roman Empire*, British Archaeological Report **S1651**

Brassington, M., 1971 A Trajanic kiln complex near Little Chester, Derby, 1968, *Antiquity* **51**, 36–69

Brassington, M., 1980 Derby racecourse kiln excavations 1972–3, *Antiquity* **60**, 8–47

Breeze, D. and Dobson, B., 1972 Hadrian's Wall: some problems, *Britannia* **3**, 182–208

Breeze, D. and Dobson, B., 2000 *Hadrian's Wall*, (3rd edn), London

Brickstock, R. J., 2003 The coins, in Hodgson 2003, 200–8

Briscoe, T., 1983 A classification of Anglo-Saxon pot stamp motifs and proposed terminology, *Studien zur Sachsenforschung* **4**, 57–71

Brodribb, G., 1987 *Roman Brick and Tile*, Gloucester

Bruce, J. C., 1863 *The Wallet Book of the Roman Wall*, London & Newcastle upon Tyne

Buckland, P. C., 1986 *Roman South Yorkshire: a Source Book*, Sheffield

Buckland, P. C. and Dolby, M. J., 1980 *A Roman Pottery Kiln Site at Blaxton Quarry, near Doncaster*, Archaeology of Doncaster **4/1**

Buckland, P. C., Hartley, K. F. and Rigby, V., 2001 The Roman pottery kilns excavations at Rossington Bridge 1956–1961, *Journal of Roman Pottery Studies* **9**, 1–96

Bulmer, W., 1955 Roman glass vessels in the Corstopitum Museum, Corbridge, *Archaeologia Aeliana* 4 ser. **33**, 116–33

Bushe-Fox, J. P., 1912 *First Report on Excavations on the Site of the Roman Town at Wroxeter, Shropshire*, Oxford

Bushe-Fox, J. P., 1926 *First Report on the Excavation of the Roman Fort at Richborough, Kent*, Oxford

Bushe-Fox, J. P., 1949 *Fourth Report on the Excavations on the Roman Fort at Richborough, Kent*, Oxford

Callender, M. H., 1965 *Roman Amphorae*, Oxford

Campbell, D., 1986 Auxiliary artillery revisited, *Bonner Jahrbucher* **186**, 117–32

Carlton, R., 1988 Ethnoarchaeological study of pottery production in Dalmatia, *University of Newcastle upon Tyne and University of Durham Archaeological Reports for 1987*, 50–55

Caruana, I., 1997 Ceramic building material, in Wilmott, T., *Birdoswald. Excavations of a Roman Fort on Hadrian's Wall and its Successor Settlements: 1987–92*, English Heritage Archaeological Report **14**, London

Casey, P. J., 1974 The interpretation of Romano-British site finds in Casey, P. J. and Reece (eds), *Coins and the Archaeologist*, British Archaeological Report **4**, 37–51, Oxford

Casey, P. J., 1984 Roman coinage of the fourth century in Scotland, in Miket, R. and Burgess, C. (eds), *Between and Beyond the Walls: Essays on the Prehistory and History of the North of Britain in Honour of George Jobey*, 295–304, Edinburgh

Casey, P. J., 1986 *Understanding Ancient Coins*, London

Casey, P. J., Davies, J. L. and Evans, J., 1993 *Excavations at Segontium (Caernarfon) Roman Fort, 1975–1979*, Council for British Archaeology Research Report **90**, York

Cessford, C., 1995 Torcs in early historic Scotland, *Oxford Journal of Archaeology* **30**, 229–42

Charlesworth, D., 1959 Roman glass in northern Britain, *Archaeologia Aeliana* 4 ser. **37**, 33–58

Charlesworth, D., 1961 Roman jewellery found in Northumberland and Durham, *Archaeologia Aeliana* 4 ser. **39**, 1–36

Charlesworth, D., 1963 The granaries at Hardknott Castle, *Transactions of the Cumberland & Westmorland Antiquarian & Archaeological Society* n. ser **63**, 148–52

Charlesworth, D., 1966 Roman square bottles, *Journal of Glass Studies* **8**, 26–40

Charlesworth, D., 1972 The glass, in Frere 1972, 196–215

Charlesworth, D., 1975 The commandant's house, Housesteads, *Archaeologia Aeliana* 5 ser. **3**, 17–42

Charlesworth, D., 1976 The hospital, Housesteads, *Archaeologia Aeliena* 5 ser. **4**, 17–30

Chenet, G. and Gaudron, C., 1955 *La Céramique sigillée d'Argonne des IIe et IIIe siècles*, *Gallia* Supplement **6**, Paris

Christison, D., 1896 Account of the excavation of Birrens, a Roman station in Annandale, undertaken by the Society of Antiquaries of Scotland in 1895, *Proceedings of the Society of Antiquaries of Scotland* **30**, 81–204

Clarke, D. V., 1970 Bone dice and the Scottish Iron Age, *Proceedings of the Prehistoric Society* **36**, 214–32

Coggins, D., 1979 Durham: Binchester, *Medieval Archaeology* **23**, 236

Collingwood, R. G., 1930 Romano-Celtic Art in Northumbria, *Archaeologia* **80**, 37–58

Collingwood, R. G. and Richmond, I. A., 1969 *The Archaeology of Roman Britain*, London

Compton, J. and Webster, P. V., 2000 The coarse pottery, in Evans, E., *The Caerleon Canabae: Excavations in the Civil Settlement 1984–90*, *Britannia* Monograph **16**, 198–264

Cook, J. M., 2004 *Early Anglo-Saxon Buckets*, Oxford University School of Archaeology Monograph **60**, Oxford

Cool, H. E. M., 1990a The problem of third century

drinking-vessels in Britain, *Annales du 11e Congrès de lAssociation Internationale pour lHistoire du Verre*, Amsterdam, 167–75

Cool, H. E. M., 1990b Roman metal hair pins from southern Britain, *Archaeological Journal* **147**, 148–82

Corcoran, J. X. W. P., 1952 Tankards and tankard handles of the British Early Iron Age, *Proceedings of the Prehistoric Society* **18**, 85–102

Corder, P., 1930 *The Defences of the Roman Fort at Malton*. Roman Malton & Distirict Research Report **2**, York

Corder, P., 1933 Ballista balls at wall turrets, *Proceedings of the Society of Antiquaries of Newcastle upon Tyne* 4 ser. **2(1)**, 36

Corder, P., 1937 A pair of fourth-century Romano-British pottery kilns near Crambeck, *Antiquaries Journal* **17**, 392–413

Corder, W. S., 1903 Wallsend (Segedunum), *Proceedings of the Society of Antiquaries of Newcastle upon Tyne* 3 ser. **1**, 42–72

Corder, W. S., 1912 Segedunum – the last phase, *Proceedings of the Society of Antiquaries Newcastle upon Tyne* 3 ser. **5**, 204–12

Cramp, R., 1983 Anglo-Saxon Settlement, in Chapman, J. C. and Mytum, H. C. (eds), *Settlement in North Britain 1000 BC – AD 1000*, British Archaeological Report **118**, 263–97, Oxford

Cramp, R., 1988 Northumbria: the archaeological evidence, in Driscoll, S. T. and Nieke. M. R. (eds), *Power and Politics in Early Medieval Britain and Ireland*, 69–78, Edinburgh

Croom, A. T., 1994, Small finds, in Bidwell and Speak 1994, 177–205

Croom, A. T., 1995 A hoard of Roman military equipment from South Shields, *Arbeia Journal* **4**, 45–53

Croom, A. T., 2003 The finds and North African style pottery, in Hodgson 2003, 183–230, 246–9

Croom, A. T., 2007 *Roman Furniture*, Stroud

Croom, A. T., McBride, R. M. and Bidwell, P. T., 2008 The coarse wares in Cool, H. E. M. and Mason, D. J. P., *Roman Piercebridge: Excavations by D. W. Harding and Peter Scott 1969–1981*, Architectural & Archaeological Society of Durham & Northumberland Research Report **7**, 208–30, Durham

Crow, J. G., 1988 An excavation on the north curtain wall at Housesteads, 1984, *Archaeologia Aeliana* 5 ser. **16**, 61–124

Crow, J. G., 1989 *Housesteads Roman Fort* (English Heritage Guidebook), London

Crow, J. G., 2004 *Housesteads: A Fort and Garrison on Hadrian's Wall*. 2 edn. Stroud (first pub. 1995 *English Heritage Book of Housesteads*. London)

Crummy, N., 1979 A chronology of bone pins, *Britannia* **10**, 157–64

Crummy, N., 1983 *The Roman Small Finds from Excavations in Colchester 1971–9*, Colchester Archaeological Report **2**, Colchester

Cunliffe, B., 1968 *Fifth Report on the Excavations of the Roman Fort at Richborough*, Oxford

Curle, J., 1911 *A Roman Frontier Post and its People: the Roman Fort of Newstead in the Parish of Melrose*, Glasgow

Curwen, E. C., 1937 Querns, *Antiquity* **11**, 133–51

Dale, R., 1987 *The Price Guide to Black and White Pot-lids*, Woodbridge

Daniels, C. M., (ed.) 1978 *Handbook to the Roman Wall with the Cumbrian Coasts and Outpost Forts*, 13 edn, Newcastle upon Tyne.

Daniels, C. M., 1980 Excavations at Wallsend and the fourth-century barracks on Hadrian's Wall in Hanson, W. S. and Keppie, L. J. F. (ed.), *Roman Frontier Studies 1979*, British Archaeological Report **S71**, 173–193 Oxford

Daniels, C. M. (ed.), 1989 *The Eleventh Pilgrimage of Hadrian's Wall*, Newcastle upon Tyne

Daniels and Rankov, N. B. (ed.) 1982 'Roman Britain in 1981: I. Sites explored' (Wallsend Fort interim note), *Britannia* **13**, 340–42

Dannell, G. B., 1971 The samian pottery, in Cunliffe, B., *Excavations at Fishbourne, Volume II: the Finds*, Report of the Research Committee of the Society of Antiquaries of London **27**, 260–316, London

Dannell, G. B. and Hartley, B. R., 1974 The samian pottery, in Ainsworth, C. J. and Ratcliffe, B. A., Densham, Spectroscscopy and a Roman cremation from Sompting, Sussex, *Britannia* **5**, 312–15

Dannell, G. B., Hartley, B. R., Wild, J. P. and Perrin, J. R., 1993 Excavations on a Romano-British pottery production site at Park Farm, Stanground, Peterborough, 1965–1967, *Journal of Roman Pottery Studies* **6**, 51–93

Davies, R. W., 1971 The Roman military diet, *Britannia* **2**, 122–42

Davison, D. P., 1989 *The Barracks of the Roman Army from the 1st to 3rd Centuries A.D.*, British Archaeological Report **S472**, Oxford

Dearne, M. J. and Lord, T. C., 1998 *The Romano-British Archaeology of Victoria Cave, Settle*, British Archaeological Report **273**, Oxford

Delort, E., 1953 *Vases Ornés de la Moselle*, Nancy

Dickinson, B. M., 1984 The samian ware, in Frere 1984, 175–97

Dickinson, B. M., 1986a Samian pottery from the civil settlement, Doncaster, in Buckland, P. C. and Magilton, J. R., *The Archaeology of Doncaster*. British Archaeological Report **148**, Oxford

Dickinson, B. M., 1986b Potters' stamps and signatures on samian, in Miller, L., Schofield, J. and Rhodes, M., *The Roman Quay at St Magnus House, London*, London & Middlesex Archaeological Society Special Paper **8**, 186–98, London

Dickinson, B. M., 1988 The stamped and decorated samian, in Thomas, G. D., Excavations at the Roman civil settlement at Inveresk 1976–77, *Proceedings of the Society of Antiquaries of Scotland* **118**, fiche 1: A7–14, B1–14

Dickinson, B. M., 1996 Samian pottery, in May, J., *Dragonby. Report on Excavations at an Iron Age and Romano-British Settlement in North Lincolnshire*, Oxford

Dickinson, B. M., 2002 The samian, 139–48, in Snape, M. and Bidwell, P., Excavations at Castle Garth, Newcastle upon Tyne, 1976–92 and 1995–6: the excavation of the Roman fort, *Archaeologia Aeliana* 5 ser. **31**, 1–250

Dickinson, B. M., 2003 The samian ware, in Hodgson 2003, 189–93

Donaldson, G. H., 1988 Thoughts on a military appreciation of Hadrian's Wall, *Archaeologia Aeliana* 5 ser. **16**, 125–38

Doppelfeld, O., 1966 *Romisches und Frankisches Glas in Köln*, Cologne

Dore, J. N., 1989 *Corbridge Roman Site*, London

Dore, J. N., 2010 *Haltonchesters: Excavations directed by J. P. Gillam at the Roman Fort, 1960–61*, Oxford

Dore, J. N. and Gillam, J. P., 1979 *The Roman Fort at South Shields: Excavations 1875–1975*, Society of Antiquaries of

Newcastle upon Tyne Monograph **1**, Newcastle upon Tyne

Dövener, F., 2000 *Die Gesichtskruge der römischen Nordwest-provinzen*, British Archaeological Report **S870**, Oxford

Driel-Murray, C. van, 2009 Ethnic recruitment and military mobility, in Morillo, A., Hanel, N. and Martin, E. (eds), *Limes XX. Estudios sobre la Frontera Romana/Roman Frontier Studies*. Anejos de *Gladius* **13** (III), 813–22, Madrid

Dungworth, D. B. and Starley, D., 2009 The metalworking debris in Rushworth, A., (ed.) *The Grandest Station: Excavation and Survey at Housesteads Roman Fort by C. M. Daniels, J. P. Gillam, J. G. Crow, D. J. Smith and the RCHME 1954–95*, English Heritage Archaeological Report, 579–88, Swindon

Durand-Lefebvre, M., 1963 *Marques de Potiers Gallo-Romains Trouvées à Paris et Conservées Principalement au Musée Carnavalet*, Paris

Eckardt, H., 2002 *Illuminating Roman Britain*, Monographies *Instrumentum* **23**

Edmonds, M., 1995 *Stone Tools and Society. Working Stone in Neolithic and Bronze Age Britain*, London

Egan, G. and Pritchard, F., 1991 *Dress Accessories 1150–1450*, Medieval Finds from Excavations **3**, London

Eggers, H. J., 1966 Römische Bronzefässe in Britannien, *Jahrbuch des Römische-Germanischen Zentralmuseums Mainz* **13**, 67–164

Eiden, H., 1949 Untersuchungen an den spätromischen Horrea von St Irminen in Trier, *Trierer Zeitschrift* **1949**, 73–98

English Heritage 1991 *Management of Archaeological Projects*, London

Esperandiu, E., 1913 *Recueil Général des Bas-reliefs de la Gaule Romaine* **5**, Paris

Ettlinger, E., 1973 *Die Römishen Fibeln in der Schweiz. Handbuch der Schweiz dur Römer- und Merowingerzeit*, Bern

Evans, J., Jones, R. F. J. and Turnbull, P., 1991 Excavations at Chester-le-Street, *Durham Archaeological Journal* **7**, 5–48

Evelein, M. A., 1928 *Beschrijving van de verzamelung van het Museum G. M. Kam. De Römeinsche Lampen*, S'Gravenhage

Feachem, R. W., 1951 Dragonesque Fibulae, *Antiquaries Journal* **31**, 32–44

Ferris, I., 2010 *The Beautiful Rooms are Empty: Excavations at Binchester Roman Fort, County Durham 1976–1981 and 1986–1991, Part 1 and 2*, Durham

Fleming, S. J., 1997 *Roman Glass: Reflections of Everyday Life*, Philadelphia

Fölzer, E., 1913 *Die Bilderschüsseln der ostgallischen Sigillata-Manufakturen*, Bonn

Ford, B., 1991 Two vessels in pink grog tempered ware from the Roman Fort at Cramond, Scotland, *Journal of Roman Pottery Studies* **4**, 55–6

Fowler, E., 1960 The origins and development of the penannular brooch in Europe, *Proceedings of the Prehistoric Society* **26**, 149–77

Fox, C., 1958 *Pattern and Purpose*, Cardiff

Fremersdorf, F., 1958 *Das naturfarbenes Glas in Koln*, Die Denkmäler des römischen Köln **4**, Cologne

Fremersdorf, F., 1962 *Die römischen Glaser mit aufgelegten Nuppen*, Die Denkmäler des römischen Köln **7**, Cologne

Frere, S. S., 1972 *Verulamium Excavations, Vol. I*, Report of the Research Committee of the Society of Antiquaries of London **28**, London

Frere, S. S., 1974 Review of Baatz 1973, *Britannia* **5**, 494–6

Frere, S. S. (ed.) 1977 Roman Britain in 1976: I. Sites explored (Wallsend Fort interim note), *Britannia* **8**, 371–2

Frere, S. S. (ed.) 1983 Roman Britain in 1982: I. Sites explored (Wallsend Fort interim note), *Britannia* **14**, 289–90

Frere, S. S. (ed.) 1984 Roman Britain in 1983: I. Sites explored (Wallsend Fort interim note), *Britannia* **15**, 277–9

Frere, S. S., 1984 *Verulamium Excavations* III, Oxford University Committee for Archaeology Monograph **1**, Oxford

Frere, S. S. (ed.) 1985 Roman Britain in 1984: I. Sites explored (Wallsend Fort interim note), *Britannia* **16**, 268–70

Frere, S. S. and Tomlin, R. S. O., 1992 *The Roman Inscriptions of Britain, Volume II, Fascicule 4*, Stroud

Funari, P. P. A., 1996 *Dressel 20 Inscriptions from Britain and the Consumption of Spanish Olive Oil*, British Archaeological Report **250**, Oxford

Gallagher, D.B., 1987 The Anglo-Saxon cemetery of Hob Hill, Saltburn, *Yorkshire Archaeological Journal* **59**, 9–27

Gentry, A. P., 1976 *Roman Military Stone-Built Granaries in Britain*, British Archaeological Report **32**, Oxford

Gidney, L., 2003 The animal bones from the hospital and barrack XII, in Hodgson 2003, 231–40

Gillam, J. P., 1958 Roman and native, AD 122–97, in Richmond, I. A. (ed.), *Roman and Native in North Britain*, Edinburgh

Gillam, J. P., 1970 *Types of Roman Coarse Pottery in Northern Britain* (3rd edn), Newcastle upon Tyne

Going, C. J., 1987 *The Mansio and Other Sites in the South-Eastern Sector of Caesaromagus: the Roman Pottery*, Chelmsford Archaeological Trust Report **3.2**, Chelmsford

Goodburn, R. (ed.) 1976 Roman Britain in 1975: I. Sites explored (Wallsend Fort interim note), *Britannia* **7**, 306–8.

Goodburn, R. (ed.) 1978 Roman Britain in 1977: I. Sites explored (Wallsend Fort interim note), *Britannia* **9**, 419.

Goodburn, R. and Grew, F., 1984 The non-ferrous metal objects in Frere 1984, 19–67

Green, M., 1976 *A Corpus of Religious Material from the Civilian Areas of Roman Britain*, British Archaeological Report **24**, Oxford

Green, M., 1978 *Small Cult Objects from the Military Areas of Roman Britain*, British Archaeological Report **52**, Oxford

Greenwell, W. (ed.), 1872 *Feodarium Prioratus Dunelmensis*, Surtees Society **58**, Durham, London & Edinburgh

Greep, S., 1995 The worked bone, antler and ivory, in Blockley, K., Blockley, M., Blockley, P., Frere, S. and Stow, S., *Excavations in the Marlowe Car Park and Surrounding Area, Vol. 2: the Finds*, Archaeology of Canterbury **5**, 112–52, Canterbury

Gregory, A. K., 1996 Romano-British Pottery, in May, G., *Dragonby. Report on Excavations at an Iron Age and Romano-British Settlement in North Lincolnshire, Volume 2*, 513–85, Oxbow Monograph **61**, Oxford

Grew, F. O. (ed.) 1980 Roman Britain in 1979: I Sites explored (Wallsend Fort interim note), *Britannia* **11**, 355–8.

Grew, F. O. (ed.) 1981 Roman Britain in 1980: I Sites explored (Wallsend Fort interim note), *Britannia* **12**, 322.

Griffiths, W. B., 1992 The hand-thrown stone, *Arbeia Journal* **1**, 1–11

Griffiths, W. B., 1993 Excavation to the north-east of Wallsend Roman Fort – 1993, *Arbeia Journal* **2**, 25–37

Griffiths, W. B., 1994a Excavation summary: Wallsend, Buddle Street, *Arbeia Journal* **3**, 58

Griffiths, W. B., 1994b Excavation summary: Wallsend, Rawdon Court, *Arbeia Journal* **3**, 58–9

Griffiths, W. B., 1994c Throwing stones, in Bidwell and Speak 1994, 204–5

Griffiths, W. B., 2003 The throwing stones, in Hodgson 2003, 230

Guido, M., 1978 *The Glass Beads of the Prehistoric and Roman Periods in Britain and Ireland*, London

Guiraud, H., 1988 *Intailles et Camées de lEpoque Romaine en Gaule, Gallia* Supplement **48**, Paris

Hagen, H., 1937 Kaiserzeitliche Gagatarbeiten aus den Rheinischen Germanien, *Bonner Jahrbucher* **142**, 77–144

Hair, T. H., 1844 *Views of the Collieries in the Counties of Northumberland and Durham*, London

Harcourt, R. A., 1974 The dog in prehistoric and early historic Britain, *Journal of Archaeological Science* **1**, 151–75

Harden, D. B., 1962 Glass, in R.C.H.M., *An Inventory of the Historical Monuments of the City of York, Volume 1: Eburacum*, 136–41, London

Harden, D. R., 1977 Report on the glass bowl, in Partridge, C., Excavations and fieldwork at Braughing, *Hertfordshire Archaeology* **5**, 102

Harden, D. R., 1979 Glass vessels, in Clarke, G., *Pre-Roman and Roman Winchester part II: the Roman Cemetery at Lankhills*, Winchester Studies **3**, 209–20, Winchester

Harden, D. B. and Price, J., 1971 The glass, in Cunliffe, B., *Excavations at Fishbourne 1961–1969*, 317–68, London

Harding, D. W. and Scott, P., 2008 *Roman Piercebridge*, Architectural & Archaeological Society of Durham & Northumberland Report **7**, Durham

Hartley, B. R., 1970 The dating evidence for the end of the Saalburg Erdkastell, in Schönberger, H., Die Namenstempel auf glatter Sigillata aus dem Erdkastell der Saalburg, *Saalburg-Jahrbuch* **27**, 28–30

Hartley, B. R., 1972a The samian ware, in Frere 1972, 216–62

Hartley, B. R., 1972b The Roman occupations of Scotland: the evidence of samian ware, *Britannia* **3**, 1–55

Hartley, B. R. and Dickinson, B., 1977 The samian ware, in Rogerson, A. *Excavations at Scole, 1973*, East Anglian Archaeology **5**, 155–72, Dereham

Hartley, B. R., Pengelly, H. and Dickinson, B., 1994 Samian ware, in Cracknell, S. and C. Mahany, C. (eds), *Roman Alcester: Southern Extramural Area: 1964–1966 Excavations*, Council for British Archaeology Research Report **97**, 93–119, York

Hartley, K. F., 1984 The mortaria, in Breeze, D. J., The Roman Fort on the Antonine Wall at Bearsden, in Breeze, D. J. (ed.) *Studies in Scottish Antiquity Presented to Stewart Cruden*, 32–68, Edinburgh

Hartley, K. F., 1985 Mortaria, in Wheeler, H. North-west sector excavations 1979–1980, *Derbyshire Archaeological Journal* **105**, 38–153

Hartley, K. F., 1994 The mortaria, in Rollo, L. *Iron Age and Roman Piddington: the Mortaria 1979–1993*, Upper Nene Archaeological Society Fascicule **2**, Northampton

Hartley, K. F., 1999 The stamped mortaria, in Symonds and Wade 1999, 196–211

Hartley, K. F., 2000 The mortarium stamps, in Rush, P., Dickinson, B. Hartley, B. and Hartley, K. F., *Roman Castleford Excavations 1974–85, Volume 3: the Pottery*, York Archaeological Service **6**, 186–90, York

Hartley, K. F. and Webster, P. V., 1973 Romano-British pottery kilns near Wilderspool, *Archaeological Journal* **130**, 77–103

Haselgrove, C, 2002 The Later Bronze Age and the Iron Age in the Lowlands, in Brooks, C., Daniels, R. and Harding, A. (eds), *Past, Present and Future: The Archaeology of Northern England.* Architectural & Archaeological Society of Durham & Northumberland Research Report **5**, 49–69, Durham

Haselgrove, C. C. and Healey, F., 1992 The prehistory of the Tyne-Tees Lowlands: some recent finds, *Durham Archaeological Journal* **8**, 1–24

Haslam, J., 1993 Glass vessels, in Margeson, S., *Norwich Households: the Medieval and Post-Medieval Finds from Norwich Survey Excavations 1971–1978*, East Anglian Archaeology **58**, Norwich

Haverfield, F., 1913 Inscriptions, 263–71, in Forster, R. H. and Knowles, W. H., Corstopitum: report of the excavations in 1912, *Archaeologia Aeliana* 3 ser. **9**, 230–80

Hawkes, S. C. and Dunning, G. C., 1961 Soldiers and settlers in Britain: with a catalogue of ornamental buckles and related belt fittings, *Medieval Archaeology* **5**, 1–70

Hayes, R. H., Hemingway, J. E. and Spratt, D. A., 1980 The distribution and lithology of beehive querns in northeast Yorkshire, *Journal of Archaeological Science* **8**, 297–313

Henig, M., 1970 The veneration of heroes in the Roman army, *Britannia* **1**, 249–65

Henig, M., 1976 Intagli, in MacGregor 1976, 6–10

Henig, M., 1977 Death and the maiden: funerary symbolism in daily life, in Munby, J. and Henig, M. (eds), *Roman Life and Art in Britain*, British Archaeological Report **41**, 347–66, Oxford

Henig, M., 1978 *A Corpus of Roman Engraved Gemstones from British Sites*, British Archaeological Report **8**, 2nd edn, Oxford

Henig, M., 1980 The gemstones, in Frere, S. S. and Wilkes, J. J., *Strageath Excavations within the Roman Fort 1973–86, Britannia* Monograph **9**, 179–80, London

Henig, M., 1988 The chronology of Roman engraved gemstones, *Journal of Roman Archaeology* **1**, 142–52

Henig, M., 1993a Copper-alloy and non-ferrous metalwork, in Woodward, P. J., Davies, S. M. and Graham, A. H., *Excavations at Greyhound Yard, Dorchester 1981–4*, Dorset Natural History & Archaeological Society Monograph **12**, 117–32, Dorchester

Henig, M., 1993b Intaglio, in Casey, P.J., Davies, L. J. and Evans, J., *Excavations at Segontium (Caernarfon) Roman Fort 1975–79*, Council for British Archaeology Research Report **90**, 206, York

Henig, M., 1997 Intaglios, in Marvell, A. G. and Owen-Jones, H. S., *Leucarum: Excavations at the Roman Auxiliary Fort at Loughor, West Glamorgan 1982–4 and 1987–8, Britannia* Monograph **12**, 395–6, London

Henry, F., 1933 Emailleurs d'Occident, *Prehistoire* **2(1)**, 65–146

Henry, F., 1936 Hanging bowls, *Journal of the Royal Society of Antiquaries of Ireland* **66**, 209–46

Hermet, F., 1934 *La Graufesenque (Condatomago)*, Paris

Herrmann, F. R., 1969 Der Eisenhortfund aus dem Kastell Künzing. Vorbericht, *Saalburg-Jahrbuch* **26**, 129–41

Heslop, D. H., 1987 *The Excavation of an Iron Age Settlement at Thorpe Thewles, Cleveland, 1980–1982*, Council for British Archaeology Research Report **65**, London

Higham, N. J., 1986 *The Northern Counties to AD 1000*, Harlow

Hodder, I. and Hedges, J. W., 1977 'Weaving combs': their

typology and distribution with some introductory remarks on date and function, in Collis, J. (ed.), *The Iron Age in Britain: a Review*, 17–28, Sheffield

Hodgson, J., 1840 *History of Northumberland, Part 2, vol. III*, Newcastle upon Tyne

Hodgson, N., 2003 *The Roman Fort at Wallsend: Excavations in 1997–8*, Tyne and Wear Museums Archaeology Monograph 2, Newcastle upon Tyne

Hodgson, N. (ed.), 2009 *Hadrian's Wall 1999–2009: A Summary of Excavation and Research prepared for the Thirteenth Pilgrimage of Hadrian's Wall, 8–14 August 2009*, Kendal

Hodgson, N. and Bidwell, P. T., 2004 Auxiliary Barracks in a new light: Recent discoveries on Hadrian's Wall, *Britannia* 35, 121–57

Hoffmann, D., 1969 and 1970 *Das spätrömische Bewegungsheer und die Notitia Dignitatum.* (2 vols) *Epigraphische Studien* 7.1 & 2, Dusseldorf

Holbrook, N., 1984 *Some Pottery from the Roman Fort at Wallsend*, unpublished BA dissertation, Newcastle upon Tyne

Holbrook, N., 1991 A watching brief at the Roman fort of Benwell-*Condercum* 1990, *Archaeologia Aeliana* 5 ser. 19, 41–5

Holbrook, N. and Bidwell, P. T., 1992 Roman pottery from Exeter 1980–1990, *Journal of Roman Pottery Studies* 5, 35–80

Horsley, J, 1732 *Britannia Romana*, London

Howe, M. D., Perrin, J. R. and Mackreth, D. F., 1980 *Roman Pottery from the Nene Valley: a Guide*, Peterborough

Hull, M. R., 1963 *The Roman Potters Kilns of Colchester*, Report of the Research Committee of the Society of Antiquaries of London 21, London

Isings, C., 1957 *Roman Glass from Dated Finds*, Groningen

Isings, C., 1971 *Roman Glass in Limburg*, Groningen

Issac, B., 1990 *The Limits of Empire*, Oxford

Jacobi, L., 1897 *Das Römer Kastell Saalburg bei Homburg vor der Höhe*, Hamburg

Jacobs, J., 1912 Sigillatafunde aus einem römischen Keller zu Bregenz, *Jahrbuch für Altertumskunde* 6, 172–84

Jarrett, M. G., 1969 *The Roman Frontier in Wales*, Cardiff

Janssens, P. and Vanderhoeven, M., 1974 Glass, in Roosens, H. and Lux, G. V., Gallo-Romeinse Tumulus te Helshoven onder Hoepertingen, *Archaeologia Belgica* 164

Jenkins, F., 1957 The cult of the Dea Nutrix in Kent, *Archaeologia Cantiana* 71, 38–46

Jenkins, F., 1958 The cult of the Pseudo-Venus in Kent, *Archaeologia Cantiana* 72, 60–76

Jobey, G., 1963 Excavation of a native settlement at Marden, Tynemouth, *Archaeologia Aeliana* 4 ser. 41, 19–35

Jobey, G., 1970 An Iron Age settlement and homestead at Burradon, Northumberland, *Archaeologia Aeliana* 4 ser. 47, 51–96

Jobey G., 1982 The settlement at Doubstead and Romano-British settlement on the coastal plain between Tyne and Forth, *Archaeologia Aeliana*, 5 ser. 10, 1–23

Jobey, G., 1986 Millstones and millstone quarries in Northumberland, *Archaeologia Aeliana* 5 ser. 14, 49–80

Jobey, I., 1979 Housesteads ware: A Frisian tradition on Hadrian's Wall, *Archaeologia Aeliana* 5 ser. 7, 127–43

Jobst, W., 1975 *Die römischen Fibeln aus Lauriacum*, Forschungen in Lauriacum 10

Johnson, A., 1983 *Roman Forts*, London

Johnson, J. S., 1983 *Late Roman Fortifications*, London

Johnson, J. S., 1993 *Chesters Roman Fort*, London

Jope, E. M., 2000 *Early Celtic Art in the British Isles*, Oxford

Juhász, G., 1935 *Die Sigillaten von Brigetio. Dissertationes Pannonicae* ser. 2 3, Budapest

Karnitsch, P., 1955 *Die verzierte Sigillata von Lauriacum (Lorch-Enns)*, Forschungen in Lauriacum 3

Karnitsch, P., 1959 *Die Reliefsigillata von Ovilava*, Linz

Keller, E., 1971 *Die Spätrömischen Grabfunde in Südbayern*, Munich

Kenyon, K. M., 1934 The Roman theatre at Verulamium, St Albans, *Archaeologia* 84, 213–61

Kenyon, K. M., 1948 *Excavations at the Jewry Wall Site, Leicester*, Oxford

Kiernan, P., 2009 *Miniature Votive Offerings in the Roman North-west*, Ruhpolding

Kilbride-Jones, H., 1938 Glass armlets in Britain, *Proceedings of the Society of Antiquaries of Scotland* 73, 366–95

Knorr, R., 1907 *Die verzierten Terra-sigillata Gefässe von Rottweil*, Stuttgart

Knorr, R., 1939 Frühe und späte Sigillata des Arcanus, *Germania* 23, 163–8

Kunzl, I. C., 1982 *Medizinische Instrumente aus Sepulkralf unden der römischen Kaiserzeit*, Bonn

Lander, J., 1984 *Roman Stone Fortifications: Variation and Change from the First Century A.D. to the Fourth*, British Archaeological Report S206, Oxford

Lassus, J., 1981 *La forteresse byzantine de Thamugadi, I: Fouilles … Timgad 1938–1956*, Etudes d'Antiquites Africaines – CNRS, Paris

Leach, J., 1962 The smith god in Roman Britain, *Archaeologia Aeliana* 4 ser. 40, 35–45

Leach, J. and Wilkes, J. J., 1962 Excavations in the Roman fort at Housesteads, 1961, *Archaeologia Aeliana* 4 ser 40, 83–96

Lindgren, C., 1980 *Classical Art Forms and Celtic Mutations*, Park Ridge

Lloyd-Morgan, G., 1977 Roman mirrors in Britain, *Current Archaeology* 58, 329–31

Lloyd-Morgan, G., 1981 *Description of the Collections in the Rijksmuseum G. M. Kam at Nijmegen. X. The Mirrors*, Nijmegen

Lloyd-Morgan, G., 2000 The Venus shrine, in Ellis, P. (ed.), *The Roman Baths and Macellum at Wroxeter: Excavations by Graham Webster 1955–85*, English Heritage Archaeological Report 9, 141–2, London

Loeschcke, S., 1911 *Beschreibung römischer Altertümer, gesammelt von Carl-Anton Niessen. Keramik und Terracotten*, Cologne

Loeschcke, S., 1919 *Lampen aus Vindonissa*, Zürich

Lomas, R. A. and Piper, A. J. (eds), 1989 *Durham Cathedral Priory Rentals I. Bursars Rentals*, Surtees Society 198, Newcastle upon Tyne

Longley, D., 1975 *Hanging Bowls, Penannular Brooches and the Anglo-Saxon Connexion*, British Archaeological Report 22, Oxford

Longstaffe, W. H. and Booth, J., 1889 *Halmota prioratus Dunelmensis*, Surtees Society 82, London, Durham

Loveluck, C., 2002 The Romano-British to Anglo-Saxon transition – social transformations from the Late Roman to early medieval period in northern England, AD 400–700, in Brooks, C., Daniels, R. and Harding, A. (eds), *Past, Present and Future: The Archaeology of Northern England*. Architectural & Archaeological Society of Durham & Northumberland Research Report 5, 127–48, Durham

Ludowici, W., 1927 *Stempel-Namen und Bilder römischer*

*Töpfer, Legions-Ziegel-Stempel, Formen von Sigillata und anderen Gefässen aus meinen Ausgrabungen in Rheinzabern 1901–1914*, Munich

Maaskant-Kleibrink, M., 1878 *Catalogue of the Engraved Gems in the Royal Coin Cabinet, The Hague. The Greek, Etruscan and Roman Collections,* The Hague

Maaskant-Kleibrink, M., 1986 *The Engraved Gems in the Rijksmuseum G. M. Kam,* Nijmegen

Macdonald, G. and Curle, A. O., 1929 The Roman Fort at Mumrills, near Falkirk, *Proceedings of the Society of Antiquaries of Scotland* **63**, 396–575

Macdonald, G. and Park, A., 1906 *Roman Forts on the Bar Hill,* Glasgow

MacGregor, A., 1976 *Finds from a Roman Sewer System and an Adjacent Building in Church Street,* Archaeology of York: the Small Finds **17/1**, York

MacGregor, A., 1978 Industry and commerce in Anglo-Scandinavian York, in Hall, R. A. (ed.), *Viking Age York and the North,* Council for British Archaeology Research Report **27**, 37–58, London

MacGregor, M., 1976 *Early Celtic Art in North Britain,* Leicester

MacLauchlan, H., 1857 *The Roman Wall and Illustrations of the Principal Vestiges of Roman Occupation in the North of England,* (Atlas volume), London

Mackreth, D. F., 1993 The brooches, in Hands, A. R., *The Romano-British Roadside Settlement at Wilcote, Oxfordshire. I. Excavations 1990–92,* British Archaeological Report **232**, 27–37, Oxford

Mackreth, D. F., 1994 Copper alloy and iron brooches, in Cracknell, S. and Mahany, C (eds), *Roman Alcester: Southern Extramural Area 1964–1966 Excavations, Part 2: Finds and Discussion,* Council for British Archaeology Research Report **97**, 162–77, York

Manning, W. H., 1976 *Catalogue of Romano-British Ironwork in the Museum of Antiquities, Newcastle upon Tyne,* Newcastle upon Tyne

Manning, W. H., 1985 *Catalogue of the Romano-British Iron Tools, Fittings and Weapons in the British Museum,* London

Marchant, D. J., 1991 *Roman Weaponry in the Province of Britain from the Second Century to the Fifth Century AD,* unpublished PhD thesis, University of Durham

Marsden, E., 1969 *Greek and Roman Artillery: Historical Development,* Oxford

Marsh, G., 1978 Early fine wares in the London area, in Arthur, P. and Marsh, G. (eds), *Early Fine Wares in Roman Britain,* British Archaeological Report **57**, 119–223

Martin, M., 1976 *Das fränkische Gräberfeld von Basel-Bernerring,* Basel

May, T. and Hope, L. E., 1917 Catalogue of the Roman pottery in the Museum, Tullie House, Carlisle, *Transactions of the Cumberland & Westmorland Antiquarian & Archaeological Society* 2 ser **17**, 114–97

McBride, R. M., 2003 Tile, in Hodgson 2003, 186–9

McBride, R. M., 2010 Roman pottery from 59 Denhill Park, Benwell, *Arbeia Journal* **9**, 161–3

McWhirr, A. (ed.), 1979 *Roman Brick and Tile: Studies in Manufacture, Distribution and Use in the Western Empire,* British Archaeological Report **S68**, Oxford

Mensch, P. J. van, 1979 A Roman soup kitchen at Zwammerdam?, *Ber Rijkdienst Oudheidkundig Bodemonderzoek* **24**, 159–65

Miket, R., 1980 A restatement of evidence from Bernician Anglo-Saxon burials, in Rahtz, P., Dickinson, T. and Watts, L. (eds), *Anglo-Saxon Cemeteries 1979,* British Archaeological Report **82**, 289–305, Oxford

Milne, J. S., 1907 *Surgical Instruments in Greek and Roman Times,* Oxford

Monaghan, J., 1987 *Upchurch and Thameside Roman Pottery,* British Archaeological Report **173**, Oxford

Monaghan, J., 1997 *Roman Pottery from York,* Archaeology of York **16/8**, York

Morris, E. L., 2007 Making magic: later prehistoric and early Roman salt production in the Lincolnshire fenland, in Haselgrove, C. and Moore, T. (eds) *The Later Iron Age in Britain and Beyond,* 430–43, Oxford

Morris, P., 1979 *Agricultural Buildings in Roman Britain,* British Archaeological Report **70**, Oxford

Mutz, A., 1972 *Die Kunst des Metalldrehens bei den Römern,* Basle

Myres, J. N. L., 1977 *A Corpus of Anglo-Saxon Pottery of the Pagan Period,* Cambridge

Myres, J. N. L. and Southern, W. H., 1973 *The Anglo-Saxon Cremation Cemetery at Sancton, East Yorkshire,* Hull Museums Publication **218**, Kingston upon Hull

Nash-Williams, V. E., 1930 The samian potters' stamps found at Caerwent (Venta Silurum) in Monmouthshire, *Bulletin of the Board of Celtic Studies* **5**, 166–85

Németh, M., 1991 Aquincum: Erschlie ungen in den Jahren 1981–88, *Budapest Régiségei* **28**, 97–106

Nieto Prieto, J., 1989 *Excavacions Arqueologiques Subaquatiques a Cala Culip 1,* Girona

Oelmann, F., 1914 *Die Keramik des Kastells Niederbieber,* Frankfurt

Oldenstein, J., 1976 Zur Ausrüstung römischer Auxilareinheiten, *Römisch-Germanische Kommission des Deutschen Archäologischen Instituts Berichte* **57**, 51–285

Oram, R., Griffiths, W. B. and Hodgson, N., 1998 Excavations at Wallsend Colliery B Pit, 1997, *Archaeologia Aeliana* 5 ser. **26**, 115–60

O'Riordain, S. P., 1940 Excavations at Cush, Co. Limerick, *Proceedings of the Royal Irish Academy* **45C**, 83–181

Oswald, F., 1931 *Index of Potters' Stamps on Terra Sigillata ("Samian Ware"),* Margidunum

Peacock, D. P. S., 1980 The Roman millstone trade: a petrological sketch, *World Archaeology* **12(1)**, 43–53

Peacock, D. P. S and Williams, D. F., 1986 *Amphorae and the Roman Economy: an Introductory Guide,* London

Peck, C. W., 1964 *English Copper, Tin and Bronze Coins in the British Museum 1558–1958,* London

Peeters, J., 2003 *Housesteads Ware on Hadrian's Wall. A Continental Connection,* Undergraduate dissertation, University of Amsterdam

Perrin, J. R., 1981 *Roman Pottery from the* Colonia: *Skeldergate and Bishophill,* Archaeology of York **16/2**, York

Perrin, J. R., 1990 *Roman Pottery from the* Colonia: *Tanner Row and Rougier Street,* Archaeology of York **16/4**, York

Perrin, J. R., 1999 Roman pottery from excavations at and near to the Roman small town of Durobrivae, Water Newton, Cambridgeshire, 1956–58, *Journal of Roman Pottery Studies* **8**, 1–141

Peter McGowan Associates, Crow, J., Rushworth, A. and Renshaw, J., 2002 *Housesteads Roman Fort, Conservation Plan,* **1**: *Report* and **2**: *Gazetteer,* Newcastle upon Tyne

Philp, B. and Henig, M., 1985 Roman gemstones from Dover, *Antiquaries Journal* **65**, 463–5

Philpott, R., 1991 *Burial Practices in Roman Britain: a Survey of Grave Treatment and Furnishing AD 43 – 410*, British Archaeological Report **219**, Oxford

Piboule, A., 1977 Catalogue destampilles de la région de Néris-les-Bains, *Revue Archéologie du Centre* **16**, 131–45

Pilar Lapuente, M., unpublished The petrography of some Roman pottery from the Roman fort of South Shields, Tyne and Wear

Pirling, R., 1974 *Das römische-fränkische Gräberfeld von Krefeld-Gellep 1960–1963*, Berlin

Potter, T. W., 1979 *Romans in North-west England: Excavations at the Roman Forts of Ravenglass, Watercrook and Bowness on Solway*, Cumberland & Westmorland Antiquarian & Archaeological Society Res **1**, Kendal

Price, J., 1978 Trade in glass, in Plat, J. du and Cleere, H. (eds), *Roman Shipping and Trade: Britain and the Rhine Provinces*, Council for British Archaeology Research Report **24**, 70–8, London

Price, J., 1980 The Roman glass, in Lambrick, G., Excavations in Park Street, Towcester, *Northamptonshire Archaeology* **15**, 63–8

Price, J., 1985 The glass, in Bidwell 1985, 206–14

Pringle, D., 1981 *The Defence of Byzantine Africa from Justinian to the Arab Conquest*, British Archaeological Report **S99**, Oxford

Proctor, J., 2009 *Pegswood Moor, Morpeth: A Later Iron Age and Romano-British Farmstead Settlement*, Pre-Construct Archaeology Monograph **11**, London

Rackham, D. J., 1986 Assessing the relative frequencies of species by the application of a stochastic model to a computerised database of fossil or archaeological skeletal material, in Wijngaarden-Bakker, L. van (ed.) *Database Management and Zooarchaeology*, PACT **14**, Rixensart

Radford, C. A. R., 1932 Small objects in metal, bone, glass etc, in Bushe-Fox, J. P., *Third Report on the Excavation of the Roman Fort of Richborough, Kent*, 76–93, Oxford

Radnóti, A., 1938 *Die Römischen Bronzegefässe von Pannonien*, Budapest

Rae, A. and Rae, V., 1974 The Roman fort at Cramond, Edinburgh: excavations 1954–66, *Britannia* **5**, 163–224

Raffald, E., 1970 *The Experienced English Housekeeper*, London

Rankov, N. B. (ed.), 1982 Roman Britain in 1981: I. Sites explored (Wallsend Fort interim note), *Britannia* **13**, 340–2.

Reinach, S., 1921 *Catalogue Illustré du Musée des Antiquités Nationales au Château de Saint-Germain-en-Laye*, tome 2, Paris

Richardson, W., 1923 *History of the Parish of Wallsend: The ancient townships of Wallsend and Willington*, Newcastle upon Tyne

Richmond, I. A., 1930 Birdoswald fort, *in* Richmond, I. A. and Birley, E., Excavations on Hadrian's Wall, in the Birdoswald-Pike Hill Sector, 1929, *Transactions of the Cumberland & Westmorland Antiquarian & Archaeological Society* n. ser. **30**, 169–75

Richmond, I. A., 1934 The Roman fort at South Shields, *Archaeologia Aeliana* 4 ser. **11**, 83–102

Richmond, I. A., 1936 Roman leaden sealings from Brough-under-Stainmore, *Transactions of the Cumberland & Westmorland Antiquarian & Archaeological Society* 2 ser **36**, 104–25

Richmond, I. A., 1950 Excavations on the Roman fort at Newstead, 1947, *Procseedings of the Society of Antiquaries of Scotland* **84**, 1–37

Richmond, I. A. and Birley, E., 1930 Excavations on Hadrian's Wall, in the Birdoswald-Pike Hill Sector, 1929. *Transactions of the Cumberland & Westmorland Antiquarian & Archaeological Society* 2 ser. **30**, 169–205

Richmond, I. A. and Gillam, J. P., 1950 Excavations on the Roman site of Corbridge 1946–49, *Archaeologia Aeliana* 4 ser. **28**, 152–201

Ricken, H., 1934 Die Bilderschüsseln der Kastelle Saalburg und Zugmantel, *Saalburg-Jahrbuch* **8**, 130–82

Ricken, H., 1948 *Die Bilderschüsseln der römischen Töpfer von Rheinzabern, Tafelband*, Speyer

Rickman, G. E., 1971 *Roman Granaries and Storebuildings*, Cambridge

Rigby, V. and Stead, I. M., 1976 Coarse pottery, in Stead, I. M., *Excavations at Winterton Roman Villa and other Roman Sites in North Lincolnshire 1958–1967*, Department of the Environment Archaeological Report **9**, 136–90, London

Riha, E., 1979 *Die Römischen Fibeln aus Augst und Kaiseraugst*, Augst

Rivet, A. L. F. and Smith, C., 1981 *The Place-names of Roman Britain*, 2nd edn, London

Robertson, A. S., 1975 *Birrens (Blatobulgium)*, Edinburgh

Robinson, H. R., 1975 *The Armour of Imperial Rome*, London

Rodriguez, J. R., 1997 *Heeresversorgung und die wirtschaftlichen Beziehungen zwischen der Baetica und Germanien*, Stuttgart

Ross, A., 1967 *Pagan Celtic Britain*, London

Roth, H. L., 1918 Studies in primitive looms, *Journal of the Royal Anthropological Institute of Great Britain & Ireland* **48**, 103–44

Rowley-Conwy, P., 1998 Improved separation of Neolithic metapodials of sheep (*ovis*) and goats (*capra*) from Arene Candide Cave, Liguria, Italy, *Journal of Archaeological Science* **25**, 251–8

Rush, P., Dickinson, B., Hartley, B. and Hartley, K. F., 2000 *Roman Castleford. Excavations 1974–85, Volume III: the Pottery*, Yorkshire Archaeology **6**, York

Rushworth, A., 2009a *The Grandest Station: Excavation and Survey at Housesteads Roman Fort by C. M. Daniels, J. P. Gillam, J. G. Crow, D. J. Smith and the RCHME 1954–95*, English Heritage Archaeological Report, Newcastle upon Tyne

Rushworth, A., 2009b Franks, Frisians and Tungrians: Garrisons at Housesteads in the 3rd Century AD, in Morillo, A., Hanel, N. and Martin, E. (eds), *Limes XX. Estudios sobre la Frontera Romana/Roman Frontier Studies. Anejos de Gladius* **13** (III), 1147–56, Madrid

Schaetzen, P. de and Vanderhoeven, M., 1964 *De Terra Sigillata te Tongeren* II, Tongeren

Schönberger, H., 1967 Ein Eisendepot, römische Flossfesseln und andere Funde im Bereich des Kastells Heilbronn-Böckingen, *Fundberichte aus Schwaben, Neue Folge* **18(1)**, 131–51

Schönberger, H., 1969 The Roman frontier in Germany: an archaeological survey, *Journal of Roman Studies* **59**, 144–97

Scott, I. R., 1980 Spearheads of the German *Limes*, in Hanson, W. and Keppie, L. J. F. (eds), *Roman Frontier Studies 1979*, British Archaeological Report **S71**, 333–43, Oxford

Sherlock, S. J. and Welch, M. G., 1992 *An Anglo-Saxon Cemetery at Norton, Cleveland*, Council for British Archaeology Research Report **82**, York

Sherlock, W., 1992 The Anglo-Saxon pottery, in Sherlock and Welch 1992, 54–5

Silver, I. A., 1969 The ageing of domestic animals, in

Brothwell, D. and Hoggs, E. (eds), *Science in Archaeology*, 283–302, London

Simon, H. G., 1965 Die Römische Fund aus dem Grabungen in Groß-Gerau 1962–3, *Saalburg-Jahrbuch* **22**, 38–99

Simpson, F. G. (ed.) 1976 *Watermills and Military Works on Hadrian's Wall: Excavations in Northumberland 1907–1913*. Kendal

Simpson, F. G. and Richmond, I. A., 1933 Birdoswald, in Report of the Cumberland Excavation Committee for 1933: Excavations on Hadrian's Wall, *Transactions of the Cumberland & Westmorland Antiquarian & Archaeological Society* n. ser. **33**, 246–62

Simpson, F. G. and Richmond, I. A., 1937 The Roman fort at Halton, *Archaeologia Aeliana* 4 ser. **14**, 151–71

Simpson, F. G. and Richmond, I. A., 1941 The Roman fort on Hadrian's Wall at Benwell, *Archaeologia Aeliana* 4 ser. **19**, 1–42

Simpson, G., 1953 The figured samian ware, in Richmond, I. A. and Gillam, G. P., Buildings of the first and second centuries north of the granaries at Corbridge, *Archaeologia Aeliana* 4 ser. **31**, 242–53

Simpson, G., 1977 La marque SACER.F in *tabula ansata* et quelques oves de Sacer de Lezoux, *Revue Archéologie du Centre* **61/2**, 85–88

Smith, C. R., 1880 *Collectanea Antiqua* **7**, London

Smith, D. J., 1968 Housesteads: south-east angle and a note on the water supply. Typescript, Museum of Antiquities, University of Newcastle upon Tyne

Smith, R. A., 1922 *A Guide to the Antiquities of Roman Britain in the Department of British and Mediaeval Antiquities*, London

Snape, M. E., 1992 Documentary Research on Benwell and Wallsend, *Arbeia Journal* **1**, 37–40

Snape, M. E., 1992 Excavation summary: Wallsend-Buddle Street and Wallsend-Fort Ditches, *Arbeia Journal* **1**, 58–62

Snape, M. E., 1993 *Roman Brooches from North Britain*, British Archaeological Report **235**, Oxford

Snape, M. E. and Bidwell, P. T., 1994 The *Vicus* of the Roman Fort at Wallsend, Tyne and Wear, *Arbeia Journal* **3**, 13–33

Snape, M. E. and Bidwell, P. T., 2002 Excavations at the Castle Garth, Newcastle upon Tyne, 1976–92 and 1995–6: the excavation of the Roman fort, *Archaeologia Aeliana* 5 ser. **31**, 1–249

Spain, G. R. B. and Simpson F. G., 1930 The Roman Wall from Wallsend to Rudchester Burn, in Hope Dodds, M., *A History of Northumberland* **13**, 484–564

Stallibrass, S. M., 1991 Animal bones from excavations at Annetwell Street, Carlisle, 1982–4. Period 3: the earlier timber fort, English Heritage Ancient Monuments Laboratory Report **132/91**, Portsmouth

Stallibrass, S. M., 1993 Animal bones from excavations in the southern area of The Lanes, Carlisle, Cumbria, 1981–1982, English Heritage Ancient Monuments Laboratory Report **96/93**, Portsmouth

Steiner, P., 1911 *Xanten-Sammlung des Neiderrheinischen Altertums-Vereins*, Frankfurt

Stewart, I. H., 1955 *The Scottish Coinage*, London

Stokes, P. R. G., 1992 *Observations on the Roman Military Diet and Culinary Practices from the Commandant's House, South Shields*, unpublished B. A. dissertation, University of Durham

Stokes, P. R. G., 1996 Debris from Roman butchery, *Petits Propos Culinaires* **52**, 38–47

Strong, D. and Brown, D., 1976 *Roman Crafts*, London

Swan, V. G., 1992 Legio VI and its men: African legionaries in Britain, *Journal of Roman Pottery Studies* **5**, 1–33

Swift, E., 2003 *Roman Dress Accessories*, Princes Risborough

Symonds, R. P. and Wade, S., 1999 *Roman Pottery from Excavations in Colchester 1971–86*, Colchester Archaeological Report **10**, Colchester

Taçon, P. S. C., 1991 The power of stone: symbolic aspects of stone use and tool development in western Arnhem Land, Australia, *Antiquity* **65**, 192–207

Thomas, J., 1991 *Rethinking the Neolithic*, Cambridge

Thomas, M. D., 2003 Lorica Segmentata, *Volume II: a Catalogue of Finds*, Journal of Roman Military Equipment Studies Monograph **2**, Oxford

Todd, M., 2006 Excavations in the *praetorium* of the Roman fort and *vicus* at Chester-le-Street, 1960–63, *Archaeologia Aeliana* 5 ser **35**, 39–47

Tolan-Smith, C., 1996 The Mesolithic/Neolithic transition in the Lower Tyne Valley: a landscape approach, *Northern Archaeology* **13–14**, 7–15

Toller, H., 1977 *Roman Lead Coffins and Ossuaria in Britain*, British Archaeologial Report **38**, Oxford

Tomber, R. and Dore, J., 1998 *The National Roman Fabric Reference Collection: a Handbook*, Museum of London Archaeological Service Monograph **2**, London

Tomlin, R. S. O., 2003 Inscription on stone, in Hodgson 2003, 183

Tyers, P., 1996 *Roman Pottery in Britain*, London

Vago, E. B., 1971 *Aussrabungen in Intercissa (1957–69) Abba Regia*, Budapest

Vanderhoeven, M., 1974 *Funde aus Asciburgium*, Duisburgh

Vaughan, J. E., 1987 Knives and knife handles, in Harbottle, B. and Fraser, R., Black Friars, Newcastle upon Tyne, after the dissolution of the monasteries, *Archaeologia Aeliana* 5 ser **15**, 23–149

Vermeule, C. C., 1959 *The Goddess Roma in the Art of the Roman Empire*, Cambridge, MA

Waddington, C., 1998 *A Landscape Archaeological Study of the Mesolithic–Neolithic in the Milfield Basin, Northumberland*, unpublished PhD thesis, University of Durham

Walke, N., 1965 *Das Römische Donaukastell Straubing-Sorviodurum*, Limesforschungen **3**, Berlin

Walters, H. B., 1908 *Catalogue of the Roman Pottery in the Departments of Antiquities, British Museum*, London

Warry, P., 2006 Tegulae: *Manufacture, Typology and Use in Roman Britain*, British Archaeological Report **417**, Oxford

Watkin, J. and Mann, F., 1981 Some late Saxon finds from Lilla Howe, N. Yorks., and their context, *Medieval Archaeology* **25**, 153–7

Watson, G. R., 1973 *The Roman Soldier*, London

Waugh, H. and Goodburn, R., 1972 The non-ferrous objects from Verulamium, in Frere 1972, 115–62

Webster, G., 1944 A Roman pottery at South Carlton, Lincs., *Antiquaries Journal* **24**, 129–43

Webster, G., 1989 Deities and religious scenes on Romano-British pottery, *Journal of Roman Pottery Studies* **2**, 1–28

Webster, G., 2002 *The Legionary Fortress at Wroxeter. Excavations by Graham Webster, 1955–85*, English Heritage Archaeological Report **19**, London

Webster, J., 1989 Objects of stone, in O'Leary, T. J., *Pentre Farm, Flint 1976–81*, British Archaeological Report **207**, 86–8

Welfare, A., 1985 The milling stones, in Bidwell 1985, 154–64

Welsby, D. A., 1982 *The Roman Military Defence of the British Provinces in its Later Phases*. British Archaeological Report **101**, Oxford.

West, S. E., 1985 *West Stow. The Anglo-Saxon Village,* East Anglian Archaeology **2**, Ipswich

Wheeler, R. E. M., 1926 The Roman fort at Brecon, *Y Cymmrodor* **37**, 20–68

Wheeler, R. E. M., 1943 *Maiden Castle, Dorset,* London

Wheeler, R. E. M. and Wheeler, T. V., 1932 *Report on the Excavations of the Prehistoric, Roman and Post-Roman Site in Lydney Park, Gloucestershire,* Oxford

Whitworth, A. M., 2000 *Hadrian's Wall: Some Aspects of its Post-Roman Influence on the Landscape,* British Archaeological Report **296**, Oxford

Wild, F., 1979 Samian ware, in Potter, T. W., *Romans in North-West England,* Cumberland & Westmorland Antiquarian & Archaeological Society Research Series **1**, 269–91, Kendal

Wild, F., 2010 The samian ware, 89–98, in Snape, M., Bidwell, P. and Stobbs, S., Excavations in the military *vicus* south-west of the Roman Fort at South Shields in 1973, 1988 and 2002, *Arbeia Journal* **9**, 43–132

Wild, J. P., 1970a Button-and-loop fasteners in the Roman provinces, *Britannia* **1**, 137–55

Wild, J. P., 1970b *Textile Manufacture in the Northern Provinces,* Cambridge

Williams, D. F., 2002 The amphorae, in Snape and Bidwell 2002, 150–1

Willis, S., 2005 The context of writing and written records in ink: the archaeology of samian inkwells in Roman Britain, *Archaeological Journal* **162**, 96–145

Wilmott, T., 1997 *Birdoswald. Excavations of a Roman fort on Hadrian's Wall and its Successor Settlements: 1987–92,* London

Wilmott, T., 2001 *Birdoswald Roman fort. 1800 Years on Hadrian's Wall,* Stroud

Wilmott, T., Cool, H. and Evans, J., 2009 Excavations at the Hadrians Wall fort of Birdoswald (*Banna*), Cumbria: 1996–2000 in Wilmott, T. (ed.), *Hadrian's Wall: Archaeological Research by English Heritage 1976–2000,* 203–395, Swindon

Young, W. H., 1933 The Municipal Museum, Gateshead, *Proceedings of the Society of Antiquaries of Newcastle upon Tyne* 4 ser. **6**, 117–21

Zalkin, V. I., 1960 Metapodial variation and its significance for the study of ancient horned cattle (English summary), *Bulletin of the Moscow Society of Naturalists, Biological Series* **65**, 109–26

Zienkiewicz, J. D., 1986 *The Legionary Fortress Baths at Caerleon: the Finds,* Cardiff

Zwart, A. J. M., 1998 A bridled horse burial from Beuningen (NL), *Journal of Roman Military Equipment Studies* **9**, 77–84

Zwierlein-Diehl, E., 1991 *Die Antiken Gemmen des Kunsthistorischen Museums in Wien 3,* Munich

# INDEX

Bold numbers are the volume number, followed by the page number. Further numbers are catalogue numbers. Page numbers in italics are figures; with 't' are tables.